Louise Cairoli

MAN as MAN

MAN as MAN

The Science and Art of ETHICS

Rev. Thomas J. Higgins, S.J.
LOYOLA COLLEGE, BALTIMORE, MARYLAND

REVISED EDITION

MILWAUKEE
THE BRUCE PUBLISHING COMPANY

IMPRIMI POTEST:

GULIELMUS F. MALONEY, S.J.
Praep. Prov. Marylandiae

NIHIL OBSTAT:

JOANNES A. SCHULIEN, S.T.D.
Censor librorum

IMPRIMATUR:

✠ ALBERTUS G. MEYER
Archiepiscopus Milwauchiensis
May 20, 1958

Library of Congress Catalog Card Number: 58–11856

MARIAE, MATRI DEI ET MEI

PREFACE TO REVISED EDITION

Since the first publication of MAN AS MAN I have found that there is less disagreement among writers on ethical subjects than one might be led to think from surface appearances. Thus, few people would really balk at accepting the statement of Rader: "The real center of value is the personality-in-society, and this social personality, as a dynamic of forces, is the whole man. Only an ethics that does justice to every essential side of man's nature, as both individual and social, as mind and body, as thinking, feeling, and desiring, is complete and complex enough to be the basis of valid social ideals" (*Ethics and Society*, 367–368). For "personality-in-society" substitute "member of the mystical Body of Christ" and the case is adequately stated. Basis of agreement exists because, after all, a common human nature and a fundamental decency and appreciation for things human unite those who write about man as man. The one serious obstacle to better understanding lies in one's attitude toward metaphysics. True, the hand of positivism still lies heavy on the land but that metaphysics will not always be an object of scorn seems assured by the progress made of late by Natural Law theories. If Natural Law revives, metaphysics cannot be far behind. Positivism declines and one of these days the bright young men are going to rediscover metaphysics.

I sincerely thank Miss Nellie Merrick and the Misses Elizabeth J. and Margaret M. Eichelberger for their clerical assistance in the preparation of the manuscript.

THOMAS J. HIGGINS, S.J.

Loyola College
June 10, 1958

CONTENTS

BOOK TWO

PRINCIPLES OF INDIVIDUAL ETHICS

BOOK THREE

PRINCIPLES OF SOCIAL ETHICS

BOOK ONE

GENERAL PRINCIPLES OF MORALITY

Chapter I PRELIMINARY NOTIONS

I. THE IMPORTANCE OF THIS STUDY

1. The subject of this study is man. The entire man is studied, man as man — not a partial aspect of him, not a view of certain fields of human activity interesting to specialists but of no concern to the rest of men. We consider rather the essentially human things which interest all men, not because they are physicians, barbers, or housewives, but solely because they are men. Other disciplines aim at making good engineers, good dietitians, good speakers; ethics intends to form good men. Not everybody aspires to be a good dentist, machinist, or beautician. Dentists, machinists, and beauticians can quit their avocation, or at least forget at times their professional capacity, and no great harm is done. No one, however, ceases to be a man, nor can anyone, without grave hurt to himself, ever seriously forget he is a man.

2. While other disciplines, psychology, for example, also consider the total man, our study views him in a way that is of surpassing importance. Ethics answers the most vital questions: What is man for? What ought man to do to accomplish what he is for? These answers outline the right way to live and offer the means of becoming a successful human being, namely, one who attains the ultimate purpose of life. Hence, in the words of Socrates, "we are discoursing about the way in which we should live — a topic of consuming interest even to a man of mediocre intelligence."[1] Ethics then should have a peculiar attraction for all. It has a distinctive nobility surpassing that of all studies except those which deal with God, the apex of all things.

II. WHAT IS MAN?

3. Before explaining ethics we must first explain man. Modern science describes man in various ways — as *homo sapiens*, the erect and comparatively hairless animal closely related to the ape; as an extremely com-

---

[1] Plato, *Gorgias*, 500.

plicated chemical formula not yet worked out to its last constituent; as a species of electron-proton complex; as a reflex mechanism; as an assemblage of stimulus-response relationships; as a psychoanalytical ego motivated by *libido* or basic physiological drives. Man may be all these but he is much more. For an adequate description of man we turn to the established findings of the other branches of scholastic philosophy.

4. We summarize man by means of Aristotle's four causes — material, formal, efficient, and final. Man is a unified whole, a complete substance formed from the coalescing of two widely differing constituents. One of these is the material element, the undetermined and determinable part of him. In common speech we call it his body; but strictly this material element should not be conceived as an organized body but as matter not yet determined to be any specific thing.

5. By union with a formal or determining cause, this material element is vivified into a human body so that the resultant of this union is a rational animal. This formal cause or soul is a vital principle, the ultimate internal reason why man can perform his vital actions. Man's soul is a simple, spiritual, incomplete substance endowed with immortality. The soul is the source for all of man's activities, sensory and immaterial, knowing and appetitive. The two highest powers or faculties of the soul are the intellect and the will. Through his intellect man is capable of immaterial knowledge; in certain of his acts, which he exercises through his will, man is free.

Thus psychology teaches that the *intrinsic causes* of man are his material body and free, spiritual, and immortal soul.

6. Man's *extrinsic causes* are his efficient and final causes. All contingent beings, of whom man is one, owe their origin to the Self-Subsisting Being who produced them out of nothing. God the Creator, then, is the ultimate efficient cause of man.

7. The ultimate final cause of the universe is likewise God. This statement applies to two distinct sets of activity: on the part of God, the motive inducing Him to create; and on the part of creatures, the goal in which all their activities rest.

What moves God to create cannot be some finite good He is to get from creation. God is not to be imagined as a celestial contractor who invests in a universe which is to supply Him with something He lacks. Being infinitely perfect, He has all things; being immutable, nothing can be added and nothing taken away from Him. Since He cannot acquire He can only give. The reason, then, why He creates is *His own infinite goodness*. Good is diffusive of itself — it tends to share itself. God creates because, loving His own infinite excellence, He desires to communicate something of that infinite reality to things outside Himself. However, He is not compelled to do this, for, being infinitely perfect, He is likewise free. Therefore, the ultimate motive of divine activity in the universe is the infinite goodness and liberty of God.

8. Regarding the end toward which all created activity must tend, a distinction is made between an end which is to be acquired and an end-result which is to be produced. The end to be acquired is God, who is to be possessed according to the capacity of each thing. God, therefore, is the absolutely ultimate end of all things. The end-result in which the universe's activity is to culminate is the *extrinsic glory of God*. This is a created thing. It is not the motive inducing God to create, but God cannot create without willing it because an inescapable law of order demands that all created activity conclude therein.

God's *intrinsic glory* is the knowledge and praise which He has in the depth of His own Being, of His own infinite excellence. A dim resemblance to this is the extrinsic glory rendered Him by the works of His hand. This is twofold, namely, the fundamental glory of God and the formal glory of God. God communicates finite reality to His creatures thus manifesting His goodness. All created things from the simplest atomic structure to the most complex animal are patterned after, and in every way are dependent on, God. Since each is something and does something imitative of the Divine Being and His infinite activity, each shows forth something of God excellence. This manifestation of the divine excellence constitutes the *fundamental glory of God*. Every creature by its mere existence and activity renders God this glory.

9. But a creation, no matter how beautiful, which would merely reflect but never consciously acknowledge the bounteous Creator, would be a very imperfect imitation of the glory God has in Himself. It would be a symphony no ear but God's would hear, a loveliness that would ravish no eye but its Maker's. Hence God enlarges the diffusion of Himself by making intelligent beings, images of Himself with intellect and will, who not only manifest the divine reality communicated to them but acknowledge it, and freely and intelligently subordinate themselves to Him. This is the *formal glory of God*. This must be the over-all end to be produced by a universe in which created intelligences exist; and as man is part of the universe, the apex and mouthpiece of visible creation, the final and absolute end of human activity is rendering God this extrinsic glory. Creation will have given God His glory and fulfilled the divine purposes for it when finally nonintelligent things shall have fittingly subserved created intelligences and these in turn are perfectly subordinated to God so that He is all in all.

We legitimately postulate this essential picture of man; it is proved elsewhere. Upon it as on a foundation stone rests the structure we rear in this study.

III. WHAT IS ETHICS?

10. The denial of metaphysics has led to serious misconceptions of ethics. To understand, therefore, that ethics is the science and art of man as man, let us consider the name of ethics, its subject matter, point of view, function, and ultimate purpose.

11. The name ethics. The word is a transliteration into English of the Greek *ἤθικα,* which is equivalent to our term *morals.* Although the root of *ἤθικα* is *ἤθος,* which means customary way of acting, we may not say that ethics is a mere historic or anthropologic record of human customs. To admit this is to confuse entirely manners and morals. A civilization has its prevailing tone of living to which manners and morals contribute: manners represent changing aspects of conduct like the forms of etiquette, recreation, and dress; morals reflect patterns of behavior which have an unchanging aspect like the rearing of children, reverence to parents, regard for truth. They[2] who would identify manners and morals say that morals are simply the "mores" or prevailing customs. It is widely held that ethics is the manner of acting which a particular society approves or disapproves as helpful or harmful to the common interest, that these patterns admit of no explanation except a historical one and are to be accepted as mere facts. Ethics, however, is neither sociology nor history; its essential function is to establish and explain the proper norms of conduct. These include universal, immutable moral laws which are as valid as the laws of chemistry or physics.

Ethics is sometimes used in the sense of a code of honor, of accepted procedure in some particular field of human activity. Thus people talk of medical or business ethics. We use the term, however, in the unrestricted sense of applying to all men. Ethics is not just a code one must live up to under penalty of offending against good taste or of incurring the displeasure of others but the rule of conduct to be observed by all men under penalty of incurring the ultimate of human evil.

12. The subject matter of ethics is the characteristic act of man. Since man has a nature which is specifically different from all other beings, he has an activity which is peculiar to him alone. This distinctive act proceeds from man's characteristic faculty in a distinctive human way, that is, from man's will illumined by rational knowledge. It is the

[2] Cf. W. G. Sumner, *Folkways.* Boston, Ginn, 1950.

free deliberate act. To prove the freedom of the will, however, is not an ethical but a psychological problem.

13. Point of view. Several sciences deal with the human act: economics and political science rather remotely; law and sociology more intimately. Sociology regards the human act as it promotes or destroys desirable social relationships; political science, as it constructs useful or harmful political institutions; economics, as it fosters the material welfare of people; law, as it helps or hinders the State. No sciences, however, treat it more closely and thoroughly than do ethics and psychology. Psychology sets forth the *physical* nature of the human act, that is, its physiological and psychic perfection, without however referring this to some absolute value. Ethics considers the *moral* or peculiarly human aspect of the act. The moral aspect of the act is its relationship to man's absolute value. The act will have *moral rectitude*, and will be morally right, when it promotes that value; it will have moral turpitude, and will be morally wrong, when it hinders that value. We shall show that man's absolute value is his supreme good, which is beyond comparison with any other human value. Quite properly, then, ethics appropriates as its own the terms right and wrong. For that is pre-eminently right which leads to the supreme good; that is absolutely wrong which frustrates that good. Clearly, then, of all studies based on reason and dealing with the human act, ethics is pre-eminent.

14. Has ethics the function of serving as the philosophic science of morality? Some empiricists say that ethics is not a science at all. These authors, awed by the spectacular success of the physical sciences, restrict the term "science" to them on the ground that only those studies are sciences whose findings can be tested by observation and which can make verifiable predictions. Underlying this position is the false assumption that deduction from analytic concepts is not a legitimate source of knowledge. It is narrow-minded to claim that the methods which proved successful in investigating the actions of irrational agents are the only methods which may be applied to the free unpredictable actions of men. Furthermore, a normative discipline like ethics need not be interested in predicting future generalizations. For if it correctly establishes its proper norms, these are principles capable of solving new problems. Hence there is no cogent reason for abandoning the traditional view that science is the knowledge of a thing through its causes. Therefore, any systematized body of truth with a proper subject matter and a distinctive point of view is a science. Since ethics has a subject matter, the human act, which it studies from the point of view of moral rightness and wrongness, it is a science.

15. Still greater confusion regarding the function of ethics has been engendered by the view of the logical positivists that the function of philosophy is merely to submit the language of science to logical analysis and to refine its concepts. Their cardinal principle is that only two classes of propositions can be true: (1) the propositions of logic and mathematics whose truth is independent of experience, and (2) facts and empirical hypotheses which can be verified by observation. Consequently ethics does not enter the realm of intellect. Ethical concepts are pseudo concepts and ethical propositions have no cognitive meaning. They are mere expressions of emotion. According to Ayer,[3] if I say, "Stealing is wrong," I am uttering neither truth nor falsity; I am emitting an interjection, evincing feelings of disapproval, which, indeed, I may also try to arouse in the hearer.

The bald assertion that ethical sentences are nonsensical has been modified by other logical positivists. Thus Stevenson[4] says that ethical sentences have a descriptive as well as prescriptive meaning and distinguishes between moral beliefs, which are cognitive, and moral attitudes, which are emotional. The function of ethics is to resolve ethical dispute by persuading others to change their beliefs and assume one's own moral attitudes. Thus ethics becomes a form of rhetoric. Toulmin[5] and others[6] agree with Ayer that "philosophy is a department of logic"[7] and hold that the central question of ethics is, What is the correct mode of reasoning in ethical problems? According to Hare ethics is "the logical study of the language of morals"[8] and the meaning of fundamental moral concepts is to be taken from the standard dictionary. Even among non-positivists a common view is that the task of ethics is the explanation of the fundamental moral concepts. Hill says: "What interests ethical theories . . . is not why [ethical judgments] are made or whether or not they are true, but what is meant by the moral terms used."[9]

16. The assertion of logical positivism that only logical, mathematical, and empirical statements are cognitive has no basis. Since it cannot be included among the three classes mentioned, it falls by the very principle it appeals to.[10] The assertion that ethical statements have no meaning is a piece of skepticism which the experience of mankind denies.

[3] Alfred J. Ayer, *Language, Truth and Logic*, p. 107. London, Gollancz, 1956.
[4] C. L. Stevenson, *Ethics and Language*. New Haven, Yale, 1953.
[5] Stephen Toulmin, *The Place of Reason in Ethics*. Cambridge, 1953.
[6] Paul Edwards, *The Logic of Moral Discourse*. Glencoe, Free Press, 1955.
[7] Alfred J. Ayer, *op. cit.*, p. 57.
[8] R. M. Hare, *The Language of Morals*, p. v. Oxford, Clarendon, 1952.
[9] T. E. Hill, *Ethics in Theory and Practice*, p. 14. New York, Crowell, 1956.
[10] Cf. Rudolph Allers, "On Emotive Communication," in *Symbols and Values: An Initial Study*. New York, Harper, 1954.

In the course of this study we hope to demonstrate the *truth* of fundamental ethical judgments. Philosophy is not a branch of logic nor is it highly developed grammar. Assuredly the language of ethics should be precise and its reasoning processes exact but logic and grammar are only a preparation for ethics. To say that the ethician should analyze ordinary discourse and find therein the solution of ethical problems is to make the man in the street the final judge in philosophical issues. Philosophy is not a mere inquiry into meaning. If ethics has only a semantic function it is merely the history of moral thought and is not what philosophy should be — an endeavor to answer the ultimate questions. It is well to "inquire systematically what people mean by each of the major moral terms, and what ordering of the disclosed meanings renders man's moral experience most intelligible."[11] But ethics goes beyond this inquiry. It assumes that moral words have meaning and it rejects false meanings. It shows that moral concepts are valid by indicating the realities they express. Then it formulates these concepts into the norms upon which the right and wrong of conduct rest. Since any theory of semantics must, consciously or unconsciously, rest upon a metaphysic, semantics can only be a tool of ethics.

We, therefore, define ethics as the philosophic science which establishes the right or moral order of human acts, that is, in the light of first principles, ethics determines the absolutely necessary norms of free acts whose realization in practice truly makes us men.

17. Ethics is a *philosophic* science, first, because it treats of the *ultimate* principles of conduct. To be a part of philosophy, or even a science at all, ethics must rest on metaphysics, the science of being-in-general. This is the ultimate science of self-evident principles which tests and validates the principles and postulates of all sciences. Without a grounding in metaphysics no science is properly anchored in reality and may prove to be delusion. Once ethics, by means of metaphysics, shows that it is rooted in the bedrock of reality, then it becomes the metaphysics of the human and social sciences. Since ethics explains the ultimate principles of conduct, it can criticize as morally right or wrong pronouncements of law, sociology, anthropology, economics, and the political sciences.

18. Ethics is philosophy for the added reason that it bases its conclusions on *unaided reason*. In this respect it differs from moral theology. Both ethics and moral theology treat of morality, the direct relation of human acts to man's supreme good. Moral theology treats the whole range of morality; ethics does not. Ecclesiastical law and the sacraments

[11] T. E. Hill, *op. cit.*, p. 17.

figure largely in moral theology; ethics says nothing of them. For the most part, moral theology is concerned with practice, leaving to ethics the formulation of theory. Moral theology views man as destined to a supernatural end and bases its conclusions on both reason and revelation. Ethics prescinds from man's supernatural status and draws its conclusion from reason alone.

Moral theology clears up some doubts which unaided reason might not be able to solve. We might not know for certain that lewd desires were wrong if Christ had not said: "Anyone who glances at a woman with a lustful intention has already committed adultery with her in his heart."[12] The function of revelation, however, in the field of morals is chiefly confirmatory. It is the anchor which holds reason to its moorings when passion would sweep it loose. We shall show in due time that man's weakness requires such confirmation (see § 331).

19. Since it is confined to the limits of reason, ethics cannot tell the whole truth about man as man. It labors under the unavoidable handicap of regarding man *as he would be if he were not elevated to a supernatural status.* No contradiction between legitimate ethical conclusions and the word of God is possible. For God is the Author of reason and revelation and upon nature He builds grace. There is, however, a danger of ethics drifting from reality unless it is supplemented, as occasion requires, by revealed truth. Thus, students should not be left under the impression that man's end is merely *natural* beatitude, that in his magnanimous man Aristotle describes the highest type of person. Furthermore, it should be helpful to remind them of that corruption of human nature which theology calls concupiscence, and whose cause is original sin. Concupiscence, or an inclination to evil, is the reason why people experience difficulty in accepting some ethical conclusions. Aristotle pointedly says: "A young man is not a proper hearer of lectures on ethics; for . . . since he tends to follow passion, his study will be vain and useless. . . . It makes no difference whether he be young in years or youthful in character; the defect does not depend on time, but on living . . . as passion directs. For to such persons, as to the incontinent, knowledge brings no profit." But lest young people be discouraged from this study, he adds: "To those who desire and act in accord with rational principles knowledge about such matters will be of great benefit."[13]

20. If we try to correlate ethics with the other parts of philosophy, let us say that the matter of philosophy falls into two divisions: that

[12] Mt. 5:28.
[13] *Nicomachean Ethics,* I, 3, 1095a.

which is and that which ought to be. Metaphysics is the ultimate explanation of all that is; logic, of all that ought to be in the field of intellect; ethics, of all that ought to be in the field of will. Ethics does not summarize what human conduct is but establishes the norms of what it ought to be.

21. The purpose of this study is that by acquiring the science of ethics one become skilled in the art of ethics. Art is the systematic application of knowledge resulting in the acquisition of skill in the production of some desired result. Ethics is the art of human living and its result should be ease in being the good man in every circumstance. Only a barren pedagogy would permit students to be content with a take-it-or-leave-it explanation of the laws of moral behavior. As logic aims at imparting skill in producing correct acts of the intellect, ethics should impart skill in performing good acts of the will. To aim at virtue, however, does not deny the intellectual character of this investigation but shows that we esteem prudence more than science (cf. § 290). The final outcome of both the science and the art should be that a man, having learned to live aright, attain the full stature of human perfection.

IV. THE BACKGROUND AND DIVISION OF THIS STUDY

22. Although the moral experience of the race supplies ethics with its data, not all this experience is equally valuable in the formulation of an ethical system. Emotions, like indignation at one man's conduct or satisfaction with another's, are too subjective to be reliable guides in establishing objective norms. But that which men are generally agreed upon as morally true or false can serve as a starting point — or better, a common-sense background — for the science of ethics. There is quite general agreement that all men — except the sophisticated few — differentiate between moral right and wrong, that all nations distinguish between good men and bad men, that all languages have words to express virtue and vice, that certain acts are obviously good and others obviously wrong, that a man should do the obvious good and avoid the obvious evil, that they who do good deserve praise and those who do evil deserve blame. One brings to this study an amount of natural certitude. Men begin their study of right and wrong at an early age and they have a facility for making some sound moral judgments. Surrounding this core of agreement and natural knowledge, however, there hovers, like the old wives' remedies which used to infest the art of

healing, a body of misconceptions and prejudices. By the application of metaphysical principles we separate the wheat from the chaff, rejecting what is false and converting natural certitude into formal certitude.

23. Our study proposes to establish what is orderly conduct and it falls into three main parts: (1) *general ethics,* or ethical theory, which studies the principles underlying all morality. This is followed by special or practical ethics. This includes: (2) *individual ethics,* which sets forth the good and evil which a man is to do and avoid as an individual; and (3) *social ethics,* which explains what is good and evil conduct for man as a social being.

24. General ethics can be summarized as the exposition of five great principles: End, Good, Law, Conscience, and Virtue. Each embodies the answers to a fundamental inquiry. *End* answers the question, what is that in which human conduct should terminate? *Good* solves the problem, What kind of activity will terminate in man's natural end? *Law* solves the problem, Why ought a man seek his natural end by doing good and avoiding evil? *Conscience* answers the question, How does each man know the good he is to do and the evil he is to avoid? Finally, *Virtue* answers the question, What internally helps a man readily to do good and avoid evil? Properly integrated these answers form an ethical system and offer an ultimate explanation of the norms of human conduct.

READINGS

St. Thomas, *Summa Theologiae,* I, 75, 76, 83, 90, 91.
——— *Contra Gentiles,* III, 17–22.
American Catholic Philosophical Association Proceedings, Vol. 25 (1951).
Aristotle, *Nicomachean Ethics,* I, 1–5.
Bednarski, F., "Propria principia ethicae methodo axiomatica ordinandae," *Angelicum,* 32 (1955), 3–20.
Berdyaev, N., *The Destiny of Man,* 1–83. London, Bles, 1948.
Cauchy, V., "A Defense of Natural Ethics," *American Catholic Philosophical Association Proceedings,* Vol. 29 (1955), 206–218.
Cobb, J., "The Possibility of a Universal Normative Ethic," *Ethics,* 65 (1954–1955), 55–61.
D'Arcy, M. C., *Christian Morals,* 3–39. London, Longmans Green, 1937.
Deploige, S., *The Conflict Between Ethics and Sociology,* 90–116, 264–280. St. Louis, Herder, 1938.
Heard, G., *Morals Since 1900.* New York, Harper, 1950.
Hill, T. E., *Contemporary Ethical Theories.* New York, Macmillan, 1950.
Klubertanz, G. P., "Ethics and Theology," *The Modern Schoolman,* 27 (November, 1949), 29–39.
Messner, J., *Social Ethics,* 3–52. St. Louis, Herder, 1949.

Newman, J., "The Ethics of Logical Analysis," *Studies*, 42 (1953), 303–320.
Reinhardt, K. F., *A Realistic Philosophy*, 90–107. Milwaukee, Bruce, 1944.
Semper, I. J., "On the Dignity of Man," *The Month*, 13 (May, 1955), 292–301.
Todd, J. M., ed., *The Springs of Morality*, 8–21, 313–327. New York, Macmillan, 1956.
Tsanoff, R. A., *Ethics*, 8–22. New York, Harper, 1952.
Wild, J., *The Challenge of Existentialism*, 116–150, Bloomington, Indiana, 1955.

Chapter II THE END OF MAN

I. MAN'S SUBJECTIVE END

25. Backed by the common sense of mankind we assume that moral right and moral wrong exist. Is this conviction of right and wrong to be explained as a mere subjective attitude on the part of some men, or is there in the objective world something to validate our assumption? Rightness implies order; wrongness, disorder; and order implies a principle of direction toward an end. We say that there is a right way and a wrong way of playing a game, of running a telephone system, of conducting a university, but we cannot say which is the right way and which is the wrong way unless we know the purpose of the game or of a telephone system or of a university. Since order is the fitting together of many things unto a given end, end is the fundamental principle of order, of all rightness and wrongness. Therefore moral right and wrong will be real and objective if man as man has an end; if he has not, moral right and wrong are meaningless. If we deny end to man, we deny all ethics. Without an end to achieve, human conduct is neither orderly nor disorderly; it just *is*, as existentialists claim. Furthermore, if we claim a false end for man our system of morality will founder in grievous error. We cannot exaggerate the importance of this discussion. That so many modern ethical systems shy away from the question of man's end is indicative of grave weakness.

In § 9 we postulated that man exists for the glory of God. This is an end which he has in common with the universe. But has not man an end proper to himself? If human nature is distinct from all other natures, has it not its own specific end? This then is our first problem, *Has man a peculiar and distinctively human purpose?*

A. What Is an End?

26. As a contingent being — one which exists but need not exist — man is subject to cause. End is the most elementary of causes. Without an end nothing could be caused, nothing contingent ever exist; for end is *that on account of which anything begins to be*. The end is always a good, that is, something which is capable of conferring some suitable perfection, advantage, or value. Once good is apprehended as such and is sought, it becomes an end. Initially, then, the end is the mental representation of some object or result conceived as desirable; intermediately steps are taken to realize it; ultimately the end is the possession of the good sought.

An end has certain characteristics: (*a*) *it is sought for its own sake* precisely because it is apprehended as good. Consequently, it differs from a *pure means*, which is sought only that a true end may be attained. However, a particular good may be sought both for its own sake and also as a means of attaining some further good. Hence there are proximate ends, intermediate ends, and ultimate ends. Moreover (*b*) *other things are sought on account of the end*. What we conceive of as leading to the desired object we seek solely that we may secure it. Finally (*c*) *end is first in the order of intention, last in the order of execution*. First is the mental representation of a good which arouses the appetite to desire it, then the ordering of means to secure it, and last of all the satisfaction of desire in the possession of the end obtained.

B. Has Man a Distinctive End?

27. Aristotle answers this question in the following way: "Are we then to suppose that while carpenter and cobbler have certain works and courses of action, man as man has none but is left by nature without a work? Or would one rather hold that as eye, hand and foot and in general each of his members has manifestly some work; so too the whole man as distinct from these has some work of his own?"[1] On the other hand Dewey, a typical representative of relativism and the trend to distort fundamental concepts, says: "The abandonment by intelligence of a fixed and static end was the necessary precondition of a free and progressive science both of things and morals."[2] According to him we must give up the idea of a final good for "a belief in a plurality of changing, moving, individualised goods and ends."[3] "The end is no longer a terminus . . . to be reached. It is the active process of transforming the existent situation. Not perfection as a final goal, but the ever-enduring process of perfecting, maturing, refining, is the aim of living."[4]

We can prove that man has an end which is not an interminable

[1] *Nicomachean Ethics*, I, 7, 1097b.
[2] Cited by Sedgwick, *History of Ethics*, 6th ed., p. 325.
[3] John Dewey, *Reconstruction in Philosophy*, p. 162. New York, Holt, 1920.
[4] *Ibid*., p. 177.

process by these considerations: (*a*) *Man acts for an end in all his human acts.* Man's characteristic act, which we call a *human act,* proceeds from his will. The will acts solely for a good, and a good which is sought is precisely what we mean by the term *end.* What is done without purpose is irrational, and hence is not a human act. (*b*) *In man's acts there must be some end which is final.* It is not enough that man seek an end in particular actions; his total activity must be for an over-all end. An infinite series of intermediate ends without a final end is as meaningless as a short-range series of acts without purpose. If man's activity led to an endless series of intermediate ends without a final end, man would never begin to act. Since the end of an activity is first in the order of intention, it is only the apprehension of a last or final end which can give man the impulse to make his first will act. The impulse would have to traverse an infinite medium if there were no final end of human activity. Hence "as in the process of reasoning, the principle is that which is naturally known, so in the process . . . of the will, the principle must be that which is naturally desired which . . . is the last end."[5] Since end is last in the order of execution, man would go on seeking without ever coming to rest if there were no final end. Therefore the denial of a final end involves the contradiction that man could never start to will and could never cease to will. (*c*) *Man can have but one final end.* The last end of anything is that which fills its capacities; beyond it there is nothing which the thing may achieve or tend to achieve. (*d*) *The last end of all men is one and the same.* Since all men have the same nature, they must have the same end. Human nature, which is common to all men, is directed to an end common to all men. Unity of nature demands unity of end.

Men therefore, exist in order to attain a final end; otherwise their life-movement would be irrational. Human reason does not devise this end but discovers it existing in nature, that is, planned by nature and set before each to accomplish. Hence "just as there is naturally one last end for all men, so the will of each should be oriented to one last end."[6]

C. In What Does Man's Last End Consist?

28. We distinguish a natural end (end of work) from an arbitrarily chosen end (end of agent). A natural end is that result toward which a being or an activity is directed by its nature. The end of the eye is seeing; of the feet, locomotion. An arbitrarily chosen end is one which a free agent selects to pursue. This may coincide with some natural end,

[5] St. Thomas, *Sum. Theol.,* I–II, 1, 5.
[6] *Ibid.*

as when a boy plays ball for fun, or it may not coincide. For example, laughter, whose natural end is the outward expression of delight, may be used to conceal pain or to annoy one's listener.

We are not inquiring into the arbitrarily chosen goals toward which different persons shape their lives but into that one good which nature offers all men.

29. A natural end may be intrinsic or extrinsic. An intrinsic natural end is a good realizable within the being itself. An ultimate intrinsic end is that crowning state of completeness which is attained by the proper exercise and fullest development of the being's natural capacities. An extrinsic natural end is a good realizable outside the nature of the being and consists in the well-being of that superior thing to which the being must contribute by nature's design. Thus a plant, over and above its own well-being, serves as food for brutes; brutes are intended for the use of man.

Man has no ultimate *extrinsic* end. For, although his completed nature must be subordinate to God, man can give God no true good or even utility. While this end differs conceptually from the extrinsic glory of God, in reality the two ends are one. Man glorifies God by attaining his own perfection.

30. What, then, is that peak of well-being to which nature directs man? To the pantheist it is absorption into the absolute, but pantheism has been thoroughly rejected elsewhere. To Schelling,[7] Hegel,[8] Von Hartmann,[9] and Wundt[10] it is the evolution and perfection of the race as a race to which the good of the individual is completely subordinated. But it is contrary to the immortal worth of the individual, the image of God, to exist for the utility of anything.

THESIS I. Man's natural end is perfect happiness. Man is perfectly happy only when his rational appetite is satisfied.

31. In creation the divine purpose is the communication of reality to, and the manifestation of God in, created beings. Each creature has a principle of activity whereby it moves to its destiny which is a limited participation in the divine excellence. The creature's good and the divine purpose are identified. Hence to insure the creature's movement toward

---

[7] F. Schelling, *Sämmtliche Werke*, Vol. I, p. 313 ff. Stuttgart, 1856.

[8] G. Hegel, *Werke*, Vol. VII, p. 312 ff. Berlin, 1833.

[9] Edward von Hartmann, *Phänomenologie des sittlichen Bewusstseins*, pp. 710, 711, 870. Berlin, 1879.

[10] Wilhelm Wundt, *Ethics — The Principles of Morality and Departments of Moral Life*, trans. Washburn, Chap. 2, p. 87. London, Swann and Sonnenschein, 1901.

the divine purpose, the Creator implants in each a natural appetite for its proper good.

32. *Appetite*, then, is the tendency of a natural agency toward some action for the securing of some good. This motion may be vital or nonvital, conscious or unconscious. An *elicted appetite* is the tendency toward a good apprehended by previous knowledge. Thus, a hungry squirrel seeks acorns. An *innate appetite* is the tendency toward a truly fitting good springing from the nature of the being and operating with or without previous knowledge. Thus, a salmon tends to spawn, a man to preserve his life.

When the natural appetite of a being is filled to capacity, the being is complete. In man this completion is called happiness or the conscious realization of all *befitting* desire, the pleasant state of satisfied tendencies. We are not now investigating the exact nature of happiness nor inquiring how or by what act happiness is attained but we simply assert that in happiness alone all human tendencies rest.

PROOF OF PART I

33. **Man's natural end is perfect happiness.** Since an end is a good, the final end must be the highest good. Man's highest good is perfect happiness because, (*a*) as experience testifies, all other ends — honor, wealth, fame, power — are sought on account of it; (*b*) it is the one good which, as Aristotle says,[11] is self-sufficing, that is, it makes life complete and lacking in nothing.

PROOF OF PART II

34. **Man is perfectly happy only when his rational appetite is satisfied.** Since man moves toward an end, he is incomplete. An incomplete being attains its end when its appetitive capacity is exhausted. As a rational being, man exhausts his appetitive capacity only when his will is satisfied. Although he has many appetites, these are subordinated to one dominant appetite, the will; otherwise he would not be one being. It is the will which seeks happiness and it cannot rest until it finds it.

[11] *Nicomachean Ethics,* I, 7, 1097b. Plato teaches the same doctrine; for example: " 'What does he gain who possesses the good?' 'Happiness,' I replied. . . . 'Yes,' she replied, 'the happy are made happy by the acquisition of good things. Nor is there any need to ask why a man desires happiness; the answer is already final.' " *Symposium,* 205–A. And again: "The being who possesses the good always and everywhere and in all things has the most perfect sufficiency, and is never in need of anything else." *Philebus,* 60.

Therefore, "since good is the object of the will, the perfect good of man is that which entirely satisfies the will of man. Consequently to desire happiness is nothing else than to desire that one's will be satisfied."[12]

35. Corollary I. Being perfectly happy is man's subjective end and highest perfection. The happy man is complete and has what nature intends him to have.

Corollary II. By natural impulse all men seek happiness even though all may not know in what happiness consists.[13]

Corollary III. In all his human acts, a man seeks happiness, if not by an actual, certainly by an interpretative, intention (cf. § 71).[14]

II. THE OBJECT OF HAPPINESS

36. "To say that happiness is the chief good seems a platitude."[15] Hence the challenging question is, What will fully satisfy the reasonable appetite of man and make him happy? Man's completion is obtained through *the possession of some object.* Just as we cannot know without knowing *something,* so we cannot be perfectly happy about nothing. We must be happy about something. What is that thing?

37. Some confused people say that we can never know what will make us happy. *But the object of our happiness must be knowable.* Lesser beings pursue their natural ends through blind instinct, but man's very nature would be disorganized if his total being moved toward an end of which he could have no knowledge. The rational being *qua* rational seeks something which is known.

38. Hence arises our next problem about man's end: What will make all men happy? This was the riddle of the ancients and is still a point of radical departure. A good deal of the clash of opinion on various problems of ethics can be traced to disagreement on this fundamental question. The chief answers will now be considered.

39. 1. *Finite external goods.* Many people of all ages, either because they cannot grasp that man has an immortal soul, or because they are completely engrossed in getting their happiness *now,* maintain, or at least act as though they did, that money, fame, and worldly power can make us perfectly happy. This belief is false because the object which sates out craving for happiness must (a) *exclude the possibility of unhappiness;* (b) *give us all we can desire;* (c) *not of itself make us unhappy.* Experience, however, shows us that an abundance of external goods is

[12] St. Thomas, *Sum. Theol.,* I–II, 5, 8.
[13] *Ibid.*
[14] *Ibid.,* I–II, 1, 6.
[15] Aristotle, *Nicomachean Ethics,* I, 7, 1097b.

(*a*) often accompanied by unhappiness; (*b*) leaves much to be desired; and (*c*) frequently brings misery.

40. 2. *Corporal beauty and bodily well-being.* The Epicureans held that man's highest good is the maximum of bodily well-being and the minimum of bodily pain. No combination of beauty, health, and strength, however, can constitute the perfect human good because man's body is only a part of him — and the inferior part at that. Since man is more excellent than the brute, his highest good must pertain to that wherein he excels the brute.

41. 3. *Pleasure.* The Hedonists, whose prototype is Aristippus, contend that the primary object of the will is pleasure. Complete happiness is complete pleasure.

Hobbes says: "We all measure good and evil by the pleasure or pain we either feel at present, or expect hereafter."[16] "The felicity of this life consisteth not in the repose of a mind satisfied. For there is no such *finis ultimus*, utmost aim, nor *summum bonum*, greatest good, as is spoken of in the books of the old moral philosophers. . . . The cause whereof is, that the object of man's desire, is not to enjoy once only, and for one instant of time; but to assure for ever, the way of his future desire."[17]

Bentham says: "In all this chain of motives, the principal or original seems to be the last internal motive in prospect. . . . This motive . . . is always some pleasure, or some pain; some pleasure, which the act in question is expected to be the means of continuing or producing: some pain which it is expected to be the means of discontinuing or preventing."[18]

For Spinoza "blessedness is nothing but the peace of mind which springs from the intuitive knowledge of God."[19] J. S. Mill says: "Pleasure and freedom from pain are the only things desirable as ends."[20]

These authors confuse the state produced in man with the object producing that state. Perfect pleasure is the consequence of having attained the most pleasure-giving object; therefore it cannot be that object. Since pleasure is a subjective quality, it cannot be the prime object of the will. First, pleasure can be experienced only after some object has been attained. Second, the primary object of the created will

[16] Thomas Hobbes, *Philosophical Rudiments Concerning Government and Society*, Chap. XIV, 17. Molesworth's English edition, Vol. II, p. 196. London, 1841.

[17] *Leviathan*, Chap. XI, *ed. cit.*, Vol. III, p. 85.

[18] Jeremy Bentham, *An Introduction to the Principles of Morals and Legislation*, Chap. X, 2, pp. 101–102. Oxford, Clarendon, 1917.

[19] Benedict de Spinoza, *Ethics*, trans. White-Stirling, p. 241. New York, Macmillan, 1894.

[20] John Stuart Mill, *Utilitarianism*, p. 17.

must be something outside itself. Only the divine Will has within Itself Its own sufficiency. We cannot be happy without pleasure, but happiness is only partially identified with pleasure. Happiness is right action with its connatural satisfaction: pleasure can result from either right or wrong action.

42. 4. *Knowledge, love, or virtue.* The Stoics held that virtue or wisdom was the perfect good of man. These, however, are subjective and as such cannot be completely satisfying because their ability to satisfy depends on the thing known or loved. The will's object must be outside itself.

43. 5. *Man himself.* Kant postulates a God who is merely the disinterested spectator of human life, the indispensable orderer and harmonizer of the physical universe.[21] Taking its cue from Kant who plainly says that man is an end unto himself,[22] a perverted humanism considers man as an absolute being. This may be understood of man the individual or man the race.

The individual. Nietzsche held that "life itself is *essentially* appropriation, injury, conquest of the strange and weak, suppression, severity . . . and exploitation."[23] To him, "'exploitation' does not belong to a depraved or imperfect society; it belongs to the *nature* of the living being as a primary organic function; it is a consequence of the intrinsic Will to Power, which is precisely the Will to Life."[24] Pushing this notion to its logical conclusions, he evolved his theory of the superman to whom any act is permissible because he has the will to power.

According to T. H. Green[25] and F. H. Bradley,[26] Hegelian pantheists, the end of every man is self-realization or the perfection of his natural capacities and faculties. The human self is one of the many subjects in which one divine mind partially reproduces itself. It achieves self-realization only as a member of the social community, the highest manifestation of the evolving Absolute.

The race. A perfect nation or a perfect human race is the destiny of each man. According to melioristic ethics the end is to "leave the universe a whole lot better than it would have been without [one's] life."[27]

---

[21] *Critique of Practical Reason*, trans. T. K. Abbott, pp. 221–222. London, Longmans Green, 1898.

[22] *Ibid.*, p. 229.

[23] Friedrich Nietzsche, *Beyond Good and Evil*, trans. Helen Zimmern, p. 199. New York, The Modern Library, 1937.

[24] *Ibid.*, p. 200.

[25] T. H. Green, *Prolegomena to Ethics*, p. 189, 3 ed. Oxford, Clarendon Press, 1890.

[26] F. H. Bradley, *Ethical Studies*, pp. 64–81, 2 ed. Oxford, Clarendon Press, 1927.

[27] E. T. Mitchell, *A System of Ethics*, p. xiii. New York, Scribner's, 1950

Others combine this idea with the self-realization theory of Green. Tsanoff says that the goal is "harmonious, integral realization, perfectibility, fulfillment of personality, achievement of a sound, sane, just, free, humane, creative civilization."[28]

Although the realization of human potentialities, either of the individual or of the race, is an end, it cannot be the final end or the object which satisfies human desire. For man cannot finally be satisfied with himself. If he could he would be his own end and a necessary, all sufficient being. But he can never be other than contingent. God alone is absolute. Furthermore, the force of man's appetite is such that no created good can satisfy it. Satiety, as we shall presently see, can come only from possessing the all-good, the universal good.[29] Therefore, the object of human happiness must be something beyond humanity itself.

44. 6. *Progress.* The attenuated remnant of evolutionary doctrine which now claims that man's end is merely progress or function is like a stream of water disappearing in sand. Dewey says that "growth itself is the only moral end";[30] Holmes,[31] that the only worthwhile thing in life is the struggle to live. These opinions contain the irrational supposition that we aim just for the sake of aiming and not to hit a target, that we journey, not to arrive somewhere, but to go through endless motions.

THESIS II. The sole object capable of satisfying our appetite for happiness is God. Man possesses God by acts of perfect knowledge and love.

PART I

45. Analysis of the human appetite reveals that the only thing capable of satisfying it is God, the uniquely necessary and infinite Person. St. Augustine gives eloquent voice to this truth: "Thou hast made us for Thyself, O God, and our hearts are restless until they rest in Thee."[32]

46. Proof. *God alone is capable of satisfying our rational appetite.* The will has: (*a*) an innate appetite for all good since good is the formal object of the will; (*b*) an elicited appetite for all good because

[28] R. A. Tsanoff, *Ethics*, p. 122. New York, Harper, 1947.
[29] *Sum. Theol.*, I–II, 28, 8.
[30] John Dewey, *Reconstruction in Philosophy*, p. 177. New York, Holt, 1920.
[31] *Vide infra*, § 908.
[32] *Confessions*, Bk. I, Chap. 1.

the intellect can conceive of a perfect good and present it to the will as desirable. Hence our appetite will not be satisfied until it shall have attained a perfect good. There is only one perfect good and that is God.

PART II

47. St. Thomas explains how God is the end of all things: "Things are ordained unto God not as an end for whom something is to be acquired but that they may acquire from Him Himself."[33] How does man acquire God? It must be by an act. Since potency is less perfect than act, happiness must be act. Man is not perfected by merely having the *power* of acting perfectly or by having something very pleasant done to him, but by *his doing something excellently*. Aristotle says: "The good of man comes to be a working of the soul in the way of the best and most perfect excellence in a complete life."[34] He calls this *Eudaemonia* which consists in complete well-being of life and its activities and is found in man's distinctive function. It is the highest energizing of man's rational life in conformity with the laws of its excellence, and the delight flowing therefrom.

48. **Proof.** *Man possesses God by acts of perfect knowledge and love.*

Any being attains its final objective and enters its perfect state by the highest acts of its characteristic tendencies. Since the highest acts of man's characteristic tendencies are perfect knowledge and perfect love, man attains God, his final end, by such acts.

N.B. Perhaps Aristotle did not appreciate the full significance of his words when he wrote: "If then the understanding is divine in comparison with men, the life of understanding is divine in comparison with human life. We must not take the advice of those who tell us, that being men, one should cherish the thoughts of a mortal, but as far as in us lies, we must play the immortal and do all in our power to live by the best element in our nature."[35] Even in a natural order man's perfect life is imitation of God's life.

49. **Corollary I.** Thus we answer the first over-all question of ethics, "What is that in which human conduct should terminate?" (Cf. § 24.)

Corollary II. Therefore moral right and wrong exist. Moral right is that which leads to final possession of God; moral wrong, that which hinders our final possession of God.

---

[33] *Contra Gentiles,* III, 18.
[34] *Nicomachean Ethics,* I, 7, 1097b.
[35] *Ibid.,* X, 7, 1177b.

III. THE ESSENCE OF HAPPINESS

50. What is happiness in the possession of God like? No phenomenological description of it is available. The Scholastics call it beatitude, the full and enduring possession of a supreme and perfect good. In beatitude we find: (*a*) *absence of every evil* — the happy man has no defects to mar the fullness of his well-being; (*b*) *presence of all good connaturally possible*; Boethius says it is "a state made perfect by the aggregate of all good things";[36] (*c*) *certitude that this will last*. Beatitude, however, does not make one infinite. Our happiness is limited by our nature and the preparation we have made for the last end.

51. The doctrine of Nirvana, which holds that happiness is utter cessation from all activity, compels us to emphasize the active nature of happiness. We may, however, speak of it as a state on account of its permanency. We carve "At Rest" on tombstones to signify that the struggle with evil and the toil for the end are over. Once the end is achieved, however, we shall not be placidly inert, onlookers at the most sublime spectacle, but we shall be active to the very depth of our being. St. Thomas says: "In that state of happiness man's mind will be united to God by one, continual, everlasting operation."[37]

52. If we seek the precise act in which happiness consists, we find a variety of opinions. The Scholastics agree that in happiness there is the act of knowing God, the act of loving God, and the joy resulting therefrom; that no one could be perfectly happy if he lacked one of these. But which of these acts constitutes the essence of happiness? Aristotle, describing the imperfect happiness of this life, says it must flow from the most perfect human power which he identifies as the speculative intellect.[38] St. Thomas accepts this doctrine, and applying it to the supernatural order says that the essence of beatitude in the next life is the vision of God[39] and that the will acts are mere consequences.[40] While this opinion is quite widely held, it is not unchallenged. Scotus[41] holds that beatitude consists in the act of love; St. Albert the Great,[42] St. Bonaventure,[43] and Suarez[44] say that it consists in both knowledge and love.[45]

---

[36] *De Consolatione Philosophiae*, III, 2, PL 63, 724.
[37] *Sum. Theol.*, I–II, 3, 2.
[38] *Nicomachean Ethics*, X, 8, 1178b.
[39] *Sum. Theol.*, I–II, 3, 8.
[40] *Ibid.*, I–II, 3, 4.
[41] *In IV*, d. 49, q. 4.
[42] *In IV*, d. 49, 6.
[43] *In IV*, d. 49, 1, 5.
[44] *De Ultimo Fine*, d. 7, s. 1, n. 24 ff.
[45] In many circles "voluntarist" is a bad word. But even at the risk of being called a voluntarist we offer the opinion that knowledge of God is not something ultimate but is further ordained unto the love of God. Men do not know merely to

53. Besides the knowledge and love of God which make up *essential beatitude*, the perfected man will enjoy minor blessings, which constitute *accidental beatitude*. Thus, since he is a social being he will enjoy God not in lonely contemplation but in the company of other men.

Does the body play an essential or accidental part in beatitude? It is argued that the soul after death is in an unnatural state of separation, that, as the form of the body, it longs for reunion with the body, and hence it will not be perfectly happy until it is reunited to the body. The answer is that while the soul needs the body in this life, once this life is over it can exist, operate, and be happy without the body. A spirit, by nature, must be able to exist and function independently of matter. Since the body exists for the soul, the body will have fulfilled its essential function once the soul reaches its end. Hence reunion with the body does not belong to the essence of beatitude but rather to the fullness of its perfection.[46]

Revelation assures us of the resurrection of the body. In the glories of a risen body we shall find the chief items of accidental happiness.

54. It must be emphasized that the beatitude just described is a purely *natural beatitude* which corresponds to man's natural capacities. It is not the happiness which a man can enjoy in this life but that which would be his after death if he lived in a purely natural order and attained the last end. Natural possession of God is by knowledge and love of Him as

---

know; but in order that the object known may be embraced or rejected by the will. St. Thomas argues that just as gold is the end of the miser so that when he has it in his hand the will can only rejoice, so when the intellect lays hold of God, our last end, all that the will can do is to rejoice. However, the objective end of man is not a thing but a Person. After that Person is grasped by the intellect, there remains the nobler act of love whereby *the man gives himself to God*. Unless man did this, God would be subordinate to man as the gold is to the miser and the best love he would have for God would be love of concupiscence. Furthermore, quest of the end is desire for union with it; attainment of the end is actual and most perfect union with it. St. Thomas admits that "the union caused by love is closer than that caused by knowledge" (I–II, 28, 1, ad 3). Since, then, a more perfect union remains after intellect has laid hold of the end, and since happiness is perfection, it would seem that the essence of happiness is not the less perfect union of knowledge but the more perfect union of love. This conclusion seems confirmed, first, by human experience according to which love — the mutual giving of self on the part of lover and beloved — is the perfect action. Furthermore, God has revealed Himself, not as intelligence, but as love. God is charity, says St. John. In these disputed questions, however, it should be kept in mind that it is possible to pose the question in such a way that one's opinion turns out to be the right answer. Thus St. Thomas says that the essence of beatitude is the act by which the end is laid hold of. What is that act? The act of the intellect! But the question may be put another way. Since happiness is man's perfection, what is the most perfect act of man? Love of God!

[46] *Sum. Theol.*, I–II, 4, 5.

He is reflected in creatures. This knowledge is analytic and discursive for it is not natural for man to look upon the face of God. This discursive process would be an ascent of the mind, as described by Plato,[47] from the individual to the universal, a step-by-step ascent up the grades of reality from a contemplation of bodily beauty to intellectual and moral beauty until we reach a Beauty eternal and immutable, the Fount of all beauty and the Reality upon whom all other beauties depend, while it is independent of them.

There is another beatitude which arises from the clear, immediate vision of God. It is knowing God as He knows Himself — without any intervening medium. This is *supernatural* beatitude, a finite sharing in the very life of divinity. Through the divine bounty man is *actually destined* for this alone. No student of ethics should be under the delusion that he is meant for merely natural beatitude. In either case God alone is the object of our happiness, but there is a vast difference in the way God is known and loved. In one case we are but servants before a kind Master; in the other we are lifted from the status of hirelings to that of sons by a loving Father.

Man's natural end is completely contained in his supernatural destiny. In ethics, however, we consider man's final end exclusive of its supernatural elements.

The question has been raised, Has not the soul a natural desire for the beatific vision? Would it not be ultimately frustrated without this vision? An affirmative answer seems to destroy the essential difference between the natural and the supernatural orders and to say that God could not create intelligent beings without destining them for the beatific vision.

IV. ATTAINMENT OF HAPPINESS

A. Is Happiness Attainable?

55. Normal beings regard an end as a goal one reaches or misses, not as an interminable process. Kant, however, says: "Now, the perfect accordance of the will with the moral law is *holiness*, a perfection of which no rational being of the sensible world is capable at any moment of his existence. Since, nevertheless, it is required as practically necessary, it can only be found in a *progress in infinitum* toward that perfect accordance, and on the principles of pure practical reason it is necessary to assume such a practical progress as the real object of the will."[48]

[47] *Symposium*, 210–211.

[48] *Critique of Practical Reason*, p. 218.

Nor does a future life hold out any more certain hope of realization. For "one who is conscious that he has persevered through a long portion of his life up to the end in the progress to the better . . . may well have the comforting hope, though not the certainty, that even in an existence prolonged beyond this life he will continue steadfast in these principles; . . . he may have a prospect of a blessed future; for this is the word reason employs to designate perfect well-being . . . which like holiness is an idea that can be contained only in an endless progress and its totality, and consequently is never attained by a creature."[49] Man, then, desires a holiness and a happiness he never achieves, a perfection "whose margin fades forever and forever as I move."[50] This we deny.

THESIS III. Happiness in the possession of God is actually realizable.

PROOF

56. Happiness is actually realizable, because:

It would be contrary to *divine wisdom* to put in us an inescapable tendency toward an end that would not be realized.

It would be contrary to *divine fidelity* to lure us on by a promise which is impressed on our nature but which would not be consummated.

It would be contrary to *divine goodness* to stimulate us by an appetite of which we are conscious but which would never be satisfied.

B. When Do We Get Happiness?

57. According to their answer to the inevitable question, When should a man have his happiness? all men fall into two categories: those who insist on happiness *now*; those who are willing to wait for happiness *hereafter*. According to the happiness-now theory the only life which counts is the here and now. There may not be another life, and, even if there is, it cannot be of much importance. Hence, if one misses happiness now, he is a fool. The second view is that perfect happiness is impossible in this life; that whatever imperfect happiness is now obtainable must always be kept subordinate to permanent, substantial happiness hereafter.

THESIS IV. Perfect happiness is impossible in this life.

58. Proof. The universal experience of mankind testifies that there is no one who does not experience an abundance of evil and a lack of many good things at all stages of life. Death, inevitable for all men,

[49] *Ibid.*, p. 220, note.
[50] Tennyson's "Ulysses."

precludes the hope of permanently possessing any good. God is known and loved only vaguely and remissly. Our mortal happiness, therefore, must be imperfect.

V. THE PURPOSE OF THIS LIFE

59. Happiness is real and realizable. If, then, we cannot get it in this life, it must be obtainable in a future life. Hence this most important question is left: *What is the purpose of this life?*

THESIS V. The purpose of this life is preparation for perfect happiness hereafter. The attainment of this purpose depends on the moral character of one's will acts.

PART I

60. **Proof.** *The purpose of this life is preparation for happiness hereafter, because:*

The end of this life is either the actual enjoyment of happiness or preparation for it. For man's final end is also his *chief good.* Now the chief good of any being is that toward which all things pertaining to that being tend. Hence all things human — this life included — must tend either to happiness itself or to direct preparation for it.

Perfect happiness is impossible in this life, as we have just proved.

Corollary. Man disposes himself for happiness by ordering and directing his whole life to knowing and loving God, the sole object of his beatitude.

PART II

61. **Proof.** *The attainment of this purpose depends on the moral character of one's will acts.*

A finite, contingent being who has not yet reached his final perfection may, if he is free, choose to reject it. Because he is free, man can perform acts which perfect his nature and acts which degrade it. It is impossible that the latter should conduce to his happiness. Therefore, if man insists on acting in a way which degrades his nature, it is impossible that he arrive at perfect happiness or even at a state approximating it. Therefore his attaining a state of preparation for beatitude depends on the moral perfection of his will acts.

62. **N.B.** What constitutes adequate preparation for beatitude? Is there further opportunity for preparation after death? Neither of these

problems can be solved by reason with certainty. However, revelation unmistakably tells us that the sole disposition requisite for beatitude is the state of sanctifying grace at death; that there is one mortal life and one death. Hence the practical meaning of life is reduced to this: the necessity of dying in the state of sanctifying grace.

63. Corollary I. Mortal life is essentially a probation.

Corollary II. Man's ultimate intrinsic end, his beatitude, is not absolutely but only *conditionally* decreed by God. The ultimate end of the universe, the glory of God, has been absolutely decreed. Even with regard to those who fail to win their happiness, God will work His purposes and obtain His glory.

Corollary III. Moral values have supremacy over all else in life. Every activity or happening in the life of every man has enduring value only in so far as it leads him to his final end. For upon his judicious use of this life depends the character of his future life. Hence, as a prudent man, he must endeavor to use the things of life in so far as they lead to a happy life hereafter and should abstain from whatever hinders the accomplishment of life's purpose. One cannot exaggerate the seriousness of human life.

Corollary IV. Except the perpetual loss of beatitude, there can be no greater misfortune than ignorance of the meaning of this mortal life. The pall which hung over Hellenic civilization when it was at its height arose from doubt and uncertainty about life's meaning. Euripides sums it up in the lines:

> O'er all man's life woes gather thick;
> Ne'er from its travail respite is.
> If better life beyond be found
> The darkness veils, clouds wrap it round;
> Therefore infatuate fond to this
> We cling — the earth's poor sunshine-gleam:
> Naught know we of the life to come
> There speak no voices from the tomb
> We drift on fable's shadowy stream.[51]

Like doubts and uncertainty are producing a similar pessimism among modern men.

[51] *Hippolytus,* 190–198.

READINGS

St. Augustine, *De Beata Vita,* tr. L. Schopp as *The Happy Life.* St. Louis, Herder, 1939.

St. Thomas, *Summa Theologica,* I–II, 1–5.

——— *Contra Gentiles*, II, 46; III, 16–22; 24–53.
Brosnahan, T., *Prolegomena to Ethics*, 90–137. New York, Fordham, 1941.
Bruehl, C. P., *This Way Happiness*, 35–46. Milwaukee, Bruce, 1941.
Buckley, J., *Man's Last End*, 54–95. St. Louis, Herder, 1949.
Cicero, *De Finibus*, Bk. I, cc. 9–11; 17–19; Bk. IV, cc. 6–18.
Farrell, W., *A Companion to the Summa*, Vol. II, 1–20. New York, Sheed & Ward, 1945.
Garrigou-Lagrange, R., *Beatitude*, 33–129. St. Louis, Herder, 1956.
Gilson, E., *Moral Values and the Moral Life*, 15–51. St. Louis, Herder, 1941.
McAllister, J. B., *Ethics*, 2nd ed., 33–59. Philadelphia, Saunders, 1955.
MacIver, R. M., *The Pursuit of Happiness*, 15–40; 162–174. New York, Simon and Schuster, 1955.
Messner, J., *Ethics and Facts*, 75–135. St. Louis, Herder, 1952.
Moore, T. V., *A Historical Introduction to Ethics*, 89–120. New York, American Book, 1915.
Mullaney, T. V., "The Natural, Terrestrial End of Man," *The Thomist*, 18 (July, 1955), 373–395.
O'Connor, W. R., *The Eternal Quest*. New York, Longmans, 1947.
Reinhardt, K. F., *A Realistic Philosophy*, 108–123. Milwaukee, Bruce, 1944.
Renard, H., *The Philosophy of Morality*, 11–59. Milwaukee, Bruce, 1953.
Scheeben, M. J., *Nature and Grace*, tr. C. Vollert. St. Louis, Herder, 1954.
Seneca, *Epistulae Morales*, 65, 71, 92.
Smith, G., "Philosophy and the Unity of Man's Ultimate End," *American Catholic Philosophical Association Proceedings*, 27 (1953), 60–84.
Titus, H. H., *Living Issues in Philosophy*, 2 ed., 274–290. New York, American Book, 1953.

Chapter III THE HUMAN ACT

64. Man, an incomplete being, achieves completeness or happiness by a succession of proper acts. Since he has a distinctive nature, he seeks his end by a distinctively appetitive act — the human act. Human acts alone constitute the field of ethics. However, before studying human acts from their moral aspect or their direct relation to the end, we should know their psychological make-up.

I. THE PSYCHOLOGICAL NATURE OF THE HUMAN ACT

A. What Is a Human Act?

65. Not every act of man is a human act. Since man has a complex nature, he performs acts which are the same as those of (*a*) *minerals* — should he fall upon a mountainside he would roll down like any stone; (*b*) *plants* — like them he digests food and grows; (*c*) *brutes* — like them he can feel hot or cold. These are not human acts because they do not proceed from man's will and confer no perfection which is distinctively human.

Although the will is man's characteristic appetite, not every act of the will is a human act. There are spontaneous reactions of the will which are not rational choices. These are not human acts because man is not master of them. He is master only of those acts of which he has previous knowledge. These are called voluntary under one aspect and free under another aspect. Acts are voluntary if they proceed from an internal principle with knowledge of the purpose of the act. An act is free if it proceeds from a self-determining agent.

66. Are all voluntary acts free? Man is master of all his voluntary acts except one — that highest act by which he embraces his Supreme Good. When the intellect adequately presents the Perfect Good to the will, the will is unable to reject it. This act is perfectly voluntary because it proceeds with full knowledge, approbation, and willingness; but it is not free. By his nature man is determined to elicit this act because it is the end of the will. While the created will is free with respect to the means to the end, it is not free as regards the end. However, since this act will not take place in this life, and since ethics deals with the proper ordination of human acts toward their last end, we may say that man is master of his voluntary acts, that his voluntary acts are free.

The human act, therefore is the *free, deliberate act*, the act of man as man.

67. Three elements enter the human act: (*a*) motion of the will; (*b*) intellectual knowledge of the purpose of the act; (*c*) freedom. Obviously without motion of the will no human act is possible. The weakest form of volition is the *velleity*, the motion of the will toward an unrealizable object merely as an object of complacence. It is a human act: our secret desires and daydreaming present moral problems. Intellectual knowledge is not a mere condition or accompaniment but a co-cause of the human act. Sometimes the imagination presents a proposed act as totally good or totally evil. When it does so it causes the will to accept or reject the act in a nondeliberate way. Deliberation is possible only after the intellect presents the act as partially good or partially evil. Man deliberates only about that which has some goodness, real or apparent, which attracts the will, along with some admixture of evil, real or apparent, which repells the will. After deliberation, prolonged or instantaneous, the will makes a free choice and it is the making of free choices which marks man as a moral agent.

If knowledge or free choice is totally lacking, the act is *involuntary*. An involuntary act may be performed without advertence to the purpose of the act, as when a stroller taps the pickets of a fence as he passes. It may be done with knowledge against the choice of the will, as when a man emerging from an anesthetic talks foolishly but is unable to control his words.

B. The Object of the Human Act

68. The human act has to have an object or term; for, as a rational choice, it is the choosing of *something*. It is the object which gives the will act its specific character not only psychologically but ethically. We do not substantially evaluate the will act by its subjective intensity or remissness but by the thing willed. This object may be direct or indirect.

69. The *direct object* is that which *immediately* terminates the will act. Anything at all can be the direct object of the will, for there is no limit to the will's capacity to act. What immediately terminates the will act may be (*a*) the object of a purely internal will act, such as a friend who is loved or an enemy who is hated; (*b*) the activity of

another faculty placed at the will's command, such as drinking medicine or singing a song. This is a *commanded act* and is physically distinct from the act of the will. If nothing further is sought than the exercise of that faculty, as when one decides merely to walk or swim, that activity is the will's object. If the act is commanded in order to secure some further object, as when the mind sets out to memorize a poem or the hands to seize a coin, the object (c) to be attained by the commanded act is likewise the will's direct object. The commanded act and the act of the will, though physically distinct, form a volitional unity; for the commanded act is the means used by the will to attain its desired object.

The truly human act, however, is *always and only the inner act of the will.* It alone is free. The commanded act is spoken of as free only because it falls under the influence of the will.

70. The *indirect object of the will* is an effect which is not intended but is foreseen, at least confusedly, as following from what is directly intended. Thus, I take a horn away from a noisy child and he cries. I foresee but do not intend his crying. Should I intend it, it would become a direct voluntary object.

To be called voluntary in any way, an unintended effect must be known to some extent. Unintended effects which are not knowable have no measure of voluntariness. Noe's drunkenness was probably wholly involuntary because he had no means of knowing how the wine would affect him.

The indirect object is called *voluntary in cause* for its voluntariness is to be sought in its cause, the directly willed action of which it is the effect.

C. Kinds of Human Acts

71. On a basis of completeness we distinguish: (*a*) the *perfect voluntary act*, in which there is full knowledge and consent; (*b*) the *imperfect voluntary act*, also called semideliberate, in which there is incomplete deliberation or consent.

The voluntary act is a motion toward an object, the production of an effect. It is aptly termed intention. From the point of view of the object sought we distinguish: (*a*) *positive intention*, which is directed toward a positive action; (*b*) *negative intention*, whose object is the omission of an act.

Since an intention may be required for the fulfillment of an obligation we distinguish: (*a*) *actual intention*, a will act which here and now produces a given effect; (*b*) *virtual intention*, a will act which has been placed and has been interrupted but morally continues and produces a given effect. The difference between these two intentions lies in the awareness of the agent. A virtual intention is an actual intention which has moved from the focus of attention to its extreme verge; (c) *habitual intention,* a will act which has been placed and, since it has never been revoked, is regarded as extending to a given effect; (d) *interpretative intention,* a will act which is not actually placed but would be if it were thought of and hence is regarded as productive of an effect.

We offer this illustration: I walk to town to buy my father a certain brand of tobacco (actual intention). On the way I meet a friend and forget why I am going to town but in virtue of my original intention I continue on my way (virtual intention). In town I visit a church and say some indulgenced prayers. I had once formed and never retracted the intention of gaining all possible indulgences (habitual intention) and although I am not now thinking of indulgences, I qualify for one. At the store I buy my father a different brand of tobacco because I find an extraordinary bargain. I prudently interpret that such would be my father's intention if he knew of this (interpretative intention of my father).

When a human act is necessary for the fulfillment of an obligation or the placing of a valid act, a virtual intention is the least that will suffice. Certain types of obligation may be fulfilled by a habitual intention. Certain courses of action may be justified by appeal to interpretative intention.

The qualifications, *good, bad,* and *indifferent,* do not apply to the psychological but only to the moral aspect of the human act.

D. Responsibility

72. From the psychological nature of the human act we are able to draw an immediate quasimoral conclusion regarding responsibility, or imputability. An act is imputed when it is charged to one as its responsible agent. The person who is responsible for an act must answer for its consequences, that is, assume blame if these consequences are unsatisfactory or receive credit if these are satisfactory.

THESIS VI. Man is responsible for his human acts.

73. **Proof.** Man is responsible for those acts of which he is master. But man is master of his human acts. Therefore man is responsible for his human acts.

N.B. All men agree that we are chargeable for the acts under our control. Our human acts attach themselves to us and are ours in a peculiarly personal way. They are the stuff out of which our human destiny ultimately is composed. What is accredited to us or blamed on us depends upon the objects of our will acts.

II. THE MODIFICATION OF THE HUMAN ACT

74. The voluntariness of our acts depends on intellectual knowledge and free consent. Responsibility is proportionate to voluntariness. Therefore, whatever hinders or enhances the will's freedom or the mind's knowledge will likewise affect one's responsibility for acts performed under such modifying influences. There are five such modifying factors: ignorance, passion, fear, habit, and violence.

A. Ignorance

75. Ignorance is absence of knowledge in one capable of knowledge. What is said here regarding ignorance applies to error, mistake, inadvertence, and the like.

Ignorance is an obstacle to voluntariness because one does not will what one does not know.[1] Does it destroy all voluntariness and hence all responsibility? That depends on whether one's ignorance is itself voluntary or involuntary.

Ignorance is involuntary when it is unavoidable either absolutely or relatively. It is not the result of conscious and willful neglect. This is *invincible ignorance* which means that, despite the care and diligence proportionate to the circumstances, the knowledge is beyond the grasp of this person. What constitutes proportionate care and diligence depends on the importance of the matter, the age, mental development, and even the health of the person. *There is no responsibility in the case of invincible ignorance.*

Ignorance is voluntary either when we choose to be ignorant (affected ignorance) or when by conscious failure we do not obtain knowledge within our grasp. There exists a previous obligation to know which has been consciously slighted in whole or in part. If no effort has been made to obtain the knowledge, the ignorance is crass; if a feeble but inadequate effort has been made, the ignorance is simply vincible. The difference between invincible and vincible ignorance consists in this: in the former there is no previous obligation to know; in the latter such an obligation must exist and must be willfully neglected.

Vincible ignorance diminishes but does not destroy voluntariness. Hence wrongs done through vincible ignorance are chargeable not as

[1] Aristotle, *Nicomachean Ethics*, III, 1, 1110a.

directly willed but as *voluntary in cause*. For they are foreseeable results of voluntary neglect. The degree of culpable responsibility depends on the culpability of the causative neglect. There is, however, a certain type of affected ignorance which may be said to increase voluntariness and manifest greater malice, namely, where one is determined to act, law or no law, and his plea of ignorance of wrongdoing is but an added motive for acting.

Ignorance of law is lack of knowledge concerning the existence or correct meaning of a law or moral principle. In civil law ignorance of law generally does not excuse one from the consequences of action contrary to the law. The courts presume it to be the duty of all to know the law. Where a law prescribes the conditions for the validity of an action, invincible ignorance of the law will not render valid an action which does not meet the required conditions. Thus, if the law requires the signature of the testator for the validity of a will, one's ignorance of this requirement would not make his unsigned testament a good will.

Ignorance of fact, taken as the correlative of the above, is lack of knowledge concerning some circumstance pertinent to the application of a law or moral principle. Thus, while a boy knows that stealing is wrong, he may walk off with another's lunch, thinking it to be his own. In American law ignorance of facts is a recognized defense where knowledge of certain facts is essential to a civil offense like burglary, but no defense where a statute makes an act indictable, irrespective of guilty knowledge, as in the sale of liquor to minors.

Moral responsibility for ignorance of law or fact must be judged by the norm of vincibility or invincibility.

B. Passion

76. Because he has an animal nature, man has instinctive tendencies toward or away from what he apprehends as sensible good or evil. In modern terminology, an intense motion of this kind is a *passion;* it is accompanied by a more or less noticeable change in the bodily organism. Thus, under stress of fear the face pales; in anger, blood rushes to the brain and face. It is because the body *suffers* these changes that these motions are called passions. While they can and do interfere with free activity, in themselves they are neither morally good or evil but an indestructible part of man's psychic make-up. We treat here also of those feebler motions which only slightly disturb the rational agent.

Passions differ from sentiments, which are the elicited acts of the will. One may have a passion of love and a sentiment of love, a passion of hatred and a sentiment of hatred, and so forth. Passion blends with sentiment, and sentiment stirs up passion because the sensitive appetite and will are rooted in the same vital principle, the human soul.

77. **Varieties of passion.** Psychologically passions stem from a fundamental motion which we call sensible love — the yearning for union with that which pleases the sensitive appetite. Because of a difference in the object sought for or avoided, two types of passions are distinguished, concupiscible and irascible. In the case of *concupiscible* passions, no special difficulty attends the attainment of good or the avoidance of evil. They include the passions of desire, joy, aversion, sadness, and hatred. In the case of *irascible* passions, there exists such a special difficult. They include passions of hope, fear, daring, despair, and anger.

For the purposes of ethics we distinguish spontaneous passion from stimulated passion. The former arises without premeditation or incitement by the will. Thus, struck by a snowball, I flare into resentment and profane language. Stimulated passion is either deliberately stirred by the will as when I deliberately work myself into a rage against one whom I greatly dislike, or it accompanies a strong sentiment of the will, as when a deep sentiment of love for one of the opposite sex arouses carnal desire.

78. Passion affects voluntariness and hence responsibility in the following ways:

a) *Spontaneous passion diminishes the freedom of the will.* First, it increases the inclination of the will toward one particular object. For perfect freedom, the will should not be inclined by any influence outside of the illuminating intellect more one way than another. Second, passion renders calm deliberation more difficult, since it causes the intellect to give a one-sided view of reality.

b) *Spontaneous passion may destroy the freedom of the will.* Experience shows that extremely violent fits of anger or fear can make a man incapable of reasoning. Hence, acts performed under the influence of such passion would in themselves be blameless. But a man may well be antecedently blameworthy in that he is not the master of his passions. Passion in an adult of sound mind is hardly strong enough, of itself and wholly without the will, to effect any considerable outward action. If passion does overwhelm an adult, the reason is that the will for a long time has been yielding its supremacy to passion and permitting it to range unchecked.

c) *Stimulated passion*, far from lessening responsibility, increases it, or better, is a sign of the will's intense inclination toward its object. The will and sensitive appetite are rooted in the same soul. Hence, when the will's desire for some object is so intense that it kindles strong emotion toward the same thing, we conclude that the will act is exceedingly strong. Such passion makes a good act better and a bad act worse. For St. Thomas says that "he who gives an alms with greater pity, merits more, and he who sins with greater lust, commits a greater sin; for this is a sign that the motion of the will is stronger."[2]

d) *Wrongs foreseen as the result of stimulated passion are indirectly voluntary and imputable.* They are foreseen, at least confusedly, as effects flowing from a directly voluntary act. Thus, if I nurse my indignation against another, realizing that if I do not stop, I may hurt him; and then a final burst of passion moves me to assault him, I am responsible for the injuries I inflict.

The chief practical result of the study of ethics should be the formation of the reasonable man. Nothing is more reasonable than that passion always be under our control. Neither the delight of forbidden pleasure nor the difficulty of what is reasonably enjoined should deter us from fulfilling our duty. Hence the chief moral end of education is the acquisition of self-control. Our passions are like children or horses — they will run away with us if they are not constantly kept in check. Over and above the habit of temperance, of which we shall speak in due time, we must practice self-denial. We practice self-denial when, upon due occasion, we refuse the sensitive appetite even what it might lawfully have, so that in the time of temptation it will have learned to yield to the dictates of reason.

C. Fear

79. Fear is the shrinking of the appetite from some evil difficult to avoid. We are not speaking of the emotion of fear, which affects voluntary acts in the same way that any passion does, but of the sentiment of fear. We are not discussing actions done *with* fear, for example, a man applies for a position fearful that he will be rejected. Our discussion is of choices taken *on account of* fear. The mind apprehends some disagreeable outcome and the will, to avoid it, makes certain decisions. Fear is grave if the threatened evil is great, imminent and difficult to avoid; if one of these elements is lacking the fear is slight. Fear may be absolutely grave, such as to affect the average person, or it may be relatively grave to a particular person on account of age, infirmity, timidity, or the like. Our main problem is, Are the choices made on account of fear voluntary or involuntary?

The answer is that actions motivated by fear are *voluntary acts and hence are imputable*. The knowledge and freedom sufficient for a human

[2] *De Malo*, 3, 11.

act are present. Thus, to avoid the displeasure of his wife, a man lies about his activities of the night before. Lying is apprehended as the lesser of two evils and is chosen as the efficacious means of avoiding a worse evil. Therefore, it is a truly volitional act and is imputable.

In these choices there is generally a nonvoluntary element, reluctance, an implied or explicit wish that one did not have to do this thing. Thus, to save his property a man perjures himself, reluctantly, wishing some other means were available.

Since the passion and the sentiment of fear often blend together, there is a lessening of responsibility whenever fear excites the mind rendering a calm, reasoned decision difficult.

Although fear is never an excuse to do that which is everywhere and always wrong, nevertheless, fear of extreme evil usually exempts us from immediate compliance with human law for the human legislator is rightly considered as not wishing to impose too grievous a burden. Sometimes, however, the human legislator can demand the heroic: thus even under threat of death, a priest is forbidden to reveal the secrets of the confessional, a captured soldier to betray information vital to the security of his nation. In such instances, however, the human legislator is merely reiterating the prohibition of the Natural Law.

Positive law invalidates or declares rescindable certain acts performed under pressure of grave fear unjustly imposed by some external, rational agent. The reason is not that such acts are not voluntary but that otherwise the law would be approving an injustice and the common good would suffer. Vows, wills, renunciations, and marriages are invalid under these conditions; oaths and many contracts are rescindable.

D. Habit

80. Habit requires a longer explanation than would be feasible here. It is treated in Chapter IX (see § 307). As an obstacle to the human act it operates as does spontaneous passion.

E. Violence

81. Violence is an abuse of force, applied from without and tending to compel a reluctant agent against his choice. No amount of force can directly touch the elicited act of the will. Not even God can force the will and at the same time leave it free. Violence, then, affects our commanded acts, that is, actions of the external faculties, such as being compelled to sign a perjurous affidavit at the point of a gun; or of the imagination and sensitive appetite, such as being tempted by the evil one to commit a sin of thought against one's will.

Two problems at this point arise, responsibility for acts performed under duress and resistance to violence.

Concerning *responsibility* there are three important considerations. First, under any kind of stress one can and always must withhold *internal* consent to what is wrong. Should there be consent, it would be voluntary though with proportionately diminished responsibility. Second, where violence is *irresistible*, neither the moral nor the positive law holds us responsible for the external act. Third, where the external pressure is not *irresistible*, responsibility is diminished in proportion to the force brought to bear and the acquiescence of the will.

Is any *further external resistance* demanded beyond the resistance of the will? (*a*) If the oppressor alone does the wrong and the oppressed is but a spectator, as in a robbery, no resistance is demanded. (*b*) If some passive kind of participation in a wrong act is required of us, we must offer enough resistance to prevent internal consent or obvious scandal. (*c*) If a threat of force is employed to induce one *actively* to perform an act always and everywhere wrong, one may not comply irrespective of the consequence. Thus, prisoners of the N.K.V.D. given a choice between masturbating and a bloody beating had to choose the beating.

READINGS

St. Thomas, *Summa Theologica*, I–II, 6, 8, 9; 12–17; 22–48.
Adler, M., *A Dialectic of Morals*, 12–30. Notre Dame, Review of Politics, 1941.
Aristotle, *Nicomachean Ethics*, III, 1–3.
Arnold-Gasson, *The Human Person*, 462–492. New York, Ronald, 1954.
Black, V., "Good Reasons and Reasonable Acts," *Journal of Philosophy*, 52 (March 31, 1955), 181–189.
Conway, W., "Grave, Unjust and Extrinsic Fear in Canon Law," *Irish Ecclesiastical Record*, 84 (1955), 343–346.
De Letter, P., "Venial Sin and Its Final Goal," *The Thomist*, 16 (1953), 32–70.
Ford, J. C., "Criminal Responsibility in Canon Law and Catholic Thought," *Bulletin of the Guild of Catholic Psychiatrists*, 3 (December, 1955), 3–22.
Gannon, T. J., *Psychology: The Unity of Human Behavior*, 384–409. Boston, Ginn, 1954.
Garrigou-Lagrange, R., *Beatitude*, 133–254. St. Louis, Herder, 1956.
Gilson, E., *Moral Values and the Moral Life*, 52–133. St. Louis, Herder, 1941.
——— *The Christian Philosophy of St. Thomas*, 251–286. New York, Random, 1956.
Holaind, R., *Natural Law and Legal Practice*, 71–94. New York, Benziger, 1899.
Lottin, O., *Morale Fondamentale*, 45–103. Paris, Desclée, 1954.
Lucey, L., "Free Will in Law," *Thought*, 9 (March, 1935), 623–637.

Oppenheim, F. E., "Rational Choice," *Journal of Philosophy*, 50 (June 4, 1953), 341–350.

Renard, H., *The Philosophy of Morality*, 60–193. Milwaukee, Bruce, 1953.

Rimaud, J., "Psychologists vs. Morality," *Cross Currents*, Winter, 1951, 26–38.

Royce, J. E., *Personality and Mental Health*, 207–231. Milwaukee, Bruce, 1954.

Strecker-Appel, *Discovering Ourselves*, 2 ed., 71–196. New York, Macmillan, 1951.

Sullivan, R. P., *Man's Thirst for Good*, Westminster, Newman, 1952.

VanderVeldt-Odenwald, *Psychiatry and Catholicism*, 22–43. New York, McGraw-Hill, 1957.

Chapter IV THE GOOD

82. The first basic question in ethics was concerned with the final end of all human activity, which consists in the endless possession of God through knowledge and love. Now we are asking: What kind of activity will lead man to his final end? We have just seen that this activity consists in what we call human acts. Having described the nature of the human act — the properties which make it specifically human — we turn to its morality or moral aspect. As the voluntary act is *the act* of man, so its morality is its paramount aspect.

What Is Morality?

83. Morality is the relation of the human act to man's absolute value. By absolute we do not mean absolute in itself, as God is absolute, but absolute to man. Up to the present, men have agreed that morality has to do with some absolute value, but the impact of evolutionary doctrine on modern thought has resulted in the denial of all absolute values, especially in the field of morals. Here we are concerned with showing the absurdity of a morality which is ever changing.

84. Since there is an absolute value in human life and since morality is the relation of conduct to that value, we ask what that value is. It must be something which is supreme for man, that for which the whole man exists. Since man is not all-sufficient but a contingent, incomplete intelligence, he exists that he may accomplish some end. Therefore, man's absolute value is that end and his supreme business is directing himself toward it. The word *moral*, then, signifies whatever has a direct bearing on man's perfect happiness, and the moral aspect of his human acts will be the direct relationship of these acts to his final end.

85. Since man is free, he can choose to disregard his end and hence to miss it. His acts, then, can have the quality either of moral rightness if they lead to the end or of moral wrongness if they lead away from the end. The problem, therefore, is, What ultimate principle differentiates between the right act and the wrong act? If a man should actuall

attain his end, the rightness of his conduct would be proved beyond dispute. Now we could know the right way to New York through personal experience or expert instruction. Have we similar knowledge regarding human conduct and attainment of the end? We have not attained the end nor do we know anyone who has. "There speak no voices from the tomb."

86. But even though experiential knowledge is lacking we can solve the problem. For the difference between right and wrong in our acts is revealed by a more fundamental quality of goodness or badness. The right act is good and the wrong act is bad. The reason is this. Since an end is a good, the final end is the supreme and universal good. In every human act we choose a particular partial good or a particular partial evil. If we persevere in choosing partial goods, eventually we reach the supreme good; but if we insist on choosing evil, we must finally miss the supreme good. Hence by choosing a particular partial good we do right and advance toward the final end. Similarly by choosing a particular evil we do wrong and to that extent move from the end or at least fail to advance toward it. Therefore, the problem of differentiating right from wrong becomes the problem of distinguishing between human good and human evil.

87. Hence we raise the all-important question of *what is the ultimate difference between moral good and moral evil?* The answer will be a principle directing us to that which leads to the end and warning us against that which leads away from the end. To give a full answer to the problem which lies at the heart of all ethical speculation, we must give an adequate account of the ethical good. We approach this task by asking: (*I*) What are good and evil *in general?* (*II*) What are good and evil for *man as man?* (*III*) Is the difference between moral good and evil arbitrary or natural? (*IV*) What is the ultimate explanation of moral good? (V) What particular factors determine a human choice to be good or bad? (*VI*) To what things do the designations *good* and *bad* apply?

I. GOOD AND EVIL IN GENERAL

A. The Nature of Good

88. Our exposition of the good is broadly equivalent to what modern authors call axiology, the study of values. A non-Scholastic philosopher asks: "Are values, as distinct from facts, in any sense real or present in the world, and if so, what is their nature and status?" To this clear question his colleagues give hopelessly contradictory answers. First, some say that you cannot know what good as such is.[1] Second, naturalists

[1] Cf. H. D. Aiken, *Ethics*, LXIV, p. 25.

contradict intuitionists. For when naturalists say that good is "some natural quality or relation, such as pleasantness or capacity to arouse and satisfy desire, that can be observed or inferred from experience,"[2] the intuitionist retorts that good is a "non-natural" property which cannot be analyzed or defined but only intuited.[3] Third, when the subjectivist says that good depends entirely upon one's own thought, will, or feelings, he is contradicted by the objectivist who says that good exists independently of the agent's thoughts or feelings.[4] Finally, the logical positivists (who are called emotivists in this context) say that all four of the above-named disputants are wrong in thinking that good is an object of knowledge or that ethical sentences impart meaning. Expressions about the good are merely interjections,[5] imperatives,[6] or gerundives.[7] In this last view, "there is nothing distinctly moral in the world to be cognized,"[8] and one is back to the skeptical opinion of Hume.[9] However much these authors may disagree about their understanding of good, they are united in a common disdain for metaphysics. "Metaphor," says Toulmin, "gives birth to metaphysics."[10] But it is only by recourse to metaphysics that this deadlock can be resolved.

89. Metaphysics, the bedrock of all science, teaches that the good is coterminus with being, that every being is one, true, and good. When we say that a being is one, we look at it in itself and see that it is undivided, just itself. When we say that it is true we look at it in relation to intellect and see that it is intelligible. When we say that it is good we look at it in relation to appetite and see that it is desirable. In this sense all existent beings, from God to the most tenuous particle, are good, both to themselves and to other beings. The goodness of a being, considered without reference to another thing, is its absolute goodness; when we consider it with reference to another thing, we have its relative goodness. Goodness, then, is not something accidental to things and limited to only this or that aspect of reality; like being it transcends all categories.

On the level of created being Aristotle[11] says that the good is that at which all things aim. He means that whenever a being desires, it seeks

[2] P. B. Rice, *On the Knowledge of Good and Evil*, p. 28. New York, Random, 1955.
[3] G. E. Moore, *Principia Ethica*, p. 21. Cambridge, 1956.
[4] Cf. S. Toulmin, *The Place of Reasoning in Ethics*, pp. 9–45. Cambridge, 1953.
[5] A. J. Ayer, *Language, Truth and Logic*, p. 107. London, Gollancz, 1956.
[6] R. Carnap, *Philosophy and Logical Syntax*, p. 24. London, 1935.
[7] S. Toulmin, *op. cit.*, pp. 70–72.
[8] E. W. Hall, *Mind*, Vol. 64, p. 320.
[9] *The Philosophical Works of David Hume*, Vol. IV, pp. 192–193. Edinburgh, 1826.
[10] S. Toulmin, *op. cit.*, p. 116.
[11] *Nicomachean Ethics*, I, 1, 1094a.

only good. Hence the good is what satisfies appetite. Appetite arises because the created being suffers a want: the thing desired is seen as the means of fulfilling this want. The created being suffers want because it does not, at the beginning of its existence, possess the fullness of its well-being; but toward that well-being, as toward its natural end, it moves through the urge of its appetites. It desires its perfection, which consists of all those elements which make it what it is fully capable of being and which render it capable of faultless action proportionate to its place in the hierarchy of being.

90. Goodness, then, is the capability of a given object to satisfy an appetite. But why is this object capable of satisfying appetite? Because it suits the appetent being! There is another universally understood meaning of good, namely, a thing is good if it is well adapted to its purpose. Thus a hammer, sentry, or teacher is good when each satisfactorily fulfills the function of hammer, sentry, or teacher. Since natural beings tend toward an end of completion, they are good insofar as they are adapted toward that end and move toward it. Thus one is a good man if he prepares his being for happiness and advances toward his perfect well-being. "For things directed toward an end are not said to be good except in relation to the end."[12] Incomplete beings naturally seek that which will complete them. These objects of desire, then, are good because their attainment will complete the being. But why can they help the being realize its end? Because they suit the being, they fit in with it. Hence the ultimate explanation why the good is desirable is that it is suitable or fitting to the agent seeking it.

B. The Nature of Evil — privation

91. Evil is understandable only in terms of good, for evil is the lack of goodness or being. It is not, however, a mere lack. If it were, then everything but God would be bad because God alone lacks no reality. Badness, then, is the lack of something which *ought to be present* within the being. A dog is not a bad dog because he cannot speak, but he would be if he could not run. A lawn-mower is a bad lawn-mower if it will not do what it is supposed to do — cut grass. Evil, then, is a privation, the absence of good which ought to be present.

What is this privation of good, an entity or a nonentity? Just as some people erroneously regard moral good as the remote or mystic, so they consider evil a positive thing, something repulsive like a wart or a discolored growth. Inasmuch as evil inheres in some actual being it is said

[12] St. Thomas, *Sum. Theol.*, II–II, 23, 7.

to be positive. But evil as evil — the privation of good — can no more be a positive entity than can a hole in the ground. First, every positive entity is good for the reason that it has real being. Second, if evil were a positive thing, God, who is the cause of all positive beings, would also be the cause of all evil. This conclusion, however, involves God in the contradiction of willing and not willing the same thing under the same aspect.

Evil, the privation of good which ought to be present, is not natural to any being. Evil is brought about by a cause which destroys or hinders some being. But all efficient causes are real beings and, as such, are good. Therefore evil is caused by good but not directly. Only good can be the object of appetite. That which is sought is always good but the production of a particular good may bring with it a privation which is an evil. Thus the cat's dinner is the mouse's death. Evil, then, is sought under the guise of good. Conscious beings seek evil not as evil but as that which appears to be good.

II. THE GOOD AND EVIL OF MAN AS MAN

A. The Good of Man as Man

92. A conscious being can seek some object of desire not only because it is suitable but also because it is pleasant or useful. Hence we distinguish perfective good, delectable good, and useful good.

93. *Perfective good* affords a suitable perfection. It is good in the true and more proper sense because, once it is had, it becomes a perfection of the appetent being. An example of a perfective good is knowledge. It adds more reality to the being and is desirable both for its own sake and because it helps the being to its final end.

The chief perfections of man are his substance with its faculties, his acquired skills, and all activity which enhances his substance, faculties, and skills. His perfective goods or intrinsic values are, therefore, those objects of desire whose attainment will make him a better man: toward them nature gives him a kind of natural inclination. We call them the upright, the righteous, the honorable: they are primarily the ethical good. We should understand that morally we make ourselves by our choices: eventually we become what we choose. For, as St. Thomas says, "Good exists in a thing in so far as that thing is related to the appetite, and hence the aspect of goodness passes on from the desirable thing to the appetite."[13]

---

[13] *Ibid.*, I, 16, 1.

The science of ethics points out what things are choice-worthy and the order and measure in which they are to be sought. The art of ethics makes us skilled in attaining them.

94. In acquiring an object of desire a conscious being experiences satisfaction or delight. On the lowest level this consists in the passing of an appetite from a state of discontent to one of repose. On a higher level this consists in the positive enjoyment of the thing possessed. Satisfaction or delight is also a good because, once it has been experienced, it too becomes an object of desire. We call it *delectable good*, the satisfaction of the conscious appetite in the fulfillment of desire. While it may be sought for itself, it is not good in the same way that perfective good is, for it cannot exist of itself. As a subjective state of the appetent being its existence depends upon possession of some perfective good, real or apparent.

Nature intends perfective good to produce suitable satisfaction and it does so unless the being is distracted by a more powerful delight or dissatisfaction. Delectable good is nature's inducement to conscious beings to seek the fullness of their well-being in their proper perfective goods. Although this good has a worth of its own in that a man should not be without some measure of it, nevertheless, its chief value should be estimated by the object whose possession brings it into existence.

The great problem of delectable good is learning not to make it the chief object of desire. It may not be prized above perfective good. To do so is unreasonable; it is to live by emotion. Delight is only a part of happiness.

95. In seeking true human values we find things which are helpful though not desirable for their own sakes. Their acquisition does not necessarily improve us. They are only instruments. They are *useful goods* and are desired because they are a *means* to what is desirable for its own sake. The useful is good only by extrinsic denomination. Examples of useful goods are money and popularity.

It is a serious error to mistake what is merely useful for what is perfective or to degrade the perfective to the role of the useful.

Delectable and useful goods are ethically good when we consciously seek them in due subordination to perfective good.

96. Crowning all perfective goods is the Supreme Good, which is suitable in the highest degree and which completely satisfies all appetency. The *supreme perfective good* of man is God, knowable, lovable, and glorifiable. The *supreme perfection* of man is his perfect act of intellect and will possessing God. Man's *supreme pleasure* is the delight consequent upon the possession of God.

B. The Evil of Man as Man

To grasp the evil of man as man we must understand the difference between real good and apparent good and between physical evil and moral evil.

97. Since a being can desire only good, and since man has a natural inclination to his proper good, why does not man automatically tend to and attain his supreme good? Unintelligent beings unerringly seek their natural ends and do no wrong because they are directed by an unerring Intelligence. Man, however, directed by his own intelligence, can do wrong because he can mistake *apparent good* for *real good.* This distinction is most important because without it ethics would not exist; there would be no problems of good and evil for man. St. Thomas states the difference between real and apparent good thus: "Just as the end is twofold, the last end, and the proximate end, so also is good twofold, one, the ultimate and universal good, the other proximate and particular. The ultimate and principal good of man is the enjoyment of God. . . . Man's secondary and, as it were, particular good may be twofold: one is truly good, because, considered in itself, it can be directed to the principal good which is the last end; while the other is good apparently and not truly, because it leads away from the last end."[14] Real good perfects the whole being as such: it is suitable to a unitary nature or to a faculty duly subordinated to that nature. Although apparent good is an object of desire, it does not perfect the whole being. It is indeed suitable to some faculty of man, but not as that faculty is duly subordinated to man's unitary nature. Thus, to sing perfects a man vocally. If the song is praise of God, the whole man is perfected; if the song is lewd, the whole man is hurt.

98. But man's evil arises not only from mistakes of intellect but especially from wrong choices of the will. In these alone do we find moral evil which is quite different from physical evil. *Physical evil* is the privation of a natural good in a unitary being. In man it is some lack of physical or psychic completeness like death, pain, disease, loss of limb. *Moral evil,* which can be wrought only by an intelligent being, is the privation of goodness in human acts. Since the good of an incomplete being is found in its operations, so also is its evil. Hence the evil of man as man consists in no defect of his physical or psychic being but in a defect in his voluntary choices. This defect is lack of rectitude; the evil act cannot lead to the last end. Nevertheless, this is not an ultimate explanation. What we must determine is *why* some acts have rectitude

[14] *Sum. Theol.,* II–II, 23, 7.

and why others lack it. The answer lies partially in Section III where we ask whether the difference between moral good and evil is natural or arbitrary; it is found more fully developed in Section IV where we state the ultimate difference between good and evil.[15]

III. IS THE DIFFERENCE BETWEEN MORAL GOOD AND EVIL NATURAL?

A. Moral Positivism

99. The difference between moral good and evil is natural if it derives from the nature of things so that this act is good and that bad whether one wishes they were or not. Just as a circle is what it is not by the choice of anyone, so a good act is good not because someone has labeled it good but because the eternal fitness of things makes it so. The difference between good and evil is arbitrary if it depends on someone's free choice and designation. The system which rejects a natural difference is Moral Positivism, which may be viewed as Classical Positivism, Naturalism, and Logical Positivism.

---

[15] Although we do not substitute "value" for "good," we should give a brief explanation of the terminology of the Value-Theorists. They say that value, in general, is that which is significant or preferable — that which we want. Value is had by one's personal response to experience. The noun "value" is both abstract and concrete. The abstract noun means goodness, the quality of being choice-worthy. Its opposite is often called "disvalue." Sometimes value is made to include both good and evil. Then good is positive value and evil is negative value.

The concrete "value" is, first, a pleasing emotion or satisfactory reaction to experience. According to some authors, value is nothing but a subjective state. Russell opines that " 'values' lies wholly outside the domain of knowledge. That is to say, when we assert that this or that has 'value,' we are giving expression to our emotions, not to a fact which would still be true if our personal feelings were different." This value resembles delectable good. Most moderns, however, are beginning to reject the ethical skepticism which results from Russell's doctrine and are asserting objective values — existent things which are 'good reasons' which should guide our choices. They distinguish intrinsic values — things desirable for their own sake (perfective goods) — from extrinsic or instrumental values (pure means). The chief values are utility, beauty, meaning, validity, truth, health, play and social, moral and religious values. The all-inclusive value is moral whose highest type is religious value.

Furthermore, value is used in two contrasts. In one, it is the assertion of value which differentiates the value judgment from the factual statement. Hence value represents that which ought to be as opposed to that which is. The second contrast is made by the Deontologists who rigidly distinguish good from right. They associate good with value, right with obligation, but deny that value belongs to ethics.

The verb "value" means either the act of evaluating or a habitual attitude of valuing.

The criterion of value varies with the philosophical system. It may be quantity of pleasure for the individual or the group, biological survival, insight into preference, a system of ideal norms. The problem is the same as our problem of the norm of morals. *Vide infra*, §§ 111 ff.

100. 1. According to *Classical Positivism* moral differences depend either upon the sole will of God, or the law of the State, or the customs of people. Ockham,[16] Gerson,[17] and Pufendorf[18] taught that there is no intrinsic necessity why one act should be good and another bad: God's good pleasure decides. Descartes piously avers that just as the three angles of a triangle equal two right angles for the sole reason that God wants it that way, so all moral distinctions depend on His arbitrary will.[19] Following the lead of Kierkegaard but drawing their original inspiration from Luther and Calvin, some Protestant theologians, like Barth[20] and Brunner[21] in Switzerland, Heim in Germany, Niebuhr[22] and Tillich in the United States, teach that the basis of the good is simply and solely the will of God. It is wrong to say that anything can be good in itself because all goodness and all essences are the product of the divine will which man can know only in part. Hence human ethics is at sixes and sevens because the will of God cannot be captured and fitted into general principles. Consequently a man cannot know anything to be right or wrong except that which God approves or disapproves for him in this particular time, place, and circumstance. "God establishes the order of good and evil — and breaks through it where He wishes, and does so from person to person."[23]

Hobbes put the origin of morality in civil authority,[24] saying that right and wrong do not exist before civil law determines them.[25] For Rousseau, the social contract is the source of morality.[26]

According to Comte ethics is but the record of how men actually conduct themselves.[27] As the physical scientist examines the phenomena of nature to discover the physical laws of nature, so by a like objective study of human behavior the moralist arrives at the generalizations which

---

16 *Super IV libros senteniarum*, Lib. II, q. 19, ad 3 dubium.

17 *Tertia pars operum Joannis de Gerson*, LXI, E and F.

18 *De jure et gentium*, Lib. I, c. 2, § 6.

19 *Meditationes de prima philosophia*, "Appendix continens objectiones, etc.," Resp. VI, n. 6 et 8.

20 Karl Barth, "The Problem of Ethics Today," in *The Word of God and the Word of Man*, tr. Horton, pp. 136 ff. London, Pilgrim Press, 1928.

21 Emil Brunner, *The Divine Imperative*, tr. O. Wyon, p. 111 ff. Phila., Westminster Press, 1947.

22 Reinhold Niebuhr, *An Interpretation of Christian Ethics*, pp. 43–62. New York, Living Age, 1956.

23 Martin Buber, "The Suspension of Morals," *Moral Principles of Action*, p. 223, ed. by Ruth Anshen. New York, Harper, 1952.

24 *Leviathan*, Chap. XIII. Molesworth's English edition, Vol. III, p. 115.

25 *Ibid.*, pp. 157–158.

26 J. J. Rousseau, *The Social Contract*, p. 18. London, Dent, 1935.

27 L. Levy-Bruhl, *The Philosophy of Auguste Comte*, tr. F. Harrison, p. 307. New York, Putnam, 1903.

are moral laws. These generalizations will fluctuate from generation to generation because morality derives from practice and custom. "Custom," says Paulsen, "forms the original content of duty."[28] There are only mores — moral laws founded on metaphysics are an offense to modern enlightenment.

Comte and Durkheim[29] make ethics a branch of sociology. Following the master's lead, Nordau says: "If the individual had been able to live alone morality could never have come into being. The concepts of Good and Bad characterize those actions which society feels to be beneficial or harmful to itself."[30]

Mores arise, says Westermarck,[31] from the emotions of the group. Hence the *Encyclopedia of Social Sciences* defines morals as "the sum of taboos and prescriptions in the folkways. . . . Right conduct is what the group approves of, wrong conduct what the group disapproves of."[32]

Positivism is clearly relativistic, as Levy-Bruhl placidly confesses: "Being positive, this morality will be relative."[33] One prize-winning author[34] calls ethics *parontology* (from *παρῶν*, "to become") — the science of things that are about to be. The smart ethician is the one who best predicts the shape of the new mores.

101. 2. *Naturalism* holds that the visible world is the whole of reality, that it has no ultimate explanation, that freedom, purpose, or transcendental destiny do not exist within the course of nature. Naturalists espouse empiricism — the epistemology which has come down from Hume — assert that knowledge is limited to experience, and deny the existence of absolute truths. Hence moral phenomena are purely natural phenomena and ethics is a positive science whose sources are observation and introspection. Ethical goodness is a natural physical property inherent in some object and of the same type as color, shape, or feeling. It is called the V-property by naturalists who, however, disagree as to what constitutes the V-property. Some hold an affective or subjectivistic theory; others, a conative or objectivistic theory. According to the first explanation good is physiological, the pleasant titillation of nerves. Prall

[28] F. Paulsen, *A System of Ethics*, tr. Thilly, Vol. I, p. 345. New York, Scribners, 1903.

[29] Emile Durkheim, "Determination du fait moral," *Bulletin de la Societé française de philosophie*, Vol. VI, pp. 113–212, 1906.

[30] Max Nordau, *Morals and the Evolution of Man*, p. 83. New York, Funk & Wagnalls, 1922.

[31] Edward Westermarck, *The Origin and Development of Moral Ideas*, Vol. I, pp. 5–20; Vol. II, p. 738. London, Macmillan, 1912.

[32] "Morals," Vol. X, p. 643, reissue of 1937.

[33] *The Philosophy of Auguste Comte*, p. 307.

[34] Henry Lanz, *In Quest of Morals*, p. 163 ff. Stanford, Stanford University Press, 1941.

says: "Values are based on nothing deeper or more fundamental, nothing more absolute and eternal, than just the nature of our motor-affective apparatus."[35] Being scientific, this kind of naturalist tries to find physical or chemical processes going on in an agent's body with which he may identify ethical goodness. A slightly different variant is that morals is a matter of personal taste or preference. Santayana says: "The ultimate intuitions on which ethics rests . . . are not opinions we hazard but preferences we feel."[36] The present tendency, however, is that for occurrent feelings, which are transient, one should substitute attitudes or permanent likes and dislikes.

Akin to the affective theory and yet partaking in the objectivistic view is the interest theory. Value is "that special character of an object which consists in the fact that interest is taken in it,"[37] says Perry. And interest is "a state, act, attitude or disposition of favor or disfavor,"[38] explainable in behavioristic terms. Value becomes moral good when it is integrated with all of one's interests and with those of the community. According to Parker good "is the satisfaction of any interest in any object."[39] Hence the supreme good is the harmonious satisfaction of all of one's desires. The doctrine means that things are good because we want them and bad because we dislike them.[40] Insofar as an object is made good by the agent's feeling concerning it the interest theory is subjectivistic.

Many naturalists, however, think that the founding of goodness on feeling or attitude is too slippery a basis to make their theory scientific. Hence, in place of an affective theory, they hold a conative theory according to which good is a function of striving. Good is whatever I should bring into being. Some say that conduct is good when it maintains accord with the cosmic process;[41] others, when it advances organic evolution;[42] or when it advances the life-process or the will to live.[43] James says the good is that which works, that is, helps the ongoing social process.[44]

102. The *Pragmatism* of James was developed by Dewey into *Instru-*

---

[35] D. W. Prall, *A Study in the Theory of Value*, p. 269. Berkeley, 1921.
[36] G. Santayana, *Winds of Doctrine*, p. 144. New York, Scribners, 1926.
[37] R. B. Perry, *General Theory of Value*, p. 116. New York, Longmans, 1926.
[38] *Ibid.*, p. 115.
[39] D. H. Parker, *Human Values*, p. 21. New York, Harper, 1931.
[40] J. L. Mothershead, *Ethics*, pp. 92–93. New York, Holt, 1955.
[41] O. Stapledon, *A Modern Theory of Ethics*, 224 ff. London, Methuen, 1929.
[42] C. H. Waddington, *Ethics and Science*. London, Allen & Unwin, 1942.
[43] A. Schweitzer, *Civilization and Ethics*, p. 244. London, Black, 1929.
[44] William James, "The Moral Philosopher and the Moral Life," *Essays on Faith and Morals*. New York, Longmans, 1947.

mentalism. A judgment of value is a prediction about the future enjoyability of given objects. The good satisfies a need and gives a satisfactory result; for "the hypothesis that works is the true one."[45] When Dewey says, "This course of action is good," he means that it has been found enjoyable in the past and people expect it to be satisfactory in the future. The proposition, however, is only a generalization; for one may apply it to a new situation and find it bad. In that event one makes a reappraisal either of the goal he has in mind or of the means selected to achieve the goal. All doctrines are man-made and of no eternal value. A doctrine is an instrument for the improvement of life and when one fails to work, you drop it and try to forge a more suitable tool. The needs and desires which a doctrine should satisfy are both personal and public. Obsessed with the idea that man and his situation always changes, the instrumentalist holds that ethical rules are the result of trial and error and merely the techniques which a civilization has adopted to solve its particular problems. Moral good, then, is that which the men of this place and time have rightly or wrongly thought would benefit them; that which in the long run produces the greatest enjoyment by resolving social tensions.

103. 3. *Logical Positivism* quickly disposes of our problem by saying it is a bogus problem. To discuss the difference between right and wrong is meaningless because ethical concepts cannot be verified; they tell us nothing of the world of experience. We cannot talk of ethical norms because value or normative statements "have no objective validity whatever. If a sentence makes no statement at all, there is obviously no sense in asking whether it is true or false. And we have seen that sentences which express moral judgments do not say anything at all. They are pure expressions of feeling and as such do not come under the category of truth or falsehood. They are unverifiable for the same reason as a cry of pain or a command is unverifiable — because they do not express genuine propositions."[46]

B. Rejection of Moral Positivism

104. 1. The *Logical Positivism* which denies the present problem on the alleged grounds that ethical proposition can neither be true nor false is moral nihilism. Reichenbach frankly admits: "The desire to establish moral directives by an act of moral cognition appears understandable;

[45] John Dewey, *Reconstruction in Philosophy*, p. 156. New York, Holt, 1920.
[46] A. J. Ayer, *Language, Truth and Logic*, 2nd ed., pp. 108–109. London, Gollancz, 1956.

but the scientific philosopher must forego the quest for moral guidance."[47] This assertion is contradicted by a universally verifiable desire on the part of man for moral knowledge. So universal an instinct cannot be in vain. There must be moral knowledge. Furthermore, these exaggerations exclude "not only moral, aesthetic, metaphysical, religious, and all other statements involving introspection but also statements in terms of which in the last analysis the findings of science must be verified."[48] Finally, such skepticism repudiates man's rational nature according to which choice follows knowledge. For this doctrine says that in his most important choices man can never *know* whether he is right or wrong. Hence, for man no real difference between right and wrong exists and morally he is no different from a beast.

105. 2. The *Naturalist* is wrong in general when he accepts the universe and says one cannot explain it; when he denies freedom, finality, and the supernatural; when he adopts an epistemology which rules out the existence of God. In particular, the subjectivist banishes reason from morality when he makes its basis personal feeling or attitude. By saying that there are as many moralities as there are individuals, this doctrine denies the unity of the human race and makes social life unending conflict. The objectivist errs when he says the basis of morality is the cosmic process, or evolution, or life. For, since the human act is peculiar to man alone, the criterion of its goodness should be that which is peculiar to man and to no other being.

106. As for *Instrumentalism,* we admit that it is only the truth which in the long run works but we may not say that that which works is true. The instrumentalist either gives an ultimate explanation of moral good or he does not. If he does not, one must seek it outside of Instrumentalism. If he does, and in reality he attempts to do so, then his definition of moral good is unsatisfactory. For if he says with the utilitarian that the good is the enjoyable, there remains the more ultimate question, But why is it good to seek the enjoyable? If he says that human welfare decides, then one must ask him, In what does human welfare consist? If he judges the goodness of human acts by their consequences, he should have an exact idea of what these consequences should be. In some phases of behavior like eating and the relief of bad pain we have immediate perception of what a good result is but in the total field of human choices how do we know from the data of instrumentalism what are suitable results?

107. 3. All forms of positivism are rejected in the following thesis.

[47] Hans Reichenbach, *The Rise of Scientific Philosophy*, pp. 305–306. Berkeley, University of California, 1951.

[48] T. E. Hill, *Contemporary Ethical Theories*, p. 28.

THESIS VII. There is a natural difference between moral good and moral evil.

Some acts are such that of themselves they must always and everywhere be suitable or unsuitable for men. They are good or evil in themselves. Their goodness or badness comes from no factor external to them but solely from the fact that in themselves they promote or defeat a human end. They do so from their nature. Therefore nature draws the line between moral good and evil.

We do not say that every good act is intrinsically good and every bad act intrinsically evil. There is an extrinsic source of morality but it is not the fundamental source. An act or omission may be wrong because the law forbids it, for example, failure to report income. Remove the law and the omission is no longer wrong. But there are some acts which would always be good, though no positive law commanded them; and others would still be wrong, even though no positive law forbade them.

108. Since positivism is really repudiation of the human intellect, the indirect refutation of this doctrine is the assertion of the full function of the intellect to possess abstract knowledge, the demonstration that there are essences, natures, universal ideas, and propositions universally valid. Positivism cannot remain a part of philosophy because it is denial of philosophy. Fortunately, "The positivistic approach to knowledge has been rotting from the top, losing self-confidence."[49] However, the news of the decline of positivism has not yet penetrated to the social sciences or to all classrooms.

PROOFS

109. 1. There is a universal conviction among men that certain acts, such as parricide, mass murder of the innocent, cruely for cruelty's sake, are always and everywhere wrong; that other acts, such as filial reverence, mercy to the afflicted, fidelity to one's word, are always and everywhere good.[50] Now a universal and constant effect demands a cause equally universal and constant. The only cause as universal and constant as these effects is a common human nature revealing a common goodness or badness in these acts. What is always and everywhere adjudged good or evil cannot be attributed to convention but to the nature of things.

2. If custom, law, or the arbitrary will of God were the origin of moral differences, they could make that which is forbidden permissible

---

[49] *Time*, March 9, 1953, p. 60.

[50] Cicero, *De Finibus*, Bk. V, c. 22; *De Lege*, Bk. I, cc. 10–11.

and forbid that which is now commanded. But certain acts, like lying, theft, and murder must always be forbidden; certain commanded acts like obedience to proper authority, reverence to parents, help to the needy can never be forbidden. If such a reversal were made human life would become impossible. Since certain actions are necessary to a human existence, law makes them obligatory; since certain others make a human existence impossible, law forbids them and not vice versa. No custom, not even God, can make what is destructive of human ends obligatory or even permissible. Therefore, moral differences arise not from convention but from the nature of things.

110. Corollary I. *Some actions, independently of any will, human or divine are of their very nature morally good or bad.*

Corollary II. *There is an unchanging difference between moral good and evil because of the nature of things.*

N.B. I. Not all morality is intrinsic. Much is extrinsic, based on precept but this is valid only inasmuch as it is derived from principles eternally true (cf. § 238 ff.).

N.B. II. People's ideas on certain moral issues may change:[51] (*a*) One generation may erroneously look upon card playing, horse racing, gambling, dancing, drinking, and the like as *totally* wrong. A subsequent generation repudiates this view. (*b*) Social custom may change that which constitutes a proximate occasion of sin. Thus a manner of dress, provocative when first introduced, may cease to allure when people have grown used to it. (*c*) Genuine ill will, followed by a wish to justify one's wrongdoing, will sanction as right what is truly wrong as is seen in the modern approval of divorce.

IV. THE NORM OF MORALS

111. Since the basic difference between moral good and evil is natural, we seek the natural thing which causes the difference. This will necessarily be the norm of morals. A norm is a rule of measurement, an authoritative standard. In the National Bureau of Standards there is a bar of platinum-iridium which is the standard for all linear measurements. Objective standards exist for judging aesthetic, athletic, literary, military performance: *a fortiori* moral standards exist. The norm of morals then is that to which we compare the human act to see if it is good or bad.

Before proceeding to identify this norm, we must first deal with a view which discards the notion of a norm on the grounds that we do

[51] Cf. Roger Burlingame, *The American Conscience*. New York, Knopf, 1957.

not compare the human act with any objective standard: we just look at it, and immediately we see or feel whether it is good or bad. Thus intuitionism.

A. Intuitionism

112. Shaftesbury (1671–1713) said that moral acts are sentiments or emotional tendencies to good or evil. We differentiate between them by means of a moral sense, innate but distinct from reason. "Sense of right and wrong therefore being as natural to us as natural affection, and being a first principle in our constitution and make-up there is no speculative opinion, persuasion or belief, which is capable immediately or directly to exclude or destroy it."[52]

Subsequent writers explain the moral sense in various ways. Rousseau said it is the heart: we distinguish right from wrong by sensible attraction to the good and sensible aversion from evil.[53] Herbart[54] said it is a kind of moral taste: ethics is a branch of aesthetics. Reid calls it "an original faculty" whereby "we perceive certain things to be right, others to be wrong."[55] This intuitive perception operates like our senses so that our moral sense distinguishes right from wrong in much the same way as vision knows red from blue or taste tells bitter from sweet. "All moral reasoning rests upon one or more first principles of morals, whose truth is immediately perceived without reasoning."[56]

Without assuming a specific moral faculty, Adam Smith[57] held a theory of moral sentiments. Morality is propriety or the fitting of sentiment and emotion to all situations of life. The propriety of one's conduct is measured by sympathy[58] so that those acts which evoke sympathy and approbation are good; those which arouse antipathy and condemnation are bad. However, since those who may judge the value of actions may be prejudiced, and since the danger of prejudice is greatest when one evaluates his own actions, Smith appeals to the disinterested spectator. Hence his axiom, Always act in such a way that the impartial onlooker can sympathize with, and approve of, you. From this position it was an easy step to the view that public sentiment or Mrs. Grundy is the basis of morals. Victorian Mrs. Grundy survives in the phrase, "What will the neighbors think?"

---

[52] *Characteristicks of Men, Manners, Opinions, Times*, Vol. II, p. 44.
[53] *Emile*, tr. Foxley, pp. 250–252. New York, Dutton, 1933.
[54] Johann F. Herbart, *Sämmtliche Werke*, Vol. 8, 4–212. Leipsic, 1851.
[55] Thomas Reid, *Essays on the Active Powers of the Human Mind*, p. 236. Edinburgh, Bell, 1788.
[56] *The Works of Thomas Reid*, Vol. I, p. 481. Edinburgh, 1863.
[57] *The Theory of Moral Sentiments*, pp. 479–480. London, Bell, 1880.
[58] *Ibid.*, pp. 4, 205–206.

According to G. E. Moore, the banner-bearer of modern intuitionism, it is foolish to seek a single criterion of right and wrong before we "first know what things are right and wrong."[59] These we know by intuition. The essential concept of ethics is intrinsic value or that which ought to exist for its own sake. But this is indefinable for " 'good' is a simple notion, just as yellow is a simple notion . . . just as you cannot explain to anyone who does not know what yellow is, so you cannot explain what good is."[60] His ethical system rests on principles which are incapable of being established inferentially.

According to Max Scheler, the phenomenologist of the Husserl school, notions of right and good are "irreducible phenomena of emotional intuition."[61] We do not need a norm of morals because an act has either a negative (evil) or positive (good) value, which one immediately sees, not by an operation of intellect, but by an emotional act of "value-appreciation."[62] A similar operation recognizes an objective hierarchy of values, which, like the difference of negative and positive values, is found by comparing the values among themselves and not by measuring them against an abstract norm of goodness. For the making of such evaluations there is present an "intuitive 'preference-evidence' for which no logical deduction can be substituted."[63]

113. Criticism. Since certain aspects of morality are very evident, one can see why some men claim to have intuition of them; but it does not follow that these things cannot be justified by reason. Furthermore, since the moral act is *the* act of man, there is little wonder that it is accompanied by emotion, but to say that this act is all emotion and that morality stems from emotion is denial of man's nature according to which appetite should follow reason.

Concerning any type of intuitionism, we hold that the existence of a moral sense distinct from reason is gratuitously asserted.

The older type of intuitionism is pure subjectivism. For if the ultimate explanation of a good act is that it affects one's moral sense in a favorable way, there can be no verification of the correctness or incorrectness of a feeling. Hence the same objections which were brought against subjective naturalism are valid against this position (cf. § 105).

A false impression is given by the modern intuitionists when they say we have an immediate intuition of value. While we have an immediate

59 *Principia Ethica*, p. 223. Cambridge University Press, 1956.

60 *Ibid.*, p. 7.

61 *Der Formalismus in der Ethik und die materiale Wertethik*, 4th ed., p. 278. Bern, Franke, 1954.

62 *Ibid.*, pp. 88, 188–190.

63 *Ibid.*, p. 87.

intuition of psychological states which are pleasing or displeasing, we do not have intuition of what is morally right and wrong. This we learn from instruction and experience. Instruction calls for norms and norms must be validated by reason. While it is sensible procedure in any science to accept first principles as self-evident, nevertheless, these principles must somewhere be shown by reason to be noncontradictory. Such is the function of metaphysics. We do not deny, however, that after one is experienced and well instructed he can, in obvious matters, make intuitive judgments of right and wrong.

Since intuitionism is too naïve an account of basic morals, there must be a norm and the central problem in any ethical theory will always be: what is the thing to which we compare the human act in order to discover if it is good or bad. The outstanding answers to this question are now set forth.

B. Utilitarianism

114. Utilitarianism holds that the morality of an act consists in its utility to serve as a means to some end.[64] This system, first, denies the distinction among perfective, delectable, and useful goods. Bentham says: "Pleasure is . . . the only good; pain is . . . the only evil."[65] Second, the vast majority of utilitarianists hold that the end is some kind of temporal happiness. Hence those acts are good which conduce to the attainment of temporal well-being; those are bad which hinder it. Two types of utilitarianism are distinguished: individual (hedonism) and social (altruism).

115. Hedonism. The norm is the greatest pleasure of the individual which may range from purely sensual pleasure to the delight consequent upon possession of God.

Democritus (460–370 B.C.) taught that delight (εὐθαμία) is the highest good. This he identified with equable and imperturbed temper of mind (συμμετρία) to be obtained by moderation of desire. Aristippus (435–354 B.C.) held that the supreme good is the present pleasure of the body. Epicurus (341–270 B.C.) taught that no pleasure is to be foregone except for its painful consequences and no pain to be suffered except as a means to greater pleasure. However, the pains and pleasures of the mind are more important than those of the body. The wise man is he who strikes a true balance of pleasure over pain by keeping his mind free from disturbing fears for the future. This thought Horace re-echoes in his *nil admirari*.

---

[64] Cf. John Stuart Mill, *Utilitarianism*, pp. 9–10.

[65] Jeremy Bentham, *Principles of Morals and Legislation*, p. 102. Oxford, Clarendon, 1907.

Hobbes was the first great Christian writer to revive the pagan concept of the good. "Everyman, for his part, calleth that which pleaseth and is delightful to himself, good; and that evil which displeaseth."[66] The encyclopedists, Diderot[67] and Helvetius;[68] the materialists, Holbach and Feuerbach,[69] revived the doctrines of Aristippus in a stark, crude form. The advice of Holbach on how to choose among pleasures and how to give passion its head is worthy of Lucretius Caro, the Epicurean. Drake told his students at Vassar: "To men everywhere it feels bad to be in severe physical pain. . . . It feels good to taste an appetizing dish. . . . All differences in value, including all moral distinctions, rest upon this disparity in the immediate worth of conscious states."[70]

116. Altruism. Actions are good or bad insofar as they advance or impede the happiness of society. Pufendorf taught that God gave man the kind of nature He pleased.[71] God laid on man, as the supreme law of his nature, sociability:[72] what conforms to this prescription is good; what contravenes it is bad. According to Bentham[73] and Mill,[74] an act is good insofar as it promotes the greatest amount of pleasure for the greatest number of people (and animals too!). Comte, who coined the word "altruism" from the Provençal, *altrui*, "other," demands such devotion to neighbor and humanity that we cease to love ourselves. One's egotistic acts, if not bad, are at least amoral. "Live for others"[75] was his supreme motto. Wundt[76] maintains that the end of human acts is the progress of culture; hence only the act which advances culture is good. Marxism goes by this norm: whatever advances world-wide revolution is good; whatever retards it is bad. The evolutionist, Spencer,[77] attempted to reconcile egoism with altruism by his doctrine of sympathy, which today has passed into the limbo of forgotten theories.

Schopenhauer said this world is the worst conceivable and the best we can achieve is the absence of pain. As misery is only increased by progress the end of life is a kind of Nirvana or cessation from desire. "Peace, Rest and Bliss dwell only where there is no where and no

---

66 *Human Nature*, Ch. VII, 3. Molesworth's English edition, Vol. IV, p. 32.

67 *Oeuvres de Denis Diderot*, "Pensées Philosophiques," Tome I, 197–278.

68 *De L'esprit*, pp. 99–113. Paris, Lavigne, 1845.

69 Ludwig Feuerbach, *The Essence of Christianity*.

70 Durant Drake, *Problems of Conduct*, 75–76. Boston, Houghton Mifflin, 1935.

71 *De Jure Naturae et Gentium*, Lib. I, c. II, p. 18.

72 *Ibid.*, Lib. II, c. III, 15, pp. 142–144.

73 *Morals and Legislation*, pp. 2, 310.

74 *Utilitarianism*, p. 17.

75 L. Levy-Bruhl, *The Philosophy of Auguste Comte*, p. 319.

76 Wilhelm Wundt, *The Principles of Morality and Departments of Moral Life*, tr. Flag-Washburn, p. 90. London, Swann Sonnenschein, 1901.

77 Herbert Spencer, *Data of Ethics*, pp. 244–257.

when."[78] He conceived two levels of morality. One is ordinary virtue, built upon sympathy, whose purpose is to diminish suffering by compassion. However, in ordinary sympathetic conduct some trace of the fundamental error of the will to persist as an individual remains. Hence one does not rise to the truest reaches of morality until he shall have achieved complete self-mortification.[79] Only thus does one see through the delusions of individuality and so be absorbed in the Supreme Will which is the sole reality.

117. **Criticism.** Utilitarianism is correct in saying that a good act will lead to happiness but its notion of happiness is false.

1. Its fundamental error is misconception of man's end. Utilitarianists hold either the "happiness now" theory or the theory that the individual or humanity is an end in itself.

2. Its second error is confusion of useful, delectable, and perfective. The delectable is only part of happiness: good and useful are not synonymous.

3. It establishes a norm which is inconstant and variable. However, to be reliable, the standard whereby other things are measured should itself be unchanging. A variable standard is no standard. The heirs of utilitarianism admit that moral values and standards are in a state of perpetual flux but a relativistic, ever changing morality is absurd.

C. Kant's Autonomous Reason

118. According to Kant there is a moral law, inspiring as the starry heavens and independent of any nonhuman lawgiver. This law consists of dictates of the Practical Reason — categorical imperatives — whereby one must do this and avoid that. Reflecting on these imperatives, Kant found in them the notes of universality and necessity. Whence do these come? Not from outside me, thought Kant, because outside me all things are singular and contingent. Therefore, they come from my rational nature as such. Since these categorical imperatives cannot be subordinated to anything outside man, Kant called them autonomous. Man has his own law within himself and is an end unto himself.[80] In Kant's view, God exists not as supreme lawgiver and judge of human conduct but as a kind of Divine Atlas, propping up the universe and making it go, so that those who obey the dictates of the Autonomous Reason may have their happiness.[81]

---

[78] Arthur Schopenhauer, *Parerga und Paralipomena*, Vol. II, p. 46. Berlin, 1862.

[79] *The World as Will and Idea* in Durant's edition of *The Works of Schopenhauer*, p. 238. Garden City, 1928.

[80] *Critique of Practical Reason*, trans. Abbott, p. 229.

[81] *Ibid.*, p. 222.

Do these dictates of reason form the norm? Not quite. The one rational thing which is simply good is good will. The will is simply good not through what it effects nor through its fitness for any given goal but when through willing it is *good in itself*.[82] It becomes such, materially, when one wills what duty prescribes. But this is not enough for one may will what the law prescribes out of natural inclination or expectation of personal advantage. The morally determining element of the will, then, is its motive. The will act is simply good when its motive is solely that of duty done for duty's sake. Now duty is the necessity of acting from respect for the law.[83] Law and law alone should determine the will. Neither this nor that particular prescription of law but law in general — this alone is to serve the will as principle.[84]

How, finally, does one determine that a given act possesses this required conformity to law? Only when one's motive for acting can be converted into a law for all rational beings. Therefore, Kant frames this most fundamental of all imperatives: So act that thy maxim may become a universal law. This is the source of all particular imperatives. He illustrates his principle by promise breaking and lying which must be wrong because one could never will that his motive (to extricate himself from a difficulty by a lying promise) should ever become a law for all men.[85] Such a law would be self-defeating.

119. Criticism. 1. Kant's description of a good will is incomplete if he means to exclude from the category of good all acts which aim at a result to be effected or an advantage to be gained. What he is trying to say is that a will act can be good even if the effect it seeks is not accomplished. The will is good whenever it seeks a good object (§ 132). A good object certainly may be the effecting of a desirable result, for example, regaining the favor of God. Nor are all acts which seek an advantage for the agent outside the sphere of the morally good. While most self-love is reprehensible, there is a reasonable self-love.[86] Thus, to repent of one's sins out of fear of hell is good.

2. Surely duty done for duty's sake is noble, but we cannot admit that only such acts are good. There are higher motives than duty. Kant fails to distinguish good that we must do from good that we are counseled to do. We are seldom obliged to do the heroic, but whoever, through the pure love of God, does the heroic over and above the call of duty assuredly does what is good. Such an act is better than one done for duty's sake. It is possible to transcend duty. No one would claim that a

---

[82] *Ibid.*, p. 10.
[83] *Ibid.*, p. 16.
[84] *Ibid.*, p. 18.
[85] *Ibid.*, p. 19.
[86] Cf. Aristotle, *Ethics*, IX, 8, 1168b. Cf. *infra*, § 334 ff.

girl is obliged to surrender her earthly prospects to devote herself to the service of the aged poor but all mankind would call her act good.

3. Kant's ultimate criterion of goodness, namely, Act only on that maxim whereby thou canst at the same time will that it should become a universal law, does not fit all cases. From his examples of deceitful promises and suicide we gather that each moral law must be self-consistent, applicable to human nature as such, and hence that reasonableness is the soul of morality. To that one can agree. But the Kantian criterion has universal application only if *all good is obligatory.* When we apply it to works of supererogation it becomes absurd. A man could will to quit society for the sake of divine contemplation but he could not will that all men do the same. One may virtuously choose to be celibate but a universal law of celibacy would be evil. Simeon Stylites sitting on his pillar was an object of awe and veneration but it would be impossible for everyone to imitate him. These courses of action are morally good but only on condition that they do not become universal laws.

4. Have the dictates of the practical reason objective validity? Since they are offered as embodiments of reasonableness, and as reasonableness to be such must be valid for all rational beings, they appear to be objective. Kant says they are valid for all men.[87] He deduces them from the autonomy of the will, and freedom, he says, is the key which explains the will's autonomy.[88] The freedom of the will, the immortality of the soul, and the existence of God are postulates of Kant's practical reason. What Kant calls practical reason is the will[89] demanding obedience to moral law: what we call intellect, he calls the speculative reason. Kant denies that his postulates are known by the speculative reason. "The above three ideas of speculative reason are still not in themselves cognitions."[90] If there be any reality behind them we do not know and cannot know. He plainly says: "How a categorical imperative is possible can be answered to this extent that we can assign the only hypothesis on which it is possible, namely, the idea of freedom . . . but how this hypothesis itself is possible can never be discerned by any human reason."[91]

If, then, the dictates of the practical reason are deduced from the freedom of the will, and if the intellect cannot validate the freedom of the will, how can these dictates be validated? If the basis on which they rest are unprovable assumptions, why are not also they?

The root of the difficulty is Kant's epistemology, according to which the intellect can know only the appearances of things, the phenomena, but it can never penetrate to the thing as such, the noumenon.[92] As a

[87] *Ibid.*, p. 105.
[88] *Ibid.*, p. 65.
[89] *Ibid.*, p. 60.
[90] *Ibid.*, p. 232.
[91] *Ibid.*, pp. 81–82.
[92] *Ibid.*, p. 70.

consequence, Kant has handed on a God-idea which is only a hollow shell, the content of which is whatever anyone chooses to make of it. He has done the same for moral principles.

D. Is the Norm Man's Last End?

120. Some Scholastic authors[93] say that since a good act leads to man's last end, the last end is the norm of goodness. The argument may be put in the following syllogism:

Human acts are means to the ultimate end.
But means derive their goodness from the ultimate end.
Therefore human acts derive their goodness from the ultimate end.

That human acts are means arbitrarily chosen to the end, we deny. That good human acts are such that of their very nature they must be chosen as means to the end, we admit. Applying the distinction to the minor premise, we admit that means arbitrarily chosen derive their goodness from the end, for example, a proper ticket with relation to admission to a game; but we deny that those things which must be chosen as means derive their goodness from the end, for example, outstanding athletic ability with regard to forming a team. In other words, the human act is not good because it leads to beatitude, but because it is good, it leads to man's end. Before the act is actually ordered as a means to man's end, it already has a fundamental good, a *bonitas primitiva*, as St. Thomas says.

E. Our Doctrine on the Norm of Morality

121. Morality is both subjective and objective. Subjective morality is the moral status of the human act as it appears to the agent; objective morality is the moral status which the act has apart from the agent's view of it. Although there is, as we shall prove, a subjective norm — conscience, this presupposes an objective norm. First, if there were only a subjective norm, there would be as many norms as there are men. Consequently there would be no true norm, valid for all men. This is borne out by contemporary facts. Relativistic morals makes men despair of formulating an ethical system. As Brunner says: "The picture presented by natural ethics is that of a heap of ruins. The original truth of God has been split up into a thousand fragments, and each of these fragments . . . is itself . . . distorted into a caricature of the original."[94] Second, a moral standard without objective validity would mean the blind following of impulse. Advocacy of such a theory is subversion of man's

[93] Cf. C. Macksey, *De Ethica Naturali*, p. 161. Romae, Univ. Greg., 1914.
[94] *The Divine Imperative*, p. 67.

rational nature. Therefore, the norm of morality must be objective.

122. An objective norm may be manifesting, constitutive, and obligating. (a) A *manifesting norm* designates an act as good, another bad but it does not make them so. The universal testimony of mankind is such a norm. It tells man that ordinary drunkenness is wrong but it does not tell why. This is the function of the constitutive norm. (b) A *constitutive norm* is that criterion by relation to which an act is *made* good or bad. Our sole inquiry is: what is the constitutive norm of morals? (c) An *obligating norm* not only distinguishes the good from the bad but also enjoins the doing of good and the avoiding of evil. Goodness must not be confused with obligation. Goodness is suitability to a given nature; obligation, determination or constraint to one act or course of action. Obligation will be dealt with later.

THESIS VIII. The norm of morality is man's rational nature adequately considered.

123. **What is human nature?** A nature is the essence of a being considered as the source of its operations. To deny the existence of essences is to deny the function of the intellect. When the intellect is presented with an object, its natural tendency is to ask what it is and answer in terms of essence. If there were no intelligible essences our knowledge would be limited to the sort of thing found in our primers: "I see the cat; the cat sees me." Contingent essences or natures are destined for ends to be attained by proper activity. When we say that man's nature is the norm of his acts, we do not mean that just as we have a standard platinum-iridium bar to which all foot measures may be compared, so we have in the concrete an ideal human nature, as Plato seems to have held.[95] By rational nature we understand the reality which underlies the universal term "rational animal." This reality is found in every human being and makes him a man. Although it does not exist in the abstract manner in which it exists in the mind of a philosopher, it is real and actual. It is the common bond unifying all men, although in each man it is actually united to his individual characteristics.

124. **What is human nature adequately considered?** We would be wrong if we said the norm of morals is man's rationality exclusively considered. Man is a complex being in whom are many elements fused to form a unitary whole. He is virtually vegetative and sentient but formally rational. Hence the norm is not a partial aspect of his nature

[95] *Phaedrus*, 247. Whether Plato really held this doctrine on universals or merely had it imputed to him by Aristotle is disputed. According to St. Augustine, Plato was referring to the *ideae exemplares* in the Divine Mind.

but its totality. Therefore, an adequate account of his nature must take into consideration his essential relations, intrinsic and extrinsic. The extrinsic relations must be included because he is not an isolated being but destined by nature for contact with many other beings.

Intrinsically and essentially man is a composite, the inferior parts of which must be subordinated to the superior element. Otherwise the order of a unitary nature would not be maintained. Order requires that the vegetative and sentient be *subordinate* to the rational. Vegetative and sentient goods, however, are proper objects of the rational appetite because man is by nature vegetative and sentient and the reasonable fostering of these values promotes his well-being. However, excessive attention to man's lower needs disturbs the order of his nature and hence is harmful to the entire man. On the other hand, actions which directly promote rational life may be bad for the entire man if, sought to excess, they do not take into account the reasonable demands of the lower man. Hence, a primary need of man is due subordination of part to part to secure the welfare of the whole.

Extrinsically yet essentially man is a contingent, social, and proprietary being. As a *contingent being,* man is a creature completely dependent on God. Any assertion of human independence from God is a false view of human nature. As a *social being,* man is intended by nature to develop and attain his last end in the company of his fellow men. This relationship is one of equality except where the common good demands that an individual participate in God's authority and thus be superior to some of his fellows. As a *proprietary being,* man is intended by nature to have dominion over irrational creatures which are pure means to assist man to attain his end. Since God cannot abdicate His absolute dominion over these things, man is their steward.

If, therefore, a human act disturbs any one of these relationships, it is unsuitable to human nature and bad. To be morally good, the act must promote one of these relationships and at the same time not disturb any of the other three. For it is axiomatic that "evil results from any single defect, but good from the complete cause."[96]

125. § 124 contains a key description. If it is wrong our practical ethical conclusions will be wrong. We assume, however, the correctness of most of our description from valid metaphysics and psychology. That man is essentially social and proprietary we shall prove later.

This is the strategic point where we ground ethics upon metaphysics. The norms of conduct flow from man's essential relations which in turn

[96] *Sum. Theol.,* I–II, 18, 4, ad 3.

are founded upon man's being. *Agere sequitur esse* — activity follows nature. Morality founded on the being of man is universally valid and in force wherever man is found. Since the being of man is changeless it is the root of changeless universal norms.

PROOF

126. **The norm of morality is man's rational nature adequately considered.** The norm of morality is that to which we compare the human act to see if it helps or hinders man as man. Since moral goodness is man's perfection as a unitary whole, then the norm of morality is the standard to which the human act is compared to determine whether or not it perfects man as a unitary whole.

This standard of comparison must be: (*a*) man's *nature* because every nature is a principle of activity. Hence to determine whether an act proceeding from this nature is suitable or not, we must compare the act to the nature; (*b*) man's *rational* nature, for man is rational; (*c*) man's rational nature *adequately considered,* for man's nature is complex. Hence the *total* nature is the norm. Otherwise we could not measure the act as good or bad for the total man, for man as man.

127. **N.B.** We follow the same line of reasoning in appraising things other than human acts. Should an egg have the fragrance of a lily? That depends on the nature of an egg. If I should ask the owner of a pet shop, "Is spinach and celery good for my pet?" he will reply, "What kind of a pet have you?" If I ask, "Are bananas good for a monkey?" to give a sensible answer, he will compare bananas to the nature of a monkey. In determining human goodness we do just that.

128. **Corollary I.** Since evil is the privation of good, what indicates the good indicates the evil.

Corollary II. Acts conforming to man's rational nature adequately considered are those which will lead him to his last end. Thus is solved the second general problem of ethics.

129. Against this proposition, fundamental to our ethical theory, positivism argues that since no one can tell what is normal human nature, human nature cannot be the norm of morals. It is, however, quite possible to answer the question, "What is man?" To deny that we have inherited from the past an essential outline of man is to assert the futility of all philosophy. Furthermore, without reference to the past, we can arrive at certain knowledge of the objects of human desire which are desirable for their own sake. We can find an ultimate end and good of human

life and the chief subordinate ends and goods which conduce to the ultimate end. From knowledge of ends, desirable for their own sake, and of the appetites by which man seeks them, we can know the nature in which these appetites are rooted.

Again, the positivist derides statements about ends and goods as value-judgments which do not express objective reality but only subjective desires and individual emotions. He says that every estimate of good is purely subjective, incapable of objective tests. The assertion means that either objective standards of human goodness do not exist, or they are so elusive that the individual can never be sure of them. Everyone, then, in his estimate of the good, is on his own. Either alternative, however, is a denial of man's rational nature. If we say there are no objective standards of *human goodness*, we are confronted by objective standards of many other kinds of goodness. Objective standards abound for judging good presidents, good linguists, good ball players. The army has definite standards as to what constitutes a good captain, a good mortar man, a good sentry; the individual is not left to his emotional estimate in regard to these things. Assuredly it is more important that there be good men than that there be good presidents, good linguists, good soldiers, or good anything. If, however, there are no objective standards of human goodness, it follows that: (*a*) a most essential element of order has been omitted from the world; (*b*) God has made most inadequate provision for men; (*c*) no one can lead a rational life, that is, seek a *known* human good. If, on the other hand, we say that objective standards are so elusive that individuals can never be sure of them, we say that the human intellect is of no value. If it cannot be relied upon in a matter so personal and important, it cannot be relied upon for anything. If, in his estimate of good, man is merely emotional, then he does not follow reason but impulse. He does not choose a good which is *known*; he is the sport of likes and dislikes for which no justification in reason is possible. True, some men and women act in this manner but to say that this is true of all men is to say that no one is rational.

F. The Ultimate Norm of Morality

130. We have discovered that the basic ethical norm is human nature adequately considered. If we seek to discover why human nature is what it is, we pass from the realm of ethics to that of metaphysics. And it is quite proper to regard the ultimate source for human nature being what it is as the ultimate norm of morality. This ultimate reason is, of course, God. But God under what aspect? We say that it is not the divine will or the divine intellect but the divine nature, archetype and exemplary cause of all created being, which is the last reason why human nature is what it is.

There is one important ethical conclusion from the statement that the divine nature is the ultimate norm, namely, the rejection of *independent morality* or the theory that moral distinctions have no relation to God. Morality is based upon the nature of man and the nature of man upon the nature of God, the fount of all reality. The experience of mankind, especially of ancient Greece and Rome and contemporary life, shows that where due regard for God decays, true morality withers.

V. THE SPECIFIC DETERMINANTS OF MORALITY

131. In establishing the norm of morality we have solved the main problem relative to the nature of the moral good. Two subsidiary points remain. The first is to account for the peculiar or specific morality of the human act. The second is to see what are the things which may be designated morally good or morally evil (cf. § 87).

132. The human act is generically good or bad because of its relation to the norm. But no act is merely good or merely bad; it has a specific kind of goodness or badness. There are moral species or categories — virtues and vices — just as there are categories of natural things. Thus almsgiving has a kind of goodness different from that of obedience or mercy: perjury differs in evil from adultery or sacrilege. How do we account for both the generic and the specific morality of the act?

If we consider merely the physical aspect of an action, we may call the act good or bad because of the skill or ineptitude with which it is performed. Thus we speak of a good catch or a bad throw meaning that the player performed expertly or inexpertly. In considering the moral aspect of an action we view the will as it chooses some object. Will acts are good or bad not because of their ease or difficulty, but because of the object chosen. Hence the human act is good when one wills a good object and in that object are the factors which determine the total morality of the act. In other words, the generic and specific morality of the act are explained by (*a*) what a man does and (*b*) why he does it.

Considering the *complete* term of the will act or the total good as known and willed, we discover in it these elements contributing to the morality of the act: (*a*) *the act as it is in itself* (sometimes called the object in the more restricted sense); (*b*) certain *moral circumstances* which modify the act; (*c*) the motive or reason why it is done (often called the end of agent). The first two constitute the *what* of the will act; the third the *why*.

These three elements are the sources of the act's morality or its *specific moral determinants.* They are the factors which determine not only the conformity or nonconformity of the act with the norm but also the specific nature of its conformity or nonconformity. They are the reason why the act has its specific relation to the norm.

In order that an act may be good, both what a man does and the reason why he does it must conform to the norm. If one or the other factor does not accord with the norm, the whole act is bad according to the axiom: *evil results from any single defect, but good from the complete cause.*

A. The Moral Object

133. The determinants of morality are more easily understood from examples than definitions. This is particularly true of the object. We may describe this element in simple terms by calling it the action in the abstract, that is, action stripped of its motive and circumstances, and say that ethics and law deal with moral acts such as lying, murder, theft, etc.

We may also consider the analogy between the moral object and the "end of work" described in § 28. An end of work is that result in which an activity by its nature terminates. This applies primarily to physical actions. Applied to moral acts, it means that moral result in which the human act naturally culminates. This moral result bears a single relationship to the norm of morality. It must be single because the moral act, like a physical thing, cannot specifically be two things; it can only be one. Thus, taking the life of an innocent person, whether by stabbing, shooting, or strangling, is one moral result in which the human act ends. We designate the result by a single label, murder. Another act may terminate in compliance with a superior's order, another in relief of a neighbor's want. The former is an act of obedience, the latter an act of charity.

The moral object may be identified with a single physical act such as an interior act of the love of God or hatred of one's enemy. Usually a series of physical acts constitute one will object because they are the necessary means to fulfill a single intention of the will. This collection of physical acts known and willed is a unit because between it and the norm of morality there is a single relation. Thus, "taking what belongs to another against that person's reasonable will" is a single moral result; it has one specific relation to the norm, and to it we apply the single term "stealing." Many distinct physical acts may be involved, for example, influencing others, signing a check, changing records. But we are not so much interested in the physical character and number of these actions as in the result in which these actions terminate and *the relation which this result has to the norm of morality.* This result, desired, achieved, or only approved, standing in a definite relation to the norm of morality, is the *moral object* of the will act. This morally specifies the will act and gives it its first status in the moral order. It is the moral core of the human act, *its primary moral aspect.* Hence many authors define the moral object as that to which the will directly and immediately addresses itself.

134. The relation between this moral result, or moral object, and the norm may be one of conformity, difformity, or neutrality.

1. The relation may be one of *conformity* either because:

a) The moral object so conforms to the norm that its contradictory is positively out of accord with the norm, for example, love of God, obedience to one's parents. Such actions are intrinsically good.

b) The moral object does not so conform to the norm that its contradictory would *of itself* positively degrade human nature but solely because it is that commanded by positive law, for example, payment of income tax or compliance with military draft. Such acts are good but not intrinsically good.

2. The relation may be one of *difformity* either because:

a) The result is an abuse of the faculty from which it proceeds and hence is always out of accord with the norm, for example, a lie or blasphemy. Such will objects are *intrinsically* evil.

b) The result, while not an abuse of a faculty, contravenes some positive law and thereby is out of accord with the norm. If the law which forbids this act ceases to be a law, the act is no longer bad, for example, the eating of meat on Friday or failure to register for the draft.

3. *Neutrality.* Sometimes neither the object nor its contradictory is out of accord with the norm. Such acts of their nature are *morally indifferent,* for example, riding a bicycle, taking a Sunday walk.

There are moral objects, therefore, which are good, bad, and indifferent. To will a bad object is always morally evil no matter how good the motive may be. To will a good object does not necessarily make the act good — the motive must also be good. In the case of an indifferent object, the morality of the action must be judged from the motive (cf. § 139, 4).

B. Moral Circumstances

135. The moral value of a human act primarily depends upon the substantial relation of the act to the norm. The moral quality of an act, however, may be further affected by *moral circumstances,* that is, those accessory conditions which modify the substantial morality which the act already possesses. To strike one's brother is worse than hitting a stranger; it is better to pray for ten minutes than for five.

Accidental circumstances may surround an act which in no way affect its morality, for example, to steal with the right hand or the left, to save the life of a Frenchman or an Englishman. Only those circumstances are moral which modify the *moral status* of the act. This modification can only be accidental for the substantial morality of the act depends on its moral object. Moral circumstances do not give the act its first and essential morality but merely modify what morality it already possesses.

The phrase, "circumstances alter cases," should be carefully understood. There are certain physical concomitants which change an act indifferent in itself into one that is good or bad. To walk in the morning is indifferent in itself. For a child to walk when he ought to be in school is wrong. The circumstance of time certainly alters the case. It is not, however, a moral circumstance of the act but pertains to its moral substance. It is a decisive factor making the act disobedience. A moral circumstance is never the altering factor that makes the act substantially good or bad.

136. Moral circumstances can alter the status of the human act in two ways: (*a*) To an act which is already good or bad from its object they can add a new relationship to the norm, or give it a new moral angle. To steal a cup is theft. If the cup is a consecrated chalice the act is sacrilege. Those circumstances which involve the practice or violation of some additional virtue add a new species to the act. Thus adultery violates not only chastity but also justice. An alms given to one's parents is not only an act of charity but of piety. (*b*) Within the same moral species (virtue or vice), circumstances can increase or diminish the goodness or badness of the act. It is one thing to steal five sheets of blank paper and another to take five bonds. One may extort information by cruelty which can be greater or less. The fervor or remissness with which one performs his act is the accidental circumstance which is wholly subjective.

C. The Motive

137. Some persons confuse motive and object. Motive is the objective, if you will, that is, the reason for acting. It is the good, freely chosen by the agent, which he wishes to accomplish by an act. It is the original source of the whole act because an act, with its object and circumstances, is the means taken to accomplish the end in view. Since the end is loved more than the means and hence is more voluntary, motive usually exer-

cises the greatest, but not necessarily the primary, influence upon the morality of the total act.

No man is better than his motives. Men are characterized virtuous or vicious accordingly as they act from good or evil motives. Weak men are they who sometimes choose evil means to secure good ends. All our motives should be reducible to the absolutely ultimate end of human activity, the glory of God. In this conjunction one may inquire if pleasure is a good motive. The Stoic said it was not and the Puritan has agreed with him. But pleasure is a good so that if one acts from a motive of pleasure or convenience in a reasonable manner he performs an act of temperance (cf. § 297). However, to act *merely* for pleasure, that is, to the exclusion of any perfective purpose, is irrational. To dedicate one's life to the quest of pleasure is a very serious disorder.

Motives are not usually single and simple but multiple and complex. This is one of the reasons why self-examination is so difficult. There are proximate and ultimate motives as in the case of a person giving alms to obtain a favor from God. The proximate end is to relieve one's neighbor, the ultimate end is to dispose God to grant the favor sought.

Several motives each of which is sufficient to move the agent are partial motives. A primary motive is one of two motives which would move the agent without the other; the other is a secondary motive.

138. How the motive influences the morality of an act is clear from the following:

1. If the motive coincides with the object, as in giving an alms to relieve another's necessity or playing a game for recreation, the action's morality is judged from its object.

2. If the object is indifferent, as running, the action will be good if the motive is good, as in running to assist another. A good end ennobles an indifferent means — which is poles apart from saying that the end justifies the means. If the motive is bad the action is bad as in running to steal. If the motive is indifferent, the action will be good or bad according to § 139, 4.

3. If the object is bad, *no amount of good intention will render the act good.* No one may perjure himself to escape unjust condemnation. The will may never will evil. However, such an act is not as evil as an act in which the motive is also bad. In some cases motive really plays the role of the moral object inasmuch as it gives the act its fundamental morality. Usually, however, we consider the act as already possessing a primary morality from its object or moral nature. We then inquire what moral effect motive produces.

4. If the object is good and the motive bad the morality of the action will vary under the following conditions:

a) If there is only one motive and that bad, the entire act is vitiated. All actions chosen as a means to an evil purpose, though good in themselves, are tainted by such motivation. If I visit a sick man to discover where his valuables are kept so that I might later steal them, such a visit is part of my act of theft.

b) If there are several motives, one good and one bad, these conclusions will follow: (1) If the bad motive is grievously wrong, even though it is only a secondary motive, the entire act is vitiated. For example, if a man were to assist a woman in a tangled legal predicament, his chief motive being one of kindness yet accompanied by hope of seduction, the entire act would be wrong. The agent is turned completely away from God his last end. (2) If the bad motive is only secondary and merely venially wrong, the whole act is not vitiated. In this there are really two moral actions, a substantially good act with an evil concomitant. For example, if I make a substantial donation to charity out of true pity for the afflicted and at the same time experience a feeling of vain complacency, such vanity does not destroy the substantial goodness of my act.

SUMMARY

139. 1. *What is a moral act?* An act which proceeds from man's free will with intellectual awareness of the moral goodness or badness of the object chosen.

2. *What is a morally good act?* The choice of that which is known to be morally good. The good is the suitable. Having established the end of man, we say that the suitable act is the right act, one properly directed to man's end. Having set up the norm of morals, we say that the act is right because it befits human nature adequately considered. Formally, rectitude is the correct relation of the act to the end; goodness, the relation of conformity of the act to human nature. But that which is good is always right and vice versa. Finally, consideration of the specific determinants of morality shows that the good act is one that conforms to human nature both in its moral object and circumstances as well as in its motive.

3. *What is a morally evil act?* The choice of that which is known to be morally evil. It lacks the suitability it should possess because the agent wills what is unbecoming his nature. The unsuitability may be either in his motive or in the act itself. Whoever so acts is not tending to his last end.

The act is *formally evil* whenever the agent chooses that which he thinks is wrong — even though objectively it is right. The act is *materially evil* when the agent chooses as right an object which objectively is wrong (cf. § 250).

An act is *grievously evil* when the agent wills what is so unbecoming his nature that he is completely turned from his last end. He chooses a created good and subordinates himself to it as to a last end. Such an act is a total denial and overthrow of the order of his nature.

An act is *venially evil* when it is directed away from the last end but not so as to destroy the agent's habitual tendency toward it. The act is not a total subversion of his nature.

4. *What is a morally indifferent act?* It is an act which has a neutral relation toward the norm, for example, bathing or running. Viewed in the abstract, these acts are neither morally good nor evil, but as they actually happen they must be good or bad. In the concrete no truly human act can be morally indifferent. This is clear from analysis of a man's intention when he acts. A man intends what is morally good or morally bad or morally indifferent. To intend moral good is a good act. To intend moral evil is a bad act. To intend what is morally indifferent must be either a good act or a bad act. For the morally indifferent is sought either reasonably or unreasonably. When a person seeks it reasonably, he is directing his act at least interpretatively toward the last end. Such direction to the end suffices to give it proper rectitude and to make it good. If the agent seeks the morally indifferent unreasonably, his act is not directed toward the last end and is bad.[97]

VI. THE EXTENSION OF MORALITY

140. The last question concerning moral goodness is to determine its extent. To how many things do the terms moral good and evil apply? Since the good of an incomplete being is to be found by and in its operations, we look for the good or evil of man as man in his deliberate choices.

A. Direct Objects of the Will

141. 1. Moral goodness and badness primarily belong to *the elicited act of the will*. The act may be desire, love, hope, content, or their opposites, and even if it is in no way externalized, it is still *the moral act* because it alone is the free act (§ 69).

2. *The commanded act of any faculty* placed in obedience to the

[97] St. Thomas, *Sum. Theol.*, I–II, 18, 9.

will is good or bad by extrinsic denomination. For, strictly speaking, only the will act is good or bad. However, in common speech it is the external act, such as heroic rescue or theft, which is called good or bad rather than the will act commanding them. For, when the external act is the immediate object of volition, it gives moral character to the will's inner act. Furthermore, in some divine laws and in all human laws the external act alone is mentioned.

142. Though physically distinct, the inner act of the will and the commanded act of some other faculty form one moral action, the controlling factor of which is the will act. Hence, if the will decides on a good or bad act, the person is worthy of praise or blame even though the act is prevented. Thus, one who has offered to be a blood donor and is refused has certainly acted well. A young man who has determined to see a lewd show but is stopped from entering the theater is guilty not of seeing a lewd show but of intending to do so.

It may be argued that once a man has resolved to commit an evil act, he may as well go through with it even though in the interval between his evil resolution and its execution his conscience bids him to desist. Since he is already guilty of a wrong act of the will, he will be no worse off if the external act is performed. This is fallacious because: (*a*) The most general moral principle is that a man should avoid evil as far as he can. If he stops before the external act is accomplished, he has avoided the evil of the external act — he is guilty only of a bad internal act. (*b*) Many bad external acts result in scandal or injustice to others. If a bad external act is not accomplished, there is no obligation to repair scandal or make restitution. (*c*) Positive law, civil or ecclesiastical, can punish only for the external act.

What, then, does the external act add to the inner act of the will? Morally, it adds nothing essential. However, it does add an accidental fullness of perfection because the intention is realized. Greater effort and intensity of will is required to externalize the act; there is longer and more intense dwelling on the good or evil. The difference between the will act realized and the will act unrealized is merely quantitative, that is, one of degree.

B. Indirect Objects of the Will

143. The direct object of the will whether internal or both internal and external makes the will act good or bad. Does the indirect object, the voluntary in cause, affect the will act? Is the will act made good or bad because of foreseen but unintended effects?

Unintended good effects do not affect the will act. If one foresees that certain good effects will follow from his will act but one does not intend them, these effects do not add to the moral goodness of his act. He has not willed good when he could have done so; he has not done good as far as he could.

I may do a notable kindness to a sick man, which has the further effect of relieving the anxiety of his wife. If foreseeing this effect, I do not also intend it I cannot be credited with doing her a charitable deed.

144. Is the will act bad because some evil but unintended effects result? An act in itself innocent may become bad when all the following conditions are present: (*a*) some evil effect is foreseen at least confusedly as resulting from it; (*b*) one is free to place or not to place the act; (*c*) *there is an obligation to omit the act precisely to avoid this evil effect.* To prevent scandal or immediate co-operation in another's evil act one is forbidden to do various things innocent in themselves (cf. § 668 ff.). To proceed to do them is to be guilty of wrongdoing.

145. But many evil though unintended effects may follow from one's will acts. Must one, therefore, refrain from acting whenever an evil though unintended effect will follow, according to the axiom that one must avoid evil as far as he can? We are to avoid evil unintended effects *as far as we can.* However, if one had to avoid every act which had any sort of evil effect, one would be reduced to almost complete inactivity. To determine, therefore, when a will act that is followed by a bad effect is permissible, we make use of the principle of double effect.

146. The Principle of Double Effect. A will act followed by two effects, one good and one bad, is permissible under the following conditions:

1. *The initial voluntary act must itself be good,* for the will can never directly tend to evil.

2. *The good effect must follow as directly as the evil effect.* This sequence is not one of time but of causality, that is, the evil effect cannot be the cause of the good effect. If it were, the agent would have to will the evil effect directly to attain the good. Evil, however, may not be willed under any circumstances, irrespective of the good that may be obtained.

3. *There must be a proportionately grave reason for placing the act and permitting the evil effect.* It would not be reasonable to allow a grave evil for a relatively insignificant good.

4. *The evil effect must never be intended,* otherwise the will would directly tend to evil.

Points 1 and 4 above are not difficult to understand and apply. The heart of the principle is contained in 2 and 3. Unless one can grasp how two effects can follow with equal directness from one act and what would constitute a sufficiently grave reason for allowing some effect, he cannot apply this principle.

147. The following is an example of the application of the principle. A pregnant woman is suffering from a cancer of the womb. May a surgeon perform a surgical operation which will remove the cancerous womb and at the same time result in the death of the unborn child?

First condition. The initial act, the removal of the cancerous womb, is not a morally bad act. It is justifiable mutilation, because a part may be sacrificed to save the whole.

Second condition. Two effects follow from this act: a good effect, the correction of the mother's dangerous pathological condition; and a bad effect, the death of the foetus. Both effects follow with equal directness because the surgical operation removes the womb both with its cancer and its foetus. It would be different if the surgeon were to kill the foetus in order to afford the mother relief. In this case the evil effect would be directly intended as a means to the good effect.

Third condition. There is a sufficiently important reason for allowing the foetus to die, namely, saving the life of the mother.

Fourth condition. The surgeon does not intend the death of the foetus but merely permits it.

READINGS

St. Thomas, *Summa Theologica*, I–II, 7, 18–20.

——— *Contra Gentiles*, III, 1–16.

Adler, M. J., *A Dialectic of Morals*, 31–107. Notre Dame, Review of Politics, 1941.

Anderson, C. A., "Human Nature: the Common Concern of the Humanistic Disciplines," *Ethics*, 64 (April, 1954), 169–185.

Aristotle, *Ethics*, II, 5–6; IX, 8.

Connolly, M., "The Claim of Morality," *Studies*, 42 (1953), 395–406.

Conway, W., "The Act of Two Effects," *Irish Theological Quarterly*, 18 (April, 1951), 125–137.

Hall, E. W., *What Is Value?* New York, Humanities, 1952.

Hawkins, D. J. B., *Nature As the Ethical Norm*. Blackfriars, 1951.

Herring, F. W., "What Has Reason to do with Morality?" *Journal of Philosophy*, 50 (November 5, 1953), 688–698.

Hildebrand, D., *Christian Ethics*, 64–78, 129–190. New York, McKay, 1953.

Lafleur, L. J., "The Meanings of the Good," *Philosophy and Phenomenological Research*, 15 (1954–1955), 210–221.

Lamont, W. D., *The Value Judgment*. Edinburgh, University Press, 1955.

Leclercq, J., *Les Grandes Lignes de la Philosophie Morale*, 225–255. Paris, Vrin, 1954.

Lottin, O., *Morale Fundamentale*, 229–295. Paris, Desclée, 1954.

Mangan, J. T., "An Historical Analysis of the Principle of Double Effect," *Theological Studies*, 10 (1949), 41–46.

McAllister, J. B., *Ethics*, 15–32. Philadelphia, Saunders, 1955.

O'Connor, W. R., "The Nature of the Good," *Thought*, 24 (December, 1949), 637–654.

Osbourn, J. C., *The Morality of Imperfections*, 99–146. Westminster, Carroll, 1950.

de Raeymaeker, L., *The Philosophy of Being*, 212–235. St. Louis, Herder, 1954.

Rockey, P., "The Morality of the Exterior Act," *Modern Schoolman*, 31 (1954), 213–221.

Simon, L. M., "Substance et circonstance de l'acte morale," *Angelicum*, 33 (1956), 67–79.

Siwek, P., *The Philosophy of Evil*, 21–103. New York, Ronald, 1951.

Vann, G., "What Is Natural?" *Commonweal*, December 18, 1953, 274–276.

Ward, L., *Values and Reality*, New York, Sheed & Ward, 1935.

Wild, J., "Ethics as a Rational Discipline and the Priority of the Good," *Journal of Philosophy*, 51 (November 25, 1954), 776–788.

Chapter V LAW

148. We began our explanation of what orderly conduct ought to be by establishing its ultimate principle, namely, the final end of happiness. Next we saw that, on account of human freedom, we had to find a principle to distinguish between good acts which tend to the end and bad acts which do not. This principle is the norm of morality, human nature in its essential relations.

From consideration of the end and the good it is clear that man can be happy. The next inquiry might be: How does man become happy, that is, what are the specific good acts which prepare us for happiness, what are the specific bad acts which prevent happiness? These are the particular questions of axiology or value-ethics but they are not as yet in place because one final constituent of basic morality has not been explained. The notions of the end and the good must be complemented by the notion of obligation. For it is these three, end, good, and obligation, which are the objective foundation upon which all morality rests.

While we shall shortly prove that moral obligation exists, we may now safely say that its existence is as certain as motherhood. Just as all men see that there are good acts and bad acts, so they also acknowledge some kind of compulsion to do the good and avoid the evil. Everyone has a code according to which certain good things are to be done, certain evil things to be avoided. Thus in the eyes of an English gentleman cheating at cards or going back on one's word is simply not done. We call this compelling force duty or moral obligation. Everyone is conscious of it except the few who do violence to their rational nature.

We express moral obligation in terms of "ought." For just as "is" is the connective in logical propositions, so "ought" has the same function in ethical statements. "Ought" can mean wishful thinking, probability, expediency, propriety, and necessity, either conditional or unconditional. The first four meanings are represented by a prudential nonethical ought: only in the last meaning may we seek the ethical ought. This expresses a unique thing — moral necessity, whose definition we leave to the end of this chapter.

149. **What is the basic problem regarding moral obligation?** Meli-

oristic ethics[1] — a modern system which says that value is a comparative thing of better and worse so that what men call good is really the better and what men call evil is really the worse — finds itself without any problem of moral obligation. For the meliorist, duty or ought is not a fundamental concept but merely a traditional term to which passing reference suffices. If the meliorist is asked, "Why ought I do this rather than that?" he answers, "Because this is better."[2] He is at such great pains to identify the good with the better and to say that the right act is that which is productive of the maximum good that understandably he bypasses the notion of obligation. He dare not say that we are *obliged* to do the better or to produce the maximum good.

150. Sometimes the problem of moral obligation is put in this way: Is moral obligation conditional or unconditional? John Gay (1669–1745) says that obligation is the necessity of doing or omitting an action in order to be happy. If this is the full truth, obligation is equivalently one's desire to have that to which the obligatory act conduces. J. S. Mill accepts this position and says that the source of obligation is motive and sanction. Kant, on the other hand, says that obligation is categorical. And this is the view of the common man. When he says that "Fathers must support their children" or "Do not steal or cheat" he attaches no "and's," "if's," or "but's" to the injunction. However, this method of putting the problem does not seem to highlight the most fundamental issue.

151. Our exposition of ethical theory has brought us to this conditional obligation, namely, if one wishes to be happy one must do good and avoid evil. Is this the end of the matter, as the silence of many ethicians would lead one to conclude? Suppose one is not interested in the end! *Is there any compulsion to seek the end and choose the necessary means to the end?* This is the third over-all problem, mentioned in § 24 and it introduces what some authors call deontology (from δέον — "it is necessary").

To give a complete answer to the main problem we put four subsidiary questions: (I) What is the source of obligation? (II) Where does one find obligation? (III) How far does obligation extend? (IV) What is the nature of obligation?

I. THE SOURCE OF MORAL OBLIGATION

Whence does obligation arise? What would automatically entail the cessation of obligation if it ceased to exist itself?

[1] From the Latin *melior* meaning "better."
[2] E. T. Mitchell, *A System of Ethics,* p. 175. New York, Scribners, 1950.

A. Unsatisfactory Answers

152. The force theory. Hobbes held that all moral distinctions and hence obligation arise from the law of the State which is purely an accumulation of physical might.[3] Spencer says that evolving man was first conscious of an internal restraint, the foreseen usefulness or harmfulness of a proposed act;[4] later, as he began to lead a less simple life, an external pressure was brought to bear upon him, the fear of political, religious, and social penalties. Out of this dread of social consequences has evolved the notion of moral obligation.[5] This in turn will disappear the higher man mounts in the moral scale.[6]

The statement of Holbach, that "moral obligation is the necessity of doing or avoiding certain actions in view of the well being we seek in social life,"[7] is elaborated upon by modern sociologists who say that what people experience as moral obligation is fear of the coercive power of society. Because the group resents certain actions, it forbids them. If indirect coercion is sufficient to induce conformity to its taboos, well and good. If not, the dominant group forces its will upon the nonconformers. The boldest upholder of the theory of social coercion is Holmes, who says law is physical force, a "statement of the circumstances in which the public force will be brought to bear upon men through the courts."[8]

153. Criticism. If a man goes counter to his nature and acts like a brute, force may be necessary to bring him to reason. However, it is a subversion of human nature to hold that man should be directed to happiness by physical compulsion. This is to deny the freedom of his nature, to make of him a mere brute.

154. The theory that autonomous human nature is the source of obligation. According to Kant, the obligation of observing the moral law originates in human nature. He reasons that only that will act can be simply good which is posited without hope or fear of anything consequent thereupon. Hence, to be good the will cannot be determined by anything outside itself. Therefore it is autonomous. "What else," he asks, "can the freedom of the will be but autonomy, that is, the property of the will to be a law unto itself?"[9] And Kant is the first

[3] Thomas Hobbes, *Leviathan*, Chaps. XIII and XVII, Molesworth's English edition, Vol. III, pp. 115, 157–158. London, Bohn, 1841.

[4] Herbert Spencer, *Data of Ethics*, pp. 120–121.

[5] *Ibid.*, p. 126.

[6] *Ibid.*, pp. 127–128.

[7] *La Morale Universelle*, Tome I, p. 2. Paris, 1820.

[8] O. W. Holmes, Jr., *Holmes-Pollock Letters*, ed. M. O. Howe, Vol. II, p. 212. Cambridge, Mass., Harvard University Press, 1941.

[9] *Critique of Practical Reason*, trans. Abbott, p. 65.

discoverer of this principle. "Looking back now on all previous attempts to discover the principle of morality, we need not wonder why they all failed. It was seen that man was bound by duty, but it was not observed that the laws to which he is subject are *only those of his own giving* . . . and that he is only bound to act in conformity with his own will; a will, however, which is designed by nature to give universal laws."[10]

Man, then, is a legislator obliging himself to live in accord with his nature.

155. Criticism. The commands of morality cannot originate in man. If the autonomous reason is the sole source of obligation, man is both a superior who imposes a command and an inferior who is bound by it. But in a contingent being, there is no self-binding principle. Only the Necessary Being whose end is wholly in Itself can compel Itself to act in conformity with Its nature. Man is neither a necessary being nor an end unto himself. Therefore, moral obligation originates outside of man. Reason discovers and enunciates it but reason cannot be identified with it.

156. The theory of essential order. Vasquez[11] seems to hold that the objective order of our human nature, apart from or antecedent to any divine command, compels us to do good and avoid evil. Janet says: "Moral obligation is based on the following principle: 'Every being owes it to himself that he should attain to the highest degree of excellence and of perfection of which his nature is capable'. . . . It is not because a higher power desires our good that it is incumbent on us to seek it; it is because we inevitably desire it ourselves."[12]

157. Criticism. Order — the disposition of means to an end — imposes a hypothetical obligation on the mind, that is, "you must do good and avoid evil if you wish to attain your final end," but it is not sufficient to bind the will. The will can be bound only by some orderer. To say that this orderer is human nature is to say that a contingent nature can bind itself categorically. This is impossible as we have seen.

158. The tendency of modern non-Scholastic authors is either to ignore our present problem or thoroughly to attenuate the stern notion of duty left them by Kant. It is like jousting with windmills to try to summarize what they say on this topic. This much, however, is discernible. They agree in calling the act which is of obligation the right act. The majority then proceed to say that the right act is founded on

[10] *Ibid.*, p. 51.

[11] *Commentariorum, ac Disputationum in Primam Secundae S. Thomae, Tomus Secundus*, q. 90, disp. 150, cap. 3. Ingolstadii, 1606.

[12] Paul Janet, *Theory of Morals*, trans. M. Chapman, pp. 170, 173. New York, Scribner's, 1898.

the good. Their idea of obligation will vary as does their concept of the good. Thus to Dewey duty is what is owed by the partial self to the ideal self. The source of duty then would be "progress," the needs of "the growing self."[13] Hill says: "The relation of 'intrinsic good' and 'ought' is then best expressed by saying . . . that each type of experience tends to produce an obligation to bring it into existence that is proportional to its intrinsic goodness. . . . What ought to be done is presumably that which will bring about the most intrinsic good altogether."[14]

The British deontologists, on the other hand, claim that the fundamental concept of ethics is not the good but the right, that the right does not depend on the good. "The rightness of an act cannot be deduced . . . from the goodness of its consequences."[15] An action may be right even though it does not bring into being as much good as some other action possible to the agent in the circumstances. In actual situations we have an immediate rational intuition of right and duty: these "immediate judgments neither need nor can be demonstrated."[16]

159. Criticism. The best which the first-mentioned theories can show is a weak hypothetical obligation, that is, if you want progress or the maximum good you must do thus and so. Such an obligation might be efficacious with well-intentioned people but what of those who are not interested in progress of the self or in the maximum good? Is one to say that no obligation exists for such persons? That would make ethics wholly relativistic, and we have shown the untenability of relativistic ethics.[17] Or is one to say that the obligation of making progress or achieving the maximum does rest on us? To this alternative we answer that progress and the maximum good have as much capacity to produce a categorical obligation as has the essential order of human nature. None of them can account for a categorical moral obligation.

Concerning deontological theories we grant that after considerable experience an upright man can make intuitive judgments about the right thing to do in obvious situations. However, to say that an act is right because one sees it to be right is no ultimate answer. The right act can, and if necessary, should be demonstrated to be such by reduction to first principles. Otherwise ethics would be an autonomous discipline — a statement which cannot be made about any science. While the deontologist may have grounds for rejecting the melioristic theory of the maximum good, it is not true that the right is independent of

[13] Dewey-Tufts, *Ethics*, pp. 362–363. New York, Holt, 1908.
[14] T. E. Hill, *Ethics in Theory and Practice*, p. 226.
[15] E. F. Carritt, *The Theory of Morals*, p. 71. London, Oxford University, 1928.
[16] *Ibid.*, p. 84.
[17] Cf. § 121 where we show that the norm of morals must be objective.

the good. The right must be based on the good; otherwise there could be an obligation to that which is not good.

160. Our answer to the problem of the source of obligation is that **the ought of obligation arises only from the reason and will of a superior embodied in law.**

B. The Eternal Law

161. Law essentially involves order and necessity. Order is the intelligent and efficient disposition of means to a chosen end. Military, civil, and ecclesiastical law manifest the order men must observe to secure the purposes of the armed forces, the State, and the Church. An orderly process, however, does not become law until a superior makes it obligatory. True law compels obedience to the order prescribed. Hence St. Thomas defines law in the most general sense as "a kind of rule and measure of acts according to which one is induced to act or is restrained from acting."[18]

Military, civil, and ecclesiastical law are instances of activity, order, and law in limited fields. Is there an all-inclusive activity, order, and law? There is certainly a universal activity and order — *the order of the universe*. In creating the universe God had in view a supreme and focal purpose which the whole of creation — angels, planets, rocks, men, brutes — was to accomplish. He had in mind also more particular ends which particular classes of creatures and individuals were to attain as parts of this general scheme of things. The means whereby the general end and all particular ends were to be achieved were evident to Him. The sum of these means converging upon a grand purpose, the activity of a universe directed toward one supreme end — this is the order of the universe.

Does God will that this order be necessarily carried out? If so, there is a universal law, and the divine guidance and compulsion of creatures unto the end of the universe constitutes *The First Law*, the prototype and source whence all other law must proceed.

THESIS IX. There exists in God an Eternal Law directive of all creatures unto the end of the universe.

162. Law may be considered as existing in three ways: (*a*) *actively*, as it exists in the mind of the legislator — a pattern of order — and in his will — the determination that this order be executed; (*b*) *passively*, as it exists in the minds of those who are to obey it; (*c*) *significatively*, as it

---

[18] *Sum. Theol.*, I–II, 90, 1.

exists in some external sign, some book, tablet, or inscription, whereby it is conveyed to its proper subjects.

St. Augustine defines the Eternal Law as the *mind and the will of God commanding the natural order of the universe to be observed, forbidding it to be disturbed.*[19] It is law in the *active sense* and consists in the decree of the divine intellect devising the means that make possible the attainment of the divine creative purpose and in the decree of the divine will making mandatory the following out of this order. All things that are moved must be subject to the Prime Mover.

An adumbration of this doctrine is apparent in ancient classic literature. In *Oedipus Rex*, Sophocles speaks of laws ordained on high, without mortal birth, deathless.[20] In *Antigone* he says, "No man can override the unwritten and undying laws of the gods."[21] In the *Gorgias*, Plato quotes Pindar, "Law is king of all, of mortals as well as immortals."[22] Cicero says: "For reason did exist, derived from the nature of the universe, urging men to upright conduct and restraining them from evil. Now this reason did not first become law when it was written down, but when it first came to be; and it came to be simultaneously with the divine mind. Wherefore the true and primal law, capable of command and prohibition, is the right reason of supreme Jupiter."[23]

163. **Proof.** *There exists in God an Eternal Law.* It is not enough that God create, giving creatures their substantial being; by suitable providence He must lead them to their final end and supreme good. It would be a glaring defect in God not to care for His creatures. Unless He directs them to their destiny by law God fails to make suitable provision for them. Therefore (*a*) in God's mind there must exist the over-all purpose of creation, the final ends of all classes of beings, and the pattern of action required of creatures for the attainment of these purposes. If these purposes did not exist or if God did not know how they could be realized, He would not be infinitely wise. Therefore also (*b*) in God's will there exists the efficacious decree that this activity of creatures be forthcoming. God must will the purpose of creation, the final ends of His creatures, and the means of achieving them. If not, then either creatures are too much for God or God is careless and indifferent about them.

This act of the divine intellect and will constitutes a law for it is the norm whereby creatures are properly directed to act toward the common end of the universe and are forbidden from acting contrary

---

[19] *Contra Faust.*, Lib. XXII, cap. 27.
[20] *Oedipus Tyrannus*, 863–869.
[21] *Antigone*, 454–455.
[22] *Gorgias*, 484b.
[23] *De Legibus*, Lib. II, n. 4.

to it. It is an Eternal Law because whatever is in God must be eternal.

164. But it is objected there can be no Eternal Law because: (*a*) there are no subjects existing from eternity, (*b*) nor is there an eternal promulgation or outward sign manifesting the law.

In answer to the first objection we say that while there is no community of subjects *actually* existing from eternity, nevertheless, following the decree of creation, it does exist as known and *preordained* by God.

In answer to the second objection we say that there certainly can be no terminative promulgation, no actual manifestation of law to creatures until such time as they begin to be. Such terminative promulgation is requisite for the passive existence of law in the subjects whom it binds. Is such promulgation requisite for the active existence of law in the mind of the legislator? In the case of a human legislator, such promulgation is necessary, but not in the case of the Divine Legislator. The reason is that after the human legislator has determined to enact a law, he may change his mind during the interval between his decision and actual promulgation. Hence such a determination is regarded as an intention to frame a law, which intention does not acquire the fixity of law until it is outwardly signified to those to whom it pertains. With God, the Divine Legislator, it is different. He is unchangeable. Therefore, once God has absolutely determined to legislate, the thing is done — nothing more is required for a law in the active sense. God will not alter His determination and the terminative promulgation infallibly will occur at its appointed time.

165. Corollary I. *God absolutely wills the end of the universe* — the divine extrinsic glory, which is the communication of reality by God to creatures according to their capacity to receive it and the manifestation and acknowledgment of the same by creatures. This is the primary decree of God's will pertaining to creation and in it every species of obligation is rooted. Paley[24] rightly derives obligation from the divine will but mistakenly deduces it from the divine will to reward the observers of the law and punish its violators. Certainly the predominant motive why most men keep the law is fear of punishment and hope of reward, but the meting out of punishment and rewards are but subordinate ends to God — means to the primary end, the maintenance of universal order.

Corollary II. In accordance with the nature of each, *God wills the supreme good of all classes of beings* and ordains that all things act according to their kind. Hence man is obliged by God to seek the last end.

[24] William Paley, *The Principles of Moral and Political Philosophy*, Vol. I, Bk. II, Chaps. II and III, pp. 57–62. London, Faulder, 1791.

Corollary III. *Moral obligation exists and is unconditional.* A natural compulsion is imposed on man to co-operate with the divine purposes by seeking his end and choosing the necessary means to attain it.

II. WHERE MORAL OBLIGATION IS FOUND

A. The Existence of a Natural Law

166. Law, in the general sense just established, extends to all created things. To produce its effect, the Eternal Law must issue from the Divine Legislator and be received by all who are to be directed by it. God communicates His Law *naturally,* that is, He directs His creatures in a way that is suitable to the nature of each. Any other way would frustrate the divine intent.

The natural way whereby God impresses His mind and will on creatures is through principles intrinsic to them. Experience shows that beings operate through their own internal principles. Hence God does not direct His creatures toward their destined ends by external force, as a child pushes his sailboat, but by intrinsic principles rooted in their natures. Hence creatures are subjected to and participate in the Eternal Law *naturally*. This involves two things.

First, the Eternal Law, communicated to and existing within the creature, is the divine guidance for that being. This impress of the divine mind constitutes the specific law of each creature's nature. Second, the law exercises its compulsion upon the creature *naturally*. In irrational beings the law functions blindly: the compulsion brought to bear is sheer physical necessity. A set of necessary tendencies irresistibly moves these beings to observe the order divinely appointed for them. These tendencies give rise to constant and uniform modes of action which men express in convenient formulae known as the *physical laws of the universe*. However, since law is a function of reason and as these beings have no reason, the impress of the divine mind and will upon them can be called law only metaphorically.

In man, however, the Eternal Law cannot operate as a blind impulse. If it did, it would violate human nature, whose chief glory is self-direction. Although we have an innate appetite for happiness, it must be guided by our intellect which has the power to judge what is orderly and must be done, what is disorderly and must be left undone. Hence the Eternal Law's compulsion of man cannot be physical. It can only be moral, that is, manifested to his reason and imposed on his free will. Although man has the physical freedom to act contrary to the Eternal

Law, he is aware of its mandates and realizes that they oblige him categorically.

167. Law, which operates by appeal to reason and through moral necessity, is *moral law*. This alone is law in the true sense and is defined by St. Thomas as "an ordination of right reason toward the common good, promulgated by him who has the care of the community."[25]

"An ordination of right reason" means: (*a*) a competent directive proceeding from the mind of the legislator; (*b*) a command to obey this directive issuing from the legislator's will. Because law causes a true obligation it differs from mere *counsel*. "Toward the common good" means that the end of law is the good of a perfect community, a good for many, to be obtained by the collective effort of many, and when obtained shared by many. Hence law differs from *precept*, which is given to an individual or group of individuals. "Promulgated" means that the law must be so proposed that it can readily come to the knowledge of those whom it is to direct. Hence promulgation is the authoritative manifestation of the law as binding. "By him who has the care of the community" means that to ordain authoritatively to an end belongs to the one in whose care the end is.

168. These explanations are preparatory to the key statement of our whole ethical theory, namely, that the Eternal Law exists and operates in man and as such is called the Natural Law, which is law in the passive sense and is defined by St. Thomas as the rational creature's participation in the Eternal Law.[26] It is man's awareness that certain conduct is necessarily good, certain other necessarily evil; that God commands the former and forbids the latter. The mind of man must clearly mirror the Eternal Law for man.

Since angels, oxygen, trees, cats, etc., have a part to play in the universe and are provided for in the Eternal Law, one could speak of the natural law of angels, oxygen, trees, cats, etc. Similarly we could speak of a natural *moral* law for men. However, since our interest is solely in the divine law as it touches man, we appropriate the term "natural law" and apply it to man alone.

THESIS X. Man participates in the Eternal Law by the Natural Law.

PROOFS

169. 1. The Eternal Law must apply to man and exist in him; otherwise man is not the object of God's providence. Divine providence over

[25] *Sum. Theol.*, I–II, 90, 4.
[26] *Ibid.*, 91, a. 2.

the rational creature demands that God supply man with proper direction to his final end and impose a fitting necessity of following such direction. That which supplies the direction and imposes the necessity constitutes a Natural Law. It has to be a *law* because (*a*) a mere counsel would not be enough to insure attainment of the end in view. (*b*) The imposition, however, of physical necessity would not comport with man's free, intelligent nature. (*c*) The law must be *natural*, that is proposed to man's reason and binding his free will, because God must deal with His creatures according to their natures.

2. The experience of the human race testifies that men everywhere perceive that certain actions are right and certain other actions are wrong and that they are bound to avoid the wrong actions and to do the right actions. The only reasonable explanation of so universal an experience is a Natural Law existing in human reason and reflecting a divinely imposed order of conduct. For in these commands men are conscious of an Authority, distinct from themselves, higher than any human authority, identified with the Author of their being. They perceive that these commands are binding even when their violation leaves nothing to be feared from other men. In the light of these commands they judge the rightness and wrongness of the actions of the highest human authorities. They are the norms by which they judge human law; by them the most unlettered man is able to distinguish between justice and injustice. If men obey these commands they experience peace of conscience; if they transgress them they have feelings of guilt. Men refer these feelings of guilt to a supreme Arbiter of conscience because men endeavor to get rid of them by placating the Divinity.

170. Corollary I. The Eternal Law's injunctions for man constitute the specific law of human nature.

Corollary II. Man finds moral obligation in the Natural Law.

B. What the Natural Law Is

171. The Eternal Law as it pertains to man, constituting *the law* of his nature and existing in his reason, is the Natural Law. What exactly is this?

THESIS XI. The Natural Law consists in practical universal judgments which man himself elicits. These express necessary and obligatory rules of human conduct which have been established by the Author of human nature as essential to the divine purposes in the universe and have been promulgated by God solely through human reason.

172. When we say that the Natural Law consists in universal judgments we do not mean that it is just a psychological act of man. Obviously our emphasis is upon the content of these judgments as revelatory of the Eternal Law.

Just as man formulates principles of knowledge, such as the principle of contradiction, and mathematical and physical formulae, so also he forms judgments concerning his moral behavior. Reflecting upon the world about him, he arrives at general conclusions regarding human action, such as, Children must obey their parents. These judgments express two things: (*a*) a norm of human conduct; (*b*) an obligation to follow the norm.

These judgments, then, are a law because they convey to man a pattern of action and an obligation to conform thereto, both of which originate in a Supreme Legislator, the Author of his nature. We must note, though, how differently each of these proceeds from the Divine Legislator.

173. **The norms of conduct.** Does God arbitrarily command certain acts which He might have forbidden? Are these basic rules of conduct framed by whim? Not at all. What these rules command or forbid does not depend on God's free choice; it ultimately arises from the nature of things. For example, the obligation of reverence for parents arises from an essential relation of human nature (cf. § 124). But all essential human relations, all created essences are what they are and are unchangeably such because they are so many possible imitations of the divine nature (cf. § 130). God's will cannot change the essences of things. Even if, by an impossibility, God were to order otherwise, two and two would always make four, blasphemy would be evil. In His governance of the universe, God is not like the artist of Donald Duck, contriving by caprice; rather, He follows a law of order which is the immutable order of His own Divine Nature. Hence the ideals of conduct, embodied in the Natural Law, depend not on the divine will but on the divine nature.

These norms of human conduct concern *activity which necessarily promotes or frustrates man's last end.* When we proved that there is a natural difference between good and evil (cf. § 109), we saw that an action intrinsically good of its nature perfects man, that an action intrinsically evil degrades man. At that point of our investigation we discerned in such acts logical necessity touching the mind but not the will. Logical necessity means that a man ought to do thus and not thus if he wishes to be reasonable. But suppose that he does not wish to be reasonable? Law then intervenes imposing obligation on the will.

174. **Obligation.** The Divine Legislator commands man to be reason-

able: he orders man to attain his final end. A true necessity falls not merely on the mind but on the will, on the total man, to frame his conduct in accordance with these ideals.

Knowing that certain acts necessarily perfect man, God must command man to do them; knowing that others degrade man, He must forbid man to do them. Once God determines to create man, He has no choice but to prohibit murder, injustice, lying, and the like, since they violate human nature. Since God absolutely wills the end of the universe and efficaciously desires man's good, He must convey to man not merely the desirability of doing what is good and avoiding what is evil but He must oblige him to act accordingly without, however, physically constraining him.

What God so wills constitutes *the most necessary and obligatory norms of conduct*. They are necessary because they either enjoin goods so fundamental that the minimum fullness of human well-being is impossible without them or forbid evils which are totally subversive of human well-being.

The Natural Law, then, is nature moving us to those real values without which we cannot be happy, forbidding those apparent goods which destroy happiness. The particular contents of this law flow directly from human nature, ultimately from the divine nature of which ours is a reflection. Its obligatory character comes from the will of God commanding every creature to live according to its kind.

175. How has God promulgated this law? God must manifest it so that man recognizes it as the authentic pattern of behavior demanding his conformity. Rhetoricians say that God inscribes the law in the heart of man. This metaphor means that God enunciates His law through our nature, that is, *the sole instrument of promulgation is human reason.*

The promulgation of the Natural Law has two aspects. On His part, God gives man reason endowed with a tendency to formulate these necessary rules of conduct. This tendency is like the imprint of Divine Reason on irrational beings. For "what the impression of an inward active principle is to natural things, so the promulgation of law is to men; because by promulgation law imprints on man a directive principle of human actions."[27] On his part, man, in virtue of this guiding tendency, uses his reason to discover the law. Training and experience lead him to formulate the law, at least in general outline. He is not born with innate ideas of the law nor does he find it in any book or upon tablets of bronze or granite. No archaeologist is going to unearth an

[27] *Ibid.*, 93, 5, ad 1.

original copy of this law. It exists in the mind of God and in the enlightened moral consciousness of the race.

176. Cicero has well said that the Natural Law is right reason.[28] In summary, then the Natural Law is (*a*) *virtually* the human reason sharpened with the tendency to formulate judgments as to what a man must and must not do. (*b*) *Formally* the Natural Law consists in these judgments. They are a true law — in the passive sense — existing in man's consciousness whereby he regulates his behavior. (*c*) *Fundamentally* the Natural Law is the objective reality giving validity to those judgments — that essential order of human nature explained in § 124 now made obligatory by the will of God commanding.

It is largely a matter of words when one asks whether the Natural Law consists in the judgments (*b*) or the realities (*c*) behind the judgments. If we say that the Natural Law consists in the judgments, we understand that these judgments are based on reality and have objective validity.

177. Proof. *The Natural Law consists in practical universal judgments, elicited by man himself, and expressive of the essentially necessary and obligatory rules of human conduct because:*

The Eternal Law, as it pertains to man, must be promulgated to him naturally. The law of his nature must be disclosed to him in a way suitable to that nature.

The only natural way in which the Eternal Law can be promulgated to man is that he himself elicit practical, universal judgments which express the essentially necessary and obligatory rules of human conduct. The reasons for this are:

a) The natural way of promulgating law to man is through his reason;
b) It is not natural that God implant judgments in his mind;
c) Nature has not written this law in any natural *external* sign for man to read.

Hence the only way remaining is that *man himself elicit judgments revealing this law.* This truly suits a being whose chief dignity is self-direction toward his last end. These judgments must be practical, universal, and expressive of the essentially necessary and obligatory rules of human conduct; otherwise the law is not *promulgated.*

The Eternal Law naturally promulgated is called by men the Natural Law.

Corollary. Therefore we define the Natural Law as right reason reflecting the divine command that man do certain good acts and avoid certain evil acts.

[28] *De Re Publica,* III, 22.

C. Objections Against the Natural Law

178. Since positivists and relativists have strenuously objected against the concept of Natural Law, the center of our ethical system, it is worthwhile to examine a number of their arguments.

1. The original attack upon the Natural Law began with the denial of philosophy along with ends, natures, essences, and metaphysical principles. To this cruder sort of positivism one replies by vindicating metaphysics, the science of the fixed and universal principles underlying all reality and all knowledge. The existence of metaphysics is demanded: (1) by the need of unifying all knowledge; (2) by the need of validating the assumptions of all particular sciences; (3) as the basis in reality without which rational knowledge is impossible.

179. 2. Against a philosophy based on metaphysics is pitted the philosophy of change. According to Dewey, a metaphysical philosophy "is the expression of a provincial . . . point of view, a culture that is pre-scientific."[29] The intellectual battle of today, avers the same prophet, lies between fixity and change. Fixity is the villain in the piece, for on its side are ranged dogmatism with its intolerance and persecution of dissenters, and religions which breathe the spirit and methods of the prescientific period. On the side of change, is light, progress, democracy, and all the bright new world.

There are many ways of refuting the philosophy of change. One is by proving the existence of an unchanging God. Another refutation, more appropriate to ethics, is the demonstration that human nature is unchanging. All men have in common an essential something which puts them in the man-class, just as all trees have that which puts them in the tree-class. If any individual man did not have human nature, he would not be a man. That essential something which makes many belong to the same species has to be unchanging, since it is that which makes a thing to be what it is. If human nature, which makes men to be men, should change, then a man would be a man — by supposition — and he would also be that other thing into which his nature has been changed. But a thing cannot belong to two essential classes any more than one individual can be identified with another individual. If a thing had two essences, it would be two things and its necessary unity would be destroyed. The problem of man's mode of origin, whether by direct creation of both soul and body or by evolution, does not really pertain here. The claim that man evolved from lower species has been made but to date it has not been established. But even if the claim is

[29] "Challenge to Liberal Thought," *Fortune*, August, 1944, p. 180.

valid, it would still be true that man is a rational animal and being such he could not *at the same time* be also a subman or an ape. The concept "rational" excludes the concept "irrational." If then human nature should be changed, men are no longer men; they have become something else. One nature excludes another nature so that a thing cannot at the same time be both a duck and an oak. So also a man cannot be both a man and something other at the same time. If he should become something other he would cease to be a man. Essences are changeless. A triangle is no triangle if you give it four sides. A duck is not a duck if it becomes a fish. So man is no longer man if you add or subtract from his essential nature. Furthermore, if we appeal to the great scientific criterion of "the facts," the only factual man of whom we have record is a rational animal. The men and women of Homer are suspiciously like the men and women of today. We must, then, await the display of facts which will show us men who are something other than rational animals. Dewey would have done well to ponder the paradox of La Rochefoucauld: "*Le plus ça change, le plus ça reste la meme chose.*"

180. 3. Some advocates of the Natural Law have offered as its basis a "state of nature" — an imaginative fancy as to how men lived before society was organized. Hobbes said this was a state of general warfare; Rousseau, an idyl by a woodland stream. When these various states of nature were rejected as myths, so too was the law which was supposed to have flowed therefrom. The answer to this objection is that the assignment of a false basis for the Natural Law does not destroy the Natural Law but emphasizes the need of finding its true basis. The Scholastics never plumped for a state of nature as did the Contractualists of the eighteenth century. While there must have been a time when men lived by the Natural Law alone, we know nothing about it. A state of nature is something purely incidental to the Natural Law. Although it may have been a passing phenomena connected with the Natural Law, it cannot be its basis. The basis is human nature — something quite different from a state of nature.

181. 4. Kelsen says: "Something is just or unjust for the individual for whom the appropriate norm of justice exists, and this norm exists only for those who . . . wish what the norm prescribes. It is impossible to determine the norm of justice in a unique way. It is ultimately an expression of the interest of the individual who pronounces a social institution to be just or unjust. But that is something of which he is unconscious. His judgment claims to assert the existence of a justice independent of human will. This claim to objectivity is particularly evident when the idea of justice appears under the form of the 'natural law.' According to the doctrine of 'natural law,' the norm of justice is immanent in nature — the nature of men or the nature of things — and men can only apprehend but not create or influence this norm. The doctrine is a typical illusion, due to the objectivization of subjective interests."[30]

The doctrine of the Scholastics concerning the objective validity of truth and goodness has had its effect. When they argue for an objective hierarchy of natural human goods, a positivist has no better retort than to say that they are suffering from delusion! How spurious is the claim of Kelsen that Natural Law justice is "an objectivization of subjective interests" or that justice is "an ideal inaccessible to human cognition" is clear from certain recent facts: Stalin kills 4 to 5 million peasants to collectivize the Ukraine; Hitler kills 5 to 6 million Jews; the NKVD holds some 15 million people for slave labor. According to Kelsen's explanation the protests of these people against being killed or enslaved are *mere* expressions of self-interest and an illusion; there is nothing objective in their claims which can be sustained by the intellect. The citation of Kelsen's statement in this context is its own refutation; for all mankind must cry out that these deeds are monstrous and destructive of human values, that these victims were denied something which all men are entitled to — a conclusion which can be sustained by the intellect anywhere, any time, any place.

182. 5. The positivist says that the Natural Law has no content. Kelsen declares: "None of the numerous natural law theories has so far succeeded in defining the content of this just order in a way approaching the exactness and objectivity with which science can determine the content of the law of nature. . . . That which so far has been put forth as the natural law . . . consists for the most part of empty formulas."[31]

The first answer is that the objector forgets he is dealing with free acts. If I release a stone from my grasp, it has no choice but to fall to the ground. It cannot leap up or jump sideways but it does as it has to do. It is different with the human agent. The complicated situations created by human freedom are not so easy to discern and evaluate as are those which arise from the activity of necessary agents. The norms of free conduct cannot always be expressed with the precision of a formula in physics or chemistry.

Second, in our exposition of special ethics we shall show that the precepts of the Natural Law have sufficient content and precision. Indeed

---

[30] Hans Kelsen, *General Theory of Law and State*, pp. 48–49. Cambridge, Harvard, 1949.

[31] *Ibid.*, pp. 9–10.

the content of prohibitions against lying, stealing, adultery, suicide, etc., is quite precise; they allow no exceptions. Whatever is objectively a lie or theft or adultery is always and everywhere forbidden. For some people these precepts have too much content. We shall not have accomplished our purpose in special ethics unless we set forth the precise limits of the outstanding Natural Law precepts.

Third, it is only in the light of human ends and hierarchic goods that the Natural Law precepts take on their proper meaning. We have just seen that the over-all command of the Natural Law is, Attain human destiny. Hence the particular precepts aim at attaining lesser values required for the ultimate end. Hence there is a specific precept forbidding every action which defeats a truly human end and a specific command for every action whose omission would frustrate a human end. A list, therefore, of human ends desirable for their own sake along with the actions which always defeat these ends and the actions necessary to promote them cannot be meaningless and without content.

Finally, if one will study in special ethics the commands and prohibitions which the Natural Law lays upon individuals, families, and states, he will find all the definiteness and content requisite for *fundamental* norms. It is absurd to demand of the universal and fundamental norms the same quality of definiteness which one seeks in the less universal norms provided by human authority.

183. 6. The positivist says that while the Natural Law may be a system of moral principles, it is not law because it does not issue from visible authority and no coercive penalties enforce it.[32]

This objection merely points out the difference between Natural Law and civil law. The latter flows from visible authority and makes uses of force whereas the former does neither. The conclusion is that the two differ, not that the only kind of law is civil law. To have valid law neither visible authority nor coercive penalties are necessary.

That something be law it must issue from genuine authority, be a reasonable directive leading men to the end of a self-sufficing community, and be so authoritatively declared that men recognize it as imposing obligation on them. The precepts of the Natural Law fulfill these requirements. Not only are they law, they are primeval law, coeval with the human race, ineffaceable, valid forever. St. Thomas says: "Every human law has just so much of the nature of law, as it derives from the natural law. But if at any point it deviates from the natural law, it is no longer law but a perversion of law."[33]

---

[32] Thomas E. Holland, *Jurisprudence*, 13 ed., p. 54. Oxford, Clarendon, 1937.
[33] *Sum. Theol.*, I–II, 95, 2.

III. THE EXTENT OF MORAL OBLIGATION

184. We see from the foregoing how moral good — that which is perfective of human nature — is transformed by law into duty. How far does duty extend? The first duty is attainment of the supreme good. Next, one must seek those human ends, desirable for their own sake, without which one cannot lead a good life and attain his last end. Does this mean that every morally good act is obligatory? By no means. First, while affirmative laws always bind, they do not press us at every moment but only when the occasion arises for their observance. Second, there is good of supererogation, which never becomes obligatory; that is, it is not required for the attainment of the last end.

There is a great deal more, however, to the moral life than aiming at the last end. Morality is a wide field which contains some truly sublime objectives. Theoretically, moral theology covers the whole field but in practice it restricts itself to that which is required of the faithful to lead an upright Christian life. Ascetical theology is addressed to those who desire the fullest control of self and passion. Mystical theology has in view chosen souls who desire perfect union with God now. These two disciplines do not speak of the obligatory since they are treating with those who press far beyond the obligatory: rather their field is the generous, the unusual, the sublime. Ethics, however, stands at the beginning of the moral process. Like Pizzaro, drawing a line with his sword on the sands of Panama to separate the fainthearted from the adventurous, ethics draws a hard and fast line between what is obligatory and what is not obligatory. He who steps over that line commits sin and forfeits, or at least endangers, the last end.

The distinction between good of obligation and good of supererogation is essential to an understanding of duty. As we shall shortly see, categoric moral obligations are referrable only to the last end. There is a least common denominator of good. This indicates what is requisite for attaining the last end and is the measure of categoric obligation, as our Lord pointed out to the rich young man.[34]

The ethical perfectionism, upheld by Emerson and Green, obscures, if it does not destroy, the notion of obligation. Green says that the will of a man should be directed toward "something, he knows not what, which he may and should become."[35] To seek in this life the highest perfection of our nature is noble and praiseworthy but it is not obligatory. One can attain the last end without acquiring perfection now.

---

[34] Mt. 19:16 ff.

[35] *Prolegomena to Ethics*, 5 ed., p. 221, 1924.

Indeed it is a delusion to determine to follow counsels of perfection habitually unless one has solid mastery of his obligations.

185. We also see how moral evil — that which degrades man — becomes sin, the deliberate violation of God's will. While the obligation of doing good has limits, that of avoiding sin has none. Although the command to avoid evil does not always extend to all the evil but indirect consequences of one's acts, it certainly includes all acts wherein one directly chooses what he knows to be wrong, for of such choices a man is master. The Natural Law forbids every morally evil act, mortal or venial.

Sin alone is wrong and unnatural. In the truest sense it is the sole evil for by it alone can beatitude be lost. The world is full of physical ills — pain, hunger, disease, death. These things, however, are not contrary to nature; they come by defect of nature, the inevitable falling short of beings who do not possess the plenitude of reality. But the flouting of the divine command by sin is no mere shortcoming or lack of further perfection. It is a positive turning against nature. It alone is a breach of Eternal Law. It is the one thing which defeats nature's purpose and disturbs the order of the universe. However, as we shall presently see, this check is only temporary. God, through the sanctions attached to His law, can undo the evil of sin.

IV. THE NATURE OF MORAL OBLIGATION

186. The over-all question, *Is there any compulsion to seek the last end and choose the necessary means to the end?* has been answered by saying that the obligation to do this arises from the Eternal Law and is found by man in the Natural Law. Seeking the last end and choosing the means necessary to reach it marks the limits of categoric moral obligation. It remains now to speak of its nature.

Obligation involves four elements: (*a*) one who binds, namely, God absolutely willing the final purposes of the universe; (*b*) one who is bound, namely, man — his free will which bears the burden of duty; (*c*) that to which man is bound or the commands and prohibitions which must be laid on him that he fulfill his part in the universe; (*d*) obligation, or duty, looked at in itself or formally. Our final inquiry here is: *What is the essential definition of duty?*

187. Moral obligation is a form of necessity, and necessity is a determination unto one. Consequently obligation is a relation. One term of the relation is the free will of man bound to do or omit some act. What is the other term? Since the necessity here involved is moral and final,

we have a free being determined to an end which must be reached. What is that end for the sake of which duty compels the free act or omission? This is the other term of the relation of obligation.

The problem may be put in more concrete terms as follows. In the Natural Law we recognize a categoric necessity: children must reverence their parents; parents must nourish their children. Why are they so compelled? Because they thereby live according to their nature. But why must they lead reasonable lives? Because God so commands them. Why does God so command? Because this act or omission is necessarily connected with that end which God has decreed simply must be attained. Is this end our beatitude? No, *de facto* some do not attain beatitude. What, then, is that ultimate goal which man must reach by divine decree? It is giving external glory to God. Among all ends proposed to man only one is supreme, unique, and absolutely to be attained. God has decreed that all creatures give Him external glory and He will obtain it both from the just who attain beatitude and the unjust who do not. When human probation is over the divine goodness communicated to man will be fittingly manifest, and God will be all in all.

188. The necessary way of accomplishing his unalterable purpose in the universe is for man to perform good acts and refrain from evil acts. Since doing good and refraining from evil are necessary means to an absolutely obligatory end, these means are also obligatory. The reason is that whoever is determined to an end is likewise determined to the unique means conducing to that end.

Moral obligation, therefore, is the necessity, imposed by God and manifested to man, of performing or refraining from acts which inevitably conduce to or hinder the attainment of the absolutely ultimate end of man.

189. It is not necessary that man perceive the connection between his act or omission and the glory of God in order that he be actually obligated. He may at first see only the nexus between the act or omission and its suitability to his nature. In this case he is not adequately conscious of obligation. If, however, he once perceives that God truly desires the act or omission, he then becomes adequately subject to obligation even though he has only a confused knowledge of why God wants it. This, of course, requires knowledge of God, at least as the Supreme Lawgiver. Whether a man can without fault lack this knowledge of God and hence this knowledge of moral obligation, is one of the first questions of *special ethics* (cf. § 326).

READINGS

St. Thomas, *Summa Theologica*, I–II, 90–94.
——— *Contra Gentiles*, III, 111–114.
Aumann, J., "The Theology of Venial Sin," *Catholic Theological Society of America Proceedings*, 1955, 74–96.
Broad, C. D., *Ethics and the History of Philosophy*, 195–217. London, Rutledge, 1952.
Constable, G. W., "The False Natural Law," *Natural Law Forum*, 1 (1956), 97–103.
d'Entrèves, A. P., *Natural Law*, London, Hutchinson, 1951.
Doolan, A., *Order and Law*, 5–41. Westminster, Newman, 1954.
Fuchs, J., *Lex Naturae: Zur Theologie des Naturrechts*. Dusseldorf, 1955.
——— "De Valore Legis Naturalis in Ordine Redemptionis," *Periodica*, 44 (1955), 45–64.
Gilson, E., *The Spirit of Medieval Philosophy*, 324–342. New York, Scribner's, 1936.
Hare, R. M., *The Language of Morals*, 150–179. New York, Oxford University Press, 1954.
Hillenbrand, M. J., "Dharma and the Natural Law — A Comparative Study," *Modern Schoolman*, 27 (1949), 19–28.
Kenealy, W. J., "Whose Natural Law?" *Catholic Lawyer*, 1 (October, 1955), 259–266.
Maritain, J., "Natural Law and Moral Law," *Moral Principles of Action*, 62–76, ed. R. N. Anshen. New York, Harper, 1952.
——— *The Rights of Man and the Natural Law*, 58–64. New York, Scribner's, 1951.
McNabb, V., *St. Thomas Aquinas and Law*. Blackfriars, 1955.
Murray, J. C., "Natural Law," *Great Expressions of Human Rights*, 69–104, ed. R. M. MacIver. New York, Harper, 1950.
O'Donoghue, D., "The Thomist Concept of Natural Law," *Irish Theological Quarterly*, 22 (April, 1955), 89–109.
Ortiz-North, "A Return to the Natural Law," *Thought*, 30 (Winter, 1955–1956), 525–536.
Pius XII, "The Nobility of Law," *Catholic Mind*, 50 (1952), 632–637.
Stevens, G., "The Relations of Law and Obligation," *American Catholic Philosophical Association Proceedings*, 29 (1955), 195–205.
Suarez, *De Legibus*, Bk. I, c. 12; Bk. II, cc. 1–7. Confer *Selections From Three Works*. Oxford, Clarendon, 1944.
University of Notre Dame Natural Law Institute Proceedings, Vol. I (1947) and Vol. II (1948).
Wild, J., "Natural Law and Modern Ethical Theory," *Ethics*, 63 (October, 1952), 1–13.
——— *Plato's Modern Enemies and the Theory of the Natural Law*, 64–234. Chicago, University of Chicago, 1953.
Wu, J. C. H., "Law," 6 sect., Supplement II, *The Catholic Encyclopedia*, 1955.

Chapter VI SANCTION AND MERIT

190. Law is not an end in itself but a means to a common good. The Natural Law is the sole way whereby man is to attain the ultimate purpose of existence. Since the end has been willed absolutely, the same is true of observance of the law. However, law is proposed to a free being who is capable of disregarding it. Some effective means, therefore, are necessary to assure satisfactory observance of the law and adequate attainment of its purpose. A reasonable motive for observance is reward for obedience and punishment for disobedience. Whatever measure of due observance is finally lacking will be compensated for by the infliction of just penalties whereby the end absolutely desired will be attained. Hence, there can be no complete consideration of the law without a discussion of the good in which observance of the law issues and of the evil which attaches to its violation. We shall consider first the sanction of the law and then its reward.

I. SANCTION

191. The word "sanction" derives from the Latin *sancire,* which means "to render holy and inviolate." Technically, to sanction means to affix to the law definite rewards and punishments in order to insure observance. In ordinary use its punitive element is connoted rather than its character as a reward. A sanction then is either the decree of the lawgiver assigning a reward for observance and a punishment for violation, or the reward promised or the punishment threatened.

192. Sanction has an immediate and an ultimate end.

1. The immediate end of sanction is to provide for the law's observance. Before a person decides to keep the law or violate it, he sees that punishment awaits the offender. The threat of punishment is intended to be an effective motive to induce persons to observe due order. Hence the first purpose of sanction is to promote observance of order and prevent violation of the law. *Sanction is a preservative of moral order.*

Considered from this aspect, sanction is a stimulant or corrective for man's inconstant will. The threat of punishment which we know will be carried out serves as a moral prophylaxis. A person who has run afoul of the law and incurred its penalties is not so eager to embark on further violations. Then, too, the punishment of the guilty is a deterrent to others. However, it would not be just to pick out an innocent person and punish him merely to frighten others from violation.

The immediate end, or preservative aspect, of sanction has to do with the good of subjects, for sanction serves as a *corrective* for the individual and a *deterrent* for the community. This is so because the observance of the law and the good of individuals are identified.

2. The ultimate end of sanction is the realization of the final purpose of the law, that is, man's rendering to God the glory He desires from him. Consequent upon man's free determination either to obey or disregard the law, sanction provides for the stabilization of objective justice by giving the observer the reward promised and by meting out adequate punishment to the violator. Therefore *sanction is finally a restoring or a vindication of moral order.*

193. Materialists, atheists, and many of our so-called advanced thinkers scoff at the notion of punishment as a relic of the dark ages or a hangover from old-fashioned, hell-and-brimstone religion. They contend that the threat of punishment is unworthy of human dignity and that henceforth "men are to be emancipated from heaven and governed by love alone." Others, while admitting that the corrective aspect of sanction has some value, vigorously denounce the idea of retribution. If you say God is so good, they cry, how can He take delight in human pain. Just as man may not take vengeance, neither may the Supreme Lawgiver.

Such persons forget that man's universal craving for retributive justice is a natural inclination, which is in itself good. Man instinctively recognizes that they who do evil must suffer evil in return. Vengeance, however, is forbidden the individual man because he is unable temperately and impartially to right the wrongs done him. But our instinct says that someone must — someone who is sufficiently impartial and competent. If this were not the case, man would have an essentially evil instinct. Our nature, however, can have no such flaw.

Second, such objectors blind themselves to the malice in every serious violation of the Natural Law. They fail to see how evil it is for man to reject the Creator's will, to prefer a creature to the Creator, and by such choice despise the Creator. This is dishonoring an infinitely lovable Person and the overthrow of essential order.

Nor must we anthropomorphize God as seeking petty vengeance upon the despisers of His commands. His punishment is not vengeance: it is vindication of order. As Universal Provider and Ruler, God has the infinite knowledge, power, and perfect equity to do what no human could do, namely, restore perfectly the balance of moral order disturbed by wrongdoing. God not only can do this but He must — His infinite sanctity demands that no creature prefer himself to the Creator and benefit thereby. In vindicating order, God does not will evil. He wills the punishment conditionally before the law's violation; after the violation He wills it absolutely, *not however as an evil, but as a good,* that is, a necessary restoration of order. Men, blinded by pride and passion, may not conceive the necessity for restoration of the moral order violated by sin. One must contemplate the infinite goodness of the Creator and the utter dependence of the creature to appreciate this fundamental truth.

194. As the preservative function of sanction has to do with the good of subjects, so its vindicative (not vindictive) function pertains to the good of the lawgiver, the establishment of perfect justice, and the attainment of creation's purpose. Both of these aspects of sanction are natural and essential. Which is the more important?

If we consider the immediate good to be effected, the prevention of moral evil and the preservation of the moral order here and now, the preservative function of sanction would appear of first importance. But since man is prone to evil, no sanction is absolutely efficacious as a deterrent of evil. There must be recompense for man's lapses: the divine glory which these actions did not render must be realized. Therefore, bearing in mind the final purpose of creation, we see that the vindicative function of sanction is paramount. Only as a restorative of order is sanction completely efficacious, for it is only by equitable apportionment of rewards and punishments that creation's purposes are ultimately obtained. Revelation alone tells us there will be a day of general judgment given over to vindicative justice. Reason, however, acclaims it only right and fitting that there be some final reckoning, a righting of wrongs, and an acquittal of debts so that at some future time there will be a final equilibrium of perfect justice.

195. Kinds of sanctions. 1. By reason of its *efficacy,* a sanction is: (*a*) *sufficient,* when it constitutes a motive sufficient of itself to induce the rational will to obey the law; (*b*) *insufficient,* when of itself it is not sufficient to induce obedience.

2. By reason of its *proportion to merit and demerit,* a sanction is either just or unjust. It is (*a*) *just* when there is true proportion between the observance of the law and the reward, between the violation of the law and the punishment. "To make the punishment fit the crime" is not a

mere saying but an ideal of distributive justice. (*b*) A sanction is *unjust* if such proportion does not exist.

A *perfect* sanction is both sufficient and just. Such a sanction promises a good which outweighs any evil resulting from observance of the law and threatens punishment surpassing any advantages gained by violation of the law.

3. By reason of its *origin* a sanction is (*a*) *positive*, that is, established by the free will of some legislator, for example, fines, imprisonments, excommunications; (*b*) *natural*, that is, the inevitable result of actions conforming to or contravening the Natural Law.

196. Has the Natural Law appropriate sanctions? There are three main spheres or orders of moral activity: individual, social, and universal. In each order there are corresponding sanctions.

1. *The individual order.* This is the moral order of man's activity in regard to his personal individual good. The law of this order is that the appetites of the individual must be subject to reason. To enforce this order, nature establishes appropriate sanctions — approbation of conscience and tranquillity, or disapproval of conscience and remorse; health of mind and body or diseases; the freedom of self-control or slavery to concupiscence. Every hospital bears testimony to the existence of such sanctions. One who gives rein to his passions must pay the price nature exacts.

2. *The social order.* Man is a social being and from living in the company of his fellow man, a complicated activity arises. The law which governs these activities is that man must do unto others as he would have them do unto him.

Here, too, nature applies her sanctions such as domestic peace or strife; friendship and neighborly relations or enmities and friction; prudent management of public resources or national bankruptcy; prosperity and peace in national relations or war, penury, and social disturbances. Love begets love; hatred, hatred. As you sow, so shall you reap.

Many people, however, believe only in such sanctions. They say that if they observe the physical laws of their nature they will be rewarded with good health; if they are industrious and work hard they will achieve success, perhaps riches; if they are neighborly and keep the law of the State, they will be secure and well thought of. But a mere Horatio Alger view of life is not complete; temporal success and happiness is not the end; it is only a means to the true end of man.

3. *The universal order.* This is the complete moral order of man as man in relation to his *last end.* It is supreme and contains within itself all other relations. Its law is that every man is obliged to seek his last end.

Are the sanctions of this order one or many?

THESIS XII. The Natural Law has a perfect sanction, realizable only in a future life and consisting in the perpetual loss or attainment of beatitude.

PROOF OF PART I

197. **The Natural Law has a perfect sanction,** because its Author is infinitely holy, wise, omnipotent, and just.

1. Since He is wise and holy, He must attach *some sanction* to His law; otherwise He is indifferent to the law's observance. His infinite sanctity forbids that He be indifferent to that which concerns His external glory.

2. Since He is wise and omnipotent, He will employ means sufficient in themselves to assure the purpose for which the law was promulgated. Hence the sanction of the Natural Law is *sufficient.*

3. Since He is just, His rewards will be proportionate to man's observance of the law; His punishment, to man's violation of the law. Hence the sanction of the Natural Law is *just.*

PROOF OF PART II

198. **The perfect sanction of the Natural Law is realizable only in a future life** because experience amply testifies that the sanctions of the Natural Law in this life are imperfect. Many observe the Natural Law and receive no proportionate reward; others constantly flout it and suffer little punishment.

PROOF OF PART III

199. **The perfect sanction of the Natural Law is the perpetual attainment or loss of beatitude,** because it is the sole sufficient sanction and it is adequately just.

1. *The sole sufficiency of this sanction.*

a) A sufficient sanction offers as a reward a good that outweighs any advantage to be had by breaking the law. Only beatitude is such a reward.

b) The sufficient sanction must threaten a penalty greater than any evil which may come from keeping the law. Since death sometimes is necessary for observance of the law, the only evil conceivably greater is the perpetual loss of beatitude. Besides, if violators of the law are some day to attain perfect happiness, no other sanction can possibly deter them from evil. They may sin with the assurance that some day all will be well with them.

2. *The justice of this sanction.*

a) It is *most natural* that observance of the Natural Law, which is intended solely as a means to man's last end, should result in perfect happiness and that those who refuse to obey the law should not obtain their last end.

b) There is *just proportion* between good acts and the attainment of beatitude and bad acts and the loss of beatitude. The first is evident because good acts, of their nature, must terminate in man's ultimate perfection.

It is argued, however, that there is no proportion between bad acts and the perpetual loss of beatitude. We answer that God must fix a limit beyond which the probation of man may not be protracted. Otherwise God might have to wait forever upon man's good pleasure, which is impossible since God is Master of man.

At the conclusion of this probation a man is either substantially in accord with the Natural Law or substantially in a state of rebellion against it. In the former case, he is substantially prepared for beatitude, which must be an eternal possession for unless he has no fear of losing it, he could not be completely happy. In the latter case, a man is to be either (1) annihilated, (2) granted another probation, (3) admitted to beatitude, (4) given a temporal punishment after which he will be admitted to beatitude, (5) eternally deprived of beatitude.

The first possibility is rejected because annihilation frustrates God's purpose in creating this man. Thereby God would forever be deprived of the glory He decreed to obtain from this individual. The second is absurd in the supposition that the man has come to the end of all probation. The third is contrary to the justice and holiness of God. He cannot grant beatitude to one who is a rebel against Him. The fourth is inadequate. Turning from an infinite good constitutes an infinite evil. No temporal punishment is adequate for an infinite wrong.

200. N.B. I. There is a stark simplicity about this sanction. For, since the law is the sole way to happiness, he who does not follow the way will not reach the end.

N.B. II. God is not *unjust* in punishing with eternal pain bad acts that were but momentary in their execution. The reason is that the guilt of sin is measured not by the duration of the act but by its gravity. Every seriously sinful act of man is a total turning away from his last end which is infinite good. Natural equity demands that each one be deprived of that good against which he acts, for thereby he shows himself unworthy of it. Second, each sin, being a rejection of the divine will, is an insult to an Infinite Person. Hence its guilt is infinite, and it deserves an infinite penalty. But since pain cannot be infinite in intensity, it can only be everlasting in duration.

N.B. III. Nor is the decreeing of such punishments contrary to divine *goodness*. God does not delight in these as an evil to man but He wills them as a good required by the order of the universe. Order demands that no one enjoy the divine good who is unworthy of it. The person who violates the Natural Law proves himself unworthy of the divine good; hence order demands that he should not enjoy it. Punishment is the withholding of good from one who is unworthy.

N.B. IV. The *sanctity* of God demands that He deny beatitude to one who ultimately rebels against His law. The reason is found in the necessity for God's concurrence in the acts of contingent beings. The sinner denies that God is his last end. Therefore, if God were to concur in the perpetual happiness of the unrepentant sinner, He would co-operate *forever* in a lie, for He would approve the falsehood that something other than God can be man's last end.

The man who concludes his mortal probation in a condition of serious sin has chosen some creature and rejected the Creator as his last end. Since the opportunity of changing that choice by repentance has passed, God must accept as irrevocable the choice the sinner has made. Since the sinner has irreparably chosen something other than God, it is now impossible that he should ever have God. God accepts as final the sinner's fateful choice. Since the sinner is hardened in evil, God cannot communicate beatitude to him for he has no capacity to receive it.

N.B. V. It is objected that the threat of the loss of beatitude does not induce all men to observe the law and hence is an inefficacious sanction. We reply that as a motive it has everything necessary to induce observance and that it is only *per accidens* inefficacious because: (*a*) men refuse to advert to the existence of the sanction; or (*b*) they do not think its imposition is imminent.

N.B. VI. Reason cannot give a certain answer to a number of important questions on this problem. For the whole truth one must turn to revelation. The following, for example, are some questions and the answers that are obtainable only from revelation. (*a*) What constitutes immediate preparation for entering upon one's final beatitude? Possession of sanctifying grace. (*b*) What moral state entails loss of final perfection? Death in the state of unforgiven mortal sin. (*c*) How many probations is a man granted? One and only one.

II. MERIT

201. The notion of merit might have been introduced at the end of the treatise on good by establishing that man's good actions will ultimately terminate in a deserved reward and that therefore man's supreme good is an object of merit. Merit, however, is included in our treatment of law because it becomes more understandable when considered in conjunction with law and the sanction of the law.

Even the most uncivilized men know that man is a responsible being, the master of his acts (at least of some). Consequently they understand why his bad acts deserve denouncement and should be punished, why his good acts are worthy of praise and perhaps should be rewarded. What is the basis of this universal conviction? In treating sanction we demonstrated that the ultimate of human blame and punishment is loss of beatitude. What is the ultimate praise and reward that can be bestowed on him? As there are natural punishments for evil conduct culminating in a supreme punishment, are there likewise natural rewards for good conduct terminating in an ultimate reward?

Man's attainment of beatitude may be viewed under two aspects. First, it may be regarded as a natural climax of a good life. A man performs such and so many good acts acquiring thereby such human perfection that he connaturally attains to a state of ultimate perfection. This ultimate good is the natural crown of many particular good acts. Second, we may look on man performing his good acts as one freely fulfilling an onerous obligation which is of advantage to the Supreme Lawgiver and consequently is deserving of a suitable return from Him. Is this second view valid? Is beatitude bestowed on man as a reward? Do man's good works entitle him to a reward which may not be denied him?

Although the question is a familiar one, it is difficult. Revelation has familiarized us with the notion of eternal reward. Considering man as elevated by grace to a supernatural status and hearing the clear and oft-repeated promises contained in Scripture of a forthcoming reward, we conclude that the relationship of true merit can exist between God and His adopted sons. But if man were not raised to a supernatural plane, if he were never to become a son of God but were to remain merely a servant of God, could man merit? To understand the difficulty let us first see what merit is.

202. Merit is that quality in a free act which renders the agent deserving of some reward. We also speak of a merit as any free act possessing this quality. Merit can also be used to designate either reward or punishment. It is commonly restricted to the former and the term "demerit" is used to signify the latter.

Three conditions must be fulfilled for the human act to be meritorious.

1. The act must be *free:* the agent must be the master of his act. Only on this condition may the act be called imputable, that is, truly belonging to the agent and rendering him deserving of praise or blame. Necessary acts are not meritorious. No dog, horse, or any animal may receive a reward in the true sense.

2. The act must benefit another, bestow on him some *favor* or *utility.* The agent, however, must not be bound in justice to confer the good because of benefit or reward already received.

3. The recipient must *freely accept* the favor. Thus, if someone does me a favor, for example, cuts my lawn without my knowledge or presumed consent, I am not strictly obliged to give him anything in return. If this were not the case, I could become the victim of unlimited imposition. Acceptance can be explicit or implicit and can be signified in different ways, for example, contract, mutual understanding, silence, or even the very nature of things.

When all three of these conditions are simultaneously present an act deserves reward. What is the reason for this? Is it something exclusively within the act itself or may it also be something outside the act? To answer this question we must distinguish between condign merit and congruous merit.

203. Condign merit alone is merit in the strict sense. It exists when the act is in some way equal to the reward: the act itself, in the estimation of both God and men, entitles the agent to proportionate reward. Note that we say "in some way." The most obvious case is that of *strict justice;* of such sort is all condign merit between man and man. The refusal to concede a reward so due is a violation of commutative justice and involves a consequent obligation of restitution. However, not all condign merit urges from justice. It can be founded on a promise given and the need to be faithful to it.

Congruous merit is merit by analogy. It exists when the reward proceeds from the generosity of the giver, while the intrinsic value of the act is not proportionate to the reward. For example, in a competition, only one prize may be offered, but the runner-up may come so close to winning that a prize is also given to him. For extraordinary services to the State great generals have been granted pensions and gratuities. Rewards given because of congruous merit are not due by way of strict justice. The conferring of such rewards may be based on some kind of equity, distributive justice, gratitude, or friendship. Withholding them is not a violation of commutative justice, although it may offend against decency or gratitude or involve personal discrimination.

204. The difficulty now is clear. How can man benefit the infinite God who already has all things? If no benefit is conferred, no relation of merit is possible. The answer is that while man cannot add to God's intrinsic perfections, he can give God external glory. But how can man ask a reward for giving God what actually belongs to God? All the external glory which man's good acts can proffer is God's possession. Why should man be rewarded for rendering God His due? The answer is, that, although God has an absolute claim to all of man's activities, man can merit if God wills to reward man for fulfilling his obligations. We shall prove that God does so will and hence that *man can merit.*

205. What can man merit? Man can merit beatitude, the only good really worth earning. If, then, man can merit beatitude, is it by congruous or condign merit?

How can man attain beatitude by condign merit if all condign merit is based on strict justice and if strict justice cannot exist between God and man? It is true that commutative justice cannot exist between God and man because: (a) it presupposes equality and independence between the two parties and (b) the object matter of commutative justice (§ 305) consists of goods which of themselves could belong to either one or other of the parties. But there is no equality between the finite and the Infinite; contingent being depends absolutely upon the Necessary Being. Furthermore, God has prior claim of absolute ownership upon whatever man can make or possess. Hence the relation of commutative justice cannot exist between man and God. Therefore, is man's merit before God merely congruous merit? No, we shall prove it to be condign, based not on justice but on the divine fidelity.

THESIS XIII. Man can condignly merit beatitude from God. This merit rests not on justice but on God's fidelity.

206. In a condignly meritorious act we distinguish between remote exigency and actual exigency for a reward. The *intrinsic value* of the act as a benefit to another constitutes *remote exigency; acceptance* by the one benefited of an act that has been *performed* constitutes *actual exigency* for a reward.

To prove the relation of condign merit between man's good acts and beatitude we must show first *their remote exigency for beatitude.*

Once that it is admitted that man's acts can have a remote exigency for a reward, they can also have an actual exigency if (a) God has promised to reward good acts and if (*b*) man is on good terms with God both when he performs the good deeds and when he claims the reward.

PROOF OF PART I

207. **Man can condignly merit beatitude.** (*a*) As we have noted already, the intrinsic value of an act benefiting another constitutes remote exigency for a reward. Consequently, if man's morally good acts have an intrinsic value precisely as benefiting God, they can constitute a remote exigency for beatitude as their fitting reward. To show this the following considerations are in order.

Man's final end is a double good: a divine good, the glory of God; and a human good, man's happiness. By perfecting himself man glorifies God; man benefits God by contributing to His glory and God benefits man by conferring happiness upon him. But man can attain his end only by morally good acts. There is a true proportion, then, between these acts and the divine glory and human happiness. They are the sole and necessary means whereby God obtains what He desires from man. The intrinsic value of human acts is the basis for their merit. An additional but not essential feature is that it is often onerous and difficult to keep the law and render God glory.

(*b*) An actual exigency for reward exists because (*i*) God has promised to reward good acts with beatitude. This promise is implicitly contained in man's natural urge for happiness. God has given man an irresistible desire for happiness and imposes on man an inescapable obligation to perform actions which lead to his last end. (*ii*) In addition, man can actually do good and avoid evil and thereby enjoy the favor of God.

Consequently morally good acts have an intrinsic value, confer a benefit on God which He freely accepts, and contain within themselves something proportionate to the reward He promises. Hence the merit which these acts gain is not congruous but condign.

PROOF OF PART II

208. **This merit rests not on justice but on God's fidelity.** Merit between God and man is based either on justice or on God's fidelity. There is no other conceivable basis. It cannot be based on justice because God cannot be bound to man. Whatever man has or can have already belongs to God. To hold that God is bound to man would imply that some sort of equality existed between Creator and creature, but this is

impossible. Therefore, merit between God and man rests on God's fidelity.

209. If God has promised a reward for obedience to His law and man obeys it, God necessarily is obliged to give him beatitude. God does not owe man this reward in justice. God cannot be so bound: this would entail the subordination of God to man. Rather, because of His divine perfection, God must be faithful to His promises and the order He established in the universe. Let us suppose, however, that the impossible did happen and that God withheld the reward, would wrong be done? Yes, but no injustice would be done to man, for man has no rights before God; there would be the greater disorder of God failing to act in accordance with His divine attributes.

210. In § 204 we called the glory of God an "external benefit" given by man to God for which man is rewarded with beatitude. How is man's submission to the divine will a good as far as God is concerned? It adds no intrinsic perfection to God nor is it useful for the acquisition of such. The universe and all the glory it renders God could cease and God would be perfectly happy and unchanged. Hence Suarez, though admitting that some call the glory of God His "extrinsic good," mildly deprecates the use of the term with reference to God, because "among men these extrinsic denominations would not rightly be called a good unless they were useful for what is internal; since, therefore, this glory affords God no utility, it cannot properly be called any good of His."[1]

Is it not haggling over words to restrict the term *good* to internal perfections and to that which conduces to their attainment? Provided we realize the significance of our speech, why cannot we call a thing good which is completely external and can in no way be an intrinsic perfection of the person to whom it is attributed? The word would be used analogically, just as terms are used that we apply to both God and creatures. The inadequacies of language force us to call such a thing good. After admonishing us not to call God's glory an extrinsic good, Suarez proceeds to call it a befitting good of a sort, becoming the majesty of God[2] which God can intend and acquire. While this can in no way affect God, it is something — a divine advantage — demanded by the nature of things and which God in creating cannot renounce. It is the very last result in the whole concatenation of produced causes and results: the fact that God is known, loved, and glorified.

Comparison of the tenuousness of this divine advantage to the tremendous reward of beatitude reveals the boundless munificence of God.

---

[1] *De Gratia,* L. VIII, c. L, no. 13; *editio Bert.,* tom. IX, p. 312.
[2] *Ibid.*

By way of intrinsic good God gets nothing, man everything; God gives all, man nothing. Because man is primarily the beneficiary of creation, St. Thomas says: "God seeks His glory not on account of Himself but of us."[3] As Cajetan explains, this does not mean that we are the ultimate end of the creative act but they for whose *utility* God seeks His glory.

Who then is the ultimate beneficiary of creation? In the sense that internal benefit is gained, it is man; in the sense that perfected man must be subordinated to God, it is God. The divine operation must of necessity ultimately terminate in God; otherwise He is less than His handiwork.

[3] *Sum.Theol.*, II–II, 132, 1, ad 1.

READINGS

St. Augustine, *De Libero Arbitrio*, tr. D. M. Pontifex as *The Problem of Free Choice*, 58–67, 178–189. Westminster, Newman, 1955.
Fagothey, A., *Right and Reason*, 180–197. St. Louis, Mosby, 1953.
Heiney, D., "Mythos and Ethos," *The Personalist*, 35 (1954), 152–159.
Houselander, C., *Guilt*, 1–150. New York, Sheed & Ward, 1951.
Leclercq, J., *Les Grandes Lignes de la Philosophie Morale*, 313–325, 426–433. Paris, Vrin, 1954.
Massimi, M., *Catholic Morality*, 58–62. Paterson, St. Anthony's Guild, 1943.
McAniff, J. E., "Natural Law: Its Nature, Scope, and Sanction," *Fordham Law Review*, 22 (1953), 246–253.
Plato, *Crito*, 48–54. Republic, X.

Chapter VII PROPERTIES OF THE NATURAL LAW

211. Having established the existence of a Natural Law with a perfect sanction and a fitting reward, we turn to its permanent characteristics. There are three distinct problems. (I) Is this law one and unchangeable for all men of all times? Or is it rather a set of flexible directives that may be discarded or replaced as varying circumstances may suggest? (II) Is it a code whose tenets all normal men readily come to know? Or is morality something of itself so elusive that men can have no certain knowledge of it? (III) Is it both so explicit and comprehensive as to assure adequate guidance for the whole range of human conduct? Or is it only a broad outline the further particulars of which must be supplied from some other source?

I. DOES THE NATURAL LAW ADMIT OF CHANGE?

212. The doctrine of perpetual change is prominent in modern philosophy and its ramifications are found in modern ethics. Just as man is the product of slow evolution, so too are moral directives. The code that sufficed for us as we were emerging into the subhuman ape that walked erect was quite different from the moral norms acceptable to the cave man of the late Pliocene Age. According to Durant Drake, "morality is not static but a set of experiments, being gradually worked out by mankind, a dynamic, progressive instrument which we can help ourselves to forge."[1] The relativist Lanz maintains that "moral principles change, not because the social and economic conditions compel them to change but because under different conditions they logically mean different things and practically call for different patterns of behavior. . . . The old formulas, which we still regard as holy commandments . . . become empty words because they no longer fit the trend of the time."[2] Evidently, if human nature is gradually changing into

[1] *Problems of Conduct*, p. 38. Boston, Houghton Mifflin, 1935.

[2] Henry Lanz, *In Quest of Morals*, pp. 161, 162, 166. Stanford University Press, 1941.

something different, then the fundamental laws governing human conduct must change too. Contrary to this most prevalent modern opinion we establish *Thesis XIV*.

THESIS XIV. The Natural Law is one, universal, and both intrinsically and extrinsically unchangeable.

213. Part I — Unity. There is one body of moral truths. This fact can be established by two proofs:

1. Although the law contains many commands and prohibitions, all of these are derived from, and are reducible to, one principle (§ 224). The fact that there is disagreement as to how this fundamental rule of life is to be expressed does not invalidate this argument.

2. All men possess the same specific nature and are destined to one ultimate end. Since the end is one, the ordination to that end is likewise one. The Natural Law is the outward expression of that one ordination.

214. Part II — Universality. The law is not only one in itself but it binds all men imposing on each the same obligation of observing the due order leading to man's last end. The reason is that all men have the same specific nature and tend to the same end. Although the law may not actually oblige this or that individual because of insanity or lack of development, nevertheless, each, inasmuch as he is a human being and has an intellect, falls under the law at least as its potential subject.

Furthermore, all human acts of every individual are governed by this law. There are no areas of personal or public conduct which lies outside the jurisdiction of the Natural Law. Every human act as a motion toward a particular good can be such only if it is also a motion toward the supreme good. Man seeks his happiness in each human act. But what governs man's motion to his last end is the Natural Law.

Under the same conditions of person, place, time, and circumstance the same rule of conduct holds for all men.

215. Part III — Immutability. It is necessary to distinguish between the changeable and unchangeable in morals. Subjective changes, even on the part of large groups, are common enough. In Massachusetts in 1700 cooking on Sunday was a sin; slaveholding, however, was permissible. In 1840 the vast majority of American colleges frowned on dancing as the invention of the devil. Card playing, smoking, drinking, horse racing were sins to many Evangelicals whose grandchildren ridicule the notion. Such subjective changes do not concern us.

Objective changes, however, are also possible. Social custom may change a proximate occasion of sin into a remote occasion. The ordinary man now is not lasciviously affected by women wearing shorts. People have become accustomed to them. In 1905 such dress would have been a proximate occasion of sin. Again, positive law commanding or forbidding under pain of sin may be revoked. The very rigorous laws of fasting are an example.

The *genuine* commands and prohibitions of the Natural Law cannot be changed. To this objective body of moral truth nothing can be added, nothing taken away. A projected change in the law would be made either by addition or loss of binding force.

216. Addition. May some new and fundamental rule of conduct be added to the law? Certainly by study and reflection we can learn more about the law, but no one will discover new fundamental commands or prohibitions. This is contrary to Bertrand Russell's statement: "Perhaps when we know more we shall be able to say that the best sexual ethic will be quite different in one climate from what it would be in another, different again with one kind of diet from what it would be with another."[3] Even though we move into an atomic age of the most unforeseen developments, we shall not need a new moral code. The Natural Law concerning man's behavior to the State was valid though inapplicable in the days before States existed. So too were its precepts concerning international relations when these were of the sketchiest sort. If completely undreamed-of circumstances of life unfold, so too will nature's precepts concerning them. These will not be new precepts. They will always have been in nature's code. The fact is that the occasion for their application will never have arisen before.

217. The more likely way that we may conceive of a change taking place in the Natural Law is that it lose its binding force even though the conditions of persons and circumstances remain unchanged. The change would be either intrinsic or extrinsic. If the change were *intrinsic*, the law would break down from within. Thus "the Everlasting's canon against self slaughter"[4] or adultery would lapse because neither of these prohibitions any longer promoted human welfare. An *extrinsic change* would be one initiated by the lawgiver. He might *abrogate* the law, that is, render it null and void in its entirety; he might *derogate* from the law, that is, cancel a part of it while the remainder retained its force; or he might *dispense* from the law, that is, exempt some individual or individuals while the law continued to bind everyone else.

218. Our position is that the Natural Law will never lapse nor has

[3] Bertrand Russell, *Marriage and Morals,* p. 6. New York, Liveright, 1929.
[4] *Hamlet,* Act 1, Scene 2.

God, the Supreme Lawgiver, the power to cancel the law in whole or in part or even to dispense one individual so as to render good or at least permissive what the law forbids.

To some this may be an extreme point of view. It contradicts all modern opinion which does not admit the existence of a Natural Law. It also apparently contradicts the older scholastics and theologians who held that the Natural Law is immutable in its primary precepts but admits of a few rare exceptions in some of its secondary precepts. This, however, is but a dispute about words.

Ockham[5] is certainly an adversary when he says that God may, if He chooses, permit actions which contradict any natural precept. Scotus[6] held that the precepts on the first tablet of the Decalogue were immutable; those on the second admitted of exceptions. Durandus[7] held that God could dispense from the affirmative precepts.

PROOF OF PART III (a)

219. The Natural Law is intrinsically immutable, because its prescriptions cannot in whole or in part become useless or harmful.

Whatever becomes useless or harmful ceases to be binding and hence to be law. It would no longer promote the common good.

That the precepts of the Natural Law cannot become useless or harmful follows from the fact that they express essential relationships of human nature. Relations flowing from the essence of a thing can no more change than the essence itself. A change in an essence would argue a change in the Immutable Essence of God in which created essences are founded.

PROOF OF PART III (b)

220. The Natural Law is extrinsically immutable, because God must always forbid what is intrinsically evil and command what is intrinsically good. Intrinsically good and evil acts are the matter of Natural Law. If God must always command one and forbid the other, He cannot possibly change the law. The sanctity of God and the absolute need of His upholding the order of the universe forbid that He should ever cease to prohibit what is intrinsically evil and command what is in-

---

[5] *Super IV libros sententiarum*, L. II, q. 19, ad 3 dubium.

[6] *Sum. Theol.*, IV, 94, a. 5. Vol. 4, pp. 614–617 (Doctor, Oxon. 3, disp. 37). Romae, 1902.

[7] *Super sententias Petri Lombardi, etc.*, Lib. I, distinct. 47, quaest. 4.

trinsically good. The unseen Lawgiver fixes His law once and forever: He does not return to amend it.

221. **N.B.** To answer difficulties one should grasp (*a*) the precise meaning of each precept of the law and (*b*) the nature of an intrinsically evil action. Our basic position is that *the Natural Law forbids only actions intrinsically evil and commands only actions intrinsically good.*

One source of difficulty is that the Natural Law is expressed in general formulae which do not always designate the precise limits of the law. Some have the impression that the law commands and forbids what it does not intend to command or forbid. We formulate the law, "Thou shalt not kill." This does not mean that all bloodshed is wrong but only the shedding of innocent blood on human authority. We say, "You must not take the property of another." Not every instance of taking another's property is wrong, but only that which is contrary to his *reasonable* will (see § 535). We have the formula, "Deposits are to be returned," but this does not express the exact sense of the law, namely, that deposits are to be returned when justly and reasonably sought. When each precept is expressed in exact language it will be evident that no exceptions are permitted. However, the briefer formulae are in general use, because they are simple and apply to the vast majority of cases.

A second source of difficulty is that one does not always understand what an intrinsically evil act is. We may distinguish two types of evil acts: (*a*) Some acts are in themselves so totally destructive of human ends that they are never tolerated. Lying, blasphemy, perjury, and masturbation are such acts. (*b*) There are others which are not good but are not in themselves so completely destructive of human ends as never to be permissible. Divorce and polygamy are cases in point. Both of them render difficult, but do not frustrate, the ends of matrimony.

That the Supreme Legislator for a grave reason and under controllable circumstances could tolerate the latter practices as the lesser of two evils is conceivable. A grave reason would be some pressing supernatural good, and circumstances would be controllable if special providence would prevent the evils normally resulting from these practices. God, the Universal Provider, could exercise such providence. Since man cannot, it would always be wrong for him to assume these practices of his own accord. Since the attainment of created ends is ultimately the care of God, He could permit man to take the more rather than the less difficult means to the end of a natural institution. Man could not presume to do this. Thus the will object which is intrinsically evil is not "plurality of wives" but "plurality of wives without divine permission." This latter the Natural Law forbids and to it there is no exception.

222. If the matter remains the same, the Natural Law is always unchanged. Every act intrinsically evil must always be forbidden. But certain acts which otherwise would be intrinsically evil are not such and do not fall into the category of evil acts because of an act of God's supreme dominion. When God told Abraham to slay Isaac, the Israelites to take the precious vessels of the Egyptians, Osee to take to himself an adulterous woman, He was not permitting a violation of the laws against murder, theft, or adultery. As master of life He could end Isaac's life in the manner He chose; as owner of all things He could dispose of the Egyptians' goods; as custodian of matrimony He could cancel a previously existing matrimonial bond. Hence the acts commanded were neither murder, theft, nor adultery. Therefore they were not prohibited by the law. If the matter is changed, the law does not apply.

At this point we note a tremendous difference between Natural and positive law. In the latter, the lawgiver determines the matter of the law; in the Natural Law, the matter determines the law. A state may decree that driving a car at a speed greater than forty miles an hour is a civil offense. Because adultery is of its nature wrong, it has to be forbidden by the Natural Law. In positive law, the matter remaining the same, the law can be nullified. For example, a state may void its speed laws. In the Natural Law, however, the matter remaining unchanged, no change is possible in the law. What objectively is adultery must forever be forbidden.

II. IS THE NATURAL LAW EASILY KNOWN?

223. Since the Natural Law is the basic moral code of the human race, all men should know it with sufficient correctness. But do they? Are some men ignorant of it? Is their ignorance culpable or inculpable? To give a satisfactory answer, we classify the various precepts of the law according to the clarity of the objective evidence giving them validity. Some precepts are easier to grasp than others because some are more important for the welfare of men.

224. Primary principle. All the precepts of the law are reducible to a single formula. In the past, especially toward the close of the eighteenth century, many writers have tried to sum up all moral obligation in one compact phrase.[8] Hobbes' dictum was: "Every man ought to endeavor peace, as far as he has hope of obtaining it; and when he

[8] See Neubauer in *Wirceburgenses*, Tractatus de Legibus, Vol. 5, c. 1, a. 4, pp. 216–222. Paris, 1880.

cannot obtain it, . . . seek, and use, all helps, and advantages of war":[9] This is another way of saying: "Self-preservation is the first law of life." Pufendorf's summation is: "Every man . . . should cultivate and preserve toward others a sociable attitude which is peaceful and agreeable to the nature and end of the human race."[10] Fichte says: "Do at each time what thou art determined to do or always fulfill thy destination."[11] Destination according to Fichte appears to be the subordination of all things to one's Ego which constantly moves toward absorption into infinitude — which it will never completely accomplish. Comte says: "Live for others."[12] According to Liberatore the basic principle of Thomasius is: "Do what makes the life of man as long-lasting and happy as possible: avoid the opposite."[13] We have already commented on Kant's doctrine: "Act only on that maxim which you can will to become a general law" (see § 118). Herbert Spencer submits: "Every man is free to do what he wills, provided he infringes not upon the equal freedom of any other man."[14] According to Lanz, "the highest law of morality may be expressed in the form of the norm: Be free, or negatively: 'Do not be a slave to forces which tend to compel you to act as they command.' "[15]

The falsity, or at least the inadequacy, of these summations is clear from our explanation of morality. Some have presented the truth, but in too vague a fashion as Epicurus when he said, "Follow nature," or the Stoics who advise us, "Live according to nature."

Some Scholastics have summed up moral obligation as follows: "Love God as your end and everything on account of Him," or "Live conformably to human nature considered in all its essential aspects."[16] Berti says: "All the precepts of the natural law are reduced to two, love of God and one's neighbor."[17] Meyer puts it: "Observe the right order

---

[9] *Leviathan*, Chap. XIV. Molesworth's English edition, Vol. III, p. 117.

[10] *De jure naturae et gentium*, Lib. 2, c. 3, § 15.

[11] Johann G. Fichte, *The Science of Ethics*, trans. A. E. Kroeger, p. 159. London, Keegan Paul, 1897.

[12] Levy-Bruhl, *The Philosophy of Auguste Comte*, p. 313.

[13] Matt. Liberatore, *Institutiones Philosophicae*, Vol. III, ed. 5. Neapoli, Giannini, 1871. *Ethica*, n. 102, p. 119.

[14] *The Principles of Ethics*, Part IV, Chap. 6, n. 272, Vol. II, p. 46. New York, Appleton, 1898. Though he offers this as a supreme principle of justice yet in view of his social philosophy one can take this as his over-all principle of morality. Compare Appendix A of the same work, pp. 437–439 of Vol. II and his *Social Statics*, Chap. 6, 1, pp. 67–68.

[15] Henry Lanz, *In Quest of Morals*, p. 148.

[16] Cited by T. Brosnahan, *Adversaria Ethica*, p. 97. Woodstock, 1902.

[17] Jo. Laur. Berti, *De Theologicis Disciplinis*, T. 2, lib. 20, c. 4, prop. III, pp. 6–7. Venetiis, 1750.

of rational nature sanctioned by God."[18] However, no one better resolved it philosophically or expressed it more aptly than St. Thomas: "Good is to be done and sought for, evil is to be avoided."[19] Like Suarez[20] we may syncopate the phrase of the Angelic Doctor and thus epitomize the whole law: "Do good and avoid evil." Primary precept of Nature L

This principle does not mean that every possible good must be done but every good the omission of which would be evil. Reason tells us that any human act which is necessary for man to obtain the proper goods and the end of human life must be performed; that any act which prevents him from obtaining the same is forbidden.

This principle holds the same primacy among moral truths as the principle of contradiction among speculative truths. In the latter the subject is something immediately known and from consideration of the subject we necessarily infer the predicate. In the first principle of the moral order the subject is not something immediately known but once a person, however young, comes to know, either through his own efforts or the instruction of others, what moral good and moral evil are, he immediately forms the judgment that good is to be done and evil avoided.

225. Secondary principles are those conclusions which immediately or by easy inference follow from application of the primary principle to the essential needs and situations of human life. Since good is to be done, parents must rear their children; children must reverence their parents. Since evil is to be avoided, one must not steal or commit murder.

226. Tertiary principles are those more difficult conclusions which by a more involved process of reasoning are deducible from the primary and secondary principles and for which the evidence is not so strikingly clear, for example, the evil of polygamy, divorce, dueling, and contraception.

THESIS XV. No man whose reason is developed can in any way be ignorant of the primary principle of the Natural Law. While he cannot be invincibly ignorant of the secondary principles, he may at times be invincibly ignorant of some tertiary principles.

227. Since there can be misunderstanding about the phrase "a man of developed reason," let us take it in our main discussion in the sense in which the Scholastics are agreed, namely, the average mature adult whose development of reason has not been hindered by physical defect and has been assisted by parental and social influence.

---

[18] T. Meyer, *Institutiones Juris Naturalis*, Sect. 1, Lib. 3, c. 2, a. 6, Vol. I, p. 253.
[19] *Sum. Theol.*, I–II, q. 94, a. 2.
[20] *De Legibus*, Lib. II, c. VII, n. 5.

PROOF OF PART I

228. No man whose reason is developed can in any way be ignorant of the primary principle of the Natural Law.

The universal experience of mankind proves this. No one has ever become so depraved as to accept that evil is to be done and good avoided. No man has ever sincerely said with Milton's Satan, "evil, be thou my good."[21] No thinking man has ever actually believed the natural is to be avoided, the unnatural to be done. While depraved men have considered the unnatural to be natural, no one contends on principle that the unnatural is to be done.

There is also an *a priori* proof. If invincible ignorance of the primary principle of the Natural Law were possible, this contradiction would follow. The normal man would be equipped with everything necessary to attain his end and at the same time he would *not have knowledge* of the most fundamental norm for attaining it.

Moreover, the formal object of the will is the good and man has an innate tendency to his own good. To contend that a normal person could ever fail to perceive that good is to be done and evil avoided, is to say that the human mind can know no moral truth. This contention is one step removed from universal skepticism.

PART II

229. No man of developed reason can be invincibly ignorant of the secondary principles of the Natural Law.

When a child reaches the use of reason, he does not at once know the moral truths which immediately follow from application of the primary principle to the facts of life. Rather, in the course of normal development he gradually gains this knowledge so that by the end of his formative years he knows the commands and prohibitions of the Decalogue. Failure to attain this knowledge is blameworthy provided he has a sound mind and has had a normal social education.

230. A number of difficulties are brought against this position. Ethnological facts are cited to prove whole people's ignorance of the fundamental laws of morality. The "lowest races" have no religion,[22] not even a name for divinity.[23] Darwin[24] and Bridges[25] said the Fuegians

[21] *Paradise Lost*, Book IV, 110.

[22] Lord Avebury, *Marriage, Totemism and Religion*, p. 138. London, 1911.

[23] Charles Darwin, *The Descent of Man*, Part I, Chap. III, pp. 93–94. New York, Appleton, 1886.

[24] Charles Darwin, *Journal of Researches Into the Natural History and Geology of*

had no knowledge of God. They should have said they saw no evidence of such knowledge. So sacred did these primitive people regard their religion that they jealously guarded it from all strangers. Years later missionaries[26] who won their confidence found them true monotheists.[27]

Again evidence of ignorance is offered which is not ignorance of Natural Law but false application of the law. Thus, a barbarous people knowing that theft is forbidden steal from strangers under the impression that this is not theft.[28] Others, knowing well that they should honor their parents and not kill, put their parents to death under the mistaken idea that this is not murder but rather the conferring of a needed favor on them.[29]

Furthermore, some people have rejected one moral principle through inability to reconcile an apparent conflict of true moral principles. Thus, Indian widows felt obliged to commit suicide upon the death of their husbands; families have engaged in blood feuds.

PROOF OF PART II

231. No man of developed reason can be invincibly ignorant of the secondary principles of the Natural Law. For otherwise the Natural Law would not be sufficiently promulgated.

If the Natural Law were insufficiently promulgated, God would be guilty of folly or inefficiency. The Natural Law is intended to direct man

---

the Countries Visited During the Voyage of H.M.S. Beagle (*Round the World, Under the Command of Capt. Fitz Roy, R.N.*), pp. 214–215. London, Murray, 1845, 2 ed.

[25] Thomas Bridges, "Manners and Customs of the Firelanders," *A Voice for South America*, Vol. XIII, p. 181 ff. London, 1866.

[26] Ivan Kologriwof, S.J. (ed.), *God, Man, and the Universe*, p. 263. London, Coldwell, 1937. Wilhelm Schmidt, S.V.D., *Der Ursprung der Gottesidee*, Vol. II, p. 867 ff., 917 ff. Münster, Aschendorf, 1929.

[27] Andrew Lang's change of opinion is noteworthy. In his *Myth, Ritual and Religion* (Vol. I, pp. 34–39. London, 1887) he espoused the view of Tylor that the first form of religion was a mere animism which excludes any notion of morality and a Supreme Being. After reading the reports of the Benedictines of New Norcia, Western Australia, and pursuing his own investigations of Australian aborigines, Bushmen, Adamanese, Zulus, North American Indians, he reached the conclusion "that there are two chief sources of Religion, (1) the belief . . . in a powerful, moral, eternal omniscient Father and Judge of men; (2) the belief . . . in somewhat of man which may survive the grave." (*The Making of Religion*, p. 301. London, 1909, 3 ed.) Long ago Plutarch denied that any traveler has come across a city destitute of temples, gods, or sacrifices (*Adversus Coloten*, c. XXXI). The more patiently ethnographic investigation is pursued and the evidence sifted, the more the conclusion is re-enforced that there are no peoples without religion. See Wilhelm Schmidt, *op. cit.*, Vol. II.

[28] Edward Westermarck, *The Origin and Development of Moral Ideas*, Vol. II, Chap. 28, p. 20. London, Macmillan, 1917, 2 ed.

[29] *Ibid.*, Vol. I, Chap. 27, p. 390.

to his last end but it could not do so if it were inadequately promulgated.

The sole means of promulgating the Natural Law is man's intellect. Therefore, the mind eliciting the judgments which form the outstanding precepts of the law must be *naturally infallible*. If it were not, man would not be participating in the Eternal Law. Hence, if man through no fault of his could be ignorant of these principles, there would be a defect not in his willing co-operation but in his very nature, in his intellect. If his intellect is deficient, the Natural Law cannot be promulgated to him.

232. N.B. What shall we say of amoral people, persons who appear to have no knowledge of, or feeling for, the common moral principles? First, some of them once had the knowledge and allowed it to be lost. This results when conscience is throttled. One leads an evil life and yielding to passion forms habits contrary to reason. The protests of conscience are gradually stilled, and because of the desire for self-righteousness, the mind is perverted to agree that no wrong is being done. This ignorance is very culpable.

Second, others are victims of exposure to false doctrines and bad example in youth. Can they be invincibly ignorant of the common moral principles and at the same time intelligent in other matters? Billot[30] seems to think so. Others say a man might be a mathematical genius and yet a moral moron. Cathrein thinks that a whole people might be more or less invincibly ignorant of secondary principles[31] if their degeneracy has reduced them to a kind of brutish state.

One hesitates to make a hard and fast conclusion concerning such cases. However, if the mind is normal in other respects, invincible ignorance in moral matters is hardly admissible. First, the mind is not composed of parts, one of which knows financial truth, another aesthetic truth, and still another moral truth. If the mind can know some truth, it can know all natural truth. If then it functions normally in other respects, its failure to understand moral truth is not due to intellectual incapacity.

Second, these moral truths are obvious. If the minds of these persons are shown to be normal by their grasp of other truths, the cause of their ignorance must lie in the will. Thus if a man knows languages very well but is totally ignorant of mathematics, the reason is not that he is incapable of understanding mathematics but that he is not interested in, or dislikes, the subject. So also, if an intelligent person does not know simple moral truths, the reason must be attributed to bad will. No one has better expressed this fact than St. Paul: "As they liked not

---

[30] *Etudes*, December, 1920, Vol. 165, p. 515.
[31] Victor Catherein, *Philosophia Moralis*, 10 ed., p. 172.

to have God in their knowledge, God delivered them to a reprobate sense."[32] Finally, to say that a mature functioning man could be inculpably ignorant of these things is like saying that a chemist could blamelessly be ignorant of the formula for salt or a physician of the simplest medical procedures.

Therefore, even the victims of a perverted rearing are blamable, though with diminished guilt, if they do not know the obvious truths of the Natural Law. The normal mind, as long as it is normal, does not confound the natural with the unnatural, the obviously evil with the good. It is able to differentiate between good and evil and even in the midst of untruth arrive at truth.

PROOF OF PART III

233. A man of developed reason may at times be inculpably ignorant of some tertiary principles of the Natural Law, because under certain conditions knowledge of them would be morally impossible.

One is inculpably ignorant if knowledge is morally impossible.

Since the tertiary principles are conclusions of rather involved processes of reasoning, the ordinary person who grows up in surroundings where these conclusions are commonly rejected would not have sufficient opportunity to arrive at the truth. Thus he might conclude that divorce and polygamy are allowable. Such ignorance would not be incompatible with nature's purposes because, despite it, the ends of human life could be sufficiently attained.

III. IS THE NATURAL LAW SUFFICIENT?

234. Some have thought that the Natural Law is sufficient to direct man in all his problems. They drew up a set of Natural Law principles and in an *a priori* manner attempted to deduce therefrom a civil code complete in detail and applicable to all times and places. This was a mistake.

THESIS XVI. The Natural Law is insufficient. Its inadequacy is supplied for by positive law which must be based on the Natural Law.

PROOF OF PART I

235. Since the tertiary principles of the Natural Law are not always

[32] Rom. 1:28.

readily discovered, some authority is needed to declare them. While the ordinary man may know the common precepts of the Natural Law, he may not always know how they apply to all cases. Hence it should not be left to each one to determine what in the concrete constitutes theft, assault, defamation of character, perjury, and the like. Further refinements of the Natural Law are necessary to prevent conflicting opinions and to insure harmony among men. Thus, since the Natural Law does not specify how the citizen is to support the State, some other law must. Finally, there is need of some temporal sanction for the enforcement of the Natural Law over and above that which it provides.

PART II

236. No one denies that the law which supplements the Natural Law is *positive law*. This is a rule of action freely chosen by a competent authority for the common good and promulgated not in the nature of the subject but in some external sign. *Positive* comes from *positum* or "given." In this context it means law given by a determinate lawgiver at a determinate time, place, and occasion. Its promulgation is a historic event. The competent authority is divine or human. Divine positive law proceeds from God, the Author of the supernatural order, but since ethics is primarily concerned with the natural order, we speak merely of human positive law.

237. How does positive law differ from Natural Law?

1. The *matter* of Natural Law consists of acts intrinsically good or evil; the matter of positive law is chiefly acts intrinsically indifferent.

2. The obligation of Natural Law arises from God's will hypothetically necessary. If God decrees to create man, He must make obligatory the precepts of the Natural Law. The obligation of positive law derives from the free will of a human lawgiver.

3. The *promulgation* of Natural Law is effected by nature and the unaided intellect; of positive law, by some external sign expressly chosen for the purpose.

4. As to *source*, Natural Law proceeds from God immediately as the Author of nature; positive human law, from man immediately, from God mediately; positive divine law, from God the Author of the supernatural order.

5. As to *extension*, Natural Law applies to all men; positive law does not necessarily apply to all. Natural Law is immutable and inseparably bound up with human nature; positive law is not.

PROOF OF PART III

238. Positive law must be based on the Natural Law, because otherwise it would not lead man to his last end.

All law must lead man to his last end. All things in the universe less than man are for man and were created to assist him in the prosecution of his last end.

The *sole* norm indicated by nature directing man to his last end is the Eternal Law naturally promulgated to man. Any other law would not lead him to his last end.

239. Positive law is based on the Natural Law in either of two ways: the matter of a positive law may be the same as that of the Natural Law, or where the matter is different, the obligatory force of positive law is derived from the precept of the Natural Law that the laws of legitimate rulers are to be obeyed. Therefore positive law may be declarative and determinative.

Positive law is *declarative law* inasmuch as it commands or forbids what is commanded or forbidden by the Natural Law, or more clearly applies the Natural Law to specific cases, or enjoins what is necessarily deducible from the Natural Law as requisite for good living. Both the content and the binding force of such law comes immediately from the Natural Law and is positive only in its mode of promulgation and the special sanction — if any — which attaches to it. Such is the moral law — not the liturgical law — given to Moses on Mount Sinai as well as the common law defining fornication, perjury, robbery, homosexuality, and providing civil penalties for the same. The greater part of the criminal codes of nations is but a more definite enunciation of the Natural Law.

Positive law is *determinative law* which enjoins what is not an evident deduction from the Natural Law. It is human authority commanding or forbidding actions in themselves morally indifferent but whose presence or absence are here and now deemed necessary or useful to the common good. An example is the provision of our Constitution that the function of sovereignty be distributed among three departments of government. While the Natural Law commands that the State be financially supported, it does not determine that this should be done by a levy on real estate or by a tax on income. Any further discussion of positive law is the province of special ethics.

READINGS

St. Thomas, *Summa Theologica*, I–II, 94–96.
——— *Contra Gentiles*, III, 122.

Bertke, S., *The Possibility of Invincible Ignorance of the Natural Law*, Washington, Catholic University, 1941.
Cathrein, V., *Philosophia Moralis*, 10 ed., 171–182. Friburgi, Herder, 1915.
Constable, G. W., "What Does Natural Law Jurisprudence Offer?" *Catholic University Law Review*, 4 (1954), 1–21.
Del Vecchio, G., *Philosophy of Law*, Washington, Catholic University, 1953.
Fagothey, A., *Right and Reason*, 157–168, 198–208. St. Louis, Mosby, 1953.
Goodhart, A. L., *English Law and the Moral Law*, 3–37, 147–151. London, Stevens, 1953.
Petrazycki, L., *Law and Morality*, Cambridge, Harvard, 1955.
Phelan, G. B., "Law and Morality," *Progress in Philosophy*, ed. J. A. McWilliams, 177–197. Milwaukee, Bruce, 1955.
Seagle, W., *Law, The Science of Inefficiency*, New York, Macmillan, 1952.
Suarez, *De Legibus*, Bk. II, cc. 8, 13, 14, 15.
University of Notre Dame Natural Law Institute Proceedings, Vol. III (1949) and Vol. V (1951).
Wu, J. C. H., "Christianity, the Natural Law and the Common Law," *American Benedictine Review*, 6 (1955), 133–147.
——— *Fountain of Justice*. New York, Sheed & Ward, 1955.
——— "Natural Law and Our Common Law," *Fordham Law Review*, 23 (1954), 13–48.

Chapter VIII CONSCIENCE

240. We have completed discussion of the three objective pillars of morality, namely, the End, the Norm of Morality, and the Natural Law. Since the norm of morality points out actions which of themselves promote or hinder the last end, and since the Natural Law commands the former and forbids the latter, the Natural Law is the complete and objective norm of morality. It is the complete norm because it expresses all that is contained in the notion of human nature adequately considered and adds the characteristically moral note of obligation. We turn now to consider the subjective principles of morality. Of these the first is the subjective norm of morality. This is the norm within each man which enables him to distinguish right from wrong.

241. One of man's greatest gifts is self-direction. He can direct himself because he has an intellect which enables him to discern the true way to his ultimate destiny. Intellect offers him two kinds of moral guidance. First, it sets up a moral code by disclosing general principles of morality. The habit of these principles is called *synteresis*. However, in addition to knowledge of the Natural Law, a man must know how to apply the law to particular circumstances. Herein lies the second moral function of intellect, namely, the ability so to apply the law to the daily happenings of life that one can discern right acts from wrong acts. A man must supply this moral guidance for himself. Only his own mind tells him which of his acts are right and which wrong. To reason fulfilling this function of moral guidance we give the name "conscience."

242. What conscience is not. Conscience is not *consciousness*, the intellectual awareness of our own internal acts. Nor is it *intellect*, or the light of reason. Conscience and intellect are, however, intimately connected, since intellect is the faculty of which conscience is the act. By metonomy the name of one is used for the other. Nor is it *synteresis*, habitual knowledge of moral principles. Conscience is not a habit but an act.

243. What conscience is. In a *broad sense* conscience includes all intellectual acts which discern the goodness or badness of a concrete human act either past, present, or future.

Concerning past or present acts conscience acts as witness or judge testifying that what I am doing or have done is worthy or unworthy. Thus, preparatory to confession, a Catholic examines his conscience, judging which of his past acts are morally bad. A man may feel the sting of remorse for years after doing a particularly sordid deed. In the very act of wrongdoing one may experience an uneasy conscience. The tranquillity of conscience following our good acts is the perception of the spiritual delectable good consequent upon acts that truly perfect us. We give the name *consequent conscience* to the moral judgment concerning what we have done or are doing. Since it follows the human act which it judges, consequent conscience cannot serve as the moral guide to that act.

244. In the *strict sense* conscience is the last practical judgment concerning the moral goodness or badness of a human act here and now to be performed. Conscience, as guide, is not concerned with past or present acts but only with future acts. It is not concerned with acts of the remote future which may never present themselves for decision. Conscience is called a practical judgment because it is concerned not with speculation but with action. It is, however, a practical application of speculative truths already possessed. It is called the "last" judgment because it immediately precedes the resolution of the will to act or not to act. It is that immediate intellectual light shed upon the proposed act without which the act would not be a human act. We call it *antecedent conscience.*

Immediately prior to the will's free determination, the mind elicits a judgment — which is conscience — informing the agent that the act he contemplates or its omission is one of the following: (*a*) necessarily good and commanded, and hence to be done; (*b*) good but not commanded, better than its opposite and therefore counseled; (*c*) bad and therefore forbidden; (*d*) neither commanded nor forbidden, to be done or omitted as one chooses.

245. The fourth over-all problem of general ethics is, How does each man know the good he is to do and the evil he is to avoid? The answer is, By means of his conscience! There is no need of an explicit proof that *antecedent conscience* is the guide of our moral actions. Since it is the knowledge requisite to make the will act a human act, no one denies that it is the light which guides the will in its moral choices.

Four problems, however, arise concerning conscience: (I) How is conscience formed? (II) What obligation is there to obey conscience?

(III) What degree of certainty is sufficient to induce obligation? (IV) How does one attain the necessary degree of certainty?

I. HOW IS CONSCIENCE FORMED?

246. A novel answer has been proposed by the advocates of *situational ethics,* a system which is partially a reaction against legalistic formalism in ethics and partially a by-product of existentialism which stresses the actually existent, the value and uniqueness of the person.

In the existentialist vein, situational ethics holds that every act of conscience represents an experience which happens only once. Unique situations cannot be governed by unchanging principles. Consequently conscience is not formed by reasoning from premises but is an immediate intuition of what is right in each situation. The intuition flows from the intimate awareness which each one has of his existential good.

Since each act of conscience is self-sufficient and resembles no other act of conscience, there is no point in measuring it against an objective norm, especially against a norm like human nature. For the traditional concept of human nature is outmoded and should be replaced by the concept of "the existent person." In this concept there is very little that is absolute, much that is relative and subjective; for the paramount thing is "personal value," which differs with each one. This relegates principles and objective norms to peripheral importance. While conscience may sometimes be the same as the judgment which would result from the application of principles, it need not be; indeed sometimes it cannot. For when personal values are at stake one does not passively receive the edict of law; one actively produces the objective morality of the situation. For example, an unmarried couple may enjoy sex relations or a married couple frustrate the marriage act if the demands of the person call for it. In its total situation such action is objectively right. Not only does the person see the rightness of the act; the demands of the person have made it right.

As a protest against formalistic observance of law, situational ethics says that what counts morally is not the conformity of one's act to law but the sincerity of one's response to a situation and the uprightness of one's intention. This is necessary if we would maintain our proper relation with God, which is intensely personal — the I of man to the I of God. He is not a God of law but of love: He is our Father and we are His sons. When, therefore, a man forms his conscience he should do so face to face with God and without the intervention of any law, authority, or creed. Each man should assume a personal responsibility before God for his conduct. Hence every dictate of conscience is a personal risk, taken by the person according to his knowledge and evaluation of the situation, and in all sincerity. What God looks for is a sincere response and a right intention: He is not concerned with the act. A conscience so formed could choose divorce of one's spouse, abortion, abandonment of the Catholic faith, disobedience to legitimate authority, and the act would not be objectively wrong. This stress upon personal responsibility prevents both scrupulosity and laxity of conscience.

247. This method of forming conscience is wrong for several reasons. First, the doctrine rejects universally binding laws and holds that conscience cannot be measured against objective norms. Hence it denies the order of human nature expressed in these laws and also the rational character of moral knowledge. We have already thoroughly established the validity of universal moral principles; the rational character of the act of conscience must now be stressed.

If man as man is characterized by ability to reason, so important an act as conscience should likewise be an act of reasoning. Otherwise reasoning would not play its proper part in the attainment of the end. Hence conscience is the result of a reasoning process, the conclusion of an implicit syllogism. The major premise is a general principle, drawn from one's synteresis or habitual knowledge of morality. The minor premise is a statement of the fact which applies the general truth of the major to this particular act. The conclusion is the dictate of conscience. The following is an example.

Disobeying one's father is wrong.
But maintaining this friendship is disobeying my father.
Therefore it is wrong for me to maintain this friendship.

When one first begins to make the judgment of conscience one assuredly reasons. In time the process becomes instantaneous so that it is only in difficult cases that one is aware of reasoning. We do not say, however, that intuition never plays a part in conscience. After years of experience a conscientious person should intuit the right thing to do in obvious matters. Furthermore, our habitual knowledge of morality is sometimes increased by sudden flashes of insight. Nor is it wrong to admit that in a complex situation one should carefully scrutinize all the concrete circumstances in order to determine one's course of action. This the virtue of prudence demands (cf. § 309). But none of these admissions denies the fact that in general conscience requires reasoning from universal principles.

248. Situational ethics is open to further criticism: (*a*) it teaches that a good end — the maintenance of personal values — may justify a bad means; (*b*) while God is primarily interested in the uprightness of our motive, He desires also that the action prompted by the motive be good; (*c*) since each man is a limited individual, his personal values cannot take precedence over the good of the whole race expressed in the negative precepts of the Natural Law. These are real absolutes against which no exception is possible. Here probably is the nub of the whole matter. Historically, this doctrine seems to be the attempt of certain Europeans to salve their consciences and justify the compromises they have made with inhuman tyranny. The solution of grievous personal difficulties, however, does not lie in modification of the moral law. There can be situations wherein one must sacrifice everything, even life itself, to keep that law. The last word that can be said on this topic is that no set of difficult circumstances or accumulation of personal values will ever allow one to act contrary to the negative precepts of the Natural Law.

II. THE OBLIGATION OF OBEYING CONSCIENCE

249. Conscience may be correct or incorrect. Conscience is correct when it represents the objective moral situation. The major of one's reasoning process is the enunciation of a valid law; the minor is a proper application of the law to this case. Hence the resultant dictate of conscience is true.

When our thinking misrepresents the law or pertinent facts, or when we draw false inferences from law or fact, our judgment of conscience is *erroneous*. The failure of conscience to represent the true moral situation is due to vincible or invincible error. Our error is invincible when it is unavoidable despite the care and diligence of a good and prudent man. Vincible error is error which can and should be avoided if we make the effort commensurate with the importance of the matter. Thus, some people see no harm in cheating a railroad or public utility; some students think no moral guilt attaches to cheating in examinations.

As the moral law commands, forbids, and allows, so does conscience. What obedience must we give to it?

THESIS XVII. Whenever conscience commands or forbids, it must be obeyed both when it is correct and when it is invincibly erroneous. A vincibly erroneous conscience must be corrected.

PROOFS

250. 1. A *correct conscience must be obeyed*, because it is nothing other than the moral law applying to this particular case.

2. *An invincibly erroneous conscience must be obeyed.*

If a man is not obliged to follow an invincibly erroneous conscience, he is not obliged to follow a correct conscience. Precisely because the error is invincible a man has no means of detecting it. Hence he cannot distinguish between a correct conscience and an invincibly erroneous conscience. Both are the same to him. Hence if he must obey in one case, he must obey in the other.

The same conclusion follows from a consideration of the will act. The will act becomes good or bad inasmuch as it embraces an object, not as the object is in itself, but as the object is presented by the intellect as good or bad.

3. *A vincibly erroneous conscience must be corrected.*

One is obliged to attain necessary truth as far as he can. But whoever acts with a vincibly erroneous conscience has not attained necessary truth as far as he can. Therefore, whoever acts with a vincibly erroneous conscience has failed to fulfill an obligation. Therefore, a vincibly erroneous conscience must be corrected.

251. N.B. What obedience must be given to a vincibly erroneous conscience? The general rule is that conscience is always to be obeyed provided, as we shall see below, it speaks with certainty. However, we may distinguish between the vincibly erroneous conscience of one who here and now acts in good faith and one who does not. In the former case, the person must act according to the conscience he has: he cannot act according to a conscience which he ought to have but has not. In the latter case, the person who does not act in good faith is distorting conscience and deluding himself into approving as right that which he really knows to be wrong.

252. Corollary. Since conscience is the subjective norm of morality, each one is obliged to see to it that his conscience corresponds with the objective norm, the law. Hence, with industry commensurate with one's years, training, and state of life, one should learn what his moral obligations are — both those he has in common with all men and those peculiar to himself. This duty is especially urgent when moral doubts arise and persist. Then a person must investigate what the moral law is and how it applies to himself. To fail to take reasonable measures to solve such doubts is equivalent to assuming a state of affected ignorance, which is quite blameworthy.

III. THE REQUISITE QUALITY OF CONSCIENCE

253. Every correct or true conscience is a particular declaration of the moral order as it touches this person at this time. But how does one know that his conscience rightly reflects the objective moral order? Three states of knowledge are possible. A person may be (*a*) *absolutely certain,* that is, have no fear that his judgment is wrong; (*b*) *prudently certain,* that is, have no *reasonable* fear that the opposite is true; (*c*) *doubtful,* that is, be unable to form a certain judgment.

254. Therefore (*a*) a *certain conscience* is a moral judgment one adheres to without any fear of the opposite being true. (*b*) A *prudently certain conscience* is a firm assent in moral matters against which no positive probability militates. It represents a state of mind distinguishable from strict certitude and mere probability. In strict certitude all fear of the truth of the opposite is legitimately excluded: mere probability is accompanied by a reasonable fear of the truth of the opposite whereas prudent certitude excludes all *reasonable* fear of error. This is also called broad moral certitude and seems to participate in the nature of both certitude and probability: of certitude because firm assent is rendered; of probability because all fear of error has not been excluded. Objectively it is the highest kind of probability; subjectively, it is firm assent given where error is not absolutely impossible though it rarely occurs. (*c*) A *doubtful conscience* is an assent rendered to one of two contradictory moral propositions with a reasonable fear that the rejected proposition may be equally true. One may buy a ticket to a show guessing that it may be clean but fearing that it may not. Which of these three types of moral judgment is required for a morally good act?

THESIS XVIII. It is always wrong to act with a doubtful conscience. A prudently certain conscience suffices for upright action.

PROOF OF PART I

255. *It is always wrong to act with a doubtful conscience,* because by so acting one does not avoid evil as far as he can.

Whoever acts with a doubtful conscience has a serious suspicion that his act is wrong.

We are obliged to avoid evil as far as we can. Unless we remove the reasonable suspicion that our act is wrong before proceeding to act, we are not avoiding evil as far as we can. The reason is that whoever wills to act regardless of this suspicion, must will the law's violation, which is always wrong. If a man about to discard a cigarette packet suspects that it contains a cigarette and does not resolve his doubt, he cannot throw away the packet without willing to throw away a cigarette.

256. **Corollary I.** *A person in doubt must investigate before acting.* A person with a doubtful conscience who acts without investigation does

wrong. If direct investigation yields no solution, one may not proceed to act. The dictum of common sense — in doubt never act — also applies to the realm of conscience. However, if one is compelled to act under such circumstances, he has the equivalent of a perplexed conscience, which is treated in § 259.

Corollary II. By acting with a doubtful conscience one assumes the specific guilt of the sin about which he was in doubt.

PROOF OF PART II

257. **A prudently certain conscience suffices for upright action.** If one is always wrong when he acts with a doubtful conscience, must one have a *certain conscience?* The strict moral certitude of epistemology cannot be demanded. For, if action had to be suspended until such certitude were attained, man would be reduced to almost complete inactivity. Therefore, a prudently certain conscience suffices: it excludes all reasonable fear of wrongdoing and a reasonable standard of goodness is all that may be applied to a man.

258. From the standpoint of one's habitual mode of forming his conscience, three types of conscience may be distinguished, namely, scrupulous, lax, and tender. A perplexed conscience is akin to a scrupulous conscience.

Scrupulous conscience. Scrupulosity is a habit of mind inclining one to judge for slight reasons that moral evil exists where actually it does not. Scrupulous persons refrain from many innocent acts. In performing good acts they are tormented often by a false conscience which makes them feel that they are doing wrong; after the act they constantly worry whether or not they did wrong. They are so troubled over the past that confession becomes a torment. They are oppressed by a burden of imaginary obligations or of unforgiven sin. Scrupulosity, however, should be carefully distinguished from remorse over a wicked past.

The scrupulous person should first be made to realize that he is suffering from a form of abnormality. Scrupulosity may be the result of a naturally indecisive temperament; it may be a symptom of a mental disorder; it may be due to some physical disturbance; or it may be a special trial sent by God. Second, this person should blindly submit to a prudent adviser and boldly follow his advice. He then should endeavor to act as other good people act convincing himself that what is right for them is also right for him. It is important that he constantly exercise himself in hope and confidence in God.

259. **The perplexed conscience** is somewhat like the scrupulous con-

science. However, unlike the scrupulous conscience, it does not connote a state of doubt but only a single instance. The perplexed conscience is one to which two alternatives are proposed and both seem evil. Thus, one may be torn between the duty of not lying and the duty of parental loyalty. If he defends his father he lies; if he does not defend him he is disloyal. The victim of such a predicament suffers from an erroneous conscience which he should remedy by seeking proper advice. If he must proceed to act without advice, he should choose, in the seeming conflict of duties, the more important duty, not however as an evil, but as that which is farthest from evil. If both alternatives seem equally important, he may choose one of them upon the principle that there can never exist an obligation of committing evil.

260. **Lax conscience.** Laxity is a habit of mind which inclines us to avoid obligation for trifling and insufficient reasons. Thus, many people think there is no obligation to find the owner of lost articles; some unmarried people consider petting harmless, and some married people see no wrong in contraceptive birth control. A lax conscience is the result of too frivolous an attitude toward life, constant desire to avoid the unpleasant, the shirking of responsibility, deliberate and affected ignorance of the moral law. The truly lax conscience is at least an unconscious rejection of the law and if logically pursued leads to the conclusion that there is no such thing as wrongdoing. In the eyes of the lax person everything he does is natural and right simply because he does it. The voice of conscience is stifled to the point that the person may go to the length of sinning against the light.

261. **Tender conscience.** A person of tender conscience is inclined correctly to be aware of the smallest elements of moral evil. Too often this type of conscience is confused with the scrupulous conscience. For example we may call a man scrupulously honest when we mean that he is exactly honest. A scrupulous conscience is a false conscience; a tender conscience is exact and true.

IV. THE SOLUTION OF DOUBTS

262. A man must always be prudently certain that his act is morally good. One arrives at certain moral judgments obviously by the direct method of immediate scrutiny of the moral factors of a situation: one grasps the pertinent facts and applies the appropriate principle to them. I know with certainty that I must pay my debts as soon as I can conveniently do so. I receive my pay check and remember I owe the grocer ten dollars. I am now sure I must pay this bill without undue delay.

Sometimes, however, a doubt arises which prevents the immediate formation of a certain conscience. One may be uncertain of the moral law, for example, whether one commits a sin if he evades payment of some tax. Many people have only a confused knowledge of some moral principles and there are some moral propositions about which there will always be speculative doubt. Again one may doubt whether a fact, capable of applying the moral law to a particular case, actually exists. A man may know the law of Eucharistic fast but he may be uncertain whether three hours have elapsed since he ate that sandwich. Certainly if one knew all the facts which enter into a particular case and knew all the laws which touch upon it, he would have immediate certitude as to the course to follow. No doubt could be possible because *objectively* nothing in morals is doubtful. Objectively either a law applies or it does not; either this is a pertinent fact or it is not. But because the mind is often incapable of arriving at the truth with certainty in a complex and involved situation, subjectively one is left in doubt.

263. Some reasonable system of solving doubts is not only very helpful to one's own peace of mind but absolutely necessary for one who would offer moral advice to others. To set up a system one first should realize that doubts of conscience fall into two categories. Unless the nature of these two categories is understood and a clear-cut distinction is noted between them, one cannot formulate a workable system because the doubts of each category are solved by distinctly different methods.

A. Doubt About the Appropriate Means of Fulfilling Obligation

264. We refer here to the situation in which a person has a definite and certain obligation of *efficaciously attaining some determined end* but is in doubt about the means to attain that end. His problem is not merely whether the contemplated act is good or bad but, first, whether it will be an appropriate means to his end. The goodness or badness of his act will depend on whether it is a fitting or unfitting means to the end.

Doubts of this type are solved only by the direct method of *always choosing the safer means,*[1] that is, those which more closely approximate

[1] We do not consider this a *reflex* principle; it is contained within the problem to be solved. A reflex principle is one of a higher order, lying outside the problem to be solved, and is invoked to resolve the doubt. Its use constitutes the indirect method of solving doubts. The rigorists claimed they solved *all* doubts directly, that is, by looking at the data of the problem and choosing one of the alternatives presented by the problem. It would seem, however, that they also used a reflex principle to guide them in choosing the alternative closest to obligation. But it is of no importance whether one calls a method of solution direct or indirect.

the obligation. One may not invoke a reflex principle or use probabilities in favor of leniency. Hence, where an obligation must be safeguarded and two means present themselves, one more probably efficacious than the other, one must always choose the more probable means, the side of obligation. The soundness of this method is clear from the following cases.

1. *Salvation.* This is an end which must be insured beyond possibility of doubt. Of the means at hand, those must be chosen which most surely lead to this end. Hence, though there is a probability that an infidel might save his soul without becoming a member of the Church, he cannot rest upon such a probability but must take the safer course and enter the Church.

2. *Validity of an act.* If a person doubts whether there is a diriment impediment to a contemplated marriage, he cannot marry on the strength that no impediment exists. For if one does exist, his probable argument against its existence will not save him from an invalid marriage. Hence he must choose the safer course of making an investigation and consulting proper authority.

3. *Prevention of harm one is obliged to avoid.* A hunter may not fire at what probably is a beast but which might be a man. If I owe a man ten dollars and have two bills, one probably genuine, the other certainly genuine, I may not endanger the discharge of that debt by giving in payment what is merely probably genuine. A physician must choose between two doubtful remedies that which more probably will restore his patient to health; an agent, overseer, or lawyer must take that course which more surely will protect their principal's interests; a judge or juryman must choose the solution which is more probably just.

THESIS XIX. If a person has an absolute obligation to attain some determined end and is in doubt as to the means of fulfilling this obligation, he must follow the more probable argument and choose the safer means.

PROOF

265. The absolute obligation of attaining an end extends to the choice of means toward the end. If certain means exist, they must be chosen. If certain means do not exist and one must choose among those available, one must always choose what appears more apt. To choose what appears less apt is unreasonably to endanger attainment of the end. Therefore, in any doubt as to the means of fulfilling such an obligation,

one must always follow the more probable argument and choose the safer means.

Corollary. Whoever solves such a doubt by following the less probable argument does wrong.

B. Doubt About the Goodness or Badness of an Act

266. About the doctrine contained in Thesis XIX there is no controversy; the most rigoristic moralist would accept it. We now consider the situation of one who has no obligation of attaining a determined end but is in doubt as to the *sinfulness or nonsinfulness of his act.* It must be carefully noted that in the first type of doubt considered, obligation exists and the doubt concerns the means of fulfilling it; in the second type, the doubt is *whether an obligation exists.* Around this problem two controversies have raged: one has been settled; the other still persists.

267. The first controversy was, May a man solve this kind of doubt in an *indirect way,* that is, by using probabilities in favor of leniency and by invoking a principle which lies outside the immediate situation? The rigorist said that there is no other method of solving doubts than the direct method, that probabilities in favor of freedom from obligation are worthless, that one must always choose the side of obligation. Whenever, therefore, one suspects that the moral law commands or forbids one must always follow these suspicions until he becomes absolutely certain that he need not. Thus, if a boy doubts whether he is obliged to stop dating some girl or a woman thinks she should join a pious society, the only solution of their doubts is to drop the girl or join the society. For one must obey all doubtful promptings of law and conscience until they are utterly silenced by a clear and certain release therefrom. This doctrine is false because it holds that doubt has the same binding force as certainty and its acceptance would place an impossible burden on man. When the rigorist was rightly condemned, he changed his stand but a single pace in favor of leniency and said: "In doubt obligation always exists unless it is most probable that it does not." He then became known as the tutiorist because he claimed always to be on the safer side by choosing obligation in preference to freedom.

268. Since it is inhuman to say that in solving this kind of doubt one must always choose obligation, one may avail himself of probabilities in favor of freedom. The use of probabilities, however, does not mean that the best we are going to get is a probable opinion in favor of freedom. What is needed is a certain dictate of conscience and this will be had if one's probabilities are backed up by a reflex but *certain* principle. If the right principle is chosen, it will resolve the doubt and produce a certain dictate of conscience *under all circumstances.* We do not claim that such a principle will resolve all speculative doubts in the field of morals — some of these dubious propositions will never be settled — but it will provide the person with certain assurance that what he is about to do is morally right. This method of solving doubts is called indirect because, when all direct knowledge fails to produce certainty, one invokes a principle which is outside the situation.

269. If anyone wishes he *may* be a tutiorist in his own conduct. He may, if there is no danger of becoming scrupulous, make heroic demands upon himself and convert all probable obligations into self-assumed obligations. However, he does not have to do so. We are not discussing what may sometimes be a better thing but we are drawing a hard and fast line between obligation and freedom. Today all agree that doubts can be solved by the indirect method of reflex principles.

270. The greatly controverted question now arises, What degree of probability erases obligation. What reflex principle can solve doubt? There are four schools of thought.

1. *Probabiliorism* resolves doubts upon the principle that moral obligation exists until its nonexistence is more probable. When the argument against obligation is more probable one is free. Thus in a national crisis a youth weighs the problem, Have I a moral obligation to volunteer for military service? According to probabiliorism he would have to volunteer unless his argument for staying home had greater weight than the argument against it. This doctrine had some enthusiastic adherents in the seventeenth century. While it is no longer taught as a doctrinal system, many people are probabiliorists by temperament and unconscious preference.

2. *Equiprobabilism* holds that when an opinion in favor of the law is more probable than the opinion for liberty, the person is bound; when the opinion for liberty is more probable, the person is free. When opinions on both sides are about equal, a distinction is to be made. If the doubt concerns the coming into existence of obligation, the person is not bound; for his liberty is still in possession. If the doubt concerns the cessation of obligation, one is bound; for law and obligation are still in possession.[2]

3. *Probabilism* seeks neither a greater nor an equally probable argument in favor of liberty but simply states that any solidly probable opinion against obligation renders it null upon the principle that "a doubtful law does not oblige." This dictum holds even when the argument for obligation is more probable. Hence, in the example given above,

[2] Cf. F. J. Connell, *Outlines of Moral Theology,* pp. 44–45. Bruce, Milwaukee, 1953.

as long as the youth had a genuinely good reason against volunteering he was free to stay home even if the argument for volunteering was more probable.

4. *Laxism* holds that any tenuous trifling argument against obligation is sufficient to excuse one. For example, any opinion, expressed in print even by a young and recent author, may be dignified as probable and followed in practice.

271. Like rigorism, laxism is clearly false, for it is equivalent to denial of the moral law. The other three systems may all be used in practice. Of them, the more commonly held doctrine is that of probabilism. Primarily our concern is to show that probabilism is a reasonable system; secondarily, that, in comparison with the other two systems, probabilism is efficient and workable whereas they are cumbersome and overstrict.

THESIS XX. In solving doubts of conscience in which the sole point at issue is the goodness or badness of one's contemplated act, one may follow a genuinely probable opinion against obligation even though there is a more probable opinion for obligation.

272. Probabilism holds that if an obligation is doubtful, one may disregard it even though the argument for obligation is more probable than the argument against it. This does not mean that we may do what is *probably right* but may be more probably wrong. To believe so would be a serious misunderstanding of probabilism. No one may do what is probably wrong. What we do must be *certainly right*. What probabilism does hold is that when we act on the principle that a doubtful obligation is no obligation we are certainly right.

Probabilism is based on these epistemological truths: (*a*) what is probable cannot be certain, what is certain cannot be probable; (*b*) probability is ultimately subjective; (*c*) in a conflict of probabilities, the most probable proposition does not destroy the probability of the opposite proposition; the less probable one may objectively be the true one.

273. A *genuinely probable opinion* is one to which a sincere and prudent man may reasonably assent. If there is reliable evidence, he must necessarily assent; but if reliable evidence is lacking, he is free to choose either of two probable alternatives, provided he has reasons which are genuine, comparable, and practical. A genuine reason is one which has a sound basis and is neither frivolous nor ridiculous. It may be intrinsic — from the nature of the case, or extrinsic — from the word of a competent authority. It is comparably probable when it remains not unlikely after examination of opposing reasons. It is practical when it has taken into account the actual circumstances of the case.

When, therefore, such an opinion against obligation exists, the person is free, the reason being that the law which would impose obligation on him is here and now a doubtful law and a *doubtful law is no law.*

PROOF

274. Probabilism is reasonable because it is based on the principle that *an uncertain law can induce no obligation.* A law against which a genuinely probable opinion stands cannot be certain, for certitude and probability mutually exclude each other. If, however, an uncertain law could beget a certain obligation, an effect would be greater than its cause; for obligation is the effect of law. A person therefore is free to disregard an uncertain law even when a more probable opinion favors the law's existence.

Our proof is confirmed by St. Thomas who says: "No one is bound by a command . . . unless the command reaches him who is commanded; and it reaches him through knowledge of it. . . . As in physical things the physical agent [binds another] by contact, so in spiritual things a precept binds only by means of knowledge."[3] By knowledge or *scientia* the Angelic Doctor means certain knowledge.

275. The truth of our demonstration is thus illustrated. I am asked to give blood to an uncle who is critically ill. I argue that I should have to sacrifice important business and I am not sure if my health can stand a blood donation. On the other hand, the need of my uncle and his claims upon me are very great. I probably have no moral obligation to give the blood; it is more probable that I have an obligation. In such a conflict of probabilities one could not justly tell me that I *must* give the blood.

276. *Probabilism is an efficient and workable system* because with one sure stroke it settles doubts of conscience. Provided his reason is worthy of an honest man, the probabilist readily reaches a certain dictate of conscience. Compared with other systems, probabilism has this great advantage: whereas they demand a more probable or equally probable argument, probabilism asks only for a genuinely probable reason. In most cases the seeking for a more probable or equally probable reason prolongs the doubt. We have no nicely balanced scales to assay the value of probabilities.

Moreover, *the other systems are too strict,* when they deny that the lesser probability also erases the certainty of obligation. The logical result of this denial is rigorism. For either all probabilities — whether

[3] *De Veritate,* q. 17, a. 3.

most probable, more probable, equally probable, or less probable—destroy the certainty of the opposite proposition or no genuine probability does. It is a case of all or none. Between probability and certainty there is no middle ground. Whoever, therefore, denies the soundness of our stand should reject all reflex principles and demand certainty for release from obligation.

The overstrictness of the other systems is due to *unreasonable fear of evil.* What moved the rigorist to say that certainty alone can release one from obligation was fear of evil. All agree that this fear was ill-grounded. The same fear moved the tutiorist to demand a most probable argument and he is reckoned overcautious. The same fear moves the probabiliorist to reject a genuine though less probable reason. The probabilist, however, rightly says that one is also free of evil who follows his type of argument, that one need fear the commission of evil only when obligation is certain. He holds that one should follow reflex principles to their logical conclusions. Therefore, if probability can destroy the certainty of obligation, then every genuine probability can do so and it is illogical to refuse to go the whole way by limiting this power to the most probable, the more probable, and the equally probable reason. He refuses to yield to fear of evil until it is reasonable to do so.

277. As no one has overturned the proposition that *a doubtful law does not oblige,* so neither has anyone demonstrated that *only* a most probable or a more probable or an equally probable argument is able to render a law doubtful. Until both of these demonstrations are forthcoming probabilism stands as the humane and reasoned mode of settling the doubts we have been discussing.

Probabilism, like any other principle, may be abused. If a person imagines probabilism to be a license to pare one's obligations to the minimum and converts it into a clever scheme whereby a certain conscience can be rendered probable and obligation avoided, he is not a probabilist but a laxist. Probabilism is not an instrument to blunt the keen edge of obligation.

Nor is it to be used for the daily formation of one's conscience; it is reserved for the crisis of doubt. For the sole function of probabilism is to cut the knot of doubt and rigidly expose the extent of one's obligation. It does not pretend to counsel the better course of action. If one chooses he may assume as obligations what are only probably obligatory: one may be as strict as he chooses on himself but he may not impose uncertain obligations upon others as though they were certain.

READINGS

St. Thomas, *Summa Theologica*, I, 79, 13; I–II, 19, 20.

Davis, H., *Moral and Pastoral Theology*, Vol. I, 64–115. New York, Sheed & Ward, 1936.

De Letter, P., "In Defense of Christian Conscience," *Clergy Monthly*, 17 (April, 1953), 81–88.

Deman, T., "Dignity of Conscience," *Blackfriars*, 34 (1953), 115–119.

Flynn, F. E., "Two Kinds of Private Judgment," *Commonweal*, 55 (November 9, 1951), 113–115.

Hurth, F., "De ethica situationis," *Periodica*, 45 (June 15, 1956), 137–204.

——— "Hodierna conscientiae problemata metaphysica, psychologica, theologica," *Periodica*, 42 (1953), 238–245.

Jarrett, B., "Conscience," *Life of the Spirit*, 9 (May, 1955), 519–522.

Jenkins, J., "The Significance of Conscience," *Ethics*, 65 (1954–1955), 261–270.

Jone, F., *Moral-Theology*, tr. U. Adelman, 38–46. Westminster, Newman, 1957.

Klausner, N. W., "The Nature of Moral Deliberation," *The Personalist*, 36 (1955), 17–24.

Lacroix, J., "Religious Conscience and Political Conscience," *Cross Currents*, Fall, 1952, 14–20.

Latko, E. F., "A Psychotherapy for Scruples," *Homiletic and Pastoral Review*, 49 (1949), 617–623; 50 (1950), 906–914; 1020–1030; 1119–1124; 51 (1951), 33–38.

Lottin, O., *Morale Fondamentale*, 142–150; 297–339. Paris, Desclée, 1954.

Mailloux, N., "Morality and Contemporary Psychology," *Catholic Theological Society of American Proceedings*, 1954, 47–66.

Maritain, R., "Abraham and the Assent of Conscience," *The Bridge*, Vol. I, 23–52.

Pius XII, *The Proper Formation of a Christian Conscience in Youth*, Radio Message of March 23, 1952. *AAS*, 44 (1952), 270–278.

VanderVeldt-Odenwald, *Psychiatry and Catholicism*, 375–390. New York, McGraw-Hill, 1957.

Wack, D. J., "Moral Consciousness and Conscience," *American Benedictine Review*, Winter, 1954, 311–325.

——— *A Psychological Study of Conscience*. Washington, Catholic University, 1952.

Chapter IX VIRTUE AND VICE

278. As there is a science, so there is also an art of ethics. The supremely important result of pursuing either is that a man perform morally good acts and avoid morally evil acts. It is well to learn from the science of ethics what orderly conduct is; it is better to be skilled in the art of ethics so that a man not only do good and avoid evil but also that he acquire facility and, if possible, perfect ease in doing so. The final result should be nobility of character.

279. We come then to the final inquiry of general ethics. In the previous chapter we discussed the *subjective* principle of morality, conscience. Here we are concerned with another intrinsic principle of morality. We shall endeavor to show that there exists within man a principle which helps or hinders him in fulfilling readily the dictates of conscience, giving him a more or less permanent attitude toward moral good and evil. This inquiry introduces the topic of *habit*. Without habit a man will experience difficulty in obeying conscience. The faculties from which the human act proceed can be conditioned by habit for permanent facility in doing good or doing evil. Habit, therefore, is a subjective coprinciple of morality.

I. HABIT

280. In the most general sense, habit is a quality whereby the existence or operation of a substance is permanently affected for better or worse. Habits which affect the existence of a substance are entitative habits, such as shape or color. Those which affect its operation are operative habits. Ethics is concerned exclusively with operative habits, and these are called simply habits.

A. The Nature of Habit

281. Habit is a stable quality superadded to a faculty whereby the faculty's capacity to act in a variety of ways is channeled to produce

readily and easily a particular kind of act. Habit is difficult to change and in this respect it differs from *disposition*, which changes easily. Moods come and go; habits abide. Habit differs from faculty because habit presupposes an initial potency which it perfects. One cannot have the skill of a swimmer or gymnast if he is unable to move his limbs. Both habit and faculty are immediate principles of action, but faculty is innate whereas habit is acquired, or in the case of the supernatural virtues, infused. Habit adds an intrinsic perfection to faculty. Hence it is a real modification of the agent's nature which abides with him in the intervals between one occasion for its exercise and another. The skill of a fine surgeon remains with him even when he is playing cards or fishing. Finally, habit differs from mere routine, which of itself involves no skill. One may be accustomed to going to bed every night at ten or seeing a movie every Friday, but there is no added potency in such custom.

282. A faculty which acts in only one way cannot be modified by habit. Water will not boil faster if it has been boiled ten times before. Habit belongs to living things. It has two distinguishing features. (*a*) It presupposes *activity illumined by knowledge*. Physiological activities which are not governable by reason, such as the beating of the heart and the circulation of the blood, are not subject to habits. However, certain vegetative and sensitive activities can be sufficiently controlled by reason so that we rightly speak of good hygienic habits. Although brutes have ways of acting which resemble habits, habit is more properly a perfection of the rational nature because (*b*) *it operates under the direction of free will*. While seals and elephants may be trained to repeat certain acts, these acts are not habits in the true sense because animals have no freedom. Essentially habit is something *usable at will*. In man those habits which become mere reflex actions are routine. They are not habits ethically speaking, for the acts which proceed from them are not human acts and have no moral significance.

B. The Value of Habit

283. Habit has as *its end product a particular act easily and perfectly done*. The permanent ability to do this is well named a second nature. Habit understood in the wider meaning of custom or routine has also very practical advantages. William James aptly remarks: "The great thing is to make our nervous system our ally instead of our enemy. For this we must make automatic and habitual, as early as possible, as many useful actions as we can and guard against growing into ways that are disadvantageous to us. The more of the details of our daily life we can hand over to the effortless custody of automatism, the more our higher

powers of mind will be set free for their proper work. There is no more miserable human being than one in whom nothing is more habitual than indecision and for whom the lighting of every cigar, the drinking of every cup, the time of rising and going to bed and the beginning of every bit of work, are subjects of express volitional deliberation."[1]

One of the ends of education is the formation of proper psychological habits and the avoidance of undesirable ones. Everyone should have a system of daily living. It should not be a rigid plan but should admit of reasonable exception. Advantageous as these routines are, the less voluntary they become, the more they recede from the ambit of ethics.

C. The Origin of Habit

284. Once an act is completed, its effect on the agent is not terminated. A sort of residue, which is the tendency to repeat the act, remains in the agent. Hence habit is the act continued. Habits are caused by the repetition of the same kind of act. Ease in accomplishment comes in no other way than by doing a thing often. Aristotle puts it: "Men become builders by building and lyre players by playing the lyre; so too, we become just by doing just acts, temperate by doing temperate acts, brave by doing brave acts."[2]

The initial acts of a habit are performed with difficulty, fitfully perhaps, and by special effort. If one or other of these acts is done excellently it is due to chance — beginner's luck — and is not reproducible at will. Drudgery and repetition intervene between the first act and accomplished execution. Practice alone makes perfect. Habit is a living thing which feeds on acts and the more frequently and intensely the act is performed the deeper the habit is implanted.

Psychologists offer these valuable suggestions for the development of good habits: (*a*) To break off a bad habit or to implant a new one begin with as intense and determined an initial effort as possible, for great starting power is needed to overcome the inertia of nonmovement. (*b*) Never allow an exception, permit no small deviations from your resolve, until the new habit is securely rooted in your life. (*c*) Seize every first possible opportunity to act on every resolution formed and on every emotional prompting in the direction of the habits desired.

As habits grow by repeated acts of the same sort, so they are diminished by contrary acts. Unexercised, a habit languishes, disintegrates, and finally passes away. One forgets a language he no longer reads or speaks: the habit of chastity is utterly wrecked by constant unchaste acts.

---

[1] William James, *Principles of Psychology*, Vol. I, p. 122. New York, Holt, 1923.
[2] *Nicomachean Ethics*, II, 1, 1103a.

285. The *ethical habit* is skill in the performance of moral acts. As it is important for man to acquire corporal and psychological habits which make for efficient daily living, so it is necessary for him to cultivate proper ethical habits. These reside in man's moral faculties and are of two general kinds. Habits which are productive of acts conducing to man's last end are called *virtues.* Habits which incline him to activity leading him away from his last end are called *vices.* Virtue and vice play a large part in the loss or attainment of beatitude and may not be lightly passed over in an ethical treatise.

II. VIRTUE

286. Two of the most fascinating questions discussed by the Greek philosophers were: (*a*) *What is virtue?* and (*b*) *Who is the virtuous man?*

Virtue derives from the Latin *virtus,* which means "power." Applied to many things, virtue is the natural power or function of a thing. It is the virtue of the ear to hear, of the legs to walk. So, on the contrary, vice is a flaw, a lack of due perfection. But virtue is more than mere power to act; it is power to *work well.* "Every virtue," says Aristotle, "both brings into good condition the thing of which it is the excellence and makes the work of that thing to be well done; e.g., the excellence of the eye makes both the eye and its work good . . . therefore, the virtue of man will be a state of character which makes a man good and makes him do his work well."[3] Therefore, *human virtue is a habit perfecting man as man and inclining him to do well the proper acts of man.* St. Augustine calls this a good habit consonant with our nature;[4] and St. Thomas, a good operative habit.[5]

287. Since man is a being subject to rule, his perfection lies in conformity with the rule. Human evil consists in nonconformity with the rule by going too far or not going far enough. Virtue conforms to the rule by striking the midpoint between excess and defect. This is the *golden mean* which Horace[6] applies both to human desires and literary composition. "We often say," Aristotle remarks, "of good works of art that it is not possible to take away or add anything, implying that excess and defect destroy the goodness of works of art, while the mean preserves it; and if virtue is more exact and better than any art . . . then virtue must have the quality of aiming at the mean."[7]

[3] *Ibid.,* II, 6, 1106a.
[4] *De Diversis Quaestionibus,* LXXXIII, q. 31.
[5] *Sum. Theol.,* I–II, 55, 2.
[6] *Odes,* Bk. II, Ode X; *Ars Poetica,* 25–31.
[7] *Nicomachean Ethics,* II, 6, 1106b.

Strictly speaking there is no mean for the act of intellect; it moves by necessity to its object. Since the intellect is forced by evidence to affirm truth and since the judgment affirms or denies the identity of two objective concepts, there is no middle ground between an affirmation or denial of identity. Hence the judgment is good or bad in that it represents or misrepresents reality. The mean exists only for will acts or activities directed by the will to some good. Inasmuch, however, as some intellectual acts can be so directed, we may speak of a mean in their regard. Thus, *art*, which is an intellectual virtue, seeks the mean, as St. Thomas says.[8]

The mean in our will acts is not a thing of mathematical exactness, the center of two equidistant extremes, but that which is here and now fitting for this particular agent. Thus, virtue in the control of our emotions means that one does not check them too much or too little but permits them to be aroused at the right time, toward the right object, with reference to the right people, from the right motive, in the right measure. Modern ethics raises the problem of the mean of virtue when it seeks the exactly "right" act. In every circumstance of human activity there is always the act which is just right. What objectively determines this right act is human nature in all its essential aspects. But what manifests the mean of virtue to the agent? Sometimes it is the objective situation, as in the observance of justice. We are just toward our fellow man when we give him his own, no more, no less. But in the control of self the mean of virtue varies from person to person and circumstance to circumstance. What would be proper speech in a superior would be insolence in a subject. In these cases there is no *direct* intimation of the right act. One must rely on right reason as a man of practical wisdom would employ it. A great purpose in studying ethics is the acquiring of this wisdom or skill in making these estimates.

288. The virtuous man, therefore, is endowed with habits that incline him to act readily in accord with right reason. He is thereby correctly ordered to his last end. He is *the good man*. But how do we recognize the good man, that is, *what habits must a man possess in order to be truly good?*

289. Socrates taught that virtue is knowledge and vice is ignorance. "Those who knew," he says, "what were just and righteous acts would prefer nothing else, while those who did not know them could not do them if they would."[9] In this he is followed by Plato the whole theme of whose *Meno* is that virtue is understanding. In the *Protagoras* Plato

[8] *Sum. Theol.*, I–II, 64, 3.
[9] Xenophon, *Memorabilia*, III, c. IX, 5.

says: "No man voluntarily pursues evil, or that which he thinks to be evil. To prefer evil to good is not in human nature."[10] The Stoics, emphasizing the need of overcoming difficulty, said the good man was the brave and enduring man. Horace, expressing the doctrine of Epicurus, sums up all virtue in his famous phrase, *nil admirari:*[11] the wise man is one of undisturbed mind, cushioned against the shocks and surprises of fate by unfailing tranquillity.

The opinion of Socrates is not a mere literary museum piece. Modern literature often re-echoes the opinion of the old sage. Understanding makes human relationships, says a certain Gubsky, meaning that to get along with a man all that is required is that one know him thoroughly. *What then are good habits of mind? Do they suffice to make a man unqualifiedly* good, i.e., correctly ordered to his last end?

III. INTELLECTUAL VIRTUES

290. The intellect may be endowed with a number of good habits assisting both its speculative and practical activities. The following virtues may be distinguished.

1. *Intuition* is insight into, and facility for, grasping truths without the effort of discursive reasoning.

2. *Wisdom* is the ability to understand realities in the light of ultimate causes.

3. *Science* is the ability to grasp conclusions in some specialized department of knowledge such as mathematics, chemistry, or physics. These three habits perfect the speculative activities of the intellect. The following two perfect the practical activities of the intellect.

4. *Art* is the ability to choose efficient means to effect external productions: knowledge of how to make things, useful or artistic.

5. *Prudence* is the ability to discern the true ends of human conduct and to fashion means proper to effect these ends.

Intuition, wisdom, science, and art are *merely* intellectual virtues; they confer a facility for intellectual activity and thereby make the subject good, but since the supreme good of human life is not attained by merely intellectual activity, these habits do not make one unqualifiedly good but good only in a restricted field. Thus, one may be a good metaphysician, mathematician, or sculptor without being a good man.

291. Since prudence directly and of itself correctly orders man toward his supreme good, it is not only an intellectual virtue; it is also a moral

---

[10] *Protagoras,* 358b.
[11] *Epist.,* I, 6, 1.

virtue rendering a man unqualifiedly good. The prudent man is therefore a good man. But does the good man require anything more? Socrates says *no*. He cannot conceive how a man can know what his true good is and fail to embrace it.

But the Socratic theory contradicts human experience. Men do act contrary to their better judgment; the sinner knows he should be doing better. Ovid expresses this universal experience: "I see the better thing and approve it but I do the worse."[12] Besides, if Socrates were right, there would be no such thing as sin, for no one could do evil willfully. Hence no one could be blamed for being wicked because he could always offer the excuse that he did not know better. St. Thomas masterfully explains how it is possible for the sinner to turn his back on the light of reason.[13]

If a man is to be completely equipped to walk with readiness in the way of the moral law, other habits than those that perfect the intellect are required. The appetitive faculties must be habituated to obey the voice of reason. Hence from a consideration of merely intellectual virtues we pass to moral virtues.

IV. MORAL VIRTUES

A. Moral Virtues in General

292. What we referred to above as human virtue in general we shall now call *moral virtue*. Moral virtue is any habit operating under the direction of the will *directly* ordering man to his last end. Since human acts must be subject to the will, and since man's last end is attainable only by good volitional acts, any permanent source of good conduct must be will-directed and conducive to perfect happiness. Since it is the will's function to obey right reason, moral virtue gives man readiness to act in accord with reason. Since that which is reasonable leads to the last end, the person who possesses moral virtue is unqualifiedly good.

293. Is moral virtue one or many? There are as many moral virtues as there are specifically different morally good acts, and there are as many of these as there are specifically different moral objects which it befits a man to attain. As these are numerous, there are many virtues but all are reducible to four main categories or *cardinal virtues*. We are indebted to Greek thought for the division, to St. Ambrose[14] for the name, which comes from Latin *cardo*, a "hinge." That there are four and only four cardinal virtues is proved as follows:

---

[12] *Metamorphoses*, VII, 20.
[13] *Sum. Theol.*, I–II, 77, 2.
[14] *Expositio Evan. secundum Lucam*, Lib. V, n. 49. Migne, *P.L.*, XV, 1734.

To be steadily prompted to morally good acts in all circumstances, man must be assisted by good habits dwelling in those potencies whence the human act proceeds and in those which tend to oppose the will's dominion. Hence a habit must reside in each of the following:

1. *The intellect.* To act well, the will first must be illumined by the intellect presenting a true good to it. Hence the intellect must be habituated to discern true good from apparent good. The intellect, skilled in recognizing the reasonable thing to do in all particulars of human conduct, possesses the virtue of *prudence.*

2. *The will.* Man's will does not require a special habit to assist him to seek his own good, for innate impulse urges him to do this. However, man's will requires a special habit to dispose him to respect the good of his fellow man. This habit is the virtue of *justice.*

3. *The concupiscible appetite.* In dealing with self, however, a man may be disordered by the importunities of his sensitive appetite. Hence, a good habit must reside in the concupiscible appetite restraining it within the bounds of reason from wanton pursuit of sensible good. This habit is *temperance,* which moderates the concupiscible appetite.

4. *The irascible appetite.* A similar habit must reside in the irascible appetite and restrain man from acting unreasonably in the face of difficulty and danger. This is *fortitude.*

294. The person, then, who has acquired the moral virtues of prudence, justice, temperance, and fortitude is the good man. He is recognizable by the fact that in all situations he promptly, uniformly, and pleasurably does what is reasonable. It is the effect of good habit to do the right thing *promptly; uniformly,* because virtue is permanent; *pleasurably,* because what we do well and skillfully we do with pleasure.

295. There is a mutual relationship between the moral virtues in their perfect state.[15] The person who is perfectly just is also truly prudent, temperate, and courageous. The reason is that no real virtue can be had without prudence,[16] and prudence is impossible without justice, temperance, and fortitude. The presence of prudence implies that one's appetites are in proper order. Since man's moral judgments reflect the order or disorder in his appetites, no one can constantly make prudent judgments if his appetites are not in order.

Imperfect virtues are inclinations to right conduct resulting from natural temperament or virtues in their unformed state. They are not interconnected like perfect moral virtues. However, it is generally true that any serious attempt to develop one virtue is accompanied by growth in

[15] Cf. St. Thomas, *Sum. Theol.,* I–II, 65, 1.

[16] Thus Plato was not altogether wrong in identifying knowledge and virtue.

the other virtues. Likewise, serious collapse of a virtue often brings with it a breakdown of other virtues. A woman who surrenders to unchastity will often become unjust and intemperate. A drunken man will steal to satisfy his cravings, forget his family and his obligations.

B. Moral Virtues in Particular

296. 1. *Prudence* is the ability to discern the becoming ends of human conduct and the morally good act in all the contingencies of life. Though it resides in the intellect, it is a moral virtue for it is subject to the supreme dominion of the will. It orders man to his last end and makes clear the golden mean of the other virtues. It points out the path of justice, the measure of temperance, the limits of fortitude. Without prudence, courage becomes recklessness, patience degenerates into apathy, modesty into prudery, and meekness into pusillanimity.

The acquisition of prudence does not so much depend on one's intellectual ability as on the strength of one's will steadily focusing the mind on the true ends of life. Even a person of low intelligence can be quite prudent, for, through the influence of the will he may not permit his mind to be distracted from the genuine purpose of life. Contemplating those ends which alone are worthy of human endeavor, such persons can devise efficient means of attaining them. Brilliant persons who pursue ignoble ends possess sagacity but not prudence. To form prudent men is the purpose of this study.

297. 2. *Temperance* is that virtue which restrains within the bounds of reason the sensitive appetite seeking pleasure. Nature attaches a commensurate pleasure to all our activities. However, bodily pleasures are so vivid that they can diminish the appeal of purely spiritual pleasure. There is a danger, therefore, that we may seek bodily pleasure unreasonably. Hence, not only must the mind be endowed with prudence to discern between real good of the spirit and an apparent good of the body, but the bodily appetite must be restrained lest it overwhelm both intellect and will. The virtue of temperance is the means of moderating our pleasurable appetites.

There is no danger that man will sin by defect as far as the satisfaction of bodily pleasure is concerned. No one is so apathetic to his bodily urges that he requires a special virtue to help him seek his bodily good. Nature has taken care of this by the strength of our bodily drives.

Of all sensible pleasures none are greater than the pleasures attending those acts whereby life is conserved and new life is begotten. To conserve life we need food and drink, but an excessive indulgence in them is opposed to the Natural Law. This disorderly tendency is the capital vice of gluttony against which temperance inculcates *abstinence,* or moderation in food, and *sobriety,* or moderation in drink. A capital sin is not a wrong choice but a corrupted natural appetite which leads to many actual sins.

Nature attaches the greatest of all sensible pleasure to the activity which secures the continuance of the race. Since reproduction is a good not primarily of the individual but of the race, the individual may enjoy the pleasure only in the manner which safeguards its main purpose. Nature's dictum in this respect is set forth in Thesis XXVI, but the sexual impulse is so urgent that one is inclined to satisfy it regardless of the limits set down by reason. Against the corruption of our sexual drive temperance prescribes *chastity* whose precepts may be summarized thus: for the unmarried to seek or willfully to enjoy any venereal pleasure or for the married to seek this pleasure apart from a natural act with one's spouse is a serious wrong.

298. 3. *Fortitude* is the virtue which inclines a man to act reasonably despite the prompting of his irascible appetite. This appetite moves toward an arduous good or shuns a difficult evil. In either case it may miss the mean of virtue. Therefore, when we are inclined to avoid a danger which we ought to face, fortitude enables us to meet it. Or, more rarely, when we would injudiciously expose ourselves to harm, fortitude tempers our boldness. Its function is to restrain our fears and moderate our rashness. It seeks a golden mean between cowardice and rashness, moderating our internal motions of fear and recklessness and our external acts of flight and aggression. While there is a special moral fitness in the *reasonable* endurance of evil or the conquest of arduous difficulty, not every suffering of hardship or display of courage is moral virtue. Only that is virtue which is for a worthy end. Evil men in pursuit of crime may act bravely and perseveringly but one may not rightly ascribe this to the virtue of fortitude.

With Plato[17] we may compare the sensitive appetite to a team of horses one of which, spirited and straining ahead, needs to be checked. This is appetite striving for pleasure and requiring the rein of temperance. The other is dull and needs to be urged on. This is appetite, beset with fears, that must be whipped on by fortitude. Fortitude is the moral stimulus which enables us to overcome fear.

299. A few men fear dishonor more than death. As fortitude enables one to cope with the fear of death, a special kind of fortitude — magnanimity — disposes him to deal reasonably with dishonor.

Magnanimity is the virtue which inclines a man to great deeds and

[17] *Phaedrus,* 253D–256.

to act reasonably in the face of great honor or dishonor. Relatively, it is a great thing to use a trifle excellently but, absolutely speaking, only that act is great which is the exactly right use of a great thing. Of all goods external to man, the greatest is honor. It is the testimony of virtue and is paid to God Himself. Desire for it is man's most powerful motive. Therefore, as a man is called brave because by facing death he does what without qualification is difficult, so a man is called magnanimous because, by bearing great honor reasonably, he does what without qualification is great. What the magnanimous seeks is the great deed, but since great honor follows from his action, the perfection of his virtue is manifest in his attitude toward honor.

300. Aristotle's portrayal of the magnanimous man is truly noble. "The magnanimous man," he says, "being by hypothesis worthy of the greatest things, must be of the highest excellence since the better a man is, the more he is worth, and he who is best is worth most; it follows, then, to be truly magnanimous a man must be good, and whatever is great in each virtue belongs to the magnanimous. . . . This virtue, then, is a kind of ornament to all the other virtues in that it makes them better and cannot be without them; and for this reason it is a hard matter to be really and truly magnanimous for it cannot be without thorough goodness and nobility of character."[18]

When honor comes his way, the magnanimous man will not be wrongfully affected because he will rightfully consider it his due. Nor will he be saddened by disgrace; he will contemn it for in his case there are no just grounds for it. "As regards wealth and power, good fortune or bad fortune of every kind, he will bear himself with moderation, fall out how these may and neither in prosperity will he be overjoyed nor in adversity unduly pained."[19]

The portrait carries overtones of arrogance[20] and lacks the right touch of humble charity — deficiencies attributable to the paganism of ancient Greece. Commanding as is Aristotle's magnanimous man, he is a far cry from the perfect Man, in whom is found the exquisite tempering of all the virtues, Jesus Christ, our Lord.

301. The ordinary uses of fortitude are to enable us to persevere in well-doing despite the less spectacular difficulties. Our virtue meets opposition from men who ridicule our practices of religion and chastity. We need strength to withstand human respect. The right course of action may be most unpopular. Opposition comes also from our own

---

[18] *Nicomachean Ethics,* IV, 3, 1123b.
[19] *Ibid.,* IV, 3, 1124a.
[20] Cf. 1124b.

fickleness under drawn-out temptation. Fortitude steels us to say *no* despite our moral weariness. However, as temptation grows protracted, the insufficiency of natural virtue becomes apparent; without supernatural aid we succumb to grievous and continuing temptation. Finally, that we may remain steadfastly upright through the trials of life, fortitude supplies us with patience, the passive counterpart of boldness.

302. 4. *Justice*. There is scriptural warrant for using justice as the equivalent of virtue in general.[21] Aristotle also speaks of justice as a general virtue embracing all others.[22] As a specific virtue, however, justice regulates our conduct toward others. As temperance and fortitude perfect a man in regard to himself, justice perfects him in regard to his fellow men taken both individually and collectively. Since the primary relation among men is that of equality, justice adjusts the relations of men by securing a fitting equality. Since equality supposes two terms physically distinct, one cannot be just to himself. Hence the cardinal virtue of justice is the constant and perpetual will to render to another his due.[23]

The key word is *due* and it means that which belongs to another by right. Things which are due in a broader sense of fitness, decency, and need are not the object matter of justice but of some allied virtue like veracity, fidelity, gratitude, natural charity, friendliness, and equity. Justice deals only with what is due by strict right, and, since we distinguish what is naturally right (determined and protected by Natural Law) from what is legally right (determined and protected by positive law), we distinguish *natural justice* from *positive justice*.[24] Since the word *another* may refer to one totally separate or to one partially separate, three principal relationships arise and upon them we found three principal kinds of justice. Where the two parties are partially identified we have either the relation of social parts to the social whole and this governed (*a*) *by social justice;* or the relation of social whole to the social parts and this is governed by (*b*) *distributive justice*. Where the two parties are distinct, their relation is that of other and other and this is governed by *commutative justice*.

303. *Social justice* is the virtue which moves the individual to contribute his due share to society by promoting the common good. Since there is a quasi identification between the social part and the community, justice demands that the part support the whole in due measure. Hence

---

[21] Ezech. 3:20; 18:24; Mt. 1:19.
[22] *Nicomachean Ethics*, V, 1, 1129b.
[23] *Sum. Theol.*, II–II, 58, 1.
[24] Cf. *infra*, § 428 ff.

social justice looks toward an equilibrium of duty toward the social whole which each part must maintain. In this general sense social justice has been called *community justice*.[25]

There are as many kinds of social justice as there are distinct aspects of the common good. First, there are those aspects which are found in societies more or less organized: the family, the State, the whole human race. *Domestic justice*[26] obliges each member of a family to make a due contribution to its welfare. *Legal justice* moves individuals, both rulers and ruled, to fulfill their duties to the State. Although the good of the State can evoke the practice of very many virtues, legal justice[27] is not virtue in general (§ 302); it is a special virtue whose formal object or motive is the common *public* good. Although the human race is a real natural society, it has only begun to be organized as international society. Hence, while an individual has some obligations of fulfilling *international justice*, in the main this duty falls on States. Second, not all social needs and relationships are regulated by visible authority and as part of a distinct community. To say that society and political society are the same is totalitarianism. There are areas of social concern — cultural, recreational, economic — which are subject mostly to Natural Law. Although these interests are often inadequately regulated, yet they pertain to the *total* common good. This is especially true of socioeconomic interests. Some authors speak as if these interests alone are the object matter of social justice which they define as that species of justice which regulates the socioeconomic product for the common use of all.[28] While it is true that the phrase "social justice" originated in discussions about socioeconomic things, which belong to social justice, yet social justice is not limited to them. The end of social justice is the common good, the welfare of the community.

304. *Distributive justice* is the counterpart of social justice. As the individual has obligations to society, so society has duties to the individual. What society owes the individual is determined by distributive justice which envisions an equality between the social whole and the social parts. Here equality demands a *fair sharing* of common advantages and burdens proportioned to the needs, abilities, and merits of individuals. The obligation belongs to the community as such. Therefore, in

[25] J. Messner, *Social Ethics*, 215. St. Louis, Herder, 1949.

[26] Cf. *Sum. Theol.*, II–II, 58, 7 ad 2; and Aristotle's *Nicomachean Ethics*, V, 1, 1134b.

[27] Cf. *ibid.*, 6. It is often asked if the legal justice mentioned by St. Thomas in II–II, 58, 5 is the same as social justice. If by law in this context he means both positive and Natural Law and in the common good includes all social relationships, the answer is in the affirmative. That he means all this is not quite clear.

[28] Cf. W. F. Drummond, *Social Justice*, 55. Milwaukee, Bruce, 1955.

organized societies it will be exercised by the head of the community — by the father in the family, by the legitimate authorities in the State. Even in the unorganized areas of society the obligation of a just distribution of the common good exists and the obligation falls upon those in whose hands control rests. Should they make a faulty distribution where interests are great, enormous evils will result (cf. § 529). Distributive justice, then, is the virtue which inclines the authorities or controllers of a community to promote the social good of its members. It is violated by favoritism and partiality, the undue promotion of some interests to the neglect of others. When distributive justice takes the form of punishing offenses against the common good, it is punitive or *vindicative justice* (cf. § 194). The end of distributive justice is the welfare of the individual as a member of the community.

Since the common good aims at both the good condition of the community and the social good of the members, social and distributive justice coalesce to form one general unnamed kind of justice.

305. *Commutative justice.* Strict justice involves two things: parties adequately distinct and an object which actually belongs to someone by right. Consequently social and distributive justice are not strict justice. First, as far as social justice is concerned, the individual is not completely distinct from the community. Second, that which society demands of the individual is not yet its property. The same is true of the individual under distributive justice. Since only commutative justice involves distinct parties and concerns itself with objects *actually* belonging to one by right, it alone is strict justice. Therefore, commutative justice is the virtue which moves persons, individual or corporate, to render fully to each other what he legitimately claims as his own.

The word *commutative* comes from the Latin *commutatio*, an "exchange." A man is constantly exchanging his things — money, goods, services — for those of his neighbor. Commutative justice aims at equality in these exchanges. Equality does not mean that each should have equal possessions but that each be secure in what he has, that when he makes an exchange he get an equitable return. The object of this justice is not the common but the individual good. This is not a subjective estimate but an objective reality — the mine, the thine, the his. Hence the mean of commutative justice is an exact objective thing.

306. Since this is so, it follows that when commutative justice is violated restitution is necessary. When that which belongs to a man is wrongfully damaged or taken from him, the equality of mine and thine demands that his loss be made good.

Restitution, however, does not enter into social or distributive justice.

Thus, if a citizen withholds something due the State through social justice, though he does wrong, it cannot be said that he is keeping public property in private hands. He has failed to convert to public use some of his property but he has not stolen public property. So, too, with distributive justice. While a citizen may rightly claim that a benefit be given him, it does not become his until the State makes it over to him. Thus when the veterans of World War I were agitating for a bonus they based their claims upon distributive justice. Once Congress passed the law every veteran qualifying under the law had a claim in commutative justice to $1,600. But if Congress had not passed the law a veteran could not have surreptitiously recompensed himself at government expense.

If an obligation arising out of social or distributive justice has been neglected and the opportunity for fulfilling it passes, that particular obligation lapses; if an offense against commutative justice is committed, the obligation of restitution remains. However, in matters of social and distributive justice public officials can violate commutative justice on account of the contract by which they implicitly bind themselves to prevent damage to the State and its members. Thus, if a veteran were deprived of his legal bonus through the malice of some official, the veteran would have a personal claim against the official.

Although commutative justice aims immediately at the individual good and is buttressed with the obligation of restitution, this virtue is subordinate to the justice which aims at the total common good for "there must be one supreme virtue . . . which directs all virtues to the common good."[29]

V. VICE

A. Vice in General

307. As virtue is the inclination to act in accord with our rational nature, vice is the contrary habit disposing us to act against it. As good acts are the products of virtue, evil acts are the product of vice. Vices are formed by repetition of evil acts which becomes, in turn, a partial cause of further sinful acts. A man is called virtuous or vicious insofar as he possesses virtue or vice, but he is adjudged guilty or innocent insofar as his act is good or bad. Guilt is chargeable not to the vice but to the act.

Vices, like virtues, may become mechanical, involving no deliberation and consent. The vicious do evil by second nature. Thus the question arises, "How responsible is a man for evil acts committed under the

[29] *Sum. Theol.*, II–II, 58, 6, ad 4.

influence of a vice?" (*a*) If a person adverts and consents to a bad act, he is responsible for it, despite the presence of a vice. (*b*) If a person does not advert to a bad act as he performs it, the act is not chargeable to him as a wrong but the habit is imputed as a wrong if it is voluntary. A vice is voluntary when it has been knowingly contracted or when one neglects to break it as far as one can. It becomes involuntary when one sincerely renounces it by a definite will act. The sincerity of such a will act is manifested by the practical means one takes to implement his resolve. If no means are later taken to break a grave vice, one is guilty of grave neglect. If some measure of diligence is used, even though insufficient, one is not guilty of grave neglect.

B. Vice in Particular

308. Vice, as evil, is the privation of good — the absence of virtue. Each vice is specifically differentiated in terms of the virtue of which it is the absence and there are as many distinct virtues as there are special kinds of good. Since virtue conforms to the golden mean, vice either falls short of it by defect or goes beyond by excess. Hence there are more vices than virtues.

309. **Vices contrary to prudence.** Prudence involves (*a*) contemplation of the final end of life; (*b*) wise ordering of the details of life to that end. Opposed to the former is *prudence of the flesh*, which is repudiation of the true end of life and substitution of the enjoyment of mere temporal goods for it. The ability to secure these things may be shrewdness but it is not prudence. Some people accept the true end of life but try to strike a compromise with Mammon. Their fault is over-*solicitude for the future*, which is undue care for temporal well-being — a fault reproved in the Sermon on the Mount.[30]

As to the wise ordering of means to the end, which is the more usual function of prudence, one errs by *imprudence*, or failure to arrive at right judgments in one's moral activity. This may happen by (*a*) *negligence* or insufficient estimation of, and lack of alertness in, moral matters; (*b*) *precipitation* or allowing oneself to be carried away by impulse; (*c*) *inconsideration* or acting without taking due account of all the circumstances of the case; (*d*) *inconstancy*, that is, after having determined upon a proper course of action, one is influenced by unworthy motives to abandon it. These are errors of defect.

310. **Vices contrary to temperance.** There are no vices contrary to

---

[30] "Be not solicitous therefore saying, What shall we eat or wherewith shall we be clothed. For after all these things do the heathens seek. Seek ye first the Kingdom of God and all these other things shall be added unto you" (Mt. 6:31–33).

temperance except those of excess. These are *gluttony*, which is excess in food; *insobriety*, excess in drink; *unchastity*, excess in sexual pleasure. Our disordered inclination for food and drink is the capital sin of gluttony. In the quaint phrase of St. Thomas the daughters of gluttony are five: inept mirth, uncleanness, buffoonery, much talking, and dullness of mind. The disorderly appetite for sex is the capital sin of lust. Developing the phrase of Aristotle that "intemperance most of all destroys prudence,"[31] St. Thomas[32] enumerates the effects of lust as blindness of mind, inconsiderateness, headlong haste, inconstancy, selfishness, hatred of God, love of this world, and a horror or despair of the world to come.

The proper scope of temperance is the pleasures annexed to the senses of taste and touch. Many other pleasures both sensitive and psychic are regulated by virtues allied to temperance. Of these the chief are meekness, modesty, and humility. (*a*) *Meekness* is the virtue which enables man to control anger. The vice opposed to meekness is irascibility, better known as *anger*, or the disorderly inclination to anger and revenge. It is rightly set down as a capital vice for from it proceed brawling, turbulence of spirit, contumely, clamor, indignation, and blasphemy. (*b*) *Modesty* must not be confused with chastity. Chastity regulates venereal pleasures; modesty is that external decorum which tempers all of one's external motions — dress, speech, deportment — according to the reasonable demands of time, place, and person. It is the outward splendor of chastity and one of its surest safeguards. Much of what is called *immodesty* may well be unchastity, such as wantonness in carriage, dress, gesture, and speech. The vices opposed to modesty are *hypocrisy* by excess, and *clownishness* by defect. (*c*) *Humility* is the virtue which restrains man's natural tendency for self-exaltation. This virtue is founded on a true estimation of self. It is not incompatible with magnanimity because the truly humble recognize that of themselves they are nothing and can do nothing but with divine assistance they may accomplish even the greatest things. The contrary vice is *pride*, the inordinate seeking after excellence, which St. Augustine describes as the love of self even to the contempt of God.[33] In a certain true sense, this is the fountainhead of all vices.

311. Vices contrary to fortitude. The special function of fortitude is the regulation of fears and actions in time of danger or adversity. It is possible that one's fear may be so slight that he does not take adequate precautions to prevent harm. Aristotle takes note of this possibility

---

[31] *Nicomachean Ethics*, VI, 5, 1140b.
[32] *Sum. Theol.*, II–II, 153, 5.
[33] *City of God*, XII, 13.

remarking: "A man would be mad or insensate if he feared nothing at all . . . as they say of the Celts."[34] Persons without normal fear are few. There possibly are some people who through pride, stupidity, or prolonged exposure to danger feel no fear, but they are the exception. No special name is given to their insensibility. Fearlessness is a misnomer. The fearless man has an inward dread of death but masters it by doing his duty in the midst of danger.

Excessive fear is far more common than lack of fear. This is the vice of *timidity*. It is detrimental to soundness of mind and is the cause of many neuroses. It results in acts of *cowardice*. Thus one may prefer acts against chastity, justice, religion, etc., to avoid the thing feared. The vice of excess opposite to cowardice is *temerity* — unreasonable boldness in the presence of danger.

In categorizing the virtues regulating the tendencies of the irascible appetite, the Scholastics aligned four virtues with fortitude, namely, magnanimity, magnificence, perseverance, and patience. To the greatest of these — *magnanimity* — presumption and ambition are opposed by way of excess. *Presumption* is the attempting of great things which are beyond one's power; *ambition* is the inordinate seeking after great honor. One falls short of magnanimity by *pusillanimity*, the refusal to undertake great things which are commensurate to one's ability.

Magnificence is the virtue of making great expenditures for great works. This virtue is eminently proper where its object is honor to God. Aristotle remarks: "Those expenses are most honorable which relate to the sacrifice of the Deity."[35] One acts counter to the golden mean of this virtue by *extravagance*, which is needlessly lavish spending, or by *parsimony*, which is the unreasonable restriction of expense.

Perseverance inclines man to continue in doing good and to overcome protracted and troublesome difficulties. The excess of this virtue is *stubbornness*, or continuing to act when it is no longer reasonable to do so. The defect of perseverance is *inconstancy*, or the desisting from action when it is reasonable to continue.

Patience inclines man to endure the ordinary difficulties of life without yielding unduly to sadness. Its opposite is *impatience*, probably the commonest of human failings.

312. Vices contrary to justice. Whoever constantly violates justice is the unjust man. The unjust act may be contrary to social, distributive, or commutative justice. Only those who exercise social authority can violate distributive justice. Social justice may be violated both by those

---

[34] *Nicomachean Ethics*, III, 7, 1115b.
[35] *Ibid.*, IV, 11, 1122b.

who command and those who obey. The chief obligations arising under distributive and social justice are related in social ethics.

The epithet, unjust, is more properly applied to the person who constantly acts contrary to commutative justice. Commutative justice is violated by infringing upon some other's right. Hence acts of injustice are designated in terms of the right violated. That people form vicious habits contrary to commutative justice is clear from the number of thieves, calumniators, adulterers, etc., found in any large community.

VI. CHARACTER

313. We have seen that virtue is the disciplined, perfected ease of acting as a reasonable man. It consists in those habits of mind and will which enable one at every turn to do good and avoid evil. It is the harmonious synthesis of prudence, justice, temperance, and fortitude whereby one is adequately equipped, as far as human endeavor can achieve it, to attain life's great purpose. It is the summit of human greatness in this life. Virtue, then, is the mortal goal of human striving; character is the means to this goal.

314. *Character* comes from a Greek word meaning a "seal," an impression made in some substance such as wax or clay denoting ownership. Hence a characteristic is an individualizing trait, a significant quality distinguishing this thing from all others.

Every man is endowed by nature with individual characteristics of body, mind, and will. The general disposition of the whole man is determined by these complex factors. We call it temperament. Temperament may incline one toward mechanical skills or literary art, pugnacity or kindliness, boldness or timidity, and so on. At birth, however, temperament is unformed. It is pliable and awaits an imprint that it will bear permanently. The impression should be made by the will playing its role of mistress of the human faculties. The impression of will on temperament gives character, which distinguishes a man morally from other men.

As reason develops, the will either assumes its function of domination — and that for good or evil — or it surrenders its primacy and follows the bent of the lower appetites, giving passion free rein and being motivated merely by whim, fancy, or the opinions of others. A person's character is weak or strong in so far as the will exerts a weak or strong effort in self-formation. The wax of disposition receives a good impression if the pressure of the will is heavy and constant; a poor impression, if light and intermittent. If a man's will is weak, lower tendencies are strong and a particular one usually plays a dominant role. Such a person receives his moral designation from his prevailing passion. Thus we call him a man of irascible or gluttonous character.

315. If a man's will is strong, his character will be good, provided his moral principles are correct; if a strong-willed person's principles are incorrect, his character will be vicious. But rarely do we find a man who is totally good and never one who is totally bad. Hence the strong and good man has a bias toward a particular virtue so that he will be described, let us say, as a conspicuously honest man or a charitable man or even a meek man — for there can be a strong tendency toward the less assertive virtues. And the same applies to the strong and vicious man. He will be characterized as rapacious, proud, or domineering.

316. The person who has attained perfect virtue is one in whom all the virtues coexist in harmony. He is not conspicuous for this or that virtue because in him no one moral quality towers above another. This indeed is beauty — sublime unity amid fascinating variety. Such a person has a perfect character.

Although there has been but one perfect character in the history of man, it is worthy of special comment because it remains forever the concrete pattern after which all human goodness is modeled. It is the true ideal of human endeavor, for virtue constitutes the enduring value of life. The self-mastery and self-perfection resident in virtue are a good more desirable than wealth, power, artistic ability, athletic prowess, and the like. These things — though they are commonly the object of intense human striving — do not necessarily make one more a man. The opposite is often the case.

317. Virtue is power. First it is power for oneself. It is man's best equipment. It gives strength against "the slings and arrows of outrageous fortune." It alone gives assurance of some measure of happiness now and promise of happiness hereafter. Any acquisitions other than virtue are of little worth. Second, it wields an influence on others which no man may disdain. Parents who are outstanding not so much for beauty of body or grace of personality as for nobility of character leave the most effectual impression upon their children. How enduring can be the result of even a single man's virtue is seen among the founders of religious orders. Even evil and careless men are desirous of virtue's name for no indictment is more terrible than the simple statement, "He is not a good man."

318. How is virtue attained? First, by willing to acquire it. This does not mean ineffectually wishing for it but actually seeking it by submitting ourselves to the rigorous control of will. The will can overcome the inertia of temperament or the tenacity of acquired defect. It can produce virtuous habits contrary to natural inclination. Will power can change timidity into courage, irascibility into sweetness, lust into continence.

But such determination is impossible without a deep appreciation of virtue. No one makes strenuous efforts to possess something he does not highly value. It is precisely because most men have a more vivid appreciation of the comforts of life, or prestige, good times, and the like, that they desire these rather than virtue. Therefore, man must not only discover the value of virtue; he must constantly revert to it to appreciate it. If he does not, he will lose his desire for it.

Nor is it enough to appreciate virtue and know what it is. One must also know himself. Men have always applauded Socrates for his admonition, "Know thyself."[36] Knowledge of self is not only acquaintance with the fundamentals of human nature and the moral law; it is deep understanding of one's own peculiar abilities, tendencies, failings, and lapses. Without it, man can make little progress in the attainment of virtue.

319. It is one thing to appreciate — perhaps from afar — the attractiveness of moral beauty, it is another thing to resolve to attain it. It is still quite another thing to be faithful to such a resolve. Character comes not only from willing but from doing. One must act, act, act. Virtue comes from doing virtuous things.

Even the best-intentioned person, however, must remember that of himself he cannot do this. For man is powerless to accomplish anything in this respect without grace. This, however, belongs to the realm of the supernatural. Suffice it to conclude this subject with the advice that we are to do and act as though everything depended on our own effort and to pray and hope for God's help as though everything depended on Him.

[36] Plato, *Protagoras*, 343B; *Phaedrus*, 229E.

READINGS

St. Thomas, *Summa Theologica*, I–II, 49, 53, 61, 65, 84; II–II, 47, 123, 141.

Aristotle, *Ethics*, II, 6; III, 6–10; V, 1; VI, 5 ff.

Bourke, V. J., *Ethics*, 222–290. New York, Macmillan, 1951.

——— "Role of a Proposed Practical Intellectual Virtue of Wisdom," *American Catholic Philosophical Association Proceedings*, 26 (1952), 160–167.

Buber, M., "The Education of Character," *Cross Currents*, Winter, 1951, 16–25.

Carrel, A., *Reflections on Life*. New York, Hawthorn, 1953.

Cicero, *De Finibus*, Bk. I, cc. 14–15.

Connery, J. R., "Prudence and Morality," *Theological Studies*, 13 (December, 1952), 564–582.

Del Vecchio, G., *Justice*. Edinburgh, University, 1952.
Drummond, W. F., *Social Justice*. Milwaukee, Bruce, 1955.
Gilson, E., *The Christian Philosophy of St. Thomas*, 287–305. New York, Random, 1956.
Harvey, J. F., "The Nature of the Infused Moral Virtues," *Catholic Theological Society of American Proceedings*, 1955, 172–221.
Land, P. S., "Practical Wisdom and the Social Order," *Social Order*, 5 (July, 1955), 391–400.
Mitchell, W., *Christian Asceticism and Modern Man*, London, Blackfriars, 1955.
Nelson, L., *System of Ethics*, 70–85. New Haven, Yale, 1956.
Normandin, R., "Epines ou roses: La plaisir dans la vie chretienne," *Revue de l'Universite d'Ottawa*, 23 (1953), 7–19.
O'Donoghue, D., "The Scope of Distributive Justice," *Irish Theological Quarterly*, 21 (October, 1954), 291–307.
Pieper, J., *Fortitude and Temperance*. New York, Pantheon, 1954.
——— *Justice*. New York, Pantheon, 1955.
Plato, *Protagoras and Meno* (virtue in general); *Laches* (courage); *Euthyphro* (holiness); *Charmides* (temperance); *Georgias* and *Republic I* and *II* (justice).
Raphael, D. D., "Justice and Liberty," *Proceedings of the Aristotelian Society*, 51 (1951), 167–196.
Seneca, *Epistulae Morales*, 5, 11, 37, 66, 120, 123.
Sibley, W. M., "The Rational Versus the Reasonable," *Philosophical Review*, 62 (1953), 554–560.
Thomas, J. L., "Clothes, Culture and Modesty," *Social Order*, 4 (1954), 386–394.
Wild, J., *Introduction to Realistic Philosophy*, 67–81, 97–153. New York, Harper, 1948.

BOOK TWO

PRINCIPLES OF INDIVIDUAL ETHICS

Chapter X DUTIES TO GOD

Special Ethics

320. In our examination of general ethics, we discovered that man's primary ethical obligation is to attain his final end. The purpose of human living is for man to glorify God and be eternally happy. To achieve this end man must lead a life in keeping with his nature. This he does by obeying the Natural Law. Our study of morality, then, is completed by studying the contents of this law.

We have seen that Natural Law is nature properly inclining us to the necessary ends of human life. There are various methods for explaining the particular contents of this law. One consists in determining the ends to which nature inclines man and the contrary evils from which nature restrains him. This is the method adopted by the older Scholastics, who discussed the contents of the Natural Law within the framework of the virtues and vices.

Another method, and one which we shall follow, consists in discovering the particular obligations of the Natural Law. This method is based on the fact that the formal effect of law is obligation. The inquiry into these particular obligations constitutes special ethics, which is divided into two parts. The first is *individual ethics,* which treats of man's personal obligations in three general groups: his obligations to God, to himself, and to his fellow man. The second is *social ethics,* which studies man's obligations as a social being.

321. Although the formal effect of law is obligation, we must remember that this is not its sole aspect. To imagine that morality is only obligation, that the moral life is a heavy burden of restrictions, is completely false. Law not only commands and forbids; it also concedes. Nature is not a harsh taskmaster, merely imposing duties. Nature is very liberal to man, conferring on him great dignities and rights. Although positive law may restrict some of these, others are so sacred that no human power may deprive the individual of them. When nature commands, she urges us toward our real and compelling good. When she forbids, she is restraining us from the deceptive appearances of good, which pursued would entail the loss of all good. When she concedes, she is a wise parent giving us an ample field whereon to exercise our natural freedom. We shall examine first, what nature commands, forbids, and concedes the individual with respect to God, himself, and his fellow man.

322. **Duties to God.** In a true sense, all moral obligations are duties to God, because He is the Author of the moral law and the beginning and end of all things. In many cases, however, God is the object of our moral obligations only mediately and indirectly. By duties to God we refer solely to obligations which have God as their direct object. Whatever these duties prove to be, we may conveniently group them under a single heading — Religion.

I. WHAT IS RELIGION?

323. The term "religion" is familiar, and greatly variegated phenomena are classified under it. But what really is religion? Is it a blind instinct or emotion devoid of rational basis; a perception of the infinite (Max Miller);[1] an awareness of another world of spirits; morality touched by emotion (Matthew Arnold);[2] the opium of the masses (Marx)?[3] Before we can determine what obligations are imposed by religion, we must first know what the true nature of religion is.

324. To the overwhelming majority of mankind who conceive of religion as some kind of direct connection with God, the atheist replies — Absurd, there is no God. For an Infinite Person he substitutes blind, physical forces. There is no need to repeat here the demonstrations of natural theology proving that a necessary and infinitely perfect Being exists who is the Creator and provident Ruler of the universe; it will suffice to say with the Wise Man: "The fool hath said in his heart there is no God."[4] There is scarcely a greater perversion of the human intellect than denial of the existence of God. Foremost among modern atheists are Communists, who endeavor to root out all hitherto existent forms of religion and in its place substitute blind devotion to the party.

Agnostics claim that we do not have sufficient grounds for asserting that God exists; pantheists maintain that everything is but an emanation from one absolute being with whom everything is ultimately identified;

---

[1] F. Max Miller, *Lectures on the Origin and Growth of Religion*, pp. 21–22. New York, Scribner's, 1879.

[2] Matthew Arnold, *Literature and Dogma*, p. 21. London, Smith Elder, 1873.

[3] Karl Marx, *Selected Essays*, "Criticism of Hegelian Philosophy of Right," trans. H. J. Stenning, p. 12. New York, International Publishers, 1926.

[4] Ps. 52:1.

deists admit that God made the world but cannot be bothered to look after it. From all these, because of their errors concerning God, can come only false notions of religion.

Against this background of faith versus reason, we find four outstanding false views on religion. (*a*) Religion is emotion — a feeling of abasement before an ideal infinitely above us, of personal exaltation as we move toward, and participate in, the perfection of this idea. Schleiermacher is the voice of pietistic Protestantism when he defines religion as a *feeling* of the absolute dependence of man on the infinite.[5] (*b*) Religion has man as its object; this is the view of humanitarians. For Comte, religion is an expansive philanthropic devotion to mankind.[6] With Feuerbach[7] it is a fierce turning from God to divinize man. With Hegel and Schelling it becomes an adoration of the State as the Absolute.[8] (*c*) Religion is ethics. One is religious if he keeps the moral law, but in that law there is no explicit command to worship God. This is another of Kant's legacies to the modern world. For him, religion is the sum total of the unprovable hypotheses one must assume to explain the moral law.[9] (*d*) Religion arose from devotion to departed ancestors,[10] and has evolved into vague emotional curiosity regarding the ultimate mysteries of this world.

325. The true concept of religion. Although there is a dispute over the etymology of the term "religion," the best opinion seems to be that of Lactantius who derives it from *religare,* "to bind." "We are tied to God and bound to Him by bonds of piety."[11] This bond of piety, which determines what religion is, is both physical and moral. It is *physical* because man owes his existence entirely to God the Creator. His continuance in existence and his activity depend upon God's conservation and co-operation. He has physical being and activity solely on account of the efficient causality of God. The bond uniting man to God is also *moral.* God is not only the exemplary cause, the pattern

[5] Friedrich Schleiermacher, *Reden über die Religion.* See his *Sämmtliche Werke,* Vol. I, pp. 174, 184. Berlin, Reimer, 1843.

[6] Levy-Bruhl, *The Philosophy of Auguste Comte,* IV, 3, pp. 333–342.

[7] "We have shown that the substance and object of religion is altogether human: we have shown that divine wisdom is human wisdom; that the secret of theology is anthropology; that the absolute mind is the so-called finite subjective mind . . . there is no other essence man can think, dream of, imagine, feel, believe in, wish for, love and adore as the absolute, than the essence of human nature itself." Ludwig Feuerbach, *The Essence of Christianity,* 2 ed., p. 270. Boston, Houghton Mifflin, 1881.

[8] See § 818 footnotes 13 and 14.

[9] Immanuel Kant, *Religion Innerhalb der Grenzen Blossen Vernuft.* See Rosenkranz's edition, Vol. X, pp. 184 ff. Liepsic, Voss, 1838.

[10] Herbert Spencer, *Principles of Sociology,* Vol. I, p. 440.

[11] ***De divin. institut.,* IV, 28; *P.L.,* VI, 537.**

after which man is made, but He is man's last end. God acts on man's mind and will as final cause and supreme ruler. Therefore, God is man's beginning and end, the One upon whom man is dependent always and in everything. This is the basis of religion in the broader sense,[12] which is man's aspiration for, and willing subjection to, God in order that God may be propitious to him and that he may enjoy friendly communion with Him. The sum total of truths about the nature of God, the nature of man, and the dependence of man on God constitute *theoretical religion* or the dogmas of natural religion. Man's attempt to realize this relationship in his conduct is *practical religion.*

The ethical problem, then, is this: In what way must man approach God and submit to Him in order to commune with Him?

II. KNOWLEDGE OF GOD

326. Man's first specific obligation is to know the *one true* God. Man's subjection to God must accord with his nature: it must be a reasonable subjection, but man cannot reasonably submit to what he does not know. He must seek his last end, God, rationally; and this presupposes knowledge of God. Polytheism — which sets up creatures or fictitious beings as gods — does not satisfy this obligation. Through inculpable ignorance one could be a polytheist for a time, but ignorance of the one true God over a long period must be culpable, for constant obedience to the Natural Law results in knowledge of its Author. Absence of knowledge of the Author of the Natural Law over a long period argues to constant violations of the law. The reason for not knowing God is not lack of evidence to convince the mind but refusal of the will to recognize a Lawgiver who demands control of passion.

From knowledge of the one true God, one advances to knowledge of His chief attributes — power, divinity, and infinity. This knowledge need not be precise and scientific: the realization that God is of supreme excellence and might suffices. We shall prove that man must hope in God, worship Him, and love Him above all things — knowledge of God's chief attributes is necessary to arrive at these conclusions.

327. Knowledge of God can be acquired by reason and revelation. Natural theology is the study of God through reason. Revelation, in general, is the communication of truth by God to man. It is natural and supernatural.

1. *Natural revelation* is God's manifestation of truth to man which is due to human nature. It is the action of God whereby man is so internally

[12] In the strict sense religion is the moral virtue of religion which is explained in §§ 341–355.

constituted and so externally and naturally assisted by God that man may attain all the truths about God which lie within the natural capacity of the human intellect. The natural way for God to reveal Himself to man is through the world of nature wherein God has written the truth about Himself for man to discern.

2. *Supernatural revelation* is the action of God manifesting truths to man via formal speech. Speech is the communication of thought to another by means of arbitrary objective signs. Speech between God and man is supernatural; for it is not due to man's nature nor is it necessary either for his development or for the prosecution of his natural end. This is the sense in which the term "divine revelation" is usually understood.

The content of a revelation can be either truths which man is capable of learning by himself or mysteries which surpass his natural capacity to know. The former are supernatural only in the mode of their communication; the latter are supernatural both in their mode of communication and in their substance.

If it be objected that on account of its supernatural character revelation lies beyond the scope of ethics, the answer is that, although the relationship between them is indirect, it is sufficiently pertinent.

328. Is supernatural revelation possible? Naturalism, espousing the lay dogma that the supernatural cannot exist, denies the possibility of divine supernatural revelation. However, no proof has yet been adduced to show that God cannot do what man can do, that is, communicate His thoughts by words and signs. If such an impossibility did exist it would arise either on the part of God, or of man, or it would be due to the truth to be revealed.

Revelation could not be impossible as far as God is concerned. Being omniscient, God knows revealable truths; being omnipotent, He can devise and execute the means of presenting these truths to man so that man can know with certainty that God is speaking to him.

As for man, by nature he is able to discover truths through his own industry and from the instruction of another. Indeed, the one instructing may be an infinitely perfect Person. In fact it is but fitting that a finite mind should agree with the pronouncements of an infinite mind, that man should be able to recognize God speaking to him.

Finally, any truth which is not strictly a mystery can be proposed to, and accepted by, the human mind. Whether there are mysteries or whether these are revealable does not pertain to this investigation.

Divine revelation, then, is possible. Granted that it is possible, a hypothetical obligation arises from the Natural Law.

THESIS XXI. If God makes a supernatural revelation, the Natural Law commands man to accept it.

PROOF

329. The Natural Law commands man to accept the manifestation of One who (*a*) can neither deceive nor be deceived; (*b*) speaks precisely in order that He may be believed; and (*c*) has the right to speak and exact assent. Man would act contrary to his nature in rejecting manifest truth authoritatively proposed. Since God knows all things and cannot lie, since He has the right to speak and exact man's assent, since He would not speak unless He desired man's assent, it follows that if He were to make a revelation, the law of man's nature would oblige him to accept it.

Corollary I. From nature man has a hypothetical obligation to accept divine faith, that is to say, in the event of divine revelation, the Natural Law obliges us to believe.

Corollary II. If a doubt arises concerning the existence of a divine revelation, the Natural Law obliges man to make suitable inquiry; otherwise he would be culpably ignorant of the will of the Supreme Legislator.

330. Did God actually make a supernatural revelation? Apologetics offers irrefutable evidence that God "at sundry times and in divers manners spoke in times past"[13] to the human race. One of the demonstrations of apologetics is the ethical argument given below.

The truths of natural religion — both theoretical and practical — are of utmost importance to man; therefore he should come to know them early in life, with facility, and with certitude. Because of man's intellectual sloth and preoccupation with the necessities and pleasures of life, these truths must come easily or not at all. Again, man should have a reasonably good understanding of them early in life. Good habits are best formed in youth, but this is impossible without early knowledge of the truths of natural religion. Finally, unless man holds these truths with certitude, he will not lead an upright moral life: there could hardly be a greater impediment to the attainment of his final end than doubt about these fundamental realities.

Unaided by divine revelation, most men will not acquire the truths of natural religion easily. These truths are rather abstruse, appeal little to the imagination, and therefore are difficult to grasp. The ordinary man will not learn these things early in life. They are not only difficult to

[13] Hebr. 1:1.

grasp, but youth is so distracted and subjected to such strong emotions that he has little inclination to consider them, let alone pursue them on his own initiative. Finally, it is clear from history that only a few men of unusual ability have come to know these things late in life, and even their findings were not unmixed with serious error. The most civilized nations of antiquity, lacking such a revelation, have held gross and fantastic errors in matters of religion and morality. A few outstanding men like Plato, Aristotle, Cicero, and Virgil had a fair knowledge of these truths, but even their conclusions were unhappily mingled with error.

331. For these reasons we say that God, notably on Mt. Sinai, revealed certain moral and religious truths which man is capable of learning by himself. These truths then may be said to be naturally revealed insofar as God has given man the natural power to know them and they have also been explicitly manifested in a supernatural way. There was, however, no absolute necessity for the revelation: man could and should have known these things. Through his own fault man was ignorant of them. But the beneficence of God is not limited to giving man only the bare requisites of human existence. Even when man by sin blinds himself to religious truth within his grasp and thereby puts this truth beyond his reach, God rescues him from his folly with the light of divine revelation. Theophanies and supernatural revelation are by no means incompatible with natural religion and ethics.

III. HOPE IN GOD

332. Without hope man could not aspire to friendly communion with God. Hope is the confident expectation that God will ultimately admit us to beatitude and consequently that He will grant us in due time the means necessary to attain it.

Without hope, beatitude cannot be realized, for beatitude is an arduous good, attainable only by constant exertion and the conquest of difficulties. The enticements to ignore the Natural Law are so alluring and obedience to the Natural Law so exacting that man could scarcely undertake to keep the law or to persevere long in such an attempt without steadfast hope of reward. Without hope of attaining his end one could not perseveringly strive for it. Our present happiness is hope.

Hope is not self-confidence — reliance on one's own virtue; hope rests in God. Man's attainment of his end depends not only on his own good will but especially upon the assistance of God. Man, consequently, must reasonably expect that this divine aid will be forthcoming. He must hope for the guidance of Divine Providence and especially an effective remedy against his disordered concupiscence.

IV. THE LOVE OF GOD

333. Some people do not understand the meaning of an obligation to love God, which is distinct from acts of reverence and gratitude. They readily see that they should love their parents, wives, and children but they do not understand how they can love God even though He has revealed Himself by assuming human nature. All the more would such an obligation baffle them if they lived in a natural order without divine revelation. Does the Natural Law impose a distinct duty of loving God, even in circumstances where God is known as Spirit and Person only by the light of reason?[14] What is human love and how can God be its object?

334. In the created appetite there exists a certain bent or connaturalness toward its proper good. Whenever there is presented to the appetite a particular object, which is adapted to the appetite and therefore desirable, the object produces a change in the appetite. The object "gives the appetite a certain adaption to itself which consists in complacency in that object; and from this follows movement toward the appetible object."[15] St. Thomas goes on to explain how "the appetitive movement is circular . . . because the appetible object moves the appetite, introducing itself, as it were, into its intention; while the appetite moves toward the realization of the appetible object, so that the movement ends where it began. Accordingly, the first change wrought in the appetite by the appetible object is called *love*, and is nothing else than complacency in that object; and from this complacency results a movement toward that same object, and this movement is *desire*; and lastly, there is rest which is *joy*."[16] Essentially then love is the principle of movement toward any good which is desired.

While man can love in virtue of his sensitive appetite (cf. § 413), we speak here only of the intellectual appetite. Now the will can seek its object for two reasons. (a) *It can strive to subordinate the object to the agent's good.* This is a qualified love because the object is sought not for its own sake but for the good of the agent. We call it *love of desire.* Thus, a man can love oysters, wine, or even a person who is very useful. (b) *The will can wish good to the object loved,* which is always a person

[14] Even if there should be no revelation of the Trinity in the Godhead, yet man can and should know God as a personal being.

[15] St. Thomas, *Sum. Theol.*, I–II, 26, 2.

[16] *Ibid.*

sought for his own sake. This is love of benevolence, in which the object is loved without qualification, that is, for himself. We do not say "for himself alone," meaning to the exclusion of the good of the one loving. Indeed we agree with Aristotle[17] that love of our fellow man is based on love of self. Is love then a selfish sentiment? The exaggerated altruism of the nineteenth century, teaching that man's final end is subordination to society, exhorted man to love his fellow man with a love which excluded self. The altruists were confused because they failed to distinguish a love of self, which is laudatory because it is reasonable, from a love of self which is despicable because it is disorderly. Self-love is a term of reproach for "people who seek for themselves the greater share of wealth, honors, and bodily pleasures." But if a man seeks virtue for himself no one accuses him of self-love. And yet, "such a man seems more than the other to be a lover of self; at any rate he seeks for himself the things which are noblest and best."[18]

335. Love for our fellows stems from love of self for this reason. The end of human love is union between lover and beloved, but the person loving is more at one with himself than with any other human being. Friendship is the loftiest kind of love but we never speak of a man being friendly with himself. He has for himself what is deeper than friendship. By friendship he strives for union with other people but he is related to himself by something more fundamental than union — it is the relation of unity itself, and unity goes deeper than union for it is the very principle of union.

336. The transition from self-regarding love to benevolence occurs in this way. When I love another, I desire him to be one with me. I see him as an *alter* ego, my other self;[19] hence I put him in my place and wish him good as I do to myself. Thus maternal love, which can be so self-effacing, has its roots in love of self, because mothers see in their children the continuance of their own personalities. That one man should love another man more than himself is conceivable but we doubt if it is realizable.

337. There are many kinds of human love the noblest of which is that of friendship, or mutual benevolence between equals. It contains these elements:

1. There must be *benevolence* for the one loved is loved for his sake. Benevolence, however, cannot rest in mere good will. Unless it manifests itself in deeds it ceases. The deeds of love are to give freely. Love is a gift.

---

[17] *Nicomachean Ethics,* IX, 8, 1169a.
[18] *Ibid.,* 1168b.
[19] *Sum. Theol.,* I–II, 28, 1.

2. There is *reciprocal benevolence* or an interchange of giving. The lover wishes to give the beloved all he can give and the other can receive, and vice versa. The more perfect the love the more perfect the gifts exchanged. The greatest gift is the gift of self. St. Thomas calls this characteristic of friendship a communication of life.[20] Since, therefore, brutes cannot share in what is proper to man, namely, rational life, this kind of love cannot exist between man and brute. Furthermore, unrequited friendship cannot last; for love of friendship cannot endure without a mutual giving and receiving.

3. The mutual interchange of goods demands a *certain equality*,[21] at least of nature, which renders possible the giving and taking of what is proper to each. It is this harmony of nature which is the original source of the mutual attraction which drew one to the other. This harmony, however, does not imply that the two are exactly alike but more often that one complements the other. Fullness of life is possible to each precisely because the other fulfills his wants. This is most evident in the love of husband and wife.

4. Since the end of love is union, love in its perfect state is a *communion of mind, heart, and all things*. In perfect love there are no secrets, no reserves. Perfect love is perfect self-surrender. Seeking such union the lover always desires to be near and enjoy the physical presence of the loved one. The culmination of love is the most intense joy in the possession of one's beloved.

338. Is man obliged to love God?

1. *Man must love God with a love of desire*. Since God is man's last end, and since man cannot help desiring his perfect happiness, he must desire God. In such a love, man loves God for man's sake.

2. *Man must love God with a love of benevolence*. If man loved God merely with a love of desire, God would be subordinated to man's good. But the order of nature demands that God be subordinated to nothing whatsoever. Hence God should be loved absolutely and for His own sake. It is only in loving God thus that man truly enjoys friendly communion with him.

3. *Man must love God more than he loves himself*. A man loves his neighbor, because his neighbor is one with him in nature. But in many ways his neighbor fails to be one with him; there are many things in himself which he does not find in his neighbor. Therefore, man loves his neighbor less than he loves himself. Although God is utterly distinct from man, every perfection which is in man is also in God and to an

[20] *Ibid.*, II–II, 23, 1.
[21] Aristotle, *Nicomachean Ethics*, VI, 5, 1157b.

infinite degree. Hence God is to be loved above self. A friend is an *alter* ego but less than one's self; God is an *alter* ego but greater and hence more lovable than self. St. Thomas says that Natural Law requires man to love God more than self. "Since God is the universal good, and under this good both man and angel and all creatures are comprised, and since every creature in regard to its entire being belongs to God, it follows that from natural love angel and man alike love God before themselves and with a greater love. Otherwise, if either of them loved self more than God, it would follow that natural love would be perverted."[22]

We do not mean that God must be loved with passion or with the utmost intensity of emotion. The intensity of the will's love depends both on the adequacy of one's knowledge concerning the object and the presence of an emotional drive toward the same object. Thus a man's most intense love is for wife, parent, or child, because he can know them intimately and they can powerfully appeal to his senses. God, however, makes no appeal to our sensitive appetite. Hence it is only the will, illumined by a kind of notional knowledge, that fitfully seeks Him; not the fullness of man's being. However, when God is finally presented to the will by fitting knowledge, man will be drawn to Him with irresistible force.

Since will acts are ennobled by the excellence of the object sought, an act of the love of God for His own sake is the supreme act of which man is capable.

339. True love of friendship is naturally impossible between God and man, for between them no natural equality exists. Without equality of nature, lover and beloved cannot share what is *proper* to each. Only when God lifts man to a level above his own nature and makes him partaker of the divine nature is this love possible. God effects this divinization by the infusion of sanctifying grace. A consideration of this, however, lies beyond the scope of ethics.

340. How does man fulfill the precept of loving God? Man fulfills this precept negatively by not hating God as, for instance, Lenin did when he said: "I hate God as I do my personal enemies."[23] Hatred can also be leveled against the divine attributes, as when a hardened sinner reviles divine justice. A greater abomination than hatred of God is impossible to conceive.

Indirectly, one loves God by every act of service to Him. Whenever anyone observes the law of God, he renders God glory and makes God

---

[22] *Sum. Theol.*, I, 60, 5.

[23] Delaye-Schumaker, *What Is Communism?* p. 83. St. Louis, Herder, 1938.

manifest in his moral act. Our chief contact now with God is through His will manifest in His law.

Over and above such implicit love, man must make explicit acts of love of which God is the direct object, as occasion demands.

V. THE WORSHIP OF GOD

341. The knowledge, hope, and love of God which we have described are the natural equivalents of the theological virtues of faith, hope, and charity. These ethical obligations pertain to religion taken in the broad sense. We come now to religion in the strict sense which is the moral virtue inclining man "to show reverence to God . . . as the first principle of creation and the ruler of all things."[24] The core of this virtue is the rendering of due worship to God.

A. The Individual and Divine Worship

342. *Worship* means "worthship," the state of being worth something. The most excellent beings are persons who deserve honor or the recognition of their excellence. Honor is more than mere knowledge. It is credit which implies an act of the will referring such knowledge to another as that other's extrinsic good. Honor does not add to the person's essential excellence but it is the external adornment of personality.

If the person is of superior excellence like a father or a ruler, reverence is also due him. Reverence is the acknowledgment of another's superior dignity and power coupled with a desire of not displeasing him. As honor is due to all men because they are men, so reverence is an added tribute to those who are superior among men.

343. If it is fitting for man to honor and reverence created personalities, must he not also recognize the Uncreated Person? Man reverences God by *divine worship,* which is the recognition of the unique excellence of God together with submission of ourselves to Him. Divine worship may be explicit or implicit. Explicit worship entails three acts on man's part: (*a*) an act of the mind recognizing God's infinite excellence and judging it worthy of respect by submission to it; (*b*) an act of the will ordering some fitting token of respect to be shown; (*c*) actual manifestation of respect — this may be external, such as bowing the head, bending the knee, or saying a vocal prayer; or it may be purely internal, such as a simple act of submission of the will. Implicit worship is the honor to God contained in any morally good act (cf. § 322).

Some people say that implicit worship suffices. As long as one leads

[24] St. Thomas, *Sum. Theol.,* II–II, 81, 3.

a good clean life, there is no need of special religious observances. Observance of the Natural Law is all that God wants. However, one does not fully keep that law unless he offers God explicit worship for one of the particulars of the law is thus enunciated:

THESIS XXII. The Natural Law commands each individual to render internal and external worship to God.

344. From time to time, every man, capable of reasoning, must acknowledge within himself his complete dependence upon God and give external testimony of his dependence. Divine worship involves four things. Since God is the source of all benefits coming to man, man has a never-ending obligation of (*a*) *thanking Him* and of (*b*) *petitioning Him* for further benefits. Since God is the Supreme Lawgiver and man is constantly transgressing the law, man has need of (*c*) propitiating God and seeking to regain His favor. Finally, and above all, since God is infinitely perfect, man must (*d*) praise and reverence Him. This is adoration which would be due to God even in the impossible assumption that man were not dependent on Him. The need of adoration is the point of our proof.

PROOF

345. The Natural Law forbids man to be indifferent to or to contemn God, because man is essentially and absolutely dependent on Him as Creator, Conserver, and Co-operator. Now man would contemn or at least would be indifferent to God if he failed to render interior adoration and exterior worship to Him.

1. *Interior adoration.* If man does not acknowledge his total dependence on God, his intellect violates its natural inclination for truth; if man does not freely subordinate himself to God, his will acts as if it were independent.

2. *Exterior worship.* First, interior worship will fail if it is not externalized. Second, since man is made of body and spirit, the body too by external worship must acknowledge man's total dependence on God. God, the absolute Lord, has a right to all the activities of man, His complete servant.

346. The commonest form of divine worship is *prayer.* Prayer is conversation with God. Even apart from the dictates of religion, this ascent of the mind and heart to God is absolutely necessary for man to reach beatitude. Prayer is the efficacious instrument which disposes God to grant what we need for happiness. Its importance in man's moral life cannot be exaggerated. The man who does not know how to pray does not know his own misery and dishonor.

The most solemn and complete act of divine worship is *sacrifice*. Described in simple terms, sacrifice is the offering of a gift to God. Man, the creature, instinctively realizes that when he comes formally into the presence of his Creator he must bear with him a gift as the supreme token of his respect. This gift is some material thing of value: it is a symbol of God's supreme dominion over all things, especially over man, for whom it is substituted. To signify its return to God's exclusive possession, the gift is destroyed or altered in some way. Whenever that which has been sacrificed is eaten later by the worshipers in a sacrificial meal, we have communion with the Deity. This external communion symbolizes the inner spiritual sharing of God by man.

B. Society and Divine Worship

347. The obligation of divine worship does not only bind man as an individual; it binds him especially as a social being. Religion is not confined to the hidden recesses of the soul or the privacy of one's room. It bears a social character and obligation.

THESIS XXIII. Man must unite with his fellow man in offering God the homage of society.

By this thesis we understand that the State and the family as natural institutions have an obligation to render God external worship and that the individual must have part in such religious observances. This we call *public worship*.

PROOF

348. *Man must unite with his fellow man in offering God the homage of society*, because the family and the State are natural institutions dependent on God as (*a*) *Cause*, as is proved in social ethics (cf. §§ 707, 737, 814); as (*b*) *Conserver*. The well-being of family and State depends on man's observance of the Natural Law. As God is Author of this law, He is the Conserver and Preserver of State and family; as (*c*) *Guide* of family and State. Human authority directs these institutions to their well-being; this authority, however, is delegated by God, the supreme Lord of the universe and is a participation in His divine guidance. This is proved in social ethics, §§ 793 and 862.

Just as the individual must recognize and acknowledge his complete dependence on his Creator, so too the family and State must acknowledge a similar dependence. As the family and State are moral persons, their obligations can be fulfilled only by acts of individuals.

349. Corollary I. From the need of external worship of God, the need of liturgy follows. Liturgy, or ritual, is the natural outgrowth of repeated religious observances. The decorum attached to religious worship demands that the words, actions, costume, appurtenances, gestures, and even posture, belonging to worship be defined carefully by custom or law and not left to hasty improvisation of the moment.

Corollary II. A man cannot be a good man if he does not worship God. Neglect of this duty is *practical religious indifference.*

350. Abundant evidence for the acceptance of this obligation is furnished by the history of religions. Among all peoples there has been worship regulated by authority.

Where the family is the only social institution, the time and manner of fulfilling this obligation, as well as the necessity of individual participation, is to be regulated by the head of the family. Families did fulfill this duty. Among many people the head of the house was also the family priest until this function was absorbed by State or Church.

Where the State alone exists, that is, where there is no separate religious authority, the responsibility for public worship falls to State law. Where the Church exists, that is, where there is a distinct and separate religious authority, individual and familial participation in worship is to be regulated by that authority.

If God supernaturally intervenes and indicates a particular mode of divine worship, the Natural Law commands all men and all States to worship in this manner.

C. Manner of Worshiping God

351. The Natural Law indicates only the broadest outline of the mode of worshiping God. But there is a vast array of systems by which the one true God is worshiped. Does the Natural Law say anything concerning them? Does it leave each man free to choose whichever he fancies? Does it command him to accept what civil or parental authority dictates?

Every system of worship has a body of dogmatic truths. A creed is necessary. Religious worship cannot be mere ritual and emotion; to be worthy of God and man it must have an intellectual basis. In so far as a method of worship is also a system of religious dogmas, the Natural Law does contain precepts directly pertaining to them.

In commanding man to worship Him, God cannot oblige him to accept falsehood: man is obliged only to accept truth. Hence the Natural

Law says that man is to worship God by that system of rites which is founded on the truth and the truth alone.

352. There is a most prevalent notion to the effect that all religions are equally pleasing to God and useful to man. This is called *dogmatic religious indifference*. Since it represents God as pleased with error and implicitly asserts that error is as good as truth, it must be rejected. All known religious systems contradict one another on various points of doctrine. Consequently all cannot be right. Therefore God cannot be pleased with all religions, and it is false to say one religion is as good as another. On the other hand, all of the religions cannot be wrong, for if they were, God would receive nothing but false worship, which is absurd.

Certainly if God desires to be worshiped in a particular manner, He must intervene with supernatural revelation, for as we have said the Natural Law does not give the details pertaining to divine worship. To prove that God did make such a revelation is beyond the province of ethics.

D. Sins Against the Due Worship of God

353. Sins of defect against divine worship are classified as irreligion; those of excess, as superstition.

1. *Irreligion* is lack of reverence for God. It includes the following:

a) *Practical religious indifference* — failure to worship God when the proper occasion demands it.

b) *Tempting God* — any word, act, or omission whereby man endeavors to test one of God's attributes. It is a serious want of reverence to doubt God's power and to challenge Him to manifest it.

c) *Blasphemy* — contumely directed against God or creatures precisely because of their relationship to God. This is dishonor to God and grave perversion of human nature. To the ancient Greeks it was the worst crime.[25] So great was the reverence of the ancient Jews for the name of God that they carefully refrained from using the proper name of God, "I am who am," and substituted in its stead, "The Lord."

Even if contempt of God is not intended, it is still irreverence to use God's name as a mere exclamation or expletive. Ordinarily, frivolous and profane use of God's name is not a serious wrong. It is a serious wrong, however, to use the name of God in cursing. In cursing, one deliberately asks God to wreak evil upon another. The name of God is dishonored by being associated with a serious sin against charity.

A person who has contracted the habit of using blasphemous language

[25] Cf. Sophocles, *Oedipus Rex*, 883–893; Plutarch, *Alcibiades*, XXIII.

is obliged to rid himself of it. Even though he does not directly intend to be contemptuous of God, his evil habit dishonors God and scandalizes others.

d) *Perjury* — the violation of an oath. There is a vast difference between a mere lie and a lie under oath, for in an oath God is called upon to witness the truth of what is said. An oath is assertory when God is asked to confirm the truth of an assertion; it is promissory when He is asked to confirm a promise or resolution.

Two conditions are required for the validity of an oath: (i) the intention to swear and (ii) a proper external formula. Three conditions are required for lawful swearing: (i) truth, (ii) judgment, and (iii) justice. According to the first condition, truth, one cannot ask God to witness a falsehood. According to the condition of judgment, one must have a sufficient reason for swearing and must take an oath with proper reverence. Last, the condition of justice means that in a promissory oath, one may promise only what is morally lawful.

e) *Violation of a vow.* A vow is a free promise made to God concerning a good which is possible and a *greater good* than its contradictory. A vow is not a mere promise or resolution; it is a self-imposed obligation which binds one through the virtue of religion. It is truly an act of worship. No one is required to make any vow, but once a vow is made, the Natural Law obliges fulfillment. While one may bind himself by the extra tie of religion to that which already is obligatory, for example, chastity, the matter of a vow is usually not obligatory.

354. 2. *Superstition* is either giving a creature honor which belongs to God alone or giving God false or unsuited worship. Noteworthy among such crimes are the following:

a) *Idolatry* — explicit tribute of divine worship to a creature. History shows that no other moral evil has had such a degrading influence on man.[26] It is the most heinous sin against divine worship.

b) *Divination* — the endeavor to learn the *free future* from a source other than God. Since God alone knows what men will freely resolve to do in the future, the attempt to learn it from a creature is implicit tribute of divine honor to that creature. Man's insatiable curiosity has led him to seek for this knowledge in countless ways — consultation of oracles; inspection of cards, the entrails of men or beasts, the palm of the hand, the bumps on one's head; study of dreams; the flight of birds and the stars; messages from the spirits of the dead; use of a ouija board. To use seriously any one of these means in an attempt to learn the free future or to consult a person who seriously believes that he or she has

[26] Cf. Rom. 1:18 ff.

this power is always a grievous wrong. To attempt to learn the future from things in which one only half-believes or from persons who do not take themselves seriously is a venial wrong. To play with these things for recreation is not sinful but may be dangerous.

c) *Vain observance* — the use of means which neither naturally nor by divine authority have the power to produce the effects expected of them. In thus attributing to a creature a power which it does not possess, there is at least an implicit invocation of the creature as God. People have sought knowledge through charms, spells, the drinking of certain potions; they have resorted to talismans to ward off evil and bring good luck — a man once wore a horse chestnut in his left hip pocket during the time of his wife's pregnancy to insure the birth of a boy.

The malice of divination or vain observance cannot be adequately understood without reference to certain facts of revelation. There is a personal devil, Satan, the enemy of God and of mankind whose purpose is ever the dishonoring of God and the eternal ruin of men. Every act of divination or vain observance seriously intended contains an implicit invocation of Satan's aid. If a desired result cannot be obtained from a creature's natural powers, and if God does not see fit to grant it extraordinarily, then to choose means which are not naturally calculated to effect it, is an appeal for Satan's aid. To ask this help is to dishonor God, for everything which Satan does is directed to God's dishonor and the harm of men. Consequently, the person who believes that a desired result will *infallibly* follow from such unnatural means is always guilty of grave wrong.

If the effects to be produced by vain observance are marvelous, the practice is called *magic*. The use of magic is quite prevalent among barbarous tribes. If a wonder-worker or sorcerer endeavors to wreak evil on his neighbor, he is guilty of an additional violation against justice or charity.

There are certain silly superstitious practices which people observe for the sake of good luck or fear of bad luck. Many of these are only slightly wrong, because people do not *infallibly* expect good or bad luck from them. Through invincible ignorance, some persons see no harm in them. Others, however, comply with these practices not because they put real credence in them, but because they would be uneasy or nervous if they disregarded them.

If all superstitious intent is excluded, it is not wrong to investigate the occult powers of nature in order to widen the field of human knowledge. For example, knowledge of the influence of the mind on the body and of the body on the mind has led to progress in medicine. Again, the workings of the subconscious mind, hypnotic influence, the communication of thought directly from mind to mind (mental telepathy) may be legitimate subjects of psychological research. Scientific investigation may demonstrate that a number of seemingly marvelous or even supposedly preternatural effects have a purely natural cause. Investigation of these and similar phenomena requires utmost prudence, for experience has shown that rash dabbling may prove disastrous to health, morality, and supernatural faith.

The most prevalent of present-day forms of vain observance is *spiritism*, which is ancient necromancy (the evocation of the spirits of the dead) in modern setting. While most spiritistic mediums may be laughed at as frauds and spiritism may be considered just another shady way of making a living, not all the phenomena of modern spiritism may be dismissed as hokum. Some truly genuine effects are wrought. The explanation of some of these effects may be traced to occult but natural causes, whereas others are undoubtedly of preternatural origin — which can be due only to diabolical intervention.

355. Since religion is so basic a need of man, and since so many modern men have abandoned belief in and the practice of supernatural religion one can logically expect in our time a growing increase in superstitious practices. Man must have some religion, and when he rejects one revealed by God, he will fashion a substitute of his own contriving. How poor and crude such substitutes are, becomes quite clear in times of war and calamity. Then the old dark gods emerge from the jungle and primitive superstitions reappear. Our age of advanced thinkers, the intellectual heir of eighteenth-century rationalism, has returned to astrology, dream books, and numerology.

READINGS

St. Augustine, *Confessions*, Bk. I, cc. 1–5; Bks. IV, VII, VIII, IX.

St. Thomas, *Summa Theologica*, II–II, 81–100.

Bandera, A., "Naturalistic Spirituality," *Cross and Crown*, 7 (September, 1955), 337–347.

Bivort de la Sandeé, J. de., ed., *God, Man and the Universe*. New York, Kenedy, 1953.

D'Arcy, M. C., *The Nature of Belief*. London, Sheed & Ward, 1945.

——— "Religion and Ethics," *Moral Principles of Action*, 512–526, ed., R. N. Anshen. New York, Harper, 1952.

Dawson, C., *Religion and Culture*. London, Sheed & Ward, 1948.

De Letter, P., "Hope and Charity in St. Thomas," *The Thomist*, 13 (1950), 204–248.

Farrell, W., *A Companion to the Summa*, Vol. III, 245–300. New York, Sheed & Ward, 1953.

Festugiere, A.-J., *Personal Religion Among the Greeks.* Berkeley, University of California, 1954.

Gill, E., *The Necessity of Belief.* London, Faber, 1936.

Gilson, E., *The Christian Philosophy of St. Thomas,* 333–350. New York, Random, 1956.

Guardini, R., *The Faith and Modern Man.* New York, Pantheon, 1952.

Howell, C., *Of Sacraments and Sacrifice.* Collegeville, Liturgical Press, 1952.

Heenan, J. C., *The Faith Makes Sense.* New York, Sheed & Ward, 1948.

Joad, C. E. M., *The Recovery of Belief.* London, Faber, 1953.

Linden-Costello, *The Fundamentals of Religion.* Chicago, Loyola, 1956.

Lombardi, R., *The Salvation of the Unbeliever.* Westminster, Newman, 1956.

Maritain, J., *Approaches to God.* New York, Harper, 1954.

Moore, T. V., *The Life of Man with God.* Bruce, Milwaukee, 1955.

Nash, P. W., "Ordinary Knowledge of God and the Philosophical Demonstration," *American Catholic Philosophical Association Proceedings,* 28 (1954), 55–75.

Neil, T. P., *Religion and Culture.* Milwaukee, Bruce, 1954.

Nicholas, J. H., "Amour de soi, amour de Dieu, amour des autres," *Revue Thomiste,* 56 (1956), 5–42.

O'Brien, J. A., *Truths Men Live By,* 3–210. New York, Macmillan, 1946.

Sheen, F. J., *Philosophy of Religion.* New York, Appleton-Century-Crofts, 1948.

Stevens, G., "The Disinterested Love of God According to St. Thomas and Some of His Modern Interpreters," *The Thomist,* 16 (1953), 307–333, 497–541.

Chapter XI DUTIES TO SOUL

356. Since man must love God more than himself, his particular duties to God are of first importance. Since he is to love himself more than his fellow man, certain duties to himself are next in importance. We shall now consider these duties. Man's first duty to himself is to attain his final end. Since this life is the preparation for another life wherein ultimate perfection is granted or denied us, at the age of reason man must begin to strive for self-perfection. Man must make of himself what he can according to his ability and his opportunities. This is summed up in the phrase, *a man must love himself with a well-ordered love*. This he does in a general way when he directs his entire life to the attainment of beatitude.

More specifically, a man loves himself reasonably when he secures certain internal goods of soul and body as well as a number of external advantages. Since the spirit is of prime importance, we must know what spiritual perfection a man must acquire to assure beatitude. Man's ultimate perfection is directly promoted by the activity of his moral faculties, particularly by his will constantly embracing his real good, refusing apparent good. An essential prerequisite is that the intellect present to the will that which objectively is man's real good. A man must cultivate his intellect to the extent that he is sure of knowing his real good, and he must train his will so that he will readily choose the same.

I. TRAINING OF THE MIND

357. From our explanation of the Natural Law and of man's obligation to obey his conscience, it is clear that reason is man's supreme directive. "Follow reason" — this is one of nature's first laws. But before reason is prepared to lead, it must properly fulfill its natural function, which is to possess the truth. The so-called trained mind, in which truth and error are confused, is a human instrument of doubtful validity. Only the mind which has a clear, unwavering grasp of fundamental truth is a reliable guide.

358. The inevitable effect of erroneous principles of action is failure. From error must come disorder. With reference to material things this scarcely needs demonstration. The airplane manufacturer who uses faulty theories of aerodynamics may turn out scores of planes, but they will not stay long in the air. The same is true in moral matters, only a longer time elapses between the acceptance of error and the inevitable confusion. In the nineteenth century, Nietzsche taught the superman theory; in September, 1939, Hitler and the Wehrmacht gave a concrete demonstration of domination and spoliation. In the sixteenth century, men denied that matrimony is a sacrament of the New Law. The leaven was slow to work but today the full fruit of that denial can be seen in our sordid story of trial marriages and bargain divorces. You cannot sow the wind without some day reaping the whirlwind.

Just as we may unconsciously take on the accent or copy the grammatical mistakes of those with whom we associate, so we can absorb their erroneous thoughts. Such intellectual disease is as contagious as smallpox. Two causes operate to make this danger very real: one is as old as humankind; the other, bright as a new penny, is disguised as the offspring of human progress. The first is prejudice; the second, intellectual license.

359. *Prejudice,* or judging from insufficient evidence, is the subordination or even the very substitution of wishing for thinking. While the mind must necessarily accept the truth presented to it, it can be and is turned from the truth by undue influence of the will. As man's supreme appetite, the will can unduly dominate the mind. Thus, in solving a problem to which a conclusion has not yet appeared, the will can fix the mind's attention on reasons leading to a preferred conclusion and keep it from full consideration of opposite reasons. Even if the truth is evident, the will can turn the mind from it by having it advert to frivolous reasons. This is more easily done when one is dealing not with facts but with universal ideas. The will so acts because without sufficient reason it prefers one opinion to another. It arbitrarily fixes upon one conclusion and orders the mind to find justifying reasons for it. This is usurpation of the function of intellect and deprivation of its prerogative of being led solely by objective evidence.

360. The will can arbitrarily select one opinion rather than another for the following reasons:

1. The opinion *conforms to passion.* A person indulges in illicit pleasure. The will seeks self-justification and influences the mind to regard the object of such passion a real good. Many who practice artificial birth control cajole themselves into holding that their act is laudable.

2. The opinion promises something *more useful to one's temporal*

advantage. A man who cares little for beatitude, to be enjoyed hereafter, is deeply concerned over fortune, power, and equipment. Thus, to gain a political victory or to save himself from jail he will think it right to perjure himself.

3. The opinion is *more popular*. Living in a democracy, people can readily make an unconscious transition from public opinion as the norm of political decision to public opinion as the criterion of moral ideas. Thus, if a Gallup Poll discloses that 63 per cent of the people favor divorce, then divorce is acceptable. Fashion can dictate not only the cut of one's clothes but the style of one's ideas. Despite the spread of literacy, it is easier for most people to accept ideas ready made for them than undergo the labor of thinking. If the people of my circle consider this public figure a villain, he must be so. If the nice people of my community get drunk at parties or commit adultery, there cannot be much harm in this.

4. The opinion is a *racial or religious misconception*. To one reared in the atmosphere of the Ku Klux Klan, a given opinion can be wrong solely because it is held by Catholics. The proposal of a German is anathema to a Frenchman, and vice versa. To an anti-Semite a man stands condemned of being a knave and a trickster merely because he is a Jew.

361. *Intellectual license* generally parades as liberalism, as the opposite of prejudice. It is the creed of so-called broad-minded men, of the advanced and tolerant thinker; and it comes to this: You can think what you please. Seek truth for truth's sake but truth is simply what you think is true. Truth is not reality made manifest to the mind; it is the mind pronouncing its subjective view of reality; or worse still, the mind creating reality. Personal whim is ultimately substituted for objective reality and objective evidence. This is subjectivism gone wild in the field of intellect. It stems from the notion that man is the measure of all things. Hence each one is free to doubt, affirm, and deny what he pleases. Of course, if a man is sincere, he will not deny the existence of facts, for facts have a hard and stubborn quality. But in the field of universal ideas, each one is his own master. From this, one is naturally driven to relativism, the ultimate epistemological absurdity, the mind's last stop before out and out repudiation of the rational faculty. If the same thing can be true to you and false to another, then there is no moral order; what was moral truth to Hector and Achilles is not so to Dewey and Einstein.

362. There are high degrees of intellectual development whose attainment frees a man from all taint of prejudice and from the delusion that his own mind is the measure of truth. A liberal education aims at this rich development, which, however, cannot be obligatory on all men. What degree of mental cultivation, then, does the Natural Law demand? Let us distinguish here speculative from practical truths. By way of speculative truth, a man must have some correct notion of himself — who he is, what he is, and what he is for. This entails a knowledge of God, at least as his Maker — the Supreme Being to whom he is responsible. By way of practical truths, a man should know the primary and secondary precepts of the Natural Law and those particular obligations incumbent on him as this individual.

THESIS XXIV. The Natural Law obliges every man to cultivate his mind to the extent at least that he understand the moral duties common to all men and those special ones pertaining to his state of life.

PROOF

363. Whoever is absolutely obliged to attain to an end is likewise obliged to obtain the means necessary to that end. But man is absolutely obliged to attain his last end, and knowledge of his common and individual moral duties are a necessary means to that end. Therefore man is obliged to know his common and individual moral duties.

364. Besides knowledge of moral principles a man must also have some skill in applying principles to his conduct. His obligation in the matter of practical truths may be summarized as an obligation to seek prudence in matters of moral choice. He acquires knowledge of the right thing to do in many ways: by experience "which is the result of many memories";[1] by listening to "older people who have acquired a sane understanding of the ends in practical matters";[2] by understanding fundamental principles and by reasoning from them; by foresight about one's future conduct and by constancy in keeping one's good resolutions; by sufficient scrutiny of concrete circumstances; by caution in avoiding hindrances to upright conduct; and, above all, by doing the right thing.[3]

II. TRAINING OF THE WILL

365. The order of man's nature is maintained when man avoids false principles and possesses moral truth. What necessary perfection must he procure for his will?

[1] St. Thomas, *Sum. Theol.*, II–II, 49, 1.
[2] *Ibid.*, 3.
[3] Cf. Aristotle, *Nicomachean Ethics*, II, 1, 1103a.

1. When the mind presents man's real good, the will is obliged to accept it. As nature ordains that the mind illumine the will, she likewise commands that the will follow its guidance. Therefore, if a person disregards the voice of reason, he goes against the order of his nature which demands *the compliance of the will with the dictates of right reason.* Every sin is wrong precisely because it is a revolt against reason. The obligation to follow reason is another aspect of the virtue of prudence. For "prudence consists not in knowledge alone but also in an act of the appetite."[4] Indeed, the principal function of prudence is command or the application of knowledge to the attainment of one's desires so that prudence is lost chiefly by indulging wrong desires.

2. *The will must exercise its natural dominion over the other faculties.* This means (*a*) that the will keep the mind steady in the pursuit of moral truth; (*b*) that no subordinate appetite be permitted to seek an apparent good to the detriment of man's real good. Morally, man is a unitary whole when the will is mistress of the appetites, the custodian of the integrated personality. If animal appetites divert man from his real good, the essential order of human nature is violated. Man, then, must practice temperance and fortitude.

III. SELF-MASTERY

366. To preserve the ability of the reason to enlighten and of the will to choose, man must ever strive for mastery of his sense appetites. To prevent passion from disturbing the due order of his rational nature, he must give special attention to the control of anger and the use of right reason in eating, drinking, and sex.

A. Control of Anger

367. Anger is the motion of the irascible appetite, whose purpose is the total destruction of evil leveled against the agent. Its immediate end is to ward off the evil threatened; its ultimate end, once evil has been done, is to root out that evil totally by punishing the evildoer.

Anger in itself is good and is necessary for man. For self-preservation, he must protect himself from harm; again, it is reasonable that evildoers be punished. Righteous indignation is called for at times as a just protest against injustice or when it is the only way of correcting those for whom one is responsible. Though anger must be controlled by reason, man tends to be unreasonable when he becomes angry. The tendency to unreasonable anger is the *capital sin of anger.*

---

[4] St. Thomas, *Sum. Theol.*, II–II, 47, 16.

Anger may be unreasonable with respect to its intensity, object, and motive: (a) Anger is unreasonable in its *intensity* if it is out of proportion to the evil done. (b) Anger is unreasonable with respect to its object if the object does not deserve punishment. Effects which do not result from an evil will do not deserve punishment. Hence objects incapable of reasoning and the indeliberate faults of children should not excite anger. (c) Anger is wrong which arises from wrong motives such as pride, hatred, envy, and private vengeance. The individual man may not punish wrongs which are purely private, for only a superior having lawful authority may punish.

B. Right Reason in Eating and Drinking

368. The orderly use of means is determined by the end for which they are intended. Since food and drink are the natural means of preserving life, and since the Natural Law obliges man to preserve his life, man must eat and drink. The use of food and drink is orderly if it promotes or at least does not endanger one's health and life; it is unreasonable if it imperils health or shortens life.

The misuse of drink is a vastly greater moral evil than excess in eating. Modern man has a special problem to solve here.

Drunkenness is the imbibing of alcoholic drink to the extent that one loses the use of reason without a justifying cause. Two elements in this definition require special note: namely, loss of reason and lack of justifying cause. Loss of reason may be partial or complete. Indications of complete loss of reason are conduct that is totally different from one's normal behavior, inability to distinguish right from wrong, failure to realize that one actually is drunk.

Not every instance of the loss of reason involves moral wrong. Sleep is a natural and necessary loss of reason. However, it would be wrong if a person drank to excess and immediately went to bed because he would be incapable of being roused if he had to be. To ease the shock of a surgical operation, one is allowed to lose consciousness. The effect produced by ordinary anesthetics may also be produced by alcohol. The essential evil of drunkenness is put down in the following thesis.

THESIS XXV. The Natural Law forbids man to deprive himself of the use of reason without a justifying cause.

PROOF

369. To deprive oneself of the use of reason without a compensating cause is patently unsuited to human nature, because:

1. All men of every age, race, and circumstance regard it as wrong.
2. Nature intends that man be self-directive. To abdicate reason even temporarily is to run counter to nature's intent. Hence nature must forbid it except when it is necessary for self-preservation.

Corollary. The same moral principle applies to the use of narcotics.

370. Over and above the essential malice stated above, drunkenness presents other evil facets. It is often the occasion of other sins such as unchastity, blasphemy, quarreling, and even bloodshed.

Again, the excessive use of alcohol is a positive detriment to health. One may learn from any standard medical textbook what damaging effect great quantities of alcohol may have on the nervous system, the liver, the digestive organs, and how it may lead to certain kinds of insanity. Alcoholism violates our obligation to preserve life and health. Wantonly to squander one's health and notably to shorten one's life for the sake of gratifying the senses is gravely wrong.

Drunkenness not only violates the rational nature of man; constant excess in drink as a rule permanently weakens the will. The alcoholic vice is a habit rooted in the body and produces a craving which the will often finds impossible to deny.

Excessive drinking is not merely a private vice; it has far-reaching social effects as well. Most drinking is done in the company of others. Drunkenness is probably the most social of all vices. One contracts the vice from the example of another, and he in turn infects others. In addition, drunkenness often leads to broken homes, poverty, and misery.

The automobile adds a new aspect to the problem of drink. Even mild indulgence in alcohol makes many people incapable of driving safely. Whoever insists on driving in a drunken condition is responsible for the damage he inflicts on innocent parties.

The alcoholic is sick in mind and body. His immediate remedy is total abstinence. Since, however, excessive drinking is often an escape from reality, the deeper therapy is psychic: the alcoholic must learn to live with himself. But an old Spanish proverb illustrates how difficult it is to remedy drunkenness: "There is no cure for the drunkard but death."

371. *Prohibition* aims by law to deprive citizens of alcohol. It is seldom an effective remedy for the evil of drunkenness. It is not effective because experience shows that it does not work but rather brings about worse evils than those it attempts to remedy. In addition prohibition rests on the false assumption that all drinking is an absolute evil. There is, however, a sober and innocent drinking which has its place in human life. It is not the use, but the abuse of drink which creates the moral evil. Furthermore, the human way to solve a moral difficulty is not by attacking human freedom, by forcibly compelling people to keep the moral law. Although the State may use force to promote the common good, it has no right to take such action in matters of private conscience.

However, if the evil of drink should become so appalling as to menace public order, health, and efficiency, the evil is no longer private and the State could justly bar all citizens from access to alcohol for the common good. The temperate citizen would then be bound in conscience to obey.

Since drug addiction is a serious menace to public health, the use of drugs must be regulated by public authority.

C. Right Reason in Sex

372. Nothing is more likely to blind the mind to man's true good or destroy the dominance of will over sense than inordinate sex. No force so frequently operates to upset the subjection of the lower to the higher faculties than this familiar form of concupiscence. Hence no man is master of himself if he cannot keep this mighty impulse within reason's bounds.

By sex is understood all activity which is directly related to the propagation of human life. To no other activity does nature attach a comparable pleasure, for the simple reason that the ultimate end of sex is not the individual good but the good of the race. If there were no need to propagate the race, sex would not exist. The sex drive is so strong precisely because its end is a good superior to that of the agent; otherwise the agent would not be sufficiently inclined toward a good other than his own.

Sex pleasure we call venereal pleasure. It is convenient to express the problem of sex in terms of venereal pleasure because: (a) this pleasure exercises so universal a lure that men are conscious of it as an acute problem of morality; (b) here more than anywhere else there is a danger of mistaking delectable good for perfective good; (c) men are drawn to use the sex faculty not so much because of its perfective good as by reason of the pleasure which attaches to it.

373. What is venereal pleasure? Pleasures of sense, especially tactile, fall into three classes: (a) *purely sensible* — the natural pleasure accompanying the exercise of the sense and in no way connected with sex, such as patting a baby's cheek; (b) *venereal* — pleasure perceived in the organs of reproduction because of activity directly tending to the reproductive act; (c) *sensual* — pleasure which stands midway between the first two and easily develops into the second, such as the pleasure of kissing one of the opposite sex.

Venereal pleasure may be perfect or imperfect. It is perfect in the male when there is an ejaculation of seed; in the female when there is a diffusion of vaginal glandular secretions. It is imperfect when the reproductive organ has not reached this consummated stage but is in preparation for it. A variety of acts — touches, looks, words — may produce these effects. From an ethical standpoint, it matters little whether the venereal pleasure be complete or incomplete, because the only natural reason for any incomplete act is that it issue in the complete act, that is, once a truly venereal act however slight is set in motion, it tends by the very impulse of nature, like a snowball rolling down a hill, to its completed perfection.

When does the enjoyment of venereal pleasure accord with nature's law? Here again the reasonable use of a means must be determined from the end. The end of sex is the procreation of children. So important a function as procreation cannot be haphazard; it must be protected by conditions which will assure that well-being of body and mind which nature designs for men. It is for nature — not men — to determine what these fundamental conditions for procreation shall be. It is for man's reason to discover them and put them in practice. In social ethics we shall prove that nature lays down two requirements for the proper use of sexual activity: (*a*) a lawful marriage between man and woman; (*b*) avoidance of any means to frustrate nature's purpose in the sex act.[5]

THESIS XXVI. Deliberately to seek or willfully to admit any venereal pleasure on the part of the unmarried or on the part of the married apart from one's lawful spouse or in any other than a natural way is a serious breach of Natural Law.

Venereal pleasure becomes the direct object of the will either when one sets out in quest of it, or when such pleasure spontaneously arises from an indeliberate source and the will approves it.

PROOF OF PART I

374. **All venereal pleasure is forbidden the unmarried,** for every sexual act is forbidden them. Since a pleasure exists solely for the perfective act of which it is the concomitant, obviously if the perfective act is forbidden, so too is the accompanying pleasure.

a) *Consummated acts.* All solitary and homosexual acts are forbidden all men because thereby nature's purpose of procreation is absolutely

[5] Reproduction is not the sole end of sex. It has a secondary end, which is the fostering of love between husband and wife. Imperfect sex acts are allowed to spouses, provided there is no danger of complete satisfaction outside the natural act.

defeated. The unmarried may not perform the natural bisexual act because nature allows it only in lawful wedlock. It is reasonable only when it takes place under conditions which make adequate provision for the *total* well-being of offspring. Any arrangement other than lawful wedlock is detrimental to the continuance of the human race. That no exception to this general law of nature is possible is demonstrated in social ethics (cf. § 709).

b) *Imperfect acts.* The only reason for imperfect acts is that they lead to, and are preparatory for the complete act. In nature's economy there is no other explanation for them. Since the unmarried may not exercise the complete act, neither may they the imperfect act.

PROOF OF PART II

375. **Venereal pleasure may be had only with reference to one's spouse.** Since only the married may willfully have venereal pleasure, and since marriage is the *exclusive* union of one man and one woman, as is proved in social ethics, venereal pleasure may be had only with reference to one's spouse (cf. § 731, Corollary).

PROOF OF PART III

376. **Venereal pleasure may be had by the married only in a natural way.** That is natural which promotes nature's end — procreation. That is unnatural which in itself defeats nature's purpose. For nature to allow what in this matter directly destroys her intent would be for her to sign her death warrant (cf. § 776).

PROOF OF PART IV

377. **All unlawful venereal pleasure constitutes a serious wrong.** To violate nature's ordinance with respect to venereal pleasure is to do that which is detrimental to the continuity of the human race.

378. **N.B. I.** The reasons why fornication, self-abuse, and positive contraception are intrinsically wrong as defeating an absolute end of nature are evident enough without the added light of revelation.

N.B. II. There are no exceptions to these basic rules for use of sex. No amount of good intention will justify a breach of them. Thus a doctor does serious wrong who asks a patient to masturbate in order to produce a specimen of semen. He should learn the morally legitimate procedures for obtaining these specimens.[6]

N.B. III. The morality of venereal pleasure which is only indirectly voluntary is adjudged from the principle of double effect. Venereal pleasure may arise unsought upon performance of certain actions of touch, sight, reading, or the like. Two considerations are important. First, how serious is the reason for placing the act which gives rise to the pleasure? Absence of a serious reason may indicate that one's motive is simply the enjoyment of venereal pleasure. Granted the reason is serious, one must always take care to withhold consent to the pleasure which arises.

[6] Edwin F. Healy, S.J., *Medical Ethics*, pp. 147–150. Chicago, Loyola, 1956.

READINGS

St. Augustine, *Confessions*, Bk. VI, cc. 11–16.
St. Thomas, *Summa Theologica*, II–II, 47, 148, 149, 150, 151, 158.
Allport, G. W., *The Nature of Prejudice*. Cambridge, Addeson-Wesley, 1954.
Boekraad, A. J., *The Personal Conquest of Truth*. Louvain, Nauwelaerts, 1955.
Buckley, J., *Christian Design for Sex*. Chicago, Fides, 1952.
Drummond, E. J., "Pursuit of Truth to Make Men Free," *Catholic Mind*, 54 (1955), 647–653.
Entralgo, P. L., "Towards a Theory of the Catholic Intellectual," *Cross Currents*, Winter, 1953, 149–161.
Flood, P., *New Problems in Medical Ethics*, Vol. I, 3–123, Westminster, Newman, 1953.
Ford, J. C., *Depth Psychology, Morality and Alcoholism*. Weston, Weston College, 1951.
Irala, N., *Achieving Peace of Heart*. New York, Wagner, 1955.
Marcus Aurelius, *Meditations*.
McAllister, J. B., "Psychoanalysis and Morality," *New Scholasticism*, 30 (1956), 310–329.
O'Brien, J. A., *Sex-Character Formation*. New York, Macmillan, 1952.
O'Connell, D. A., "Christian Liberty," *The Thomist*, 15 (1952), 209–246, 404–493.
Oldenwald, R. P., "The Problem of Masturbation," *The Priest*, 11 (January, 1955), 28–32; (February, 1955), 126–132.
Root, R., *Progress Against Prejudice*. New York, Friendship, 1957.
Staab, G., "Some Moral Aspects of Drug Addiction," *American Ecclesiastical Review*, 130 (April, 1954), 238–249.
Todd, J. M., ed., *The Springs of Morality*, 149–163. New York, Macmillan, 1956.

Chapter XII DUTIES TO BODY

379. The law of self-preservation is operative in living things. The organism by nature tends to conserve its life and faculties. Existence is the first good, and toward continuance in existence all things less than man are moved by nature. Does the same compulsion apply also to man so that there is a law of nature "by which a man is forbidden to do that which is destructive of [his] life"?[1] Is this rule ironclad or does it allow exceptions so that, for a cause, a man may dispose of his corporal members and even cut short his life? In answering these questions, we shall consider the three general cases of suicide, mutilation, and care of one's health.

I. SUICIDE

380. *Suicide* literally means the killing of self. Self-destruction can be direct or indirect. *Direct self-destruction* occurs when one's own death is the immediate object of one's will act, as when a penniless actress deliberately takes an overdose of sleeping pills. *Indirect self-destruction* follows from an action which, by its nature and the intention of the agent, can produce some effect other than death, as when an aviator destroys an enemy vessel by crashing his plane against it. In direct self-destruction life is destroyed, death is sought; in indirect self-destruction, death unsought is permitted.

Direct self-destruction could take place on the authority of a superior who has dominion over the life of the person. Such self-destruction would not be an immoral act but obedience to the command of a lawful superior. God is the master of life and death; hence if He inspired the act of those martyrs who rushed to death of their own accord, they were guilty of no wrong. Is the State also a competent superior in this matter? Could a judge order a condemned criminal to be his own executioner? It is agreed that the criminal is not obliged to obey such a command. But a command which need not be obeyed is no command. The State may command the individual to perform only

[1] Thomas Hobbes, *Leviathan*, Part I, Chap. XIV, p. 84. New York, 1947.

actions involving social co-operation; but self-destruction, which destroys one's relation to society, precludes the possibility of the individual's co-operation. Moreover, it would be abhorrent to make the criminal's wife or father the executioner: all the more abhorrent would it be to make a man his own executioner since he is closer to himself than any dear one. But could the judge *permit* the criminal to be his own executioner? Some think that if the self-inflicted death would be less painful than the death intended by the State, the criminal may be allowed to kill himself. But even this seems unlikely. For if the State cannot command self-destruction neither may it permit it. Although the State has authority to kill the criminal, it has no authority to make him or let him kill himself. The action is too opposed to the essential tendency to self-preservation and offers the criminal no social good in which he shares.

381. The suicide whose morality we are now discussing is the direct killing of one's self upon one's own authority. We are not asking if it is generally wrong — a proposition which all men seem to admit — but if it is always wrong. The ancient Stoics held that suicide was sometimes noble and honorable, a sentiment which a few moderns like Hume, Bentham, and Montaigne re-echo. According to them, a general who loses a crucial battle, the master of a foundering vessel, the victim of prolonged and incurable disease are justified in taking their lives.

THESIS XXVII. Suicide, whereby man kills himself upon his own authority, is always forbidden; but indirect self-destruction or exposure to danger of certain death is allowable for a sufficiently grave reason.

PROOF OF PART I

382. The Natural Law forbids as intrinsically evil any invasion of the exclusive dominion of God. For man to do what belongs to God alone perverts the essential order of human nature. Suicide trespasses upon God's exclusive dominion because (*a*) destruction of a thing is the ultimate act of dominion. (*b*) God has dominion over the life of man because He is man's Efficient Cause and Last End. (*c*) This dominion is exclusively God's so that it cannot be shared by man. If man were granted such dominion over himself, then God *alone* would not be man's final end, and man, the creature, would be his own end. But no created thing can be its own end.

383. **Corollary.** Man is but the steward of his corporeal life and of

all his faculties. A steward is the agent of his principal and has no independent rights over the substance which has been entrusted to him. Therefore, man may use life and body, but his use of them must accord with the will of his principal, God. Man may never on his own authority destroy his trust.

384. The intrinsic evil of suicide is clear also from a consideration of the truth, that, since God is the Maker and Last End of man, man belongs totally and essentially to Him. It is contrary to right reason to hold that one who is essentially the servant of another should determine how long he is to serve and when he is to receive the reward of his service. By suicide man overturns right order.

385. When man by suicide invades God's exclusive rights, of what in particular does man deprive God? Since God owns man absolutely, man cannot say his life is his own to do with as he chooses. He must use it as God directs through divine law. What God expects of man and has an exclusive right to exact from man are morally good acts. By morally good acts man gives God extrinsic glory. How much extrinsic glory is due from each and for how long a time it is to be rendered are matters for God to determine. Therefore, when man by his own act shortens his life, he is acting the part of God, and deprives God of that to which God is entitled, namely, further moral fruits of mortal life, a definite amount of extrinsic glory expected of probationary man.

386. Suicide as an escape from overwhelming personal disaster, an evil life, misery, frustration, or dishonor, far from being an act of fortitude, is an act of cowardice. It is a refusal to accept a severe test sent us by God. Persons who take their lives under such circumstances have the false view that happiness in this life is man's last end.

Suicide as an escape from being a burden to others also manifests the erroneous conception that the purpose of life is temporal happiness. The aged, broken, chronically infirm, and seemingly useless give others magnificent opportunities for practicing the moral virtues. God has promised eternal beatitude to those who feed the hungry, clothe the naked, shelter the homeless. How could such virtues be exercised if God did not permit appropriate opportunities?

It is lawful to wish death, that is, orderly death in conformity to the plans of Divine Providence, but we may not wish to kill ourselves.

PART II

387. Men sometimes embark on a most hazardous enterprise whence death is surely or most likely to ensue. The timid onlooker calls it

suicide. And it is suicide if self-destruction is intended. But even if they do not intend their death, if they are merely resigned to accept it if it comes, are they justified? Does the fact that they are stewards of their mortal life demand that they take every means to save their lives and avoid every proximate danger of death? No, for reason may allow, sometimes demand, exposure to imminent peril. The morality of such acts must be judged by the principle of double effect.

PROOF

388. **Exposure to danger of certain death is justified** if all of the following conditions are verified:

1. The action which results in the bad unintended effect of death and some other good effect must itself be morally good or at least indifferent.
2. The effect other than death must be morally good, as when a man plunges into icy water to save a drowning skater.
3. The intended good effect may not be caused by one's death. If it were, then one would first have to intend one's death, which is always wrong. Hence the good intended must follow from the act of exposure as immediately as does death. If exposure to death has one and only one immediate effect, namely, self-destruction, one cannot intend it without intending suicide. In such cases, the principle of double effect does not apply.
4. There must be reasonable proportion between the good intended and one's death. Death is allowed only for a gravely compensating reason. This reason could be a spiritual good, for example, avoidance of a proximate occasion of serious sin, or some notable material benefit to one's neighbor or the community.

II. MUTILATION AND STERILIZATION

389. Besides preserving his life a man must maintain his bodily faculties intact. Bodily integrity is disturbed by *mutilation*, which is the total or partial destruction of a bodily function usually effected by removing some part of the body. A *major mutilation* involves suppression of a bodily function or removal of a notable part of the body. A *minor mutilation*, like the removal of a small part of the finger or the external ear, involves only the partial suppression of a function or the removal of a less notable part of the body.

A man may not mutilate himself, because, as steward of his faculties, he must keep his trust intact. He may not dispose of his faculties at will.

This is an immediate conclusion from the nature of his relationship to his Creator from whom he has received the gift of his faculties.

Obviously an exception must be made in order to conserve life; for it is reasonable that a part be sacrificed for the sake of the whole.

390. **Are there any other exceptions?** One may not mutilate himself for the sake of avoiding sin. "Spiritual good," says St. Thomas, "can be procured by means other than the cutting off of a member because sin lies in the will. Therefore in no case is it allowed to cut off a member for the sake of avoiding any sin whatever."[2]

The discoveries of medical science raise two serious problems: the licitness of sterilization and of organic transplantation.

A. Sterilization

391. A sterile person is one who lacks the power of reproduction. Sterility may be the result of unformed organs or of a natural defect in or malformation of reproductive organs. It may be a natural cessation of fecundity because of age or it may be artificially induced. Modern sterilization is of the latter type. It renders a human being incapable of reproduction through surgical or medical means. In the male it is usually achieved by vasectomy, or the severing of the seminal ducts. In ancient times, it was done by castration, which is still practiced on brutes. Castration is the removal of scrotum, testicles, and seminal glands. Except in the rarest instances castration makes sexual intercourse impossible; this modern sterilization does not do. The female is sterilized by the operation called salpingectomy, or the severing of the Fallopian tubes. From the standpoint of the motive for sterilization, four types may be distinguished, therapeutic, punitive, contraceptive, and eugenic.

392. The purpose of *therapeutic* sterilization is the health of the individual. The removal of cancerous Fallopian tubes, ovaries, womb, or injured testicles would fall in this category. It is said that orchidectomy is a remedy against cancer. If sterilization should prove to be the proper remedy for any serious ailment, it would become legitimate mutilation, because it is just to sacrifice a part for the good of the whole.

Punitive sterilization is inflicted by the State as a punishment for crime. The argument runs that since the State can take life as a just punishment for crime, *a fortiori* it can inflict the lesser evil of mutilation. This argument is sound, and the sole point of investigation is whether sterilization is an apt sanction. Would this particular mutilation measure up to the requirements of an effective sanction?

---

[2] *Sum. Theol.*, II–II, 65, 1.

It appears that sterilization does not. Any proposed sanction to be effective must have its *deterring* value. The threatened punishment must have some power to keep prospective evildoers from crime. The fear of losing the procreative power might have some deterring effect upon peoples like Mohammedans and Chinese, who have a strongly developed sense of progeny; but sterilization to most criminals might be a rather welcome procedure, because it does not prevent sexual intercourse but rather prevents the inconvenient result of offspring. A sanction must have a *remedial*, or reformative, aspect; but since sterilization rather grants the criminal more freedom for sexual indulgence, scarcely any criminal will be improved by sterilization. Furthermore, sterilized people often experience an unhappy increase of libido. Finally, a sanction should exact *expiation* from the wrongdoer. Since sterilization involves little personal hardship, and since it takes from the offender a power he is just as pleased to be rid of, the expiatory value of sterilization is next to nothing. Sterilization, therefore, is an inept instrument for law enforcement.

Contraceptive sterilization is induced to prevent conception. The person's sole motive is avoidance of parenthood. It is not unheard of that a surgeon on the occasion of a Caesarean section will ligate or sever the Fallopian tubes so that the woman may continue sexual relations without risk of pregnancy. The mutilation in these circumstances is voluntarily accepted, although such operations have been performed without the knowledge and consent of the patient.

Eugenic sterilization has as its object the prevention of conception for the evolvement of a more perfect race.

393. "Eugenics is the study of agencies under social control that may improve or impair the racial qualities of future generations either physically or mentally."[3] It is the outgrowth of organic evolution. Natural selection, or the law of the survival of the fittest, brought man to his present level of development, but now it no longer serves him because so many of the fittest perish in war and so many of the unfit, on account of the humanitarianism of the past century, are so cared for that they too can readily propagate. The race is deteriorating because not enough superior people have sufficient progeny and too many tainted parents are passing on defective inheritance to their children.

The race cannot be substantially improved by improving the environment in which people live. Acquired characteristics are not transmissible.

[3] Paul Popenoe, *Applied Eugenics*, p. 147. New York, Macmillan, 1918. Cf. also Sir Francis Galton, *Essays in Eugenics*, p. 35. London, The Eugenics Society, 1909.

The germ plasm which passes from parents to progency is not capable of modification. So, to that age-old problem which Euripides in his *Hecuba* expresses by the question, "Is it the parents or the education?"[4] the eugenist answers vociferously that it is the parents. A man is a superior man if he comes of superior stock; he is unfit if he comes from poor stock. And that is the end of it.

Since unaided nature cannot effect the improvement of the race, the co-operation and intervention of human intelligence is required. This eugenics will supply by carrying out this simple program: let the superior element in the community, the bearers of good germ plasm, do the propagating; let the defectives, the bearers of bad germ plasm, stop propagating.

There is no danger to the race from the unfit who are now institutionalized, for the opportunity to propagate is taken from them. But it is financially impossible to segregate all potential parents of defectives. Since so many must be at large in society, let society protect itself from them by taking from them the power to propagate. Let the defective willingly submit to sterilization, but if he will not, the State should have the power to compel him.

Legislative bodies have listened to the arguments of eugenists, and it is not surprising that Nazi Germany, so loud a protagonist of the theory of superior and inferior races, should have taken extreme measures in this regard. It not only legislated that very numerous categories of the mentally diseased be sterilized, but thoroughly carried out the program. Up to January 1, 1957, thirty-two of our states had passed sterilization laws. Of these, four were declared unconstitutional. Of the remainder, only the California law has drastic provisions. In most of these states these laws are practically moribund.[5]

394. The end envisioned by eugenic legislation is admirable. Every State is interested in the birth of healthy children. Taxpayers ought not be saddled with the support of the unfit if this reasonably can be avoided. Nor is an individual justified in begetting children, if he foresees that he will have to turn them over to others for support. But are the means advocated — voluntary or compulsory sterilization — equally good? Does this kind of sterilization accord with the law of nature?

THESIS XXVIII. Voluntary contraceptive sterilization and eugenic compulsory sterilization are forbidden by the Natural Law.

---

[4] *Hecuba,* line 599.

[5] Cf. O'Hara-Sanks, "Eugenic Sterilization," *Georgetown Law Journal,* Fall, 1956, p. 43.

PROOF OF PART I

395. Voluntary contraceptive sterilization is contrary to the Natural Law because

It is unjustifiable self-mutilation. It aims only at evil. Obviously it aims at the physical evil of destroying a function. This destruction is morally justifiable only when it accomplishes a higher good. The greater physical good of the agent is not at stake because destruction of the sex faculty is not required for the health of the agent. Nor can it aim at a social good because the suppression of the faculty by which new beings are born into society is evil. For it is better to be than not to be. The intent of this action can only be positive contraception or the hindering of the union of sperm and ovum by artificial interference with natural processes. That positive contraception is always wrong is proved in Social Ethics, § 776.

PROOF OF PART II

396. Compulsory eugenic sterilization is contrary to the Natural Law because

It is an unjustifiable invasion of the State upon the integrity of the citizen's body. The State has no direct right over the faculties of citizens who are guiltless of crime. Direct dominion over an individual's faculties belongs solely to God and to the individual. To say that the State has a similar, even a superior, dominion is a gross subversion of natural purpose. Nature gives each one his faculties for *his own perfection.* They are his in the strictest sense of the word so that it is unjust to deprive a guiltless man of any of his faculties. The State may not interfere in the order established by nature between parent and child: *a fortiori* it may not interfere in the natural order existing between a man and his person. Although the common good may determine how one is to use a faculty at times, it may never deprive an innocent man of a faculty.

397. On behalf of sterilization procedures it has been urged that the organs of an individual may be removed for the benefit of society, of which the individual is a part, in much the same way as an organ is removed for the sake of the individual. The argument is fallacious on account of the difference between a physical and a moral organism.

A man is a physical unity in which the parts have no subsistence of their own and exist solely for the good of the physical whole. Hence a part may be disposed of for the good of the whole. Society is not a physical unity but a functional whole. Its parts have a subsistence of their own: so much so that ultimately society exists for the good of its members. Hence society is a moral organism and is a unity only with respect to a final purpose and action conducive thereto. Persons then are members of this moral organism only as functional parts and the moral whole can make demands on them only as regards action. As regards their physical being, persons are independent of society. Hence the moral whole can make no demands on the person in the realm of his physical being upon the grounds that the whole can dispose of its parts. This may be said only of physical unities. State sterilization then is direct intervention, not only in the sphere of action of the individual, but also and especially in the sphere of his being. But while a functional whole like the State, in which the individual is incorporated as a functional part, can regulate the actions of its functional parts, it cannot touch their being.[6]

398. **The claims of the eugenists are not even good science.**[7] The claims of the eugenists to be social *scientists* are not well sustained. First, their basic contention that "the germ plasm is incapable of improvement or deterioration"[8] is not susceptible of proof. The eugenists substitute conjecture for fact and emotionally close their eyes to the influence of environment. Second, they have no real norm for distinguishing superior stock, which may propagate, from inferior stock, which they say should be stopped from propagating; for "from vigorous and efficient parents may be produced offspring which are weak and inefficient. From defective parents may be produced offspring that are normal."[9] Third, despite numerous studies science knows comparatively little about Mendelian laws of heredity operating to produce disease among men.[10] Fourth, the eugenists have grossly exaggerated the dangers to society from increase of feeble-mindedness. For "all the statistics and the biological trends indicated by the marriage rate, birth-rate, death rate, divorce rate and fertility rate indicate that these groups are not increasing and, if anything, are declining."[11] Fifth, sterilization of all defectives would have little result in lessening the number of defectives. Since only 10 per cent of defectives are offspring of defective parents,[12] a thorough sterilization

---

[6] Confer the address of Pope Pius XII, May 14, 1956, on *Corneal Transplantation*.
[7] Confer MAN AS MAN, first edition, for fuller treatment of this material, p. 209 ff.
[8] Paul Popenoe, *Applied Eugenics*, p. 74. New York, Macmillan, 1918.
[9] H. S. Jennings, *Genetics*, p. 298. New York, Norton, 1935.
[10] Cf. Edward A. Strecker, *Fundamentals of Psychiatry*, 4 ed., p. 15; also J. H. Landman, *Human Sterilization*, p. 146.
[11] Abraham Myerson, *American Journal of Psychiatry*, Vol. 92, No. 3, p. 619, November, 1935.
[12] R. A. Fisher, *Journal of Heredity*, Vol. XVIII, p. 530, December, 1927; A. F. Tredgold, *A Text-book of Mental Deficiency*, 6 ed., p. 29. Baltimore, Wood, 1937.

program would require between two and three thousand years to reduce the number of defectives from one in a thousand to one in ten thousand.[13] Finally, the economic argument that the defective, once sterilized, need no longer be kept segregated at public expense is both shortsighted and cruel. To turn loose upon the community such persons — especially women — of low intelligence and irresponsible tendencies would give a tremendous impetus to the spread of social disease. In the long run the latter would cost the State more than the upkeep of the feebleminded.

Even if the claims of the eugenists were sensible and valid, the means which they advocate would still be morally wrong.

399. There is a sensible eugenics which consists in observance of the laws of sound hygiene and above all the moral law. The chief reason for human deterioration is disregard for the moral law. If a man disregards the specific law of his being, there is little reason for wondering why his being should suffer. The race can be improved only by improvement of the individual, and the most powerful factor that makes for the improvement of the individual is divine grace. But here again we enter the field of the supernatural.

Eugenics is another sign of the prevalent "happiness now" attitude of mind. Eugenists fail to see that "happiness hereafter" is purchasable by self-sacrificing care of the unfortunate. Divine Providence permits the unfortunate to be among us to give man an opportunity to exercise that charity which helps merit the kingdom of heaven. They scarcely deserve that kingdom who would rid us of the inconvenient presence of unfortunates by violating nature's law.

B. Organic Transplantations

400. An organic transplant is tissue taken from one living being and emplanted in a man to be part of his substance. The emplanted tissue might be from a brute. Not all biologically possible transplantations of tissue from a brute to a man are necessarily condemned. However, on account of danger of taint to offspring it is wrong to graft the sex glands of a brute on a man. But it is not wrong to take the tissue of a man who has just died, a cornea for example, and emplant it in another person. Indeed it is praiseworthy to bequeath one's corneas to a cornea bank. The burning question agitating modern Scholastics is, Is such transfer of tissue between living persons allowable? May a woman give one of her ovaries to another woman?

401. First, it is certain that one may not deprive himself entirely

[13] R. C. Punnett, *Journal of Heredity*, Vol. VIII, p. 465, October, 1917.

of a function. Such action goes beyond a man's power of administration over his body. This is indubitably clear in the case of the reproductive function. Whoever would sterilize himself for the benefit of a fellow man would be choosing a bad means to accomplish a good end. In the case of a pair of organs, however, may one share one of them with another? Some Scholastics vehemently deny the lawfulness of such action on the principle that the only reason which justifies self-mutilation is the good of one's own body. They point to the statement of Pope Pius XI as the perfect embodiment of that principle: "Private individuals have no other power over the members of their bodies than that which pertains to their natural ends; and they are not free to destroy or mutilate their members, or in any way render themselves unfit for their natural functions, except when no other provision can be made for the good of the whole body."[14] Others say that, while the principle advanced is a general one, it is not absolute, that it has been traditional to formulate the principle in an absolute way because organic transplantation was unknown until very recently; and therefore the papal condemnation is not to be extended to this type of transplant. For the lawfulness of this kind of transplant they argue from the unity of the human race and the precept of charity which bids us help our fellow man in need. They distinguish between the primary purpose of the faculty, which is the perfection of him in whom the faculty exists, and a secondary purpose, which is assistance to other man. They hold that assistance can go so far as the donation of one of a pair of organs if there is no danger of death to the donor and if a proportionate cause for the transfer exists. There are conservative authors who consider this opinion probable.

III. CARE OF HEALTH

402. The law of self-preservation obliges a man to use all ordinary means to preserve health and life. The reason is that failure to do so is equivalent to destroying life.

Ordinary means of preserving health are those which can be obtained and used without excessive inconvenience and which offer a reasonable hope of success. The difference between ordinary and extraordinary means depends on time and place. Certainly extraordinary means are those which impose a relatively intolerable burden such as great pain, horror of a medical procedure, expense notably beyond one's means.[15]

---

[14] Encyclical letter on *Christian Marriage*.

[15] Cf. G. Kelly, S.J., "Artificial Means of Preserving Life," *Theological Studies*, 11 (1950), 204–208.

Occasionally a man might be obliged to use extraordinary means if great interests such as the well-being of many people were intimately dependent upon him.

403. Hunger strike. Since no one of his own authority may refuse to use the ordinary means of sustaining life, a hunger strike can seldom be justified. Thus, if one intends unreservedly to abstain from food until he is released from unjust imprisonment, he is choosing self-inflicted death as a means to his end. For indefinite abstention from food is death. If, however, one does not intend to prolong his fast to the point of death and prudently judges that the fasting will effect his release, then if his imprisonment is unjust and if the good to be obtained is commensurate with the bodily harm he suffers, the action may be justifiable.

404. Boxing. Unusual interest has lately been manifested by moralists in an activity which the American public has accepted without question. Certainly a boxing match is not a duel even though some European moralists have called it "the American duel." It is the claim of some authors[16] that American boxing, as it is presently constituted, is immoral. One of them offers these reasons:[17] (*a*) boxing aims at a knockout which is a serious deprivation of reason without a justifying cause; (*b*) inevitably it means serious injury for contestants; (*c*) it arouses the brutishness of the spectators.

Must we accept as a general principle that a sport is seriously wrong if it aims at a loss of reason? It has been alleged that a loss of reason of even a short duration is a serious matter. This is inadmissible. In treating of drunkenness the best authors say that the time element cannot be ignored. Davis says that "intoxication . . . would not be a grave sin if the loss of reason lasted only a short time."[18] He thinks that a short time here would be something less than an hour. Actually how much loss of consciousness occurs in boxing matches? How many bouts end in a knockout and how long is the period of unconsciousness? There are no statistics available which would correlate the number of rounds fought with the resultant time of unconsciousness but to all appearances it is negligible. Furthermore, must it be said that in a professional sport there is no justifying reason which would permit this very occasional loss of reason? Making a living? Winning fame?

Concerning the other two reasons offered there can be no difference of principle. If one could not engage in boxing without giving and receiving serious injury and without arousing the brutishness of the

[16] Cf. F. J. Connell, *Outlines of Moral Theology*, p. 126. Milwaukee, Bruce, 1953. Gerald Kelly, *Theological Studies*, V. 12, 78, March, 1951.

[17] Eugene Hillman, *Theological Studies*, V. 12, 301 ff.

[18] Henry Davis, *Moral and Pastoral Theology*, V. I, 245.

spectators, then the sport is wrong. Since we are engaged in establishing *principles*, we might dismiss the matter at this point. However, while we have no fault to find with the major premises of these two arguments, we may ask if the proponents of these arguments have proved their minor premises. Their condemnation of boxing arises from their estimation of a factual situation. Is it a fact that boxing does, by and large, result in physical injury to contestants and moral hurt to spectators? Several generations ago a fight to the finish with bare knuckles was forbidden by law. Since that time the law has legalized the present form of boxing. Must now the law be made more stringent by eliminating the knockout and compelling the use of bigger gloves in order that boxing may stand within the limits of decency?

What is a realistic view of the present situation? There have been boxing fatalities and some boxers have been permanently injured. What is the proportion of fatalities and injuries to the number of bouts fought? to other contact sports like football which also has fatalities and injuries? Are serious injuries inevitable from this form of boxing? Certainly the law has been designed to prevent them. Admittedly there has been lax enforcement of the law. It is argued that a better enforcement of the law may not be expected because control of the sport has fallen into vicious hands. It is also said that even if the present laws were adequately enforced, boxing would still be injurious because any heavy blow to the boxer's head is a serious injury. This last statement, however, has not been proved, but it merits further investigation. From the evidence they present we do not think that the condemners of boxing have proved beyond reasonable doubt that there is a practically inevitable connection between the present status of boxing and serious injury to the contestants. We do not see the inevitability of the connection because one can reasonably expect better enforcement of the present law. To despair of this is to take too dim a view: public opinion is still capable of correcting flagrant abuses.

The charge that boxing brutalizes the spectators need not be taken seriously. In the knightly tourneys of the Middle Ages there was greater danger to the contestant and as much frenzied partisanship among the spectators; yet we do not read of fair ladies being denied sacramental absolution because they cheered on their favorite lances.

405. In brief, then, they who promote the sport or act as officials have a serious obligation to observe the civil law and prevent the exploitation of contestants. There is certainly room for improvement but one ought not to despair of achieving it. Furthermore, we are not convinced that the present rules are inadequate for the protection of the boxer or incompatible with human dignity. Finally, we do not see from the present status of boxing that one should conclude that it is morally wrong (*a*) for a young man to enter the fight game, (*b*) for a person to buy a ticket for a bout, or (*c*) to watch fights on TV. For serious obligations may be imposed only when their existence is certain. Since boxing has been accepted as a legitimate sport for a considerable period, the burden of proof would lie on those who might claim that the abovementioned actions are wrong.

READINGS

St. Thomas, *Summa Theologica*, II–II, 64, 5; 65, 1.
Bernard, G. C., *The Morality of Prizefighting*. Washington, Catholic University, 1952.
Connery, J. R., "Notes on Moral Theology," *Theological Studies*, 17 (1956), 557–561.
Corpus Juris, "Suicide," Vol. 60, 995–999.
Cunningham, B. J., *The Morality of Organic Transplantation*. Washington, Catholic University, 1944.
Ford, J. C., "The Refusal of Blood Transfusions by Jehovah's Witnesses," *Linacre Quarterly*, 22 (1955), 3–10, 41–50.
Kelly, G., "Catholic Teaching on Contraception and Sterilization," *Linacre Quarterly*, 21 (August, 1954), 72–79 and (November, 1954), 110–118.
——— "Pius XII and the Principle of Totality," *Theological Studies*, 16 (1955), 373–396.
Landsberg, P-L., "The Moral Problem of Suicide," *The Experience of Death*, 65–97. London, Rockcliff, 1953.
Lehane, J. B., *The Morality of American Civil Legislation Concerning Eugenical Sterilization*. Washington, Catholic University, 1944.
Lynch, J. J., "A Topical Index to Moral Problems in Medicine," *Linacre Quarterly*, 21 (August, 1954), 87–104.
McAllister, J. B., *Ethics*, 169–191. Philadelphia, Saunders, 1955.
McCarthy, J., "Direct and Indirect Suicide," *Irish Ecclesiastical Record*, 82 (November, 1954), 340–343.
McReavy, L. L., "Self-Sacrifice and Suicide — State Authorization," *Clergy Review*, 40 (1955), 534–537.
O'Donnell, T. J., *Morals in Medicine*, 69–111. Westminster, Newman, 1956.
Pius XII, "Corneal Transplantation," *The Pope Speaks*, Autumn, 1956, 198–206.
——— "Medical Ethics," *Catholic Mind*, 53 (1955), 242–252.

Chapter XIII CERTAIN EXTERNAL ADVANTAGES TO THE INDIVIDUAL

406. In considering man's obligation to love himself with an orderly love, we have seen that he must secure a minimal perfection of soul and body. The experience of the race, however, shows that the personal values we have enumerated are not enough for the good life. No man is sufficient for himself. To secure normal well-being, the individual depends on others. He needs a favorable environment. If his surroundings are not helpful, he will find it difficult to lead an upright life. For moral reasons, therefore, a man must provide himself with certain external advantages: a minimum of certain external spiritual and material goods must be at his disposal.

I. WHAT ARE THESE ADVANTAGES?

407. Five external advantages may be enumerated.

1. *Good name* — the reputation of being a good man.

2. *Personal liberty* — the moral and juridical ability of using one's faculties and goods without undue dependence on the will of others.

3. *Friendship* — mutual esteem and affection for an equal who is not related by domestic ties.

4. *Amusement* — recreation of mind and body, the relaxation of one's powers in the enjoyment of delectable good.

5. *Material resources* — a source of material good helpful to one's material life, such as money, land, or the equivalent.

II. HOW NECESSARY ARE THEY?

408. We do not say that all these things are of equal value to men or that all of them are necessary for all men and in all circumstances. Some men may dispense with one or other of these. A few heroic men

of extraordinary virtue like Simeon Stylites may do without practically all of them and lead a moral life. The point is that normally speaking a certain minimum of these things is necessary for the ordinary man to help him keep the moral law. The reason is that without this minimum of external advantages he will not preserve his dignity and avoid the proximate occasions of moral evil. The need of these things in normal circumstances is clear from the evil consequences which result when they are absent.

1. A good name is a help to the practice of virtue as a bad name is a hindrance. The man of evil reputation very often concludes that he might just as well live up to a bad name. In the company of others with similar reputation he may develop a resentment and desire for revenge on those of good reputation. Besides, as a man must seek virtue, so he must seek a good name, which stands closest to virtue and is its mirror.

2. Compulsion to wrongdoing is easily brought to bear on those who are not free. The outstanding evil of slavery is that the slave is made to do his master's bidding no matter how immoral. Freedom, on the other hand, is in harmony with the independence of human nature.

3. A man deprived of true friendship loses that solace of human companionship so helpful to weather the crises of life; he is without that moral support and encouragement which is one of the benefits of friendship. The lonely man can sink into sordid vices.

4. Nature does not intend that man be without delectable good. Mind and body suffer deeply when deprived of a minimum of pleasure. If a man is deprived of legitimate satisfaction, he will seek it in forbidden ways.

5. Without a minimum of material resources, a man lacks many means of intellectual and moral improvement. Because man has a natural inclination for these things, the abjectly poor will be willing to seize them unlawfully — they will commit crimes against chastity, truthfulness, loyalty, and the like to secure them. One of the surest breeding grounds of crime is abject poverty.

III. IN WHAT MEASURE ARE THEY TO BE SOUGHT?

409. The Natural Law commands man to acquire the minimal amount of these external advantages necessary for him to fulfill his common and individual obligations. Failure to observe this command is to be guilty of sloth.

May one seek these things beyond the minimum prescribed by the Natural Law? Nature does not restrict man to bare essentials; however, in the pursuit of the nonessential, man may not sacrifice virtue. These external advantages must always be regarded not as good in themselves but only in so far as they are means to the end of man. Possession of them does not constitute perfective human good, for no man is a better man merely because he owns five hundred acres and is respected for his honesty. These are useful goods. These things may seem to be perfective goods because men have a strong urge to secure them. But what is less than man and external to him can only be a useful good. However, these advantages do exercise so powerful an influence over most men that there is always danger that they will not be used with right reason and that they will be sought as ends in themselves.

IV. THE DANGER OF EXCESS

410. 1. In the matter of praise a man may be guilty of excess by seeking it for unworthy reasons. A man may desire the reputation of being a good man but may not be willing to practice the virtue which alone deserves it. Hence he may hide his vice under a mantle of virtue, which is hypocrisy. Or one may seek fame and reputation in many things solely for the love of such honor. This is an inordinate self-exaltation, which can lead to great excesses of pride.

2. Loving liberty, a man may be too independent and unwilling to show reverence and obedience where it is properly due. True freedom does not mean that man is entitled to think, say, and do as he chooses. One may not seek a freedom which is incompatible with his state in life. Liberty can degenerate into outright license. One can never be independent of God.

3. Too many friends or the wrong friends can be a stumbling block to man's real good. One may not sacrifice moral ideals or upright conduct to acquire or retain the friendship of any man. Too many vices have a social origin: too many bad habits are assimilated from bad company.

4. The axiom, "virtue stands in the middle ground," is nowhere better illustrated than in the case of pleasure and material goods.

It is easy to confuse pleasure and happiness and to conclude that all happiness is to be found in pleasure. Pleasure is the result of some really or apparently perfective action; happiness is the combination of the truly perfective good and the legitimate pleasure which accompanies it. If pleasure is sought for its own sake, one is little concerned whether it is the apparently or truly perfective good. The great delusion of life is founding happiness upon the pleasure of apparent good.

5. The good man is content with a modest competence. The Book

of Proverbs expresses this thought: "Give me neither beggary nor riches."[1] One may seek a surplus of material goods in a virtuous manner, but the quest presents no little difficulty. Avarice can grow unrecognized; it is fed by what one has accumulated and may develop into a craving which knows no bounds. It is a delusion to believe that a man should always seek to increase his income. Few tremendously great fortunes have been amassed by their original owners without violations of justice and charity. And once attained, great wealth can be an even greater occasion of sin than abject poverty, for the very wealthy man has at hand the ready means to satisfy every whim.

V. PRACTICAL CONCLUSION

411. Because all of these advantages are external to man, they cannot truly be called good in themselves; they are useful goods, the common sense means to man's perfective good. As Ignatius Loyola expressed it, all other things upon the face of the earth are to help man attain his last end. The reasonable way to use any instrument is to employ it in so far as it helps to attain the end for which it was made and to stop using it whenever it no longer serves our purpose. This is the way a mechanic uses the tools of his trade. No carpenter will continue to saw, merely because he likes to use a saw, when further sawing will ruin his work. However, when it comes to honor, freedom, friendship, pleasure, and wealth, men too easily invert the order of right reason, and look on helps to the good life as the good life itself, and hence will seek these things in unreasonable measure and cling to them even though by so doing they frustrate the purpose for which these things were made. The fascination of trifles obscures the good.[2] Hence, one must cultivate the virtue of prudence so as to discern the true value and purpose of these things, and above all the virtue of temperance so as not to be excessive in their use. No sounder advice was ever given the human race than this admonition in the Sermon on the Mount: "Seek ye first the kingdom of God and his justice, and all these things will be added unto you."[3]

[1] Prov. 30:8.
[2] Wisd. 4:12.
[3] Mt. 6:33.

READINGS

St. Thomas, *Summa Theologica*, I–II, 2, 4; II–II, 114; 132, 1; 168, 2, 3, 4.
——— *Contra Gentiles*, III, 121, 133.
Aristotle, *Ethics*, VIII–IX.
——— *Politics*, VII, 1–3.
Grindel, E. W., ed., *The Concept of Freedom*. Chicago, Regnery, 1955.

Keller-Lavaud, "La charité comme amitié d'après S Thomas," *Revue Thomiste*, 12 (1929), 445–475.
Leclercq, J., "Freedom as a Moral and Social Value," *Truth and Freedom*, 49–66. Pittsburgh, Duquesne, 1954.
Lorson, P., *Le plaisir sanctifié: Pour une spiritualité des loisirs*. Paris, Alsatia, 1952.
Maritain, J., *Scholasticism and Politics*, 94–113. London, Bles, 1954.
Meaney, J. W., "Propaganda as Psychical Coercion," *Review of Politics*, 13 (1951), 64–87.
Pieper, J., "The Social Meaning of Leisure in the Modern World," *Review of Politics*, 12 (1950), 411–421.
Pius XII, "The Movies and the Nature of Man," *The Pope Speaks*, II (1955), 101–112.
——— "Sports and the Christian Life," *The Pope Speaks*, III, (1956), 35–43.
——— "Sports and Gymnastics," *Catholic Mind*, 51 (1953), 569–576.
Seneca, *Epistulae Morales*, 9, 17, 35, 109, 110.
Smith, G., "The Nature and Uses of Liberty," *New Scholasticism*, 26 (1952), 305–326.

Chapter XIV OUR FELLOW MAN

412. Having viewed the individual's obligations toward God and himself, we shall now consider his obligations toward his fellow man. We sum up man's obligations to God in the phrase, God must be loved above all things. We sum up his obligations to himself by saying that he must love himself with an orderly love. What basic rule of conduct governs him in his relations to his fellow man? Can all particular obligations of this type be epitomized in the word *love?*

I. SENSIBLE AND INTELLECTUAL LOVE

413. Love is the complacency of the appetite in some object presented as good and therefore desirable. Love may be either sensible or intellectual.

1. *Sensible love* is the complacency produced in the sensitive appetite by a particular *sensible object*. Desire for the object is more or less emotional. A brute animal loves itself with a sensible love which is completely self-regarding. Every man has such a love for himself.

A man loves another man with sensible love when he is said to like him, that is, his imagination presents him as agreeable, his sensitive appetite approves of him, and consequently he seeks him with more or less intensity of emotion. It is a spontaneous attraction in which intellect plays little part. Teen-agers "adore" the current screen or TV sensation, and that is the end of it.

2. *Intellectual love* is the complacency produced in the rational appetite either by a particular object or by whole classes of desirable objects. Besides a rational love for her mother, a girl can love a person as representing an entire class of lovable beings. Thus, she loves this nun, not because of her personal attraction, but from appreciation and approval of all nuns.

Over and above sensible love of self, a man can have an intellectual type of love whereby he loves himself because he appreciates the excellence of his nature. This love overflows from self to one's fellow man because he shares that nature. Such love is not mere love of self; it is also love of race. It is not, however, the love of an abstraction — humanity — but the love of individual persons. It is practical acknowledgment that one cannot seek the completion of self unless he also seeks in proper measure the good of all other persons.

II. IS MAN OBLIGED TO LOVE HIS FELLOW MAN?

414. Does the Natural Law command sensible love of others? Since the motions of our sensitive appetite are not wholly under the dominion of the will, the Natural Law does not command us to like our fellow man. It does, however, forbid such indulgence in our natural likes and dislikes for people as will be proximate occasions of sin. Our likes and dislikes must be disciplined by right reason so that we do not offend against our fellow man in thought, word, or act.

While no man is obliged to like anyone, he is obliged to *love* all men as he loves himself. To understand this rule, which is basic to all human intercourse, let us see, first, that this is an intellectual type of love, based upon appreciation of the good to be found in all men. While it involves neither liking, emotion, nor romantic attachment, its object is always people — all people. Second, absolutely no one may be excluded from this love — neither stranger nor enemy nor foreigner. Third, the command to love our fellow man as we love ourselves does not mean that we must love him with the same intensity as we love ourselves but with the same quality of benevolence, wishing him the same goods, temporal and divine, as we wish ourselves. Our love of self is stronger than our love of neighbor, because, if love springs from likeness, much more does it arise from identity. The love we have for self is to be the pattern of the love we have for our fellow man.

Some people are not familiar with the broad sense in which we have used the word *love*. They restrict its use to very selective attachments of intense feeling like passion or natural affection. To avoid confusion, therefore, we substitute the expression *good will* for the word *love*. Man's moral obligations to other men are summarized in the following statement.

THESIS XXIX. The Natural Law commands man to accord his fellow man the same quality of good will which he has for himself.

PROOFS

415. The Natural Law commands man to accord his fellow man the same quality of good will which he has for himself because his fellow man has the same dignity of nature and final end as himself. A man must wish good to himself because of the excellence of his nature. Since all men share this same excellence, all must be accorded similar good will.

This conclusion is also demonstrable from the social nature of man. Unless this good will is obtained, social life is not possible.

416. This command of the Natural Law is expressed in the homely proverb, *Do unto others as you would have them do unto you.* This is a principle of human conduct that cannot be removed from human consciousness. What does a man wish that his neighbor should do to him? *Whatever is necessary in order that he and his neighbor should live together as human beings.* Here we again distinguish man the individual from man the social being. What social man expects of his neighbor is set down in social ethics. As one individual to another, we expect our neighbor to leave us undisturbed in what is our own. This is the fundamental law of justice from which juridical duties stem. Therefore, man's first obligation to others is to observe his juridical duties. All other duties may be called nonjuridical. Juridical duties come first; then nonjuridical duties.

READINGS

St. Thomas, *Summa Theologica*, II–II, 23, 1; 25, 1.

——— *Contra Gentiles*, III, 114.

Berenda, C. W., "The Wisdom of Love," *Journal of Philosophy*, 51 (August 5, 1954), 453–464.

Berger, M., "The Supreme Court and Group Discrimination since 1937," *Columbia Law Review*, 49 (1949), 201–230.

D'Arcy, M. C., *The Mind and Heart of Love*. New York, Holt, 1947.

Gilligan, J. F., *The Morality of the Color Line*. Washington, Catholic University, 1928.

Gilson, E., "Revelation et l' unité des hommes," *La Vie Intellectuelle*, 26 (1955), 6–24.

Johann, R. O., *The Meaning of Love*. Westminster, Newman, 1955.

La Farge, J., "Decision on Segregation," *Catholic Mind*, 52 (1954), 577–587.

——— *The Catholic Viewpoint on Race Relations*. New York, Hanover, 1956.

Mannoni, O., "The Lament of the Negro," *Cross Currents*, Summer, 1951, 1–11.

Margolis, J., "That All Men Are Created Equal," *Journal of Philosophy*, 52 (June 23, 1955), 337–346.

McKeon, R., "Love and Philosophical Analysis," *Thought, Action and Passion*, 30–53, Chicago, University of Chicago, 1954.

Chapter XV RIGHTS

417. Juridical duties are imposed by justice which is the virtue inclining a man to render to another what is his by strict right. It is the province of justice, then, to define, regulate, and preserve rights. Juridical duties can be understood only by understanding rights. A general view of rights is gained by examining their nature, origin, end, relative components, and essential attributes.

I. WHAT IS A RIGHT?

418. Etymologically, right is that which is straight, not crooked. It is opposed to wrong — that which does not conform to a given standard. Whatever leads to a given end is straight and right; what leads away is wrong. Thus we speak of right and wrong conduct as leading or not leading to man's last end. "Right" then expresses rectitude and in that sense we used the term in general ethics.

There is another common meaning of right which expresses justice or conformity with law. Because law indicates the right direction to be taken to achieve the end of the State or the universe, law and right are identified. Thus the German *Recht*, the French *droit*, and the Latin *jus* mean both law and right. Whoever keeps the law does right and is just; whoever violates the law does wrong and is unjust. It is with this second meaning of right that we are now dealing.

We are saved from the difficulty of having one word express two things because in English "a right" does not mean a law; it refers either to things possessed or to a subjective right.

419. *Right referring to things possessed* designates certain things, both material and immaterial, which belong exclusively to me. These things I call "mine." What belongs to my neighbor in like manner is "his." "Mine" and "his" appertain to us and are made sacred to us by a subjective element called a right. By metonomy, "mine" and "his," as the objects of rights, are also called rights or, better, objective rights. Thus

a man has a right to life, to a watch, to a walk in the public park. Life, a watch, a walk in the park are called rights because they are objects of subjective rights. Objective rights, then, are either possessions belonging to the individual by the bond of right, or actions, omissions, or any advantage he may enjoy because of right.

420. A *subjective right* is a legitimate and inviolable power whereby one vindicates something for himself as his own. It is a *power* or capacity in virtue of which a person *can* do something in contrast to a *duty* in virtue of which a person *owes* something. Whereas duty restricts human freedom, right confirms or enlarges it. A right is a *legitimate* power; that is, it has the approval of law. Thus a right to fish a stream does not mean that I have the strength or skill to fish but that if I choose to fish my act is lawful. A right is an *inviolable* power; that is, it is more than a permission; it promises true security from undue interference. Right first supposes that something is already mine or allows that something can become mine. Its function, then, is to protect me in what is mine. The right to fish not only permits me to fish but also protects me from being stopped if I choose to fish. If there were no possibility of anyone preventing me from enjoying what is mine — in the unrealizable situation where all would clearly know what belonged to another, and where perfect good will existed — rights would exist as legitimate powers, but there would be no need of invoking immunity on their behalf. Because this situation cannot be realized on earth, the chief function of right is to render inviolable a man's just possessions. Right *vindicates something for a man as his own* by setting up a bond of legitimacy and immunity between a man and some object in virtue of which this object falls under his exclusive control. This extends not only to what actually belongs to a man but also to what he may demand should become his. Hence it is a capacity not merely of doing or not doing, of having or holding something, but also of exacting from others. What may be done, omitted, held, or exacted because of right constitutes an objective right.[1]

421. What is the nature of this power? Is this a physical legitimacy, coexistensive with my skill and ability so that, for example, because I *can* swim therefore I may? Is the inviolability of right the same as the physical power of the individual to ward off aggression or, in the last analysis, the strong arm of the law assuring him protection? Or is right a power of a higher order? It is a moral legitimacy if it is the grant of freedom to use physical power in accord with moral law. It is a moral immunity if it operates upon the moral faculties of others, informing

[1] The French and German legalists speak of *objektives Recht* and *droit objectif* meaning "the law or the norm of right."

them that this thing is another's and bidding them not to interfere under penalty of committing sin.

422. Hobbes said: "In the natural state of man, a sure and irresistible power confers the right of dominion and ruling over those who cannot resist, insomuch as the right of all things that can be done adheres essentially and immediately unto this omnipotence thus arising."[2] Kant equates right with the power to compel,[3] and explains this power as physical power. For Holmes, a right is either a pretense: "We get up the empty substratum, a right, to pretend to account for the fact that the courts will act in a certain way";[4] or, at best, an application of force: "A right is only the hypostasis of a prophecy — the imagination of a substance supporting the fact that the public force will be brought to bear upon those who do things said to contravene it."[5] According to Kelsen a man has a right if another has a duty of acting toward him in such a way that, if the party under obligation should act in a contrary manner, a sanction may be applied against him at the request of the offended party.[6] A right then is permission from law to put some sanction in motion. According to these views right is merely force.

THESIS XXX. Right is a moral power imposing a duty or obligation in conscience to respect it.

423. Holland speaks of right as a moral power but he believes that this power consists in the force of public opinion. "Thus," he says, "if, irrespectively of a man having or not having the force or persuasion to carry out his wishes, public opinion would view with approval, or at least acquiescence, his so carrying out his wishes and with disapproval any resistance to his so doing; then he has a moral right to so act."[7]

We attach a further meaning to the moral power, which is the essence of right. A man's right binds the minds of his fellow men to recognize the object of his right as something peculiarly attaching to him, and it obliges their wills not to do anything which will interfere with, nullify, or make void what is his. A person who interferes commits a *moral wrong.*

---

[2] *Rudimentary Philosophy Concerning Government and Society,* Chap. 1, n. 14. Molesworth's Eng. ed., Vol. II, p. 13.

[3] In his *Metaphysische Anfangsgründe der Rechtslehre* (1797) Kant says: *Recht und Befügnis zu zwingen bedeuten also einerlei.* (Right and the power to compel mean the same thing.) Immanuel Kant's *Sämmtliche Werke,* ed. Hartenstein, Vol. 7, p. 29 E. Leipzig, Voss, 1868.

[4] *Holmes-Pollock Letters,* Vol. II, p. 212. Cambridge, Harvard University Press, 1946.

[5] *Ibid.,* n.

[6] Hans Kelsen, *General Theory of Law and State,* pp. 81–82. Cambridge, Harvard University Press, 1949.

[7] Thomas E. Holland, *Jurisprudence,* 86. Oxford, Clarendon Press, 1937.

PROOFS

424. 1. There is an unshaken conviction among men that rights persist even when they have been overridden by physical force, that rights exist even in those who have not the physical power to protect themselves. Nothing is more repelling to men's sense of justice than the contention that might makes right. If right is not a physical force, it must be a moral power.

2. Right is a moral power, because it appeals to intellect and constrains free will. Without respect for the things of one another men could not live together. This demand for respect cannot primarily be force or threat of force, for man is not a brute. Hence an appeal must be made to man's intellect to recognize the possession of another; and his will, under penalty of being guilty of wrong, must be constrained not to interfere with another's possession. Whoever denies that this is the fitting compulsion which should first be brought to bear upon man to insure this respect is saying that man is completely irrational.

425. Corollary I. For every right of a man there is a corresponding obligation, or debt, on the part of all men or of some individual. Otherwise right imposes no obligation in conscience and is but an empty permission.

Corollary II. That right is a legitimate moral power is deducible from the proposition just proved. This point, however, becomes more evident in our discussion of the origin of right.

II. THE ORIGIN OF RIGHT

426. Hobbes said that man originally lived in a state of nature wherein he had a right to all things he had the skill to pursue and the brawn to hold. In that antisocial world right was might. However, a condition like this cannot last long for it means the war of all upon all. For self-preservation, then, men gave up this primitive mode of existence for an artificial thing called society, or the State. Upon entering society, all cede their rights to the State, which becomes the depositary of all rights. Henceforth the State alone concedes or extinguishes all rights. Since the rights originally given to the State by man were the equivalent of physical force, the State is now the wielder of this combined might, and actually one's rights extend only so far as the State can enforce its writ.

Hobbes's views are simply the overflow into philosophy of the Calvinistic notion that man is essentially corrupt and amenable only to coercion. This view, however, is also widely held today by those who, like Holmes, deny man's spiritual nature. We have already refuted this doctrine in § 424. Right cannot have its origin in force. For, as Rousseau says, "force is a physical power, and I fail to see what moral effect it can have. . . . If force creates right, the effect changes with the cause."[8]

427. The Contractualists of the eighteenth century said that rights originate in the social contract which they claim is also the cause of the State.

As a historical fact, the social contract is a myth. But even if a contract could have caused States to arise, it could not be the origin of rights because of itself contract cannot explain its own binding force. Whence does a contract receive its power to bind and produce moral effects? Certainly not from the contracting parties; for no individual or group of individuals has the power to bind another individual or group of individuals. Of themselves all men are equal and independent. Here again one must choose between force and the Natural Law.

428. Kant's teaching has had a profound effect upon modern man's attitude toward right and justice. Kant maintains a complete separation of justice from morality.[9]

According to Kant morality proceeds from the dictates of the autonomous reason;[10] justice, from the law of the State. The end of morality is internal liberty; that is, without external coercion and without consideration of the consequences of his act, a man willingly obeys the dictates of reason out of the sole motive of duty. The end of justice is external liberty.[11] Where many live together, their conflicting liberties must be reconciled; and so *from the general notion of freedom,* Kant deduces right or the power to coerce (§ 422). Every man is compelled to cede so much of his freedom that his fellow man may be equally free. What each is to cede, how much external freedom each is to enjoy, is settled by the law of the State, whose purpose is to establish that condition of affairs wherein the acts of one are to be reconciled with the acts of every other according to a universal law of freedom.[12] No man

[8] Jean Jacques Rousseau, *The Social Contract,* Bk. I, Ch. III.

[9] Immanuel Kant, *Die Metaphysik der Sitten, Erster Theil. Metaphysische Aufangsgründe der Rechtslehre.* Koenigsberg, 1797. This contains his philosophy of right and law. It has been translated by W. Hastie as *The Philosophy of Law,* see pp. 9–58. Edinburgh, Clark, 1888.

[10] *Ibid.,* p. 23.

[11] *Ibid.,* p. 14.

[12] "Right, therefore, comprehends the whole of the conditions under which the voluntary actions of any one person can be harmonized in reality with the voluntary actions of every other person, according to a universal law of freedom." *Ibid.,* p. 45.

can trespass upon the right of another but each has the right to any line of conduct which does not limit the liberty of another.

Justice deals only with external acts, which are subject to coercion. While morals deals with internal and external acts, its primary concern is with motive. It is only indirectly concerned with justice; that is, it is a dictate of reason that one observe the juridic order.[13] Moral precepts bind in conscience, but laws of justice of themselves do not. They rely for their enforcement upon the power of the State. Morality is essentially autonomous; justice essentially heteronomous.

429. The gravest error of Kant lies, as we shall see (§ 434), in divorcing rights from morality. He is also wrong in deducing rights from the need to reconcile conflicting claims to freedom. The right of a parent to the respect of his child follows from the personal relation between them and has nothing to do with the general freedom of all. If right is an immediate derivative of freedom, then one could freely surrender any right. But there are inalienable rights which no one may surrender. A child could not give up its right to support, nor could a man surrender his right to avoid the proximate occasions of sin.

Nor is it correct to say that the object of a right is only an external act amenable to coercion. An internal act may also be the object of right. A husband has the right to the love of his wife and vice versa; a man, to the good opinion of his fellow man. But none of these can be subjected to force.

Some writers[14] describe Kant's statement that one has a right to do whatever will not injure his fellow man as pernicious. They allege, for example, that one could never acquire a right to hate God, kill himself, or commit solitary sins of impurity. In a certain sense this objection is valid but let us give Kant his due: these acts, according to him, have nothing to do with justice — the Kantian laws of justice do not touch them — but Kant would not therefore say they were allowable. To him they belong in another category entirely; they are forbidden by the dictates of the autonomous reason.

430. Reacting strongly against the *a priori* theories of Kant, Savigny[15] and the Historical School offer a purely empirical explanation. Rights, according to them, have their origin in the customs of the people. Before the acceptance of a custom by the people and before the confirmation of custom by the advent of public law, men had no true rights. They had the foundations of rights, but no real rights existed until first custom

[13] *Ibid.*, pp. 20–24.

[14] See M. Cronin, *Science of Ethics*, Vol. I, p. 648.

[15] Karl von Savigny, *The Vocation of Our Age*, trans. Abraham Hayward, p. 30. London, Littlewood, 1831, 2 ed.

and then law rose to guarantee, approve, and protect them. Rights are empirically evolved by men living in community in much the same way as speech, public manners, and art.

It is true that some rights are the result of custom as are some laws, but custom as such, that is, mere practice apart from the will of the lawgiver, can beget neither law nor right. The moral obligation existent in every right can come only from the lawgiver. A custom imposes moral obligation only through the approval, tacit or explicit, of the lawgiver.

THESIS XXXI. Rights originate in law. The Natural Law is the ultimate source of all human rights.

PROOF OF PART I

431. **Rights originate in law** because rights place a moral bond on the free will of others. The only thing capable of binding the free will is law. No man can truly bind himself; for a self-binding is no binding. Nor can he be morally bound by his fellow man as such because all men are equal. Nothing then can explain the obligatory character of right other than the law of some superior.

N.B. That various languages use the same word for law and right is understandable. This is a natural metonomy, the interchange of cause and effect.

PART II

432. No one today denies the first proposition but many, if not most, moderns deny the second. They admit no law above the law of the State and hold that the admission of a higher law, critical of State law, induces anarchy into the State. The crucial difficulty of modern philosophy, especially of social philosophy, centers around the existence of the Natural Law.

PROOF

433. The ultimate source of all rights is the Natural Law because all positive laws, including juridic laws, are subject to the Natural Law. For it is the Natural Law which commands men to live in political society; otherwise they would not reach their due perfection as men. Since political society flows from the Natural Law, so must the things necessary for the maintenance of political society, chief among which is the power to make laws. Confer also § 238.

434. Corollary I. The juridical order is part of the moral order. The juridical order is the total system of rights and justice: laws defining rights, duties corresponding to rights, and rights themselves. The moral order includes whatever is directly related to man's last end: norms, laws, obligations, human faculties, and acts whereby the last end is attained. One supreme law directs man to his end. Hence there is a *sacred oneness* to human activity so that all human acts, including external and other-regarding acts, either advance a man to the last end or withdraw him from it. Therefore even legal and juridical acts fall under the moral law.

Corollary II. Right is totally a moral power both as to legitimacy and inviolability. Therefore we define right as the moral inviolable power of vindicating something as one's own.

Corollary III. What is unjust is always immoral. What is immoral is not always illegal, that is, forbidden by positive law. What is illegal is also immoral except for the violation of a purely penal law. Confer § 928.

Corollary IV. There can never be a right to that which is immoral. For the moral law cannot grant that which is destructive of itself.

III. THE END OF RIGHT

435. From the problem just solved there arises the question, With what immediacy do rights flow from the Natural Law? Some rights come directly and immediately from civil law, for example, the right to vote. Are all our rights of this character? Provided civil law conforms to Natural Law, does the Natural Law leave it to civil law to create and determine all rights so that only that is a right which the civil law grants? As legal writers dislike to recognize as law anything other than positive law, so too they think the term *right* should not be applied to anything but legal rights. Pound claims: "The seventeenth-eighteenth century theory, however, confused the interest, which exists independently of law, and legal right, the creature of law. It confused the interest, which law recognizes in whole or in part and seeks to secure, with the right by which law gives effect to the interest when recognized and to the extent of the recognition. Natural rights simply mean interests which we think ought to be satisfied."[16]

Here, however, is more than a dispute about words. For when we claim that besides positive rights, which flow from human laws, there are also natural rights emanating immediately from the Natural Law, it is now the fashion for positivists to retort that a so-called natural right is but a subjective aspiration on the part of individuals or groups. Thus

[16] Roscoe Pound, *The Spirit of the Common Law*, p. 92, Boston, Jones, 1931.

Kelsen says that justice is only a judgment of value, that problems of right "cannot be answered by means of rational cognition. The decision of these questions is a judgment of value, determined by emotional factors, valid only for the judging subject and therefore relative only."[17] Consequently there are no principles of natural justice universally true. What has hitherto been regarded as such are merely the wish-fulfillments of a particular place and civilization. For "critical analysis always shows that they are only the expression of a certain group or class interests."[18]

436. Here is a momentous question. While the existence of natural justice and natural rights is an immediate conclusion from the preceding thesis, we wish to put proper emphasis upon the problem of positive rights versus natural rights by offering a separate explanation and demonstration. Therefore we shall establish the existence of natural rights by proving that the purpose of all rights must be the security of the human person. Since persons are real and have universal human needs which the Natural Law must protect, natural rights have an objective character and belong to all men.

THESIS XXXII. The end of all rights is the security of the human person. Apart from any positive law, natural rights exist whereby the Author of human nature protects the human person. All men are endowed with these rights.

437. The concept of natural right may be expressed in two ways. First, nature gives man his being and powers, grants him freedom in the exercise of these powers, and lays upon him the responsibility of attaining their perfection. Since he has this responsibility, he may not be interfered with by other men, not even by society, in the pursuit thereof. Hence to say that nature gives every man his proper field of activity and makes him secure in the pursuit of his final end means that nature itself has endowed him with rights.

Second, nature gives rights in order to preserve the sacredness of the human person. A person is a rational, self-active, and independent substance. Every man is a person because he has intelligence, is the ultimate responsible agent of what he does, and is not part of any other being. As an unfulfilled being, man is on his way to a sublime destiny—participation in an infinite good. Destination to such an end confers on him a unique dignity so that he is not to be prevented from attaining it by other men. To make him inviolable in working out his destiny God surrounds him with the protecting aegis of His law. This protection is

[17] Hans Kelsen, *General Theory of Law and State,* p. 6.
[18] *Ibid.,* p. 11.

natural right which exists for no other purpose than the security of man.

Are these concepts valid?

PROOF OF PART I

438. **The end of all rights is the security of the human person** because this purpose must be either the good order of society or the security of the human person. It cannot be the good order of society for in that case man as such would be subordinated to society. This cannot be, because man, as the image of God, has a pre-eminence of being over all visible created things. His destiny is extratemporal and consists in the attainment of God; unto the realization of that end all visible created things, including society, are subordinate.

PROOF OF PART II

439. **Apart from any positive law natural rights exist** because without them God has made insufficient provision for man. The Creator Himself must endow man with moral inviolable power of vindicating as his own whatever is necessary for the last end. These powers must be valid against all men and all combinations of men, including society. Otherwise a man's physical faculties would be of little use to him; for, if other men, or the State, could without moral fault and whenever it pleased hinder his use of them, deprive him of their fruit, take away his life, members, liberty, or goods, he could not live as a man. Since the providence of God does not fail, these moral inviolable powers exist. Moral inviolable powers immediately granted by the Creator are natural rights.

PROOF OF PART III

440. **All men are endowed with these rights** because all men are images of God and share one nature and destiny.

Corollary. Natural right, as a demand of human nature universally verified, cannot be a mere subjective aspiration but has as objective an existence as the nature whence it springs.

Are all men equal as to their natural rights?

441. God gives all men the same *essential* things, because He cannot give actual existence and withhold anything that necessarily belongs to

human nature. He does not, however, give the same *accidental* things to all — some have fleeter feet, others more vivid imaginations, others more brilliant minds, etc. Since the essence of right is protection by the law, our question is, Are the things of every man equally sacred to God? Indubitably. The possessions of a rich man or a native are no more inviolable than those of a poor man or a foreigner. Hence, since all men are essentially equal, so they likewise possess the same rights immediately deriving from human nature.

But each individual is not equal in every way with every other individual with respect to natural rights. Men are equal as to nature and destiny and hence as to the number and sacredness of the rights flowing therefrom. But here equality ends. These rights do not have in every individual the same extension, content, and opportunity of exercise. Nature does not distribute her gifts evenly. The order and variety of life demands diversity. As each personality differs from every other, so too do the contents of the rights deriving from these personalities. Thus the right to a livelihood or to an education will extend to a larger amount of particular goods in the case of those who have greater needs and greater capacities. A policeman has the same natural right to a livelihood as a king but the actual goods which form the content of the right will vary in either case. The right to an education for the brilliant son of a university professor and a crippled moron will not extend to the same instruments of training.

However, in every case the natural right of the individual must embrace a certain minimum of goods. What that minimum calls for depends upon a variety of circumstances, personal and social. To keep a man from that minimum is practically to suppress the right. This no one — not even the State — may do. Some persons are endowed by nature with an abundance far beyond this minimum. Justice, however, does not demand that all have exactly the same things but that each be secure in what he does have. Hence the natural rights of all are equal as to kind, number, and sacredness; but not as to content, quantity, and scope of exercise.

IV. THE RELATIVE COMPONENTS OF RIGHT

442. A right is a relation. We shall now consider the factors involved in this relation.

The term *relative* is opposed to the term *absolute*. The absolute is that which denies or at least prescinds from connection with another. The relative is that which is connected with another. Hence a relation is the connection between one thing and another, or that which makes a being a relative being.

Every relation involves (*a*) a *subject*, which bespeaks a relation to another; (*b*) a *term*, to which the subject is referred; (*c*) a *foundation*, or reason why the subject is referred to the term.

Right is not a logical but a real relation, for it exists independently of one's thoughts. While it is not a material thing, it is most actual and real, being a suprasensible moral thing.

For clarity and convenience, the three elements of a relation will, in the case of right, be divided into the following five: the subject of the relation of right is the *subject-party*; the term will be divided into the *matter* and the *object-party*; and the foundation, into the *ground* and the *title*.

A. The Subject-Party

The subject-party is the one in whom the right is vested. The question here is, Who or what can possess rights?

THESIS XXXIII. Only persons possess rights.

443. The term *person* here applies to (*a*) *natural person*, an individual human being and (*b*) *moral person*, a collection of human beings or even a collection of interests to which by a justifiable fiction of law the condition and unity of personality are attributed.

Children, the insane, and all others incapable of exercising rights have rights in virtue of their human personality which others must safeguard on their behalf. To have actual rights, however, one must actually exist, for a power without a subject in which to inhere is not a power.

444. Animals and all other inferior beings have no rights since they are not persons and exist solely for the utility of man. Hence men have no obligations *to* brutes although they have obligations *about* brutes. Man has an obligation to himself to treat brutes in a becoming way — he cannot visit upon them unreasonable anger; he cannot treat them with wanton cruelty lest being cruel to brutes he become cruel to man; nor can he abuse the bounty which the Creator puts at his disposal. Bentham,[19] however, claims brutes have rights just as men have.

PROOF

445. Only persons have rights, because moral inviolability does not attach to brutes. Moral inviolability is the essence of right. If then, brutes

[19] *Morals and Legislation,* p. 310. Oxford, Clarendon, 1907.

— which come next to man in the hierarchy of being — enjoy no such inviolability, only persons have rights.

Brutes cannot have moral inviolability, because being totally material and mortal, they must subserve men, who possess an immaterial and immortal element. The reason for their existence is man's utility. Beings whose very substance is subordinated to the utility of some other beings are merely things.

B. The Matter of a Right

446. The term of the relationship of right includes two things, the personal term and the material term. (*a*) The *personal term* is the person who has the juridic obligation to respect the right: this is the object-party of whom we treat in the next section. (*b*) The *material term,* or better, the object of right, is the "just thing," that which one may do, hold, or exact, that over which or in regard to which a person has a right. Two chief questions may be raised here.

What can be the object of right? What can a person claim as his own?

1. *Negatively*

It is of fundamental importance to establish that no person, moral or individual, can own another person.

THESIS XXXIV. The matter of a right can never be a person.

447. No one can have a right *in the person* of another. A person, as a person, cannot be subordinated as a mere means to another. The State may have a right over the goods of a citizen or over certain of his activities, as in time of war. One individual may have rights over the actions of another, as a father over a child or a master over a servant; but no one, neither individual nor State, can have such rights over a human being as to do with him as he pleases, as he would do with his goods or chattels.

PROOF

448. **No person can be the matter of a right,** because a person cannot be made to serve the mere utility of another. An attempt to do so would militate against the essentially natural equality of all persons and the reason for the existence of rights, namely, to secure the independence of the human person.

Corollary. Absolute servitude whereby one person becomes the chattel of another is contrary to the Natural Law. Even limited servitude, whereby one's total activities are permanently put at another's disposal, does not befit the dignity of human personality (§ 486).

2. *Positively*

449. In the following chapters, we set forth the chief items which can attach to the individual because of commutative justice. These form the object of right in the strict sense. What the individual may claim from society because of distributive justice and what society may claim from him because of legal justice are objects of right in a less strict sense. Their precise nature is explained in social ethics. It is sometimes said that man has a right to the assistance, friendship, benevolence, truthfulness, gratitude, and fidelity of his fellow man. That is using right in a loose sense. These do not represent juridic claims of the individual but rather duties of his fellow man toward him springing not from justice but from other virtues.

C. The Object-Party

450. The object-party is the person or persons in whom resides the juridic duty corresponding to a given right. As has been stated (§ 425), a right could not be a moral power unless it gave rise to this moral obligation.

This obligation is first *negative:* one must do nothing which will interfere with the right of another. It is *positive* when (*a*) one has bound oneself by an agreement in justice to perform certain acts, for example, a lessee to pay his rent, a judge to administer justice; (*b*) the Natural Law demands an act necessary to save the life of a fellow man, such as giving food to a starving man (cf. §§ 531–535); (*c*) one has become liable to restitution.

451. Restitution. As we have seen (§ 306), restitution attaches to all violations of commutative justice and only to them. If a person upsets the justice existing between man and man, he must restore the balance of justice by restoring the injured party to that condition of right which was his before the injury. This is a demand of Natural Law. Otherwise we would have the contradiction of the Natural Law forbidding and tolerating the spoliation of a man.

The obligation of restitution arises (*a*) from *the possession of another's goods.* The axiom of Roman law, *Res clamat domino* (the thing cries to its owner), is likewise a principle of Natural Law which may be more precisely expressed: if by accident or malice a thing passes from the possession or effective control of an owner, the thing is still his until he willingly resigns it or law makes some other disposition of it. Whether the actual possessor knows that the goods belong to another or mistakenly thinks they are his makes no difference. One cannot enrich himself by another man's goods. However, the more detailed obligations of persons having the goods of another will depend on whether they hold them in good faith, in bad faith, or in dubious faith.

The obligation of restitution arises also (*b*) from *the infliction of damage*. That this obligation be present three conditions must be met: (1) The damage must be the result of an action strictly unjust. (2) This action must be the real and effective cause, not merely the occasion or condition, of the damage. (3) The action must be formally sinful. Where there is only a legal fault and one is ordered by a court to pay, one is obliged in conscience to do so. The reason is not that the agent has been unjust but that the State may make certain disposition of private property for the common welfare. On the score of unjust damage one is obliged to repair *all* the injury which was foreseen at least indistinctly. One indeed may also be liable to restitution for both the reasons cited.

One is excused from restitution by condonation, by a voluntary adjustment, or by legitimate prescription (see § 570). Moral or physical impossibility suspends the obligation for a time.

D. The Ground and Title of Right

452. The third relative component of right is its *foundation*. The foundation is the reason why a given relation exists. Why does this person have this right? We distinguish between the ultimate reason, which is the ground of right, and the proximate reason, which is the title.

The ground of right is always some law (§ 430). Law, however, regards right only in the abstract. For a concrete right to arise, something more than law is required. While law states the general conditions under which a right is granted, some concrete fact or facts are necessary to show that these conditions are fulfilled. A law of primogeniture may state that the oldest surviving legitimate son will succeed to the entailed property of his father. In order that John Brown enter upon the entailed property of his father as heir, the fact that he is his father's oldest legitimate son must be verified. The fact of his primogeniture is the proximate reason why he acquires the estate; it is his title.

453. A *title* is some contingent fact which is the immediate cause why this particular right inheres in this person. A document which evidences such a fact is sometimes, though less properly, called a title. Title is the medium through which law confers a particular right. Every right is actuated in the concrete by some fact.

This fact can be (*a*) the mere fact of a man's existence, which is the title of all *connatural rights*, or (*b*) some other fact as in the case of *acquired rights*. Thus from the fact of generation, of matrimonial consent, of donation, various natural but acquired rights arise.

A fundamental function of civil law is to determine which facts give rise to or extinguish civil rights. Facts which give rise to rights are sometimes called investitive; facts which extinguish rights, divestitive.

V. THE ESSENTIAL PROPERTIES OF RIGHT

454. A property is that characteristic of a thing which, though not constituting its essence, is invariably found in it. If we seek the properties of right, we find they are two, limitation and coactivity. Some have said that inviolability is a characteristic, but we have shown that it is of the essence of right and enters its essential definition.

A. Limitation

455. Limitation is that quality of a right whereby its scope and exercise are restricted to given boundaries. The law that grants the power of right also determines how far that power may extend. There are no sky-blue rights. I cannot go beyond what is mine; my neighbor, beyond what is his. Rights are finite because they are adjuncts of the human personality which is limited both in itself and in its needs. As in the body the exercise of one organ is limited by the exercise of the other organs and the good of the entire body, so in the juridic order the rights of one individual are limited by the counterclaims of others and the needs of the common social good.

Periods of undue emphasis either upon the rights of individuals or of society occur. The encyclopedists of the eighteenth century attributed to the individual exaggerated rights which denied the just claims of society. State totalitarianism is the opposite extreme. It holds that the State has a right which knows no limit, that the individual has no prior and inalienable rights which the State is bound to respect. The truth, however, lies midway between the extremes. A pressing need is the accurate statement of the individual's responsibility to society and of society's obligation to the individual. This can come only from proper understanding of Natural Law doctrine.

456. The problem of conflicting claims is always with us. Civil law has definite procedures for settling conflicts. We are not concerned, however, with the due process of law but seek a moral principle by which a man may settle his conscience without recourse to authority.

THESIS XXXV. A true conflict of concrete rights is impossible. In an apparent conflict the actually existent right is determined by an examination of the relative factors in each claim.

457. A conflict of rights may be either one of these two situations:

(*a*) One person may claim the moral power to do a certain thing and another may claim the moral power to prevent him. Thus, Jones claims a right of way over his neighbor's farm; the neighbor claims the right to stop him. (*b*) Two persons claim the same thing.

PROOF OF PART I

458. **A true conflict of concrete rights is impossible** because, of two contradictory claims, only one can represent an objectively existent right. Otherwise there would be a contradiction in the Natural Law. Since all rights come from the Natural Law, an actual conflict of rights would mean that the Natural Law commands and forbids the same identical thing.

PART II

459. The second proposition is self-evident: one resolves conflicting claims by the adequate examination of both of them. Here the aim of justice is to determine which one is the actually existent right. Some say the stronger right prevails. This reply is open to misconstruction; right here might be construed to mean the stronger force. The question is not whether one right is stronger or weaker but rather which is the actual right. The solution is had by examining each claim in the light of the five relative components of right.

460. The most important component is the foundation of a right, that is, its ground and title. The ground of right is law. Hence, to interpret right, one must know the limitations implicitly contained in the law. A minor, supported by his father, might think the little wages he earns belong to himself exclusively; a wife might argue that, since she is the childbearer, she has a right to refuse the reasonable request of her husband for marital relations. Thus conflict arises because a person believes that law grants him a right which it does not concede. Accurate knowledge of the Natural Law would obviate many quarrels over conflicting rights.

Next in importance to the meaning of law comes the question, Did a fact occur which is capable of founding the alleged right? One of the great sources of quarreling is the existence or nonexistence of certain facts. Sometimes, however, it is clear that a fact took place but the nature of the fact is in dispute. A demands of *B* the return of ten dollars. *B* says A gave it to him; A says it was only a loan.

461. A solution may be reached through scrutiny of the matter of disputed rights. Since the matter is some personal good, the closer the good is to the subject and the greater his need of it, the more compelling is the bond of right attaching it to him. Thus the right to life or limb supersedes a conflicting property right. A good may be the necessary means of fulfilling an inescapable duty or one so necessary that it cannot be yielded. The right which binds such a good to a man is an *inalienable right* before which every alienable right in another gives way. As there is an objective hierarchy of values, so there is a corresponding order of preference. Goods of the soul will generally be preferred to goods of the body; the common good to an individual good; a more necessary and urgent good to one less necessary and urgent.

462. Examination of the subject- and object-party will generally yield little in deciding a conflict of rights, for justice is not a respecter of persons. When a solution is given from consideration of one party's subjective status, piety or charity rather than justice decides the issue. However, one's peculiar condition, such as an extreme danger of death, gives rise to right. Thus the right of a baker to demand money for his bread yields before the right of a penniless starving man to live.

B. Coactivity

463. *Coactivity* is the power of using force to protect the object of our right. Hegel identifies right with coactivity.[20] He is mistaken for two reasons. First, coactivity presupposes a right existing prior to itself so it cannot be that right. Thus, when I say that I have a right to defend my home from violence, I mean the home is mine, I already have a right to it. Second, there are some true rights, like the right to be thought well of by others, which cannot be secured by force.

It is easy to see how one can be confused about the identity of right and force, because in everyday life force is allied with right. The police have an apparatus of force to crush the violence of criminals. Armies exist to vindicate a nation's right to live. *How moral then is the alliance of force with right?* Basic to our whole view of rights is the statement that *men must be made to respect what belongs to another*. This is to be achieved, first, by appeal to moral obligation, as the spiritual nature of man demands. The use of force upon men becomes reasonable only when they cease to act as men and despise the appeal of moral obligation. When men act as brutes, they may be coerced as brutes, for the Natural Law allows man in defense of right to counter force with force.

[20] G. Hegel, *Philosophie des Rechts*, § 94. *Werke*, Vol. III, p. 133. Berlin, 1833.

1. The Legality of Force in Defense of Right

THESIS XXXVI. It is lawful to use force to defend certain rights. This is in essence a moral power distinct from the physical ability to coerce. The exercise thereof is normally entrusted to the civil government.

This thesis answers three questions: Is there a lawful power of defending right with force? What is the nature of this power? Who may exercise it?

PROOF OF PART I

464. The Natural Law must allow force in defense of right. For without this power rights would be almost useless owing to the malice and cupidity of evil men and their proneness to disregard moral obligation. This power, however, does not go with rights which of their nature cannot be secured by force.

465. **N.B.** Rights which have the property of coactivity are *perfect rights:* those which do not are *imperfect rights.* This does not mean that in the essential quality of right — moral inviolability — an imperfect right is inferior to a perfect right. Both equally place a moral bond on the will of another. Whoever violates the bond of an imperfect right is guilty of injustice.

A right is called perfect because it has all the means requisite to maintain itself, one of which is physical force. *Per accidens* an imperfect right is not so fully implemented, and this, not because the matter of such a right is of lesser value but because as a spiritual good or an internal act it is not amenable to force.

Rights enforceable by physical might can spring from commutative and legal justice but not from distributive justice. Piety forbids the latter. It is a grave disruption of the natural order if a member of a natural society raises a violent hand against the head to secure that which has not actually passed into his possession.

PART II

466. What is the nature of coactivity? Is it a moral license or is it one's sheer brawn? Although in its use coactivity involves physical force, it is a moral permission issuing from the moral law. However it should not be confused with inviolability, which is moral immunity from interference. Coactivity permits (*a*) *defense* — when a right is threatened, one may repel the aggressor — and (*b*) *reparation* — after an injury has been inflicted, one may forceably compel restitution. The purpose of coactivity, then, is such a defense and vindication of right as will secure this equality of justice that each one will have what is his own or, if it be taken from him, that it be returned. Coactivity, however, does not empower a man to exact vengeance or to punish the unjust.

PROOF

467. **Coactivity is in its essence a moral power,** because the right of defense is possessed by those bereft of sufficient strength to coerce. To say that the sick and aged, children and women have no right of defense because their physical strength is not equal it, is to say that might is right. If then the right to invoke force is distinct from one's physical power and can exist without it, it must be a moral power.

PART III

468. **Who possesses this power?** The obvious answer is the one who has the right. This power accompanies right. Hence the enforcement of rights flowing from legal justice belongs solely to the head of the State. As to rights springing from commutative justice, though the power of coercion primarily resides in the individual, the public welfare demands that this right be *exercised* on his behalf by the civil government. When public authority cannot or will not protect the individual, when the immediacy of the danger is such that recourse to police protection is impossible, then the individual must exercise this power for himself.

PROOF

469. **The exercise of coactivity is normally entrusted to the civil government,** because the reasonable conduct of social life demands it. Peace and order would be impossible if every man could immediately invoke force whenever his rights were imperiled. It is the natural duty of the State, as the guardian of the juridic order, to protect these rights. Hence, only when an appeal to the State would be impossible or useless may an individual forcibly protect his rights.

2. How Much Force May Be Used?

470. Only that amount of force may be used which is requisite to safeguard the right from violation or to repair an injury committed. The

harm arising from recourse to force cannot be greater than the evil involved in the disturbance of right. However, the ultimate of violence — the death of another — may sometimes be the only means available. May one go so far?

THESIS XXXVII. Under the conditions of blameless self-defense, the Natural Law allows a man in defense of life and rights equivalent to it even to slay an unjust aggressor.

We presuppose that it is impossible for the individual to invoke the aid of the State in the protection of his right.

471. The conditions of blameless self-defense:

1. *Unjust attack.* One must be the victim of an unjust aggressor. It does not matter whether the assailant is formally, that is, deliberately or culpably, or only materially unjust, such as a madman or a drunkard. A person who is justly assailed, such as an escaping criminal pursued by police, may not repel such an assault with violence.

2. *Actual aggression.* That a prospective assailant should only think of attacking one does not constitute a condition of blameless self-defense; he must actually intend and in some way initiate the attack. It would be destructive of peace if man were allowed to resort to force on mere suspicion or the remote prospect of danger. On the pretext of imaginary danger to himself, man would constantly be doing violence to his neighbor. However, at times it will be difficult to determine when an attack has begun. Certainly one may defend himself before his attacker is breaking down his door. Some make too fine a distinction between an assailant's actions which are only "means preparatory to aggression" — which would not as yet justify violent defense — and his "acts which are part of his aggression." There is considerable merit to DeLugo's statement[21] that the assailant's attack begins with his intention to harm. If a person knows that this is an *efficacious* intention, he may consider that he is in danger. An intention is efficacious if something is done to execute it. Hence, if a person is morally certain that someone has determined to attack him and has taken measures to carry out his plan, the attack has begun, and it may be violently repelled. This of course must be interpreted in the light of the remaining conditions.

3. *Last resort.* There must be no other means of self-protection. If the danger can be averted by calling for help, by frightening the assailant, by fleeing, one must do so, provided, of course, that no tremendous difficulty such as exile or a reputation for cowardice would result.

[21] "Wherefore if [the aggressor] has made ready his weapons or done anything else to carry out his determination to kill you, his attack upon you has begun and you can defend yourself." *De Justitia et Jure,* Disp. X, Sect. 7, No. 157.

4. *No more force than is necessary to repel the danger.* To inflict further harm upon the assailant after his attack has been effectively checked is to take vengeance. This is allowed to no individual. If an assailant can be stopped by wounding him, it is wrong to kill.

472. There is a dispute concerning the intention one may have. Many, following the opinion of St. Thomas[22] that only public authority can intend the death of an individual, say that a person may never intend the death of the aggressor, only self-defense. They consider this an evident application of the principle of double effect. Others, following DeLugo,[23] hold that death as death may be intended as a *necessary means* to self-defense. Since death as death is a physical, not a moral, evil, it may be intended as a necessary means to some proportionate good end. Certainly death may be intended by God; certainly by the State; why not also by an individual?

It would seem that cases may arise in which the principle of double effect will not apply. There are defensive actions which have but one end of work — death. If one chooses the act, he cannot but intend death. Thus, in a death struggle, one may manage to get his pistol to his enemy's head. To fire a pistol directly against a man's head has only one end of work — that man's death. Hence, if one intends to pull the trigger, he cannot but intend to kill. To insist that one may intend only the "quiescence" of the other party is to beget needless scruples and to utter just so many words. However, the validity of our thesis does not depend on the outcome of this dispute: it does not rest on the principle of double effect but on the principle that it is moral to counter force with adequate defensive force.

PROOF

473. The Natural Law must permit *legitimate* defense of life and rights equivalent thereunto, otherwise the grant of right is delusive. The slaying of an unjust aggressor is *sometimes* a legitimate means of defending life and similar rights. By *sometimes* we understand whenever the conditions of blameless self-defense are verified. Death of an assailant under these conditions is a means of legitimate defense because *in the conflict of rights arising the right of the innocent party prevails.* If this were not so, the right of the assailant would become more sacred precisely because of his crime; and the innocent party, placed in danger of death or spoliation by the crime of the guilty party, would be compelled to

[22] *Sum. Theol.,* II–II, 64, 7.
[23] *De Justitia et Jure,* Disp. X, Sec. 6, No. 149.

prefer the good of his assailant to his own. This conclusion is contrary to right reason.

Our argument is confirmed by the laws of all nations and by the declarations of the Roman pontiffs justifying blameless self-defense.

474. Rights equivalent to life. The loss of material goods of great value, personal liberty, chastity, and integrity of limb are commonly likened to loss of life. The least of these is material goods of great value. If by these we mean what is necessary to support life or maintain one's state in life, they may well be comparable to life itself. A further reason for the violent defense of them is added, namely, the common social good. If men were not allowed to defend these goods in this manner decent people would be at the mercy of robbers. Personal liberty, chastity, and integrity of limb are much closer to a man and can more readily be called his than external material goods.

475. Defense of the right to reputation. The defense of one's reputation presents a particular problem. It is not quite accurate to say that force is a totally inept means of defending one's reputation on the ground that one is material and the other immaterial and that consequently there is no proportion between them. Reputation is a perfect right in the sense that one can invoke the coercive power of positive law to defend it. But what can the individual do without recourse to law? He certainly may not kill a detractor or calumniator *after* the offense, for such an act would be mere vengeance. So, too, if the calumniator should refuse to restore the good name of another even under the threat of death, the carrying out of the threat would be equivalent to vengeance.

May one use force *beforehand* to prevent a loss of honor? If the prospective dishonoration is to take the form of violence to one's person, such as slapping one's face or pulling one's hat down over one's eyes, it may be repelled by force. It is lawful to answer force with force. If the assault upon one's honor is to be done by word alone, one cannot kill or maim the traducer, because (*a*) beforehand it is difficult to say how serious such an injury is going to be; (*b*) granted we are sure the worst sort of damage is to follow, *such an injury is not irreparable*. A good name may be recovered. If life and limb are endangered, one may use the utmost of violence, for otherwise the injured party would suffer an irreparable loss. Since the calumniated party does not suffer an irreparable loss, it is not equitable that he resort to irreparable damage as a means of safeguarding his right. (*c*) To allow the defense of honor by shedding blood would be destructive of public peace. Honor is a most variable and subjective thing; if one could restort to arms to defend his honor, slight resentment might result in death.

However, today when men do not habitually carry lethal weapons, to say that one may not silence a vile tongue with a blow is to deny men a protection which decency demands. In the circumstances this measure of force is reasonable.

476. What the Natural Law allows a man to do to defend his life and equivalent rights, the law of charity permits him to do on behalf of others.

Man is allowed to defend life by taking life. But is he compelled to do so? For the vast majority of people, such means are extraordinary and abhorrent. The strict obligation of preserving life extends ony to the use of ordinary means. However, a person may be so necessary to the State or his family that he would be obliged to take such extraordinary means to save his life.

477. The Natural Law allows the use of force in the defense of certain rights, yet in revelation we are *counseled* not to use force. "Blessed are the meek for they shall possess the land."[24] "If anyone shall strike thee on the right cheek, turn to him the other also."[25]

The virtue whereby man restrains his desire for revenge and the use of violence is meekness. In the matter of meekness, we may distinguish as follows between that which is obliged and that which is counseled.

1. Man is obliged to have under the control of reason all motions of anger, all manifestations of irascible passion. He is counseled sometimes to forego the natural right of using force in preserving rights.

2. Man is obliged to refrain from private revenge and personal retribution. He must forgive injury and insult to the extent that he does not will evil to anyone, even to one who has wronged him. He is counseled generally to repay evil with good. "Love your enemies: do good to them that hate you."[26]

3. The defects of other persons must be endured with patience. It is counseled that injustice be tolerated.

The virtue of prudence enables man to discern the admonitions of counsel. However, when the attack upon one's rights constitutes proximate danger of consent to sin unless forcible resistance is made, there can be no question of submission to injury. Thus, the victim of a rape must exert all force possible to drive off her attacker, for there is danger of consent to the sexual act.

[24] Mt. 5:4. [25] Mt. 5:39. [26] Lk. 6:27.

READINGS

St. Thomas, *Summa Theologica*, II–II, 57; 58; 64, 7.
Aristotle, *Nicomachean Ethics*, V.
Cicero, *De Officiis*, Bk. I.

Cohen, F. S., "Human Rights: An Appeal to Philosophers," *Review of Metaphysics*, 6 (June, 1953), 617–622.
Corpus Juris, "Self-Defense," Vol. 57, 107; "Slaves," Vol. 58, 745–768.
Cronan, E. P., *The Dignity of the Human Person*. New York, Philosophical Library, 1955.
D'Arcy, M. C., *Christian Morals*, 27–39. London, Longmans Green, 1937.
Haas, F. J., *Man and Society*, 2 ed., 29–61, 64–116. New York, Appleton-Century-Crofts, 1952.
Harding, A. L., ed., *Natural Law and Natural Rights*. Dallas, Southern Methodist, 1955.
Hart-Brown-Frankena, "A Symposium on Natural Rights," *The Philosophical Review*, 64 (1955), 175–232.
Johnston, H., *Business Ethics*, 41–77. New York, Pitman, 1956.
Kirk, R., "Burke and Natural Rights," *Review of Politics*, 13 (1951), 441–456.
Maritain, J., *The Rights of Man and the Natural Law*, 1–83. New York, Scribner's, 1951.
Mounier, E., *Personalism*. New York, Grove, 1952.
Pound, R., *Introduction to the Philosophy of Law*, rev. ed. New Haven, Yale, 1954.
Rommen, H. A., "The Genealogy of Natural Rights," *Thought*, 29 (1954), 403–425.
Ryan-Boland, *Catholic Principles of Politics*, 13–28. New York, Macmillan, 1940.
Strauss, L., *Natural Right and History*. Chicago, University of Chicago, 1953.

Chapter XVI OBJECTS OF NATURAL RIGHT

478. In an explanation of justice and right, three elements may be distinguished: (*a*) a man's possession; (*b*) the law which makes his possession inviolable; (*c*) the immunity or secure enjoyment resulting from law, which is right. We have already considered *c*, the nature of right. We have shown its origin in *b*, law. We shall now consider *a*, the object of right, or man's possession. The purpose of our investigation will be to determine the chief things which the Natural Law guarantees a man as an individual.

I. LIFE AND LIMB

479. That life and corporal members belong to the individual is so obvious that it need not be demonstrated. No human agency may directly deprive him of these unless his malicious conduct makes loss of his life or limbs necessary to preserve similar rights of others or of the State. If he is innocent of crime, the taking of his life by homicide or the invasion of his bodily integrity by mutilation is grave injustice.

The summary formula, *Thou shalt not kill,* is not an adequate statement of nature's prohibition. Homicide is the direct taking of innocent life upon human authority. This is always and everywhere wrong because it destroys the natural equality existing among all men and is an invasion of God's exclusive dominion over human life. The morality of indirect killing is judged by the principle of double effect as in the case of indirect suicide (§ 388). Although men generally recognize the heinousness of homicide, they endeavor, on convenient occasions, to avoid guilt on the claim of justifiable killing.

A. Euthanasia

480. To mask an ugly deed behind a euphemism is an age-old escape. The killing of the aged, the incurably ill, or the mortally wounded on the battlefield to bring an end to their misery is not an act of kindness but murder. Even if the painfully wounded ask for death, their request may not be granted on the pretext that no injury is done to one who willingly accepts it. More is involved than their own right to life: the superior right of God's supreme dominion is the first consideration. Doctors and nurses have a contractual obligation to use all ordinary means to keep their patients alive. Deliberately not to do so, or positively to hasten death partakes of the malice of murder. Nor may doctors use the bodies of their patients as guinea pigs in order to experiment with uncertain drugs when surer remedies can be used. When there are no sure remedies, a doctor may test the curative value of a newly discovered drug provided there is no risk to the patient.

B. Dueling

481. A duel is a fight with lethal weapons on private authority and by previous appointment. It is wholly and intrinsically wrong. An invasion of God's supreme dominion over life, it partakes of the malice both of murder and suicide. The principal in a duel deliberately endangers his life without a reasonable cause and by private authority attacks the life of his opponent.

The vicious custom of dueling arose in the early seventeenth century from a distorted notion of gentleman's honor. An insult demands satisfaction, but a duel is no substitute of satisfaction. Satisfaction is the retraction of wrong done. But the challenger, far from receiving a proper amend, allows the challenged to maintain his insult by force of arms and gives him an opportunity to perpetrate on him a more grievous wrong. After an unretracted insult honor can no longer be defended; only the opportunity for vengeance remains.

Public authority could authorize a duel which would substitute for war but it could not justify a duel for the vindication of an injury or the settlement of a private quarrel.

C. Abortion

482. The destruction of the human foetus is a most serious issue in modern ethics. The foetus is destroyed in two ways: by foeticide and abortion. Foeticide is the direct killing of the foetus in the mother's womb, after which it is expelled. This is murder just as truly as is infanticide. Abortion is *the expulsion of a living and nonviable foetus from the womb*. Since the foetus cannot live outside its mother until the completion of the twenty-eighth week of pregnancy, removal of an inviable foetus from the womb is equivalent to destroying it.

Abortion may be spontaneous, such as a miscarriage brought about by accident or disease. This would not be a human act, unless, of course, a person had been guilty of culpable neglect. An abortion is induced when it is the result of intentional interference with the foetus. A distinction must be made between directly and indirectly induced abortion.

In a *direct abortion* one intends the expulsion of the nonviable foetus and takes measures to effect it. Direct abortion is wrong whether it is sought as an end in itself — such as avoiding the consequences of moral evil — or whether it is reluctantly undertaken as a means to a good end — such as saving a pregnant woman's life. It is a direct attack upon innocent human life and is always murder.

483. It is argued that foeticide and direct abortion are allowable because a foetus, not being a person, has no rights. This contention is fallacious. The morality of the problem has no relation to the dispute over the time when the rational soul is infused into the embryo. The likeliest opinion is that this occurs when, after fertilization, a distinctly new living thing is formed. Actually, abortion is not employed until the foetus is fairly well formed and is certainly informed with a rational soul; but even if it were invoked in the early stages of gestation, the act would still be destructive of a human person. The reason is that there is direct and unbroken continuity of life from the fertilization of the ovum to the development of the embryo, foetus, infant, child, youth, and man. Any distinct and living organism, fundamentally capable of intelligence, is a human person and remains such as long as it possesses life. Every adult was once a foetus: the foetus is the first stage in the development of the human person.

It cannot be maintained that if a difficult pregnancy endangers a mother's life, the foetus as the cause of this condition becomes an unjust aggressor and hence forfeits its right to life. A foetus cannot be an aggressor — neither formally, because it is incapable of volition, nor even materially, because its existence is not the result of its own choice but of the will act of others.

It is claimed that since the mother's life is endangered by child bearing, her right to life is prior to that of the child's. The answer is that neither the mother nor the foetus has prior rights to life: they have equal rights to life, because each is equally a human person. The right of the foetus is just as sacred as that of the mother. Any action intentionally directed against the life of either is sinful.

It is exceedingly difficult to arrive at a decision in some actual cases, and in serious emergencies the solution may appear to be abortion to save the mother. The argument that an unborn baby will be missed less than a woman in her prime may seem quite compelling. Praiseworthy as the physician's intention may be, he is never justified in saving one life by directly taking another. He may argue that necessity knows no law — that he cannot stand by and see his patient die because he fears to use this last means. It is true that necessity knows no law in the sense that no man can be blamed for not doing the impossible, but no matter how dire one's necessity, an act intrinsically wrong is never justified. Moral evil may not be willed that any good, however great, may be obtained.

484. *Therapeutic abortion* is undertaken for the sake of saving the mother's life or health. In most cases this is direct abortion, but every direct attack upon the life of the foetus is a crime irrespective of the motive and permission by law. It is cynically said that an abortion is criminal if only one doctor signs for it but it is therapeutic if three sign for it.[1] Unfortunately, too many medical practitioners consider the procedures of the healing art a kind of sacred cow removed from any higher moral law. To these, whatever will effect a desirable medical end is good and beyond moral reproach. We have seen however, that the Natural Law regulates all human life and acts.

485. In *indirect abortion,* some medical treatment is administered or a surgical operation is performed for a serious purpose other than abortion but abortion results. An example would be the removal of a cancerous womb of a pregnant woman. The morality of such acts must be judged according to the principle of double effect. *Hastening of birth* after the completion of the twenty-eighth week of pregnancy is allowable for a proportionally grave reason. The foetus then is capable of living outside the womb.

II. LIBERTY OF PERSON

486. It is not too surprising to find that Aristotle not only justified but also approved absolute slavery as something intended by nature. He says, "He who would participate in reason enough to apprehend reason but not to have it is a slave by nature."[2] The medieval scholastics, seeing serfdom as an everyday fact of social existence, repeated without criticism the arguments of Aristotle favoring slavery. However, liberty of person is not merely a desirable advantage, a helpful condition of life which may be accorded or denied him as circumstances permit; it is a strict right, as we have shown in § 448.

[1] It is consoling to note that abortion no longer holds the approval once given it. There is now apparent a return to the attitude that good morals is also good medicine. Cf. *Theological Studies,* March, 1952, p. 70.

[2] *Politics,* Bk. I, 5, 1254b.

A question arises as to the morality of limited servitude. In limited servitude a man's services are wholly and perpetually handed over to a master in return for care and keep. A person who has so bound himself would still retain all his essential human rights to life, sustenance, fair treatment, marriage, and, if married, cohabitation. Although this state is less becoming the dignity of man's independent nature, yet in theory it seems that a man might be sentenced to such a life for crime or that he might freely contract for it if he felt unable to provide for himself.

Slavery, however, inevitably involves such abuses that it must be condemned. There is always the danger that the slave will be treated as a thing; his chances of intellectual and moral development are almost nil; he has no redress against injustice; he can be bent to any immoral purpose of his master. Slavery begets a slave mentality and a slave morality which has pernicious effects on slaves and slaveholders.

III. INTELLECTUAL AND MORAL INTEGRITY

487. Integrity, positively, is a condition of wholeness; negatively it is the absence of defect. A being or faculty is said to possess integrity if it actually or potentially has those things which naturally complete it. Intellectual and moral integrity means that, unimpeded by his fellow man, a man may use his specifically human powers and direct them toward their proper objects — his mind to truth and his will to moral goodness. His fellow man may not maliciously place any obstacle in the way of his mind's quest for the true and his will's appetite for the good. Otherwise he could be prevented from proper development and final perfection. Without access to truth and to moral goodness, man could not live as a man.

488. Man's right to *intellectual integrity* is violated by depriving him of the use of his mental faculties without his consent; by teaching him false doctrines; by making him the victim of false promises; by unduly deceiving him.

489. Man's right to moral integrity is violated in the following ways:

1. *By refusing him due freedom of conscience.* The right to be free to follow conscience has first a negative aspect. *No one may be compelled to do what his conscience says is wrong,* not even when conscience is invincibly erroneous. The right is *inalienable;* no one may surrender it since it is necessary in order to fulfill the absolute obligation of avoiding evil. It is *indefeasible* and may not be taken away by any authority. To do so would deprive the individual of an essential means to his last end. Masters, employers, military commanders, and the like violate this right

when they order those under their charge to violate the negative precepts of the Natural Law. But must a man always be free to do what conscience says must be done? He should be so free except when the act would militate against the common good or the equivalent good of another person.

2. *By depriving him of the necessary means of moral development.* Those to whom is entrusted the care of children, orphans, prisoners, and servants, dwelling with them day and night, must afford them suitable opportunities to cultivate their spiritual life. A law which would forbid religious instruction to children under eighteen years of age would not be a law but a moral injury. Pastors, teachers, and parents have a contractual obligation in virtue of their office to assist their charges by the good example of their lives. Bad example on their part violates not merely charity but justice.

3. *By exercising undue hypnotic influence.* Hypnosis is a somnambulistic state artificially induced wherein the patient's mind is passive but alert to the suggestions of the hypnotist. The patient's exercise of free will is impaired during such a trance but it is not clear how complete the control of the hypnotist is. Many claim that a hypnotized person will refuse to execute commands which he considers immoral when he is fully conscious. Others say that if the trance is deep enough, a hypnotized person will yield to any suggestion.

Hypnosis is not intrinsically wrong. As one may temporarily surrender the use of reason for a just cause, so also one may temporarily yield the exercise of his free will for a good reason. Hypnotism is said to have a definite curative value for people with alcoholic, gambling, and suicidal tendencies which they seem unable to resist.

Hypnosis is wrong if by means of it one (*a*) suggests immoral acts; (*b*) attempts to learn the free future; (*c*) endeavors to maintain a permanent hold on the patient's will.

One may submit to hypnosis if he has a grave reason and takes proper precautions such as having a reputable hypnotist and a reliable witness.

IV. HONOR AND REPUTATION

490. Every man is the image of God and is destined for perfect happiness. Every man deserves recognition of and respect for the excellence of his nature. This is a connatural right. Every man, irrespective of his wealth, ability, or social standing, possesses the dignity of man and to think of, speak to, or act toward him as though he were not a man is to deprive him of the honor he is entitled to by nature.

Over and above his native dignity, by industry or even by accident a man can acquire other perfections which bring additional honor. He may win credit for being a skilled architect; he may be honored as a father by his child; he may be revered for heroic virtue. All such honor is of perceptible value to a man. He may justly claim it as his own. To prevent him from acquiring this honor is usually an injustice: to deprive him of acquired honor violates his strict right.

The practice of virtue is the most praiseworthy activity of man. There is nothing a man can do that is more becoming a man than to act virtuously. A man is to be honored not only for *being* a man but also for *acting* as a man. By acting as a man, one is entitled to *reputation* or a good name. Reputation is the right of all men. It belongs to the truly good man as the natural outcome of virtue. It also belongs to the man who is only apparently good until his conduct shows that he is not. All men are to be judged good until they prove themselves otherwise. The peace and good order of society demand this attitude. If a man's reputation is genuine, his right is absolute and it cannot be taken from him against his will. If a man's reputation is only apparent, his right to it must yield to the common good, the protection of an innocent party, and his own correction and ultimate good.

491. A man's right to honor and reputation is violated by rash judgment, contumely, and backbiting.

a) *Rash judgment* is a *firm* assent of the mind whereby one judges another guilty of moral evil for insufficient reasons. It differs from rash suspicion, which does not involve firm assent. By judging rashly, man offends against his neighbor's right that he be well thought of until his misconduct forfeits good opinion. The evil consists in the will, upon insufficient grounds, compelling a *certain* judgment to the detriment of another. Justice demands that man be esteemed neither more nor less than his conduct warrants.

b) *Contumely* is the dishonoring of a person in his presence either by omission or commission. It is the contemptuous refusal to accord a man the honor which the occasion calls for, or it is open insult. Contumely is a violation of justice because it deprives one of what is due him; it is a violation of charity because it involves contempt of his person. As an offense against justice, it demands restitution; the honor denied a person must be given to him.

c) *Backbiting* is the dishonoring of a person in his absence. It takes two forms, calumny and detraction.

Calumny is false accusation of evil whereby a man's reputation is lost in whole or in part. Justice demands that the lie be retracted.

Detraction is the revelation of a true but hidden sin of another without a justifying reason. A man does not forfeit his good name except by open misconduct. Many people fail to see the injustice of detraction. They argue that if a man does wrong, he has ceased to be virtuous to the extent of his wrongdoing and thereby loses the accompaniment of virtue which is good name. Therefore, to take away the good name of such a person is not injustice, because a good name no longer belongs to him. The argument is erroneous. Secret wrong does not destroy one's reputation, because if a man possesses something — say money or reputation — he has a right to keep it until his retention of it would become an injustice to another; but the retention of a good name by one who secretly sins does not as such involve an injustice to another. Therefore, the hidden faults of others must remain secret until a reason arises for their revelation. Such a reason might be the person's own amendment, the protection of his fellows, the safeguarding of the common good.

To assess the amount of harm done by detraction, consideration must be given not merely to the defect revealed but also to the character of the detractor, the standing of the detracted, and the character of those to whom it is revealed. Since justice is violated, reparation must be made as far as possible. The truth may not be denied, but the detractor can at least endeavor to repair his victim's good name by extolling his good qualities.

V. FRIENDSHIP

492. Generically, friendship is the love of mutual benevolence. Where some special tie such as blood or marriage unites persons, we speak of *natural affection*. The virtue of piety governs this relation. In more ordinary usage, friendship means that bond of mutual esteem and good will which unites persons who are not related by blood or marriage. Friendship has this meaning here.

Aristotle points out that the motive of friendship may be the good, the pleasant, or the useful.[3] Man loves his friend for what he is — the good that is in him — or for the pleasure he affords him or the utility he finds in him. Friendships based on the latter two motives are egotistic outlets of self-love, for therein it is not the friend that is loved so much as one's own pleasure and utility. These are shallow, transient things, for such a friend may quickly cease to please or to be useful. When one values his friend and wishes him well for his own sake, and when these feelings are reciprocated, only then is true and permanent friendship

[3] *Nicomachean Ethics,* VIII, 2, 1155b.

had. True friendship is not passive. It must be fostered by habitually friendly acts; otherwise it languishes and eventually dies. Nor is it the mere acceptance of favors and affection. Aristotle said, "It is more characteristic of a friend to do well by another than to be well done by, and to confer benefits is characteristic of the good man and of virtue."[4] This idea has been more succinctly expressed by Christ: "It is more blessed to give than to receive."[5] The core of friendship is mutual well-doing, and the more excellent the benefits interchanged by friends, the nobler their friendship. To what heights of human grandeur it may rise was told for all time by Horace when he mourned for his dead friend Virgil as the other half of his soul.[6] Friendship is a rare and precious thing. It is not born in a day. Like true human excellence, it is the product of time and the constant exercise of virtue. It can flourish only between persons of true moral excellence.

493. Man has a connatural right to seek friends as the due development of his social nature. The good man has need of friends — virtuous companions, few in number, who share activities they mutually like and whose association is a help to virtue, giving life its pleasant flavor. To deny him friends is to deny him the most excellent of external goods. Once he has acquired a friend he has a right to keep him, not to be parted from him by the malicious acts of a third party. The invasion of this right is *mischief-making*, which consists in talk, not necessarily bad in itself, but bad in that it turns a man from his friend.

Is detraction a greater sin than mischief-making? To this question St. Thomas replies: "Sin against the neighbor is more grievous, the greater the harm done to the neighbor thereby. Harm again is greater, the greater the good destroyed. Now among exterior goods friendship stands preeminent, since 'none can live without friends,' as appears by the Philosopher. Hence it is said: 'Nothing can be compared to a faithful friend.' In fact, the good name that is destroyed by detraction is especially needed for this, that a man may be accounted fit for friendship. And therefore mischief-making is a greater sin than detraction and even than contumely because a friend is better than honor and it is better to be loved than be respected."[7]

[4] *Ibid.*, IX, 9, 1169b. [5] Acts 20:35. [6] *Odes*, Bk. 1, Ode 3.
[7] *Sum. Theol.*, II–II, 74, 2.

READINGS

St. Thomas, *Summa Theologica*, II–II, 64, 65, 66, 73, 74.
Barrett, E. B., *The Quest of Honor*. Milwaukee, Bruce, 1953.
Barton, R. C., *Our Human Rights*. Washington, Public Affairs, 1955.
Bonhoeffer, D., *Ethics*, 101–141. New York, Macmillan, 1955.

Bonnar, A., *The Catholic Doctor*, 81–89, 105–111. London, Burns, Oates, Washbourne, 1952.

Burch, T. K., "Patterns of Induced Abortion and Their Socio-Moral Implications in Postwar Japan," offprint from *Social Compass*, Vol. III (1956), no. 4.

De Lee, S. T., "Hypnotism in Pregnancy and Labor," *Journal of the American Medical Association*, 159 (October 22, 1955), 750–754.

Flood, D. P., ed., *New Problems in Medical Ethics*, Vol. I, 127–169; Vol. III, 263–299. Westminster, Newman, 1953, 1955.

Goodwine, J. A., "The Physicians Duty to Preserve Life by Extraordinary Means," *Catholic Theological Society of America Proceedings*, 1952, 125–138.

Heffernan-Lynch, "Is Therapeutic Abortion Scientifically Justified?" *Linacre Quarterly*, 19 (February, 1952), 11–27.

Janssens, L., *Droits Personnels et Autorité*. Paris, Vrin, 1954.

Lasswell, H. D., "The Threat to Privacy," *Conflicts of Loyalties*, 121–140, ed. R. M. MacIver. New York, Harper, 1952.

Leonard, A., "Liberty of Faith and Civil Tolerance," *Cross Currents*, Winter, 1955, 6–31.

MacIver, R. M., ed., *Great Expressions of Human Rights*. New York, Harper, 1950.

McFadden, C. J., *Medical Ethics*, 3 ed., 161–249. Philadelphia, Davis, 1953.

Moore, K. B., *The Moral Principles Governing the Sin of Detraction and an Application of these Principles to Specific Cases*. Washington, Catholic University, 1950.

Pius XII, "The Doctor's Role in War and Peace," *The Pope Speaks*, I (1954), 347–359.

Sullivan, J. V., *The Morality of Mercy Killing*. Westminster, Newman, 1950.

Chapter XVII PROPERTY

I. THE PROBLEM OF PROPERTY RIGHTS

494. Can material things be the object of right? If so, what is the nature of this right?

Men of all ages have enforced claims called property rights. Theory and practice regarding such rights alter from time to time. Thus contemporary man's views of property have been jarred to the depths by the impact of ideologies denying what hundreds of past years had taken for granted. It is of consuming importance, therefore, clearly to establish what the Natural Law commands, forbids, and allows concerning property rights, because, although these are not the most sacred of human concerns, yet they absorb a major share of man's attention. Harmonious human relations depend in no small measure upon a sound knowledge and prudent application of correct principles concerning property.

495. Ownership. At the basis of the whole matter is the concept of ownership which is *the control of a material object in one's own interest in accordance with law.*

Control is the right to possess, enjoy, and determine the disposition of a thing.

In one's own interest. A thing is at the disposal of an owner who has exclusive control of it. Exclusiveness of control is the outstanding feature of ownership; for without it there would be no appreciable difference between the mine and the thine. One who controls property in the interests of another is a *trustee*, not an owner.

Material object. The object of ownership is some material thing, or what is reckoned as such, external to the agent and capable of being exclusively controlled. Certain things like air, sunlight, and the high seas are in most respects incapable of appropriation. The term *material object* includes not merely tangible things, such as land, houses, movable goods, but also the services of another man; a variety of activities, such as a right to pasture, to hunt, to fish, to cross land, to have access to light, air, water; to have the support of land or buildings; to enter upon dignities, offices, privileges; less tangible things such as franchises, copyrights, patent rights.

In accordance with law. The right of ownership stems from the command of law that the owner shall be secure in his possession and use of a thing. But law does not undertake to protect any and every use. The Natural Law does not countenance immoral use, nor the positive law illegal use. The doctrine that an owner may do absolutely what he pleases with his possession is an error of economic liberalism. Law must fit ownership into its reasonable place in the total scheme of human rights. Hence it is for law to designate what the scope of ownership is, who is to exercise it, how exclusive and permanent an owner's control is, and when ownership must cede before some higher right.

That the Natural Law subordinates the right to own to the right of other men to live we shall show in Thesis XL. Charity demands that from one's superfluous goods help be given to the needy. The State has a right of *eminent domain.* This must not be confused with the State's own right to own things. It is its power of jurisdiction to (*a*) regulate the uses of property in conformity with the demands of the common good, and (*b*) in certain instances to appropriate private property. The justifying circumstances of the latter are the clear need of the common good and the payment of fitting recompense.

496. Ownership may be partial or plenary. Plenary ownership is a right to the fruits, use, and substance of a thing. It permits one to hold, use, gather the fruits of, change, alienate, or destroy the thing. Plenitude of control is permanent control. The thing is not merely for the owner's temporary advantage but so long as he remains the owner he determines even its future disposition. Ownership is not limited by time but solely by law.

Perfect dominion, or absolute ownership, is the right of plenary control. Imperfect dominion, or partial ownership, is a right merely to the substance or to the use or to the fruits or to the use and fruits. The English word *owner* signifies primarily one who has perfect dominion; secondarily, when it refers to imperfect dominion, it means the one who has the right to the substance of the thing. We shall use the word in its primary meaning.

497. We distinguish (*a*) *private ownership,* which is ownership by the individual. He is an absolute owner and from the control of the object owned he can exclude all others. And (*b*) *communal ownership,* which is ownership by a group such as a tribe or a State. The right does not reside in any particular individual but in the moral person, the group.

The great issue is *the validity of the concept of private ownership.*

498. The problem: the evils of private owning. For generations men had lived under capitalism which is an economic system of private owners operating for personal profit. During the nineteen-thirties the outcry against capitalism reached its peak. Great evils had grown up with it and these may be reduced to this statement: a vast portion of the wealth of the world had become the property of a few owners and the effective control of it had fallen into still fewer hands. The absorbing business of the actual directors of human affairs was a ceaseless, under-cover struggle for economic control. From time to time the heat of struggle rose beyond the boiling point and armed conflict broke out among the principal nations.

With the few controlling so much, the great mass of men had no effective protection against undue concentrations of wealth. While the common man in some communities had political freedom — he was allowed to vote — yet in no community did he have economic freedom. He lacked security. He was dependent on a wage which might cease without warning. From time to time complete or partial stoppages in the production and distribution of exchangeable goods occurred. The chief sufferer in these crises was the common man whose income was the first to be affected. When crises were prolonged vast numbers of people became dependent for subsistence upon the State.

Furthermore, there had been a multiplication of material comforts unparalleled in the history of man, but relatively few were enjoying them. The new wealth was not being equitably distributed. This was notably true in colonial areas whose people had been exploited by Europeans for centuries.

Since man in the nineteen-thirties was socially conscious and since improved communications made him aware of nearly all that was going on in the world, he vehemently demanded that something be done about economic injustices. Among the proffered solutions, two stood out notably, communism and socialism. Both held that the root of the evil is private ownership; only when it is drastically curbed or totally abolished would men begin to make right use of material goods. Many students and professors were attracted to these doctrines.

II. THE SOLUTION OF COMMUNISM

A. What Is Communism?

499. The doctrine that the only equitable way of holding property is by communal ownership is not new. From the time of Plato many have advocated it but it has never been put into large-scale practice until

now. Modern communism has a unique importance. First, on account of the great victories of Russia it has become the official doctrine of almost 900,000,000 people. Second, it is a complete way of life. It is not just a single socioeconomic tenet but a philosophy purporting to explain the whole of the universe. Since its ideological founder was Karl Marx (1818–1883) it is known as Marxist communism.

500. *Dialectic materialism* is the name which the Marxists give to their system. A dialectic is properly a method of philosophical argumentation, for example, the question-and-answer method of Socrates. Marx took his dialectic from Hegel, who propounded a form of idealistic pantheism according to which the mind makes reality, and all thought is an emanation from, and a manifestation of, one absolute idea. Hegel's philosophical procedure consists of thesis, antithesis, and synthesis. Thesis is the statement of an idea; antithesis is the denial of the statement; and synthesis, the denial of the antithesis. Hegel said that every concept contains its contradictory. Consequently, the mere positing of an idea, the thesis, necessarily brings into existence its antithesis; and the affirmation of the antithesis demands its negation, which is the synthesis. Rejecting the idealism of Hegel, Marx uses the Hegelian dialectic to explain his own purely materialistic universe. Hence the name dialectic materialism. Nothing exists, says Marx, but eternal, uncreated matter. He rejects, however, the mechanistic for the dynamic view of matter and says that all reality is matter in self-motion. The perpetual evolution of matter into newer and higher forms gives us the history of reality.

The dialectic, say the Marxists, is found in thought, in nature, and in history.

501. The *Marxist logic* summarized above is the dialectic in thought. Of late Marxism has explicitly espoused the current philosophy of change and holds that the saying of Heraclitus that all things change has now been demonstrated by modern science. Hence Marxism rejects the principle of identity and the traditional logic built upon it. For the rules of this logic are meant to be axiomatic and are "oriented on the assumption that change is a passing moment in something essentially static."[1] But such a logic cannot be "the last word in the development of a scientific method which was to become centrally occupied with change, prognosis, evolution."[2]

The dialectic in thought, say the Marxists, is but the reflection of the dialectic in nature.

---

[1] John Somerville, "Dialectical Materialism" in *Living Schools of Philosophy*, p. 430. Ames, Littlefield-Adams, 1956.

[2] *Ibid.*

502. The philosophical basis of Marxism is found in its cosmology or *explanation of nature*. Here the Marxist avers he does not invent but discovers an objective dialectic of thesis, antithesis, and synthesis. This dialectic in nature is a principle of dynamic change which the Marxist expresses in three fundamental laws of the universe.

a) *Law of the strife, interpenetration, and unity of opposites*. Whatever can be physically observed, mentally conceived, or emotionally felt consists of mutually antagonistic elements existing in an unstable unity subject to change. Without the interpenetration of its components the thing would have neither unity nor existence. Strife is essential because the elements are active, each reacting against its opposite, and generating the autodynamic motion of the thing. The formula for this law is: A is A and non-A. "It is considered evident that an A, all of whose parts are continually changing, is managing to be both A and non-A during the same instant. . . . A is never merely A, but always is what it is always becoming, namely, non-A."[3]

b) *Law of transformation of quantity into quality and vice versa*. The first law is the thesis and explains motion. The second law is the antithesis and is offered as the explanation of the increase of reality. Quantitative changes result from the negation of the thing. Thus the grain of wheat is negated and in its corruption reproduces itself a hundredfold. Communists, however, are not agreed about their explanation of qualitative changes or the emergence of new forms. The older communists said that these were effected by transformation; that is, quantitative changes went on, the same kind of thing was reproduced and reproduced until suddenly nature gave a leap and a new form emerged. A newer explanation says a new quality can arise only from the quantitative increase and decrease of existing qualities. The new form differs from that from which it evolved. It is not just the same thing on a larger scale. Thus an oak is not a larger acorn nor a man a larger foetus. A quality is an essence which is neither permanent nor unchanging. It is not opposed to matter but is something which grows out of it as part of its natural evolution.

c) *Law of the negation of the negation*. Quantitative changes and the emergence of new forms go on endlessly. Among them, however, new phases of development are discernible and each new phase is a synthesis resolving the contradictions of a previous phase and in turn producing its own set of contradictions which must later be resolved. The rise of life from inorganic matter and of thought from unconscious life are great natural syntheses.

---

[3] *Ibid.*, p. 427.

The original dialectic, however, was discovered by the Marxists in the history of man.

503. Man. In the Marxist view, man is the result of nature's leap from the brute level and he is nothing more than highly developed matter. He has neither spiritual soul nor free will and his destiny is determined by economic forces beyond his control. Individual men are always expendable: it is only Humanity or Society that counts. Men originally lived in a state of primitive collectivism wherein private property was unknown. By degrees, however, the craftier got control of the sources of production and claimed them as private property. This was the great robbery perpetrated by the first capitalists.

504. The Dialectic of History: the thesis. The historical thesis begins with a group seizing the means of production thereby producing strains in society and dividing men into the owning classes and the dispossessed masses. Ownership of productive wealth violates the equality of all men, for it elevates the owning class and makes it the exploiter of all nonowners. Here is the kernel of communist doctrine, namely, private ownership is of itself injustice and exploitation. After this first robbery or thesis, all history is the story of the *class struggle* for the instruments of production. Man is ruled by *economic determinism,* the basic fact of which is man's need of eating. This economic base of life has two features: (*a*) modes of production and (*b*) economic relations such as a system of ownership and distribution. Arising from and reflecting this economic base is a social superstructure of government, laws, arts, science, religion, philosophy, and the like. The Marxist illustrates the dependence of all human institutions upon economics by the case of the State, marriage, and religion.

505. The State did not exist in the primitive society but was devised by the owners who use it for their own class purposes. They invoke the armed might of the State to overawe the proletariat and to pass laws to confirm their spoliation.

506. There is no essential difference, say the Marxists, between the mating of men and of brutes. Hence men and women should have equal and ample sex freedom. Monogamy, which is only legalized prostitution, is an artificial device of property holders to ensure the transmission of property. Children do not belong to their families but to society which has the obligation of rearing them. In a scientific society the family ceases to be the basic economic unit. Marriage and the importance of the family will disappear with the abolition of private property.

507. Religion existed before private property but upon its rise the proprietors saw in religion another instrument of domination. Hence they supported the priests whose task it became to teach the masses its duties to the classes. The people were to be taught to be patient in suffering and want and above all their attention was to be distracted from the robbery done them in private property by holding before them an illusory hope of a better life beyond the grave. To Marx's axiom, "Religion is the opium of the masses,"[4] Lenin adds, "I hate God as I do my personal enemies." Lenin writes: "In cradling with a hope of celestial recompense him who labors all his life in misery, religion teaches patience and resignation. As for those who live from the labor of others, it teaches them to practice beneficence here, thus offering them an easy justification for their existence as exploiters and selling them cards of participation in celestial felicity at a reduction. . . . Religion is a clumsy sort of spiritual whiskey in which the slaves of capital drown their human being and their revenge for an existence little worthy of man. But the slave who has become aware of his condition and has risen to battle for his emancipation has already come half-way toward being a free man. The awakened worker of today leaves heaven to the priests and bourgeois hypocrites and turns toward the conquest of a better existence here on earth."[5]

508. The Dialectic of History: the antithesis. There is a dynamic in history, says Marx, which is leading man ever upward to a perfect society through a welter of crises which cannot be avoided. The thesis, or domination of society by the class which owns the modes of production, necessarily brings into being the *antithesis* of the nonowners who fight against their exploitation. From the struggle between thesis and antithesis results a synthesis or compromise — a combination of the good elements which had been in thesis and antithesis. Indeed there is a continuing succession of theses, antitheses, and syntheses because each new synthesis becomes in turn a thesis posing its particular stresses which must be resolved by some later synthesis. Modes of production necessarily change; therefore the economic relations established by the dominant class no longer suffice. Then the failure of the old order to meet the demands of the new situation automatically results in a revolutionary situation within which the struggle between the new challenging order (the antithesis) and the old challenged order (the thesis) takes place. Hence the class struggle is recorded in terms of the class forms which characterize the various periods of history. Thus ancient civilization is characterized by the master-slave form; the Middle Ages, by the lord-serf form; and modern capitalism, by the employer-employee relation. At

[4] "Critique of the Hegelian Philosophy of Right," *Selected Essays of Marx*, trans. H. J. Stenning, p. 12. New York, International Publishers, 1926.

[5] *New Life*, No. 28, Dec. 16, 1905. Translation also found in V. I. Lenin, *Religion*, pp. 11–12. London, Lawrence, undated.

length, however, "class war reaches its simplest phase when the capitalist is face to face with the proletariat. Capitalism, the thesis, calls into being its antithesis, organized labour, and from the resultant clash the final synthesis of a classless society will result."[6]

We are now, opine the Marxists, in the dying days of capitalism. Marx indicated as signs of speedy decay: (a) the law of surplus value[7] which purported to explain how the employer defrauds the employee with the result that the proletariat grows larger and poorer and the exploiting class smaller and richer; (b) the tendency of all businesses to become centralized in bigger and bigger firms until there will be but one firm — society; (c) periodic crises of boom and depression. The modern Marxist says that, like feudalism before it, capitalism has outlived its usefulness and its inherent contradictions are bringing on the final synthesis. Modern techniques of production are capable of producing a great abundance for all but are being defeated by outmoded economic relationships. The private ownership of capital, the hiring and firing of workers upon a basis of employer profit, and socially unplanned production must give way to the collective ownership of the sources of production and to socially planned production and distribution.

Although, in virtue of the laws of economic determinism, capitalism bears in its womb the classless society, yet individuals must hasten The Day by vigorous promotion of class warfare.

509. The Dialectic of History: the synthesis. The Marxist claims to be a scientist and asks to be judged upon the accuracy of his predictions. He is certain that a material paradise is opening before humanity and that he carries the torch which leads to the status of *pure communism.* The persuasive power of Marxism lies in its Messianic promise of an earthly felicity crudely reminiscent of the Christian description of a happy life hereafter.

The sun is now beginning to rise upon the new synthesis, the final condition of the human race, which will be distinguished by the following:

a) *Absence of government.* Under pure communism men will have no selfish notions of profit or money. They will be so accustomed to giving first consideration to the common good that they will not need a government. The State with its apparatus of power will have withered away.

[6] C. L. Wayper, *Political Thought*, p. 207. New York, Philosophical Library, 1954.

[7] For a description and refutation of the surplus-value law see MAN AS MAN, first edition, pp. 271–272 and 276–277. The surplus-value theory is a mere museum piece. Since in communistic countries the communistic State pays all wages, communists in those countries carefully suppress this piece of original Marxism.

b) *Classless society.* With private property abolished, there will be no more haves and have-nots and society will return to its primitive classless condition. This will be the millennium wherein equality and fraternity will flourish. There will be neither opportunity nor will to exploit another: no distinction between physical and mental labor, no division of interests between town and country. In this universal brotherhood the lamb will lie down with the lion.

c) *Abundance of material wealth and culture.* Communism and science will pour a horn of plenty upon an earth which will be renewed by a material Pentecost. Capitalistic restrictions upon unlimited production will be gone. All waste will be eliminated. An efficiency never before attained by man will minister to the wants of all. In this golden age of a socially planned economy and of no private possessions there will be no need of money for there will be operative the great law: from all according to his ability, to each according to his needs. Since poverty will have disappeared, so too will crime and war. Science will have mastered nature and disease; and who knows if it will not conquer death? Every avenue to education and culture will be open to each. Everybody will be an officer.

510. The Dictatorship of the Proletariat. How shall all this be done? Although the evolution of economic laws is now accomplishing the desired result, enlightened men must have part in the process. How? By the establishment of the Dictatorship of the Proletariat! The Second Internationale of 1889 was wrong when it dreamed of a peaceful transfer of the ownership of property. Reliance must be upon force, as the Third Internationale declared in 1919.[8] The privileged minorities will not yield without a struggle but must be forcibly dispossessed the world over through skillful conduct of class warfare.[9] After universal revolution a dictatorship of the proletariat will assume the function of an international State. The dictatorship will be an intermediate expedient whose purpose is to purify and uplift men for a purely communistic life. The dictatorship will do this by eliminating religion, private property, class distinctions, and all national governments.

511. The communist conspiracy. Moscow is the center of a world-embracing effort to bring about the universal dictatorship. Unto this end the whole world has been organized. Every country has been divided into suitable divisions, sections, and subsections, and in each some agent has been made responsible for the growth of communistic doctrine and

[8] Cf. *Blue Print for World Conquest,* p. 35, ed. Human Events, Washington, 1946.
[9] *Ibid.,* p. 44.

practice. At the head of the conspiracy is a very small group, the Politburo, whose orders descend through a hierarchic apparatus of power down to the communistic cell, which is the basic organizational unit. These cells, and communists on all levels of power, stand ready for any useful task. This might be the control of some labor or youth movement under cover of innocent stooges, the murder of a renegade, implanting the party line in organs of information, creating industrial unrest and strikes, turning strikes into riots and civil war, instigating colonial revolt. Each country is to be softened up by fifth-column communists so as to ensure its engulfment by the revolution.

512. The communist party. The vanguard of the revolution, the general staff directing this movement, is the communist party. For it is not the inarticulate masses which will accomplish the revolution but the party which has assumed a dictatorship over the proletariat. This party is very small, a carefully selected group whose religion is dedication to the revolution. Besides necessary qualities of efficiency and leadership, the party demands of its membership absolute obedience and obliteration of one's personality in the interests of the party. A party member can have no private life apart from the life of the party. He must steel himself against human emotion and any deviation from Marxist doctrine or the party line. He must cultivate the party virtues. He must be dynamic, forward-looking, tough-souled, atheistic, living for one only thing — to do the will of the Kremlin. He must constantly examine his communistic conscience and never be afraid to confess and amend his communistic faults.

513. Communistic tactics. The supreme tactic is that even when the party seems to retreat from pursuit of its ultimate goal, it never abandons it. Lesser tactics involve discussion of communist morality which Lenin himself thus explains: "The bourgeoisie frequently reproach us communists with having no code of ethics. It is only a maneuver to throw dust in the eyes of the people. In what sense do we deny ethics? We deny them in the bourgeois sense, according to which morality flows from the statutes of divinity. We say with assurance that we do not believe in God and we know full well that under the name of God it is in reality the clergy, proprietors and bourgeoisie who speak in order to defend their interests as exploiters. . . . We deny all morality borrowed from concepts exterior to class or even to humanity. *Our morality is entirely subordinated to the interests of the proletariat and the needs of the class struggle.*"[10]

---

[10] For another translation of the same speech, see *Religion* by V. I. Lenin. London, Lawrence, pp. 55–56.

Hence the Marxist norm of morality may thus be stated: any act is good which furthers the revolution; any act is bad which hinders it.

514. The day-to-day tactics of Marxism are those of a nation at war whose general staff will stop at nothing in order to win. Marxism is never hindered by any scruple of justice or humanity. Indeed it thinks it gains a distinct advantage by fighting outside the recognized rules of human conduct. Its disregard of accepted morality is especially shown in its attitude toward the following:

a) *Truth.* The Marxist attitude toward truth is well summarized in these words of Stalin: "A diplomat's words have no relation to actions—otherwise what kind of diplomat would he be? Good words are a mask for bad deeds. Sincere diplomats are no more possible than dry water or wooden iron."[11] The language of Marxism is Aesopian double talk.[12] It appropriates to itself all the important words of good connotation like peace, justice, democracy, patriotism, and, by giving them a communistic content, turns their definitions upside down. As a matter of policy it employs the Big Lie, assassinates the character of formidable enemies, disregards its pledged word. It wages war and calls it peace. It condemns imperialism and practices it. It feigns interest in reform in another country simply that it may disrupt it. Since it realizes that even the most despotic regime cannot forever disregard the opinions of the governed, it makes huge efforts to convince its subjects of the desirability of communism. Hence it tries to mold the thinking of all. It has rewritten history and makes scientific investigation an appendage of State policy. There is a Soviet genetics, a Soviet astronomy, a Soviet sociology. So adept is Marxism at deceit that it must warn party members not to be taken in by the party's own deceits.

b) *Human rights.* Marxism can murder millions of innocent people and call it social experiment or liquidation of counterrevolutionaries. It can sign an international pact forbidding genocide and cynically practice this crime against small nations. Its economy rests upon a base of 20 million slaves. Personal privacy does not exist in the face of universal espionage.

c) *Terrorism.* It controls its own subjects by a secret police with unlimited powers. It will overrun any noncommunist country if opportunity offers. Without a pang it destroys all opposition.

d) *Change.* It is ever ready to abandon one tactic for its opposite. Stalin reversed all Soviet policy by signing the pact with Hitler which

[11] *Collected Works of Joseph Stalin,* Vol. II, p. 277. Godizdst, Moscow, 1948.
[12] Cf. Harry Hodgkinson, *The Language of Communism.* New York, Pitman, 1955.

brought on World War II. The one thing which never changes is its determination to dominate the world.[13]

B. Refutation of Communism

1. *Summary Refutation*[14]

515. As a complete philosophy of life, Marxism clashes with sound philosophy on very many issues. Since we may suppose that the Scholastics have demonstrated their conclusions, our general criticism will consist in indicating the main points wherein communism differs. An effective refutation of Marxism is often the candid statement of its doctrines.

a) The fundamental tenet of materialism — all things are matter — is refuted by the existence of God and the spiritual human soul. Matter in motion is impossible without a Prime Mover who is Himself unmoved.[15] The Marxist makes his materialistic position more untenable by espousing dynamic materialism; for the only self-consistent theory of materialism is the mechanistic view. Marxism hopelessly confuses matter and spirit.

b) The three Marxist laws of the universe deny the principles of identity, contradiction, and causality. Although these principles are indemonstrable, their denial leads to absurdities. Denial of these principles asserts the impossibility of all reality and all knowledge.

c) Rational psychology proves the freedom of the human will.

d) The State cannot wither away because it is a natural institution demanded by the Natural Law for the well-being of men. See § 814.

e) Economic determinism is disproved by the freedom of the human will and the existence of values greater than economic ones. The perpetual warfare of classes and the dialectic of history is an unproved myth, as valid as Rousseau's "state of nature." The economic has not been the ultimate factor in historic changes; it explains much but not all. Although this issue is historical and not philosophical, it is pertinent to remark that the religious wars and the rise of Christianity and Mohammedanism cannot be accounted for on economic grounds.

f) Theodicy refutes the atheism of Marxism.

g) Class warfare and universal revolution militate against the charity we owe the neighbor.

h) The norm of morality is not utility to serve world-wide revolution.

[13] Krushchev says: "If anyone thinks that our smiles mean the abandonment of the teachings of Marx, Engels and Lenin, he is deceiving himself cruelly. Those who expect this to happen might just as well wait for a shrimp to learn how to whistle" (*Time*, September 26, 1955, p. 24).

[14] Marxist doctrines which are refuted in other parts of philosophy and ethics are here treated summarily: ethical doctrines pertaining to rights and property are dealt with more fully below. See § 516.

[15] Cf. St. Thomas, *Sum. Theol.*, I, 2, 3.

2. *Specific Refutation*

THESIS XXXVIII. Communism is forbidden by the Natural Law.

516. Communism means the politico-economic system founded on evolutionary materialism which Marxism aims at forcing on the world. The political system undermines the family, makes everybody subordinate in all things to society, envisions a classless society. The economic system denies all private property and asserts the principle: from all according to his ability, to each according to his needs.

PROOF

517. The Natural Law forbids a politico-economic system which (1) denies man a natural right and ordinary political rights; (2) is based on a false concept of human nature and human equality; (3) depends on absolute force; is opposed to (4) true liberty, (5) the good order of society, (6) the well-being of the family, and (7) an abundance of material goods. But communism is such a system. Therefore it is forbidden by the Natural Law.

1. Man's natural right to private property is proved in Thesis XLI. Communism denies people the ordinary political rights of free speech, free assembly, free elections, free communications with the rest of the world.

2. Man has a spiritual soul whose ultimate perfection is not material well-being but perfect happiness in another life. While men are equal in nature and destiny, they do not have equal gifts, abilities, rights, and duties. Nature makes women different from men. To disregard these differences is provocative of disorder. Disordered concupiscence, which will never be eradicated, together with inevitable differences of personal advantages, makes a classless society impossible.

3. To direct men solely by force is to treat them like brutes. Communism holds its own and subject peoples by naked force.

4. To deprive man of the right to own productive goods is restriction of his liberty (§ 522). *A fortiori*, in the system which does not permit ownership of consumable goods, there is no hope of his resisting tyranny. When the sources of production and the distribution of consumable goods are in the hands of the dictatorship of the proletariat, the controllers of that dictatorship could never be removed from power. The individual is then completely at the beck and mercy of his governors. It is vain to imagine that an omnipotent political power will voluntarily dissolve itself for a "stateless administration of things."

5. Distribution of goods according to needs alone is childish and unrealistic. It would result in contention and jealousy and would establish that inequality which the system seeks to remove. Complaints, disturbances, and despotic repression will follow.

6. Nature prescribes that the family and its members be immediately subject to the care and providence of its natural head, the father. The care of the aged and the sick and the rearing of the young are primarily family concerns, but in this system these functions belong immediately to the State.

7. That communism is not productive of a legitimate abundance of material goods is proved in § 523. Here it is sufficient to quote a firsthand witness, Barmine, a former high Soviet official: "Lenin's idea of socialism rested on two major assumptions: that under a collectivized economy production would rise very much higher than it can under capitalism; and that the exploited wage workers would get the main benefit of this increased production, exploitation having ceased. The Soviet economic system, together with totalitarian regime, have refuted both these assumptions."[16]

III. THE SOLUTION OF SOCIALISM

518. The terms *communism* and *socialism* may be confused for two reasons. First, between the Second Internationale and the outbreak of war in 1914 the term *communism* disappeared. The Marxists called themselves *socialists* but officially resumed the term *communist* at the Third Internationale. Second, the Marxists claim that their social revolution has reached the stage of socialism.

After winning control of Russia, the Marxists tried to put into practice the whole doctrine of Marx. They failed. They found that they could not do without the use of money. Workmen are paid wages, based not on their needs but on their usefulness to the employing State. Some private property exists. The marriage tie, the family, belief in God, and a need for religion persist. Equality of all citizens has not materialized. The people have merely exchanged one set of masters for another. The place of the old aristocrats is now filled by the communist party. The original Marxist program, however, runs counter to the plain dictates of the Natural Law in too many instances ever to succeed as such. The views of revolutionaries, penniless men on the run from the police, necessarily change when responsibility for the State and the desirable perquisites of office devolve on them. They have to turn reactionary and invoke

[16] Alexander Barmine, *One Who Survived*, p. 313. New York, Putnam, 1945.

the aid of the Natural Law at least to the extent of securing the stability of their regime. But since they have made all productive wealth the property of the State and have imposed their will on so many countries, they claim they have achieved the first or socialistic part of the Marxist program. The socialistic status they summarize in the formula: "from all according to their ability, to each according to work performed." Although the Marxist claims he has reached the level of socialism, there are, indeed, deep and fundamental differences between communism and socialism.

519. Differences between communism and socialism:

1. Whereas communism says that society should own absolutely everything, socialism distinguishes between consumable and capital goods. Consumable goods are those for use only and may not be employed to produce further wealth. Capital goods are the sources of wealth such as land, mines, factories, ships, and the like. The individual may own consumable goods but he may not own capital goods. These are to be vested in agencies which vary with the brand of socialism.

a) The *socialist* says that the State organized in democratic form shall own all productive goods. (*b*) The *agrarian socialist*, or the follower of Henry George, while allowing the individual the ownership of some productive goods, denies that he may own the soil as the primal source of wealth. (*c*) The *syndicalist* says that productive goods shall be owned exclusively by syndicals or labor unions. The goods and tools of a given trade shall belong to a corporate union and the affairs of the unions shall be governed by subordinate councils democratically selected, over which shall be a general council possessing supreme power. Some syndicalists deny the need of the State and would abolish it by force. They are (*d*) the *anarcho-syndicalists*. Others claim that the State has supreme jurisdiction over people as consumers but not as producers. These are (*e*) *guild socialists*.

2. A socialist need not hold the extremely materialistic and atheistic views of the Marxists.

3. Although socialists and communists had joined forces at the First Internationale in 1864, they split at the Second Internationale upon the question of method. The revolutionary wing, which later appeared as Marxism-Leninism, held that force alone could be successful. The socialists said that the social revolution should take place gradually and by means of parliamentary majorities.

520. We shall not discuss the feasibility of the State owning one or several sources of production but we shall confine ourselves to a discussion of classic or State socialism according to which the State, by majority vote, should take over *all* means of production and then manage production and distribution according to popular needs.

There is a preliminary question which the socialist should answer, namely, How shall this surrender of property to the State be accomplished? Since it is inconceivable that owners would willingly and gratuitously yield their holdings, will they not be forced to surrender them? Will they be expropriated in communistic fashion, or will compensation be made to them? What kind of compensation will be compatible with both justice and a socialistic regime? Is adequate compensation possible since there will be no laws of inheritance in a socialistic regime? Granted that the problem could be solved with logic and justice — which we sincerely doubt — and all sources of production and means of distribution got into the sole hands of the State, we hold that an unsatisfactory economy would result.

THESIS XXXIX. Socialism or State ownership of all productive wealth is impracticable on a large scale.

521. We shall later prove that the individual has a right to own productive goods. This nature allows. However, we are not now decrying socialism as the violation of a natural right. For it is conceivable that men could forego the exercise of this right if all men would control their greed, if each would contribute his due share to the common good. This would have been the normal thing in a state of original justice. Therein men could have entrusted to the community the exercise of their right to own property. Even today we do find instances of the surrender of this right as in religious communities and in selected groups of families the members of which are willing to have common possessions. There are sufficient safeguards to the individual to allow this practice. But when we pass from a closed, carefully controlled circle to one of national scale where men are not habitually reasonable, where they are inclined to feed their greed, and to shirk common responsibility, we must be realistic and bear in mind the shortcomings of a fallen race. To ask or compel all men to surrender the exercise of the right of owning productive wealth is to invite worse evils of tyranny and social unrest than the injustices which socialism seeks to remedy.

PROOF

The socialistic State would be unworkable, because (1) it attacks liberty and (2) diminishes production.

1. Socialism Attacks Liberty

522. Since *everyone would be an employee of the State*, the following consequences are inevitable.

a) No one may engage in business for himself.

b) Workmen may not strike against government.

c) Freedom to choose an occupation would be diminished. Since the State alone would stabilize production, it would determine the number of employees in a given industry. Once men were allocated to an industry, they would not be free to change; otherwise production would be dislocated.

d) Forced labor would be inevitable. Although some positions would be apportioned on a basis of competition, a large number of disagreeable jobs would remain which no one would want. Either many of these would go unfilled and production would suffer, or they would have to be filled by forced labor. Plato moots the same problem in his *Republic*. To the necessary question, Who will do the rough work and clean up the slops? he calmly answers, "The slaves."[17]

e) A man's place of residence is fixed by his job.

f) Where the State alone owns all capital, it alone prints the newspapers and conducts the schools. Where no private capital exists, none of these things can be in private hands. Therefore freedom of press and education must vanish. If the State owns all sources of income, totalitarianism is inevitable.

g) If each man depends upon the State for his salary, the government can work its will with him by the simple threat of cutting off that salary. In practice what secures a man in his rights is productive wealth. A man's freedom of action is in direct proportion to his economic independence. The employee of an all-powerful State has only that economic freedom which the State sees fit to grant him. His economic advance would depend not so much upon individual talent and industry as upon a *fallible and quite possibly corrupt bureaucracy*.

2. Socialism Diminishes Production

523. *a*) *It destroys man's natural incentive to labor*. The fundamental motivation for strenuous labor and productive effort is personal gain. It is idle to inveigh against the profit motive: it cannot be stamped out of mankind. A man will work without sparing himself if he knows that he will get something out of his labor for himself, whether it be

[17] *Republic*, II, 371, D.

affluence, dignified leisure, power and influence, or a comfortable old age. He desires these rewards even more so for his family.

Strenuous labor will fall off if it is not motivated by adequate rewards. In the socialistic system one of the most deeply rooted of natural incentives is taken away. Socialism forbids all laws of inheritance. Socialists say that men should and, if they are properly educated to it, will work for nobler motives than self and family — for the pleasure of virtue, the honor of a job well done, the satisfaction of having served the community. Some men will work for these motives but the ordinary man, outside of a special crisis, will do so only when his personal interests have been secured. The naïve hope that all men will constantly act out of these motives betrays a woeful ignorance of man as he actually is.

b) *It discourages the spirit of commendable thrift.* When capital is entirely in public hands it will not be conserved as when in private hands. Nothing is so neglected as common property. What belongs to everybody is treated as if it belonged to nobody. Men never will be so altruistic, so alert to the common good, as to protect and increase the goods of the State with the same zeal as they look out for their own things. It is personal interest — the hope of direct or at least ultimate gain to oneself — which explains the increase of productive goods. If all productive goods would be the common property of one hundred and sixty million people, it would be little short of madness to expect all or even the majority to take a personal interest in common property.

c) *It requires a degree of administrative ability and integrity on the part of the State officials which is morally impossible to realize.* The assumption of such new responsibilities would increase the difficulty of efficient government a thousandfold. The machinery of government would eventually break down from such an enormous and complicated responsibility. If the government were to own all productive wealth, public officials would be running all farms, the manufacturing industry, the trades, the transportation and communication systems. Socialism cannot guarantee public officials of such angelic minds as would be required to administer these industries efficiently on such a vast scale. Nor can it promise public officials of saintly probity in sufficient quantity for such a task; it would merely multiply the opportunity of plunder a thousandfold. Waste and inefficiency would be canonized, for they would be protected by a government which has no competitor.[18]

---

[18] Explaining the frequent breakdowns in Soviet industry, on page 211 of the work cited above, Barmine writes: ". . . machinery, instead of being repaired, is used until it is ruined, and then replaced. Thus the real cost of production of Soviet goods is higher than in any capitalistic country, despite the fact that the workers are paid extremely low wages. This super-exploitation should make it possible to cover most of the losses

No government should pretend to procure both the public good and the private good. We do not need an experiment to know that such an effort will fail.

524. The argument may thus be summarized: If all business is placed in the hands of government, government is either efficient or it is inefficient. Efficiency here is a reasonably abundant production and a smoothly flowing distribution of goods. If government is not efficient, the purpose of putting government into business is defeated. If it is efficient — and much of our argument proves that it cannot be — it could be so only at a price of inhuman tyranny — universal regimentation, espionage, forced labor, and the denial of natural rights. "Under socialism," Lenin grimly says, "all democracy withers away."[19]

IV. THE SOLUTION OF REASON

A. A Historical Conspectus

525. Neither communism nor socialism offers an acceptable answer to the great difficulty which we have been discussing. However, before proceeding to give a positive answer, it may be well for us to show that historically the difficulty is not so much economic as moral. Its root is greed. Society has failed to shackle individual greed, or rather has unwisely removed the bands by which an older society once contained it.

Medieval society, as effectively as human weakness can, kept men's acquisitive instincts from running wild. Western Christendom was a completely articulated, integrated society, teleologically organized upon the basis that all human action was to be directed unto an otherworldly aim, namely, the individual's attainment of eternal happiness. Hence,

---

and produce cheaply, but the incompetent bureaucratic system, wasting labor and materials, destroys this possibility. I personally observed the same thing in several other branches of industry.

"The chief trouble seemed to be that, without competition and without free trade unions, there is no stimulus to the management to use their brains. They can afford to be wasteful and incompetent because they are not under pressure from competitors to produce better and cheaper goods, and not under pressure from workers to pay higher wages. Their problem is much simpler. When the abolished capitalistic profit is not enough to compensate for their wasteful inefficiency, they cover it by cutting down on their workers' wages. That is why, in spite of the fact that workers work as hard and harder than in capitalistic countries, the Soviet industries are unable to give them the same decent standard of living. It was a basic principle with Lenin that the socialist economy would justify its existence only if it produced more and better goods than capitalism, and thus guaranteed the workers better conditions of life. This principle of Lenin's was constantly in my mind during the following years, and out of it grew irrepressible doubts as to whether we were on the right road."

[19] V. I. Lenin, *The State and Revolution*, p. 65. New York, The International Publishers, 1932.

to one supreme moral code all was subject — war, business, agriculture, government. Neither statecraft, diplomacy, nor money-making were so sacrosanct as to be laws unto themselves and immune from moral governance.

526. Making due allowances for the relative scarcity of wealth and opportunities of growing rich, the comparatively undeveloped state of commerce, and the agricultural economy which prevailed, there was an active moral force in that society which kept men's avarice within the bounds of reason. Thus, trading bore a certain stigma — not because society was governed by landowners — but for the reason stated by St. Thomas: "The trader is one whose business consists in the exchange of things. The exchange of things is twofold: one natural, as it were, and necessary, whereby the commodity is exchanged for another or money is taken in exchange for a commodity in order to satisfy the needs of life. Such trading, properly so called, does not belong to the trader but to housekeepers and civil servants who have to provide the household or the State with the necessaries of life. The other kind of exchange is either that of money for money or of any commodity for money, not on account of the necessities of life but for profit; and this kind of exchange is the business of the trader. The first kind of exchange is commendable because it supplies a natural need. The second is justly deserving of blame because considered in itself *it satisfies the greed of gain which knows no limit and tends to infinity.* Hence trading, considered in itself, has a certain debasement attaching thereto, insofar as by its nature it does not imply a virtuous or necessary end. Nevertheless, gain, which is the end of trading, though not implying by its nature anything virtuous or necessary, does not in itself connote anything sinful or contrary to virtue, wherefore nothing prevents gain from being directed to some necessary or even virtuous end, and thus trade becomes lawful."[20]

527. In their quest for a just price, the guilds did much to check unlimited gain. They considered a fair price to be that which sufficed to sustain the merchant in his station in life. What went beyond was unfair. Every State had severe laws forbidding usury. All men held that it was detestable to deprive one's neighbor of the means of his livelihood. All holding of land — from king to husbandman — carried definitely defined social obligations. The theory was that the king was not the absolute owner of the nation's land but its trustee. He held it in virtue of a contract between himself and his people. He was his people's steward and could be discharged from his office for serious violation of his coronation oath. So through the entire structure

[20] *Sum. Theol.*, II–II, 77, 4.

of feudalism, each held land on the condition of fulfilling certain social, political, and military duties. No man of substance was ever allowed to forget that he had an obligation in conscience to give of his superfluous goods to the needy. The chief barrier to greed was the universal conviction that the absorbing business of life was not the accumulation of money but the salvation of one's soul by the observance of the moral law and that the unjust possession or the wrongful use of riches was an insurmountable obstacle to that end.

528. This view of life and the organization of society upon this basis suffered a violent upheaval in the religious revolt of the sixteenth century. The unity of Christian life, manifested and made secure by the acceptance of one moral code interpreted by a supreme papacy, was rent by the rejection of papal authority. With the refusal on the part of many to accept this moral leadership, the once universally accepted code grew into disrepute, gradually but with ever increasing speed.

The first cleavage came as the logical result of Calvinism. According to Calvin, one was either predestined by God to salvation from all eternity or one was marked for damnation. Nothing a man might do could alter this immutable decree. But how could one tell if he were among the saved? The Calvinist sternly and uncompromisingly answered: only by membership in the Calvinistic Church. Since, then, the Calvinist was predestined and the prime business of life secure for him, he need not worry about salvation but could turn all his energy to something else. That something else happened to be the making of money. Thus, by the end of the nineteenth century the idea that the possession of money is the criterion of a successful life had supplanted for too many individuals the older view that until one's last breath one must work out his salvation in fear and trembling.

The factor which completed the break from the traditional, otherworld view of life and has completely reoriented modern social life was the spread of the *liberal idea* to every sphere of life. It spelled the secularization of modern life. Liberalism, like every damaging error, begins with an appealing truth — the freedom, dignity, and value of the individual. It forgets, however, that this freedom to be genuine must be restricted by the equally real claims of divine and social obligations. Luther sowed the seeds of liberalism by proclaiming the omnipotence of private judgment. The Scriptures do not mean what a divinely organized Church says their objective meaning is but what each individual finds them to mean for himself. With every man his own pope, the sixteenth century had what it fancied to be religious freedom. In the eighteenth century Rousseau enlarged upon the idea of individual freedom; it was introduced into the realm of politics, and the armies of the French Revolution carried the Rights of Man and their exaggerations into every country of Europe to the detriment of society. No sooner were the Napoleonic wars ended than the cry for economic freedom was heard. Feudalism was dead and buried. The old idea that land was held upon the condition of rendering public service had disappeared. The landed proprietor was not only the absolute owner of what his ancestors had held conditionally, but in the course of several centuries he had managed to obtain exclusive ownership of what had been the common lands of the village. Economic liberalism denuded property of any social tie. Its political slogan was free trade; and its cardinal principle was that property belongs absolutely and exclusively to its owner, that the owner is free to do with his property as he pleases provided only that he keep his contract. Society may in no way restrict one's use of his property nor demand that it serve a social purpose. The sole function of the State is to insure peace and enforce contracts.

529. Economic liberalism said that an employer was free to pay what he chose, exact whatever hours of labor he could get, demand as a price whatever the traffic would bear. Since the life of trade was competition, let competition be completely unshackled with no holds barred. While Darwin was saying that life is a struggle wherein only the fittest survived, the mill owners of England and New England were making huge fortunes from the sweat of employees working twelve and fourteen hours a day for the barest pittance. The result of such ideas and practices was the industrial slavery of the nineteenth century; the public-be-damned spirit of the barons of industry; the adoration of property rights above human rights to a decent existence. Business is business and morality does not enter into it. Unbridled competition is a form of war, and since all is fair in love and war, you can use any means within the civil law to put your competitor out of business, to rig the law for your own benefit.

530. Against this background of industrial slavery and as a protest against its injustices arose the demands of socialists and communists. Since, however, the solution of the problem of ownership does not lie in their doctrines, we seek it in the Natural Law. What metaphysical principle underlies man's relation to material goods? Upon the correct answer to this question must be based anything that is said about the use, possession, or division of material things.

Cosmology establishes that the relatively ultimate end of the material universe is the good of mankind. Nature intends that all things less than man should serve as means to his last end. The truth of this statement is clear from observation of these things and of man's needs.

Hence the primary relation between these things and man is stated thus: *Material things are ordained to serve the needs of the human race.* From a principle of cosmology we proceed to a principle of ethics: the human race has a right to use material goods; that is, because man must do it, he may.

B. The Use of Material Goods

531. Is the right of use confined to the race or does it extend also to the individual?

THESIS XL. The Natural Law grants every man the right to use material goods in order to conserve life and secure the essentials of human living. This right is connatural and in cases of extreme need it prevails over any acquired rights of ownership.

PROOF OF PART I

532. **The Natural Law gives each one the right to use material goods so as to secure life and the essentials of human living,** because, since nature gives the right to life and a human living, she cannot withhold the absolutely necessary means thereunto. Without the use of material goods, men cannot live as men.

PROOF OF PART II

533. **This right of use is connatural** because its title is the very fact of existence. At the moment a person begins to exist, the need and obligation of prolonging and fostering one's life commences. Hence also arises the right to anything absolutely necessary to satisfy this need and fulfill this obligation.

PART III

534. Goods may be classified according to a man's need of them as (a) *absolutely necessary goods* — those without which here and now he would die; (b) *gravely necessary goods* — those without which his mode of living would sink notably below the normal human level; (c) *simply necessary goods* — those which are useful for advancement. A person who lacks an absolutely necessary good is in *extreme need;* a gravely necessary good, in *grave need;* a number of simply necessary goods, in *common need.*

Man's right of use means (a) that in any sort of need he may use anything upon which no other has a claim; (*b*) in extreme need he may use any good available to stave off danger of death provided this thing is not equally needful to another in like danger who has pre-empted it. This right is so essential that any other conflicting property claim must yield to it. Therefore, to avoid imminent danger of death, one may take and use anything necessary to prolong his life and such action will not be theft. Anyone with acquired rights of ownership to such goods must cede his rights so long as the danger lasts.

PROOF

535. The right of use conflicting in cases of extreme need with any acquired rights of ownership always prevails. In this conflict of rights, the actually existing right will be the claim to *the more necessary good* (cf. § 461). Life is a more necessary good than property, a mere adjunct of life. Therefore the right of a man in extreme need to use property to preserve his life, destroys, for the duration of that need, any owner's acquired rights to that property.

536. N.B. May a person in grave need appropriate the property of another? He may in the following circumstances. The grave need must verge on the extreme, that is, one must be in danger of incurring grave and permanent harm such as captivity, mutilation, prolonged or incurable sickness; and the particular goods, necessary to escape this danger, are not equally needful to their owner. If, however, one's need verges on the common, one may not, because use in these circumstances would be destructive of public peace.

537. Corollary I. Any particular system set up by men for the further allocation, division, and distribution of material goods must safeguard the prime intent of nature regarding them, namely, that these goods are to satisfy human needs. The purpose of such a system must be the effective, peaceable, and equable realization of this natural end.

Corollary II. Any system which would defeat or render tremendously difficult the attainment of this natural purpose or which would thwart the individual's connatural right of use is forbidden by the Natural Law. Hence we condemn:

1. Socialism and communism, because they tend to create a dearth of usable goods.

2. Overrugged individualism expressed in the Liberal creed, which holds that a man may do absolutely as he pleases with his property. In using his goods a man may not disregard every consideration other than his own needs and whims. No one may abuse or destroy these

things without thought of the needs of others. No one may possess goods without accepting the social responsibility which attaches to ownership.

3. Any system which results in the concentration of wealth in the hands of the few while the great majority lack the decent comforts of human living.

C. Private Ownership of Material Goods

538. Nature commands orderly use of material goods, for such use alone will secure the end for which they were made. Since everybody cannot use everything at will, the universal right of use must be further regulated by ownership. Unless certain things are set aside as the property, at least of communities, incessant war or chaos will result. Without some kind of ownership orderly use is inconceivable.

From our refutation of communism and socialism it follows that private ownership is required for orderly use. We wish now to establish that position in a positive way.

539. We accept private ownership as a fact and seek its moral justification. Some[21] say that there is no justification of it which is universally valid, for the best that any given age has succeeded in doing is to evolve a theory of property which merely explains the current system of property holding. We think that a much more solid basis for property can be found.

540. One justifies private property by assigning to it a fitting cause. As in the case of political society (see § 846 ff.), this is not a historical investigation. We seek the juridic cause of private property. We are not interested in the historical facts which may have led men to become owners — the information is not available — but we are asking what factor in the realm of right and justice can and should be operative to produce the institution of private ownership.

541. We approach the question by distinguishing between the notion of common and the notion of proper. Common is that which is for the use of many: proper is the exclusive possession of one, either of an individual or a community. Is the bounty of nature common or proper? Everybody admits that it is common in the sense that God intends it for the use of the human race. From the certainty of common use some conclude that the bounty of nature was originally the joint *property* of all men. Some go so far even to say that it permanently remains so. This would make nature's bounty *positively common*, that is, so attached to all men that none of it could ever be the property of an individual. Such an arrangement, however, is tantamount to denial of

[21] Richard Schlatter, *Private Property*, p. 10. New Brunswick, 1951.

ownership, for if everyone were joint owners, then everyone could use everything, and we are back to chaos again. But if, to avoid this difficulty, it is suggested that civil authority should act for the joint owners and distribute from the common stock what each is to have for his exclusive use, one civil government would be required for all men, which is impossible. The doctrine is Marxism in another guise: it confuses utterly the concepts of common and proper.

542. Grotius,[22] who held that nature's bounty was the common property of all men, says that when men multiplied so that joint ownership became impracticable, men agreed to break up the common property into private holdings. The basis then of private property is contractual agreement and once the contract was made all subsequent generations are bound by it. Pufendorf[23] and Rousseau[24] subscribe to this contractual theory. The existence, however, of such a contract has not and cannot be proved.

543. Hobbes said that in the state of nature every man had a right to take and keep whatever he could prevent other men from taking from him.[25] This, however, was not ownership but struggle. When men agreed to enter society they ceded their rights to the sovereign power which their agreement created. The sovereign then became the source of all rights and private owners hold their property at the will of the sovereign.[26] Advocates of the theory of the divine rights of kings accepted the conclusion of Hobbes.[27]

544. These explanations attempt to justify private property on the ground of human convention. We maintain that private property originates in nature. We do not mean that nature gives individuals certain properties. For there are no signs of such donation. The bounty of nature, however, is *negatively common*. Although originally it is owned by no one, it can be appropriated. Communities may take from the common storehouse what hereafter they call their own. So too may individuals.

545. We justify private property, therefore, in two assertions. First, without the intervention of any human agent or human law, the Natural Law grants the individual the right to *become* an owner. When, under proper conditions, individuals exercise this right, nature approves private

---

[22] *De jure belli et pacis*, Bk. II, cc. 2, 4, 6.
[23] *De Jure Naturae et Gentium*, Bk. IV, ch. iv.
[24] *The Social Contract*, Bk. I, ch. ix.
[25] *Leviathan*, Part I, ch. xiii.
[26] *Dialogue of the Common Law*, Molesworth ed., Vol. VI, p. 29. London, 1840.
[27] Sir Robert Filmer, *Observations Concerning the Original of Government*, p. 45 ff. London, 1679.

owning. Second, the exigencies of rational living demand that in the main individuals should exercise this right and consequently private ownership is obligatory and may not be done away with.

THESIS XLI. Not only has each man an indeterminate right from the Natural Law to acquire ownership of productive goods, but some general system of private ownership is necessary.

546. In the first part we show that man has a right *to acquire* the ownership of sources of material goods without specifying what in the concrete these may be. That man has the physical power to be an owner needs no proof. It is a well-established principle flowing from the free nature of man that he has a right, the moral capacity, to do anything that lies in his physical power provided it is not forbidden by natural or positive law. In the proof of the first part we will show that there can be no natural prohibition against private owning. In the second part we will show that any positive law purporting to deny him ownership cannot be a true law.

PROOF OF PART I

547. **Each man has from the Natural Law the right to acquire the ownership of productive goods.** Permanent and exclusive control of the source of a steady supply of material goods is an act which conforms to all the essential relationships of human nature.

a) *To human nature considered in itself.* Man has recurring needs which must be satisfied by material goods and in a reasonably human way. Since he is not a wild animal, he is not to contend with his fellow man for the fulfillment of every need. Since he is not a domestic animal, his wants are to be provided for by himself. From a consideration of his free nature it follows that man is a self-provider; he himself is to procure the things he needs. But without ownership he is subject to the will, caprice, and power of others in a way that degrades the dignity and independence of his nature. Therefore, the human way for the individual to provide for his needs is by ownership of a sufficiency of productive goods.

b) *To man's relations to God.* Ownership in no way disturbs man's essential and total dependence on God.

c) *To man's relations to his fellow man.*

i) *Of individual to individual.* The control of goods for a man's own benefit without injury to his fellow man conforms to the due relation of one man to another. If the right of all men to use material goods in necessity is kept intact, no man injures another by taking to himself what antecedently had belonged to no one. Furthermore each is more content and peaceful, relations of one to another are better fostered when each has for himself his own stock of goods.

ii) *Of individual to family.* Parents have the inescapable duty of supporting, educating, and rearing to maturity all their children. Children are *immediately* dependent on their parents for these things. Parents must provide not only for immediate needs but also for future needs, that is, they must provide at least for their minor children even after their own death. The fulfillment of this duty, however, is impossible unless the head of the family may own productive goods and endow his children with these.

iii) *Of individual to society.* Private ownership is an instrument of social well-being because: nature insists that the individual provide for himself and his family and forbids that this duty be taken over by the State; every citizen should have the means of protecting himself from possible tyranny and nothing is more suitable for this than ownership of productive goods. A State will be more stable and peaceful if ownership is widely spread among its members. There is incentive to produce and conserve wealth if the rewards of personal security and ownership exist. If the production and distribution of goods is left to private initiative, the rulers of society have the leisure properly to fulfill their duty of preserving social order and providing socially necessary assistance.

iv) *Of man's relation to the material universe.* Private ownership makes man a good steward of inanimate nature, for each one is careful to preserve and increase what is his own.

PART II

548. Some general system of private ownership is necessary. Since ownership is necessary, some over-all system of ownership is requisite. In the proof of the first part of Thesis XLI we showed that men *may* own privately. Hence a system of private ownership is lawful and moral. However, that system is to be preferred which most effectively serves human needs; and, if only one system can do this, this system must be adopted. Our second proof shows that under the unalterable impact of human instincts, needs, and defects, private ownership is the only practicable system. The Natural Law, however, does not anathematize common ownership as repugnant to human nature. Common ownership can work on a small scale; and perhaps even on a universal scale if man had not been corrupted by sin. The fact of the matter is that private ownership, tempered by social control, is the one system that will work in the long run. Individuals or select groups may voluntarily surrender their right of private ownership but society is forbidden to abolish its exercise at large.

A private system is not merely one in which a few private owners are tolerated here and there; it must be an economy which takes its prevailing tone from a predominance of private owners. This would not prevent the State from owning certain goods or services wherever such ownership would better promote the common good.

Our position is not a defense of the evils of the capitalistic system. These evils are not an inevitable consequence of private ownership; they are the result of avarice, which society failed to check. These evils, moreover, are traceable to overemphasis upon the individual aspect of property to the almost total neglect of its social aspect. What social obligations attach to ownership we shall shortly explain.

PROOF

549. Some general system of private ownership is obligatory, because only under such a system can nature's purpose for material good be realized effectively, peaceably, and equitably.

a) *Effectively.* This is the only system which guarantees a sufficiency of goods because: (*i*) the individual is solicitous to preserve and *increase* only what belongs to him personally. He is incurably negligent in caring for common property. (*ii*) Man's best productive efforts can be adequately motivated only by the appeal of a personal reward. Men will make no such efforts if no such rewards are in prospect, nor will they be much concerned over the welfare of others not connected with them by a special tie.

b) *Peaceably.* (*i*) Man has a special instinct for possession, as history attests. If this instinct which is deeply rooted in man's nature is frustrated, widespread and disrupting discontent will follow. (*ii*) Nothing is so productive of friction and quarrels as joint ownership.

c) *Equitably.* (*i*) The free nature of man will resent as inequitable a status of constant and intimate dependence on the will of another, which any other system would demand. (*ii*) The obligations of parents to children demand private ownership as the necessary means of fulfillment. It would be unfair of nature to impose the obligation and withhold the necessary means of fulfilling it.

550. Corollary. The right to acquire goods is a natural right not only in the sense that nature allows a man to own privately but also in the sense that she urges him toward it. Therefore, the contention of Hobbes, Kant, and the Juridical Positivists that property rights originate in civil law is false. For if civil law instituted private property, it could likewise terminate it by introducing collectivism. But this it cannot do without destroying the peace and order of society.

D. The Actual Remedy

551. The remedy for the evils of capitalism lies in the recognition and practice of the social obligations which attach to ownership. Both the individual and society have a positive part to play in order that the remedy be effective.

552. (a) *The individual* must practice justice both in the acquisition and in the use of goods. The just means of acquiring goods are explained in the two following chapters where we speak of property titles. It is one thing, however, to acquire goods justly and another to use them properly. St. Thomas lays down this fundamental principle of use: "A man ought to possess external things, not as his own, but as common, that is, he should be ready to communicate them to others in their needs."[28] Thus he elucidates the doctrine of Aristotle that "it is clearly better that property should be private, but the use of it common; and the special business of the legislator is to create in men this benevolent disposition."[29]

553. To understand the principle that while ownership is private, use remains general, it helps if we distinguish necessary from superfluous goods. Those goods are necessary which a man needs in order to maintain the decency and dignity of his person and to fulfill his obligations as father and citizen. When goods are used in this way they fulfill their natural destination. Even these, however, are subservient to the use of another who is in extreme need.

Superfluous goods are those which are not required for the purposes just explained. It is not contrary to commutative justice that a man own superfluous goods. Social justice, however, can be violated if they are used exclusively for the advantage of the owner or neglected so that the common good suffers. For them, their primary purpose is frustrated and the reason for private ownership of them is destroyed. The purpose of private owning is to assure a responsible and orderly management of material things for the use of all. Therefore it is with regard to superfluous goods that the principle of common use should be clearly operative. But how is a man to use them so that others benefit? One

[28] *Sum. Theol.*, II–II, 66, 2.
[29] *Politics*, II, 5, 1263a.

way is by giving some of them to the needy. This is a genuine obligation of charity (see § 659). He need not, however, give them all away. For if his prudent management makes them the means whereby others obtain their living, his superfluous goods are fulfilling their natural end.

554. (*b*) *Society* must labor to spread these socioeconomic truths: that material goods are to serve human needs; that the efficient system for making goods serve human needs is private ownership tempered by social use; that the moral law governs business and politics. Justice demands that all men and nations have access to the essentials of human living; it forbids that anyone destroy the livelihood of another. Charity denies that life is class warfare and insists upon a bond of natural fellowship uniting all men.

555. Society should not merely legislate against monopolistic profiteering, starvation wages, and investment frauds, but should create conditions which will make possible three things: (1) that every man capable and willing to work be able to find gainful employment; (2) that he receive a wage which will enable him and his family to live; (3) that all men be secure in the savings which their thrift accumulates.

Such a policy will multiply the small owner and spread ownership through society as widely as possible. A society is more stable if large numbers of its citizens are economically secure. In this way there will be no undue concentration of wealth in the hands of a few with the consequent ascendancy of a selfish and irresponsible money power. However, multiplication of small owners need not mean a return to the craft age. The able and thrifty workman can be rewarded by becoming part owner of the business in which he engages.

556. To equalize the distribution of wealth, co-operative organization of society is necessary. This point will be taken up in greater detail in social ethics. Here it is sufficient to note that instead of employer associations hostilely arrayed against employee associations, there ought to be occupational associations consisting of all who make their living by the same kind of work, both owner and wage earner. If such associations were properly governed, among other things, two important results would follow. First, there would be no stoppages of the incomes of workers. Second, the management of wealth would return to its real owners. The latter would remove that evil whereby a few men, strategically placed, have been able to make world-shaking economic decisions not for the general benefit but for the interest of a few.

557. Last, society must be unsecularized. All hope of lasting improvement is a dream as long as the happiness-now attitude dominates men and nations. Civilized man must return to religion. Men are callous to the rights of their fellow man because they do not give God His due. The emphasis of life should shift from material to eternal values. The individual must reorient his life to the one end of life and convince himself that greed and injustice are insurmountable obstacles to the winning of that end. When religion again impels man to recognize his true place before God, there will be a chance that justice and charity will temper man's inhumanity to man.

But here the individual absolutely needs the help of the State. Governments themselves cannot be without religion nor can they be indifferent to the individual's efforts to attain eternal beatitude. They must realign their mighty powers to assist the over-all purpose of life. They must be rebaptized and accept again the Gospel of Jesus Christ.

READINGS

St. Thomas, *Summa Theologica*, II–II, 66, 1–2; 118, 1.
Aristotle, *Politics*, Bk. II, 3.
Bastiat, F., *The Law*. Irvington-on-Hudson, 1950.
Bochenski, I. M., "On Soviet Philosophy," *Review of Politics*, 13 (1951), 344–353.
Bray, J. F. L., *Financial Justice*. Blackfriars, 1954.
Burnham, J., *The Struggle for the World*, 57–129. New York, Day, 1947.
Chambers, W., *Witness*. New York, Random, 1952.
Cocutz, J. T., "Does Social Ownership Have Any Meaning?" *Ethics*, 64 (1953–1954), 46–50.
Cole, G. D. H., *A History of Socialist Thought*, 3 vols. London, Macmillan, 1953, 1954, 1956.
——— *The Meaning of Marxism*. London, Gollancz, 1950.
Cronin, J. F., *Catholic Social Principles*, 64–199. Milwaukee, Bruce, 1950.
De Lubac, H., "The New Man, the Marxist and the Christian View," *Cross Currents*, Fall, 1950, 67–88.
Djilas, M., *The New Class*, New York, Praeger, 1957.
Eastman, M., *Reflections on the Failure of Socialism*. New York, Devin-Adair, 1955.
Galbraith, J. K., *American Capitalism*. Boston, Houghton Mifflin, 1952.
Gurian, W., ed., *The Soviet Union*. Notre Dame, 1951.
Hazard, J. N., *The Soviet System of Government*, Chicago, University of Chicago, 1957.
Joad, C. E. M., *Guide to the Philosophy of Morals and Politics*, 664–723. London, Gollancz, 1938.
Lambek, C., *Problems of Morality and Moral Justice*, 47–86. Copenhagen, Reitzels, 1952.
Laski, H. J., *Communism*. New York, Holt, 1927.
Lippmann, W., *The Public Philosophy*, 113–181. Boston, Little, Brown, 1955.
Maclaren, D., *Private Property and the Natural Law*. Blackfriars, 1948.
Maritain, J., *Scholasticism and Politics*, 1–44. London, Bles, 1954.
Mayo, H. B., *Democracy and Marxism*. New York, Oxford, 1955.

Monnerot, J., *Sociology and Psychology of Communism*. Boston, Beacon, 1953.
Mounier, E., "A Dialogue with Communism," *Cross Currents*, Winter, 1953, 118–141.
Osgniach, A. J., *Must It Be Communism?* New York, Wagner, 1950.
Perroux, F., "From the Avarice of Nations to an Economy of Mankind," *Cross Currents*, Spring, 1953, 193–207.
Pius XII, "The Social Question in the New Order," *Catholic Mind*, 39 (June 8, 1941), 1–16.
Pontifical Academy of St. Thomas, Rome, *The Philosophy of Communism*. New York, Fordham, 1949.
Rostow, W. W., *The Dynamics of Soviet Society*. New York, Norton, 1953.
Runes, D. D., *The Soviet Impact on Society*. New York, Philosophical Library, 1953.
Sachs, A., "Rights, Promises, and Property," *Moral Principles of Action*, 228–302, ed. R. N. Anshen. New York, Harper, 1952.
Viglino, U., "The Social Function of Property and its Metaphysical Foundation," *Theology Digest*, 1 (1953), 164–168.
Voegelin, E., "The Formation of the Marxian Revolutionary Idea," *Review of Politics*, 12 (1950), 275–302.
Wayper, C. L., *Political Thought*, 194–245. New York, Philosophical Library, 1954.

Chapter XVIII PROPERTY TITLES

558. Nature gives no man any specific material goods but merely the right to acquire them. What further is required to make an individual an owner? In the general discussion of rights we saw that an abstract right, embodied in law, passes into the actual right to this particular thing through the medium of a *title.*

A *title of ownership* is some fact which concretely determines the right to own; it is the means by which the owner has the just possession of his property. This may be positive or natural. A *positive title* is some fact which the civil law defines as sufficient to create ownership. Thus, twenty years' use gives one a right of way over adjacent land. A *natural title* is a fact which by Natural Law is capable of determining ownership. This title is *original* when a thing which hitherto belonged to no one now becomes the property of some owner. It is *derived* when a new owner succeeds to property previously held.

559. Before discussing which are the facts constituting natural titles, we must first discover the most basic of these titles. This will be the *primordial title,* upon which every other title, original or derived, rests. Our question is not precisely historical but rather juridical. We are seeking the fact which ought to have been present to justify the first owner's acquisition of property. Since, however, in this instance the historical and the juridical coincide, the primordial title explains the *lawful* origin of property — how goods offered in common to all could first become the property of someone.

560. Absolutely speaking, the primordial title to material objects is *productive causality.* This is God's title to the visible universe. Man, however, cannot create. If he could create something out of nothing, it would be his, and his act of creation would be his primordial title to it. But man can only produce changes in matter already pre-existent. From this principle of productive causality a man certainly has a right to the new values he evolves by his labor, provided the matter with which he works is his. The question of primordial title, then, reduces itself to this: How does man first come to possess those materials without which he can make nothing?

I. THE PRIMORDIAL TITLE

THESIS XLII. The natural primordial title of private ownership is effective occupation.

561. Occupation is the real and permanent seizure of a thing capable of being owned with the intent to acquire original dominion over it. This demands (*a*) *on the part of the thing,* that it be physically capable of becoming someone's exclusive property and that it now belong to no one; (*b*) *on the part of the occupier,* that he intend to make this thing permanently and exclusively his own and in some appropriate way signify this intention to others. Of itself, however, a mere intention to acquire ownership and the expression of this will to others is not enough to make one an owner. There must be a real seizure of the thing — its effective occupation. A fisherman does not become the owner of an uncaught fish by pointing to it and telling his companions not to touch it; he must catch it. Hence, occupation is effective when the thing is actually subjected to the physical force of a person for his own proper use. What we cannot effectively control we cannot be said to occupy and own.

PROOF

562. The primordial title of private ownership is that fact whereby something of nature's bounty, offered to men indeterminately, may legitimately become the property of some individual. This fact can only be effective occupation. In order that things as yet belonging to nobody and capable of appropriation may pass to some private owner, effective occupation is *required.* A moral connection must be established between this object and this person which makes it evident that this thing is subjected to this person and all other persons are excluded from its ownership. But without effective occupation this is impossible. *Nothing more is required.* Since the individual has a natural right to own, he exercises this right over goods which as yet belong to no one by simply pre-empting them. Once he has effectively occupied them they are his.

563. **What can be occupied?** Man may not occupy that which is for the common good of all nor such quantities of other things which cannot be used or effectively controlled. Since everything has practically passed into the possession of some owner, occupancy is now restricted to genuinely lost articles, treasure-troves, derelicts, fish, and wild beasts.

The civil law adds further refinements to this prescription of the Natural Law and the observance of these conditions binds in conscience, at least, after judicial decision.

II. SUBORDINATE TITLES

Here we briefly examine the other facts which according to Natural Law constitute true titles of ownership. Contract is reserved for special consideration.

A. Labor

564. Labor is the exercise of bodily or mental activity. It is unreasonable to restrict this term to bodily effort. Locke and Marx said that labor is the primordial title, but this is not true in the sense that labor of itself gives one title to the material in which he works. It is true that labor, in so far as it makes occupation effective, participates in the nature of occupation.

Labor is a *natural title to its own proper fruits*, because, since man is the master of his power, he is the owner of the products of his power.

B. Gift

565. Gift is the gratuitous placing of ownership in the hands of another. That gift is a natural legitimate title follows from the very notion of ownership. That plenary control, which is ownership, is the power to dispose of the thing as one pleases — which surely includes giving the thing away. No higher law forbids this for otherwise a man could not fulfill many obligations of charity.

C. Hereditary Succession

566. Hereditary succession is legitimate succession to the dominion of a thing upon the death of the former owner. A person who prior to the death of the owner has the right to become the future owner is called an *heir*. Before the owner's death the heir has what the Romans called a *jus ad rem*, that is a right to become the owner of these goods. Upon the owner's death, the *jus ad rem* becomes a *jus in re*, or a right in or over the decedent's goods. Property so transferred is an inheritance; the right of an heir is the right of inheritance. There are two ways in which one may be an heir: (*a*) by a *will* made in one's favor and (*b*) by blood relationship to the former owner. The first way is bequest; the second, intestate succession.

Any form of hereditary succession is anathema to socialists and communists. They would introduce a collectivist regime by the simple device of suppressing all hereditary succession. Does the Natural Law approve of this mode of acquiring property?

567. Bequest, or the title obtained by a will. A *will* is the voluntary and revocable declaration of an owner concerning the final disposition of his goods to become effective at his death. How are goods actually transferred by a will? One opinion holds that the testator makes the transfer of goods at the moment of making the will but does so conditionally. There are two conditions: (*a*) that the owner not revoke his declaration before death and (*b*) that the owner die. When both of these conditions are fulfilled, the ownership of the heir which hitherto was conditional becomes absolute. According to the other opinion, the testamentary act of the testator virtually perdures until the last moment of his life, and in the moment of death his act of the will so perduring effects the transfer of dominion.

That *bequest is a natural title* is clear for these reasons:

a) *The nature of ownership*, which is stable and permanent dominion. Such absolute right of control is the right to dispose of the thing not only in the present but also to determine its use in the future.

b) *The need of social order and progress.* If a man could not name the persons who would succeed to his property, two consequences would follow. There would be strife and contention over his possessions at his death or, in the event that everything would go to the State, very few would bother to leave anything.

c) *The need of the family.* One of the chief reasons for private property is the well-being of the family. The Natural Law obliges the head of the family to provide not only for present but also for the future needs of his family. Hence he is to make provision for them for the time after his death by endowing them with a sufficiency of goods.

568. Intestate succession. When a person possessed of property dies without having disposed of it by will, he dies intestate (from the Latin *intestatus*, not having made a will), and his nearest blood relations succeed according to the provisions of civil law.

The Natural Law endows the immediate family with the right to succeed to the property of one who dies intestate. Positive law provides that blood relatives become the heirs of an intestate who has no immediate family. The reason for this prescription of the Natural Law is that if the father is obliged to bequeath sufficient of his goods to his wife and children, these dependents must succeed to his property if he dies without a will. There is no need of presuming that an intestate descendant had the will to leave his property to his family, because even if he had not intended to do so, his obligation to endow his family would bind nevertheless. They are the continuation of his personality, and in virtue of that fact they become the owners of his goods. Besides, these goods were not gathered for himself alone but for himself and the continuation of himself in his family. Since as parent he is responsible for his children coming into existence, he is likewise responsible to provide for their continuance in existence and their well-being until they can fully care for themselves.

D. Accession

569. Accession is a title whereby the owner of a thing acquires a right to the products of that thing and to whatever is united to it in a supplementary way either naturally or artificially. Taken in the first sense of a right to natural products, accession is clearly granted by the Natural Law. *Res fructificat domino:* the owner is entitled to any increase of his property resulting from its own natural activities such as the yield of plants, the offspring of animals. In the latter case, positive law usually decides that in the absence of a more specific agreement between the interested parties, where the parent animals belong to different owners, the offspring belong to the owner of the female parent.

Taken in the second sense of inseparable accessory union, accession derives from positive law which recognizes four kinds: (*a*) accretion of land to land (alluvion), for example, soil carried by a river from one bank to another; (*b*) addition of movables to land (fixtures), for example, a tree planted on another man's land; (*c*) union of movables with movables (commixture or confusion), for example, mingling one man's grain with the grain of another man; (*d*) conversion of one man's materials into another form by a man who thinks the materials are his own (specification), for example, bread baked with another man's flour. Positive law follows the principle that the total thing belongs to the owner of the principal object. The questions, then, to be settled in law and conscience are: Which substance is of principal importance? and What compensation is to be made to the owner of the accessory object?

E. Prescription

570. Prescription is a mode of acquiring (*a*) property or equivalent rights through long continued use or (*b*) freedom from juridic obligation through a creditor's nonuse of his right. In the jurisprudences founded on Roman law, the former is acquisitive, the latter liberative prescription. In jurisprudences of the English tongue, it is known as limitations.

In the acquisition of property and similar rights, prescription means that through innocent and continuous possession of a thing, a non-owner, under conditions prescribed by law, becomes its lawful owner. It is not accurate to say that the mere lapse of time extinguishes an old right or creates a new one. Only the lawgiver can erase the right of the first owner and concede his thing to the actual possessor or user.

571. The requisite conditions for prescription are five:

1. The thing must be capable of becoming private property and is *not protected against prescription by law.* Civil and canon law[1] enumerate a variety of things which may not be acquired by prescription. In the United States public property is imprescriptible: there is no adverse possession against the State.[2]

2. *A person must actually use or possess the thing as an owner.* One must so act toward the thing that other men may infer that he is the owner. One hardly acts as the owner of real property if he does not record his holdings with the proper public official. One's use or possession must be open, continuous, and peaceable. Litigation bars peaceable possession.

3. *The thing must be possessed in good faith.* In acquisitive prescription, possession is begun and continued without reasonable doubt concerning one's right to the thing. In liberative prescription, good faith means that the one being released from obligation is not aware of this obligation, or, if aware, does nothing to impede the right of the creditor. Bad faith, or knowledge that one is acting against another's right, cannot found a true title in the forum of conscience though it may in civil law if it is not discovered.

4. *There must be sufficient title.* Sufficient title is some fact, actual or presumed, which gives the prescribing agent fair reason to think the thing is his. He can have only an apparent title because, either the fact had some hidden flaw which prevented it from being a true title, or a sufficiently valid fact was thought to exist whereas it did not. His title cannot be a good title, because originally a right did not pass to him. Without some apparent title, good faith is impossible.

5. *There must be a lapse of time* sufficient to justify the prudent judgment that the former owner or creditor has abdicated his right. Diverse jurisdictions indicate varying periods of time for various rights. For realty rights in this country, the time is about twenty years; for movables, about six years. Some jurisdictions grant to one who has in good faith come into possession of a particular movable, which has not been stolen from nor lost by an owner, absolute ownership against

[1] Cf. *Codex Juris Canonici,* 1509.

[2] *Bouvier's Law Dictionary,* "Limitations," p. 726, col. 1, Baldwin's ed., 1934.

any third party.[3] This period of time, however, does not run against one laboring under an inability to sue, such as infants, married women, the insane, the imprisoned, those out of the State.

572. Reason demands that States make such laws for the peace and good order of society. Without them litigation would be endless; owners unable to prove their claims because of lost documents or deceased witnesses would be dispossessed; it would be impossible to buy land or make similar contracts for nobody would risk attempting to buy things the ownership of which would always be subject to contest. The title of prescription is rather of positive law except in the case of an immemorial holding the beginnings of which are completely unknown. Such a title is of the Natural Law.

573. To avail oneself in good conscience of statutes of limitation, one must distinguish between cases in which the law affects the title to property and cases in which it merely bars a legal remedy. In the former, if the old right is extinguished, one may in conscience take advantage thereof. This is clearly true in bankruptcy cases, for the lawgiver intends to give the bankrupt a fresh start in life. In the latter where the law merely limits the time wherein one may seek a legal remedy for damages one may also in conscience take advantage of them. For the fact that the injured party made no effort to seek redress when he might have done so within the allotted time is reasonably presumed to be a condonation. However, this does not apply to the nonpayment of money debts contracted for goods, services, and the like. For such is the conviction of men of upright conscience: American courts have ruled that in contracts for the payment of money there is no such thing as adverse possession of money, that the statute simply affects the remedy, not the debt.[4]

[3] Vermeersch, *Theol. Moral.*, Vol. II, p. 339, Bruges, Beyaert, 1924.
[4] *Bouvier's Law Dictionary*, p. 720, col. 3.

READINGS

Bouvier's Law Dictionary, articles on Title, Occupancy, Patent, Copyright, Trademark, Gift, Donatio Inter Vivos, Donatio Mortis Causa, Devise, Bequest, Will, Inheritance, Intestate, Accession, Prescription.

Brown, R. A., *The Law of Personal Property*, 1–180, 698–804. Chicago, Callaghan, 1955.

Burby, W. E., *Handbook of the Law of Real Property*. St. Paul, West, 1954.

Corpus Juris, "Accession," Vol. I, 382–390; "Gifts," Vol. 28, 617–706; "Occupation," Vol. 46, 895–898; "Prescription," Vol. 49, 1334–1336; "Wills," Vol. 68, 381–448.

Davis, H. A., *Moral and Pastoral Theology*, Vol. II, 253–265. New York, Sheed & Ward, 1936.

Holland, T. E., *Jurisprudence*, 13 ed., 216–222, 233–242. Oxford, Clarendon, 1937.
Jarrett, B., *Social Theories of the Middle Ages*, 150–180. Westminster, Newman, 1942.
Powell, R. R., *The Law of Real Property*, Vol. I. Albany, Bender, 1949.
Sparks, B. M., *Contracts to Make Wills*. New York, New York University, 1955.
Wormser, R. A., *Your Will*. New York, Simon and Schuster, 1937.

Chapter XIX CONTRACT

The most common way by which people acquire property rights is by contract. Contract is at the core of business life and is one of the chief concerns of the civil law.

I. NATURE OF A CONTRACT

574. There is a tendency among modern writers on civil law to omit all reference to right from their definition of contract and to say that a contract is "a promise or set of promises, for the breach of which the law gives a remedy, or the performance of which the law in some way recognizes as a duty."[1] The civil law's point of view is generally that of a judge settling disputes, and he views a contract as an *unfulfilled* promise which a defendant should be compelled to honor.

Although our primary concern is with conscience, we need to consider the part played by civil law. Of the many rules about contract made by civil law, some are of Natural Law; some are clarifications, necessary for the common good, of matters which are obscure in Natural Law; others have a purely positive origin. The first and second classes of rules always bind the conscience; the third, only after the decision of a judge. It is significant that the Church is careful to observe what local positive law prescribes about contract unless a given rule should violate a higher law.[2]

575. Our point of view is that of a man examining his conscience before recourse to civil law. His first problem is to determine whether an agreement he made binds from justice or fidelity. Agreements, such as social engagements, whose binding force is mere fidelity are not contracts; contract is an agreement which passes a right to a promisee and establishes an obligation in commutative justice in a promisor.

A contract is a form of juridic act. A juridic act is the external manifestation of a will which seeks to found, change, transfer, or extin-

[1] Williston-Thompson, *Selections from Williston's Treatise on the Law of Contracts*, p. 1. New York, Baker-Voorhis, 1938.

[2] *Codex Juris Canonici*, Canon 1529.

guish juridic relations in accordance with law. The act may be one-sided, wherein only one party is active, as in the making of a will. If it is two-sided, requiring the mutual assent of two or more parties, it is a contract. By Natural Law, then, a contract is a free and mutual agreement of two or more parties concerning the transfer of a right.

Our discussion will include (*a*) the nature of agreement, (*b*) the object of agreement, (*c*) the cause of agreement, (*d*) the parties to the agreement, (*e*) the effects of agreement.

A. The Agreement

576. Agreement is a consent, a coming to a mutual arrangement. This necessarily involves a thinking and a willing of the same thing by distinct parties. The agreement originates in an offer made by a promisor who expresses his willingness to be bound to a performance. The offer must be definite and communicated to a promisee. An illusory or uncommunicated offer is no offer. Nor do preliminary negotiations or an invitation to deal constitute an offer. Acceptance of the offer by the promisee, who may or may not bind himself to a commensurate undertaking, produces the agreement. Acceptance renders the deal *of itself* irrevocable. Anything which would prevent a genuine meeting of minds and wills makes agreement impossible; for no new bond of justice can rise between private parties except such as those of which they are aware and willingly assume. By Natural Law, then, agreement demands sufficient knowledge and assent of will by both parties.

577. **Sufficient knowledge.** Unless both parties have knowledge of one and the same object of agreement, they cannot agree. Such knowledge is vitiated by error or mistake. Error may be substantial or accidental.

a) *Substantial error* affects the very substance of the agreement. This happens: when the error concerns the *object* of consent; e.g., I propose to buy one car and the seller has in mind another car; when it touches the *kind* of agreement; e.g., I take money which I think is a gift but which the giver thinks a loan; when it touches the *reason* without which agreement would not be contemplated; e.g., I place an order in this store *solely* because I think I can get a discount. *Substantial error invalidates a proposed contract* because the fundamental basis of agreement is lacking.

b) *Accidental error* does not touch the substance of the thing agreed upon but only incidental points. However, that which is expressly stipulated, even though it may appear of small moment, belongs to the substance of the agreement. Accidental error does not invalidate an agreement, for there is a sufficient meeting of minds. Hence it has no effect on an unbreakable contract. If, however, one has entered a voidable contract deceived by the guile, or even the *innocent misrepresentations* of the other party even touching minor points, the one deceived may seek an annulment of the agreement.

Civil law has an important variation. It recognizes as invalidating a mutual mistake, the mistake of one party which is known to the other, but not the mistake of one party alone. The reason is that anyone could repudiate a contract by alleging he made a mistake and hence in practice all contracts would be imperiled.

578. True and internal consent of the will. A contract is a kind of private law imposing obligations in justice. Hence no one can be said to contract who does not will to accept the obligation. However, acceptance of obligation is compatible with an intention not to fulfill it.

Here is another difference between civil and Natural Law. Whereas the latter demands true internal consent for a contract, the former does not. "In some branches of the law, especially in criminal law, a person's secret intent is important, but in the formation of contracts it was long ago settled that secret intent was immaterial."[3] The civil law is justified in holding the author of a fictitious consent to a performance because "the legislator can supply for the lack of consent by authoritative decision in the interest of the common welfare."[4]

Fictitious consent, however, is no consent by Natural Law. If an innocent party suffers loss because of a fictitious consent, he must be recompensed for his loss. The effective method of doing this will often be the establishment, by true consent, of the contract which was initially defective.

If a person is prevented from making a free choice, his consent is null. *Duress*, which is irresistible, and fear, which takes away the use of reason, nullify consent. *Undue influence*, or abuse of a position of confidence or authority so as to take unfair advantage of another's weakness of mind, distress, or necessity, does not nullify consent but affords grounds for rescinding it. Grave fear, even though it is a motive *sine qua non* of one's consent, does not invalidate consent, for the act is voluntary. Such fear, unjustly brought to bear so as to exact consent, is a reason for rescinding consent. However, when one becomes free of the duress or intimidation he may ratify his original consent.

579. Consent must be mutual. Consent is mutual when (*a*) the

[3] *Selections from Williston on Contracts*, p. 20.

[4] Heribert Jone, *Moral Theology*, trans. by Adelman, p. 199, 2 ed. Westminster, Newman, 1956.

assent of one is accorded because of, or with a view to, the assent of the other. If two parties casually or coincidentally determine to do the same thing, no contractual obligation arises. Mutuality of consent requires also (*b*) that offer and acceptance simultaneously fall upon the same object. There must be an unconditional acceptance corresponding exactly to the offer. A proposal to buy a building lot for one hundred and twenty-five dollars is not acceptance of an offer to sell the same for two hundred dollars. A conditional acceptance is construed by civil law as a counterproposal and hence as a rejection of the original offer. (*c*) Offer and acceptance must be mutual in time, that is, the offer must still be open when the other party accepts. The duration of an offer depends on the will of the offeror. He may withdraw it before acceptance, but for his withdrawal to be valid it must first come to the notice of the promisee. While the offeror may rightly consider rejection the termination of his offer, he may still choose to keep it open. Besides rejection and express revocation, offers terminate by lapse of specified time or of a reasonable time if no time limit has been stated.

580. What knowledge should each party have of the other's assent? A problem of communication arises when the parties are at a distance. At what precise time does a contract arise? Is it when the second party signifies assent, when his assent reaches the offeror, or when the offeror learns of the acceptance? American law chooses the first alternative if communication is by mail. The reason is that once an offeror has embodied his mind and will in a proposal communicated to the promisee, this expression must not only stand for, but it must *be* his mind and will, as far as outward relations go, until he substitute for it another sign of his mind and will. This substitution, however, would not take effect until knowledge of the change reached the promisee. When to the mind and will of the offeror the promisee joins a definitive and communicated expression of his mind and will, an agreement is effected, even though actually the offeror has withdrawn his offer or the letter is never delivered. It is argued against this position that it does not take into consideration bilateral contracts[5] wherein both parties are promisors. According to this view acceptance is complete only when the promise of the second party reaches the offeror. The question is a thorny one to which the Natural Law has no clear answer. The first view is probably correct but in any event one must follow the ruling of positive law.

581. Consent must be externalized. Internal acceptance does not

[5] A unilateral contract is a promise for an act. After acceptance by the act obligation rests only on one party. A bilateral contract is a promise for a promise. After mutual acceptance obligation rests on both parties.

suffice. Since in a contract some right passes which can be effected only by communication, acceptance must be signified by an external act. This outward expression may be writing, words, signs, or merely one's course of action. Sometimes silence may be a sufficient sign of assent. So long as a true and mutual consent is externalized, the Natural Law does not demand any particular *form* for the validity of a contract. In some contracts positive law demands the observance of certain formalities. Failure to observe such a prescribed form can make a contract null from the beginning, as is seen in the marriage contract. As for civil contracts lacking proper form, they are probably valid in conscience before a court has passed on them.

B. The Object of Agreement

582. In a broad sense an object of agreement is that which the parties agree to do or not to do. Sometimes the term *object of agreement* indicates what the offeror undertakes, and that which the promisee contributes is called *consideration*. This discussion includes both object of agreement and consideration. What kind of thing may be the object of contract?

(1) The object of contract must be *possible*, that is, capable of realization without undue difficulty. (2) It must *exist* — either in actuality or probability, such as newly sown crops. (3) It must be *capable of precise determination*, or if in the terms of agreement it is not so determined, it is likened to the nonexistent. (4) It must be of *estimable value* — a thing, advantage, service, or omission which is useful to another. (5) The thing must be *capable of transfer* and be *the property of the one transferring it*. Accordingly, one cannot contract to give another that which already belongs to him in justice. (6) It cannot be *immoral*, that is, contrary to Natural or positive law. No one can give or acquire the right to do that which is sinful.

583. Contracts for immoral acts present a difficulty. If an immoral act is agreed upon for a price, all agree that no contract exists before the immoral act is performed. Both parties are obliged to withdraw. But if the immoral act is performed, must the price be paid? Some hold that there is no obligation to pay, that if the price has been paid it should be returned. They contend that the contract was initially invalid and remains invalid all the way through. The view of the civil law is that "agreements that are illegal or contrary to public policy are void. Courts treat them as if they never existed."[6] Public justice has no other course; otherwise it would encourage immorality. Nevertheless, most moralists say that the beneficiary of such an immoral act is bound

[6] Bergh-Connynton, *Business Law*, p. 104, 5 ed. New York, Ronald, 1956.

to pay in natural justice.[7] The reason is that, although the agreement was an invalid contract, yet it had the effect of estimating the price of the act, not as immoral but as useful, laborious, or pleasure-giving. The positing of the immoral act brings into existence, a latent contract; since the onerous part of a contract has been fulfilled, justice demands the price of it be paid.

Since, however, the opposite opinion has extrinsic probability, it follows that (*a*) one cannot be obliged to pay, because it is probable that no contract exists; (*b*) a person who has been paid may keep the price, because it is probable that a contract does exist.

584. *Bribery* is offering or taking valuable consideration for wrongdoing. It has special but not exclusive reference to the performance of public duty. If the bribe is given with the *stipulation* that a wrong act be done, the rules given above apply. If there is not even a tacit stipulation, what is offered is technically a gift, but a gift tainted by the wrong hope and intention of the giver. Could one take such a gift if he makes no promise and does not intend to do the wrong act? Theoretically one could keep the gift if doing so does not constitute scandal or proximate danger of sinning oneself. In practice, however, if one understands why the gift is offered, it is hard to see how the donee escapes co-operating in the other's sin. "With difficulty," says De Lugo, "may [the donee] be excused from a sin of scandal and uncharitableness; because acceptance is itself the reason why the other gives."[8] In the case of public officials there is the added consideration that he would compromise his freedom of acting impartially.

C. The Cause of Agreement

585. In every contract there is a *cause,* that is, an immediate and *proximate* reason why a contracting party divests himself of a right or assumes a juridic obligation. Some cause is essential to every contract; otherwise, there is no rational explanation for the surrender of a right. Because it exists within the pact, this cause is intrinsic to the contract. Thus a buyer gives or promises to give a sum of money to a seller because the latter gives or promises to give him a house. The promise or the giving of the seller is the cause of the buyer's contractual act and vice versa as far as the seller's act is concerned.

In many contracts this immediate and intrinsic cause is also the impelling *motive.* Workmen enter a wage contract to obtain the salary promised. Merchants sell their goods to receive the price. However, an

---

[7] Genicot-Salsmans, *Institutiones Theologiae Moralis,* 14th ed., Vol. I, § 584.
[8] *De Justitia et Jure,* disp. 18, n. 50.

impelling motive may be some more remote reason which stands outside the contract itself. For example, a builder may put up a public building for a sum of money (the cause) which nets him no profit, his motive in accepting the undertaking being prestige.

The cause of agreement may be consideration or liberality.

586. Consideration. The word consideration has come into the jurisprudence of English-speaking countries from the Latin. In that tongue it meant the compensation given the victim of an unfulfilled promise which the law did not recognize as contractual. The word now signifies the *quid pro quo* — that worth-while thing which the offeror is to obtain from the other party. This thing may be something of advantage to the offeror; it is always of detriment to the promisee. It consists of any abatement of one's right or any inconvenience which one agrees to suffer *with a view to obtaining* what the offeror proffers. It is the price which the offeror asks for the carrying out of his part of the bargain. When, therefore, something is done, promised, foreborne, or suffered by the promisee because of the promise made to him and at the instance of the offeror, that something is consideration.[9]

From what we saw in § 585, consideration is not to be confused with motive nor with the object of agreement (cf. § 582).

There is a distinction between *good consideration* and *valuable consideration*. The former consists of natural love and affection and the latter, money or what is reducible to money value.

Is consideration of the essence of every contract?

587. The Civil Law. Blackstone defines a contract as an agreement upon sufficient consideration to do or not to do a particular thing.[10] Sitting judges reduce the element of a contract to the bare statement — a promise for a consideration. English-speaking jurisprudence reduces all contracts to two categories: those drawn under seal, or specialty contracts,

---

[9] American legal opinion defines consideration as "that which moves from the promisee or a third person, at the request of the promisee, to the promisor or a third person designated by the promisor, at the express or implied request of the latter, in return for his promise" (in W. L. Clark, *Handbook of the Law of Contracts*, p. 147. St. Paul, West, 1931, 4 ed.). We think, in accordance with the Roman and English view of contract, that both references to a third party should be expunged because, strictly, contractual obligations fall upon, and rights accrue to, only those who are parties to the contract. The Romans clearly distinguished between the act of contract itself and obligations which arise out of contract. Rights may arise to a third party from a contractual promise: these rights the civil law may be willing to protect but they should be considered as outside the contract itself. Since consideration is a cause of contract and intrinsic to it, the concept of consideration should not include what lies outside the contract.

[10] *Commentaries*, 2, 442.

and those not drawn under seal, or simple or parol contracts. When the agreement has been drawn under seal, the law does not look for consideration; it presumes it to be present. But the presumption is rebuttable, for there are instances where agreements under seal have been nullified because no consideration was proved to exist. When the agreement is not drawn under seal, the law demands *valuable consideration.* This may not be something illegal or already due in justice. Past consideration, that is, an act performed before the agreement was entered into, is no consideration. If I promise you ten dollars for having recovered my wallet no contract exists in the eyes of the law. If I promise you ten dollars if you recover my wallet, and you do so, there is a contract. The consideration need not be adequate, that is, it need not be a commensurate return, but it must be of some value. Therefore, this general rule of civil law may be formulated: *no valuable consideration, no contract.* However, exceptional instances do exist in which the law will enforce gratuitous promises, but positive jurisprudence does not wish to call such promises contractual.

588. **The Natural Law.** Can the offeror be bound in justice by agreements wherein he obtains nothing, in the broadest sense, out of them for himself? The offeror can be bound if such is his intention. Therefore, by Natural Law we can distinguish an onerous from a gratuitous contract. In the former, consideration must exist: something must pass back to the offeror. In a gratuitous contract, obligation affects only one party: the offeror gives or promises to give; the promisee merely accepts — he neither gives nor does anything in return. Hence according to the Natural Law an agreement in which no consideration passes back to the offeror is a true contract, because a man may divest himself of a right without exacting compensation.

The civil law with good reason refuses to recognize promises as valid without consideration. If the offeror receives no benefit, and if the other party gives up nothing, may not one well question that the offeror binds himself *in justice* to perform? That he should do so for those he loves or from whom he expects affection is understandable. The cause of his transfer of right then is good consideration. But if there is no return either of affection or other value, the civil law presumes that the offeror does not bind himself in justice but in fidelity. A sound view of human nature is implied here. The fact remains, however, that men can and do bind themselves in justice without hope of return of advantage, and when they do so a natural contract arises, the cause of which is the *liberality of the offeror.* Such an agreement is binding in conscience even though unenforceable in the courts.

D. The Parties to the Agreement

589. 1. At least two distinct parties are required for a contract. No one contracts with himself, nor can a part of a corporation or moral person make a contract with another part of the same corporation. For commutative justice is always between other and other.

There may be more than one party to either side of a contract. These will be joint contractors: those who are jointly bound to fulfill the obligations of the contract are joint debtors.

2. The Natural Law demands that at the time of contract one have the free use of reason in order to be competent to contract. This excludes infants, the insane, and the drunk.

The positive law of English-speaking countries defines an infant as anyone who has not completed his twenty-first year. Recognizing that it must protect such persons from their own folly and improvidence, it holds that they are not bound to contracts which they make except those which supply necessities and that upon coming of age they may fulfill other contracts at their discretion or void them within a reasonable time. The question arises as to whether they may in conscience avail themselves of the law in their favor. Generally speaking they may, but two things are to be noticed: (*a*) they must in conscience pay for *benefits received* even through contracts void at law; (*b*) when they contract in bad faith, as when they would fraudulently misrepresent their age so as to enter a contract they intend to repudiate, they must make good the *damage sustained* by the other party. One traffics with an infant at his peril.

Up to most recent times, the contractual capacity of a married woman was practically nil, for the law looked on her civil existence as merged with that of her husband. In this country she could contract for ordinary household matters, manage her own estate, and, where a court had constituted her a feme-sole trader, engage in commerce. The tendency now is greatly to enlarge the freedom of women.

3. One must be juridically free to contract; neither the Natural nor positive law places an invalidating obstacle in the way of this person entering this contract. Thus a diriment impediment either of Natural or ecclesiastic law renders an attempted marriage contract null from the beginning. It is doubtful whether other contracts declared null by positive law are also null in conscience before a court has passed upon them.

E. The Effects of Contract

590. The effect of contract is, first, to impose an obligation in justice

of fulfilling the part each has assumed. One must carry out his part in the manner which equity, usage, and law require. It is unjust to refuse performance simply because the other party cannot prove the contract or the law bars an action. Second, one must repair damage done to the other party by sinful neglect or delay in one's performance.

The gravity of the obligation depends on the seriousness of the issue involved. Some say that primarily "the gravity of the obligation accords with the will of the parties which is the law which they arbitrarily impose on themselves."[11] However, since the mean of virtue in justice is something objective, it would seem that grave matter always calls for grave obligation. It is true that the parties could bind themselves only venially in a grave matter but they would not then be contracting. Their promise would bind only in fidelity. For, in a contract a right passes, and if the right is to something of grave matter, the obligation is also grave.

591. Obligation terminates not only upon fulfillment but also upon mutual agreement to end it, to merge one contract in another, to transfer one's rights to a third party; also, when one party rescinds the agreement for just cause; when the object of agreement has become impossible of fulfillment; when one party has substantially breached the agreement. If one party has substantially altered the terms, the other may elect either to terminate or insist upon the original agreement. The operation of law, such as laws of prescription or bankruptcy, also terminates obligation.

II. KINDS OF CONTRACT

We may classify contracts either as (*a*) *gratuitous*, if benefit accrues merely to the promisee or (*b*) *onerous*, if benefit and obligation devolve on both parties.

A. Gratuitous Contracts

592. If one so desires he may divest himself of a right without receiving anything in return. This is not a violation of justice because injustice is not done to one who willingly suffers a curtailment of what is his. The equality of justice which is demanded in a gratuitous contract is that, over and above the thing freely given by the offeror, nothing of estimable value is *exacted* by him in return. Noteworthy among such contracts are promise, gift, deposit, and loans.

593. **Promise.** A promise accepted is an offer accepted; and when the promisor binds himself in justice, there exists a true contract even though no valuable consideration is given for the promise. It is often

[11] Regatillo-Zalba, *Theologiae Moralis Summa*, Vol. II, p. 601. Madrid, 1953.

difficult to distinguish between a mere promise or intention to confer favor and a promise of contract. Usually men do not bind themselve contractually by a gratuitous promise unless they fortify the promis with a certain solemnity such as an oath, chosen witnesses, or a publi instrument of conveyance. It ultimately comes to this: What did th promisor intend at the time of his promise? In a doubtful case he nee do only what is of certain obligation.

594. **Gift** is the gratuitous transfer of property to another. It bind the conscience of the donor when the offer is accepted and any stip lated conditions are fulfilled. Title then passes irrevocably; and even the beneficiary should later prove ungrateful, the donor has no ground for recovering his gift.

595. **Deposit** is a contract whereby one accepts a movable of anothe to keep it *gratis* until the owner calls for it. The depositee is bound t safeguard it with the care and skill which any prudent man would exe cise. He must deliver it upon demand together with its increase. If it ha perished or deteriorated because of his culpable negligence, he must mak good the loss. He may not use it without the owner's consent, which however, he may reasonably presume. He may even use money, if he certain he can repay the deposit when demanded; and he may retai any profit arising from his own industry. He is entitled to recompens for any expense undergone or any damage suffered because of the deposi

When the depositee acts for pay, the contract ceases to be gratuitou and his obligation to safeguard the thing increases proportionately. W then have the contract of *caretaking.*

596. **Loans** are of two kinds, loans for use and loans for consumptio

Loans for use are contracts whereby an owner gives another gratis th use of a thing for a certain time with the understanding that this exac thing is to be returned. The borrower must bestow great care on th thing, see to its ordinary upkeep, and return it at the agreed time. If perishes through no fault of his, he has no obligation to make it goo unless such an obligation was included in the contract. Ordinaril however, this is included, especially if the thing is of great value. Th lender may not seek it before the agreed time unless some unforesee emergency arise. If the lender is paid, the loan is the onerous contrac of *lease.*

Loans for consumption are contracts whereby a fungible — a thin which is consumed in its first use — is given *gratis* to another with th understanding that an equivalent in kind is to be returned. This diffe from the first kind of loan in two ways: in the former the thing len does not become the property of the borrower and the identical thin must be restored; in loans for consumption the thing handed over becomes the property of the borrower who is not expected to return the identical thing but its equivalent in kind.

597. Can there be a similar agreement which constitutes an onerous contract? That the borrower should freely offer a price for his borrowing and that this be accepted by the lender in no way violates justice. But may the lender *demand* a price before making the loan? He may not *in virtue of the loan itself.* Once he gets back the equivalent of his thing, justice is fulfilled. Hence to charge the borrower a price for the loan is to commit the sin of usury forbidden by the Natural Law.

598. **What is usury?** People think of usury as the charging of excessive interest upon money loaned. Excessive interest is wrong but it is not necessarily the Natural Law sin of usury. Nor does usury consist in taking advantage of another's necessity. If this were so, then it would be lawful to demand usurious tribute of one who could afford to pay it. Reviving an opinion of Broedersen of the eighteenth century and of Jannet of the nineteenth century, Hilaire Belloc defines usury as "any interest however high or low demanded for an unproductive loan."[12] The inference from this opinion is that if the borrower makes a profit on a loan, the lender is entitled to a share of the profit. As far as the claims of the lender are concerned, it makes no difference whether the loan is productive or unproductive. The profit which the borrower makes from the thing lent is no reason for the lender exacting a share of the profit. To do so is to take what belongs to another, for once the thing is lent it belongs to the borrower. It increases to him alone, or it perishes to him.

Usury exists only where there is the loan of a fungible and its malice consists in a party's demanding precisely because of the loan that a greater quantity of the thing loaned be returned. A person is unjust who *lends* a case of whisky and demands back twenty-five bottles. The injustice consists in demanding back his loan and an extra something to which he has no title, namely, a price for the loan or profit from the thing loaned. First, he cannot charge for the use because the use and substance of a fungible are identified. If the seller of bread were to make two separate contracts of sale, one for the substance of the bread, the other for the use of the bread, he would be unjust because he would be selling in the second contract what does not exist. Second, both the use and the profit from the loan are the property of the borrower: one cannot claim what is the property of another. Usury, then, is the unjust price exacted for the loan of a fungible.

[12] *Essays of a Catholic,* 32. London, Sheed & Ward, 1931.

But may not the lender charge the borrower for service rendered just as a common carrier demands fare of a passenger? If making the loan costs the lender nothing, he may not charge; if it costs him something, he may. Labor and expense may be involved; the lender may lose the chance of making some profitable use of the thing; there may be danger of losing the thing entirely, a risk which the lender assumes. These reasons are extrinsic to the loan but whenever any one of them is present the lender may indemnify himself by making a reasonable charge on the borrower.

599. Is it a sin to demand interest on the loan of money? Formerly the chief way of committing usury was by taking interest on money and the doctrine on usury was developed to meet the problems which interest presented. Interest on money was a burning moral issue when money was sterile and land, which could not be purchased, was practically the sole capital good. Money was strictly a fungible: either one spent it or hid it in a strong box. But even then those extrinsic reasons, mentioned above, for asking recompense upon a loan were operative. Now it is morally lawful to take interest on money, not because the doctrine on usury has changed, but the status of money is different. Money is now a capital good and can be profitably invested. Should money return to a sterile condition the opportunity of usury revives and interest becomes a moral issue.

B. Onerous Contracts

600. The most common type of contract is that wherein rights are exchanged and benefit and burden are assumed by both parties. The moral principles underlying these contracts are in the main those found in the contract of sale, which may serve as the examplar of onerous contracts. The over-all demand of justice is that there be a true proportion between a good transferred (or a chance or hope as in aleatory contracts) and a price.

601. Sale is a contract whereby a seller transfers the ownership of a thing to a buyer for a price. There is a tremendous difference between a sale and a contract to sell. In the latter the seller binds himself to transfer the property and the buyer to accept the same at a *future time*. Only in sale does ownership actually pass. Whether one or the other agreement exists depends on the will of the parties. When the seller signifies his intention that a right of property shall pass at once and the buyer assents, then, if the goods are sufficiently identified,[13] a sal

[13] *The Uniform Sales Act* states that no property passes until goods are ascertained, i.e., identified as the particular existing chattels about which the parties are bargaining

exists by Natural Law. It makes no difference whether the goods are sold for cash or credit; to be delivered immediately or at a future date; whether they are yet to be measured or set apart; whether the seller has yet to complete them or further add to their value. These circumstances may be reasons for supposing that ownership has not yet passed, but they will not defeat an intention to do so if such an intention exists.

602. In a contract to sell the precise time when ownership does pass is important because of the axiom, "The thing perishes to its owner." Title passes and the buyer assumes the risk of goods in accordance with agreement. In the absence of specific agreement civil law lays down leading rules, e.g., title passes upon delivery of good to a carrier.

Is delivery of goods to the buyer a certain sign that ownership has passed? This was formerly assumed to be the case but installment-buying raises difficulties. Must the buyer wait until the last payment is made before becoming the owner? It is commonly agreed that in installment-buying there is a divided property interest: the buyer has an ownership which is qualified by a security interest reserved to the seller.[14]

603. There is a widespread misapprehension that in a sale one should get the advantage of the other and come away with more than he gave. The fundamental principle of justice in this matter is stated by St. Thomas: "A transaction designed for the common advantage of both should not bear harder upon the one party than upon the other; and therefore the contract should proceed on the principle of the equality of thing to thing. Now the quantity of a thing that serves human use is measured according to the price given for it. . . . Therefore, if either the price exceeds the value of the thing, or conversely the thing exceeds the price, the equality of justice will be destroyed. And therefore to sell a thing dearer or buy it cheaper than it is worth, is a proceeding in itself unjust and unlawful."[15]

The great moral problem, therefore, is *What is a just price?*

604. Price is measured by value received and value depends on a thing's capacity to satisfy needs. What a man will part with to satisfy his needs depends on what he has and the keenness of his desire. This is a purely individual estimate of value. If without deceit or undue pressure he has brought the estimate of a seller to agree with his estimate, then the two have arrived at a mutually satisfactory price. Such a price is the just price for unusual things which have no common evaluation.

---

[14] Lawrence Vold, *Handbook of the Law of Sales*, p. 270. St. Paul, West, 1931.
[15] Sum. *Theol.*, II–II, 77, 1.

The question is of things which are commonly used and exchanged. Sometimes the estimate of their value is made by law and this is the *legal price*. Observance of such law generally binds the conscience. Ordinarily, however, the value of articles in common exchange depends on a common estimate made by the buying and selling community in a given area. This is the *common price* and it is computed upon a basis of the demand for a thing (demand depending on utility) and the supply available. The *market price* is the common price except when unscrupulous buyers or sellers rig the market for their exclusive benefit. The common price of many things has a certain elasticity. Within a given margin it will vary so that we may distinguish a maximum price and a minimum price. Applying then the doctrine of St. Thomas we hold that *the seller may not sell above the maximum price nor the buyer pay less than the minimum price.*

605. Are there any exceptions to this general rule? Unusual delay or anticipation of payment is good reason for modifying the rule. *Special affection* which the seller has for the article justifies him in demanding more than the maximum price. If the total charge does not exceed the true use-value of the thing to the seller, he may ask more than the maximum price as compensation for the special loss he suffers in parting with the thing. If a seller seeks out a buyer of his own accord to dispose of an article immediately, a buyer may give less than the minimum price. For he may be suffering loss by doing this favor to the seller.

It is argued that when some special benefit will befall the buyer, either because of his crying need of it or the exceptionally profitable use he can put it to, the seller may demand more than the maximum price. This view is not acceptable. Every increase of goods, to be just, must rest on a good title. In this case when the seller receives the maximum price he has received the commutative worth of his goods. Anything above that price is pure increment. What would constitute a title to the increment? The need and desire of the buyer, it is answered. But these do not belong to the seller: one cannot profit from what belongs to another. But it is argued that the buyer is getting something for which he does not pay unless he pays more than the maximum price. Certainly he receives a special benefit but not at *the expense of the seller*. Therefore, he owes no more than the maximum price. However, he may offer the seller an extra bonus, not out of justice, but gratitude. Such is the doctrine of St. Thomas.[16] Of late there is a tendency to say that the seller may exact more, not when the buyer needs the thing, but when he will profit from it. We do not think the

[16] *Ibid.*

distinction has value. What these authors have in mind, perhaps, is that sometimes there is no market price for certain things so that the just price is what the parties arrive at. For example, it is well said of real estate that it is generally worth what one can get for it.

606. Obligation of the buyer. The buyer may not pay less than the minimum price; this he should pay at the time and place which agreement or custom determines.

Obligation of the seller. The seller may not charge more than the maximum price and he should manifest defects.

Substantial defects render the article useless for the purpose of the buyer. To conceal a substantial defect is to induce substantial error, which voids the contract.

Accidental defects make the article less suitable for the purpose of the buyer. If the defect is obvious, the seller is not obliged to make reference to it; if it is hidden and inquiry is made, the seller must reveal it or abate his price accordingly. Concealment of hidden defects is just reason by Natural Law for rescinding the contract. The axiom of civil law — *caveat emptor* — means that the buyer is expected to notice such qualities of goods to be purchased as are reasonably supposed to be within reach of his observation and judgment; should he fail to do so, the law affords him no relief.

607. Monopoly is the exclusive power to sell a given commodity or service. Exclusive control enables the controller of the monopoly to set prices. We distinguish natural and social monopoly.

Natural monopoly owes its existence to the peculiar nature of the marketable commodity; for example, things found only in one place, such as helium which is found only in Texas; things made by a secret process, such as chartreuse; a business which demands a single control, such as a telephone system.

Social monopoly results either from an act of the State (legal monopoly) or from toleration. Thus tobacco in certain countries is sold by the State alone. A copyright or patent gives the author or inventor exclusive rights to the fruits of his work. Manufacturers may give up free competition and settle among themselves the quantity of goods to be produced and the prices to be charged. Labor unions often control the supply of workingmen.

608. Monopolies are lawful when they do not violate commutative or social justice. They are sometimes necessary to build up a needed industry, to secure to the individual the fruits of his industry, to restrain waste of a nation's resources, to produce revenue necessary for the State.

609. Dangers of monopoly. The State may set up only those monopolies which are necessary for the common good. Nor may the State establish so many monopolies as would result in the abolition of private enterprise. This is clear from our refutation of socialism and communism.

Private monopolies afford opportunity for charging unjust prices. The just price here is what the price would be if there were no monopoly. This is very difficult to determine. However, one may say a price is just if it yields a moderate profit. Monopolists may more easily sin against charity, especially when the necessaries of life are involved. The State must regulate firmly and impartially all forms of monopoly.

610. **Auction** is a public sale of property to the highest bidder. A bid is an offer and a bid accepted is a sale; for then a right in the property passes. Bids, however, may be withdrawn before they are accepted. Any price arrived at is a just price if no unfair means have been used to keep it down or run it up. In American law secret bidding on behalf of the seller is fradulent; if employed, purchasers who have been deceived can avoid the sale: agreements among purchasers not to bid against each other are fraudulent with regard to the seller. If a reserve price is stated by the auctioneer, the article may be withdrawn if that price is not reached: if the auction is without reserve the article cannot be withdrawn from sale.

C. Aleatory Contracts

611. An aleatory contract is a contract of chance, one whose advantages or losses depend on an uncertain event. Two things are necessary for the maintenance of justice in this contract. The first condition touches its validity, namely, the event on which the contract hinges must be equally uncertain to both parties. It is wrong to enter this contract and render the uncertain event certain, as when having insured myself against hospital expenses I have myself hospitalized for a feigned illness. The second requisite is that the price paid be in proportion to the outcome hoped for, feared, or risked.

There are four types of aleatory contracts: insurance, gaming, betting, and lottery.

612. **Insurance** is a contract whereby one party — the insured — pays an agreed amount of money to another who promises to compensate him or his beneficiary if some specified loss should happen to him. The insured is sometimes called the assured; the insurer is called the underwriter; the consideration or money paid by the insured, the premium; the written contract, the policy; the right or interest to be protected, the insurable interest. Civil law holds that the insured must have a pecuniary interest in the event which is the object of insurance; otherwise there

is no contract of insurance but one of wager. In life insurance the uncertain event is not the fact but the time of death.

The chief obstacle to justice on the part of the insurer is fraudulent concealment. This occurs when he ostensibly offers an attractive benefit in one part of the contract which is canceled in another. The chief obstacle to justice on the part of the insured is concealment of material facts. False, even innocent misrepresentation of substantial facts voids the contract. A person who receives a policy by the suppression of material facts is guilty of fraud and if insurance money is paid, restitution is absolutely necessary. If the facts concealed are such that the company would not have insured the person, all the money received must be returned less the premiums, and the company must also be paid for the maintenance of the policy. If the company would have taken the insurance but at a higher premium, the difference must be paid.

613. **Gaming** is a contract wherein the rivals in a game of skill or change agree to pay the winner a certain prize. According to the Natural Law this is a valid contract but positive law often forbids it as the occasion of many evils. Gambling, therefore, is morally permissible provided these three conditions exist: (1) The stakes belong to one and may not be required for the satisfaction of other obligations. If one genuinely risks another's money, the winnings belong to the owner of that money. (2) There is no cheating. The rules and customs of the game distinguish cheating from legitimate deception. It is not necessary that all contestants be equally skillful, although a sense of fair play will induce the more skillful to grant odds or handicaps, which, of course, may be waived by the less skillful. (3) The constant practice does not induce bad habits such as excessive drinking, stealing, and neglect of duties.

614. **Betting** is a contract wherein persons disputing the truth of a given fact or future event agree to give a reward to whoever conjectures the truth. The same principles obtain here as in gaming. The essential note of an aleatory contract — uncertainty of event — forbids one to make a bet with certain knowledge of the outcome. However, one may take wagers as a gift if others insist on betting with him despite his protestation of knowledge.

615. **Lottery** is a contract whereby out of many depositing a price, some are chosen by lot to receive a prize. One does not pay for the prize but for a reasonable chance of drawing the prize. Fraud in the selection of the prize winners invalidates the contract.

616. To many Evangelicals, gambling, betting, and lottery are sinful in themselves. This view is incorrect: each is a valid contract, and the use thereof may be legitimate. However, these things are easily abused

and may become an incitement to sin. They can become an absorbing passion, foster cupidity, and among the ignorant encourage magic and superstition. Witness the close connection between dream books and the number's racket. It is practically impossible that a man make his living by gambling and remain honest.

Some hold that "if the civil law prohibits gambling and invalidates such contracts, the loser may in conscience refuse to pay."[17] This contradicts man's sense of natural justice and is deservedly reprobated as welshing. If it is certain that a winner under these circumstances may keep his winnings until a court deprives him of them, why is it not equally certain that the loser pay until a court frees him of the obligation? Since, however, the first opinion has its extrinsic probability, one could not insist upon an obligation in conscience to pay.

[17] E. F. Healey, S.J., *Moral Guidance*, 237. Chicago, Loyola University, 1942.

READINGS

St. Thomas, *Summa Theologica*, II–II, 77–78.

Anson, Sir W. R., *Principles of the Law of Contracts*, ed. T. H. Patterson. Chicago, Callaghan, 1939.

Brown, R. A., *The Law of Personal Property*, 226–251. Chicago, Callaghan, 1955.

Clark, W. L., *Law of Contracts*, 4 ed., 1–61, 147–166, 264–278. St. Paul, West, 1931.

Clergy Review, "A Catholic Statement on Betting," 34 (1950), 96–104.

Corpus Juris, "Depositaries," Vol. 18, 560–597; "Gaming," Vol. 27, 961–1106; "Loan," Vol. 38, 125–128; "Monopoly," Vol. 41, 76–210.

Corpus Juris Secundum, Vol. 17, "Contracts," 292 ff.

Davis, H., *Moral and Pastoral Theology*, Vol. II, 323–379. New York, Sheed & Ward, 1936.

Dempsey, B. W., *Interest and Usury*. London, Dobson, 1948.

Jankauskas, R. C., "The Morality of Basing-Point Pricing," *The Thomist*, 15 (1952), 349–373.

Johnston, H., "On the Meaning of 'Consumed in Use' in the Problem of Usury," *Modern Schoolman*, 30 (1953), 93–108.

Pound, R., *An Introduction to the Philosophy of Law*, rev. ed., 133–168. New Haven, Yale, 1954.

Robinson, E. A. G., *Monopoly*. New York, Pitman, 1949.

Stocking-Watkins, *Monopoly and Free Enterprise*. New York, Twentieth Century Fund, 1951.

Vance, W. R., *Handbook on the Law of Insurance*, 3 ed. St. Paul, West, 1951.

Vold, L., *Handbook of the Law of Sale*. St. Paul, West, 1931.

Williston-Thompson, *Selections from Williston's Treatises on the Law of Contracts*. New York, Baker-Voorhis, 1938.

Chapter XX NONJURIDICAL OBLIGATIONS

617. The first way in which we observe the general precept of loving our fellow man is by being just to him. We have seen what in the main communative justice exacts of us; the demands of distributive and social justice are presented in social ethics. Justice is the first bond that unites men: where it is lacking, their relationship is simply brutal. But justice is only a beginning of truly human order between man and man. The good man must seek the full flowering of human intercourse. To do this he must practice many virtues other than justice. These virtues we now classify in two groups: truthfulness and charity.

I. TRUTHFULNESS

618. Since men can live together in a human way only by the interchange of ideas, reason demands that the ideas exchanged be what they purport to be — the truth. Hence man has the obligation of dealing truthfully and sincerely with his fellows. This duty is partly affirmative, partly negative. On the affirmative side, justice demands that we reveal to one about to enter a contract with us all that he needs to know from us for an essential understanding of the agreement. Piety demands that parents instruct their children in the moral law. Charity may require that we warn a neighbor against impending injury, about the scandalous effects of his conduct, and the like.

We are here chiefly concerned with the negative aspect of this duty which demands that we do not say what is not true. This is lying. Everybody has the general notion that lying is wrong yet extremely knotty problems arise concerning it. We may attempt to solve these problems by treating of lying, mental restriction, and the safeguarding of secrets. To this we append a note on the positive virtue of fidelity.

A. Lying

619. Truth is a relation of conformity which may be threefold.
Ontological truth is the conformity of the object to the mind. Thus

we say, "He is a true scholar or soldier," meaning that he conforms to the normally accepted idea of a scholar or soldier. Every created being possesses ontological truth — that is, it has some measure of reality — and is what it is, because it conforms to the Divine Mind, which is the pattern of all things. Ontological truth is simply the knowable reality.

Logical truth is the conformity of the mind with the object. The mind possesses truth when it has some measure of contact with reality. This the mind has when it grasps the known object as it really is.

Moral truth is conformity between one's outward expression and one's inward thought. This is the kind of truth demanded by the virtue of veracity and which is denied by lying.

620. What is a lie? There is disagreement about the definition of a lie because different moralists in different ways solve the difficulty of reconciling the concealment of truth with the general doctrine on lying and desire that their definition be consistent with the solution they offer.

Following the footsteps of Grotius[1] and Pufendorf,[2] some writers distinguish between a lie and a falsehood, contending that the former is always wrong and that the latter may sometimes be allowed. They define a lie as the denial of truth which is due and add that its malice consists in the violation of the hearer's right to the truth. If however, the hearer — a prospective robber or murderer — has no right to the truth, or if the hearer expressly or tacitly waives his right to receive the truth, or if his right is in conflict with the stronger right of the speaker to conceal the truth, then the hearer's right to the truth is suspended and one may say to him what is not true. But such a falsehood is not a lie.

621. This definition of a lie is not acceptable for the following reasons:

1. If the right of the hearer is one of commutative justice, every time one told a simple lie he would be bound to restitution, that is, he would have to go back and tell the truth to the person to whom he had lied even in matters of small consequence.

2. If right is meant in the broader sense as that which is due to one from any source, then whoever has dominion over another's right could freely lie to him, as a parent to a child, the state to its citizens, God to His creatures. Undoubtedly no man has any kind of rights before God. Therefore, God could tell all manner of falsities to men without violating any right that they possess.

622. St. Thomas defines a lie as speech contrary to one's mind.[3] The

[1] See *Hugonis Grotii Operum Theologicorum,* Tomus Secundus, pp. 466–467. Basileae, 1732.

[2] See Samuelis Pufendorfii, *De Officio Hominis et Civis,* Lib. I., Chap. X, § 8, p. 65. Cantabrigiae, 1682.

[3] *Sum. Theol.,* II–II, 110, 1.

abandonment of that definition has ever been attended with serious consequences to the virtue of veracity. A lie, then, is the outward signification of what one thinks to be false or promising what one has no intention of doing. A statement or outward sign may be false in two ways: (*a*) *materially* when it differs from the objective truth without the knowledge of the speaker. Whoever speaks thus is not said to lie but to be mistaken; (*b*) *formally* when it is a deliberately intended misrepresentation of the speaker's mind. This is the lie. Objectively, one's speech may conform to reality, but if the speaker's judgment of this reality is erroneous, he can lie by saying what is true.

623. The full meaning of St. Thomas is best clarified by an analysis of speech. *Speech* is the uttering of words or the use of signs to one capable of understanding us in order to express judgments outwardly. The purpose of serious speech is the revelation of judgments. Hence, excluded from the category of lies are all jokes which obviously are not to be taken seriously; also the singing of songs or telling of stories since the words do not represent serious judgments but rather figments of the imagination.

624. Speech is uttered *to another*, for it is the natural medium for the exchanging of ideas among men. Hence soliloquy, or talking to oneself, is excluded from this consideration. A soliloquy is necessarily conformed to the mind of the speaker. Sometimes a soliloquizer seems to lie. For example, a man meets with a severe reverse. Naturally he does not wish this to be so. Hence under pressure of his will he forms a judgment contrary to the truth and utters it to himself, hoping thereby to solace himself and forget the distressing fact. He is not lying for he communicates nothing. He is merely wishing aloud.

625. The one to whom a person speaks must be capable of grasping what is said. Therefore, no one would say a man was lying when he talked to his dog or his horse or to a child totally incapable of understanding him. In such instances no communication of truth or falsity is possible. It would be incorrect to conclude, however, that children may be told anything one pleases. Certainly harmful truth may be withheld from children, but not by lying. They may not be told falsehoods which from the force of one's words they will rightly take to be true. A child can distinguish between fable and fact. When we purport to tell him things "for real" he does not expect a fairy tale. An example in point is the Santa Claus legend. We obtrude the story upon his belief, insisting that we are not weaving tales and commanding his acceptance — it is nothing but lying. One's intent is innocent enough, but this is a fair example of the end justifying the means. This conclusion will seem strange to American people. It will be said that we are so used to this story; our own mothers told it to us, it is surrounded by an aura of the happiest recollections. Yet it is speech contrary to one's mind. God has never and cannot so act toward man, deluding him into accepting fiction for fact. It is a wrong way to discipline young minds — eliciting good behavior by falsehood. The motive of the good should only be the true. Because of this experience, it is difficult for the young to avoid the implicit conclusion that a lie in a good cause is legitimate. For some, the awakening is a cruel disillusionment; thereafter they will be wary of the things that are told them by those whose words should be sacred.

626. **Does the intention to deceive enter into the essence of a lie?** St. Thomas says that deception pertains rather to the perfection than the essence of a lie.[4] The malice of a lie can be present where there is no intention to deceive. While in most instances the liar intends to deceive, yet one can and sometimes does proceed to lie even though he is aware that he is deceiving nobody. To save face, a superior may persist in denying a certain mistake, although everyone knows he made it and he is aware that everyone knows it. Masters in divorce cases know that petitioners are lying, and the petitioners lie despite the fact that they are aware of this.

627. **The malice of lying.** Is lying always or only generally wrong?

THESIS XLIII. Lying is both extrinsically and intrinsically evil.

PROOF OF PART I

628. **Lying is extrinsically evil** because it has bad effects on social life. Evidently it is destructive of mutual trust and good fellowship. The proper conduct of human society would be impossible if men generally were permitted to lie.

629. This proves that generally speaking lying is wrong. But as Milton asks, "If all killing be not murder, nor all taking from another stealing, why must all untruths be lies?"[5] Plato would have answered that a judicious lie is occasionally justifiable, for example, in dealing with enemies, to keep a friend in a fit of madness from hurting himself.[6] He allows the State to lie for the public good,[7] the legislator to lie to the young.[8] Perhaps the majority of mankind would agree with Plato. Our position, however, is that lying is wrong by its very nature.

[4] *Ibid.*
[5] Cited by Rickaby, *Political and Moral Essays,* p. 215. New York, Benziger, 1902.
[6] *Republic,* II, 382
[7] *Ibid.,* III, 389.
[8] *The Laws,* II, 663.

PROOF OF PART II

630. Lying is intrinsically evil because it is wrong to use a faculty in such a way as to frustrate its natural end. Evil is the privation of a good which should be present. No good is more fitting a faculty than its natural end. Hence any act of a faculty which renders impossible the end for which the faculty is intended must be an evil act. It is the privation of good that should be present.

Lying is an abuse of the speech faculty which renders the attainment of its natural end impossible. This end is the communication of ideas and judgments, as is clear from the common understanding of men. Remove that understanding, and speech would have no function either to convey information or to deceive. Deception by speech is possible solely because of the common understanding that speech is to convey thought.

631. N.B. Not even God may lie. Whatever God makes must be like unto Him. Whatever He does must mirror His perfections. Whenever He speaks His spoken word must correspond to His inward thought. Otherwise God would not be true to Himself. He would depart from Himself and so violate His own sanctity. This Plato admits,[9] at least to the extent that God does not need to lie. God cannot lie. Lying is totally unfitting the intellectual nature.

632. The seriousness of lying. The inherent malice of lying is venial. Though it is an abuse of a faculty, it does not result in a grave disturbance of the order of nature. Speech has as its purpose social use, and if by a lie the hearer were deprived of some necessary truth, and that irreparably, such a result would be a grave deordination. Lying becomes a grave wrong when to the offense against veracity there is added a grave offense against some other virtue such as religion or justice, for example, a lie under oath or a lying attack upon another's character.

Lying is not therefore a small thing. The evil of lying is demonstrated by the shame we experience on being caught in a lie. To be called a liar is a fighting matter.

Since lying is linked with most of the capital sins, a conscientious regard for the truth is stern, moral discipline. It is a difficult but sure way to strength of character and self-mastery. Truthfulness is more than a fair indication that one is practicing the other virtues. Hence its inculcation is an essential part of the education of children.

Truthfulness, however, is not the same as indiscreet frankness. There are semi-idiots who boast, "I always say what I think." Such persons are

[9] *Republic*, II, 382.

often troublemakers. Solomon observes that there is a "time to keep silence and a time to speak."[10]

633. Cheating in examinations. Examinations are (*a*) a sanction to insure the application of undergraduates to their studies, (*b*) a test to demonstrate the fitness of a person to practice a profession or hold an office.

a) Some regard the endeavor of undergraduates to frustrate the sanction as a part of a game played by teacher and pupils; at worst, a merely penal offense involving no moral fault. This is a false and damaging view. Since the natural understanding is that answers submitted are the answers of the student, he who offers the knowledge of another as his own violates veracity. He who helps him co-operates in wrongdoing. Second, the end of study is the good of the undergraduate which he implicitly binds himself to achieve in reasonable measure. Since cheating is security against neglect of that duty and an encouragement to continue one's neglect, it violates the personal good of the student and defeats the ends of education. The habitual cheat undermines his character and loses a proper sense of personal integrity. Third, wherever students are ranked one after another upon a basis of scholastic achievement, whoever cheats steals the standing of one who does not cheat.

b) Cheating in the second type of examination is always a violation of veracity; it may also offend against justice and the common good.

B. Mental Restriction

634. Some defense of a secret against importunate questioning is necessary. Sometimes silence or open refusal to answer betrays the secret. How, then, can one give an answer and at the same time conceal the truth without moral fault? Grotius says this may be done by telling a falsehood which, he claims, is not a lie. Cardinal Newman, to whom all equivocation is anathema, obliquely admits there may be extreme occasions when a lie is allowable.[11] From our preceding contention, all speech contrary to the mind is evil and never permissible. But is there not some sort of speech which is not contrary to the mind and yet protects a secret?

635. Certainly it is not wrong to use evasive speech whereby one does not answer the question asked but offers some irrelevant truth so that the questioner is distracted from what he is seeking. Nor is it wrong to use ambiguous speech — words which convey several meanings, one in-

[10] Eccles. 3:7.

[11] *Apologia Pro Vita Sua*, p. 360. London, Longmans Green, 1918.

tended by the speaker, the other gathered by the hearer — provided the meaning of the speaker is intelligible in the context in which he uses it. When he entered Egypt Abraham called his wife his sister. He used a Semitic word which meant both sister and female relative. He did not depart from the truth when he called his wife a female relative. Furthermore, words derive their power of expressing thought not only from the literal signification assigned them but also from the circumstances in which they are used. As the written word's meaning is judged not only from the text but also the context, so too the spoken word. Thus a butcher has put away his last pound of steak for his own supper. Asked by a customer, "Have you any steak?" he answers: "No." And truthfully, for in the circumstances the question means, "Have you any steak *for sale?*" Upon these observable facts of linguistics rests the doctrine of mental restriction.

THESIS XLIV. A broad mental reservation is not a lie yet its unrestricted use is immoral. However, for a sufficiently grave reason it is allowable.

PART I

636. Mental restriction is an act of the mind limiting the meaning of one's expression to some particular meaning chosen by the speaker. Such a meaning may or may not objectively be contained in the expression. Hence we speak of pure and broad mental restriction.

In *pure mental restriction* the speaker limits the significance of his expression to a particular meaning but gives no outward clue to the same. As an outward expression it fails completely to represent the speaker's mind. It is a lie, for neither the words nor signs of themselves nor the circumstances in which they are used in any way convey the speaker's thought. Thus John has just slapped his younger brother who cries. Their mother asks, "John did you hit him?" John says, "No," meaning to himself that he did not slap him yesterday.

In *broad mental restriction* the speaker limits the obvious meaning of his expression to one particular meaning chosen by himself and yet *gives some objective clue to his meaning.* He utters words which have more than one meaning: one of these meanings corresponds to his thought; by another and more obvious meaning he endeavors to conceal his thought. Hence broad mental restriction differs from a pure mental restriction in this: in the latter the speaker's meaning exists *only* in his mind; in the former it exists also in the *speaker's expression.*

637. The obvious instance of the broad mental reservation is equivocal language and certain formulae like "Not at home" or "Not guilty." The broad mental reservation, however, has a broader scope since not all the meanings expressed by language are purely literal. Contexts and circumstances can point, shade, and add new meanings to words. Thus, when John Nepomucene was asked by the Duke of Bohemia if the Duchess had sacramentally confessed to him the sin of adultery, even if she had, Nepomucene could truly answer, "I don't know" or simply, "No." The circumstances of his priesthood qualify his answer so that it objectively means, "I have no communicable knowledge on this matter." So too, lawyers, doctors, nurses, diplomats, or public officials may reply in a similar manner when questioned by busybodies concerning a matter which falls within the ambit of professional secrecy. A sensible listener can correctly interpret such denials to mean that the speaker has no information to be disclosed. Or if one who is notoriously a bad risk were to ask a person for the loan of a considerable sum, he could truthfully answer, "I haven't got it." Truthfully, because the circumstances under which the request was made clearly indicate that the reply means, "I have no money to lend you." Similarly, if someone attempts to wring a natural secret from another, the latter may answer with a flat denial. Thus, if a person were to ask, "Didn't I hear your father choking your mother last night?" one could answer, "Of course, you didn't." Such denials uttered in these circumstances simply mean, "This is none of your business."

638. When the questioner has a right to an answer, denials of this kind are lies. But they are not lies when context alters their meaning, for example, when the speaker is safeguarding a legitimate secret and the questioner has no right to the information he is seeking.

If the hearer is sensible and perspicacious, he will be aware of these circumstances and will correctly interpret the speaker to mean that he does not wish to tell him anything. Even though the hearer does not grasp the real meaning, the objective situation remains unchanged. The speaker's statement still bears a truth and imparts meaning; and although the hearer misunderstands the meaning and is deceived, this fact does not nullify the speaker's right to his secret or render him guilty of lying. Even the intention to put off one's hearer is not wrong, because not every intention to deceive is morally wrong. It is allowable for a sufficient reason.

PROOF OF PART I

639. A broad mental reservation is not a lie, because it objectively

represents the mind of the speaker.[12] A restrictive statement which in nowise represents the speaker's mind is purely a mental restriction, a lie. In a broad mental restriction either the words literally, though ambiguously, contain the speaker's thought, or the words receive, from the circumstances in which they are uttered, a true reflection of the speaker's mind and as such can be understood by the discreet hearer.

PROOF OF PART II

640. The unrestricted use of a broad mental reservation is immoral. First, the person who indulges this practice indiscriminately can easily lose regard for sincerity and truth and become a liar. Second, if it were allowable upon all occasions, the mutual trust requisite in society would be destroyed. Third, it may not be used when one deals with those who have a right to the information. Thus, it may not be used by a minor who is being corrected by his parents, the parties to an onerous contract, a person who is being interrogated by a judge or a superior within the limits of his authority.

PROOF OF PART III

641. A broad mental reservation used for a grave reason is allowable, because it is not evil either from its nature, its end, or its circumstances.

From its nature. It is not speech contrary to one's mind.

From its end. The end is to conceal the truth. This can be sometimes not merely licit but mandatory, for the good of an individual or of society can demand that certain secrets be kept.

From its circumstances.

a) The natural evil consequence, destruction of mutual trust, is avoided because wholesale use of such restrictions is not permitted but only that restriction necessary to guard a legitimate secret.

b) The evil which is permitted, namely error in the hearer, is not a moral evil for it is not deprivation of necessary truth but the absence of information to which the hearer has no right.

642. Corollary. A broad mental restriction is an extraordinary measure which may be used only when a worthwhile secret is at stake. This

---

[12] According to another explanation a broad mental reservation is not a lie because it is not speech, which is a communication. The speaker does not use words to express but to conceal thought. If the hearer is deceived, it is because the speaker has not warned him how he uses his words. Safeguarding his secret justifies the speaker in permitting the deception of the hearer.

is not any trifling matter but a truth which one fears would cause serious harm or offense if revealed.

643. N.B. I. Some say that words which appear to be untruthful are a legitimate self-defense against unjust verbal aggression. In other circumstances these words would be lies, but in legitimate defense they are not lies but acts of self-defense in which the deception of the hearer is not intended but merely permitted.

This is an inadequate explanation. According to that plea one might fabricate all sorts of stories in self-defense. Only those words constitute legitimate self-defense which taken with the circumstances in which they are uttered can objectively represent the speaker's mind.

644. N.B. II. *Mental restriction under oath.* Even in a court of law one may have an important secret to protect. One's right to guard a secret is not nullified in our American courts by the formula of the oath, "to tell the truth, the whole truth, and nothing but the truth." The reason is that this formula must be understood in the light of this natural limitation, "in so far as the law obliges me to reveal the truth." Hence a defendant at least may use a reservation to avoid convicting himself, for no one is obliged to give evidence against himself.

645. N.B. III. Mental restriction, like probabilism, may be abused. Many so-called broad mental reservations are nothing other than downright lies. But this fact is no argument against legitimate broad mental reservation. Everyday life testifies to its existence. Of course, if one cannot conceive that it is sometimes permissible to permit another man to deceive himself, that words may sometimes be used ambiguously, that words can take on added meaning from the circumstances in which they are used, this doctrine is not for him. This is often the case with the young or unlettered who confuse a broad mental reservation with lying. If, finally, persons do not solve every sort of doubt concerning truth and veracity, let us remember that when Pilate asked Christ what truth is, he received no answer.[13] Truth may long evade the mind's quest of it.

C. Secrets

646. A secret is a truth which a man has a right or an obligation to keep hidden. That the Natural Law may grant such a right is evident from the fact that concealment of the truth is sometimes necessary to preserve the life, dignity, and happiness of individuals. The nature of human intercourse sometimes obliges secrecy; if it did not, mutual trust would fail among men.

[13] Jn. 18:38.

647. Kinds of Secrets

a) A *natural secret* involves obligation which arises immediately from the Natural Law without convention or agreement, and its preservation is demanded by the nature of human fellowship. The object of natural secrecy is anyone's private affairs the revelation of which would reasonably cause injury or chagrin, for example, the fact that a dependable family head had once been in the penitentiary. Freedom of the press does not abolish natural secrets.

b) A *secret of promise* involves obligation arising from the free promise of secrecy which one makes *after* learning another's secret.

c) A *secret of trust* involves obligation arising from a pact made *before* the communication of the secret. The pact may be explicit as when a person says, "I will tell you this provided you keep it absolutely to yourself," or it may be implicit as when one confides in a priest, lawyer, or other professional person.

648. Obligation of secrets

a) *In general:* we are obliged not to (*i*) pry into another's secrets by eavesdropping, reading another's personal letters, diaries, and the like, purloining invention plans, administering a drug to obtain hidden knowledge; (*ii*) use secret knowledge unjustly obtained; (*iii*) reveal secrets.

Concerning the first, one may read another's letters if one may reasonably presume the permission of its owner or if it is necessary to prevent a grave injustice. Those who have dominative authority may do so for the correction of those in their charge. Those who have jurisdictional authority may do so for the protection of the State. The State may drug a suspect in order to discover information essential to its protection, but it may not use information so obtained to convict him of crime.

b) *In particular:* (*i*) Since the *natural secret* arises immediately from the Natural Law, it binds under penalty of grave wrong when the subject matter is serious. If revelation causes injury, justice is violated; if embarrassment only or offense results, charity alone is violated. (*ii*) A *secret of promise*, which is not also a natural secret, binds in virtue of fidelity, the quality and gravity of the obligation depending on the intention of the one promising. (*iii*) A *secret of trust* binds in justice because of an implied or explicit contract. The binding power of secrets of trust derives also from the common good. For the common good demands that people be able to seek advice and counsel in security.

649. Revelation of secrets. The obligation to secrecy ceases *in general* when the secret has been disclosed by other sources; when one may reasonably presume the consent of the holder of the secret; even though the secret is still intact, one may talk about it to another who has the same secret knowledge except, however, for the secret of the confessional.

If the obligation to secrecy binds only by reason of charity, a person is released when secrecy would result in grave *inconvenience* to oneself or the subject of the secret. Charity does not oblige at the cost of equal inconvenience to self. As for the protection of the subject of the secret, one may reasonably presume his consent to speak. *A fortiori* one is released when secrecy would result in injustice.

If the obligation to secrecy derives from justice as do all secrets of trust and some natural secrets, one is released only when grave *injury* would result to (1) oneself, (2) the subject of the secret, (3) a third innocent party, (4) the Church or State.

The revelation of professional secrets presents a delicate question. However, it seems clear enough that if *grave injury* would befall any of the above mentioned, the holder of even such a secret *may* disclose it. But *must* he? That depends on whether more good than harm would result. The violation of professional secrets would be detrimental to the common good. People certainly would be deterred from entrusting them to others if they were not held sacred. Still, there may be cases involving life and death, the security of the State, and the like in which a true obligation exists to manifest such a secret. There is one professional secret which may not be revealed under any circumstances — that of the Sacrament of Penance.

If one has promised to keep a secret at all costs, and this can be done without injury to another, one is bound to do so even at tremendous personal inconvenience.

650. N.B. Self-discipline is necessary for fulfilling one's obligations with regard to secrets. First, one must practice it by minding his own business and not prying into the lives of others. A man who is industriously intent upon his own concerns will have neither the time nor the energy to delve into the private affairs of others. Second, one must practice self-discipline in controlling idle curiosity. The wise man does not run after every passing fire engine nor does he itch for the latest gossip. There are many trifles the knowledge of which profits nothing. And finally, a man must practice it in learning to maintain a discreet silence. One is not equipped to administer efficiently or direct others if he cannot bridle his tongue.

D. Fidelity

651. The faithful man constantly and exactly fulfills his obligations. Fidelity is a note of many virtues. Thus, the constant giving of oneself to the service of God is the virtue of devotion. The relation of servant and master requires fidelity and loyalty to the latter. Here, however, fidelity refers to constancy in carrying out promises.

652. A promise is not merely the expression of a present resolution concerning some future course of conduct. A person who makes a resolution determines to do a given thing. A person who makes a promise binds himself *to another* to act accordingly. Hence a promise is made to another, gives that person a hope of performance, and carries a moral binding force which is a guarantee of execution. This binding force may be the virtue of religion, justice, or fidelity. Thus, when an alcoholic exclaims in the company of others that he will not get drunk again, he gives voice to a resolution; when he gives his wife his word that he will not drink for a year, he makes a promise. A person who does not keep his resolution is inconstant; one who does not live up to his promises is worse — he is unfaithful. A man who promises what he has no intention of doing is not unfaithful; he is a liar.

653. A promise whose binding force is religion is a vow. As we have seen in the chapter on contracts, a promise can bind in justice whenever the promisor intends to create a true right in the promisee. We deal here with promises which bind only in fidelity. Fidelity is that moral virtue which moves us to take care that our future performances respond to our promises. As veracity demands that our words correspond to our thoughts, so fidelity requires that our deeds correspond to our words. As the good of social life demands that we speak the truth, so it requires fulfillment of promises.

654. There is tribute of moral distinction in the comment, "that man's word is his bond." It manifests a person steadfast in other respects — one on whom others can rely. But its chief praise is due to the fact that the faithful man resists what is so easy to do, namely, exempt oneself from a self-imposed obligation. A person who makes a promise as it were legislates for himself and the extent and gravity of his obligation depend upon his original intention. It is not commendable — though human enough — to exempt oneself later, to pare down one's obligation. In as much as fulfillment of a promise lies within the control of the one who makes it, the promise-breaker is a paltry man.

The inherent malice of infidelity is that it dashes the hopes of the promisee; however, no right is transgressed. Its consequent evil is that one's promises are no longer trusted.

We are excused from keeping our promises when their fulfillment would constitute an immoral act or would be something notably greater than what we had originally bound ourselves to.

II. CHARITY

655. The noblest activity with regard to our fellow man is charity. From just and fair dealing, the good man rises to love or charity. Charity differs from justice in three ways: (*a*) Justice consists in rendering to another what is his; charity, in giving of one's own to another. (*b*) Justice when violated demands restitution; charity does not — the obligation of charity ceases when the opportunity to practice it has passed. (*c*) Except for the fulfillment of contracts, the obligations of justice are negative; while charity has its negative precepts, its demands are primarily positive.

656. **What is charity?** Three kinds of love may here be distinguished: love of concupiscence, love of benevolence, and charity.

a) *Love of concupiscence* (§ 334) is man's love of his fellow man solely for his own sake. Love of others solely for their usefulness or agreeableness fosters reprehensible selfishness. It is to subordinate them wholly to one's self, to fail to see the man in them. Scarcely any man is so egocentric as to have no other sort of love for at least one or other of his fellows; but because too many regard the vast majority of those with whom they deal as mere means to their pleasure and profit, men miss out on one of the chief values of life.

b) *Love of benevolence* (§§ 334, 492) is a man's love of another person for that person's sake. This entails the procurement of that other's good. The nobler the good procured, the loftier the benevolence.

c) *Charity* is man's love of God, for God's own sake. This is our rational tendency to the supremely lovable object. Benevolence for our fellow man becomes charity when we wish and procure for him every good that leads to God. This is the most excellent kind of love: we love him for his own sake and wish him the supreme good.

A. The Obligation of Charity

657. We must love God for His own sake (§ 338). We must love ourselves with charity, for we must seek those goods for ourselves that lead us to God. Since our fellow man is likewise destined for God, having the same excellence of nature as ourselves, we must cherish him with the love of charity. We must love ourselves first, then our neighbor. Charity begins at home, but it must not stay there. It must go out to all men precisely because they are men.

Supernatural charity. Reason is not capable of making known to man the richness of human relations that ought to exist. Natural charity, lofty as it is, but weakly reflects the glory of supernatural charity, known only through revelation. Destined for the immediate vision of God, man is lifted from his natural status by sanctifying grace, which is a real sharing in the very nature of God. Thereby man is divinized, made the adopted son of God, and God comes to the sanctified soul and there dwells as a lover with his beloved. In a true sense God identifies Himself with man, for Christ says, "As long as you did it to one of these my least brethren you did it to me."[14] Hence we are to love our fellow man not so much for the humanity as the divinity which is his.

What does natural charity require of us? In a positive way it requires essentially benevolence and friendliness to all men; beneficence to those in need; and, incidentally, gratitude. Negatively it forbids us to scandalize him or co-operate in his evil acts.

658. Charity daily urges in thought, word, and deed. Its obligation begins with *benevolence* whereby man always wishes his fellow man well, never evil. Our fellow man here means absolutely every man without exception. The same reason — a common humanity — which commands benevolence, commands benevolence to *all*. Hence no matter what a man's color, creed, nation, upbringing, or status, he may not be excluded from our good will.

Too many people forget that there are only accidental differences among men. Upon the level of our common humanity there can be no slaves or supermen, whites or natives. But two things sadly contribute to obscure man's remembrance of his humanity: an assumption of essential superiority or a remembrance of past wrongs either inflicted or endured. False pride of race, class, or family is often responsible for the attitude: "I am not as the rest of men" or the egregious stupidity that "niggers have no souls." It is easy to see how the oppressed will hate the oppressor; but the converse, so tersely put by Tacitus, is also true: "It is human nature to hate him whom we have injured."[15] The unreason of injury strives to find justification by claiming to find odious qualities in the victim.

So universal is this precept that we must love even our enemies. This does not mean we are to love them *qua* enemies, that is because they are injurious — for that would be most unnatural — but because they are men. Certainly we may hate the evil an enemy has wrought us, we may abominate his vicious characteristics, but his person is sacred: as long as a person is alive and is not irremediably confirmed in evil we may not wish him harm.

The command to forgive injuries means that we do not exclude the offender from our good will, that we seek no private vengeance, that we

[14] Mt. 25:40.
[15] *Agricola*, c. 42.

do not refuse him help if he is in need. If the offending party has been close to us, we must attempt a reconciliation and continue to offer him ordinary signs of good will.

The malicious opposite of benevolence is malevolence, commonly called *hatred*. It is the wishing of evil to another which is not duly subordinated to some good. It is theoretically possible to wish harm to another as a good, that is, as preventing some greater harm, as when I hope John breaks his leg before he can run off with George's wife. But in practice this is dangerous, because man so readily rejoices at the ill fortune of others. Hatred expressed in words of imprecation is *cursing*. Akin to hatred is *envy*, displeasure with the good fortune of another, which one naïvely interprets as his own loss.

B. Beneficence

659. True charity does not consist of barren good wishes. Love is manifested by deeds, and, unless, it is so proved, it dies. Thus benevolence must issue forth in *beneficence* or well-doing. To whom is one obliged to be beneficent? When a similar question was put to Christ, He replied with the parable of the Good Samaritan,[16] thereby indicating nature's law that man must help anyone who is in need.

A man's needs should be supplied because he should have the fullness of well-being. This does not mean that his every whim should be catered to but that he have what is reasonably required to live as a good man. When a person cannot supply this himself, he naturally turns to his fellow man: this is one of the basic reasons for living in society.

Coming to the assistance of another is not always a mere counsel denoting what is nice and helpful. Charity, like justice, can impose a strict command. It does so when *a given person alone can supply the need and his doing so does not expose him to a like difficulty*. If others will not or cannot help, then I must if I can; and I can unless I would create the same need in myself. The reasonableness of the qualification is clear from the fact that charity begins at home. Hence when there is question of a prospective helper's equal need, he may prefer himself.

Since we are faced by a world of needs, we require, besides the basic principle stated above, more detailed guidance to direct our beneficence. This is given us in the *order of charity* which regulates our helping according to (*a*) the severity of need, (*b*) the needful person, (*c*) the good which is needed.

660. Severity of need. Three degrees of need may be distinguished:

1. *Extreme need* is spiritual when one is in immediate danger of losing

[16] Lk. 10:25–37.

his soul and *has not the means of helping himself.* It is temporal when one is in danger of losing his life or what closely approximates life.

2. *Grave need* is spiritual when one is in serious moral danger and can help himself only with great difficulty. It is temporal when temporal goods of great value such as one's fortune, status, or authority are at stake.

3. *Common need* means that one is threatened with a slight evil, spiritual or temporal, or with a great one which can easily be avoided.

661. **The needful person.** If a person is in extreme spiritual need, any temporal good requisite must be sacrificed to rescue him. However, there must be a proportion between the certainty of losing the good risked and one's hope of benefiting the neighbor. Even at the risk of death, one should go to an infant who would otherwise surely die without baptism (unless some greater harm to the Church was involved). If a person is in extreme temporal need, he must be helped even at the cost of grave inconvenience. Thus, one would be obliged to pick up the victim of a hit and run driver on a lonely road, although complications with the police would result. If a person is in grave need, he must be helped but not at the cost of grave inconvenience. As for those in common need, general assistance offered from time to time suffices, as when one contributes to the support of the poor in general.

Those who are closest to us should be helped first. The order of preference is as follows: husband or wife, children, parents, blood relatives, friends, benefactors, fellow countrymen, strangers.

662. **The good which is needed.** There is a natural hierarchy of goods so that in rendering assistance the spiritual good of the neighbor is to be preferred to his temporal good, the common good to the individual good, necessary goods to unessential goods, one's own good to that of the neighbor. One is obliged to prefer himself if his *necessary* spiritual good is involved. Thus, one could never risk his own salvation to save another. Nor may one commit the slightest sin to procure any benefit whatever for another. However, a person may, and sometimes should, sacrifice his own spiritual but unessential good to secure the *necessary* temporal or spiritual good of another. He may even have to postpone the fulfillment of a positive precept, as when he omits Sunday Mass to help a person who is desperately ill. As far as purely temporal goods are concerned, one may if he elects prefer his neighbor to himself. Such an act is usually consummate wisdom.

C. Friendliness

663. Our fellow man is not always in difficulty; how does charity require that he be treated in normal circumstances? The general answer

is — with *friendliness*. Does this mean one must be a friend of all men? Since friendship can be had only with a few, it is impossible to be a friend to all. A friend is another self. There are few things more revolting than fulsome protestations of insincere regard.

There is, however, a level whereon all men may be said to be friends in the wider sense — the level of our common humanity. That general love which we are bound to have for all should be externalized in respect and graciousness of behavior which is due even the stranger.

Just as men could not live in society without truth, so neither can they without the pleasure of social intercourse. As Aristotle says: "No one can spend his days in company which is positively painful or even not pleasant; since to avoid the painful and aim at the pleasurable is one of the most obvious tendencies of human nature."[17]

Therefore a man is bound by natural propriety to be pleasant, human, and agreeable in his dealings with his fellows, "unless," as St. Thomas wisely qualifies, "for some reason it be necessary at times to make others sorrowful to good purpose."[18] Put in the phrase of Newman, a man must always be a gentleman, a person who never *needlessly* gives pain. On this principle every code of etiquette should rest. Genuine good manners are a simple acknowledgment of the dignity of our fellow man.

There is a certain minimum of courtesy and good fellowship due to all men. The closer anyone is bound to me by duty, association, or blood, the greater must be these evidences of fellowship. The nature of human intercourse indicates a level of decency and humanity that must be observed by those who eat at the same table, are partners in the same firm, officers in the same company, monks in the same monastery, members of the same family, and so on, under penalty of being seriously at odds with the Natural Law.

D. Gratitude

664. Physics tells us that every material action has an equal and opposite reaction. Charity tells us that a kind act requires reciprocation. The return of good is an act of gratitude consisting in acknowledgment and requital of a favor done. It need not be proved that those who gratuitously do good to others should receive good in return. Though all men perceive the necessity of gratitude, it is a rare virtue.

In a favor done two things are distinguishable: the act of beneficence and the good will prompting it. Good will is sincere — and the bene-

[17] *Nicomachean Ethics*, VIII, 5, 1157b.
[18] *Sum. Theol.*, II–II, 114, 2.

faction genuine — when it flows from a conviction of humanity, fellowship, or compassion; it is fictitious when it proceeds from a feeling of superiority, a person's looking down upon his fellow man in need. From the latter comes the saying, "Cold as charity." So too the act of gratitude must contain a sentiment of good will toward one's benefactor as well as the external act of requital.

Some people with feelings of superiority dislike being in need of a favor. Hence a favor done them may be an affront to their pride. So far from being well disposed toward their benefactor, they come in time to resent him. Samuel Johnson acridly says: "There are minds so impatient of gratitude that their gratitude is a species of revenge and they return benefits, not because recompense is a pleasure but because obligation is a pain."[19] Such people make haste to repay favors lest they be under obligation to anyone. Of these Seneca says: "If he seeks to pay too quickly, he owes unwillingly; and he who owes unwillingly, is ungrateful."[20]

But every inward acknowledgment of gratitude ought not to involve humiliation. No man is self-sufficient; every man has a universe of wants. It is virtue to be humble and admit the poverty of our human condition. Without that, no grateful sentiment is possible.

But many people have no superiority complex making them averse to receiving favors. Their gratitude is really the hope of future favors: it is that mother of flattery and sycophancy, as La Rochefoucauld expressed it: "Gratitude in most men is only a strong and secret hope of greater favors."[21] Robert Walpole is reported to have said: "The gratitude of place expectants is a lively sense of future favors."[22]

The least requital that gratitude demands is an outward expression of an inward grateful sentiment. The habit of saying "thank you" is a sign of civilization. A salient feature of gratitude is opportuneness, that is, the returning of good when and in a manner in which it coincides with the benefactor's need. The perfection of gratitude means that one repays more than he received. Since the benefactor was gratuitous in giving what he was not obliged to give, and since the recipient to be gratuitous also must make a gratuitous recompense, it would seem that his recompense would not be gratuitous unless it exceeded the quantity or quality of the benefit received.

---

[19] *The Rambler*, January 15, 1751.

[20] Quoted by St. Thomas, *Sum. Theol.*, II–II, 106, 4.

[21] Duc de la Rochefoucauld, *Maximes*, No. 298, p. 108. Paris, Froment, 1823.

[22] William Hazlitt in *Wit and Humor*. See his Collected Works, ed. Waller and Glover, Vol. 6, p. 17. London, Dent, 1903.

E. Scandal

Besides forbidding hatred, revenge, and envy, charity imposes two especial negative precepts: man may not scandalize his fellow man nor co-operate in his evil.

665. Nature of scandal. Many people confuse scandal with detraction or with uncharitable gossip. Scandal means more than misuse of the tongue.

Scandal derives from the Greek, *σκάνδαλον,* which means a stumbling block. One becomes a scandal or a moral stumbling block to his neighbor when he unreasonably offers him the occasion of wrongdoing. The law of benevolence obliges man to wish his neighbor every good that conduces to his last end. Since sin alone can deprive him of his final good, it is a violation against benevolence to will that another do evil or even permit him to do so when it could reasonably be prevented. The motive for avoiding scandal is clear enough, but the precise extent of this obligation requires more exact determination.

1. One Who Gives Scandal

666. Scandal involves two parties, one who gives scandal and one who receives it.

From the viewpoint of the one who gives scandal, scandal is any word, act, or omission which is likely to induce another to do wrong. Not every act or omission which gives scandal is evil in itself, although such acts generally are. Some innocent acts also may scandalize. Certain manifestations of affection between man and wife could be a scandal to an unmarried pair. The essence of scandal is inducement or enticement to sin resulting either from the mere placing of an act — such as an older brother's stealing, which results in his younger brother's stealing — or from persuasion, command, solicitation, or other similar means designed to lead another into evil.

In the first instance scandal is not the *cause* of another's evil act; it is the occasion. The cause is the other person's free but defective will. In the second instance the scandalizer is a *moral co-cause* or co-operator in the sin.

To be guilty of scandal it is not necessary that another person actually do wrong; one is guilty of scandal if his action constitutes an inducement to sin. Thus there is scandal in unsuccessful solicitation or in an attempt to show pornographic post cards to a young man even though he refuses to look at them.

Scandal presupposes that the will of another has not yet been determined to evil. Hence the very wicked and the one who has already made up his mind to do evil is seldom scandalized. Thus, Jones's failure to attend Sunday Mass is not a scandal to his roommate because he decided the night before that he was not going to Mass. Nor is scandal given to one who would in no way be influenced by example. Thus a cursing father is a scandal to his growing son but not to his pious wife.

667. There are two types of scandal, direct and indirect. In *direct* scandal a person intends the evil action of another. The evil action may be intended for two reasons. First, it may be willed as an end in itself, for example, a person may wish that his neighbor sin precisely because it involves his spiritual ruin or is direct dishonoring of God. Christian virgins have been judicially condemned to brothels; atheism and sexual aberrations have been taught the young with that end in view. This is the nadir of ill will to another and is aptly called *diabolical*. Usually, however, one does not desire the evil action of another as an end in itself, but as something useful or convenient to oneself. Thus one engages in lewd kissing for personal satisfaction, not for the moral harm of another. All direct scandal has a twofold malice. First, it is a violation of charity because by it we fail to render our neighbor the love due him; second, as a direct co-operator, one also assumes the guilt of the evil act of the one scandalized.

668. Scandal is *indirect* when another's evil act is not intended but foreseen as inevitable or likely. Thus, one invites a friend into a bar although he knows the friend is likely to drink too much. If the scandal-giving action is itself sinful, one is responsible for its foreseen consequences. Thus, a perjured father knows his daughter will imitate his perjury when she makes out her income-tax returns. If scandal is only indirect, one violates charity, but one does not assume the guilt of the sin which the scandalized person commits. This is an important fact, because in a matter of justice the obligation of restitution may not be imposed upon one who gives indirect scandal.

669. If a scandalous action is innocent in itself, the principles governing the voluntary in cause given in §§144–147 must be applied. Circumstances may oblige one to omit an innocent act precisely because scandal will follow. Thus, two doctors ought not discuss certain gynecological cases in the hearing of young people who would be venereally excited. To act in circumstances in which scandal is likely to follow, one must have a reason proportionate to the circumstances. The sufficiency of one's reason may be determined by considering (*a*) how certain and how grave the other person's sin will be; (*b*) how close the connection

is between one's act and the other's sin; (c) how grave an inconvenience is involved in the omission of the act.

2. *One Who Takes Scandal*

670. From the standpoint of the one who takes it, scandal is the evil which one does upon the occasion of the scandal-giving action of another. Since man is amenable to suasion and is naturally prone to imitate the example of those around him, there is a certain level of scandal which is a danger to the ordinarily peccable man. However, there are two classes who have an extraordinary susceptibility to taking scandal. The sin which these commit is either pharisaical scandal or scandal of the weak.

Pharisaical scandal arises from the malice of one who wrests another's good action to his own hurt by perverse misconstruction. Thus the sight of a young couple departing for innocent recreation occasions rash judgments in a busybody next door. The term is derived from the fact that the miracles of Christ were the occasion of the Pharisees' sinning against the light. Scandal of this sort should simply be spurned.

Scandal of the weak is the wrong which one commits through ignorance or frailty upon the occasion of another's good act. Thus, a tourist stopping at Havana on a Friday sees his Catholic companions eat meat and does the same, thinking it to be a sin.

671. To what extent one is obliged to avoid the scandal of the weak may be judged from the foregoing (§ 669). If the scandal flows from ignorance, the ignorant party should be instructed. Thus the tourist in Havana should be told that it is lawful to eat meat in a Spanish-speaking country on a Friday. Sometimes, though, instruction is ineffective and the scandal becomes pharisaical.

If a person is particularly weak, special consideration must be given to the problem. However, it is never permissible to do that which is intrinsically wrong to avoid even a greater sin by another. Thus, one could not steal to prevent another from committing adultery. Positive precepts necessary for salvation may never be omitted for the sake of preventing moral evil on the part of another. A wife could not neglect to have her child baptized in order to prevent her husband from blaspheming. Positive precepts not necessary for salvation, even though they bind gravely, *may* but need not be omitted to keep another from serious wrong. A girl could but is not obliged to omit Sunday Mass because her presence there will rouse the passion of a libidinous youth.

F. Co-operation

672. Co-operation is physical activity (or its omission) by which a person assists in the evil act of another who is the principal agent. Moral concurrence in the evil act of another is suasion and the like mentioned in § 666. Co-operation may be formal and material.

673. In *formal* co-operation one intends the evil act of another. The person who co-operates joins the other *in his evil intention*, as when a messenger delivers an insulting note and rejoices in the hurt it causes. Formal co-operation is always wrong for two reasons. It violates charity and takes on the specific guilt of the sin in which one has co-operated.

674. In *material* co-operation one does not join the principal agent in his evil intent but nevertheless assists him by an act not in itself wrong. Thus one student gives notes to another who will use them to cheat in an examination. The general law of morality is that man must avoid evil as far as he can and the specific law of charity bids him to prevent his neighbor from doing wrong to the best of his ability. May a man therefore ever have a nonvoluntary part in another's sin? Generally speaking, he may not, but at times the principle of double effect may be applied. Since the material co-operator does not intend the evil of the principal's act, whenever his own act is good or indifferent and *he has a proportionately grave reason for acting, his co-operation will be licit.*

675. Two things must always be considered. First, it must be determined whether the proposed co-operative act is intrinsically wrong. In making a decision on this point, one must bear in mind that there are simply no circumstances in which the act could be good. As this principle applies to the making of things, the question is not whether the thing made will be put to a bad use but whether it has no good use whatever. There are few such things. When the co-operative act is intrinsically evil, one may never proceed to act, irrespective of one's ostensible intention, irrespective of the pressure brought to bear on one. A person who so acts becomes a formal co-operator because, since the act has only one end of work and that evil, one cannot choose to do it without intending its evil end of work. Thereby one is conjoined to the evil intention of the principal agent. Even though he thought it a joke, a shipwrecked sailor could not take an *active* part in the religious ceremonies of pagans; the spectator of a lynching could not help pull on the rope which draws the victim off the ground even though his doing so is necessary to save himself from lynching.

The second point to be considered is whether the good one seeks by his co-operative act outweighs the evil he allows in his neighbor's bad act. Some may ask whether there can be a justifying reason for permitting moral evil since there is an obligation to prevent it. The obligation of preventing another from doing wrong derives from charity, but charitable obligation does not bind when it is disproportionate to the good which will result from it.

676. In judging the sufficiency of one's reason for acting when one's co-operative act is not intrinsically wrong we distinguish three sets of circumstances: (*a*) *Where serious harm would result to Church* or *State*, material co-operation is never allowed, because private good must yield to the common good. Even to avoid torture or death one could not take even a material part in treason. (*b*) Where an *injustice* would be done to an innocent third party, the sole excusing reason would be threat of *equal damage* to the co-operator. One could not tell a thief where his neighbor has concealed his car unless silence would result in the loss of his own car. (*c*) Where there is no question of the first two sets of circumstances but solely one of preventing any other serious sin, the issue is decided upon the proximity of one's co-operation and the gravity of the evil to be avoided by the co-operator.

677. In terms of the proximity of one's co-operation, it may be immediate and mediate.

In *immediate* co-operation one has part in the very act of another's wrong, as in fornication. In the overwhelming majority of cases immediate co-operation is intrinsically wrong and hence forbidden. An exception are those acts in which a person has a purely passive part, as in a rape to which one does not consent. It is also possible to play an immediate part in certain sins against justice. Thus under threat of death one could have an active part in a theft because the one so constrained is in extreme need and this use of his neighbor's goods becomes a unique means of saving his life.

In *mediate* co-operation one places an act which is preparatory to another's sin, such as selling a murderer poison. Mediate co-operation may be *proximate* or *remote* according as it approximates concurrence in the sin. It is one thing to tell a youth where he can buy pornographic post cards, another to drive him to the place of purchase, and still another to sell them to him. The ultimate of proximate co-operation is *necessary co-operation*, without which the sin could not take place.

678. If one's co-operation is quite proximate and necessary, an extremely grave reason is required. Such would be fear of probable death, serious infamy, the loss of some important organ. If co-operation is less

proximate, a grave reason is required. Such would be fear of great pain or loss of a considerable sum of money. If co-operation is remote, slight inconvenience excuses. Proportionately graver reasons are required in the case of parents, teachers, pastors, and the like, who have a special obligation from piety or justice to prevent others from doing evil.

679. The general principles governing co-operation are clear enough, but they present troublesome difficulties in application. It is often difficult to distinguish formal from material co-operation (which must always be one's first consideration); and if material co-operation be established, to determine if there are sufficient grounds for allowing it. The science of casuistry takes up those cases most likely to happen — it solves cases for servants, merchants, innkeepers, workmen, book sellers, and so on. But since the variety of human conduct is practically infinite, it does not help too much to have memorized the solution of stock cases. One repeatedly is forced to use his own judgment to decide whether one may proceed or must desist. When one cannot rely on his own prudence to apply these principles, he must seek the advise of a wise counselor.

READINGS

St. Thomas, *Summa Theologica*, II–II, 23, 26, 31, 43, 106, 109, 110.

Bezzina, E. E., *De Valore Sociali Caritatis*. Neapoli, D'Auria, 1952.

Clergy Review, "Lies and Terminological Inexactitudes," 40 (1955), 681–683.

Costello, J. A., *Moral Obligation of Fraternal Correction*. Washington, Catholic University, 1949.

De Marino, A., "Why Lying is Forbidden," *Theology Digest*, 4 (1956), 9–12.

Flood, D. F., ed., *New Problems in Medical Ethics*, Vol. II. Westminster, Newman, 1954.

Gardiner, H., "Moral Principles for Discerning the Obscene," *Catholic Theological Society of America Proceedings*, 1954, 126–139.

Gilleman, G., *Le Primat de la Charité en Théologie Morale*, 101–182. Louvain, Nauwelaerts, 1952.

Hildebrand, D., *Fundamental Moral Attitudes*. New York, Longmans Green, 1950.

Hodges, D. C., "Ethics and Appearance," *Journal of Philosophy*, 51 (August 19, 1954), 481–490.

Humbert, A., "The Notion of 'Scandal' in the Synoptics," *Theology Digest*, 3 (1955), 108–112.

Kelly, G., *Guidance for Religious*, 85–127. Westminster, Newman, 1956.

Medico-Moral Problems, "Cooperation in Illicit Operations," 33–35. St. Louis, Catholic Hospital Association, 1951.

McCarthy, J., "The Morality of the Use of the 'Truth-Drug,'" *Irish Ecclesiastical Record*, 71 (1949), 361–365.

Mouroux, J., *The Meaning of Man*, 196–266. New York, Sheed & Ward, 1948.

Nelson, L., *System of Ethics*, 145–161. New Haven, Yale, 1956.

Regan, R. E., "Problems of Professional Secrecy," *Catholic Theological Society of America*, 1955, 152–171.

Seneca, *De Beneficiis*.

Wertham, F., *Seduction of the Innocent*. New York, Rinehart, 1954.

BOOK THREE

PRINCIPLES OF SOCIAL ETHICS

Chapter XXI MAN A SOCIAL BEING

680. Up to the present we have considered the rights and duties of the individual man and even where we have seen him dealing with other men, his relationship to them has been that of individual to individual. We have touched on certain aspects of social life in our treatment of communism and socialism, but the emphasis has been upon the good or evil status of the individual. However, it is clear that man is more than an individual. History emphatically testifies that men do not live isolated lives but have ever acted as members of some group. Hobbes's[1] description of the original man, a lone marauder whose hand was against every other man, has never actually been verified. Homer's scorn for the "tribeless, lawless, hearthless man"[2] stresses the abnormality of asocial man. The facts of history show that man has been and is social. Hence the moral question arises: Does inclusion in a social organization impose on men duties and rights specifically different from those they bear as individuals? If so, what is their origin, nature, and extent? Before examining the norms of social conduct, we should establish the (I) nature, (II) causes, and (III) naturalness of society.

I. WHAT IS A SOCIETY?

681. These elements are to be found in any society. First, there must be a common good, an end which is to be pursued by many so as to be of help to many. Thrown completely on his own, the individual finds that he is unable to realize countless values. To acquire learning, bridge a river, adequately protect his family, cross the seas, or even to amuse himself, he must unite with other men. Their combined effort will put advantages otherwise inaccessible within reach of the individual. These advantages are a common good to be obtained by co-operative effort, an orderly working toward the desired end. Co-operative action does not imply that all do the same things but that each has an activity helpful to the end.

[1] *Leviathan*, Chap. XIII, Molesworth's English edition, Vol. III, pp. 112–113.
[2] *Iliad*, IX, 63.

Second, a society requires a plurality. Without at least two persons association is impossible. A group of individuals, however, does not become a society by mere local juxtaposition. A crowd of strollers on the boardwalk is not a society. The plurality must be fused into a union. A society is an *ordered* group, one consciously aiming at a definite good by mutual effort.

Furthermore, not every casual or temporary pooling of human effort makes a society. When a farmer calls his neighbors for corn-husking, they do not constitute a society. A society is a *permanent* union, though not necessarily perpetual. The apparatus of a society is not set up to attain momentary or chance goods but those whose achievement demands considerable time and are of lasting importance.

Finally, a society of men differs from a herd of animals. It is a working together of human beings as human beings, a thinking and a willing of the same thing. Hence the members of a society must know in general the good which they seek by their union and the chief means leading to it; and they must desire both the end and the means. The tie, then, which binds together a social organization is moral, the tie of intellect and will.[3]

682. Therefore we define a society as *the permanent moral union of two or more persons striving for a common good by co-operative activity.* Since this moral union is regarded as possessing rights similar to those of an individual, it is aptly called a moral person. Because a society demands subordination of part to part and of all parts to the whole, it is called an organism. It will be helpful for future explanations of particular societies to apply to the general notion of society the four Aristotelian causes, but we must keep in mind that this application is only analogous.

II. CAUSES OF A SOCIETY

683. The material cause of society is the plurality, the multitude, which is socially united. The efficient cause is an agent whose juridical action gives the multitude the moral unity of a society and determines the existence of a society. His action is juridical, not physical, because the effect to be produced, a society, is not a physical but a juridical unit. Hence, when treating of the origin of particular societies

[3] Purely spiritual substances do not live a social life in the human sense because they contain within themselves all the means necessary to fulfill their potentialities. Each angel is a species exhausting the potency of its form. The potency of the species "rational animal" is exhausted only by all men.

we shall not talk of an efficient but of a juridical cause. This cause will always be some person or persons endowed by law with the right to form a social union with this or these persons. The question of *final* and *formal* causes requires fuller treatment.

A. Final Cause

1. *The Social End*

684. The final cause can only be a common good. Although a common good may include a great variety of things — making money, educating children, saving one's soul — it must always be something worthy of human striving. Men may not band together for an end forbidden by the moral law. A society must promote human happiness. Hence associations to foster wrongdoing, such as Murder, Inc., or gangs of auto thieves, bear only an outward resemblance to a society.

Granted the end is worthy of human effort, it becomes a *common* good not merely because many seek it together, but principally because it is a source of advantage to many. If no benefits accrue to the members, there is simply no common good. But in order to benefit its members, a society must be a going concern; it must seek its own conservation and improvement. In no society could benefits be shared among its members unless it were first in good condition. But if a society should seek its own prestige to the detriment of its members, it would become perverted. For a society is of less importance than its membership. Societies are for men: men do not exist for societies.

As the end varies so, too, will the nature of the society and the kind of activity requisite to achieve the end. *The end specifies the society.* Since a bridge club has a different purpose than a business partnership or a State, the form of these societies and the kind of social activity required of the members will differ.

2. *Social Activity*

685. A discussion of the end of a society is incomplete without a consideration of the means whereby the common good is attained. These means can only be social activity — ends are attained by proper action. What, then, is social activity? In a preliminary sense, we may call that activity social whereby a social organism is established, for example, the action of the founding Fathers writing the Constitution of the United States. Once a society has been duly erected, social activity is (*a*) the actions of the society operating as a social unit, such as Japan's signing a fisheries' treaty with Russia, or (*b*) the acts of its members

performed in virtue of their particular duty or capacity to promote the common good, such as the proclaiming of Thanksgiving Day by a governor, the quelling of a disturbance by a policeman, a citizen's paying his taxes.

686. Two fundamental requirements underlie all social activity. The first is the concrete steps that the organization takes to secure its social goal. What must a golf club do to provide its members with facilities to enjoy the game of golf? How is a state to protect its citizens? Where many minds and possible opinions are involved, there must be agreement as to the means to be selected, the practical steps to be taken. Otherwise, confusion results: the social end could never be attained. Besides, as there will necessarily be a diversity of social functions, so there must be agreement as to which members fulfill the various functions. Otherwise they would not be done.

The second requirement is that a society must see to it that its various functions are fulfilled. Here difficulty is always encountered for some members will be unwilling to do their allotted share. Some may co-operate at first, but after a spurt of initial activity they lapse into inactivity. Evidently, then, since men are inconstant, there will not be a constant and efficient movement toward the common good unless the society has the power to compel continuous co-operation.

This twofold power men call *authority*, which we define as the legitimate power to direct and compel the members of a society to act in accord with the proper end of a society.

687. **How necessary is authority?** To the ordinary man this is a senseless question, but there always has been the rebel to whom the yoke of authority is heavy and who strives to throw it off. In our time Bakunin (1814–1876),[4] one of the greater gods of the social democrats, both in word and act rejected as much authority as he could. Proudhon (1814–1865),[5] the brains of modern anarchism, denied the State much of its essential authority. Communism has woven a dream of a happy day when by natural evolution State authority will have ceased (§ 509). Among the ancients, Zeno and Carpocrates advocated a stateless society. What perhaps the modern and ancient anarchist has in mind is that the State does not constitute a true society. That question we shall resolve later. But when he decries all authority, the anarchist is actually protesting against the abuse of authority which commonly consists in

[4] See Emile de Laveleye, "L'Apôtre de la Destruction Universelle — Bakounine," *Revue de Deux Mondes*, Juin 1, 1880, Vol. 39, pp. 546–582.

[5] See *La Revolution Sociale, Oeuvres Completes de P. J. Proudhon*, Vol. 7. Paris, Libraire Internationale, 1868. *De La Capacité Politique Des Classes Ouvrières*. Paris, Dentu, 1865. *De La Justice Dans La Revolution Et Dans L'Eglise*. Bruxelles, 1868, 1869, 1870.

rulers using the society to advance their own private interests. The great enemy of the common good is the unreasonable private good. However, in all this the anarchist is not quite sincere. When he says that he hates his rulers and would abolish all rule, he really means that he wants to rule. His abolition of authority is only a temporary expedient preparatory to his own rise to power.

688. Our contention is that you cannot have a society without authority. This seems a self-evident proposition, yet it has been at least verbally denied.

THESIS XLV. Authority is at least an essential property of any society.

We do not say whether or not authority pertains to the essence of a society but simply that wherever you have a society you must also have authority.

PROOF

689. Authority is an essential property of a society, because without it a society could not attain its end. A society essentially involves co-operative and constant activity toward a common end. Without some power to *direct and compel* movement toward the end, the end is unrealizable. The reasons are: (*a*) There must be harmonious agreement on the choice of social means. Otherwise there would not be order but chaos. Therefore a society must have the power to select the social means leading to the common good. (*b*) Since men are selfish, they will often be unwilling to forego their private interests for the common good. Hence there must be some power to compel co-operation. Since men are fickle, there will not be permanent co-operation without the power to compel. This necessary social power to direct and compel is authority.

690. **Corollary I.** The necessary unity of any society demands that it have *one and only one supreme authority*. This is vested in some individual person or group of persons. Whoever bears this authority is not a master but a superior. A master is obeyed by servants or slaves; a superior by subjects. A master may command what is for his own private good; a superior only what is for the common good. The obligation to promote the common good falls first upon the superior who fulfills this duty by devising and executing those particular measures conducive to the society's end. Secondarily, it falls upon subjects who fulfill their duty by obeying the directions of authority.

Corollary II. The sole kind of activity which *directly* falls within the sphere of social authority are external acts amenable to external direction and coercion. Social authority may not command purely internal acts, because it can neither direct, judge, nor compel them. However, if an internal act is necessarily involved with an external act, such as internal consent in a contract, one may be obliged to place it not in virtue of social authority but of the Natural Law.

B. Formal Cause

691. The formal cause is that determined and determining thing which converts a plurality into a society. What is that thing, analogous to the physical form in entities physically one, which makes a society a society?

Two opinions are offered by scholastic authors. According to both of these, a society is essentially a moral union: the individuals comprising a society are welded into the state of oneness. This unity is completely moral. It is caused and preserved by activity of intellect and will. Since moral union is the essence of a society, what determining form gives the multitude the moral oneness of a society?

692. The first opinion contends that this is *authority*. Hence, as a being is made a man by the union of matter and a rational soul, so a multitude becomes a society when the stamp of authority is imprinted on it.

The second opinion holds that this moral union is the formal effect of a *moral and juridic bond*. The formal cause of society is a bond, because each individual in the group is united to every other individual, each to the society as such, and the society in turn to each. It is a moral bond consisting in the knowledge of, the desire for, and the striving after a common good precisely as it is common to all. It is a juridic bond, comprising the sum total of rights and duties which each member has with respect to the common end. This is aptly called the *social bond*, and once it exists and as long as it lasts, a society exists. Only when it dissolves does the society cease to be.

693. Although the first opinion is easier to understand, the second seems more probable. The second opinion is preferable because we can form an essential concept of a society without including authority therein but not without including the social bond. This is clear in the case of conjugal society. Therefore, if authority does not constitute the essential form of conjugal society, it is not the formal cause of any society. Authority flows from the social bond, not vice versa. Authority is necessary that a society attain its end; it is not necessary that a society exist. Therefore, authority is an essential property of a society but not its formal cause.

Our opinion is confirmed by the fact that in societies there is a fusion of the formal and the final causes. For the content of the moral and juridic bond depends on the end in view. As the end varies, so also does the bond (cf. § 684). Authority neither determines nor pre-exists this end; it pursues it. In natural societies the end is fixed by the Natural Law; in artificial societies, by the society itself.

III. SOCIETY A DEMAND OF NATURE

694. The phenomenon of human association is universal. The American pioneer on his lonely farm hungered for an outlet for his social cravings. Today, Junior builds his clubhouse in the back yard, sister has her sorority, and mother her discussion club. The history of mankind is the record of the rise and fall of States. How do we explain social intercourse? Is its origin in nature or in the arbitrary will of man?

695. According to Hobbes, man is by nature antisocial. His primitive status was one of perpetual readiness to attack his fellow man. Hobbes mourns that this life was "solitary, poor, nasty, brutish and short."[6] But since universal contention will eventually destroy man, man ought to live at peace with man. Men have agreed to do so by means of a social contract (cf. § 865) which is the basis of all society. It is the origin of all law, right, justice, and even of morality. This arrangement had to be irrevocable and men have now grown accustomed to it. Human sociability, then, is an artificial thing, a mere human invention.

Marx goes to the opposite extreme when he says that the nature of man is the product of social forces at work upon it.[7]

Following the lead of Spencer,[8] evolutionists say that the social order has been evolved and established in its present state by physical laws acting with iron necessity.

696. Our explanation is that social life is natural to man, not in the sense that teeth and fingernails are natural as nature's direct donation, but in the sense that it is required if man is to attain his end. Individuals cannot realize the potentialities of their natures and integrate the human self through attainment of its proper ends without social life. Anxious for their well-being and spurred by their wants, men listen to the urgings of their incompleted selves and freely obey the law of nature by entering into social relations with their fellows.

---

[6] *The Leviathan*, Chap. XIII, Molesworth's English edition, Vol. III, p. 113.

[7] *A Contribution to the Critique of Political Economy*, Preface, 1859.

[8] Herbert Spencer, *The Principles of Sociology*, Vol. I, pp. 3–104, 609–618. London, Williams, 1877.

THESIS XLVI. Man is by nature a social being.

PROOF

697. Man is by nature a social being, because (*a*) he has a natural aptitude for society; (*b*) he has a natural and compelling inclination for it; (*c*) outside of society he labors under the moral impossibility of attaining his proper well-being.

a) Man's aptitude for society is proved by his faculties of hearing and speech. These constitute natural equipment for social life.

b) Man's tendency to society is evident from the fact that men dislike solitude. They want to share their joys and sorrows and welcome pity and sympathy.

c) It is morally and sometimes even physically impossible for men to attain the fullness of well-being without social organization. First, the race could not continue without the family. As an infant and an old man, a person absolutely requires the help of others. Second, any appreciable intellectual, moral, and aesthetic development is possible only in society. It is a characteristic mark of man that he seek to improve himself and his surroundings and advance toward civilization. St. Thomas sums up the argument: "man needs to be helped by other men in order to attain his proper end."[9]

Therefore a tendency, inclination, and a need so universally verified must be rooted in human nature.

Corollary. A man is by nature a member of human society.

698. **N.B. I.** *What is Society?* According to those who think that sociability is only an accidental advantage of the individual, society is a fiction, merely another name for all individuals. This view is false because, as man is by nature social, society must be real. Since the time of Hegel there has been a tendency among German philosophers to go to the opposite extreme and give society a mysterious subsistence of its own. This view is also false because society is not a substance. The truth stands in the middle ground: society is all men standing together in a real and *essential relation* of mutual help.

Messner says that "society has a supraindividual being . . . but it cannot be concluded . . . that it has any being independently of its members."[10] To illustrate, he compares society to a house "which likewise possesses a being distinct from the mere sum of its components of

---

[9] *Contra Gentiles,* III, 117.
[10] J. Messner, *Social Ethics,* p. 109. St. Louis, Herder, 1949.

wood and masonry."[11] Among men, being an individual and being social are equally natural. Both are rooted in the nature of man: individuality does not flow from society as the collectivist theory holds; nor does sociability flow from individuality, as the individualist theory holds.

This supraindividual being is explained by various analogies. Taking the analogy from metaphysics we call society an accident inhering in the substance, man. Taking the analogy from psychology we call society an organism — a being capable of performing vital activities of itself through the co-operation of mutually dependent parts. Therefore we attribute to society a moral form like unto the form of things physically one. The basis in reality for this attribution is (*a*) man's essentially social character; (*b*) the conspiration of human wills toward human perfection; (*c*) the dependence of individuals upon groups, of groups upon all men; (*d*) the unity of the human race and the natural disposition toward its end implanted by the Creator; (*e*) the order which follows from this unity and the quest of means to realize the end, which is the common good.

699. **N.B. II.** *What is the common good?* It is now possible to distinguish *the common good* from a common good. The latter is the end of a particular society; the former is that which answers the social wants of all men. In what does the common good consist?

The individualist and collectivist theories say that there is no substantial difference between the individual and the common good but each doctrine reaches this conclusion from opposite premises. Thus Adam Smith[12] held that the common good is that which would result automatically if everyone sought his individual good to the highest degree. It was this "harmony of interests" or canonization of selfishness which was the philosophic background of industrial slavery. The Utilitarianists said that the common good is the greatest good of the greatest number. The Nazis and Communists said that the individual good was only a minuscle share in the collective good. Both views are wrong.

The common good is the sum total of conditions, made possible only by co-operative effort, which must be present that individuals may attain their due perfection. The common good is the well-being of society at large and the help it affords the individual. These helps taken collectively make up the common good. They are the benefits produced by institutions like the family, the local community, the State, the community of nations, and a variety of associations based on freely chosen ends. The common good includes not only economic, cultural, military,

[11] *Ibid.*

[12] *Wealth of Nations,* p. 14, Modern Library ed.

and political service but also every good for whose attainment man requires the help of his fellow man. Hence it is moral and ethical consisting of proper standards and influences of honor and rectitude, morality and justice. Indeed at its core is the ethical good because the final purpose of society is that men attain their eternal destiny. The end of social activity is such a cultivation of these common helps that in any given place and time human beings can develop to the greatest possible degree compatible with the good of the whole group.

The immediate principle which orders men toward this sublime goal is justice which aims that all men, in accord with their needs and merits, may share in the helps which society affords them for the realization of their existential ends.

The common good is being sought and *society* is supplying the individual with adequate help when all necessary social institutions exist and are active. Perennial, universal needs are met by enduring social institutions. Sometimes, however, areas of the common good, like the aesthetic, economic, or international good, may scarcely be organized. Organization means that the social goal has been clarified and the means of attaining it are operative. In a free society some items of the common good are under private control; in a collectivist society every item is State controlled.

700. N.B. III. *How do we interpret the phrase, "The common good comes before the individual good"?* In the individual we distinguish between his personal good and his social good. The former is his physical being and his need to complete it in perfect happiness. His social good is the help which he is entitled to from society for the attainment of his personal good. The common good is the help afforded all men by society. Evidently the social good of an individual is subordinate to the social good of many or of all. As a social part an individual is subordinate to the social whole, for the whole is greater than any of its parts. But this principle is universally applicable only to things which are physically one. The relation of the individual to the race is not that of physical part to physical whole; the race is not one physical substance. Men form a moral unity, that is, a unity of wills and action with respect to a common end. As a physical whole directed to his perfect happiness, the individual is not subordinate to the moral whole, the race. For the moral whole exists precisely to help him to his perfect happiness. True, the common good can and does subordinate to itself the temporal happiness of the individual but it may not do so in such a way as to impair his perfect happiness. His supreme eternal good is superior to his social good, even to the common good of all. For a physical unity which is immortal is more excellent than a moral unity. No one, therefore, may be compelled to sacrifice his supreme good nor even to risk it by sin, even though he would thereby confer the most tremendous benefits on any society. However, certain societies such as Church and State are so necessary to all men, so completely equipped to promote man's real good that there never could be a true conflict in which an individual would have to choose between his supreme good and the genuine good of one of these societies. That which promotes the real good of these societies must eventually promote the good of the individual.

701. N.B. IV. The command of the Natural Law that men live in society applies to men collectively, not disjunctively. Therefore, if some individual, for the sake of supernatural contemplation, were to live a completely solitary life, he would not violate the Natural Law. Aristotle[13] well says that he who, by deliberate choice and not a mere accident of fortune, is free of all social bonds is either a very wicked man or better than man. St. Thomas adds that "social life is necessary for the acquiring of perfection; solitude is for those who have become perfect."[14]

[13] *Politics*, I, 2, 1253a.
[14] *Sum. Theol.*, II–II, 188, 8.

READINGS

Aristotle, *Politics*, I, 1–2.

Banner, W., "The Natural Law and Social Order," *The Return to Reason*, ed. J. Wild. Chicago, Regnery, 1953.

Byrnes, R. F., "Pobedonostev's Conception of the Good Society," *Review of Politics*, 13 (1951), 169–190.

Copland, D., "Authority and Control in a Free Society," *Studies*, 42 (1953), 275–292.

Domenach-Ricoeur, "Mass and Person," *Cross Currents*, Winter, 1952, 59–66.

Garrett, T. M., "Saint Augustine and the Nature of Society," *New Scholasticism*, 30 (January, 1956), 16–36.

Gilby, T., *Between Community and Society*, 105–213. New York, Longmans Green, 1953.

Grindell, C. W., "Individual Rights as a Limitation of the Common Good," *American Catholic Philosophical Association Proceedings*, 27 (1953), 127–142.

Kamiat, A. H., *The Ethics of Civilization*. Washington, Public Affairs, 1954.

Kelly, G., "The Common Good and the Socio-Economic Order," *Catholic Mind*, 51 (1953), 524–542.

Letwin, S. R., "Rationalism, Principles, and Politics," *Review of Politics*, 14 (1952), 367–393.

Marc, A., "Personne, Société, Communauté," *Revue Philosophique de Louvain*, 52 (1954), 447–461.

Maritain, J., *The Person and the Common Good*. New York, Scribners, 1947.
Martin, C., "Responsibility in Society," *Studies*, 43 (1954), 51–60.
Messner, J., *Ethics and Facts*, 216–254. St. Louis, Herder, 1952.
——— "Freedom as a Principle of Social Order," *The Modern Schoolman*, 28 (January, 1951), 97–110.
——— *Social Ethics*, 99–143. St. Louis, Herder, 1949.
O'Connor, D. A., *Catholic Social Doctrine*. Westminster, Newman, 1956.
O'Toole, G. B., ed., *Race: Nation: Person*. New York, Barnes & Noble, 1944.
Riesman, D., *Individualism Reconsidered*, 15–120. Glencoe, Free Press, 1954.
Rommen, H. A., "Natural Law: Man and Society," *Fordham Law Review*, 24 (1955), 128–140.
Sheed, F. J., *Society and Sanity*. New York, Sheed & Ward, 1953.
Sturzo, L., *Inner Laws of Society*, 3–29. New York, Kenedy, 1944.
Thought, "The Common Good," 30 (1955), 63–80.
Walsh, C. J., "Economic and the Common Good," *Thought*, 29 (1954), 7–31.
Whyte, W. H., *The Organization Man*. Garden City, Doubleday, 1957.

Chapter XXII CONJUGAL SOCIETY

702. Man's social nature urges him to form whatever societies his needs require. There are two outstanding types of society, natural and artificial. An *artificial society* is one whose existence, end, and nature are determined by man's free choice. Here the common good is some incidental good, appealing to some classes of men but not to all men generally. Little boys do not care for bridge clubs. A *natural society* is one whose existence, end, and nature have been determined by the Natural Law. Nature ordains man for such a society because without it he could not attain the due perfection of his nature. The common good here is an essential good appealing to all men generally.

We shall now consider which societies are natural and how nature intends that they operate.

I. THE EXISTENCE OF THE CONJUGAL UNION

703. The first good of man and of society is existence. What provision has nature made for the continuance of the race? This purpose is not merely more human life — not any sort of deficient or backward human beings — but more human beings who are normal and sound. To effect this end, it is not enough that nature endow men with the faculty of reproduction, for not any haphazard or arbitrary use of this faculty will suffice for nature's purpose. Orderly use of this faculty is requisite.

Nature provides for the orderly reproduction of brutes through the operation of blind instinct. But it is contrary to his rational dignity that man be required to co-operate blindly with nature; his co-operation in the reproduction of his kind should be by way of willing acceptance of a pattern of orderly sexual activity proposed to his reason. Therefore man's use of the power of reproduction is regulated by law. Because of man's social nature, this law requires a natural society or institution as the prime instrument of its operation.

THESIS XLVII. The Natural Law demands a permanent union of man and woman for the proper continuance of the human race. This conjugal union is a true and natural society.

704. The procreation of new human life requires the carnal union of male and female. Does a temporary, casual union wherein fertilization is effected suffice for nature's purpose, or is a more permanent union necessary? By permanent we mean that the partners in this union live together at least until their offspring are physically, intellectually, and morally capable of proper human living. Here we do not ask whether this union should last until the death of one of the partners.

PROOF OF PART I

705. **A permanent union is necessary.** The Natural Law demands a permanent union of man and woman because *only* such a union can fittingly realize nature's purpose regarding the propagation and rearing of human beings.

Casual, temporary unions do not make for sufficient propagation and fitting rearing.

a) These unions do not make for sufficient propagation because they tend to result in the sterility of the woman and the impaired physical well-being of the offspring. Furthermore, their purpose is not offspring but self-gratification.

b) They are not apt to provide for the proper rearing of children. Even among brutes, parents remain together until their young can care for themselves. No animal is as helpless and for so long a time as the human infant. Since nature intends the well-being of the young, it demands that human parents remain together until their offspring are capable of an adequate human life. Since the task of raising children is so onerous, only parents, definitely known and permanently united, can exercise that care without which the suitable physical, intellectual, and moral development of the child is impossible.

PROOF OF PART II

706. **This union is a true society.** In the conjugal union are present all the necessary elements of a society, namely, several persons working together in a stable, moral union for a common good to be achieved by mutual co-operation.

PROOF OF PART III

707. This society is natural. The reasons are:

a) Nature has destined men for conjugal society (*i*) *physiologically,* because men and women not only have faculties for reproduction but a strong impulse to use them; (*ii*) *psychologically,* because men and women are the natural complements of one another. They are everywhere attracted to this union and see in it the natural framework on which to build their happiness.

b) That this society is morally necessary for a universal human good is proved in § 705.

708. Corollary I. Nature forbids all transient, casual unions of the sexes because they are essentially destructive of her purpose regarding human propagation. The partners in every act of carnal intercourse must be prepared *beforehand* to assume complete responsibility for the possible consequences of the act, namely, adequate care of the new *person* who may result therefrom. If nature allowed the act under circumstances which do not provide this guarantee, she would countenance the deterioration of the human race. Even though these unions conceal their real identity under pleasant-sounding names, like companionate marriage, they are a blatant substitution of passion for reason, of delectable good for perfective good.

709. Corollary II. Nature demands that sex activity be restricted to the conjugal union. Only persons united in this society may perform the generative act. Therefore fornication is always wrong. The reason is that the indispensable guarantee of the offspring's good is the bond of this union. This is the rule of nature: no conjugal bond, no sex activity.

Is any exception possible? There is an exception to the general rule that no one may kill or take the property of another. May a similar expection be found in this matter on the ground that a particular unmarried couple will certainly educate any offspring begotten, or that their intercourse will certainly be sterile?

While preservation of innocent life calls for an exception to the general rule about killing and stealing, no similar reason can be urged against the rule regarding sex. Reason indeed demands that none be tolerated. To admit any exception here would destroy the general rule. It would be tantamount to legalizing promiscuity, because concupiscent man, as in the case of divorce, would soon use any reason as an exception. Besides, if the sex appetite could be lawfully satisfied outside of marriage, too many would abstain from assuming its burdens to the consequent detriment of the race.

710. **Corollary III.** The contention of evolutionists that the human race originally lived in a state of sexual promiscuity is false.

When the first flame of evolutionary doctrine was lighted in the nineteenth century, many were captivated by it — here at last was the all-embracing principle which explained all things. Accepting an hypothesis as a principle, the evolutionists cast about for facts to substantiate it. To fasten a purely animal status on primitive man, any and every sort of analogy was seized upon; seeming facts which pointed in the direction of evolution were pronounced indubitable facts. One of these was the alleged fact of original promiscuity.[1] An imposing array of scientific names plumped for it.

The argument ran: (*a*) ancient and modern primitive peoples living in promiscuity are survivals of a once universal condition; (*b*) certain customs can be explained solely in the light of primitive promiscuity.

On the first point, later researches show there are no substantiated instances of wholesale promiscuity, and the more scientists investigate primitive peoples, the more conclusive is the evidence that the family is the basis of social organization. Westermarck cites all the ancient and modern evidence offered and concludes: "Even if there really are or have been peoples living in a state of promiscuity, *which has never been proven*, and is exceedingly hard to believe, these people do not afford any evidence whatever for promiscuity having been the rule in primitive times."[2]

On the second point, among the customs cited are various sexual aberrations such as prenuptial unchastity, religious prostitution, and exchange of wives. However, one can find similar instances of sexual aberration in the great cities of modern Western civilization, and by a parallel argument one might conclude that our ancestors of three thousand years ago lived in a state of promiscuity except that the facts of history forbid such a conclusion. Modern aberrations are instances of degeneration from a loftier ideal. So too the aberrations of primitive peoples can more reasonably be explained upon the same basis.

The outstanding proof offered for promiscuity is that of the matriarchate, or mother right, the argument being that because descent was reckoned from the mother, therefore paternity was uncertain, and therefore a state of promiscuity once prevailed. But no proof has ever been

[1] Herbert Spencer, *Principles of Sociology*, Vol. I, pp. 661–671.

[2] Edward Westermarck, *The History of Human Marriage*, Vol. I, p. 125. London, Macmillan, 1921.

offered that the matriarchate ever universally prevailed or that it preceded the patriarchate. Where the matriarchate flourished among primitive people, descent through the mother is reasonably explained in some cases by the fact that the new husband went to live with his wife's family and hence he was counted as a member of that family. But the best explanation is that where polygamy prevails, it is more convenient to reckon descent from the mother than the father.

The *Encyclopedia of Social Sciences* clearly accuses evolution of missing the mark on this point and sums up the modern findings thus: "In social organizations it was shown by Starcke, Westermarck and the anthropologists in the United States that the individual family was the one ubiquitous social unit, the most primitive as well as the most persistent."[3]

Westermarck concluded his case against promiscuity, arguing that male jealousy would not tolerate a system of promiscuity. A valid enough argument. But the stronger argument is, that, since promiscuity results in infertility and venereal disease, the human race could not have survived a state of original promiscuity.

II. THE NECESSITY OF CONJUGAL SOCIETY

711. Conjugal society is necessary for adequate and proper propagation of the human race. The Natural Law, therefore, commands marriage. This command falls directly and primarily upon the race and not upon particular individuals, since propagation is primarily a good of the race, only secondarily a good of the individual. Hence this obligation directly presses an individual only when the race is in danger of dying out. Tilling the soil, gathering the fruits of the field, providing clothing and shelter are needs of the race; but it does not follow that every man should be a farmer, a builder, and a weaver. Only when there is an insufficiency of these things is the individual commanded to procure them himself. So too with conjugal society. From the way men act and have acted through history it is safe to assert that there will always be enough persons who will desire the married state and assume the function of procreation. Hence there will be little danger of this obligation falling directly upon particular individuals.

However, *per accidens*, an individual may be obliged to marry for family reasons, or reasons of state, or because otherwise he could not lead an upright life. As the Apostle says: "It is better to marry than to burn (with concupiscence)."[4]

[3] *Encyclopedia of Social Sciences*, "Evolution, Social," Vol. V, p. 660.
[4] 1 Cor. 7:9.

But so vehement is the urge to procreate, so rooted in human nature is the inclination to use the faculty of procreation that one may well ask whether a man does not go counter to his nature if he refuses to marry. As we shall see in discussing the purposes of matrimony and the education of children, the conjugal tie requires practice of great virtue. Is not, then, the full perfection of one's personality, the completeness of one's natural life thwarted when one abstains from matrimony? Many authors have stated that voluntary celibacy is contrary to the Natural Law and that therefore all who are physically and socially capable of marriage ought to marry. This position we reject.

THESIS XLVIII. Individual celibacy is not contrary to the Natural Law. If it is undertaken from motives of virtue, it is a nobler state than matrimony.

712. Celibacy or virginity is not only abstention from matrimony but from all use of sex. Its material element is bodily integrity and freedom from venereal pleasure; its formal element, rendering it specially virtuous, is the safeguarding of it for God's sake. Some people may not marry for selfish reasons. We are not discussing virginity compulsorily but grudgingly borne but virginity freely chosen for reasons of religious worship, contemplation, or the service of mankind. St. Augustine says: "We do not praise virgins for being virgins, but, because their virginity is consecrated to God by holy continence."[5]

PROOF OF PART I

713. **Celibacy is not contrary to the Natural Law.** Celibacy would be contrary to the Natural Law if the Natural Law commanded each individual to marry. There is no such command, for (*a*) the good of the race does not require it, as proved in § 711, and (*b*) nor does the good of the individual. The precept might be necessary if celibacy were impossible to observe, but many who are prevented from marrying and others who freely choose celibacy do actually observe it. The advantages necessary for the physical, intellectual, and moral development of the individual can be secured outside the married state.

PROOF OF PART II

714. **Celibacy, undertaken from motives of virtue, is a nobler state than matrimony.**

[5] *De Virginitate,* XI.

N.B. The argument presupposes that there is a sufficiency of propagators. If this were not so, celibacy could not be chosen from motives of virtue. That this condition has held and still holds is well put in the words of St. Augustine: "The means of filling up the number of the elect abound in all nations."[6]

Celibacy, undertaken for God's sake, is a nobler state than matrimony because it subordinates a lesser good to a higher good. It sacrifices a vehement bodily inclination for the higher good of religious worship or the common good of society in the practice of the corporal and spiritual works of mercy. It liberates man from many earth cares[7] so that he may give a more undivided attention to God and draw closer to Him. "It is a virtue," says St. Thomas, "which exceeds the common run of human goodness for it likens men to God in a very peculiar way."[8]

715. Among ancient and modern people evidence abounds of celibacy, certainly of religious celibacy, being accorded greater respect than matrimony. The Romans demanded virginity of the Vestal priestesses whose prestige was beyond compare.[9] At Sena among the Gauls there were similar virgin priestesses.[10] At the time of Christ the Jewish sect of the Essenes dedicated themselves to perpetual chastity.[11] Tertullian exhorts his Christian hearers to be content with a single marriage by pointing to the chastity of the pagan priestesses of Juno and of African Ceres.[12] He cites the virgins of Apollo in Ephesus and of Egyptian Thebes;[13] he refers to the dedicates of Scythian Diana and Pythian Apollo.[14] Arnobius[15] mentions the votaries of the same Phrygian Cebele to which Lucian[16] refers. Herodotus speaks in awe of a woman consecrated to Baal in Babylon, of another sacred to Theban Jupiter.[17] The cult of Ephesian Artemis[18] and of Syrian Astarte[19] demanded eunuch priests. Passing by the tremendous tradition of Christianity, we find the Mexicans, immediately prior to the time of Cortez, compelling under penalty of death the

---

6 *De Genesi ad Literam*, IX, 7.
7 Cf. 1 Cor. 7:32–34.
8 *Contra Gentiles*, III, 136.
9 Dionysius of Halicarnassus, *Antiquitates Romanae*, Bk. II, n. 67.
10 Pomponius Mela, *De Situ Orbis*, Lib. III, Chap. 6.
11 Loeb's Classical Library, *Josephus*, Vol. II, "The Jewish War," II, 119–161.
12 *Ad Uxorem*, I, 6. *P.L.*, I, 1284.
13 *De Exhortatione Castitatis*, 13. *P.L.*, II, 928.
14 *De Monogamia*, XVII. *P.L.*, II, 953.
15 *Adversus Gentes*, V, 7. *P.L.*, V, 1094 ff.
16 *De Dea Syria*, 15.
17 I, 181–182.
18 Strabo, XIV, 1, 23.
19 Lucian, *De Dea Syria*, 50 ff.

priests and priestesses of their most sacred divinities to be celibate.[20] Chastity enjoyed peculiar honor among the Incas of Peru.[21] In India among the Jains,[22] among the Todas[23] of South India, in Ceylon among the Buddhists,[24] in Tibet[25] and China among both Buddhists[26] and Taoists[27] celibacy is demanded from all aspirants to true holiness and is proportionately revered. Mohandas K. Gandhi, the late spiritual leader of 300,000,000 Hindus wrote to Viscount Wavell, viceroy of India: "We (Gandhi and his wife) were a couple outside the ordinary. It was in 1906 that by mutual consent and after unconscious [*sic*] trials we definitely adopted self-restraint as the rule of life. To my great joy this knit us together as never before."[28] Gandhi's conduct was a practical assent to the statement of St. Thomas: "If a man abstain from bodily pleasures, in order more freely to give himself to the contemplation of truth, this is in accordance with the rectitude of reason."[29]

III. THE NATURE OF THE CONJUGAL UNION

716. We explain this natural society in the light of its four causes. Since the formal cause of a society depends on the end, we explain the nature and function of the conjugal union in this third part where we treat of its final cause and essential properties. In the fourth part we deal with the efficient cause. Where we discuss the requirements for matrimony in the fifth part the material cause is explained. In the sixth part we discuss the current evils endangering matrimony.

A. The Ends of Matrimony

717. To the all-important question, What does nature intend to accomplish through matrimony? we have already (§§705–706) given an oblique answer. We have shown it to be a natural institution, designed

[20] Francisco Saverio Clavigero, *The History of Mexico*, trans. Charles Cullen, Vol. I, Bk. VI, Sect. 15–17, pp. 274–277. London, Robinson, 1787.
[21] Garcilasso de Vega, *The Royal Commentaries of Peru*, trans. Sir Paul Ricaut, Part I, Bk. IV, Chap. I–VII, pp. 99–106. London, 1688.
[22] Edward W. Hopkins, *The Religions of India*, p. 294. Boston, Ginn, 1898.
[23] *Ibid.*, p. 537.
[24] Malte-Brun, *A System of Universal Geography*, corrected by James Percival, Vol. I, Bk. XLIX, p. 504. Boston, Walker, 1834.
[25] Andrew Wilson, *The Abode of Snow*, pp. 189–191. New York, Putnam, 1886.
[26] Sir John F. Davies, *The Chinese*, Vol. II, p. 81. London, Knight, 1836.
[27] *Ta Tsing Leu Lee, The Fundamental Laws etc. of the Penal Code of China*, trans. Sir George T. Staunton, CXIV, p. 118. London, Cadel, 1810. The Taoist priest who took a wife was to be punished with eighty blows and expulsion from his order.
[28] *Time*, September 4, 1944, p. 43.
[29] *Sum. Theol.*, II–II, 152, 2.

by nature to procure the proper birth and rearing of the human offspring. But is this the only end of matrimony? Are there other goods, of less, equal, greater importance, which nature also intends?

We are not concerned with the personal motives which induce people to get married. These may be good, bad, and indifferent. A man may enter upon the office of president of the United States for reprehensible reasons. His doing so would not alter the fact that this office had a juridical end and function fixed by the Constitution. So too with matrimony. While varying motives induce different people to enter upon it, the Natural Law has already determined its end and function.

Observation and analysis reveal that matrimony offers the human race three distinct blessings.

718. **Mutual advantages of a life totally in common.** It is not good for a man or a woman to live alone. Both naturally crave companionship, especially of the sort that opens up to them the fullest possibilities of personal development. They perceive the great utility of casting their lots together, because their temperaments and abilities will complement one another and an agreeable harmony of life will result. The inducement is not merely the pleasure of each other's company, the protection and providence of the husband, or the home-making of the wife. Matrimony affords the opportunity of a total interchange of all human goods — physical, mental, and moral — from which a man and woman may expect what reasonable felicity this mortal life can provide.

Hence by the exchange of physical conveniences and social amenities a man and woman can rise to real communion of mind and heart — a deep, wholehearted, and affectionate love. This is more than carnal desire, a passing fire of passion; it is the decent, uplifted, and even exalted yearning of the rational appetite, nobly seeking the true good of the object of its affection, deepening and purifying itself of selfishness with the passing of the years. Where this kind of love is patiently cultivated, each shares with the other not only a common domestic economy but the loftier reaches of the spirit; each helps the other to become a better person, to acquire virtue and every advantage that leads to God, their supreme felicity. As far as personal moral benefit is concerned, matrimony is the ordinary but potent instrument whereby the adult attains his last end. Therefore, it is folly for one to choose a partner who would lessen rather than improve his or her opportunities of attaining the last end.

719. **Remedy for concupiscence.** Nature has given men and women sexual faculties and a strong inclination to use them. Yet nothing is more obvious than concupiscence, man's tendency to abuse these. That this is the immediate result of sin and the inclination to repeat sin, both

revelation and experience testify. However, the fundamental cause of concupiscence is found in the duality of man's nature: he is both spirit and body; the drives of the body are more compelling and alluring, and man is more inclined to satisfy his carnal urges than to restrain them in accordance with the dictates of reason. Therefore, to obviate the evils of lust, nature provides a natural, safe, and dignified means of satisfying the sex instinct. This matrimony offers in the carnal union of man and wife, which is the ultimate expression of their mutual love. Thereby two are made one flesh. The marriage act, as the ultimate expression of conjugal love, is sacred; as ordained by God, it is naturally holy.

720. Procreation and education of children. A man and woman usually enter matrimony because of mutual love. This love finds its natural expression in the marriage act, which in turn naturally issues in the birth of a new being which must be protected, reared, and guided unto its proper perfection.

721. No labored proof is required to show that matrimony is capable of producing these three benefits and that nature intends it should do so. Also obvious is the fact that there is a clear and natural connection between these three functions of marriage. However, *which one is first and most important in nature's plan?* This is a vital question: upon its correct solution depend the essential characteristics and the fundamental laws of matrimony, so that matrimony will be one kind of thing if its primary end is the good of the spouses and quite another thing if that primary end is the good of children.

THESIS XLIX. The primary natural end of matrimony is the proper procreation and education of children.

PROOF

722. Among the natural ends of matrimony the proper procreation and rearing of children is primary because unto this all other matrimonial goods are subordinated *by nature.*

a) All the activities of matrimony naturally and ultimately issue in the birth and rearing of children. The ultimate result of the activities of a natural institution constitute its end of work.

b) To say that nature subordinates the birth and rearing of children to the good of the spouses is equivalent to saying that nature does not care whether that end be attained at all. From the history of civilizations, ancient and modern, wherever the notion prevails that matrimony is primarily for the good of the spouses, the race is insufficiently propagated. A declining birth rate has ever accompanied this idea. Hence, since the selfishness and weakness of men are so great, nature simply could not afford to prefer the convenience of the spouses to the propagation of the race. If the primary end of matrimony is not the birth and rearing of children, then nature has inadequately provided for the continuance of the race.

c) There is a difference of sex, and hence a mutual attraction between the sexes, and hence a need for allaying concupiscence, primarily because new human beings are to come of the carnal union of the sexes. If nature had chosen some other way for the propagation of the race — which is conceivable — there would be no difference of sex. Since the conjugal union is nature's sole provision for the carnal union of the sexes (§ 709), the primary end of the conjugal union must be the propagation of the race.

B. The Properties of Matrimony

723. The essential characteristics of matrimony are those qualities which flow from its nature and impart to it its enduring form. What form, then, is the conjugal union to take? Is it one or several? Does nature offer a pleasing variety or does she insist on only one matrimonial system?

Since we have rejected casual temporary unions as destructive of the race and in no way measuring up to the requirements of conjugal society, there is no sense in which promiscuous unions can be called a form of marriage. Hence only these four forms of marriage are conceivable: (a) *group marriage*, a tie among a small closed group of men and women each of whom would have either simultaneously or successively marital rights with one another; (b) *polyandry*, the union of one woman with several men; (c) *polygyny*, the union of one man with several women; (d) *monogamy*, the exclusive union of one man and one woman.

724. Group marriage need not detain us. The actual practice of it is rare, being found among a few peoples such as Eskimos,[30] Todas,[31] and Australian aborigines.[32] This arrangement supposes each man in the group to have his own wife upon whom he has pre-emptive claims; it merely affords him legal toleration of access to the other men's wives under certain specified conditions, for example, when he travels he is

[30] Waldemar Bogoras, *The Jesup North Pacific Expedition, Memoir of the American Museum of Natural History*, Vol. VII, "The Chukckee," Chap. XIX, pp. 602–609. Leiden and New York, Brill, 1909.

[31] W. H. R. Rivers, *The Todas*, pp. 522–523. London, Macmillan, 1906.

[32] B. Malinowski, *The Family Among the Australian Aborigines*, pp. 30–89, 113–115. London, 1913.

supplied by his host with connubial comfort; circumcision brothers often have access to one another's wives. It is a debased form of monogamy. Its morality depends upon the conclusions we reach concerning polyandry and polygyny.

1. *Polyandry*

725. The practice of one woman having several husbands at the same time is quite rare and is found only among savage or degraded peoples in Tibet,[33] somes places in India,[34] Africa, and the South Sea Islands.[35] Its usual form is fraternal, that is, several brothers agree to have one wife. The main reason for the arrangement is poverty; since each brother is too poor to have his own wife, they agree to have one in common. Another reason is that since the husband must be away from home for a long period of time in a land where it is not safe to leave a woman alone, he agrees with other men to act as husband to his wife during his absence. In Madagascar[36] and Ashanti,[37] polyandry seems to be a special privilege accorded a reigning queen or the sisters of a king. However, it is held in abhorrence by the overwhelming majority of mankind.

THESIS L. Polyandry is contrary to the plainest dictates of the Natural Law.

PROOF

726. Polyandry is execrated by the Natural Law because it is a simulation of matrimony which renders impossible the primary end of matrimony.

a) The polyandric woman tends to become sterile.[38]

b) The offspring of such unions will generally have to provide for themselves, because the paternity of the child can be very dubious. None of the men involved is likely to nurture and rear a child that may not be his own.

c) Such an arrangement is an inevitable source of bitter jealousy, strife, and domestic discord. The home has no natural head. No child could be properly reared in such an atmosphere.

---

33 Andrew Wilson, *The Abode of Snow*, pp. 183–189. New York, Putnam, 1886.

34 Rivers, *op. cit.*, pp. 515–521.

35 Urey Lisiansky, *A Voyage Round the World*, Chap. IV, p. 83. London, 1814.

36 Grandidier, cited by Westermarck, *History of Human Marriage*, Vol. III, p. 151.

37 W. Winwood Reade, *Savage Africa*, p. 47. New York, Harpers, 1864.

38 Cf. St. Thomas, *Sum. Theol.*, *Suppl.*, 65, 1, ad 8. Regatillo-Zalba, III, 589. Davis, IV, 58. Noldin-Schmidt-Heinzel, III, 439.

2. *Polygyny*

727. It is by no means as unusual or abhorrent for one man to have several wives at the same time as for a woman to have several husbands. Before adjudging the morality of polygyny let us note several facts. The first recorded instance of polygyny is that of Lamech,[39] who was also a fratricide. It has been and still is practiced by many races but never by any race enjoying a high level of civilization. It is found among people of a rude or a debased civilization, and the actual practice of it among these people is not nearly so widespread as some suppose. For polygyny is a prerogative of wealth: the ordinary man cannot afford more than one wife.

Even in the polygamous family there is an imitation of monogamy, for the man does not equally consort with all his wives but lives with a favorite. When she ceases to please him, he makes another his favorite.

Nor is polygyny so effective for reproduction as is monogamy. Wherever reliable records are kept, it is apparent that the number of male and female births is approximately equal. Where polygyny is practiced the demand for wives will exceed the supply. The older and wealthier will have plenty of wives: many of the younger and healthier men, more capable of propagating, will have none. Since the polygamous husband will live with his favorite wife, the rest of his wives will suffer neglect so that very few of them will bear the number of children they might have borne in a monogamous union.

THESIS LI. The Natural Law forbids any human authority to legalize polygyny.

728. The same evil does not inhere in polygyny as in polyandry. Hence we do not claim the polygyny — and the same holds for divorce — is intrinsically wrong, as blasphemy, perjury, and contraception are. These actions are utterly destructive of human ends. But neither polygyny nor divorce is *absolutely* opposed to the good which matrimony intends. The primary end of matrimony is still attainable despite them, though with difficulty. However, on account of the difficulties which they beget in domestic and civil life, these practices are such hindrances to the secondary ends of matrimony that the Natural Law must forbid any human power to introduce or legalize them. Therefore, polygyny and divorce, *instituted by human authority*, are intrinsically wrong, and forbidden by the Natural Law.

729. But are they not of themselves, *in se*, contrary to the Natural

[39] Genesis 4:23.

Law? There is a tendency among modern authors — Castelein,[40] Joyce,[41] Leclercq[42] — to say that they are evil *in se*. When it is asked how God could have allowed polygyny to the Patriarchs and divorce to the Jews, they reply that God did not give a dispensation in either case, that He merely tolerated an evil in much the same way as the State might tolerate prostitution without approving it.

However, one must admit more than mere divine toleration. If polygyny is *in se* evil, the Patriarchs lived a good part of their lives in grave sin. But this is inadmissible. Their sin could not have been formal, because Holy Writ lauds their sanctity and holds them up as models of virtue. Nor could it even have been material sin. We should have to suppose that these men lived in invincible ignorance that polygyny is *in se* wrong. But in the case of holy men who received so many divine lights, inspirations, and revelations, the supposition is absurd.

Moreover, the moral code of the Mosaic law is a positive enunciation of the Natural Law. If polygyny and divorce are *in se* evil, Moses should have legislated against them. But he did the contrary. He takes polygyny for granted as an accepted institution and legislates concerning it.[43] He explicitly allows divorce,[44] to which fact Christ Himself testifies.[45]

730. It is, therefore, a plausible conclusion that polygyny and divorce are not *in se* evil. Since it is not the existence (*esse*) but the well-being (*bene esse*) of matrimony which these practices oppose, the Divine Lawgiver may, for grave reasons, permit them. This no human legislator can do. The reason for the difference is that God by His omnipotence and universal providence can do what the human legislator cannot, namely, prevent the evils usually consequent upon these practices. That God exercised this special providence seems clear, because (*a*) polygyny ceased among the Jews by the time of the Babylonian captivity; (*b*) from the time of Moses to Christ divorce among the Jews never rose to be a serious social menace as it did in contemporaneous Rome and Greece. To preserve the true religion among His chosen people

[40] A. Castelein, *Institutiones Philosophiae Moralis et Socialis*, pp. 416–417. Bruxelles, Société Belge de Libraire, 1899.

[41] George H. Joyce, *Christian Marriage*, pp. 22, 30. London, Sheed and Ward, 1933.

[42] Jacques Leclercq, *Marriage and the Family*, pp. 89–90. New York, Pustet, 1941.

[43] "If a man have two wives, one beloved and the other hated; he may not make the son of the beloved the first born, and prefer him before the son of the hated" (Deut. 21:15).

[44] "If a man take a wife and have her and she find not favor in his eyes for some uncleanness; he shall write a bill of divorce and give it in her hand and send her out of his house" (Deut. 24:1).

[45] "He said to them: Because Moses by reason of the hardness of your hearts permitted you to put away your wives: but from the beginning it was not so" (Mt. 19:8).

by allowing them to follow the marital customs of the surrounding nations appears to be a sufficiently grave reason to justify the permission. It were better that God should grant them a dispensation from the original unity and indissolubility of the marriage tie, rather than that they should take it upon themselves and thus lapse from the true religion. That this divine license does not constitute an exception to the Natural Law has already been pointed out (§ 221).

However this dispute may be settled, our contention is sound — the Natural Law forbids *men* to introduce and legalize either polygyny or divorce.

PROOF

731. No human authority can legalize a practice which militates against the adequate ends of matrimony, for man may not lawfully hinder the essential purposes of nature. Polygyny militates against the adequate ends of matrimony, which include the good (*a*) of the spouses, (*b*) of the children, (*c*) of the State. In polygyny there is an *essential inequity* which runs counter to the good of all three.

The good of the spouses. *a*) Matrimony demands reciprocal attachment. This is impossible in a situation where a wife cannot give her whole heart to a husband for the reason that he can give her but part of his divided affections. Love of friendship can exist only between equals.

b) The polygynous arrangement lacks the equity which a permanent contract like marriage demands. Since polyandry is intrinsically wrong, a woman must give herself *exclusively* to a husband. What excuses the husband from a like exclusive giving? Polygyny does not provide a complete remedy for concupiscence for all the wives, whereas the man is artificially stimulated to more and more sexual indulgence.

c) Wherever this practice prevails, woman's condition is servile.

The good of the children. Polygyny naturally begets discord, jealousy, and contention in the family. This must react against the proper rearing of children. Children should regard their mother as an object of reverential love, the ideal of all that is good and noble. Instead she is but a servant, a person of small consequence.

The good of the State. Because the number of males and females born is approximately the same, where polygyny flourishes many men will have no wives. Poverty dooms to enforced celibacy many younger men who must either become eunuchs or engage in intrigue with another man's wives.

Corollary. *Monogamy* — the union of one man with one woman —

is the rule of nature. Nothing more simply indicates this than the fact that the birth rate of males and females is about the same.

3. *Divorce*

732. We have established the unity of the matrimonial bond. We have already shown that a certain stability must attach to the conjugal union (§ 705). Does it last until the death of the spouses and admit of no exceptions in any particular case? Or, granting a general need of permanence, may we admit exceptional cases wherein the conjugal tie may occasionally be broken?

Divorce is opposed to the permanency of the marital union. It may be perfect or imperfect. (a) *Imperfect divorce* is a relaxation of the major obligations of the matrimonial contract without a severing of the bond. This is called a separation from bed and board. The separated parties may not remarry. (b) *Perfect divorce* is a severing of the bond itself and allows the parties to enter new marriages.

It is strongly contended today, and in many quarters taken for granted, that if a marriage has so completely failed with a decent person being reduced to misery by the infidelity, insanity, cruelty, or drunkenness of one's mate, an efficacious remedy should be provided. Since it would mean an intolerable loss of happiness for the innocent party to wait until the death of the other for the dissolution of the union, a perfect divorce should be granted.

THESIS LII. The Natural Law forbids perfect divorce upon mere human authority.

733. The Natural Law does not condemn divorce as an evil in itself which is to be always and everywhere prohibited. Divorce is not good, but, since the primary end of marriage is attainable despite it, it is not totally evil. Therefore, the Divine Lawgiver Himself may allow it as the lesser of two evils and under controllable circumstances. It has already been mentioned that He made this exception in favor of the ancient Jews. Revelation also testifies that a similar permission exists in the Church today. Thus there are circumstances wherein a pagan converted to the faith may be released from an existing marriage and permitted by the Church to remarry. The Church may also cancel the marriage of two baptized persons which has never been consummated. This severing of the bond, however, is not an exercise of mere human authority; it is done through an explicit grant of divine power.

The fact that divorce may be granted upon divine authority does not indicate that the Natural Law is subject to change. For the Natural Law does not say: "Do not grant divorces," but "Do not grant divorces unless the Supreme Lawgiver approves."

PROOF

734. The Natural Law forbids any human power to introduce into matrimony a practice which foments enormous evils.

Divorce renders the primary end of matrimony more difficult to attain. *a*) A child's education requires the guidance of both parents. Both have their unique contributions for the upbringing of their offspring.

b) The child of divorced parents can scarcely have an equal love for both parents. Reverence and filial affection ought to be the foundation stone of his character, but these qualities can be destroyed in circumstances which lead to contempt or even hatred of one of his parents.

c) Divorce conduces to the avoidance of children, because the presence of a young family renders future unions more difficult.

Divorce militates against the good morals of husband and wife. *a*) The possibility of obtaining a divorce tends to destroy that complete union of mind and heart between husband and wife which marriage demands. In this union there should be no fear of a future rift. If divorce is envisioned even as remotely possible, this fear will be present, at least in some degree. Such a fear may grow, give rise to suspicion, jealousy, and eventually to a desire for someone else.

b) The possibility of divorce fosters selfishness and removes a potent motive for the practice of virtue. Successful marriage demands mutual forbearance, the spirit of give and take. Where divorce is possible, the thoroughly selfish party will refuse to curb his willfulness, knowing that he can get out of a bad situation by divorce. Where divorce is impossible, the parties are compelled to practice many virtues to maintain a union which usually constitutes their only chance at matrimony.

c) Besides rendering needless that prudent care in the selection of one's partner which so serious a step demands, the possibility of divorce actually incites to crime. If a person is anxious to get a divorce, the sole legal grounds for which are the commission of a crime, he will willingly enough commit that crime.

Divorce militates against the good of society. Since the family is the fundamental organic unit of the State, the well-being of the State depends in large measure upon the well-being of the family.

Divorce promotes discord in families, tends to restrict the birth rate, incites to crime, prevents the proper training of future citizens, belittles the practice of self-control, patience, faithfulness, and other virtues, which in the citizen are of estimable value to the State.

735. The foregoing argument proves that as a *general rule* matrimony should be dissolved only by death. Two arguments prove that this is a universal, ironclad rule admitting of no exceptions.

1. In practice it would be impossible to limit divorces only to grave and exceptional cases. *Either divorce will be granted for every reason or it must never be granted.* This is a matter of all or none. The only way that the indissolubility of marriage can be maintained is by absolute indissolubility. If one loophole is allowed, inevitably, like the first breaching of a dike, the whole barrier will be swept away. In little more than one hundred years, the legal reasons for divorce have multiplied enormously; whereas formerly divorce could be had only by a special act of parliament for the reason of adultery, it is now to be had for the asking. Give men an inch and they take a mile. The scholastic writers who held that our position on divorce could not be proved from the unaided light of reason would have changed their opinion if they had seen the proceedings of a Mexican or Parisian divorce court or the spectacle of States competing with one another to make divorce as easy as possible so as to attract the tourist divorce trade.

2. The main reason for divorce in an exceptional case is relief for the victim of an indissoluble tie. However, under a system of divorce — and there would inevitably be a system, for divorce cannot remain an exceptional and isolated phenomenon — the number of victim cases would not be fewer but infinitely greater and the chief victim would be the woman, the weaker party. The evils which follow from divorce affect the whole of society; those incidental upon indissolubility are purely personal and do not affect society at large, any more than do the pains of the sick in a hospital. Now matrimony has as its end the good of the race; this end determines its characteristic of indissolubility, which may not be altered or impaired because of accidental hardships to the individual. Hence the common good reasonably demands that individuals bear the trials incidental to an indissoluble tie rather than let loose upon society the vast evils entailed in divorce.

IV. THE ORIGIN OF MATRIMONY

736. The problem of the origin of conjugal society presents two questions. The first may be framed thus: *What cause determined that such an institution should exist?* Evolutionary writers say that it originated in the same sort of paternal and maternal instinct to protect one's young and hence to live together as that which keeps male and female chimpanzee together.[46] This instinct was the root of a habit: in time it grew into a custom imposing moral obligation, which — in the language of those who offer this explanation — means that public opinion would disapprove of, and public authority would punish, the husband who abandons wife and children.

737. We deny as a gratuitous assumption the contention that man has ever been other than a rational animal. Whether man ever had subhuman ancestors is beside the point; we are establishing the specific law of rational animals, and in that law we find a need for conjugal society. That public sentiment is not the constitutive norm of morality, that moral law does not originate in mere mores and customs, we have disposed of in general ethics. Hence conjugal society is not an accidental arrangement which men stumbled upon and became accustomed to. It is not the result of chance or experimentation. It is divinely appointed. From the preceding sections in which we proved conjugal society to be natural and necessary, it is clear that it originated in a command of the Natural Law. God, then, is the Author of conjugal society. As Universal Ruler and Provider, He has in view the proper conservation and increase of the race and has chosen conjugal society as the sole means to this end. In order that His divine purpose be realized and this instrument for human good be made use of, God implants in men and women a strong desire to enter the married state and presents to their reason the truth that their chief hope of temporal felicity lies therein. The fact that some persons listen to the prompting of nature and marry, while others flout it by homosexuality or like excesses, does not interest us now. Our point is that conjugal society is a divinely established institution.

738. The second question which the problem of the origin of matrimony presents is this: *What cause produces every actual conjugal society?* Is there a direct divine intervention in the setting up of each conjugal union according to the homely adage that marriages are made in heaven? Obviously not: there are no signs of such divine intervention. Besides, it would be bordering on the impious to blame God for the folly of mismated marriages. It is the way of God with men to indicate the general pattern of essential human institutions and then to leave it to the discretion and choice of men to fill in the particulars. Since, then, men and women are not born married, how are they brought together,

[46] Herbert Spencer's explanation is typical. See *Principles of Sociology*, Vol. I, pp. 621–640. Cf. also Edward Westermarck, *The History of Human Marriage*, Vol. I, p. 26 ff. London, Macmillan, 1921.

what causes the union of each particular married couple? To answer, we must distinguish between (*a*) the historic origin and (*b*) the juridic origin of each particular union.

A. Historic Origin

739. Every conjugal union has some factual beginning. Some accidental and variable set of facts culminated in this man's marriage to this woman. These antecedent facts in the main fall into two general patterns: one, called a courtship, wherein the man woos his prospective bride; the other, and more customary in human history, a nuptial agreement wherein parents or other parties arrange the union. What these diverse facts may have been or now are, is for the social historian to say. At present we are not directly concerned with these facts except to say that they are merely dispositive and not the causative factors in the resultant union.

B. Juridic Origin

740. Since the conjugal union is a true society, its creation means the endowing of the parties concerned with obligations and rights which they previously did not possess. A conjugal society is a moral person possessing a definite juridic standing. What in the juridic order is capable of producing the juridic effect of this man's now becoming the husband of this woman? This thing — fact, happening, disposition, legal edict, or whatever it be — will constitute the proximate efficient cause — or better — the juridic cause of every actual conjugal society.

THESIS LIII. The proximate juridic cause of every actual conjugal union can only be the free and mutual consent of a man and a woman.

PROOF

741. Each particular conjugal society must arise from a juridic cause which is in keeping with man's rational nature and with the peculiar character of this society. Such a cause can only be the free and mutual consent of a man and a woman.

a) *This cause must be in keeping with man's nature.* On entering the married state a man disposes of his person for life. Assuredly, the significant act of a man's career whereby he disposes of his person, and that for life, must be a free act. For to be responsible for his person, he must be free in the disposal of it. Second, nature does not determine who is married to whom. Since no individual is compelled to marry, it is left to the free choice of each to enter this society as he chooses and with the partner of his choice.

b) *The cause must be in keeping with the peculiar character of this society.* A union so intimate demands mutual love, which certainly cannot be extorted by force, fear, or command. Second, this state entails tedious burdens which no individual is, *per se*, obliged to assume, much less in the company of this particular partner. Hence the very nature of this society demands that one enter it solely by free choice.

742. N.B. It may not be argued that in the past almost universally, and even now generally among savages, the marriages of women have been arranged by parents or other responsible persons. This fact need not imply that the girl was married against her will. Since she desired matrimony, and since the only way to it was to accept the spouse of her parents' choosing, she would willingly enough acquiesce. If her wishes were not directly consulted, she was not without the means of making her inclination known and her influence felt. Even among savage tribes today, if the girl is unwilling, she is not forced to marry a particular man. Even though parents have married off their children with little consideration of their happiness, and young people have been mated unwillingly, consent is still an essential requisite. These examples are but instances of practice falling short of law. Although many persons lie and steal, it does not follow that there is no moral law against lying and stealing.

Corollary. *The marriage rite as the constitutive act of matrimony is a contract.* For this act, consisting in the free and mutual consent of two parties to give and accept rights concerning one and the same object, fulfills the requisite conditions for a valid, bilateral contract.

V. THE MARRIAGE CONTRACT

743. The contract of betrothal must not be confused with the contract of marriage. Betrothal is a mutual promise of marriage, binding in commutative justice, and severable at the will of the parties. It pertains to a *future* giving and acceptance of marital rights. The marriage contract is the mutual handing over of such rights here and now. It is more than a promise to exchange rights; it is the actual exchange of rights, and it is not severable at the will of the parties. We shall now consider the marriage contract in detail in the light of (*a*) matrimonial consent; (*b*) the matter of this consent; (*c*) the parties to the contract; (*d*) the relation of this contract to other contracts.

A. Matrimonial Consent

744. Consent is so essential to the marriage contract that no human power can replace it. If it is wanting, conjugal union is impossible. Matrimonial consent must be genuine, deliberate, mutual, externally manifested, and given by a man and woman capable of making this contract.

Genuine consent is true agreement; outward pretence of agreement is not consent. A person who has manifested fictitious consent is not married, although positive law rightly considers such a person married until he offers juridical evidence that he did not consent. Fictitious consent, however, may be validated by the proffering of a properly sanating consent. If the withholding of consent was *purely internal*, the marriage contract could be validated by the mere eliciting of true consent, provided the consent of the other party remained. If the withholding of consent was external but *could not be juridically proved*, an external but private manifestation of consent could validate the contract. If the withholding of consent was external and *could be juridically proved*, an external manifestation of consent, satisfactory to social authority, is required for convalidation.

Deliberate consent is given with full advertence of the mind and perfect agreement of the will. No one assumes grave obligations without knowing them and being willing to accept them.

Mutual consent is given by each party because of and with a view to the consent of the other. An onerous bilateral contract requires the agreement of both parties. However, their agreement need not be simultaneous; the consent of one party may be given for the first time, even a long time, after the other party has agreed. If the consent of the first party remains, this delayed consent produces a valid marriage.

Consent must be *externally manifested*. The manifestation of agreement is essential in any contract. The Natural Law only requires that each party outwardly signify agreement to the other. However, since the conjugal union is of such importance to society, and since very great evils would arise if this contract were concluded in total secrecy, positive law can and usually does prescribe that this manifestation of agreement accord with a prescribed form, such as the presence of certified witnesses.[47] The Natural Law commands compliance with these forms even when positive law prescribes them under penalty of nullity of contract. However, where compliance with these forms would be impossible and a couple might otherwise be compelled to forego matrimony

[47] *Codex Juris Canonici*, 1094.

forever, or for a very long time, the positive law would lapse by *epikeia* and the merely natural form of contract would be permissible.

Consent must be given by *a man and woman capable of contracting.* The elements which constitute capability for making the contract will be taken up presently.

745. Conditional consent. It is possible to render a conditional consent. A careful distinction should be made between a true condition (a condition precedent) and a modal condition. The latter leaves the matrimonial consent intact and sets forth circumstances under which the contract will be carried out, as when a man marries with the understanding that he will continue a seafaring life.

A true condition is a circumstance upon which a party makes his consent depend so that it is given absolutely or withheld according as the circumstance is verified or not.

a) *Condition concerning the future.* (1) If the condition is something lawful, the marriage will be suspended until the condition is verified. (2) If the condition is something necessary, impossible, or unlawful but not contrary to the substance of matrimony, the presumption is that the condition was not seriously intended. (3) If the condition is contrary to the substance of matrimony, consent is invalid. Therefore, if one consents only on condition that (i) no true right of intercourse be given, or (ii) only a right to contraceptive intercourse be given, or (iii) one be at liberty to marry other wives or to break up this union and marry some other person, or (iv) one is free to commit adultery, he does not consent to marriage but to a sham of marriage. In concrete cases, however, a very difficult problem arises of determining what is the prevailing intention of parties who thus qualify their consent. If their stipulations are real conditions precedent, consent is invalid; but if the parties intend to marry as other people do and have a further intention of abusing matrimony or of not fulfilling its obligations their consent is valid.

Only a reason of extreme gravity justifies a conditional consent. The condition should be stated so as to be capable of juridic proof. It is a serious injustice to affix a condition to one's consent without the knowledge of the other party.

B. The Matter of Consent

746. What exactly forms the object of the matrimonial consent, or better, what right does one party transfer to the other in this contract? The man who enters this contract transfers to a woman the exclusive and permanent right to use his body for acts proper to procreate children.

By acceptance of this right, the woman is constituted the wife of the man. Similarly, the woman transfers to the man the exclusive and permanent right to use her body for acts proper to procreate children. By acceptance of this right, the man becomes the husband of the woman.

That a right to natural copula alone is the essential object of the matrimonial consent follows from the primary end of matrimony. The rights of cohabitation, of mutual love, of a certain community of goods, of the wife to protection and support, and of the husband to obedience, are merely consequences of this essential point. Cohabitation pertains not to the essence but to the integrity of matrimony; mutual love is the practical condition requisite for the happy outcome of the matrimonial venture; a community of goods is a condition necessary for the reasonable bearing of the obligations of matrimony.

That this right is permanent follows from the indissoluble permanence of this union (§ 735). That it is an exclusive right follows from monogamistic character of matrimony (§ 731, Cor.). Once this right is mutually exchanged, each party is bound in commutative justice so that any sexual contact with a third party violates justice in a serious matter.

747. To the inexperienced, the realization that a right to carnal intercourse is the primary object of the matrimonial consent is sometimes a shattering of youthful ideals. If after marriage one subconsciously clings to the notion that intercourse is an earthy evil at best to be tolerated, he or she seriously endangers the success of marriage. Though this attitude reminds one of Manicheism, which taught that the flesh is essentially evil, yet it is the outcome of a chaste upbringing. However, a little reflection must show that this act is wholesome and praiseworthy. For it is the ultimate expression of mutual love and is ordained by God as the sole means of fulfilling a divine purpose. It lapses into the indecent only through its unholy imitation in the form of fornication, adultery, and contraception.

748. In the exercise of marital rights both parties are absolutely equal. Although the man is the head of the family, in this fundamental respect he has no priority over his wife. Nor has the wife over the husband, even though the burden of childbearing falls on her. Neither is subordinate to the other. Each is bound to accede to the other's *serious* request for marital relations so that refusal is a grave violation of justice. The causes which excuse from sin in a refusal are the other party's complete loss of reason, the adultery of the other party, grave danger to one's health, grave spiritual harm, continuing refusal of the man to support wife and children. Failure to fulfill this fundamental obligation with alacrity and charity are the roots of marital discord and disunion.

749. *Artificial insemination* is the fertilization of a woman by means other than natural intercourse. Obviously no unmarried woman may receive seed. The exclusive character of matrimony forbids a wife to receive any but her husband's seed. Furthermore, a wife may not be impregnated by her husband's seed except through natural intercourse. The plan of nature is that children should be the fruit of a personal union whereby two are made one flesh. The right which is exchanged in the matrimonial contract is not the right to be a parent but the right of natural sexual congress. It is lawful, however, to use various artificial means to assist the natural act attain its purpose of fruitfulness.

C. Parties to the Consent

750. Parties to consent are a man and a woman physically and juridically capable of matrimony.

1. *Physical Capacity*

Physical capacity means that each party has (*a*) the age and unimpeded use of reason requisite for true matrimonial consent; (*b*) the ability to perform the generative act in the natural way. Because of physical incapacity, therefore, the Natural Law excludes from matrimony persons with any of the following six deficiencies:

751. a) *Lack of age.* The natural age for matrimony is that age at which a person has sufficient knowledge and discretion to give true matrimonial consent. Positive law usually presumes that a person is not so qualified before the age of puberty and hence prohibits marriage before that age. Canon Law[48] invalidates the attempted marriage of a male before the completion of his sixteenth year and of a female before the completion of her fourteenth year.

752. b) *Lack of the use of reason.* Infants or lunatics, intoxicated, drugged, or hypnotized persons are incapable of making a contract.

753. c) *Defective knowledge.* A valid contract requires sufficient knowledge of the object of consent. The absence of this knowledge precludes the essential agreement, which is contract. What, then, is that bare minimum of knowledge for lack of which a person is incapable of this contract? From our explanation of the matrimonial consent (§ 746) it follows that one must know at least that matrimony is a permanent society between man and woman for the procreating of children through some sort of bodily communion. It is by no means necessary that one know the precise mode and nature of carnal intercourse, generation, and birth, but one has to know, at least vaguely and in general,

[48] *Codex Juris Canonici,* 1067.

that one hands over and acquires a right to some sort of bodily conjunction whence children are begotten and which is peculiar to matrimony. It is confessedly difficult to draw a hard and fast line which would accurately define where sufficient knowledge exists and where an invalidating ignorance begins. Certainly a person would be invalidatingly ignorant who thought matrimony a mere friendly, temporary alliance or the *mere* setting up of a common ménage, or who was totally and absolutely unaware of the need of some kind of corporal intercourse. Positive law — as Canon Law[49] — presumes that this sort of ignorance does not exist after one has reached the age of puberty.

754. d) *Mistake*, or error, in this matter, has to do with (1) the person of the other party, or (2) some essential quality of matrimony.

(1) *The person of the other party.* Mistake of person, for instance, John marries Anna thinking her to be Sarah, her twin sister, invalidates consent. It constitutes substantial error. Mistake concerning some quality in the person — as when Mary marries Paul thinking him to be wealthy whereas he is not — does not affect consent. The error is only accidental. In two cases, however, a mistake of quality is equivalent to a mistake of person. First, the quality may be definitive of the person, as when George marries Marjorie Wilson thinking her to be *The* Marjorie Wilson, President Wilson's daughter. Second, one may marry upon the explicit condition of the existence of a given quality, as when Charles tells Louise that he will marry her provided she is of pure Caucasian blood.

(2) *Some essential quality of matrimony.* In § 753 we discussed the knowledge essential to consent, but a related and quite knotty question may arise. Unity and indissolubility are essential properties of matrimony. Does ignorance of this truth vitiate consent? For example, a Mohammedan, marrying his first wife, may vaguely hope to take more wives when his financial condition improves; many Americans marry believing in divorce. Do their wrong notions invalidate consent? Usually they do not. Mistaken notions about polygamy and divorce can coexist with true consent because ordinarily these ideas do not affect that which the parties will. These persons intend to marry as other people do: the object of their intention is true matrimony, not a simulation of it. When, however, such error *actually* influences consent so that a person by positive act of the will excludes some matrimonial property, he does not validly consent.

755. e) *Duress and fear.* Duress is irresistible violence to which one unwillingly submits. It is a bar to any contract. Canon Law[50] safeguards

[49] *Ibid.*, 1082, 2.
[50] *Ibid.*, 1074.

freedom to consent by providing that no marriage is possible between an abductor and a woman forcibly taken or detained with a view to matrimony until such time as she is restored to a place of safety and freedom.

A person who enters matrimony induced by grave fear performs a human act and has true consent, but is such consent sufficient for the matrimonial contract? First, Canon Law[51] declares null from the beginning consent extorted by grave fear arising from a source external to the agent and unjustly inflicted so that one embraces matrimony to escape the threatened evil. Many civil codes have similar prescriptions. But does the Natural Law also invalidate such a consent? There is a sharp cleavage of opinion here. Those who answer in the affirmative say that if an ordinary contract is entered into under pressure of such fear, the contract is later rescindable, but since the matrimonial contract, once validly formed, cannot be rescinded, such consent must be initially invalid. Otherwise, one would suffer an irreparable injury by being morally forced into a permanent state through fear of injustice. On the other hand, it is more reasonably contended that an act elicited even under grave, external, and unjust fear is still a human act, a free choice. Since neither slight fear, nor fear arising from a source internal to the agent, nor just external fear invalidates matrimonial consent, no fear does. Either all fear invalidates a contract or no fear does. Nor may an exception be urged in the case of unjust external fear on the ground that it causes irreparable injury. For one may be led into matrimony by deceitful or even fraudulent misrepresentations and suffer a similar injury, yet no one claims that such consent is initially invalid.

The practical conclusion is that when nonbaptized persons enter matrimony induced by fear in a place where the civil law does not nullify such consent, then by Natural Law such a marriage is to be looked on as valid, according to the maxim that a juridic act is presumed valid unless its invalidity is certainly established.

756. *f*) *Impotence.* Since the right which passes in the matrimonial contract is the right to use one's body for acts proper to procreation, nature must prohibit from matrimony persons incapable of such acts. If an act is impossible, no right to that act can be given or accepted. The object of contract is nonexistent; hence no contract is possible. Anyone, therefore, who before matrimony is *perpetually* incapable of performing the generative act in the natural way either with this person or with all persons is barred by nature itself from marriage with this person or with all persons. A male has this incapacity if he lacks seed,

[51] *Ibid.*, 1087, § 1.

or the ability to eject seed, or the ability to eject it into the body of a woman. A female is impotent if she cannot receive seed.[52]

Impotence must carefully be distinguished from *sterility* which is inability to generate. Sterility is not a bar to matrimony. This is evident from consideration of the material object of consent which is only the generative act, not generation itself. This ultimately does not depend on the choice of the agent. Nor may one be prohibited from marriage because of impotence unless the disability is clearly certain. Artificial insemination does not remove impotence.

2. *Juridic Capacity*

757. Juridic capacity means that a person otherwise physically able is not prevented from matrimony by some juridic obstacle established by Natural or positive law. This juridic obstacle is some external circumstance affecting a person and legally rendering him temporarily or permanently incapable of matrimony.

But if one is mentally and physically fit, why should law specify further requisites. Is not matrimony a private affair and entrance into it but the response of an individual to one of the most primal of human instincts? Since matrimony antedates the State, and since the right to marry is an immediate concession of nature, why should this right be abridged by social authority?

Matrimony, however, is not entirely a private affair. It has such wide-reaching social effects that the well-being of society depends in no small measure upon the well-being of the conjugal union. Since the sexes can consort in a way that runs counter to the social good, social authority may determine these detrimental circumstances and forbid and even nullify marriage where they are verified.

758. Natural juridic capacity. The Natural Law prohibits matrimony because of (*a*) consanguinity and (*b*) an existing marriage tie. A person who attempts to marry despite these impediments contracts an invalid marriage.

a) *Consanguinity.* Marriage between a parent and a child is unnatural because it would destroy the essential relation of inequality between a child and its parent established by nature itself; all consanguine marriages tend to be detrimental to the offspring: *a fortiori* these evil consequences would follow from a marriage in which the blood relationship is the closest possible.

Unless it is absolutely necessary to carry on the human race, the marriage of brother and sister is likewise forbidden by nature. That

[52] T. J. O'Donnell, *Morals in Medicine,* 182 ff.

special relation of love and confidence between brother and sister which is of such value to both would be destroyed and turned into a source of evil rather than good if they were free to marry. Unless nature herself forbade all hope of carnal intercourse between offspring of the same parents, the peace and purity of family life would be destroyed. Mentally and bodily defective persons come from such unions. A third reason may be added: the marriage of brother and sister would not establish those new bonds of friendship and relationship which the marriages of unrelated persons provide.

These evils militating against the good of the offspring, the sanctity of family life, and the strengthening of social ties, are found in the marriage of closely related cousins, though of course to a lesser degree. The Natural Law does not prohibit such unions; it is rather left to positive law to regulate them so that these evil effects are prevented.

b) *An existing marriage tie.* Monogamy is the law of nature. Therefore once a person has entered a valid conjugal union, no human authority can allow him to enter another union until the death of his partner will have severed the existing marital tie.

759. Positive juridic capacity. Since mention has been made of positive law establishing invalidating matrimonial impediments, it is well to make clear the nature of this power and the reason for it. Besides clarifying the conditions under which the Natural Law disqualifies a person from contracting marriage, positive law may determine that there are other conditions wherein matrimony would be harmful to the social good. Since matrimony affects the common good in so many ways, and since the Natural Law is not sufficiently explicit regarding all possible contingencies, there is need of positive legislation to establish, as necessity requires, other impediments and salutary laws that will secure the good estate of matrimony. As we shall presently see (§ 765), matrimony has a naturally sacred and religious character.

Hence any further regulation must devolve upon religious authority. Therefore it is for the Church to legislate for the marriages of baptized persons, not only because of the naturally religious character of matrimony, but especially because the marriage ceremony of the baptized is a sacrament. To the Church alone is entrusted the care of the sacraments.

It has been contended by some Christian writers who hesitate to give the State its full due, that in the case of nonbaptized persons, the State has no jurisdiction over marriage itself except to clarify and enforce the impediments of the Natural Law. But the need of further legislation for the common good is apparent, and since among the nonbaptized there is no religious authority competent to do this, the task must fall upon the State. However, such civil impediments must, as any other laws, be reasonable, capable of being observed, and promotive of good morals; otherwise, they have no force.

3. *The State and Christian Marriage*

760. Since the so-called liberal movement of the eighteenth century States have been legislating about the validity and lawfulness of Christian marriage. Such legislation is usurpation because the State has no direct power over Christian marriage or its inseparable effects such as the legitimacy of the children. The reason for the State's lack of authority is that Christian marriage is a sacrament and to the Church alone belongs the care of the sacraments.

Indirectly, as a result of some other legal act, the State may affect the marriage of Christians, as when by perpetual imprisonment or the segregation of persons infectiously diseased, the State would take away opportunity to marry. By application of the principle of double effect the State may do this, provided a proportionately grave cause is at hand to offset so grave an effect as curtailment of the right to marry.

761. No difficulty exists where the civil law merely repeats the prohibitions of the Natural Law, where the Church explicitly accepts as a canonical impediment some civil impediment such as that which arises from legal adoption,[53] or where the State issues reasonable regulations in the interests of public order. The State can legislate concerning the *merely* civil effects of Christian marriage, that is, effects which are separable from the contract itself, such as dowry, succession to titles and property, use of the husband's name by the wife. Under the head of reasonable regulation would also come the need of recording marriages with a public official and of a soldier to secure his commanding officer's permission before marrying. Real difficulty arises, however, when the State declares null or voidable the marriages of Christians who (*a*) have not gone through a civil ceremony, or (*b*) are of different races, or (*c*) who have not secured a certificate of medical fitness.

762. Civil ceremony. Insistence on a civil ceremony for recognition of a Christian marriage is a remnant of the anticlerical effort to destroy Christian marriage.

Miscegenation. A number of states in the United States forbid very strictly marriage between a white person and a person of color (black or yellow). The law is founded on race prejudice and is not promotive of good morals.

763. Medical certificates. Many States require a certificate attesting

[53] Cf. Canon 1080.

that one is free from venereal disease before one can marry. The intent of such legislation — the stamping out of these diseases — is admirable but in pursuing its aim of good health the State may overstep its proper bounds.

As guardian of public health, the State may demand examination of prospective spouses, advise remedies, and suggest cures. It may segregate the venereally afflicted for a time *if* segregation is a reasonable means of cure. But the State may not prohibit or nullify a Christian marriage. To do so would be usurpation of authority and would be equivalent to the State's saying who could or could not receive the other sacraments of the Church.

In defense of eugenic legislation it may not be alleged that the venereally afflicted are prohibited from marriage by the Natural Law. As such, disease is not a Natural Law impediment. This we gather from the silence of the Church. Careful and detailed as her legislation is, she has never said that communicable disease is an impediment.

In general, prudence demands that the baptized conform to this kind of legislation. They are bound to submit to examination and to undertake reasonable means of cure; but if for an urgent reason — avoidance of concubinage or legitimation of children — a healthy party were willing to marry a syphilitic, the parties could proceed in good conscience. Such a marriage could be contracted as a remedy for concupiscence, a secondary end of marriage. The physical evils to offspring and healthy consort which once were normally expected are now, in the main, preventable. But even if dire physical consequences should happen, these are an immeasurably lesser evil than a single grave sin which such a marriage could prevent.

764. May the State make disease a matrimonial impediment for nonbaptized persons?[54] That human authority should do something so drastic as to annul the right to marry, a very grave reason is required. Two reasons are here conceivable: the good of society and the protection of the innocent party. Concerning the good of society, we may admit in the abstract that if society were being overwhelmed by a staggering increase of subnormal children due to the marrying of diseased persons, the Natural Law would approve of civil legislation curbing such marriages. However, this state of affairs does not exist. Furthermore, the State has at hand sufficient means of control and cure of disease without resorting to an absolute and permanent prohibition of marriage to diseased persons. Such enforced celibacy would be too great a burden

[54] Cf. J. P. O'Brien, *The Right of the State to Make Disease an Impediment to Marriage*, 122 ff. Washington, Catholic University Press, 1952.

for these people to bear. A temporary prohibition, however, say for the few months necessary for the cure of gonorrhea, would be within the right of the State. But the exercise of the right by prohibitory laws would be inexpedient. For such laws foster common-law marriages and sexual promiscuity. The addition of a single formality to the celebration of marriage is, among certain people, enough to bring about a decrease of marriages. The second reason alleged for the State's power to make disease a matrimonial impediment is the protection of the other party from the danger of contracting the disease. The diseased party has a grave obligation to disclose his situation to the other party and the State may see fit to urge this obligation by legislation. But this legislation ought not to impede marriage but simply assure that both parties are aware of the physical condition of the other.[55]

D. The Relation of Marriage to Other Contracts

765. The marriage contract differs from all other contracts by reason of its end, matter, unalterable terms, and intimate connection with religion.

End. The end intended by nature in the marriage contract is not primarily the good of the individuals contracting but the good of the race. While persons who enter matrimony consider it the chief source of their temporal happiness, nevertheless this personal good in nature's intent is subordinate to the good of the human race. When this natural order is reversed and the majority of people act as though the primary end of matrimony were the good of the spouses, dire evils follow. In this misconception are rooted divorce, birth control, and trial marriage.

Matter. In all other contracts the matter is external and inferior to man. Here the contracting parties dispose of their very persons.

Unalterable terms. The terms and duration of many contracts are determined by the parties themselves. This is not the case in the marriage contract. This contract sets up a natural institution; and once the contract is formed, the resultant union cannot be dissolved by the mutual consent of the parties, nor can they determine anything contrary to the essential constitution of this union which has already been fixed by the Author of nature and placed beyond the tampering of men.

Intimate connection with religion. The matrimonial contract is especially related to God because its ultimate end is the procreation of rational beings wherein God concurs in a very special way by the creation of spiritual souls. It initiates conjugal life whose purpose is the increase of immortal beings, destined for eternal beatitude. Besides, the

[55] Cf. *Massachusetts Annual Laws,* 1944, Supplement, c. 207, 28 A.

burdens of this state are so heavy that they can reasonably be borne only with the help and solace of religion.

The natural matrimonial contract is not an explicit act of religion; but, because of its close connection with God's purpose — the procurement of His external glory — it is naturally sacred and holy. However, we know from revelation that the contract between baptized[56] persons is a sacrament and hence an explicit act of supernatural religion.

VI. MATRIMONIAL EVILS

766. Anything which militates against the integrity of matrimony or renders difficult the attainment of its ends is a matrimonial evil. It deprives this institution of a good that should be present. From our discussions of companionate marriage, forced consent, polyandry, polygyny, and divorce, it is evident how these things are destructive of the good of matrimony. Several further points deserve attention.

A. Evils Contrary to the Good of the Spouses

767. Marital love, the rock on which husband and wife build their happiness, is impossible of realization, or if had, is destroyed by certain heedless or sinful acts.

Unwise choice of one's partner. Passionate haste, which is but a fire of the body, drives into wedlock many young people wholly unsuited to each other. Passion dies and there is no loftier bond to takes its place. Young persons ought not to be motivated solely by romantic illusions and physical beauty. To be sensibly realistic, they should ask themselves, What will my dream man be like ten, twenty years from now? How well can we bear the years together? It is an ancient wisdom which says — marry your own kind. This advice has special reference to religion. Marriage intends to make two one flesh, but if there is a profound difference in a couple's philosophy of life — and religion is the basis of a philosophly of life — a complete union of mind and heart is next to impossible. The saddest result of such mismating is that so often the children grow up without any religion.

Selfishness is at the bottom of domestic quarreling, nagging, the pursuit of habitual sins which, like drunkenness, make family peace impossible. Love is surrender, giving — not demanding always, always taking. The man or wife who habitually puts self first will certainly fail at marriage.

Adultery known and uncondoned can be sufficient reason for the perpetual cessation of marital life. It is the heinous rupture of the

[56] See *Codex Juris Canonici*, 1012, 1.

communion of body whereby two are made one flesh. It is caused by the grudging fulfillment of marriage duties, and desire for variety, excitement, and sensual friendship of a third party. It is not jealousy or narrow-mindedness but simple common sense which forbids married persons such friendships.

B. Evils Contrary to the Good of the Child

768. Abortion and sterilization, which we have considered, are obviously contrary to the good of offspring. Impediments to the proper rearing of the child are dealt with in the next chapter. Here we come to grips with an outstanding problem of modern times — birth control.

1. *What Is Birth Control?*

769. In general, birth control is planned limitation of offspring. In many periods of history, for economic or religious reasons, men have desired as numerous a progeny as possible. In a simple pastoral or agricultural economy, the rearing of children is inexpensive. A man's wealth depends on the number of children who will work for him and his renown upon the number of descendants who will revere his memory. But when civilization becomes urbanized and a large family becomes an economic liability, the tendency to limit its size arises.

The English parson, Thomas Malthus (1766–1834), raised a "scare problem" on a world-wide scale. He contended that where the reproductive instinct was uncontrolled, the population increased in geometric proportion (1–2–4–8–16).[57] Since the products of the earth increased only in arithmetic proportion (1–2–3–4–5),[58] the number of births must be radically curbed to prevent overcrowding of population and shortages of food. The remedy he suggested was late marriage and voluntary continence in marriage.[59]

This economic, or rather demographic, problem, as it is now called, is quite a live one. Some authors[60] paint a gloomy picture of a world soon to be crowded with starving people; others[61] scoff at this notion and point to the earth's increase of fertility because of scientific advances. The desirability of limiting offspring has taken firm hold and is carried

[57] T. R. Malthus, *An Essay on the Principle of Population.* London, Johnson, 1803.

[58] *Ibid.*, Bk. I, Chap. 1, p. 8.

[59] *Ibid.*, Bk. IV, Chaps. 1–2, pp. 483–503.

[60] William Vogt, *Road to Survival.* Fairfield Osborn, *Our Plundered Planet.* Harrison Brown, *The Challenge of Man's Future.*

[61] *Report of FAO, 1955.* Eugene Holman, "Our Inexhaustible Resources," *Atlantic Monthly*, June, 1952. Robert Salter of the U. S. Agricultural Research Administration, *Time*, November 8, 1948. C. L. Swanson of Connecticut Agricultural Experiment Station, *Time*, January 18, 1954.

out extensively. Motives and methods have changed since the time of Malthus. He appealed to the common good and advocated chaste self-restraint. Today, the appeal is on a more personal basis and scarcely any modern advocate of birth control preaches self-restraint but only positive contraception.

770. We have two problems: one of end, the other of means. The problem of end is this: *Is it wrong for a married couple to desire no children?* This will object is not intrinsically wrong. For the obligation to propagate falls directly on the race and not on the particular couple; when the race is in danger of extinction, the obligation falls on individual couples. However, since the obligations of society are fulfilled by individuals, whoever enters the married state assumes an obligation toward the primary end of marriage. You cannot enter an important society and be indifferent to its main purpose. But the obligation is not so absolute that one may not be released from it for cause. The gravity of the excusing reason depends on whether the by-passing of marriage's primary end is temporary or perpetual.

771. The desire to have no children on the part of the married is dangerous. First, it may invalidate consent. If one yields no right of intercourse, or fails to grant a perpetual right, or agrees only to an abuse of intercourse, his consent is invalid. He is not agreeing to true matrimony. A person who wishes matrimony must be willing to accept parenthood. However, the intention of not having children is compatible with valid consent if a person's prevailing intention is to enter the married state and to this intention is joined a subsequent intention either to abuse matrimony or wholly to refrain from its use. One may validly consent and intend to abuse it, because one may assume obligations which he does not intend to fulfill. This is always grievously wrong. If the intention is not to use matrimony, we distinguish several possibilities: (*a*) The resolution or vow of one party to preserve chastity does not invalidate consent provided he gives and accepts matrimonial rights because he can acquire a right even though he does not intend to exercise it. (*b*) If beforehand both parties compact not to use matrimony so that the consent of one is given only on condition that the other agrees to perpetual chastity, their agreement invalidates consent. (*c*) If both parties agree unconditionally to exchange marital rights and then subjoin to their matrimonial consent the modal condition of not using matrimony, the consent is valid. To marry and intend not to use matrimony is a procedure to be justified only by a most extraordinary reason: matrimony is not the milieu for keeping a vow of chastity.

Second, the desire not to have children is dangerous because one is strongly tempted to use illicit means to carry out the intention. What are licit means of limiting offspring?

772. **Abstention from marital relations.** The effective method of preventing conception is abstention from intercourse. Is it wrong for a couple to abstain?

The obligation which each party assumes is to render the marital debt upon the other's request, but there is no obligation from the nature of the contract to request relations. First, there is no need of a moral obligation because the proximate end intended by nature — sufficient use of generative faculties — is adequately assured by the driving urge to use these faculties. Second, requesting relations is a privilege, and no one is *ex se* obliged to use a privilege. Therefore there is no obligation in justice to request relations, although at times one may arise from charity, that is, to prevent a rift of love or to avoid the incontinence of the other party.

If both of them are willing, a couple may abstain either for a time or even altogether and do no wrong. Their resolution in this respect should accord with what they prudently feel able to accomplish.

773. **Restriction of intercourse to infertile period.** The rhythm theory advanced by Latz and others holds that in the menstrual cycle of most women there is a definite period of sterility which may be accurately computed and forecast. If the sterile period of the wife can be determined, is it wrong to confine intercourse to that period?

First, a danger of invalid consent may arise if "one of the parties in contracting matrimony had the intention to restrict matrimonial right, and not only its use, to the periods of sterility; with the result that the other party would not even have the right to request intercourse at other times."[62] The contractual right which the parties exchange is not only permanent but uninterrupted.

Second, since no act against nature is committed, restriction of intercourse to the sterile period is lawful, *if one has a proportionate reason.* As the Holy Father declared, "upon couples who perform the act peculiar to their state, nature and the Creator impose the function of helping the conservation of the human race. . . . The individual and society, the people and the state, the Church itself depend for their existence on the order established by God in fruitful marriage. Therefore, to embrace the married state, continuously to make use of the faculty proper to it and lawful in it alone, and, on the other hand, to withdraw

[62] Address of Pope Pius XII to the Italian Catholic Union of Midwives, October 29, 1951.

always and deliberately with no serious reason from its primary obligation, would be a sin against the very meaning of conjugal life."[63] It is wrong, therefore, to adopt this practice for no serious reason, for example, for the mere inconvenience of having children. The excusing cause is determined in the light of whether the couple already have children, the length of time the practice is to be followed, and the difficulties to be overcome. Certainly a proportionate reason would be serious danger to the wife, inability to support more children, the fact that children would be defective or stillborn. Whether it would be a serious sin for a couple who have no children to adopt the practice perpetually without a sufficient reason is not quite certain.

774. Positive contraception. This in interference by artificial means with the marriage act so as to prevent the union of sperm and ovum.[63] It is always wrong.

2. *The Malice of Positive Contraception.*

THESIS LIV. Every act of positive contraception is intrinsically wrong.

775. Since this demonstration is so important, the basis upon which it rests must be clearly grasped. We recall that the good is the suitable, and nothing is more suitable to a faculty than its natural end. Evil is deprivation of a good which ought to be present. Perfective good is that which is suitable because it affords the faculty a due perfection or removes an imperfection. Delectable good is desirable inasmuch as it is the satisfaction consequent on the attainment of perfective good. Nothing so perfects a faculty as attainment of its natural end; this end attained is the perfection of the faculty.

Nature urges man to his due perfection through the use of his faculties. To ensure sufficient use of these faculties, and attainment of the fullness of human well-being, nature attaches delectable good to the use of a faculty. Hence to set a faculty in motion, to enjoy its pleasure, and to allow the action to proceed to its natural term — that is the orderly use of the faculty. However, to set a faculty in motion, to enjoy its delectable good, and then so to distort the act that its natural end is made impossible — this is always evil because it is deprivation of a good which ought to be present, namely, the possibility of issuing in its natural end. This is perversion of a natural process, and the gravity

[63] Physiologic control of fertility is the taking of drugs so as to render one or both parties sterile or to induce abortion. Cf. article by Gibbons-Burch listed on page 401.

of the evil done is measured by the importance of the good which is frustrated.

We apply this doctrine to the sex faculty. The natural end of sex is a tremendous good; and because this ultimate perfective good is not so much a good of the individual as it is a good of the race, nature has attached to this faculty the most appealing of all sense pleasures. Hence, to set this faculty in motion, to cull the pleasure, and then deliberately to prevent conception and destroy the ultimate perfective good for which the faculty exists, is a foul perversion, a disorderly use of the faculty, a frustration of nature in a matter of the utmost moment. The unreason lies not only in the subordination of perfective to delectable good but in the total abolition of the perfective good. If that is not evil, nothing is evil.

PROOF

776. To use an important faculty so as to prevent it from its natural end is intrinsically wrong. But in positive contraception one uses the important faculty of sex so as to prevent it from its natural end. Therefore positive contraception is intrinsically wrong. The major premise of this argument is proved in § 775.

If it be argued on behalf of contraception that satisfaction of the sex impulse is also a natural end of the sex faculty, the answer is that this end is secondary, and that the Natural Law forbids us to destroy the primary end of a faculty in order to enjoy a secondary end.

Corollary. The only legitimate means of limiting offspring is *virtuous* continence.

777. Though generally the guilt of contraception falls equally upon both parties, this crime may be committed so that one party alone sins, as when the man interrupts the act or the woman resorts to lotions after the act. The innocent party has a grave obligation in charity to admonish and to take serious steps to deter the other. If no heed is paid to these warnings, the innocent party does not sin by proceeding with marital relations.

3. *Excuses for Contraception*

778. **Health motive.** Women are worn out before their time by too frequent childbearing. Births should be more properly spaced for the good both of child and of mother. The American Birth Control League propagandizes with a doleful picture of wan, depressed mothers harried by a brood of noisy children, typified in the letter quoted by

Bromley: "We have been married three years and have four children, and I have lost my health. I am so nervous I can hardly do my work. The doctor tells me it is because I have given birth to children too often."[64]

But this is far from the normal situation. Certainly births ought to be properly spaced and this nature takes care of when the mother herself nurses the child. Of course conception is not impossible during the time of natural nursing but it is exceptional. Apart from the use of contraceptives or abstention, there is usually a natural interval of two years between births — an interval which widens as the woman grows older. Considering the age at which women marry in urban civilization and the incidence of their menopause, one may forecast that their normal expectancy of children will range from four to six — by no means the intolerable burden depicted by the American Birth Control League. It should be noted that among the poor it is not the mere bearing of children which wears out women but the dreadful living conditions they have to endure. The remedy lies not in offering them contraceptive knowledge but in procuring a living wage for the heads of families. Medical science is beginning to return to the position that nature, not man, is the best spacer of births.

After studying 38,087 obstetric patients, Dr. Nicholson J. Eastman[65] of the Johns Hopkins Medical School found these conclusions inescapable: (*a*) Infants born within two years of a previous viable delivery have at least as low a stillbirth and neonatal mortality as infants born after longer intervals. (*b*) The longer the interval between births, the more likely the mother is to suffer from some form of hypertensive toxemia of pregnancy. The incidence of this complication is lowest when the interval is twelve to twenty-four months, significantly higher when it is twenty-four to forty-eight, and much higher when it exceeds four years. (*c*) In patients who had a previous hypertensive toxemia, the likelihood of repetition becomes progressively greater as the intervals become longer.

He found it quite probable that the chances of neonatal mortality increase as the interval widens. His figures were 1.5 per cent for the "Brief" interval group, 2.2 for the "Moderate" interval group, and 2.6 for the "Long" group.

He concludes that physicians recommending child spacing for the

---

[64] Dorothy B. Bromley, *Birth Control: Its Use and Misuse*, p. 16. New York, Harper, 1934.

[65] N. J. Eastman, "The Effect of the Interval Between Births on Maternal and Fetal Outlook," *American Journal of Obstetrics and Gynecology*, April, 1944, pp. 445–463.

health of mother and child often overlook the most potent factor favoring the mother, namely, youth. Child spacing means maternal aging and after the early twenties maternal aging involves greater risks. Whatever advantage is had by a rest period of several years is offset and often more than counterbalanced by the aging factor. Youth is a better ally of childbearing than child spacing.

If a woman is able to bear a child every year, her fertility may not be checked by intrinsically wrong means. Nor may such means be resorted to by one who has been told with the utmost certainty that another pregnancy will be fatal to her. Medical directives are not the over-all law of human activity.

One of the principal preoccupations of the advocates of birth control is the recommendation of "safe" contraceptive methods, that is, methods which are not only effective but cause no injury to health. But they carefully conceal the fact that constant use of any contraceptive over a long period can be dangerous to the woman's health. The female body is intended by nature to absorb the sperm and receive an increase of vitality from that which is the bearer of life. Hence, if the body is constantly excited sexually but starved of the sperm, it is small wonder that physical and psychic disorders result. That such ills result is another indication of the primacy of the moral law, which may not be transgressed with impunity.

779. Good of the child motive. Many parents, otherwise upright and devoted to their duties but without the courage to be continent, practice contraception because they wish fewer children who will be brought up better and left in a more comfortable situation than they were by their parents. But this attitude is really exaltation of material goods above spiritual values.

One or two children will have more material advantages than six — more toys, more amusements, better clothes, more spending money. But normally a large family is a better educative milieu than a small one. A child has better opportunities for development in a large family than in a small one. The larger the number of children, the more closely parents are knit together and the less danger of their separating. To provide for a larger family, man and wife must exercise more moral virtue — more providence, more industry, a graver sense of responsibility, and above all more unselfish devotion. The special effort which they must constantly exert cannot but react favorably upon their children. Hence, these parents will make a better home — better, not in the sense of hardwood floors, refrigerators, and television, but in the sense of human contact, affection, and moral tone. The father must be alert to provide the means of subsistence; the mother will have neither inclination nor opportunity to spend the best of her time and energy outside the home. Children grow up in an atmosphere of sacrifice; they learn "to wait their turn." There is little danger of their being pampered. The rough edges of their character are constantly being worn off in daily interplay by their brothers and sisters.

780. The economic motive. A common reason offered for birth control is: "Oh, we would love to have more children but we cannot afford them." The expenses attendant upon childbirth have risen enormously within a generation, and worse, the economic burden of raising children has become heavier. The reason is not precisely that it costs more to live today, but that everybody is expected to have more. Many wants are artificial; they are demands for so-called necessities which a few years ago were dream luxuries. While the scale of living adapts itself to the average family, unfortunately the average family is now the restricted family. Hence, raising a large family is either beyond the financial resources of the normal parent or the large family tends to become underprivileged.

There should be social co-operation to lessen the expenses of childbirth. Since society has an appreciable stake in the birth of its future citizens, it ought to see to it that these expenses never become an obstacle to a sufficient birth rate.[66]

As to the larger problem of maintenance, two observations are in order. First, society must make it possible for heads of families to secure an income sufficient to support a normal family in human decency. Second, and this is the practical crux of the difficulty, the individual has to solve correctly the problem of every period of high civilization — the problem of choosing between material goods and moral goods. Margaret Sanger pithily puts the problem: "Which would you rather have — a child or a car?"[67] But is it reasonable to seek an increase of material comforts at the price of moral dereliction? As always, so now all larger social and economic problems verge upon the moral, and their ultimate solution is not to be found in rejection of the Natural Law.

The facts of history are plain: a rising birth rate has always been an index of national vigor, and a falling birth rate of national decline.[68] Since wealth is the product of human industry and ingenuity, it cannot come from cutting down the population. This is true even in an indus-

[66] See F. J. Corley, "Family Allowances: U. S. Plan," *Social Order*, 3 (April, 1953), 145–156.

[67] See Leclercq, *Marriage and the Family*, p. 215, translator's footnote, 9. New York, Pustet, 1941.

[68] See Rousseau, "Marks of a Good Government," *Social Contract*, Bk. III, c. 9.

trial civilization which depends on the size of its markets, which in turn depend on the number of nonproductive consumers. Children are the nonproductive consumers and the more the number of children is curtailed, the more markets must shrink. No nation will remain vigorous whose family heads settle down to the enjoyment of comfort instead of devising new sources of subsistence.

Acute problems of too many mouths to feed do arise on a national scale in particular areas, but we may not accept the implication of the Neo-Malthusians that there is not a living in the earth for mankind. God gave the earth for the support of mankind and He did not miscalculate. He expects of course the co-operation of men so that when science increases the span of life it also discovers new means of living. Men will find a living if they use their industry and ingenuity. Sometimes, however, more is required, namely, the practice of international justice and charity so that all peoples have access to the means of a decent living.

781. The pleasure motive. Parents can live a pleasant life at a minimum of inconvenience. They can have the pleasures of love and escape its difficult consequences: one or two children, easy to raise and take delight in, rather than six or eight who would be a stone upon one's back. Sex is stamped in bold, harlot colors across the face of contemporary life because contraception has opened up to the unmarried a high, wide, and handsome promiscuity.

But there is no greater sign of the softness and imbecility which civilization can generate. The softness is apparent. The Natural Law offers the stern dilemma: be continent, or assume greater responsibilities. Nevertheless, the easygoing modern evades the law because he loves his comfort. The choice he makes is imbecility. For the contraceptive addict foolishly thinks that here is the one case where a man can have his cake and eat it too. But he forgets two truths. One, that the substantial goods of life — growth in virtue and eternal beatitude — are to be purchased at a price, the endurance of difficulty. The other, that whoever spurns perfective good for the sake of present delight is a fool. Whoever honestly and consistently seeks perfective good must eventually find delight; whoever puts delight first, finishes with neither.

782. Finally, contraception is another instance where reasons of natural goodness, valid and conclusive in themselves, are not enough to persuade men to upright conduct. Only the mind and will, illumined and inspired by supernatural grace, can resist so alluring an evil. One must have supernatural faith to choose between a momentary difficulty and an eternal reward, between the enticement of present convenience and the substantial reality of an eternal punishment; supernatural hope,

confidently and blindly to put one's trust in God and appreciate that the same Divine Lawgiver who imposes the burdens of parenthood likewise gives abundant strength to bear them; supernatural charity, to love God and the manifestations of His will above all things seen and unseen. The Psalmist assures us, "I have not seen the just forsaken, nor his seed seeking bread."[69]

[69] Ps. 36:25.

READINGS

St. Thomas, *Contra Gentiles*, III, 122–126.

——— *Supplementum*, QQ. 44–66.

Bennett, M. K., *The World's Food*, 3–57. New York, Harper, 1954.

Brittain, R., *Let There Be Bread*. New York, Simon and Schuster, 1952.

Brown, B. F., "The Natural Law, the Marriage Bond and Divorce," *The Jurist*, 15 (January, 1955), 24–51.

Callahan, E. R., "Divorce — A Survey," *American Catholic Sociological Review*, 9 (1948), 162–172.

Canavan, F. P., "The Finality of Sex," *Catholic World*, 178 (1954), 278–283.

Cavanaugh, J. R., *Fundamental Marriage Counseling*. Milwaukee, Bruce, 1956.

Conway, J. D., *What They Ask About Marriage*. Chicago, Fides, 1955.

Ennis, E. P., "The Ends of Marriage," *Clergy Review*, 37 (May, 1952), 270–281.

Gibbons-Burch, "Physiologic Control of Fertility: Process and Morality," *American Ecclesiastical Review*, 138 (1958), 246–277.

Good-Kelly, *Marriage, Morals and Medical Ethics*. New York, Kennedy, 1951.

Healy, E. F., *Medical Ethics*, 146–169. Chicago, Loyola, 1955.

Keenan-Ryan, *Marriage: A Medical and Sacramental Study*, New York, Sheed and Ward, 1955.

Kelly, G., "Rhythm," *Linacre Quarterly*, 19 (1952), 111–117.

Lattey, C., "Divorce in the Old and New Testament," *Clergy Review*, 35 (April, 1951), 243–253.

Lynch, J. J., "Fertility Control and the Moral Law," *Linacre Quarterly*, 20 (1953), 83–88.

McCarthy, J., *Problems in Theology*, Vol. I, 342–433. Westminster, Newman, 1956.

McInerney, G. K., "Greater Esteem of Virginity," *Catholic Mind*, 53 (1955), 656–663.

McLaughlin, S., "The New Malthusianism," *Irish Theological Quarterly*, 18 (July, 1951), 281–288.

Messenger, E. C., *Two in One Flesh*. Westminster, Newman, 1950.

Mihanovich-Schnepp-Thomas, *A Guide to Catholic Marriage*. Milwaukee, Bruce, 1954.

O'Donnell, T. J., *Morals in Medicine*, 177–228. Westminster, Newman, 1956.

O'Sullivan, D., "Toward a Spirituality of Marriage," *Studies*, 43 (1954), 17–30.

Pius XI, encyclical letter, *Casti Connubii*.

Pius XII, address to the Italian Catholic Union of Midwives, October 29, 1951. *Catholic Mind,* 50 (1952), 49–64.

——— Encyclical letter, *De Sacra Virginitate.*

——— "Marriage and Parenthood," *The Pope Speaks,* Autumn, 1956, 191–197.

Thibon, G., *What God Has Joined Together.* Chicago, Regnery, 1952.

Thomas, J. L., *The American Catholic Family,* 33–95. Englewood Cliffs, Prentice-Hall, 1956.

Werth-Mihanovich, *Papal Pronouncements on Marriage and the Family,* 1–117. Milwaukee, Bruce, 1955.

Chapter XXIII THE FAMILY

783. The primal social unit, the one closest to life and nature, is the family. Herein man's social needs and tendencies are first, though inadequately, satisfied. The term *family* may apply to the union of husband and wife; parents and children; parents, children, relatives, dependents, and servants dwelling under a common roof. To the last mentioned pertained Aristotle's definition of the family — the association established by nature for supplying man's everyday needs.[1] In the familial union three human relationships stand out: the relationship of husband and wife; the relationship of parents and children; the relationship of master and servant. The first has been discussed in the preceding chapter. The second and third are taken up here, with emphasis upon the second.

I. PARENTAL SOCIETY

784. Parental society is the moral union of parents and children. It is obvious that this is a natural society, because children are the natural fruit of the conjugal union. Our purpose here shall be to determine the adequate end of this society and the chief ways of realizing this end.

A. The End of Parental Society

785. Immediately upon the birth of a child an enormous want with subsequent human problems arises. Here is a new human being, with the potencies and essential rights of human nature but completely helpless. Since he has a right to go on living as a human being, he must be protected until he can care for himself. He must be taught how to live efficiently and reasonably. The process by which he acquires the skill of reasonable living is *education*, which is not synonymous with schooling. Schools may or may not share in the educative process and, when they do, their contribution is only partial. Education begins at

[1] *Politics*, Bk. I, 2, 1252b.

the birth of the child and continues until the child reaches full maturity and is fully prepared for self-direction and further self-development. It is a process of tutelage which gradually fuses into a process of self-perfection.

Education is the proper and harmonious development of the total youth which renders him capable of living as a man and equipped for the attainment of his final end. Training is an absolute necessity. The blind promptings of natural instinct do not suffice, as in the case of brutes, to lead the child to the proper and skillful use of his human faculties. He must acquire this knowledge from the instruction of others. Those who guide him must see that all his faculties — physical, intellectual, and moral — receive proportionate attention. None should be neglected lest a disintegrated personality result. Attention, however, should be given to each faculty in proportion to its value to the whole man. The training of the body ought to be duly subordinate to the development of the intellect, which in turn is of less importance than the training of man's will. Hence any system of education which ignores moral discipline and religious training is not worthy of the name which it bears.

786. The immediate end of education is a competent person, that is, one who in accordance with his natural endowments and place in life discharges his functions as a human being with efficiency and independence. Competence is not perfection of the money-making instinct or possession of a haphazard assortment of information. Competence rather is action in accordance with right reason, which supposes possession of right habits and skills. Thus equipped, he can, without unduly leaning on others, live an adequate human life, fulfill his general and particular obligations, and completely take over the task of self-development which should culminate in the attainment of his final end.

787. That every child has a natural right to a good education requires no special proof. It is included in his right to live as a human being. The point of dispute concerns the agent who has the right to educate him. One hundred years ago this would have been considered an idle question. Anyone would have answered that by the common consent of mankind this is the task and the right of parents, for the training of children is the principal end of the family.

But because the family has to such a great extent invoked the aid of society in this matter, and exaggerated notions of the right and competency of the State have taken hold in many places, there is a tendency today to disrupt, by State intervention and monopoly, the order established by nature between parent and child and to give the State rights in education which it cannot have. Communism thus claims the right to take children from parents and raise them in State nurseries and State schools.

THESIS LV. To parents alone belongs the inherent right to educate their children.

788. A most intimate union between parents and children is established by nature and founded on the fact of generation. This union is natural, as the following facts show: (*a*) the strong love, at first instinctive and later rational, which children have for parents; (*b*) the unwearied devotion of parents to the interests of their children, the untiring energy to supply, even at the sacrifice of their own personal convenience, all that is necessary for their development; (*c*) the natural inclination of children to seek the means of their development from their parents alone, spurning the intervention of outsiders. These facts, verifiable every day in the normal family, indicate nature's intent that parents, first and foremost, should be the educators of their children.

PROOF

789. **To parents alone belongs the inherent right to educate,** because: Those upon whom before all others the Natural Law has imposed an inescapable obligation to educate alone have the right to educate. For an inescapable obligation to perform a given task carries with it a right to fulfill that obligation. If the obligation falls only on one party, that party alone has the consequent right.

Upon parents alone and before all others the Natural Law has imposed the inescapable obligation of educating their children for these reasons:

a) From the *fact of generation* it is clear that:

(1) By reason of a most peculiar kind of causality, children belong to their parents and in a way that no citizen belongs to the State. Children are part of their parents' bodies, the extension of their parents' personalities. If all created things belong absolutely to God because of His divine causality, children belong to their parents under God since parents alone are with God cocauses of these children. The care of persons, like the care of things, redounds primarily to those to whom they belong.

(2) Man is responsible for the natural and foreseen results of his free acts. Since children are in a state of complete physical, intellectual, and moral helplessness because of the generative act of their parents, parents are responsible to provide them a suitable education.

(3) If there is a good absolutely intended by nature (such as the good of education) the natural and special aptitude to attain that good argues to an obligation to do that for which the aptitude is given. Parents have an aptitude to educate their children, which is shared by no one. This aptitude is founded on their knowledge of them, their selfless love of them, and their strong inclination to procure their well-being. In education nothing can replace these qualities.

b) There is no indication that the Natural Law has imposed this obligation upon the State or anyone else.

790. Corollary. The essential end of parental society is the good of the child; its secondary end is the well-being of the family itself which arises from the mutual love of all its members and the practice of the domestic virtues. Its remote end is the good of the State which is founded on the family.

791. N.B. I. An analysis of the right to educate.

The *subject party* is parents and parents alone. The obligation to educate falls on them jointly, so that, if one is lacking or utterly deficient the entire obligation falls on the other. Teachers, tutors, educational officials are the delegates and assistants of the parents. How much they share in this right depends upon the explicit or implicit delegation of the parents.

The *object party* is the child to be trained.

The *matter* is all necessary and useful instruments of education such as doctrine, information, and especially discipline — whatever will reasonably promote the true good of the child.

The *ground* is the Natural Law imposing on parents an inescapable obligation to care for their children until they can care for themselves.

The *title* is the fact of generation. As parents are one principle of generation, so they form one efficient principle of education.

N.B. II. The State has definite rights in education. That this is a subsidiary right will be better shown after the function of the State has been explained. (Cf. § 992 ff.)

B. The Means of Education

792. For the task of rearing children successfully parents must have a deep sense of responsibility. Children, as human beings, have an immortal worth; and no matter how much assistance or how many subsidiary agencies parents may summon to their aid, they alone are chargeable with the good or evil upbringing of their children. To acquit themselves of so indefeasible an obligation nature provides the essential means of domestic authority and family affection. Those educational

helps which the ordinary family cannot secure of itself are included in our discussion of the state's part in education (cf. § 982 ff.).

THESIS LVI. The Natural Law confers on parents social authority to guide their children to the proper ends of the family. The primacy of this authority resides in the father.

PROOF OF PART I

793. Nature confers domestic authority upon parents.

The Natural Law must confer upon every natural society authority for the attainment of that society's end and upon those who alone are capable of wielding it. But the family is a natural society, and in it parents alone are capable of wielding authority. Therefore the Natural Law confers authority upon parents.

PROOF OF PART II

794. The primacy of domestic authority resides in the father.

The unity of the family demands that it have one head. The reason is that in the partnership of mother and father one of them must bear the responsibility of making decisions. Natural indications point to the father as being this head, because he generally has the proper qualifications — greater prudence and constancy, greater strength and protective ability. Moreover, nature disqualifies the wife for this position because of her natural function of childbearing and her consequent need for protection.

795. Corollary I. *Education is an authoritative process.*

Anyone who knows anything has a right to teach it to another who is willing to listen; but no one has a duty to listen to instruction, much less submit to discipline, unless the one teaching has authority to instruct, compel attention, and exact obedience.

Corollary II. *Children have an obligation of filial reverence to their parents,* as the holders of legitimate authority. As we shall presently see, all human authority is a participation in the divine authority.

Corollary III. *Children and wives have an obligation of obedience.*

C. Familial Obedience

1. Wives

796. The Natural Law commands a wife to obey her husband in everything that pertains to the reasonable conduct of the family and is compatible with her dignity as a human being and a wife. She is a beloved companion, not a child or a slave. If in some cases the wife has more influence than the husband, the Natural Law is not necessarily overturned. Because of this man's incapacity or this woman's outstanding capacity such an arrangement may be the only one that makes for peace and security in a particular family.

While the civil law and especially social custom today give married women a social and economic freedom they never enjoyed before, nevertheless this so-called emancipation of women should never be such that "the husband suffers the loss of his wife, the children of their mother, and the home and whole family of an ever watchful guardian."[2] There are but few remains of that ancient Christian chivalry whereby men once elevated their wives to a pedestal as queen and mistress of the household. She was looked on as better than man — more religious, more moral, more God-fearing and was deferred to accordingly. Modern woman, somewhat after the fashion of the dog in Æsop's fable who saw in the water the reflection of himself carrying a bone, is snapping after delusive emancipation; and if she completely descends from the regal throne she once enjoyed to go down into the hurly-burly of everyday life to contend with men for a false equality, she will get hurt. And badly. "She will soon be reduced to the old state of slavery (if not in appearance, certainly in reality), and become as amongst the pagans the mere instrument of men."[3]

2. *Children*

797. From the fact of parental authority it follows that children must obey their parents. Only the obedient child is the educated child. Parading under a variety of names, for example, progressive education, there is a modern trend which would tone down the place of authority in education and which looks askance at absolute obedience as breeding inhibitions and dwarfing the child's personality. To offset this trend it is necessary to distinguish truth from falsity in parental authority.

798. *a*) It is possible to tyrannize children. To prevent such action, the motive of any command should be the child's good, not the selfish convenience of parent or teacher. No child should be overwhelmed with a torrent of do's and don't's. To be genuine a command must be reasonable, but all reasonable commands should be carried out. The youngest child should be made to see that disobedience is never tolerated.

799. *b*) Because the child is incapable of self-direction, it must be

[2] Pius XI, Encyclical on Christian Marriage.
[3] *Ibid.*

guided to its true good; but some have a mistaken notion of the child's true good. The child's true good is ultimately a supernatural good; and since all men are tainted by original sin, a child will have great difficulty in recognizing its true good. It is absurd to give children the initiative in their education, because they lack that supernatural gift of integrity whereby lower appetites are completely subordinate to reason. Hence left to their own whims and fancies, they become the victims of their own blind pride and concupiscences. All education must transcend the natural and realistically appreciate the downward trend of a nature debased by sin. The uninhibited child is usually a willful, spoiled, undisciplined brat. As children advance toward maturity, a larger initiative and greater freedom must be accorded them; but to deal with elementary or high school pupils as though they were matriculated in a university is a woeful lack of realism.

800. c) Even though there is danger of suppressing good tendencies or even of cruelty on the part of unworthy parents, correction has its essential place in child training. And correction *necessarily* implies corporal punishment. For all authority must have the power of coercion, physical as well as moral. The young child in many ways is inclined to act like an animal rather than a rational being. When he persists in acting irrationally by continued disobedience, physical pain is the only effective corrective. Spare the rod and spoil the child is as true today as it was in Solomon's time.

801. *d*) To issue commands that advance the child's true welfare and prudently to enforce them requires of parents a loving understanding of the child as an individual. They must recognize that each child is a unique personality, different from all others and possessing differing capacities, hopes, and problems. Parents must be willing to give time and attention to things which primarily are of interest to the child. This demands eternal vigilance, thorough knowledge of his comings and goings, especially of his companions. It may be injected here that too early and too free a mingling of the sexes is bad. Nature isolates young boys to themselves — so also immature girls. This wall of separation should not be artificially broken down, for thereby sexual desires may be awakened too early and grave harm will result since a long period of time must elapse before these stirrings can be satisfied by marriage.

The supreme test of parental wisdom is adolescence. In this period of growth intellect is awakening, habits though still fluid are in the process of hardening, the freedom of manhood is just around the corner. It is no longer possible completely to possess children as in earlier years, to do all their thinking and deciding for them. If they are confronted with freedom and responsibility too suddenly, they may not be able to cope with the situation. Pre-eminent skill is needed to guide them over what are often the rough waters of their late teens into the assured ability to think and act as adults.

802. Here again we must depart from the field of ethics and have recourse to the supernatural. Mere considerations of natural goodness and merely natural helps are insufficient to heal the wounds of original and actual sin. Divine grace is the ultimate remedy. Hence the child must be taught to live a sacramental life, to practice not merely the natural virtues of prudence, justice, temperance, and fortitude but also the supernatural virtues of faith, hope, and charity. His moral training should be intertwined with the cultivation of supernatural religion, which should have first place in the home. The effective means of accomplishing this is personal example.

803. Filial obedience, however, is limited both as to scope and duration. The end of parental authority — the good of the child — determines the scope of obedience. Hence a child must not obey when commanded to do what is patently sinful. The choice of a *fixed* state in life is also outside the parent's command. Parents may not forbid their children to embrace the true faith. Nor even to enter religion or to marry. Children are obliged to seek the advice and counsel of their parents and sometimes to defer temporarily such a step because of parental indigence; but since the permanent conduct of their adult life is involved, the choice must ultimately be their own. Therefore, when youth is capable of self-direction, parental authority ceases. The child is emancipated; his education is finished. If civil law does not specify the precise time when this is effected, it surely happens when he leaves the paternal home to assume his place in life. Should he remain in the paternal home after he has attained his majority, he is still subject to his father in what pertains to domestic order.

D. Family Affection

804. Authority in the family must be tempered by love. Between members of a family exists a special kind of love — piety. While a son's obligation to obey ceases in time, his obligation of love, reverence, and gratitude never does. The love which parents have for children should be well ordered and efficacious. It is *well ordered* when it is (*a*) impartial — unreasonable partiality toward a favorite may offend distributive justice — and (*b*) when it seeks both the spiritual and temporal good of the children in due proportion. Parental love is *efficacious* when it

actually procures for the children the goods which befit them. Love is not sentimentality but good will manifested in deeds. The first of such deeds on the part of the father is providing the means of living for wife and children. The spiritual welfare of the children must be given precedence over any material advantage. Those parents are guilty of serious wrong who, for the sake of enhancing their social prestige, or otherwise advancing their worldly prospects, send their children to schools where their supernatural faith is endangered and their eternal beatitude imperiled. When parents grow old and cannot support themselves, piety demands that their children take care of them. Brothers and sisters have a similar obligation of assisting one another in grave need.

II. SERVANT SOCIETY

805. Servant society is the union existing between the blood members of a family and their domestic servants; parents, children, and domestics constitute the family in the most complete sense. A domestic, then, is an outsider who agrees to serve a family upon condition of sharing proportionately in its advantages. He differs from a workman laboring for the employer in that the workman is not admitted into the family of his employer.

806. Is servant society natural? This society is not natural in the sense that it fulfills an imperative need of nature. Nor may it be called natural with reference to a situation in which the domestic is something less than a man, the chattel of a master. However, we may call servant society natural in the sense that the Natural Law countenances it because in a human way it answers a mutual need constantly present among men, namely, (*a*) of parents for domestic assistance and (*b*) of persons of small means for a living which they could scarcely otherwise provide for themselves.

That this mutual need will perdure seems clear enough. Because of the number of children, the importance of their other occupations, their age, or physical disability, many family heads will always require assistance in the orderly conduct of their home. Although numerous household goods formerly produced by familial labor are now procured outside the home, and although modern inventions have made domestic work far less difficult, the need of help in the home will never completely disappear. So too, because of personal inclination, dearth of initiative, lack of training, or opportunity for more lucrative situations, there will always be those who gravitate toward domestic work.

Servants may contract to work for the family but remain outside the family circle or they may make their home with the family as members of the family. In either case there are advantages and disadvantages for both parties. The chief advantage of the first arrangement is that the worker retains his independence and can have a family of his own. In the latter arrangement there is a fuller and more human relation of man to man, of a member of the family to the head of that family.

807. In the servant-master relation, the chief tie binding the parties is commutative justice. The master is obliged to give his servant a just wage and a commensurate living. Those holes in garrets and odd corners which until quite recent times were provided as sleeping quarters for servants could scarcely measure up to the requirements of a decent living. The servant, on the other hand, obliges himself to make an adequate return of service — both as to the time, quality, and quantity of his labor.

But a more human tie — a tie of piety — binds them. The master should act as a father who takes a human interest in the physical and spiritual welfare of those in his care, treats them with paternal kindliness, endeavors to correct their moral defects, sees to it that they fulfill their religious duties, provides for their old age after they have given him a lifetime of service. On their part, servants owe their master a quasi-filial reverence; loyalty and fidelity in looking after the interest of the family which goes beyond the mere letter of a contract; and obedience not only in the matter of service but also of personal conduct.

READINGS

St. Thomas, *Summa Theologica*, II–II, 101, 104, 105.

Aristotle, *Politics*, Bk. I, cc. 3–13.

Connell, F. J., "Juvenile Courtships," *American Ecclesiastical Review*, 132 (March, 1955), 181–190.

Dawson, C., "Education and Christian Culture," *Catholic Mind*, 52 (1954), 193–203.

Drinan, R. F., "Parental Rights and American Law," *Catholic World*, 172 (October, 1950), 21–26.

Firkel, E., *Woman in the Modern World*. Chicago, Fides, 1956.

Fitzpatrick, E. A., *How to Educate Human Beings*. Milwaukee, Bruce, 1950.

Fitzsimons, J., "Relationship in the Family Community," *Clergy Review*, 41 (1956), 69–81.

Fullam, R. B., *The Popes on Youth*. Buffalo, America Press, 1956.

Gabriel, A. L., "Educational Ideas of Christine de Pisan," *Journal of the History of Ideas*, 16 (1955), 3–21.

Irish Ecclesiastical Record, "Obligation of Householders Regarding the Spiritual Welfare of Their Domestic Employees," 80 (October, 1953), 267–268.

Jaeger, W., *Paideia: The Ideals of Greek Culture*, Vol. I, 2 ed. New York, Oxford, 1945.

Kane, J. J., "The Changing Roles of Father and Mother in Contemporary American Society," *American Catholic Sociological Review,* 11 (1950), 140–151.

Kriekemans, A., *Principes de l'education religieuse, morale et sociale.* Louvain, Nauwelaerts, 1955.

MacIver, R. M., *The Web of Government,* 22–38. Macmillan, New York, 1947.

McAllister, J. B., *Ethics,* 2 ed., 352–368. Philadelphia, Saunders, 1955.

Mullaney, J. V., "The Natural Law, the Family and Education," *Fordham Law Review,* 24 (1955), 102–116.

O'Doherty, E. F., "The Adolescent," *Studies,* 42 (1953), 83–89.

Pius XI, encyclical letter, *On the Christian Education of Youth.*

Pius XII, "The Dignity of Woman," *The Pope Speaks,* III (1957), 367–375.

Sattler, H. V., *Parents, Children and the Facts of Life.* Paterson, St. Anthony's Guild, 1952.

Seneca, *Epistulae,* 9, 10.

Thomas, J. L., *The American Catholic Family,* 127–271. Englewood, Prentice-Hall, 1956.

Werth-Mihanovich, *Papal Pronouncements on Marriage and the Family,* 118–153. Milwaukee, Bruce, 1955.

Chapter XXIV THE STATE

808. "Human society," says Suarez, "is twofold: imperfect or domestic; and perfect or political."[1] Man's social instincts find their first outlet in the family. Although this is the basic social unit, it cannot satisfy all the needs of human nature. Therefore, a more perfect social organization is required.

Aristotle notes how the family naturally grows into the village and "when several villages unite in a single complete community, large enough to be nearly or quite self-sufficing, the state comes into existence, originating in the bare needs of life, and continuing in existence for the sake of the good life."[2] He goes on to say that the end of social organization is the production of the perfect or self-sufficing society, one fully capable of ministering to the needs of human nature. This is political society, which he identifies with the city-state of his time.

809. We come then to examine the concept of the ultimate social unit or the perfect society. A perfect society is one which seeks a universal human good and possesses, or at least is responsible for supplying, the full means of attaining that end. In the supernatural order the Church is the perfect society because it seeks the salvation of all men and it has all the means necessary for procuring that end. In the natural order the State has, up to the present, been accepted as the perfect society.

The identification of the State as the perfect society has been questioned in our time. Modern States, it is said, lack two requisites of self-sufficiency. Scarcely any one of them is economically self-sufficient; all are, in this respect, mutually interdependent. Second, States are subordinate to a higher international law. Do these limitations of the modern State argue that man's social development is as yet incomplete? that some day there will be a political organization more perfect than the State? The existence of these limitations are undeniable, but no one can say with certainty that we are going to have a more perfect political

[1] *De Legibus*, Bk. III, ch. 1, § 3.
[2] *Politics*, I, 2, 1252b.

society. Until now the State has served as the perfect social unit and so we must consider it until an organization more perfect appears. We accept the State as a perfect society because it alone has the organization and the responsibility for providing for the all-round social needs of a people. These needs, however, the State need not supply exclusively from its own territory.

810. What is the State? Kelsen identifies the State with a particular law. Thus France, Spain, and Switzerland are simply French, Spanish, and Swiss law.[3] Duguit says that the State is a fiction devised to conceal the social preponderance of particular persons or groups.[4] But men mean by the State much more than these narrow views indicate. They understand a community of governors and governed who occupy a particular territory and under some independent form of political rule seek by public action what is deemed socially necessary for the good life.

Mere local juxtaposition or common language is not enough to make a people into a political society. Such unity can derive only from a common social bond and a common authority. This authority must be independent of any similar authority on the same level. If it is not independent it is part of an organization which is independent; and this is the ultimate social unit. The need for a proper territory follows from the need to be independent.

Four elements are found in every State: end, people, territory, and authority.

I. IS THE STATE A NATURAL SOCIETY?

811. Is the State a natural institution or merely an artificial device like a business partnership?

812. As we have shown (§ 695), Hobbes held that the State is an artificial invention, the product of a human compact. Rousseau accepts Hobbes's main contention with some peculiarities of his own. According to the French philosopher, "the most ancient of all societies and the only one that is natural, is the family."[5] Before the State appeared, man lived in a state of nature — he was a noble savage, living an idyllic life by streams and woodland fastnesses, completely free and subordinate to no one. Whenever life in that state becomes impossible, men have to band together in some form of association. The instrument which sets

[3] *General Theory of Law and State*, p. 181.

[4] Leon Duguit, *l'Etat, Le Droit Objectif et La Loi Positive*, p. 18. Paris, Thorin, 1901.

[5] *Social Contract*, Bk. I, Chap. 2.

up this association is a social contract whereby each man agrees to give up all his rights to govern and protect himself on the condition that all the others do the same. "At once, in place of the individual personality of each contracting party, this act of association creates a moral and collective body . . . receiving from this act its unity, its common identity, its life and its will. This public person so formed by the union of all other persons formerly took the name of *city* and now takes that of *Republic* or *body politic*."[6]

813. According to communism (§ 505), the State is unnatural because it arose from the need of the exploiting classes to keep the exploited masses subservient. It will die out when all class distinctions have been abolished. "The State, which is in truth only organized coercion, has inevitably risen at a certain degree of development of society when the latter was divided into irreconcilable classes and could no longer subsist without some power placed above them and separated from them."[7]

THESIS LVII. The State is a natural society.

PROOF

814. The State is a *natural society* because: Men have a natural aptitude for political society and a compelling need for it.

a) *Aptitude.* Men not only desire the fullness of the good life but they have a native ability to band together and procure it. They have a mutual benevolence whereby they can wish good to all who are willing to co-operate. They have a natural endowment for such co-operation: they have the power of communication, an inclination to obey authority, and some have the ability to command.

b) *Need.* The State is necessary for the full temporal happiness of man. The family cannot supply for its members everything physical, intellectual, and moral required for their proper development. Innumerable advantages are impossible unless man sets up a social organization capable of procuring them.

Whatever answers so universal an aptitude and need must be natural. As Aristotle argues: "The state is by nature clearly prior to the family and to the individual, since the whole is of necessity prior to the part. . . . The proof that the state is a creation of nature is that the individual,

---

[6] *Ibid.*, Bk. I, Chap. 6.

[7] V. I. Lenin, "Karl Marx," *Encyclopedie Russe.* See also V. I. Lenin, *State and Revolution*, p. 8. New York, International Publishers, 1932.

when isolated, is not self-sufficient; and therefore he is like a part in relation to the whole."[8]

Furthermore, whatever terminates man's social propensities must likewise be natural. As Aristotle says: "If the earlier forms of society are natural, so is the state, for it is the end of them, and the [complete] nature of a thing is its end. For what each thing is when fully developed, we call its nature. . . . Besides, the final cause and end of a thing is the best, and to be self-sufficing is the end and the best."[9]

815. **Corollary I.** Man is by nature a political animal.

Corollary II. The Natural Law compels men to form States.

II. THE SPECIFIC END OF THE STATE

816. A few men like Haller[10] have said the State has no specific distinctive end. However, since the State is a natural, not an artificial entity, it must have a natural end prescribed by the Author of nature. Nature does nothing in vain.

817. As a natural thing it is different from every other natural unit physical or moral. Its natural end is common to all States, because as natural institutions they have a common essential statehood. Hence Montesquieu[11] is wrong when he says that each State has its own specific purpose which differs from that of other States and has in common with others merely the general purpose of its own conservation. Self-preservation cannot constitute a distinctive end because this is common to too many things which differ essentially.

Since the State is a true society, its distinctive end will be some form of common good. It is agreed to call this the Public Good. What then is the Public Good for whose attainment States exist?

A. The Totalitarian View

818. The State is a superentity, adequately distinct from and superior to the body of citizens. The individual exists for the State, not the State for the citizen. Society and the State are identified; in a totalitarian State there is no free society. The Public Good, then, will be solely the good estate of this superentity, that is, the fulfillment of arbitrary ends chosen by the rulers.

---

[8] *Politics*, I, 2, 1253a. Aristotle speaks here of logical priority and juridical unity.
[9] *Ibid.*, 1252b.
[10] Charles L. de Haller, *Restauration de la Science Politique*, Vol. I, Chap. XVII, pp. 552, 554. Lyon, Russand, 1824.
[11] Baron de Montesquieu, *The Spirit of the Laws*, trans. Nugent-Pritchard, Bk. XI, Chap. IV, p. 181, Vol. I. New York, Appleton, 1900.

Plato held as a supreme but admittedly unrealizable end a commonwealth wherein absolutely everything was held in common.[12] The commonwealth was "a greater man" to which each citizen was subordinate as the hand or foot is to the whole body. This "greater man" has an end similar to that of the individual, namely, to live according to virtue.

Hobbes's conception of the Great Leviathan, an accumulation of irresistible force and the origin of morality, laws, and rights, has given fresh impetus to the totalitarian idea in modern days. Some pantheists like Schelling[13] and Hegel[14] have gone to the extreme of identifying the State with God — the State is the absolute being, the all-sufficient one whose end is itself.

Modern totalitarianism takes the form of national socialism or communism. Whereas in the ancient tyrannies the end was enhancement of the power and riches of the despot, today the totalitarian end is collectivistic. Thus the end of national socialism is the aggrandizement of the nation-state, its fulfillment of a historic mission; the end of communism is the subordination of the individual to humanity and the establishment of the material paradise.

819. The modern totalitarian State is characterized by these marks: the power of government extends to all phases of social and individual activity; no individual has any rights against the State; he is, does, and has as the State wills; the State is a single party affair; the political will of the State is formed by the person or group which heads the party; a parliament is merely a group to receive the will of the executive whose power is unlimited; no expression of contrary opinion is tolerated and all dissidents are summarily disposed of; the police terrorize the citizens, scrutinizing all their actions and even their thinking; to make the will of the government palatable citizens are subjected to ceaseless propaganda.

THESIS LVIII. The Natural Law forbids that any State be an end completely unto itself.

---

[12] *Republic,* Bk. V, 458.

[13] Friedrich W. J., von Schelling, *Neue Deduktion des Naturrechts.* See his *Sämmtleche Werke,* Vol. I, pp. 247–280. Stuttgart, 1856. See also *System des transcendentalen Idealismus* in the same set, Vol. III, p. 583.

[14] Georg W. F. Hegel, *Grundlinien der Philosophie des Rechts.* See his *Werke,* Vol. 8, Nos. 257–272. Berlin, 1833. In No. 258 he says: "It is the course of God through the world that constitutes the State. Its ground is the power of Reason actualizing itself as will. When conceiving the State, one must not think of particular States, not of particular institutions, but one must much rather contemplate the *Idea,* God as actual on earth, alone."

PROOF

820. The State cannot be an end unto itself, because:

A means to the good of individual men cannot be its own end. By nature the State is a means to the good of individual men. A State is not a physical unity. Of itself it has neither soul, consciousness, will, nor eternal destiny. It is only a moral unity having a temporal existence. Therefore in the hierarchy of objective values it is something less than individual men. All things less than man are for the utility of man.

821. Corollary I. The Public Good must be something which redounds to the real good of individual men.

Corollary II. There is scarcely any social doctrine more offensive to human dignity, or more degrading to the human person, than the dictum that man exists for an omnipotent State which can do with him as it wills.

822. Granted, then, that the ultimate beneficiary of the Public Good must be the individual, how many and what kind of advantages should the State offer men? How broad or narrow is the scope of the Public Good? The precise answer to this question will be a summary statement of the natural functions of the State. Of the three answers given, the first interprets the scope of the Public Good very narrowly, the second very broadly, the third moderately.

B. The Laissez-Faire View

823. The opposite of totalitarianism is *laissez faire,* or individualism run wild. It teaches that the sole function of the State is to stop the war of all upon all. This it does by securing the individual rights of the citizen but it may not assist him in procuring the good life. This is strictly his own affair and he is not entitled to any social assistance.

Kant was the first to express this view and he arrived at it from his notion of rights. Maintaining a complete cleavage between an internal moral order and an external juridical order, he claimed that the State, as the external force, had nothing to do with morality; its end was to procure and safeguard such external conditions that the rights and liberties of all might harmoniously coexist (cf. § 428). Hence it exists to prohibit those external acts which would disturb that harmony of liberty. Nothing more.

The economic liberals of the Manchester school, who held that "the economic man" should act solely in his own interests, claimed that society would be ideally prosperous if there were free trade and unlimited competition. For them the State is merely a policeman who keeps order and sees to it that contracts are observed.

THESIS LIX. The purpose of the State cannot be restricted to mere safeguarding of the juridic order.

824. The pernicious effects of this doctrine we have already noted (§§525–529). Laissez faire really means the State must stand by while the little man is exploited by the big man. The atrocious evils of industrial slavery were the inevitable consequences of the laissez-faire doctrine.

PROOF

825. *a*) Liberalism is an insufficient declaration of the purpose of a natural institution. It is absurd that a natural institution have but a negative function — the prevention of violations of commutative justice. As the family has a positive function of providing for the welfare of its members, *a fortiori* must the State wherein man expects to realize completely his social tendencies. The positive function of the State is set forth in § 833.

b) Since the State may create rights, for example, a share in the goods of a distantly related intestate, set up corporations, and so on, its function cannot be the mere safeguarding of rights.

c) It is the common conviction of men that the State has a wider and ampler function.

C. The Paternalistic State

826. As the old-fashioned father provided his family with the means of life, so the State directly cares for its citizens from cradle to grave. As children have turned to their fathers for the things they need, adults should now consider that the State owes them a living.

The old conviction that a man should face the world and wrest a living from it should be modified: a large part of that responsibility can be transferred to the State, which is to secure him against the age-old fears of sickness, poverty, unemployment, pauperism in old age. Hence the State undertakes to guarantee the individual proper prenatal care, a decent creche, a happy childhood, an education, remunerative employment, recreation, hospitalization when ill, a sufficient pension when he reaches sixty — all this without too much embarrassing consideration of personal co-operation and deserving. When nature has handicapped him by physical weakness or lack of talent, the State will come to his aid with special assistance that will level him with his fellow citizens. As social evolution has taken from paternal power its right of life and death, the office of family priest, so now in great measure the State will take over its job of family protector and provider.

827. A bright new world is being blueprinted wherein all the old scourges of mankind will be absent. State action is to produce a land flowing with milk and honey, suspiciously similar to the communistic millennium. Precious little mention is made of any increase of moral goodness — of valor, endurance, self-sacrifice, faith, hope, or love of God.

The delusion in paternalism is twofold, namely, that mankind can be so renovated by direct State action that the effects of original sin will be eradicated and that man lives by bread alone.

828. The reality of paternalism is this: at best it is a benevolent socialism. If the State is to take direct care of its citizens, it must have that measure of control over them demanded by socialism. At worst it is a fraud whereby those who currently hold governmental power in a democracy hope to establish themselves therein indefinitely. An individual or a group can hold power indefinitely if it can destroy those sound safeguards which a democratic people possess against unlimited governmental control, that is, their fundamental political liberties. Hence the people are to be deceived into surrendering these liberties upon the specious promise of economic security. An ancient device, it succeeded before in the twilight days of a dying democracy — the Roman populace gave up their liberties upon the assurance of bread and games.

THESIS LX. The Natural Law forbids the State to take direct, complete, and perpetual care of its citizens.

829. We do not deny that some measure of direct and perpetual care is involved in safeguarding the juridic order, which we shall prove to be the first purpose of the State. Nor is it unreasonable that in a grave crisis such as earthquake, flood, or war a State should temporarily take over complete care of its citizens. However, when a great part of the citizenry is perpetually dependent for its livelihood directly on the State, it is a sure sign of a diseased commonwealth. It entails the overthrow of the order of human life established by nature.

PROOF

830. The State cannot have a purpose which if realized would make the citizen less a man. If the State were to take direct, complete, and

perpetual care of its citizens, they would become worse men. Paternalism would be destructive of the moral fiber of citizens indirectly and directly.

Indirectly paternalism would tremendously lessen the value and importance of the family. Every indication of nature is that the *family first* is to take care of its young, sick, and aged. To transfer this duty to the State as a prime obligation is to destroy a natural function of the family. If the family is weakened, harm will inevitably come to the individual and society.

It is argued that since the family has not taken adequate care of its sick and aged, the State must. It is true that if a family is unable to provide for itself, the State should come to the rescue. But the State must not directly intervene until every reasonable private means has been resorted to and none has been successful. Put a living wage at the disposal of family heads and the family can and will care for its sick and aged. And better than the State.

Directly paternalism would be destructive of the moral integrity of the individual. Nature intends that the adult be self-directive and self-providing; but if the State assures him that his needs will be satisfied, he will not develop a sense of responsibility and it will not be necessary for him to practice human virtue. Inevitably paternalism begets laziness, shirking of duty, and an inhuman sense of dependence. There would be little need for providence, thrift, and courage in the face of difficulty.

831. **Corollary I.** The State must not do for the citizen what he can reasonably do for himself.

Corollary II. No government owes its citizens a living.

Corollary III. The State should not inject itself into matters which pertain strictly to the Individual Good. For it to do so means ultimately harm to the Public Good.

832. **N.B.** Paternalism interferes with the operation of the sanctions of the Natural Law: in order to procure the means to lavish such benefits on its citizens, the State must take from the alert, provident, and thrifty, who are thereby penalized for their success by being compelled to support the shiftless and improvident.

"If any man will not work, neither let him eat."[15] This is both inspired writing and a dictum of the Natural Law. A situation in which a man is permitted to squander his earnings in prosperous times and neglect to provide for the leaner years ahead because he is sure of direct State aid is an encouragement to foolish living and ultimately a burden upon the more restrained and virtuous. Truly the State ought to protect the

[15] 2 Thess. 3:10.

common people — who necessarily are of limited means — from the exactions of a monied power, but this must not be done by handicapping talent and industry and rewarding ineptitude and sloth. It is quite absurd to imagine that nature has delegated the State, as it were, to follow up after her and compensate the mediocre and dull witted for nature's initial but uneven distribution of her gifts.

D. The Scholastic View of the State's Purpose

833. Most scholastics steer a middle course between the narrow concept of the Public Good according to laissez faire and the exaggerations of the paternalistic State. For them two elements compose the Public Good. They are peace and public prosperity.

Peace is tranquillity of the juridic order. The outstanding purpose of the State is the maintenance of commutative justice, making individuals and families secure in the peaceful possession and exercise of their natural rights. It is impossible for a man to realize his potentialities if most of his energies are consumed in the defense of himself or his family. To live and develop as a man he requires an atmosphere of security which can be provided only by a State itself secure from internal and external disturbance. Our federal Constitution aptly expresses this purpose in its preamble: "to establish justice, insure domestic tranquillity, provide for the common defense."

Public prosperity. Prosperity, in general, means an abundance or at least a stable sufficiency of those things required for man's *temporal well-being*. This includes not only material goods such as food, clothing, shelter, property, personal freedom, and physical and mental health but also immaterial goods such as good reputation, culture, and moral and religious training. Prosperity does not so much consist in having many things but in having the right things, chief among which are a material competence and the moral virtues. A very clear distinction should be made between private and public prosperity.

a) *Private prosperity* is the possession by the individual of a sufficiency of requisite goods. Private well-being is an individual or at most a family concern and the securing of it is the chief temporal preoccupation of each individual or family head.

b) *Public prosperity* refers to the sum total of those helps and facilities which must be available to put private well-being within reach of all: it is an abundance of social, economic, and industrial *opportunities* which will help all classes of citizens to use their initiative and industry and thus secure a desirable competence for themselves. The State does not assume responsibility for each one's individual good, nor should it, as a father does his children, endow its citizens with the goods of prosperity, but it ought to offer all a fair chance of self-help.

Since neither the individual nor the family is all sufficient, co-operative effort must supply whatever else is needed for human welfare. This is summed up by the term, *social opportunity*. The manner, measure, and mode of social opportunity to be provided by the State will depend on many factors of time, place, climate, custom, and complexity of economic development. But every State, no matter how rude and barbarous, must, over and above the defense of the juridic order, provide its members with some measure of collective opportunity. In an industrial civilization, the State has achieved one goal of public prosperity when it has produced a general situation wherein a man can find employment and by his industry secure for himself and his own a decent sufficiency of temporal advantages.

The collective opportunities offered by the State, however, are not limited to economic ones but may embrace all avenues of human development. Thus Edmund Burke, who surely was no collectivist, describes the State as "a partnership in all science, a partnership in all art, a partnership in every virtue and in all perfection."[16]

This aspect of the State's purpose is touched upon in our federal Constitution by the words: "promote the general welfare and secure the Blessings of Liberty to ourselves and our Posterity."

THESIS LXI. The specifying and proximate end of the State is the public good of peace and public prosperity.

PROOF

834. The proximate and specific end of the State is some good which men seek to obtain by uniting into States and which they can neither efficiently nor permanently obtain outside the State. Since the State is a natural society, nature intends it to be the answer to definite human needs. Therefore its specifying end will be that particular good which fulfills these needs. When it is asked what men naturally seek in the State, the correct answer will be a statement of the natural purpose or specifying end of the State.

In virtue of a natural impulse men unite in States because

a) *primarily* they wish to be secure as regards their persons and homes and in the enjoyment of their rights. They want peace.

b) *secondarily* they desire the means of self-betterment. Preserving

[16] Burke, *Select Works*, ed. E. J. Payne, Vol. II, 114. Oxford, 1921.

their rights and independence, normal men wish, relying on their own effort, to have the advantage of opportunities for physical, intellectual, and moral advancement — opportunities made possible only by co-operative effort. Such opportunities we call *public prosperity*.

Outside the State neither permanently nor efficiently can be realized

a) peace and security in one's rights. If the State is destroyed, anarchy and confusion result.

b) innumerable opportunities for human development. The progress of mankind has been achieved through the peaceful intercommunication of men. Without the State this has been and will be impossible. By the institution of the family man can manage to live, but without the institution of the State he could never live well.

835. Corollary I. This end — peace and the public welfare — is the measure of the reasonableness of all the State's activities.

Corollary II. When a given society by and large is no longer capable of promoting peace and the public welfare it automatically ceases to be a State.

III. THE FORMAL CAUSE OF THE STATE

836. Having established the most important of all truths about the State, namely its specific purpose or final cause, we now examine its remaining causes. We shall touch briefly on its formal and material causes, and more fully on its efficient cause.

In § 691 ff. we showed that the formal cause of any society is a moral juridic bond. According to this principle, the formal cause of the conjugal union is the peculiar bond of love and justice which makes man and wife one. The members of a family are made a unity by the bond of love, piety, and commutative justice. A State is formally made a State not by civil authority but by the civic bond which unites a plurality of families into a political union.

837. What is this civic bond? Civic justice directs men and institutions to the common *public* good. It touches all three forms of justice mentioned in §§ 303–305: social and distributive justice directly; commutative justice indirectly. It calls upon the exercise of social justice when it indicates to the citizen what he must do on behalf of political society. Inasmuch as this obligation of citizens is prescribed by law, natural or positive, we call it the obligation of *legal justice*. Civic justice also obliges the heads of the State to administer distributive justice. Civic justice is deeply concerned with commutative justice because it is its natural guardian, but commutative justice is not a formal constituent of civic justice. It is, therefore, those obligations of citizens to uphold the State by observing legal justice and of the State to promote the general and individual social welfare by observing distributive justice which constitute the bond of civic justice. The equality which this sort of justice envisions is that of the citizen toward the public good and of the public good toward the citizen. Hence the total complexus of rights and duties flowing from civic justice constitutes the social bond which is the formal cause of the State.

IV. THE MATERIAL CAUSE OF THE STATE

838. The material cause of a society is the plurality which is socially united, that is, those component parts upon which the juridic bond of society directly falls. In the conjugal union, the family, and like simple societies, the material element is always individual persons.

Is the same thing true in the State? There are two opinions. According to one — which has behind it the practice of the past few centuries — the material element of the State is the mass of individual citizens. This view is called either the *theory of social atomism,* or the *mechanistic theory* of *society.* According to the first explanation individuals are bound together in the State in much the same way as atoms in a mass of matter. According to the second explanation the State is a mechanical contrivance of many wheels and cogs — the individual citizens — which are geared together and are powered by a central motor — social authority. Nothing stands between the individual and the supreme authority of the State.

839. The opposite view considers the State an organism, that is, an entity similar to a living body composed of various organs, each of which has a distinct function, and all of whom are directed to the good of the whole. In an organic society there is a graded hierarchy of social units, one dependent on the other but each flourishing with an autonomous life and function of its own. Hence, the *citizen is not the material element of the State* but some imperfect society is, the family, the municipality, or the province, depending on the complexity of the State's development. Aristotle, whose ideal was the city-state, defines the State as the union of several villages in a single complete and self-sufficing community.[17] By villages he explicitly means households or enlarged families — children, grandchildren, and the like.

As States expand there is an increase in the number of political sub-

[17] *Politics,* Bk. I, 2, 1252b.

units having some measure of autonomy under the supreme authority of the State. Yet no matter how large the State grows, men always have the natural tendency to satisfy their first political needs by local self-government. Where States are large and economic problems complex, private or semipublic associations founded on men's work or profession will arise. The purpose of such occupational groups — which are not mere labor unions but associations of all, employers and employees, engaged in the same occupations — ideally is the common interest of all in that group, sought of course in harmony with the public good. The State should foster such associations, grant them sufficient authority to advance their purposes and to make friendly arrangements with similar associations. These were once called guilds; now their proponents call them corporations. A State which has subordinate societies — municipalities, corporations, and families — leading a vigorous and efficient social life of their own, is *organized;* it leads a truly organic life. If subordinate societies are merely tolerated and most of their functions absorbed by the State, that State is not *organized* but merely *administered.*

840. The atomistic view of the State must be rejected. It arose as a corollary of the eighteenth-century doctrine of the rights of man and economic liberalism. It led at first to rugged individualism, that overemphasis upon individual freedom which in practice means that the strong and cunning are given full opportunity to oppress the weak. Some react to the evils of economic liberalism by an appeal to socialism; others call upon government to regulate all the relations of the individual to the State. This is that interventionism now practiced by some present-day democracies. In either case the final result is that all intermediate social units having been destroyed or absorbed by the State, the State must needlessly interfere in the private concerns of its citizens and thus assume a bewildering and impossible burden.

841. Very aptly Pius XI writes: "Things have come to such a pass that the highly developed social life which once flourished in a variety of prosperous institutions organically linked with each other, has been damaged and all but ruined, leaving thus virtually only the individual and the State. Social life has lost entirely its organic form. The State, now encumbered with all the burdens once borne by associations rendered extinct by it, is in consequence submerged and overwhelmed by an infinity of affairs and duties. . . . It is an injustice, a grave evil and a disturbance of right order for a higher and larger organization to arrogate to itself functions that can be efficiently performed by smaller and lower bodies. This is a fundamental principle of social philosophy, unshaken and unchangeable. . . . Of its very nature the true aim of all social activity should be to help individual units of the social body but never to destroy or absorb them."[18]

"The State should leave to these smaller groups the settlement of business of minor importance. It will thus carry out with greater freedom, power and success the tasks belonging to it, because it alone can effectively accomplish these, directing, watching, stimulating and restraining. . . . Let those in power be convinced that the more . . . a graded hierarchical order exists between the various subsidiary organizations, the more excellent will be both the authority and the efficiency of the social organization as a whole and the happier and more prosperous the condition of the State."[19]

THESIS LXII. The material cause of the State is the family. Between the family and the State other subordinate societies should be hierarchically arranged.

PROOF OF PART I

842. The material cause of the State is the family. The State is composed either of a union of individuals or a union of families. It is not composed of a union of individuals. In the obvious economy of nature, there are three social units — the individual, the family, and the State. Nature directs the individual to the family union, the family to the State. To say that individuals are immediately directed by nature to the State, means that nature decrees the social extinction of the family.

The family is the cell of society, biologically and morally; that is, future citizens are prepared for life in society by the family. Because the functions of the family are closer to nature and more responsive to man's essential needs, the family is first among natural societies. It exists prior to the State and has rights which the State cannot take away. Therefore, to deprive the family of its natural place as the basis of political society is seriously to weaken the State. The good condition of the State depends upon the good condition of the family.

843. Corollary. The bond of civic justice falls essentially and immediately upon the heads of families and only accidentally upon independent, unmarried persons. Children are immediately subject to paternal authority; mediately to civil authority.

---

[18] *Quadragesimo Anno.*
[19] *Ibid.*

PART II

844. **Between the family and the State other subordinate societies should be hierarchically arranged.** In the organic concept of the State, the State is a moral organism. An organism is a living structure made up of distinct parts, each having its separate function, joined one to the other by a unifying vital principle so that all work unto the good of the whole body.

The State as a moral organism will be made up of heterogeneous and autonomous parts arranged in a hierarchical order based on social function and united by an intrinsic social principle — conspiration toward the public good.

Besides the obvious difference of physical and moral union, these further differences between a physical and a moral organism should be noted. In living bodies the parts have only an *apparent* autonomy and they exist *entirely* for the sake of the body; hence their activity is pointed *directly* to the good of the body. In the State, the parts have real autonomy and all have their particular ends; some of them, that is, the human persons, have an *existence which is independent* of the State and in some respects work only *indirectly* for the common good.

Where life is simple and social needs few, the organic structure of the State will be simple. There may be no need of other societies except the family and State. Where the community is large and human needs are diverse and complicated, other subordinate societies, notably locally self-governing bodies and occupational groups, ought to be formed. As Pius XI expresses it: "For as nature induces those who dwell in close proximity to unite into municipalities, so those who practice the same trade or profession, economic or otherwise, combine into vocational groups. These groups in a true sense autonomous, are considered by man to be, if not essential to civil society, at least its natural and spontaneous development."[20]

PROOF OF PART II

845. The Natural Law demands the organic structure of the State because that type of organization better promotes the common good.

It makes for a more flourishing condition of the family since it does not interfere with the family head in matters which are strictly of private concern.

---

[20] *Ibid.*

The smaller items of the social good are better promoted by individuals organized in small groups in which they take an intelligent interest.

The heads of the State, freed from the minutiae of smaller business, have the leisure and energy to promote the over-all interests of the community.

V. THE EFFICIENT CAUSE OF THE STATE

846. In the physical order an efficient cause is an agent whose physical action unites the formal cause to the material cause thus producing the new being. Applying this analogously to the moral entity of the State, we ask, What agent brings together the formal and material elements, that is, imposes on the aggregated families the bond of civic justice so that they are transformed into a State?

However, there is danger of confusion in such terminology since the State is a moral, not a physical, thing. Hence the question is better phrased as follows: *What is the proximate juridic cause of any actually existent State?* A similar question was raised in § 738 concerning the conjugal union.

847. To avoid ambiguity it must be recalled that we have already proved that the State originates in a dictate of the Natural Law. Hence the present issue of *proximate cause* is not with Hobbes, Rousseau, the communists, or positivists but solely with philosophers who admit a Natural Law origin of the State. The point of dispute here may be obscured for two reasons. The first reason is failure to distinguish the question of the origin of the State from that of the origin of political authority. To those who maintain that political authority is the formal cause of the State, these two questions must necessarily be one. To those of us who hold that civic justice is the formal cause of the State, two distinct though intimate questions are involved. Hence we shall deal first with the origin of the State and then with the origin of political authority. The second reason for misunderstanding is failure to distinguish between a juridic cause and a historic cause which is merely dispositive. Nor is this question one of idle speculative interest; very practical moral consequences depend upon the settlement of this point.

848. A *juridic* cause is one which *validly* produces a real effect in the juridic order. Since the juridic order is the total assemblage of justice, rights, and juridic duties, a juridic effect will be some right, some duty, or a complex combination of both which is granted, abolished, or modified. Statehood is a juridic effect, for with its establishment there begins to exist a tremendous aggregation of rights and duties which were non-

existent beforehand. Hence our question is, *What creative thing in the realm of justice produces statehood?*

849. This cause is always twofold: one ultimate, the other proximate. The ultimate ground of every right is always some law. Hence *some law is always the primary juridic cause of any juridic effect.* In the case of the State, the cause is the Natural Law commanding families to unite in the civic union. This we have proved against Hobbes and all who claim the State is an artificial device of man (cf. § 814).

But no law creates a concrete right without the intervention of some contingent fact. Such a fact in virtue of law actuates in the concrete a definite juridic effect. With reference to the creation of a right, we have called this fact a *title.* This fact or title is a juridic cause, though secondary and proximate.

Our question reduces itself to this, What secondary and proximate juridic cause operating in virtue of the Natural Law can create a State; what fact or facts constitute a valid title to statehood? Note the term, "valid title." We are not asking what facts *actually* lead men to form States. This is a historical question. Our difficulty is ethical, namely, what are the fact or facts which *ought to be* present *legitimately* to induce statehood?

850. Scholastics give two general answers.

a) The sole fact capable of producing a State is the consent, at least tacit, of the multitude.

b) While the consent of the multitude is sometimes the proximate juridic cause of the State, this is the exceptional case. Many other facts may constitute title to statehood. It is usually the very force of circumstances which demands the establishment of the State without any reference to the consent of the multitude. Since the formal cause of the State is public authority, the same fact which designates the holder of this authority is likewise the juridic cause determining the origin of the State. Chief among such facts, as cited by the proponents of this theory are the following:

1. *Propagation from one family stem.* The State naturally grew out of the family. It grew in size and importance so that its needs could no longer be satisfied by mere domestic organization. For this, political organization was gradually substituted. As the patriarch was head of the family organization he naturally assumed the headship of the nascent State.

2. *Natural ability of the territorial proprietor.* A number of unrelated people occupy the same territory controlled by one proprietor. Gradually the need of a protector against hostile outsiders, of a judge to settle

their disputes, of a lawgiver to direct their economy calls for political organization, the setting up of a ruler. Since no one else has qualifications comparable to those of the proprietor, he is naturally designated as the wielder of authority and his assumption of civil rule brings the State into being.

3. *Victory in a just war.* Factually many States rose from the power of the sword. If the victory was won by one who had justly entered the war, he could afterward rightly subject to himself the vanquished for reasons of just compensation, of self-defense, of military security, of provision against future harm.

Our criticism of this view is: (i) there is a confusion of historical cause with juridical cause; (ii) the alleged ethnographic, historical, economic, or military facts may well have disposed the people to become apt material for the fullness of the civic bond, but (iii) apart from consent they cannot *validly* induce the status of civil society.

851. Concerning our first observation. Cronin argues for this second position very acutely when he writes: "The head of the village community became imperceptibly, as the community expanded and took on wider and wider functions, the head of the State. Henceforth his authority was more than domestic; it became political as well. And in this way and not through compact, political authority came first to be vested in the supreme ruler in the case of most States. Such is the testimony of history and of all recent sociological inquiry into the origin of political rule amongst primitive peoples. Here is no trace of anything in the nature of a social compact. The first political rulers derived their authority at a time when such a compact would have been unthinkable, a period when any attempt to superimpose upon the family or tribal organization based upon the tie of blood another organization based upon a wholly different principle, viz., popular election to power, would have been exceedingly difficult, if not impossible. And yet in those days the rulers of States wielded the scepter on titles as legitimate and with an authority quite as effective and convincing as any ruler of the present day."[21]

852. This citation argues that history shows one principal cause of the State. Therefore this had to be a juridic cause, that is, the patriarch assumed rule; he could not have done wrong in so acting. Now a similar investigation into the history of marriage might reveal few traces of the consent of the parties to be married; it might show that the vast majority of marriages were arranged by parents who were little concerned about the consent of their offspring. Such a fact, if proved to be a fact, would not overthrow the ethical conclusion that consent alone is capable

[21] *The Science of Ethics,* Vol. II, p. 503.

of forming the conjugal union. We would not conclude that parental arrangement was the juridic cause of matrimony but simply that whoever did not give his consent was not validly married. So too, even if history affords small evidence of consent in the formation of States, this fact would not rule out the moral necessity of consent. For ethics is not the record of how men *have acted* but a pattern of how they *ought* to.

853. One may question whether scientific history confirms the facts to be such as alleged by Cronin. As far as prehistoric peoples are concerned, we can only conjecture: examined with sufficient scrutiny, the nations known to history do furnish enough evidence to the effect that consent entered into their founding. But even if the facts are as cited; even if the patriarch did everywhere assume political authority, the ethical question is, *Was he justified in doing so without the consent of the heads of the families under him?* Suarez argues: "The son by the attainment of reason, liberty and adult age is emancipated, freed from paternal power and becomes *sui juris.* Wherefore if he has his own family he has his own domestic authority over it equal to that which his father has over his family; nor is he obliged by the very nature of things to form one civic union with his father; nor from the very nature of things does any higher sort of jurisdiction lie between them."[22] The adult who is free of another becomes subject to him only by willingly agreeing to it. Certainly the fact could well have been that the only practicable thing for the children and the grandchildren of the patriarch to do was to agree to his political rule. They may even have had a moral obligation to agree. But suppose one or other did not? Would the patriarch have been justified in forcing them? He could not, because antecedent to their political subjection to him he did not have political coercive power over them. Hence if he compels his rule by force, his authority rests on force, and force of itself cannot beget political authority.

Concerning our second observation. One must not imagine that by "the multitude" we mean a mere mass or unorganized conglomeration of people; rather we have reference to an aggregation of families composing something approximating a moral unity, almost but not perfectly united in the civic union.

There is quite a deep juridic gulf between the status of one large family or collection of families living in the same neighborhood and that of statehood. In that initial stage the authority of family head suffices. As the family grows into the sept or clan, as the unrelated families are bound closer together by intermarriage, trade, religion, or

[22] *De Opere Sex Dierum,* Bk. V, Chap. VII, No. 14.

self-defense, their public problems become more complicated and the people must develop a further organization of life to solve them. Historically it was a gradual process: the occasional acceptance of a judge to settle their disputes, of a war chief for defense, of a priest for permanent religious guidance, of a spokesman to represent their interests before other groups and make commercial deals in their name. As each step was taken, custom cemented it: prudence demanded its permanency. Not that they originally had before them a complete design of civic order outlined by some philosopher toward which they consciously strove; but out of their own and their ancestors' experiences handed on by tradition, they worked out an economic, military, and juridical organization whose ultimate term was a self-sufficient community, a State, a juridic existence essentially different in its duties and rights from that whence the evolution began.

854. Many factors assisted in this upward process. The blood tie, the family organization, the authority of family heads, common language, religious rites, the outstanding ability of certain persons to serve the public interest, the fact that one group was subjugated by another—these in varying measure played an influencing or disposing part in the end result that these families formed with these other families a self-sufficing community. As the full scope of statehood emerged, as the super-familial authority took on more and more of the attributes of sovereignty, and the family heads submitted more and more to a common public rule the sole juridic factor making the distinctive steps of the process *legitimate* could only have been the agreement of the family heads involved.

THESIS LXIII. The proximate cause of any actually existing State can only be the consent, at least tacit, of the multitude.

855. By a multitude we understand a somewhat organized group of families, apt material to become a civic organization and looked at, at least conceptually, prior to its assumption of the *total* civic bond whereby it is fashioned into a particular State.

By consent we mean the free agreement whereby families accept in general the duties and rights necessary to constitute a sovereign State. To be valid this agreement must be physically free though it may not always be morally free, for circumstances may be such as to produce an imperative command of the Natural Law obliging these people to unite into this State.

It is easy to understand how a man and woman consent to form the conjugal union but how a similar consent on the part of the multitude operates to produce the State may not be easy to grasp. A multitude is more complex: it requires more time for agreement.

856. There is no difficulty understanding explicit consent such as that had in the formation of the American Republic. Consent is certainly manifested by cheerful subordination to, and co-operation with, public authority. Consent may be complete and spontaneous or it may come about gradually, in other words, all the people may consent at the same time, or group after group may yield its consent only over a considerable period of time. The people may consent to the entirety of the bond, as would be the case now; or they may only gradually assume the obligations of civil life, as in primitive times. Indirect consent may be shown by readiness to accept a definite person or group as ruler: tacit consent is shown by the omission of all protest and repudiation when such action would have been effective or a matter of duty. Hence whether it be expressed or tacit, direct or indirect, we can best denominate this necessary element as *natural consent*.

This consent, however, is worlds apart from the Social Contract of Hobbes and Rousseau. These differences will be more evident after we have investigated the origin of political authority (cf. § 877).

PROOF

857. The proximate juridic cause of the State is that fact which in virtue of the Natural Law validly produces the State by imposing the bond of civic justice on the multitude. For the multitude is transformed into a State when it is bound not by ties of friendship, blood, or commutative justice but solely by the bond of civic justice. As the ultimate cause of the State is the Natural Law, so its proximate cause is some fact imposing civic justice on the people and approved of by the Natural Law.

The sole fact which may validly produce this effect is the consent, at least tacit, of the multitude. For a group of families not as yet formally constituting a State to have the bond of civic justice imposed on it the Natural Law requires their consent.

a) *Their consent is required*, because:

i) Just as nature does not designate who is married to whom so, *before the actual formation of the State*, neither does nature designate the members of a definite State. Hence, antecedent to the rise of a State, each man is politically free and independent of others. Adults possessing the use of reason and free will unite into States because they see that such unions are morally necessary and because they intend to reap the benefits of such association. Such an intention is explicit or implicit consent.

ii) If the multitude does not freely assume the bond of civic justice when a State is formed, it is forcibly imposed on them. There is no other possibility. But force cannot create those social rights which constitute the State. In the juridic order force may protect and repair a right: it cannot produce a valid and positive effect.

iii) Of its very nature the bond of civic justice demands the agreeing of many wills toward the common public good. But an agreement is necessarily consent. Since the object of agreement here is a common good, this consent must be a free consent. The reason is that, in order that a man, hitherto not obliged to seek a good in which *others* are to share, now be obliged to do so, he should freely agree to it.

b) *Nothing further is required.* Once men have agreed to strive after the common public good, they have assumed the bond of civic justice and the State is formally constituted.

READINGS

Aristotle, *Politics*, Bk. I, cc. 1–2; Bk. II; Bk. VII, cc. 1–12.

American Catholic Philosophical Association Proceedings, "The Philosophy of the State," Vol. XV (1939).

Azpiazu, J., *The Corporative State*. St. Louis, Herder, 1951.

Bluntschli, J. K., *The Theory of the State*, 3 Eng. ed., 283–326. Oxford, Clarendon, 1921.

Burgess, J. W., *The Foundations of Political Science*, 3–93. New York, Columbia, 1933.

Ebenstein, W., *Modern Political Thought*. New York, Rinehart, 1954.

Friedrich-Brzezinski, *Totalitarian Dictatorship and Autocracy*. Cambridge, Harvard, 1956.

Gettell, R. G., *Political Science*, rev. ed., 19–119, 375–424. Boston, Ginn, 1949.

Gierke, O., *Natural Law and the Theory of Society*, tr. E. Barker. Cambridge, University Press, 1934.

Hoffman, R., *The Organic State*. New York, Sheed & Ward, 1939.

Lecler, S., *The Two Sovereignties*. New York, Philosophical Library, 1952.

Leclerq, J., *L'Etat ou La Politique*. Namur, Wesmail--Charlier, 1948.

Leo XIII, encyclical letter, *Immortale Dei*.

Maritain, J., *Man and the State*. Chicago, University of Chicago, 1951.

Martin, T. O., "The State: Its Elements," *American Ecclesiastical Review*, 125 (September, 1951), 177–195.

Marx, H. L., *The Welfare State*. New York, Wilson, 1950.

Messner, J., *Social Ethics*, 463–504. St. Louis, Herder, 1949.

Murray, J. C., "Leo XIII on Church and State," *Theological Studies*, 14 (1953), 1–30, 145–214, 551–567; 15 (1954), 1–33.

Nisbet, R. A., *The Quest for Community*. New York, Oxford, 1953.

Philbin, W. J., "The Individual and the State," *Irish Ecclesiastical Record*, 79 (January, 1953), 3–19.
Pius XII, Christmas Allocution, December 24, 1942, *Catholic Mind*, 41 (January, 1943), 45–60.
——— Christmas Allocution, December 24, 1944, *Catholic Mind*, 43 (February, 1945), 65–77.
Plato, *Republic III*, 386–402; *Laws*, 817 (on the cultural function of the State).
Powers, F. J., ed., *Papal Pronouncements on the Political Order*, 58–99. Westminster, Newman, 1952.
Rommen, H. A., *The State in Catholic Thought*, 248–358. St. Louis, Herder, 1955.
Scott, J. B., *Law, the State and the International Community*, Vol. II, 173–238. New York, Columbia, 1939.
Scott, M., "A Philosophy and Theology of the State," *Dominican Studies*, 6 (1953), 171–179.
Wayper, C. L., *Political Thought*, 1–41. New York, Philosophical Library, 1954.

Chapter XXV THE AUTHORITY OF THE STATE

858. Since some Scholastics hold that authority is the formal cause of the State, to them the question of the origin of the State is identified with the question of the origin of political authority. Though we do not admit that the State is formally constituted by authority, nevertheless, these two questions are so closely interwoven that an adequate discussion of the nature of the State is impossible without consideration of the nature and origin of authority.

859. **What is political authority?** It is the legitimate power of the State to direct and compel its members to co-operate toward the attainment of the common public good. This is sovereignty, a power which is supreme, one, total, and constant (cf. § 1063).

Supremacy. Every State is independent and its authority originates of itself; it is not derived from any political superior; it is above every political agency within the State; it extends to the full control of its own internal and external affairs. However, this supremacy does not imply freedom from natural, divine-positive, and international law.

Unity. Being supreme and independent, every State is one. Although there may be many subordinate agencies within the State possessing some measure of authority, there can be only one which is supreme. The unity of the State demands this. There will be as many States as there are supreme authorities. The unity of sovereignty does not demand that it be inseparably attached to one person or one group.

Totality. This supreme power is a total power, that is to say, it consists in *all* the rights and powers which any State must have to achieve its purposes.

Constancy. Sovereignty is a constant quantity. Its *legitimate* power is the same in every State, large or small, ancient or modern. Just as the totality of parental power never fluctuates so too the content of sovereignty does not change. Rickaby, however, says there is "far more authority in the England of today than in the England of the Heptarchy."[1]

[1] *Catholic Encyclopedia*, "Authority," Vol. II, p. 138.

It is obvious that the amount of authority may appear to fluctuate because strong rulers sometimes go beyond the just limits of their authority and weak rulers fail to use their power to the full. But it may not be so obvious that new and variegated needs do not add to sovereignty powers which it never had in simpler ages. Each power which the State now exercises was always there, but there may have been no need to exercise it in this specific way. New circumstances do not confer fresh powers but merely summon the exercise of old powers in a new way. Should civilized States lapse into barbarism, sovereignty would lose none of its powers. It would merely mean that the occasion to exercise many specific powers which a complicated civilization now demands would no longer be present.

I. THE ORIGIN OF AUTHORITY

860. A most general question is proposed here. We are not asking from what particular source this king or president, this parliament or congress received its authority, for we are not as yet interested in the person or persons who hold authority. Our inquiry is more fundamental: whence come State authority as such? Is it from men or God?

A. Ultimate Origin

861. According to materialistic evolutionary doctrine, humanity is in a process of unending evolution which is governed by ironclad laws operating with physical necessity. At the proper time and in the required state of development, civil authority directly and totally proceeded from humanity. According to communism, authority arose from the need of the exploiting classes to keep the masses in subjection (cf. § 505). According to another evolutionary variant, authority rose out of public opinion enforcing tribal customs and taboos.

THESIS LXIV. Supreme political authority has an ultimate divine origin.

PROOF

862. That is ultimately from God which exists because of a peremptory command of the Natural Law. Since God is the Supreme Legislator who speaks through the Natural Law, whatever that law commands is the command of God.

Supreme political power exists because of a peremptory command of the Natural Law. States must exist because they are demanded by the Natural Law for human welfare. Therefore, an essential property of the State, civil authority, is likewise demanded by the Natural Law.

B. Immediate Origin

863. Authority may come from God in a variety of ways. He could be merely the *mediate* author. First, He could give men a general impulse toward it and a wide authorization to do whatever conduces to social welfare. Then, in virtue of this impulse and fortified with this permission, men hit upon authority as an instrument of social betterment. God sanctions it. Thus the Church by a general grant of divine power may erect such corporations or take whatever steps may more readily lead to man's eternal welfare. In virtue of this delegation she has instituted sacramentals and set up religious orders. Is the same true of the State and its authority?

864. Second, in a much vaguer and more general way God could allow men to solve their human difficulties in the manner that seems good to them and give His approval to whatever does not contravene His explicit law. Thus, after the Black Sox scandal of 1919, the owners of the big league baseball teams formulated a code and set up Commissioner Landis with complete power to keep baseball clean. One could hardly say that the rules of organized baseball and the power of Commissioner Landis were from God — this is true only in the remote sense that God approves what is sensible and decent.

865. The contractualists explain the origin of political authority in almost parallel terms. The great writers among them — Hobbes, Locke, Rousseau — believed in God. God is in the background of their social scheme, but to them authority is *immediately from men:* it is a concession yielded by men willing to be ruled; it is divine only very remotely.

866. According to Hobbes, society arose from a compact men made among themselves for self-preservation and peace. However, even in society men are still vain, contentious, revengeful, and self-seeking. Hence a mere covenant does not suffice to keep men peaceable and orderly, because "covenants without the sword are but words and of no strength to secure a man."[2] There must be some visible power to keep them in awe and tie them by fear of punishment to the performance of their agreements. Hobbes thus evolves his argument: "The agreement of men is by covenant only, which is artificial; and therefore it is no wonder if there be somewhat else required, besides covenant, to make their

[2] *Leviathan,* Chap. XIII. Molesworth's English edition, Vol. III, p. 154.

agreement constant and lasting: which is a common power to keep them in awe. . . .

"The only way to erect such a common power . . . is, to confer all their power and strength on one man, or upon one assembly of men, that may reduce all their wills by plurality of voices, unto one will; which is as much as to say, to appoint one man or assembly of men, to bear their person; and everyone to own, and acknowledge himself to be the author of whatsoever he that so beareth their person, shall act or cause to be acted, in those things which concern the common peace and safety; and therein to submit their wills, every one to his will, and their judgments to his judgment. This is more than consent, or concord: it is a real unity of them all, in one and the same person, made by covenant of every man with every man, in such a manner, as if every man should say to every man, *I authorize and give up my right of governing myself, to this man* or *to this assembly of men, on this condition, that thou give up thy right to him, and authorize all his actions in like manner*. This done, the multitude so united in one person, is called a commonwealth. . . . This is the generation of that great Leviathan, or rather, to speak more reverently, of that *mortal* god, to which we owe under the *immortal God*, our peace and defense."[3]

867. Locke was primarily interested in vindicating the Protestant rebellion of 1688 whereby the propertied middle class, acting through parliament, overthrew the monarch, James II. According to Locke man originally lived in a state of nature, or the natural community of all mankind, wherein he has independence, equality with all others, and the right to punish invasions of Natural Law. He leaves this natural community for "a private or particular politic society" by *explicit consent*. His reason is that he wishes his property to be safe. "The great and chief end, therefore, of men's uniting in commonwealths . . . is the preservation of their property."[4] Since law provides this security, "the first and fundamental positive law of all commonwealths is the establishing of the legislative power. . . . This legislative is not only the supreme power in the commonwealth, but sacred and unalterable in the hands where the community have once placed it."[5] Here was the identification of Natural Law and the facts of contemporary political life with a vengeance!

868. Rousseau accepts the Social Contract because he sees in it the only answer to this difficulty: man must finally associate with other men

[3] *Ibid.*, Chap. XVII. Molesworth's English edition, Vol. III, pp. 157–158.
[4] *Second Treatise of Government*, Chap. IX, § 124.
[5] *Ibid.*, Chap. XI, § 134.

in society, but how can he do this and still retain his liberty? "The problem," he says, "is to find some form of association which will defend and protect with the whole common force the person and goods of each associate, and in which each, while uniting himself with all, may still obey himself alone, and remain as free as before."[6] The answer is a formal compact whose terms are in essence these: "Each of us puts his person and all his power in common under the supreme direction of the common will, and, in our corporate capacity, we receive each member as an indivisible part of the whole."[7] Each and every man by totally alienating himself and his rights to the community has created a general will of which he is an inseparable part. This general will is *Authority*, the Sovereign. Since his will is an indivisible part of the general will, and since he is at one with the Sovereign People, in obeying the general will the individual is still obeying himself.

The contractualist opinion is thus summarized: individuals had a natural liberty and rights over their own acts; when by formal agreement they yielded this power to the community, political authority arose. Posterity is ever after bound by this contract. Authority, therefore, immediately arose from the will of man.

869. We repudiate any explanation of sovereignty which attributes to it a merely human origin, immediate or remote. Certainly, since mere artificial societies derive totally from the arbitrary will of man, the directive authority they possess emanates from a human source. Thus, since a school is not a natural institution, it receives its authority over its pupils from the explicit or implicit delegation of parents. But in natural societies — the marital union, the family, and the State — the case is different. The authority exercised therein is totally divine. It is in no way the composite resultant of many human choices; it may not be construed as the general will of many agreeing to obey it nor as the accumulated might and right of many men.

THESIS LXV. In the erection of any given State the original possessor of supreme political authority receives it directly and immediately from God.

870. God does not merely approve of political authority or only will it to exist through man's direct contriving. He is its *immediate cause,* that is to say, whenever a new State arises and hence a new authority comes into being, it is God who directly confers this authority upon its first possessor without the mediation of any man. Certainly the

[6] *Social Contract,* Bk. I, Chap. VI.
[7] *Ibid.*

intervention of man is required for the erection of the State; but once a new State begins to be, authority derives from no man or collection of men but directly from God. The same is true of parental authority. Human activity is required for a man and woman to become parents; but once parental society is formed by the birth of children, the parents receive authority over their children not from any human source whatever but directly from God.

PROOF

871. That power comes solely and immediately from God which (*a*) must be present in the State whether man wills it or not; (*b*) cannot be augmented or diminished by human power; (*c*) contains prerogatives which no individual or collection of individuals possesses. Political authority is of this nature because:

a) To will the existence of the State and to will it not to have authority is a contradiction, for the absence of authority is the dissolution of the State. God *alone* provides those things which are essential and indispensable to a natural institution.

b) The specific powers which attach to sovereignty are determined not by human choice but by the natural end of the State. For men to add to these powers is to induce tyranny. To diminish these powers is to deprive a natural institution of a means necessary to its end. This no man may legitimately do.

c) The State can bind the consciences of many (Thesis LXVIII) and punish with death (Thesis LXXIV). As such, no individual or any group of individuals possesses these powers even rudimentarily. Therefore the State could not have received them from individuals surrendering them.

872. Corollary I. The person or group that wields legitimate civil authority holds the place of God and can exact obedience in those things which fall within the scope of civil jurisdiction.

Corollary II. Those subject to such jurisdiction have an obligation in conscience to obey. The precise limits of this duty will be discussed later (cf. §§ 924 ff.).

II. THE PRIMARY DEPOSITARY OF POLITICAL AUTHORITY

873. Granted that God is the immediate Author of authority in natural societies, the next question is, Who is the recipient of that authority? It is clear that in the conjugal union nature designates the

husband and in parental society the parents as the natural social head. What of the State? Who is the first possessor of political authority in the State? Three opinions are offered.

A. The Patriarchal Theory

874. According to those who hold that popular consent is not necessary for the legitimate erection of the State (§ 850), authority is immediately conferred by God upon that person, physical or moral, who has the greatest natural capacity to rule. This superior aptitude consists not only of personal qualifications but especially of social standing and prestige.[8] It rests upon some prior right which may be that (*a*) of the patriarch to govern his family; (*b*) of the proprietor of the land these people inhabit; (*c*) of the victor in a just war; (*d*) of a benefactor who has conferred notable benefits upon a people. Patriarchal dignity is pre-eminent and primordial among all such social qualifications. If no special individual stands out as the natural candidate to rule, there is recourse to popular choice. However, this choice does not confer authority; it merely designates the one upon whom God immediately bestows power to rule.

B. The Theory of the Divine Right of Kings

875. While some vague outline of this theory may have been voiced by one or other medieval emperor in his struggle with the papacy, it was the logical outgrowth of the action of Henry VIII of England, who arrogated to the crown of England all authority, both temporal and spiritual. It was first given articulate form by James I.[9] This theory claims for monarchy what is true of sovereignty in the abstract, that is, the sum of its power is constant and comes from God antecedent to, and irrespective of, the popular will. Just as parents receive authority over their children directly and immediately from God, so does the monarch in the beginning of the State. The mode of designation, however, is different. Parents hold authority by the natural designation of God; the monarch by the positive intervention of God, which is had either by a special act of God, as in the case of Saul, or through a permanent institution willed by God, such as election or hereditary succession. Such an institution is not a title or juridic cause of kingly power but a mere condition which designates the person upon whom God immediately confers authority. The totality of sovereign power rests

[8] Cathrein, *Philosophia Moralis*, p. 399. Friburgi Brisgoviae, Herder, 1915, 10 ed.

[9] James I of England, "The Trew Law of Free Monarchies," *The Workes of the Most High and Mightie Prince, James etc.*, pp. 193–210. London, Barker, 1616.

in the king, who may call whom he chooses for assistance, yet his power is indivisible and forever inseparable from him and his successors by divine appointment. Thus is claimed for the temporal sovereign what is true of the spiritual monarch, the pope.

876. The first and second theories agree in saying that in every case God directly and immediately confers authority not upon the people but upon the rulers. They differ, however, in describing the manner whereby this authority is granted. According to the second theory, God designates the ruler by positive means — his special intervention; according to the first theory the rulers are designated by natural means.

C. The People

877. Authority first descends to the whole people united in the bonds of civic justice.

THESIS LXVI. In the beginning of every State, God confers authority upon the whole people united in the bonds of civic justice. The people may and generally ought to transfer the actual function of ruling to one person or one group.

878. There is nothing novel in the doctrine set forth in Theses LXIII and LXVI. It represents the universally accepted teaching of the scholastics from the Middle Ages[10] to the nineteenth century — whose popular expression is found in the sentence, *Vox populi est vox Dei*. The early schoolmen took this over from the Roman legists who thus explained the origin of Roman imperial power. Suarez, with whom most of all this doctrine is identified, calls it certain and common.[11]

879. Some modern scholastics, among whom are a number of avowed monarchists, condemn any explanation of authority which involves what they term a pact and which we call a consent. The term *pact* seems to be limited to an explicit contract. However, more than words are involved here. Of course, they concede that our theory of consent differs vastly from the pact of the contractualists. The main points of difference are these: (*a*) to us, the State is a natural society and we have a moral obligation to form it; to the contractualists the State is artificial and there was no moral obligation involved in its institution; (*b*) to us, many of the individual's rights come from God and nature; to the contractualists, from the Social Contract; (*c*) to us, authority comes immediately from God; to the contractualists, solely from the will of many

[10] Alfred O'Rahilly, "The Sovereignty of the People," *Studies*, March, 1921, pp. 43–46.

[11] *De Legibus*, III, c. II, 3.

individuals; (*d*) to us, once authority is transferred to a ruler, he has the right to exact obedience and his authority cannot easily and arbitrarily be recalled; to Rousseau authority so essentially and inalienably belongs to the people that they give a ruler only what they choose which they may recall at will — rulers are only paid agents of the Sovereign People; (*e*) to us, authority may take any concrete form which will promote the general welfare; to Rousseau, the only legitimate form is that of pure democracy.

880. However, we do agree with the contractualists that the State owes its proximate origin to social agreement and that political authority resides first in the whole people.

Returning to the position established in Thesis LXIII that States arise from the consent of the multitude, we further hold that when men thus unite in the bonds of civic justice, the Natural Law concedes to the moral unity so created — the Commonwealth — all rights and powers necessary for the life and function of a State. Among these powers are organization and actual government.

881. **Organization includes the powers** (*a*) to organize the State under a definite form of rulership of one's own choice; (*b*) to select individuals in whom governmental functions are to reside stably; (*c*) to determine the stable limitations of these powers by reservation of power to the community, and establish the mode of succession to these powers; (*d*) to govern the community *ad interim* either directly or by the appointment of provisional rulers; (*e*) to reorganize the government whenever a prior government disintegrates or permanently fails to function, or in new times and circumstances fails to meet the exigencies of the common good; (*f*) to be the authentic judge of conditions requiring reorganization. These are constituent powers, plenary authority to enact a fundamental law upon which governmental activity is to be based.

Actual government is the day-by-day direction of the State to the common public good by competent executive, legislative, and judicial power in conformity with the fundamental law of the land.

882. Our position is that at the beginning of the State's existence both the authority to organize and to govern devolves upon the community civilly united. If the people choose to set up a purely democratic form of government, they retain and themselves exercise all the powers of political authority.

But a pure democracy is a virtual impossibility. Only in an exceedingly small community could it work. Therefore it is almost universally necessary for the people to hand over to some individual or group the actual function of government. Thus they entrust the governing powers to appointed rulers, but retain the organizing powers for the emergency of reorganization.

883. The rulers so accepted are the secondary subjects of authority. Their authority comes mediately from God, immediately from the community. Whenever for any valid reason this secondary subject has ceased to exist, it belongs to the community to select another secondary depositary.

The people agree to this transfer in the same way that they consent to assume the bond of civic justice. This consent may be explicit, either oral or written. It may be tacit and virtual, that is, by co-operation with, or acceptance of, a given ruler, by failure to protest against a regime when a protest would be in order. The consent may be spontaneous — even instantaneous — or it may be gradual, being drawn out over a relatively long period of time. The actual transfer is accomplished whenever the people agree to accept some particular political regime other than a pure democracy.

884. When this transfer is made, may the people attach certain conditions to the exercise of such authority?

They may not limit what is essential to effective government. They necessarily transfer sufficient jurisdiction so that the established rulers have the necessary legislative, executive, and judicial authority. Above all, rulers have a full right to exact obedience; the people have an obligation to obey.

They cannot arbitrarily recall power transferred. The welfare of the people demands that the form of government be stable. Once a particular form of government is chosen, then so long as it functions with reasonable efficiency, it may not be cast aside. It must always be presumed to be operative until it manifestly becomes a permanent hindrance to the ends of the State.

885. Therefore we reject Rousseau's contention that the people remain sovereign after a form of government is adopted. According to this view, the people alone are the law-making body, and the government is but a collection of hired clerks. For Rousseau rulers are bound to carry out every behest of the people and are removable at their will. The people should convene in their sovereign capacity at definite periods established by law, the frequency of these assemblies depending on the strength of the government, "for the stronger the government the more often should the Sovereign show itself."[12] Upon the convening of

[12] *The Social Contract,* Bk. III, Ch. XIII.

these assemblies the authority of the government lapses and two questions should always be considered and voted on separately. The first is, "Does it please the Sovereign to preserve the present form of government?" The second is, "Does it please the people to leave its administration in the hands of those who are actually in charge of it?"[13] Apart from the physical impossibility of ever assembling all the people (except in a tiny city-state) to act as Sovereign, Rousseau is wrong because: (a) constant meddling with the form of government militates against peace and stability in the State; (*b*) Rousseau attributes to all the people a wisdom and capacity to make laws which the facts of experience do not support; (c) the people do give authority to their rulers, but authority means that the one possessing it has a right to command and that they who are subject to it have an obligation to obey. You cannot keep what you give away. But Rousseau insists on the contradiction of the "subject Sovereign," saying that "the words subject and Sovereign are identical correlatives the idea of which meets in the single word 'citizen.'"[14] Therefore, while rulers *become* such by the consent of the governed, they do not require the consent of the governed to *exercise* the function of ruling. Thus we interpret the phrase of the Declaration of Independence, "Governments are instituted among men, deriving their just power from the consent of the governed."

While rejecting the notion that the people are entitled to the supreme place once held by the seventeenth-century sovereign, we may, however, call the people sovereign in the sense that: (a) public action should accord with enlightened public opinion, and (*b*) the citizen enjoys a moment of sovereignty when he chooses his rulers in the voting booth.

886. Provided, then, there is no essential impairment of the function of rulership, the people may attach to their transfer of power such conditions as these:

a) A fundamental constitution either in the form of a written document or of immemorial custom may provide how the function of sovereignty is to operate: whether sovereignty shall reside in one person, one group, or several groups; what the mode of succession to these powers shall be; what relations shall be maintained among the chief bodies of the government.

b) The people may reserve to themselves the ultimate decision concerning certain specific issues, such as declaring war and changing the fundamental constitution.

---

[13] *Ibid.*, Bk. III, Ch. XVIII.
[14] *Ibid.*, Bk. III, Ch. XIII.

PROOF OF PART I

887. In the beginning of every State, God confers authority upon the whole people civilly united.

First proof.

Those particulars of social welfare which nature has not prescribed are to be settled by the free agreement of the social members. For it is inadmissible that one man or group should impose its view on others by force or fraud when nature has left the issue to be settled by men.

Nature sets up no man as natural ruler, nor does she command any particular form of government. There are absolutely no indications that nature has given political authority to any individual before the creation of a State or that nature prefers one form of government to another (§ 897).

Hence the ruler and form of government are decided by the agreement of men. But these decisions would be impossible unless political authority resided first in the whole people. The choice of a ruler and form of government is a fundamental exercising of authority. Hence the fact that the people may do this *legitimately* argues to their prior possession of authority.

Second proof.

The primary recipient of authority is the one upon whom first and necessarily rests the obligation of attaining the ends of the State. An obligation to attain an end must necessarily carry with it a right to the necessary means. Since authority is the most essential means to the common good, whoever has the primary obligation of attaining the common good has the first right to authority.

The prime obligation of striving for the common good rests upon the whole people civilly united because:

a) The nature of the State demands this. The moral person, the State, which tends to the common good is not a fragment of that society, for example, a body of rulers, but all the members united in the bonds of civic justice.

b) Whenever visible authority has ceased, the people not only can but must reconstitute it and establish another regime. This they could not do unless the obligation of attaining the common good rested primarily with them.

888. **N.B.** Ryan is incorrect when he says an original grant of authority to the people is unnecessary for their welfare.[15] Our argument shows it is necessary in order that the people may choose a form of govern-

[15] Ryan-Boland, *Catholic Principles of Politics*, p. 83. New York, Macmillan, 1941.

ment; that they reconstitute government when an old one falls to pieces; that they may legitimately reserve to themselves some portion of sovereignty. This reservation serves also this salutary purpose: it is a constant reminder to rulers that they are the bearers of a public trust to be managed not for their personal advantage but for the good of all the people. Nothing is more inimical to the welfare of the people than the failure to perceive that the State is for them, not they for the State.

PROOF OF PART II

889. **The people generally ought to transfer the actual function of sovereignty to one person or group** because the general welfare demands this. Except in a very small community it is impossible for the whole people to propose, enact, and execute the requisite laws. No large body of people could efficiently function as a ruler.

Corollary. Lincoln's words about democracy in a true sense may also be applied to government in general: *governments are of the people, for the people, and by the people.* The first, because the State *is* the people, hence, the rulers of a people *ought* to be of the people they rule. The second, because the State is *for* the people. The end of the State is the promotion of *people's* welfare. The worth of any State is measured by the human progress and achieved perfection of its people. The third, because it is from their consent that the power of sovereignty immediately flows.

READINGS

St. Robert Bellarmine, *De Laicis, Or The Treatise On Civil Government,* tr. K. Murphy. New York, Fordham.

Carlyle, R. W., and A. J., *History of Medieval Political Theory in the West.* London, Blackwood, 1903–1936.

Catlin, G. E. G., *The Story of the Political Philosophers.* New York, 1937.

Dumbauld, E., ed., *The Political Writings of Thomas Jefferson.* New York, Liberal Arts, 1955.

Haas, F. J., *Man and Society,* 2 ed., 380–394. New York, Appleton-Century-Crofts, 1952.

Joad, C. E. M., *Guide to the Philosophy of Morals and Politics,* 471–512. London, Gollancz, 1938.

Lavere, G. J., "Basis for the State in the Political Philosophy of John Locke," *Culture,* 16 (1955), 404–424.

Lewis, E., *Medieval Political Ideas,* Vol. I, 140–192. New York, Knopf, 1954.

Locke, J., *Two Treatises of Government.*

Maritain, J., *Scholasticism and Politics,* 71–93. London, Bles, 1954.

McCoy, C. N. R., "Note on the Problem of the Origin and Nature of Society," *The Thomist*, 16 (1953), 71–81.
Messner, J., *Social Ethics*, 507–539. St. Louis, Herder, 1949.
Plato, *Republic II*, 369–374; *Laws III*, 676–682.
Powers, F. J., ed., *Papal Pronouncements on the Political Order*, 17–57.
Riesenberg, P. N., *Inalienability of Sovereignty in Medieval Thought*. New York, Columbia, 1956.
Rommen, H. A., *The State in Catholic Thought*, 371–476. St. Louis, Herder, 1955.
Suarez, *De Opere Sex Dierum*, V, 3. *De Legibus*, III, cc. 1–4.

Chapter XXVI THE CONSTITUTION OF A STATE

890. Once a people accept a particular body of rulers by implicit or explicit transfer of authority, they have government, exercising actual sovereignty and guiding the State to its appointed ends. A constitution, no matter how crude, underlies every government. No government is without one, for by a constitution we do not mean merely a written document, agreed to by a sovereign, wherein he agrees to respect certain liberties of his people and follow a definite pattern in his rule. We give it a broader meaning. For our purposes we may call a constitution a fundamental system of governmental principles which indicate the form government shall take by designating those who shall hold the highest offices, prescribing the mode of the selection or creation, defining the quality and extent of governmental action, and marking the relation of the individual to his government. We shall discuss the notion of a constitution touching briefly on (*a*) the form of government and (*b*) the mode of succeeding to governmental power; and treating more extensively (*c*) governmental activity and (*d*) the citizen's relation to government.

I. THE FORM OF GOVERNMENT

891. By a government we understand that officially accepted and legitimate person, individual or moral, to whom the function of actual sovereignty is entrusted. Our problem is concerned with discovering what form of government the Natural Law commands or forbids or permits.

Some distinguish governments on the basis of the mode by which the chief magistrate is selected, that is, election or hereditary succession; the division of governmental powers; or the existence or nonexistence of a written constitution. No division, however, is more fundamental and goes more cleanly to the heart of things than that of Aristotle, which is based upon the number of persons who share in rule. During the nineteenth century there was a movement to discredit Aristotle's division as unscientific and inadequate but it came to nothing. Aristotle's is still the best because it best performs the essential functions of a good division — it resolves the thing to be studied into its simplest elements.

892. "The true forms of government," says Aristotle, "are those in which the one, or the few, or the many, govern with a view to the common interest."[1] Hence there are three simple forms: *monarchy*, in which the whole sovereignty rests in one person; *aristocracy*, in which it resides in a small class: *democracy*, in which it is exercised by the collectivity of the citizens. This last form Aristotle designates by a more generic name, a polity or constitution. "But governments," he continues, "which rule with a view to private interest, whether of the one, or the few, or the many are a perversion . . . the perversions are these: of kingship, *tyranny*; or aristocracy, *oligarchy*; of constitutional government, *democracy*."[2] Since democracy has a different connotation in modern usage, for that perverted form of popular rule which Aristotle called democracy we substitute the word ochlocracy, or *mob rule*.

893. All known forms of government either directly fall into one of these simple classes or as *mixed forms* exhibit some variant of one or other of all three. The variations of absolute monarchy, pure aristocracy, and direct democracy are many and differ according to the manner in which the powers of sovereignty — legislative, executive, and judicial — are separated and allocated partly to the one, partly to the few, and partly to the many. That may be called a limited monarchy in which the executive power rests in a hereditary king, judicial power principally in the king to whom the judges are subject, secondarily and partially in the people who serve as jurymen, legislative power partially in an aristocracy represented by an Upper House, partially in the people represented in a Lower House. That has been called a consular form of government in which legislative power resides either in the people themselves or in their representatives, or partly in a favored class and partly in the people, whereas the executive and judicial functions are vested in a consul. That is called a representative democracy in which the executive power belongs to one directly or indirectly chosen by the people; the legislative power, to representatives of the people; and the judicial power, to appointees of the executive approved of by the legislative body. To call one government a democracy merely because its chief executive is elected and another a monarchy solely because he is a

[1] *Politics*, Bk. III, 7, 1279a.
[2] *Ibid.*, 1279b.

hereditary king is not a very helpful distinction. The fundamental question is, Where is the preponderance of governmental power?

894. *Congressional government* calls for the strict cleavage of legislative, executive, and judicial powers. The idea of separation seems to have been first suggested by Montesquieu,[3] and the conscious purpose underlying it is the prevention of tyranny arising from an accumulation of unrestrained power in one person or group. One group makes the laws, one person administers them, and a third group judges according to them. By a carefully arranged system of checks each counterbalances the power of the other. At the core of the system is an executive with real power: he is independent of and not chosen by a legislature which in turn cannot be dissolved before the expiration of its contitutional term.

895. *Congressional government* rests upon the principle of diffusion of power; *cabinet government* upon the principle of concentration of power. A cabinet is a small college of ministers who are the heads of the chief departments of governmental administration. It is immediately responsible to the legislature from which it is selected by the majority party of that body. Whenever it ceases to have the confidence of the legislature, it is forced to resign; when it voluntarily resigns, the legislature is dissolved and new elections are held. It is rightly called the *government,* because it does the real governing of the State. While there is a nominal executive, he is but a figurehead, although he is a person of great dignity as the personal representative of the nation. Power resides in the cabinet, because it directly controls all administration as the supreme *acting executive,* and since cabinet members are also members of the legislature — indeed the chief men of the majority party — the cabinet controls the legislation as well.

896. Congressional government is the modern and logical outgrowth of the federal concept of the State; cabinet government is the product of the unitary type of State. By the latter is meant a State containing a single supreme government which alone controls all governmental activity and from which every minor agency of government derives its authority. Examples are England, France, and Italy, where the authority of municipalities, countries, and provinces is immediately derived from, and directly subordinate to, one central government. The federal State is a collection of semisovereignties under one supreme government: the authority of the semisovereignties is not usually derived from the central government and in many matters of purely internal interest it is completely independent of the central government. The constituent parts are rightly called semisovereignties, because there are certain matters

[3] Baron de Montesquieu, *The Spirit of the Laws,* Bk. XI, cc. X–XX.

wherein they are sovereign and to that extent may be called sovereign States but in many other matters — foreign relations — they depend on the central government. Historically the federal State has arisen from a fusion of several smaller independent States into one larger State with the result that the combining States retained something of their former jurisdiction. The United States of America and the German Reich of 1871 are outstanding examples of the federal State.

To our question, What kind of a government does the Natural Law command? we find the proponents of the theory of the divine right of kings saying the only legitimate form of government is monarchy. Rousseau makes the same claim for pure democracy.[4]

THESIS LXVII. The Natural Law neither commands nor forbids monarchy, aristocracy, or democracy but allows any form of government which is capable of attaining the ends of the State.

PART I

897. The Natural Law does not demand any of these forms of government, because there are no natural signs indicating nature's intent. Nor does the Natural Law forbid any of them, for the experience of the race testifies that States have functioned well under all three forms.

PART II

898. **The Natural Law allows any form of government which is capable of attaining the ends of the State.** What conduces to a natural good is allowed by the Natural Law. But any form of government capable of attaining the ends of the State conduces to a natural good. Therefore the Natural Law allows any form of government capable of attaining the ends of the State.

Corollary. The Natural Law forbids any form of government that operates for the private interest of rulers to the neglect of the common good of all.

899. **N.B. I. What constitutes the best form of government** is a

[4] Rousseau says: "Were there a people of gods, their government would be democratic. So perfect a government is not for men" (*Social Contract*, Bk. III, Chap. IV). Yet one must note the meaning he gives to the word *government*. In his theory, the real sovereign is always the whole people and "a government" is merely a body of administrators (Bk. III, Chap. I) selected by and directly accountable to its sovereign. The Sovereign People should meet at frequent and regular intervals to make laws and demand an accounting of their government (Bk. III, Chap. XII–XIV). This they are to do themselves, *not through representatives* (Chap. XV).

question that belongs to political science. Two remarks will suffice here. First, the best government for any particular people is that which works best for them in terms of their traditions, economic situation, level of civilization, peculiarity of temperament, and the like. Second, if we take the average run of peoples and circumstances, that form will work best which is most responsive to enlightened public opinion. This is possible only where a large and articulate middle class is found. As Aristotle says, "The best political community is formed by citizens of the middle class, and those States are likely to be well administered in which the middle class is large and stronger if possible than both the other classes . . . great then is the fortune of a State in which the citizens have a moderate and sufficient property."[5]

N.B. II. Once a form of government has been set up and accepted, *it may not be lightly changed.* For the constant turmoil consequent upon frequent change would render impossible the ends of the State. Therefore a change is to be made only when a very grave evil is to be corrected or when the true progress of the State imperatively calls for it. Zigliara[6] says the power to make this change does not rest upon the people alone nor the rulers alone but the whole society. This is generally true, though in a rare instance a radical change may be made even against the will of erstwhile rulers (see § 923).

II. TITLES TO AUTHORITY

900. In setting forth the form of government, every constitution makes clear who shall hold supreme authority. The next question is, How does one validly come to have authority?

The ground of authority has already been stated: it is the law of nature demanding the State and with it authority. A *title to authority* is some fact which demonstrates the existence of authority in this particular person or group rather than in another. What, then, are the facts which the Natural Law considers a good title to authority? As in the case of property titles, we distinguish several which are subordinate from one which is primordial, so here we have a number which are proximate and one that is fundamental.

A. Proximate Titles

901. Legitimate succession is an entry upon the authority of a

[5] *Politics,* Bk. IV, 9, 1295b.

[6] T. M. Zigliara, *Summa Philosophica,* Vol. III, *Jus Naturae,* L. II, c. 2, a. 8, p. 263. Lugduni, 1889.

predecessor in the mode and manner prescribed by the constitution. This may be by designation on the part of the predecessor, by heredity, or by election. It is presumed that the prescriptions of the constitution are consonant with right reason.

Victory in a just war. A very rare case may be verified where a justly aggrieved people finds that absolutely the sole way to its own peace and security is to deprive a hostile neighbor of its independence and assume rule over it.

Prescription. By fraud or violence, a usurper may oust the legitimate government and, though the beginnings of his rule are unlawful, he may in time become the legitimate ruler. The transition from an illegitimate *de facto* government to a *de jure* government is in this wise: (*a*) peaceful possession and efficient use of authority; (*b*) absence of all probable hope of restoring the old government without convulsing the realm.

A people must have some government; and when there is actually only one, though it be illegitimate, they are bound to co-operate with it at least in what pertains to public order and ordinary administration. When this rule has become firmly established and is actually attaining the ends of the State so that the only way to restore the old government is by public upheaval and civil war, then the rights of the old government cede to the right of the community to a peaceable existence. The public welfare is of more importance than the right of an individual, family, or party to rule. When, then, the return of the old government has become morally impossible, the *de facto* government has become legitimized.

B. Fundamental Title

902. The validity of the foregoing facts to establish authority in a particular ruler must rest ultimately upon the *permanent consent of the people*. This is a demand of the Natural Law, not a mere toleration or approval. The reasons are the same as those which show that consent is the juridic cause of the State and that the people are the primary depositary of authority. Cronin, who rejects this position, makes these significant concessions: "First we admit that the consent of the people is the best of all titles. Secondly, where consent is wanting over a long period, its absence might suffice to make a certain form of government wholly impossible, in which case a ruler might be bound to abdicate for the sake of the public good. Thirdly, the development of the republican ideal and the increasing power of the masses in the modern State are gradually rendering the consent of the governed more and more indispensable, at least as a condition of rightful rule. Fourthly, any wide acceptance, by existing rulers, of this principle of popular consent as the only title of political authority might itself confer upon the people the right of originating the form of government, which, once obtained, could not then be lawfully removed from them without their consent."[7]

Although many governments in the past have not reposed on the people's consent, the truth that they *ought to* is gradually becoming more apparent. We repeat that the State is the people; that their notion of what practically constitutes the common good most nearly approaches it; that nothing could be a greater hindrance to the common good than a government to which the people permanently refuse to give their consent.

There is no contradiction in saying that victory in a just war is a proximate title and consent the fundamental title. Thus no one will deny the right of an outraged people to destroy a pernicious foreign government and substitute one of their choice, as the Allies did to the Nazi Government in 1945. Ultimately, however, the government for the subjugated will become such that they have an obligation to accept it as did the English in Norman times or, where the victor disregards the good of the subjugated so that consent is unreasonable, his government must go, as happened to the English yoke in Ireland.

[7] *The Science of Ethics*, Vol. II, p. 538. New York, Benziger, 1922, 2 ed.

READINGS

Anderson-Weidner, *American Government*, 4 ed., 97–141. New York, Holt, 1953.

Aristotle, *Politics*, Bk. III, cc. 6–18; Bk. IV.

Barker, E., *Citizen's Choice*. Cambridge, University Press, 1937.

——— *Essays on Government*. Oxford, Clarendon, 1945.

Bodin, J., *Six Books of the Commonwealth*, trans. M. J. Tooley. Oxford, Blackwell, n. d.

Bonacina, C., "The Catholic Church and Modern Democracy," *Cross Currents*, Fall, 1951, 1–14.

Burgess, J. W., *The Foundations of Political Science*, 113–147. New York, Columbia, 1933.

Campbell, F. S., *The Menace of the Herd*, 1–137. Milwaukee, Bruce, 1943.

Corwin, E. S., *The "Higher Law" Background of American Constitutional Law*. Ithaca, Great Seal, 1955.

Dawson, C., "The Traditions of Christian Monarchy," *Month*, 195 (1953), 261–266.

Elliott-McDonald, *Western Political Heritage*. New York, Prentice-Hall, 1950.

Fowler, W. W., *The City-State of the Greeks and Romans*. London, Macmillan, 1952.

Friedrich, C. J., "The Political Theory of the New Democratic Constitutions," *Review of Politics*, 12 (1950), 215–224.
Gabriel, R. H., ed., *Hamilton, Madison and Jay on the Constitution*, 3–77. New York, Liberal Arts, 1954.
Gettell, R. G., *Political Science*, rev. ed., 244–259. Boston, Ginn, 1949.
Hammond, M., *City-State and World-State*. Cambridge, Harvard, 1951.
Heald, M. M., *A Free Society*. New York, Philosophical Library, 1953.
Hermens, F. A., "Politics and Ethics," *Thought*, 29 (1954), 32–50.
Hughes, E. J., *The Church and the Liberal Society*. Princeton, Princeton University Press, 1944.
Lewis, E., *Medieval Political Ideas*, Vol. I, 241–331. New York, Knopf, 1954.
McBain, H. L., *The Living Constitution*. New York, Macmillan, 1941.
Morris, R. B., ed., *Alexander Hamilton and the Founding of the Nation*, 94–230. New York, Dial, 1957.
Ogg-Ray, *Essentials of American Government*, 7 ed., 3–79. New York, Appleton-Century-Crofts, 1952.
Rossiter, C., "The Political Theory of the American Revolution," *Review of Politics*, 15 (1953), 97–108.
Sagar, S., "Oligarchy in Action," *Defendant*, 2 (April, 1954), 51–55.
Santayana, G., *Dominations and Powers*, 341–436. New York, Scribners, 1951.
Simon, Y. R., *Philosophy of Democratic Government*. Chicago, University of Chicago, 1951.
Spahr, M., *Readings in Recent Political Philosophy*. New York, Macmillan, 1949.
Wilson, W., *Constitutional Government in the United States*, 1–53, 173–197. New York, Columbia, 1947.

Chapter XXVII THE LEGISLATIVE FUNCTION OF GOVERNMENT

903. What must a government *do* in order to attain the ends of the State? The answer includes (*a*) what the State must do for its own people; (*b*) how it must act toward other States. The first point is treated in this and the three following chapters; the second in our treatment of international ethics.

Since authority is the power to direct and compel toward the public good, no government could direct its citizens without the power to issue directives — which is legislative power. Nor could it compel without the power to enforce its directives, which entails executive and judicial power. The functions of a government, then, are explained in terms of its legislative, executive, and judicial powers.

I. LEGISLATIVE POWER

904. Two inquiries are important here: first, the nature; and second, the extent of the State's power to make laws. The extent of this power is the subject of the two following chapters; in this chapter we shall discuss the nature of the legislative power.

Who makes law? Constitutional law, especially if it is of the customary traditional kind, is generally made by the entire society. Laws made in carrying out constitutional principles are made by the legislative, executive, and judicial arms of the government. Judges make law either by elucidating the Natural Law or by adding to the body of precedents. The executive makes what is tantamount to law — administrative rulings. The explicit function of lawmaking is exercised by the legislative power when it makes statute law. Our discussion includes any form of law.

905. To be law a directive of the State must appeal to reason and embody the sensible means of attaining some objective of political society. Anything inept, stupid, or frivolous could not be a prescription of right reason. On this point no controversy is possible.

The law of the State does more than appeal to reason by advising or suggesting. It also appeals to the will and embodies some kind of compulsion which obliges men to accept it. Every social regulation implies some kind of obligation. In artificial societies obligation can only be hypothetical; for instance, if a person consistently disregards the rules of an athletic club or a benevolent association, he is asked to leave. But a man cannot quit the State. He must live under some government. In the law of the State the note of obligation is clear, peremptory, and apodictic. What is the nature of this compelling force? Is it the physical power of the State to enforce its will? Does it impose moral obligation so that a person who disregards the law of the State incurs moral guilt?

One hundred and fifty years ago this would have seemed an idle question. All men would have answered that State law can impose an obligation on one's conscience. But the doctrine of Kant, cleaving the juridic from the moral order and denying that the law of the State has morally binding force, gave the initial impetus to a different philosophy of law which is widely prevalent today and is held by persons of quite different moral complexion. A number of causes has accelerated the acceptance of this philosophy. Three are worthy of comment.

906. The prevalence of a materialistic view of life. People who deny that man has an immortal soul and that there is a life hereafter cannot logically admit moral obligation binding conscience. If in their personal lives they substitute personal whim, expediency, or external respectability for rigorous and universally binding laws of conduct, their motive for keeping the civil law can only be fear of punishment by the State.

907. The practice of the purely secular and sometimes atheistic State. Many modern States have become so secularized that they repudiate religious obligation binding themselves, and a few States have even tried to extirpate relation. Consequently the opinion has arisen that as public religion is nonexistent so too is public morality. It is said that the State does not consider itself bound by moral principles; that it follows a policy of expedience and utility. Hence the citizen may deal with the State in the same manner, that is, even though he may have to be moral in his private conduct, no moral tie binds him to keep the law of the State. Many people argue that legislators now have no intention of binding them morally, that some expressly repudiate such a notion and rely on heavy sanctions, public opinion, and efficient law enforcement to make their laws work.

908. The theory of Holmes. Few men have had an influence on modern law comparable to that of Oliver Wendell Holmes, who held a philosophy of crude, frank, and brutal force. He was a skeptic to whom truth is completely relative and subjective. He defines truth as "the system of his intellectual limitations."[1] The test of truth for him is "a present or imagined future majority in favor of our view."[2] Hence he can boast, "To have doubted one's own first principles is the mark of a civilized man."[3] Law and morals are absolutely distinct. He wishes that "every word of moral significance could be banished from the law altogether."[4] Force is the final arbiter: he says, "Deep seated preferences cannot be argued about . . . and therefore, when differences are sufficiently far reaching, we try to kill the other man rather than let him have his way."[5] Morality is not based upon the will of a personal God and has no absolute or objective validity for "our system of morals is a body of imperfect social generalizations expressed in terms of emotion."[6] Moral principles are prejudices, that is, judgments made in advance of experience. Morals are reducible to taste so that the morally good is what Holmes likes, the morally evil what he dislikes. Holmes's approval or disapproval of Lesbian practices falls into the same moral category as liking or disliking sugar in one's coffee.[7] Tastes are due to one's environment. Although tastes keep changing, they have this practical importance that, when individuals or groups refuse to conform to the tastes of the dominant group, that is, the persons possessing the greater physical force, the holders of these dominant tastes simply put the screws on the nonconformers.[8]

Man is only a cosmic ganglion, he repeats, not a being of absolute worth. He sees "no reason for attributing to man a significance in kind from that which belongs to a baboon or grain of sand."[9] The only thing worth while in life is functioning, the struggle to live. "I know of no true measure of men except the total of human energy they embody. . . . The final test of this energy is battle in some form."[10] Human life has little sanctity: a man may easily be sacrificed in the interest of the State. The ultimate arbiter of all life is physical force so that when men disagree thoroughly and irreconcilably the final *ratio*

[1] Oliver W. Holmes, *Collected Legal Papers*, p. 310. New York, Harcourt Brace, 1920.
[2] *Ibid.*
[3] *Ibid.*, p. 307.
[4] *Ibid.*, p. 179.
[5] *Ibid.*, p. 312.
[6] *Ibid.*, p. 306.
[7] *Holmes-Pollock Letters*, Vol. I, p. 105. Cambridge, Mass., Harvard, 1941.
[8] Oliver W. Holmes, "Natural Law," *Harvard Law Review*, 1918, Vol. 32, p. 42.
[9] *Holmes-Pollock Letters*, Vol. II, p. 252.
[10] Oliver W. Holmes, *Holmes' Speeches*, p. 73. Boston, Little Brown, 1934.

decidendi is, in Holmes's own words, "We don't like it and we shall kill you if we can."[11]

Therefore the only binding force of law is physical force applied through the courts to bad men, namely, those who act contrary to the changing tastes of the dominant group. The sole semblance of legal principle is public policy. To Holmes public policy is any end which the dominant forces of the community desire so intensely as to brook no opposition to its accomplishment.[12] The clever jurist, then, is the one who can predict the shape of tomorrow's tastes and public policy. It is upon these conclusions that *legal realists* are building a jurisprudence devoid of any notion of moral obligation.

THESIS LXVIII. Civil Law not only urges a moral obligation when it declares the Natural Law, but even in matters left indifferent by the Natural Law it may impose obligation binding in conscience.

PROOF OF PART I

909. By declaring the Natural Law civil law imposes moral obligation, because:

Whatever declares the Natural Law must impose moral obligation.

The State can authentically declare the Natural Law. Some authority among men must have this power. If the State lacked it, it would be unable to make any laws.

PART II

910. In the first part we treated of *necessary* laws. When the State defines crimes, outlines fundamental obligations, or confirms certain rights it is merely enunciating the Natural Law and the consequent obligation comes directly from the Natural Law. In the second part we pass to the more proper field of human legislation, namely, those laws which are not necessary but *useful* for the common good. In general ethics we termed these determinative laws. Not only declarative laws but also determinative laws impose obligation. Thus, although the Natural Law does not determine whether the public good must be served by a publicly owned telegraph system or one privately owned — since either could be equally useful to the community — if the legislator chooses a publicly owned system, then, even though a citizen thinks a privately owned

[11] *Justice Oliver Wendell Holmes, His Book Notices and Uncollected Letters,* ed. H. C. Shriver, p. 187. New York, Central Book, 1936.

[12] *Ibid.,* pp. 187–188.

system more useful, he would be morally obliged to accept the publicly owned system.

PROOF

911. **Even in indifferent matters civil law may impose moral obligation.** A precept of the Natural Law commands man to obey the State within the proper field of its jurisdiction. As reason dictates that children must in conscience obey their parents, so reason likewise tells men that they must live under public authority and obey it. If there is widespread disregard of civil authority, social chaos results, and the promotion of human welfare becomes impossible.

The State's jurisdiction embraces many matters undeclared by the Natural Law. The nature of the State demands that it regulate matters which are not only necessary but also useful to the public good.

912. **N.B. I.** The proposition may be proved by two other reasons. (*a*) Since authority is from God, laws made in virtue of divine authority are a participation in Natural and eternal law and hence bind with similar force. (*b*) Since civil law supplements the Natural Law, it has the same *ultimate* purpose, namely, the proper direction to man's last end. Therefore it ought to operate in the manner in which the Natural Law operates, that is, by moral, not physical, necessity. Law which operates with moral necessity imposes moral obligation.

N.B. II. The fact that legislators do not explicitly advert to moral obligation when they frame a law does not prove that they wish to exclude moral obligation. Their intention is to make a true law with all the binding power which law carries.

N.B. III. The stark brutality of Holmes's doctrine on civil law is a remorselessly logical consequence of a modern jurist's erroneous view of man's nature.

N.B. IV. We have proved that, in general, disobedience to the State is wrong; that civil law can impose an obligation in conscience. A further question is, Does absolutely every law of the State bind the conscience of the citizen? This question will be solved in §§ 924–927.

II. VALID CIVIL LAW

913. What is a true law? Under what conditions does a directive of the State have the force of law and bind the conscience?

THESIS LXIX. To impose obligation, civil law must proceed from legitimate authority and be just, possible, and properly promulgated.

For a law to be valid certain conditions must be fulfilled on the part of the legislator, the matter of the law, and the promulgation of the law.

PART I

914. The *legislator* must have legitimate authority over both the citizens and the matter for which he legislates. Thus the laws which Russia made in 1940 to break up the estates of Eastern Poland were invalid, because Russia had no jurisdiction over the Poles. Similarly, the laws of the Emperor Joseph II regulating divine worship in the Austrian Empire were invalid, because the State has no jurisdiction in purely religious matters.

PROOF

915. **To impose obligation civil law must proceed from legitimate authority** because imposition of obligation is restriction of man's free will. Only legitimate authority can restrict man's freedom. Man as man has no power to bind his fellow man: all men are by nature independent. Therefore, men must have authority in order to impose their will on other men.

PART II

916. The matter must be just. The law must always ordain a prescription of right reason. No law may contradict the Natural Law. Thus an edict forbidding a father to bequeath money to his children would be void. Nor may civil law contradict divine positive law as did the laws of England which forbade the Mass. Negatively, civil law must not contravene the law of any higher authority. Positively, it must be either necessary or useful to the common good. Frivolous or silly measures, or measures which benefit only the ruler or a small class, cannot be valid laws.

PROOF

917. **To impose obligation the civil law must be just.** To impose obligation the civil law must be based on the Natural Law (cf. § 238). But what is based on the Natural Law must be just. Therefore to impose obligation the civil law must be just.

PART III

918. The matter must be possible, that is, physically and morally capable of execution by the people. Observance of civil law must not place too heavy a burden on the subject as did the old laws of imprisonment for debt. The great principle is *ad impossible nemo tenetur* — you cannot do the impossible. Therefore, heroic actions cannot generally be the object of human precept though they are sometimes the object of divine precept. Impossibility of fulfillment must be judged by concrete circumstances of place, time, climate, education, tradition, and national temperament. Thus the American draft law of 1940 could never have been enacted in 1812.

PROOF

To impose obligation civil law must be possible of observance. A law makes an action or its omission necessary, but an action or an omission which is not possible cannot become necessary.

PART IV

919. Promulgation. If law is to produce its effect, it must be so authentically manifested that the people can know that it binds them. Therefore, to give his enactment the final force of law, the lawgiver must provide that the people certainly know that the law exists, what it means, and what its binding force is. The mode of promulgation depends on the fundamental constitution of each State.

PROOF

To impose obligation civil law must be properly promulgated. A law must serve as a guide to the social actions of the people which is impossible without due promulgation.

920. Corollary. *Any edict which fulfills these conditions is a valid law without reference to popular acceptance.* If a constitution so provides, certain proposals may not *become law* until after popular ratification. This indicates that in this instance the people are part of the law-making body. But once a law has been duly established and promulgated it does not rest with the people to obey it or not as they choose. A legitimate command has been issued to them and a command necessarily calls for obedience. Acceptance or rejection of a law by the people after promulgation has no effect upon its validity.

If a law is generally disregarded by the majority of the people, these conclusions seem to follow: (*a*) the legislator may quietly allow the law to lapse. This would not be an instance of direct popular authority over established law but of tacit revocation by the lawgiver. (*b*) They certainly commit a fault who after the first promulgation of the law disobey it. When, however, the greater part of the people disobey it and it has not as yet been fully revoked, an individual person is excused from keeping it because observance in these circumstances becomes too great a burden. Suarez says, "The private observance of such a law no longer pertains to the common good."[13] (*c*) Usually widespread non-acceptance of a law is a sign that it originally had some nullifying defect.

III. UNJUST LAWS AND REBELLION

921. A law which certainly fails in any of the above-mentioned conditions is not a law but a species of violence. However, in case of doubt as to the validity of a law the *presumption always favors the existence of the law*. This presumption the common welfare demands.

922. Unjust laws. How may a people act with regard to obviously unjust laws?

a) *If it is morally impossible to obey*, that is, if obedience would impose too great a burden, the people are not bound. If, however, the law is susceptible of division and they can keep some of the law, they are not excused from the whole.

b) *If it commands what is contrary to the Natural Law or divine positive law* the people are obliged to disregard it. They must obey God rather than man. Thus, parents would have to disobey a law forbidding them to give religious instruction to their children under eighteen years of age.

c) *If it unjustly deprives them of goods or rights*, they are justified in resisting it by all legal means and also by passive disobedience. However, prudence may often dictate submission to such a law lest worse evils happen. As the seriousness of the attack upon the rights of individuals and lesser communities increases so likewise do the lawful means of resisting injustice. Resistance, however, must always be proportioned to the sacredness of the right to be safeguarded, the good to be accomplished, and the resultant disturbance.

May a people resort to armed force? They may, if the conditions of blameless self-defense against unjust aggression are verified. "As it is lawful to resist robbers, so it is lawful, in a like case, to resist wicked

[13] *De Legibus*, III, c. XIX, 13.

princes," says St. Thomas.[14] The law of self-preservation admits of no exception. As a son may strike a drunken father in order to save his life when no other means of protection are available, so likewise in order to save themselves from death, mutilation, apostasy from religion, and dangers of equal gravity, citizens may forcibly defend themselves against their government. So also may an individual. In either case, however, a just proportion must be preserved between the good to be accomplished and the resultant evil.

What begins as a measure of collective self-defense may issue in the successful vindication of rights against a tyrant. But there is a clear distinction between armed defense of rights and rebellion, which is the endeavor to oust an existing government. One, however, readily leads to the other. The ruler's government is subverted lest those who make the resistance perish as happened in the case of Cromwell and Charles I, the American colonists and George III. Therefore the question arises, May armed resistance proceed to rebellion?

923. Rebellion. a) Rebellion which is *sedition* or the attempt to overthrow a *legitimate* government is always and everywhere wrong. St. Thomas says: "Because sedition is opposed to a special good, namely, the unity and peace of the people, it is a special sin."[15] He concludes: "Since sedition is an unjust struggle against the common good of the State, it is always a mortal sin."[16] A government may abuse its power to rule and still retain a right to the loyalty of its subjects. If every abuse of authority gave citizens a right to destroy the government, civil order would be at an end. Another reason is that the power to rule comes from God, and as long as a government retains that power, an attempt to overthrow it is defiance of divine authority.

b) Rebellion *which is the overthrow of an illegitimate government* is sometimes allowable. A government may so abuse its power as to forfeit it. What are the grounds for this assertion? Some authors argue that, although abuse of authority does not destroy authority, yet it could be lost if the abuse is so great as to destroy the title upon which authority rests.[17] They say that title to rule is lost if the ruler has gained his authority by election or compact and if the conditions stipulated in the contract with the people have been grossly violated: if authority comes directly from God to the ruler, title to rule could never be lost. Since this last condition is true only of the Church and the Roman Pontiff, and since we have shown that the ultimate title of all civil

[14] *Sum. Theol.*, II–II, 69, 4.
[15] *Sum. Theol.*, II–II, 42, 1.
[16] *Ibid.*, II–II, 42, 2.
[17] V. Cathrein, *Philosophia Moralis*, 10 ed., § 708.

rule is the permanent consent of the people, we might conclude that abuse of authority which destroys the title of consent on which it rests is possible. But this is a cumbersome argument: appeal to titles of rule or broken coronation oaths is unnecessary.

It is simpler to invoke the general welfare as a means of proving that a government may be overthrown. A government ceases to be a government when it substantially ceases to direct the people to the common good. When a government becomes habitually and intolerably tyrannical, when it loses sight of the common good and pursues private interests to the manifest detriment of the people, or when from weakness, inertia, or corruption it is incapable of ruling, it ceases to be a legitimate government.

When, therefore, the common good is no longer realizable under a government, it is lawful to overthrow it, if the following conditions are fulfilled: (i) All legal and pacific means must have been tried to amend it without success. (ii) Reasonable hope must exist that the endeavor will be successful and not engender worse evils. (iii) The judgment concerning a government's incompetency is made not merely by private persons or a party but by the saner and better part of the people so that it may be considered the judgment of the community as a whole.

St. Thomas says, "A tyrannical regime is not just because it is not ordered to the common good but to the private good of the ruler. . . . Hence the assailing of such a regime has not the malice of sedition; unless perchance the assailing of the tyrannical regime is so unwise that the people suffer more harm from the consequent disturbance than they did from the tyrannical government. Rather is the tyrant seditious who fosters discord and sedition among the people that he may the more safely dominate: for that is tyrannical since it is ordained to the personal good of the ruler to the hurt of the people."[18]

To deny the community the right to destroy a thoroughly evil government is to say that the right of a person, family, or group to conduct the government is greater than the right of the community to pursue the ends of the State.

IV. PENAL LAWS

924. In Section I of this chapter we proved that civil laws bind the conscience. We now consider the quality and quantity of this obligation.

May civil laws bind under penalty of serious wrong? They may if

[18] *Sum. Theol.*, II–II, 42, 2, ad 3.

the matter is grave and the legislator intends grave obligation. That his intention is such is taken for granted unless he explicitly declares that the obligation is slight.

May serious laws bind only under venial wrong? Moralists agree that they may if the lawgiver so intends. He cannot, though, impose grave obligation if the matter is slight.

May one sometimes act contrary to civil law without committing a sin? All moralists answer affirmatively but they are not agreed upon the principle which justifies such action. The majority invoke the purely penal law theory, which we adopt.

Civil law, therefore, may be divided into *preceptive laws,* whose observance binds the conscience, and *merely penal laws,* whose observance does not bind the conscience. Three points are of importance here: (*a*) the nature of the purely penal law; (*b*) the criteria for recognizing penal law; (*c*) the number of penal laws.

A. The Nature of Purely Penal Law

925. At the heart of this problem lies the statement of Suarez that every law must impose moral obligation.[19] Certainly every divine law imposes moral obligation because this is the sole kind of obligation which the Unseen Legislator chooses to exert on men. The Unseen Legislator relies on no visible instruments to enforce His commands.

Do all human laws impose moral obligation? Ecclesiastical laws do because the Church avoids resort to force. What of the civil law? Following Suarez[20] many authors say that *all* laws impose *some* moral obligation. They then define a purely penal law as one whose morally binding force is disjunctive or hypothetical.

926. Disjunctive obligation is obligation that falls either upon the content of the law or upon acceptance of the penalty provided for violation. But it does not seem reasonable to suppose that the lawgiver offers the subject the choice of keeping the law or paying the penalty. The lawgiver cannot be said to be indifferent to the observance of law. He must desire its observance. Hypothetical obligation means that the lawgiver places no moral obligation on the content of law but solely on acceptance of the penalty if the law is broken. Nor does this explanation seem reasonable, because according to it the legislator puts moral obligation on the penalty which is the less important part of the law and puts no moral obligation on the content — the really important point.

---

19 *De Legibus,* I, c. XIV, 7.
20 *Ibid.,* III, c. XXVII, 3.

In either explanation moral obligation is whittled away to the vanishing point. There is no moral obligation to keep the precept of the law; one is not obliged to give himself up after violating the law; he may defend himself against conviction, and, if convicted, he may escape if he uses no immoral means.

927. We reject this explanation of the penal law. Indeed some moralists reject the whole theory of penal law their basic reason being fear that the doctrine undermines observance of law. Hence they insist upon the moral character of all laws, which, however, may be voided in particular instances by various exceptions. Thus, according to Ryan, "one may distinguish between the letter of a statute and its spirit, between the end at which it is directed and the means specified in its language."[21] He implies that, although the law retains its moral force, one may act contrary to its letter and commit no sin because one's act does not endanger the end for which the law was made. Others call for a generous use of epikeia (cf. § 933).[22] Another solution is that each individual have the power of self-dispensation.[23]

The moralists do seem to agree upon concrete instances wherein one may act contrary to the letter of the law. Since there is agreement about practice, the problem then is, *How shall one philosophize about the situation?* We choose the theory of penal law because it seems to fit the facts of life and, if properly expounded, is no more provocative of disrespect for law than its rival theory. The purely penal-law theory is sometimes misunderstood. It does not teach that one should violate the law whenever one may do so with impunity, or that civil-law observance is a kind of game played by subjects and law-enforcement agencies. Such a general attitude in a person would indicate low esteem of the virtue of legal justice. Furthermore, one should realize that even the penal law has its own intrinsic value and makes its proper contribution to the public good.

928. We agree with Vermeersch[24] that the purely penal law is one which binds under threat of juridic guilt and punishment but involves no moral guilt. It is contained solely within the external forum and does not touch the inner forum of conscience.

But is not this explanation the Kantian separation of justice from morals? It is not. Kant's mistake was divorcing *all* justice, especially natural justice, from morality and reducing *all* justice to the physical and external. Why should we fear to admit a partial truth in Kant's

[21] *Catholic Principles of Politics,* p. 189.

[22] Ulpianus Lopez, "Theoria legis pure poenalis," *Periodica,* XXVII (1938), 215.

[23] "Hyacinth Woroniecki,"*Angelicum,* XVIII (1941), p. 381.

[24] *Theologia Moralis,* 3 ed., Vol. I, § 172.

exaggeration, namely, that there are aspects of legal justice which do not directly enter the realm of conscience? How often does a man commit a sin by parking his car in the wrong place?

Kant denied that the juridic order pertained to the moral order (§ 428). We admit that justice is part of morality. Then it is retorted that any law of the moral order must impose an obligation in conscience. This is the whole point at issue. It is a reasonable contention that a law may belong to the moral order in two ways: (*a*) as necessary to the common good it imposes obligation in conscience because the lawgiver invokes his total power to bind; (*b*) as merely helpful to the common good it imposes no obligation *whenever the lawgiver does not choose to invoke his total power to bind.* Such law is moral in that it proceeds from legitimate authority and appeals to reason and will, but not in that it binds under pain of sin. The lawgiver *may* refrain from an appeal to conscience. First, because this is done in religious orders whose laws do not bind under pain of sin. Here the lawgiver prefers to appeal to good will and generosity rather than to impose a burden in conscience. Second, if the lawgiver can impose venial obligation where the matter is grave, why can he not denude his law of all moral obligation? He ought to do so sometimes because he has such efficient means of enforcement that he can attain the end of some laws — the mere external order of the commonwealth — without appeal to conscience. Indeed he would be unreasonable and would overburden the consciences of his subjects if he sanctioned some laws more strongly than necessary. That the lawgiver today often *does* refrain from an appeal to conscience is gathered from the fact that (*a*) he makes no provision for epikeia or dispensation; that (*b*) men of good conscience are persuaded of the purely penal character of much of modern law; that (*c*) positivistic notions of law prevail among jurists.

If, then, it be objected that the name "law" belongs only to that which imposes obligation in conscience, the dispute is purely verbal. For legislative enactments surely exist whose violation entails no direct sin.

B. Criteria for Recognizing Purely Penal Law

929. To differentiate between a prescriptive and a purely penal law it would be easy if one could directly learn the mind of the lawgiver, but in these days of parliamentary legislation this is impossible. One can use only indirect criteria.

Certainly those laws are preceptive which (*a*) declare and confirm the Natural Law; (*b*) define, create, or extinguish rights and duties in commutative justice; (*c*) *immediately* promote the common good.

One may judge the penal character of law by a number of tests. (*a*) *The matter of the law* should first be considered. This may be relatively unimportant or have little or no bearing on morals or deal with the mere policing of external order. However, one ought not to conclude that all traffic laws are merely penal. We may judge the character of law (*b*) *from the interpretation which good citizens put upon it,* or (*c*) *from the prevailing philosophy of law* which is current among lawyers, jurists, and legislators. (*d*) Laws which declare acts to be invalid unless certain technicalities are compiled with are looked on as merely penal. (*e*) If there is a vast disproportion between the penalty threatened and the violation, or if the penalty is considered a kind of compensation for the violation (fines for avoiding customs' duties), these laws are generally considered penal.

C. Number of Penal Laws

930. When it is asked how many penal laws there are, there is a great difference in the answers. European moralists incline to enlarge the number; Americans to restrict it. No general answer can be given, but merely one that is true for a particular jurisdiction. To judge, therefore, whether the laws of Maryland or the United States are preceptive or penal, one must have recourse to the above-mentioned principles and form his conscience.

V. THE MEANING AND DURATION OF THE LAW

931. To determine quality, quantity, and duration of moral obligation under law, one must first know the meaning of the law. Hence, a law, like an insurance policy, should be read in an authentic copy. This ordinary people seldom do: they obtain their information third or fourth hand. In reading a law it should be noted first whether it is addressed to and so obligates public officials or the people at large. The next consideration is what the words of the law mean.

932. Interpretation is the attempt to learn the mind and intention of the lawgiver. Since this is conveyed in his words, and since a sound interpretation of legal words demands good faith and common sense, his words are to be understood in the sense in which he used them, that is, according to their natural contextual meaning. One must assume that he is using words to convey rather than to conceal thought. *Verba* *ita sunt intellegenda ut res magis valeat quam pereat.* Technical words are to be understood in their scientifically accepted sense. When doubt arises as to the meaning of a law three courses are open. (*a*) The first is recourse to the lawgiver himself. The meaning which he gives is *authentic interpretation.* It has the same force as law itself. If sovereignty is divided, the power of giving an authentic interpretation rests sometimes with the legislative body, sometimes with the judiciary. In the United States it is the function of the supreme courts. (*b*) The second method of learning the meaning of the law is recourse to the learned in the law. The meaning given by lawyers and jurists is *doctrinal interpretation.* Its value depends on the learning and experience of the person interpreting. (c) Finally, there is *customary interpretation,* or the meaning which the law receives from the practice and conduct of the people. Moralists have always held that custom is the best interpreter of law. Since custom manifests what the people spontaneously do and what arises from natural social evolution, it should be held as the measure of the people's capacity for social co-operation and as that which is most suitable for the common good. It should receive, therefore, the approval of the lawgiver. If it does, it is authentic interpretation. However, modern lawgivers and courts do not admit the force of custom or usage either to induce or abrogate juridic obligations. "Evidence of usage is never admissible to oppose or alter a general principle or rule of law so as . . . to make the legal right and liabilities of the party *other than they are by law.*"[25] A usage of trade is not a real exception to this rule because even that must be "known, certain, reasonable and *not* contrary to law."[26] The reason for this attitude is probably because jurisdictions are so vast and people so heterogeneous that it is difficult to determine what true customs are. The disfavor which custom finds in modern law is another indication of the purely juristic character of much of it.

933. Epikeia is a mode of interpreting a law whereby an individual judges that it does not apply to this particular case so that he may act contrary to its letter. It is a kind of equity, the equitable adjustment of private good to the overdifficult demands of law. Laws are meant for the common good. When literal compliance with a law becomes detrimental to the common good, it ceases to oblige. It may happen that a preceptive course of action good and useful in most circumstances becomes harmful in others. Since the lawgiver cannot foresee and write into the law all the instances that it will touch, he proposes it in terms

[25] *Bouvier's Law Dictionary,* "Custom," p. 261.
[26] *Ibid.*

which cover the generality of cases. When, then, keeping the law harms the common good, the lawgiver is rightly understood not to wish the observance of the letter of the law. Thus law may forbid the carrying of arms, but if the life of a person is closely sought by an enemy, one may well suppose that the lawgiver intends that the innocent party should take arms and defend himself. For epikeia to be valid, one must be able to elicit with prudent certitude this judgment — this is the mind the legislator would have had if he had foreseen this case.

934. In the Natural Law there is no room for epikeia. Since the Divine Lawgiver has foreseen every possible contingency, there are no circumstances in which one may act contrary to the Natural Law. In ecclesiastical law, not only when observance of law is morally impossible but also when it causes special hardship, the lawgiver is rightly regarded as not wishing the law to press too burdensomely on the individual. Invalidating laws are an exception, namely, those which nullify acts performed contrary to their prescription. If doubt arises concerning the pertinence of an invalidating law, recourse must be had to the lawgiver who has power to *dispense*, that is, to relax the law in favor of an individual. If recourse is impossible, a person may rightly argue that a doubtful law does not oblige.

The attitude of the civil law is quite different. No court would entertain a plea of epikeia, except in a rare instance in which keeping the letter of the law would evidently and immediately impugn public policy. Civil lawgivers wish exceptions to their laws kept to the barest minimum. Even if observance works hardship on the individual, they think it better that the law be observed for the sake of example to the community. No power exists in the United States to dispense from law: the sole remedy is for the legislature to make a new law. This attitude is another indication of the purely juristic character of many modern laws.

935. Duration of law. Generally speaking laws ought to be permanent. Rickaby observes: "A law is no fleeting, occasional rule of conduct, suited to meet some passing emergency or superficial disturbance. The reason for a law lies deep down, lasting and widespread in the nature of the governed."[27] Constant changing of laws is harmful in that it makes custom impossible, and custom is the great bulwark of the observance of the law. Hence, a law should be changed only when it becomes harmful or when an evidently more useful statute should replace it.

It can be a serious mistake, however, to push the principle of stability beyond due limits and to fail to make civil law keep abreast of

[27] Joseph Rickaby, S.J., *Moral Philosophy*, p. 126.

new situations. The discoveries of science, new business conditions, and even new political conceptions have profoundly affected all nations since the end of the eighteenth century. New methods of wrongdoing must be unmasked, new social obligations require emphasis. If in an era of great change positive law, which is naturally conservative, is not correspondingly adjusted, severe tensions can be created in society.

A law binding in conscience totally ceases, first, by express repeal or introduction of contrary law; second, when the end for which it was levied has totally ceased for the community. The law then becomes useless, and the useless is unreasonable. Thus on account of an epidemic all public gatherings are forbidden; once the epidemic is over the prohibition lapses. Finally, contrary custom tolerated by the lawgiver abrogates law.

The civil law holds that a law is in force until it has been repealed or replaced.

READINGS

St. Thomas, *Summa Theologica*, I–II, 95, 96, 97.

Anderson-Weidner, *American Government*, 4 ed., 487–572.

Aristotle, *Politics*, Bk. V, 1–9.

Barker, E., "Natural Law and the American Revolution," *Traditions of Civility*, 263–355. Cambridge, University Press, 1948.

Cahn, E. N., *The Moral Decision*, Bloomington, Indiana University Press, 1955.

Catholic Theological Society of America Proceedings, "The Problem of Penal Law," 1955, 259–284.

Chamberlain, J. P., *Legislative Processes, National and State*. New York, Appleton-Century, 1936.

Chapman, S. W., "The Right of Revolution and the Right of Man," *Yale Review*, 43 (June, 1954), 576–588.

Connery, J. R., "Shall We Scrap the Purely Penal Law?" *American Ecclesiastical Review*, 129 (October, 1953), 244–253.

Dabin, J., *Theorie Generale du Droit*, 2 ed. Bruxelles, Bruylant, 1953.

Davitt, T. E., *The Nature of Law*. St. Louis, Herder, 1951.

Dumbauld, E., *The Declaration of Independence and What It Means Today*. Norman, University of Oklahoma, 1950.

Gabriel, R. H., ed., *Hamilton, Madison and Jay on the Constitution*, 80–135. New York, Liberal Arts, 1954.

Hale, R. L., *Freedom Through Law, Public Control of Private Governing Powers*. New York, Columbia, 1952.

Hall, J., *Living Law of Democratic Society*. Indianapolis, Bobbs-Merrill, 1949.

Harrington, M., "Ethics of Rebellion," *Commonweal*, 59 (January 29, 1954), 428–431.

Hayoit, P., "L'usage de l'epikie," *Revue diocesaine de Tournai*, 10 (November, 1955), 513–518.

Jessup, P. C., *Transnational Law*. New Haven, Yale, 1956.
Kessler, F., "Natural Law, Justice and Democracy," *Tulane Law Review*, 19 (1944–1945), 31–61.
MacIver, R. M., *The Web of Government*, 61–113. New York, Macmillan, 1947.
Messner, J., *Social Ethics*, 528–539. St. Louis, Herder, 1949.
O'Leary, J., "Functions of Government," *Christus Rex*, 7 (1953), 711–717; 8 (1954), 56–62.
Shotwell, J. T., ed., *Governments of Continental Europe*, 89–120, 278–285, 346–352.
Suarez, *De Legibus*, III, cc. 9, 12, 13, 16, 22, 24, 31; V, cc. 2, 3, 7; VI, cc. 1, 7, 10.

Chapter XXVIII THE SCOPE OF CIVIL LEGISLATION

936. Having examined the nature of civil legislation, we now inquire into the particular items subject to legislation by the civil power: The scope of civil legislation derives from the double purpose of the State. From its primary obligation to insure peace, *protective* legislation is deduced; from its secondary obligation to promote the general welfare, *promotive* legislation is deduced.

I. PROTECTIVE LEGISLATION

937. **Protection of the State.** The first right which the State is to defend, not so much by specific legislation as by its executive arm, is its own right to existence. For the State, as for the individual, the first law is self-preservation. That it must legislate against sedition is clear from § 923. That it may wage war against unjustly aggressive nations will be treated in § 1091.

938. **Protection of citizens.** The State must protect the natural rights of individuals, families, and lesser societies. Life, limb, and health of individuals must be safeguarded not only from the malice of other men but also from the untoward acts of inanimate agencies. A man's person must be secure from seizure and violation. A man must be free to acquire property, gain a livelihood, enter contracts, marry, set up and regulate a family. Good name must be safe from calumny and detraction. Persons must be free to worship God as conscience dictates. They must be protected from unusual inducements to vice and from the scandal of immoral teachings and publications. Private societies may call upon the State to protect them in the legitimate pursuit of their proper ends. If the State were powerless to accomplish these tasks, it could not preserve the order essential for social life. Therefore the State has the following legislative powers. (*a*) It is competent to determine natural rights and the limits of their exercise. For example, it may

fix the legal relations of man and wife, parents and children: it may determine the mode of acquiring, holding, and transmitting property as well as contractual rights and obligations. (*b*) The State may define and punish crime. (*c*) It may remove public obstacles to the exercise of private rights. For example, it may legislate against fraudulent labor contracts or offer special protection to weaker groups whose rights may be unduly endangered. (*d*) It may resolve disputes by erection of proper tribunals. (*e*) Finally, the State may determine the public duties, privileges, and relations of its citizens.

These things the State must enact into law and carry out if it is to exist at all. Woodrow Wilson called these functions constituent: they are not optional with governments for they are the very bonds of society.[1]

In individual ethics we studied extensively the existence and scope of man's chief private rights with the exception of the right to a livelihood. This right has been reserved for detailed discussion at this point because it can be understood better as a social problem and it especially requires State protection.

A. Right to a Livelihood

939. In a broad sense, a livelihood is the more or less secure possession of the means of living. That the means of life should be available to men follows from the right to live. Immunity from anxiety in the matter is not a right, for mortal man is merely on his way to final perfection. Since the probationary nature of life compels man to work out his salvation in fear and trembling, he may not say that he has a right to freedom from economic or any form of anxiety. Security is a coveted situation of well-being and comfort and is, therefore, variable and subjective. Livelihood, therefore, in the strict sense, means that a man has within reach of his diligence and prudence material means necessary for decent living.

940. A man may acquire the means of living either by (*a*) *endowment*, private or public; (*b*) *dependence* on a master or upon charity; (*c*) *exercise of his faculties*. Concerning the first, we have already established that inheritance is a natural title to property (§ 566 ff.). The right to inherit, however, is not unlimited. A wise testator will remember that for some persons enormous inherited wealth is a ready avenue to frivolous and immoral living. Unchecked inheritance can lead to the accumulation of national wealth in the hands of a few powerful families to the detriment of the people at large. For the public good, then, the State may levy inheritance taxes, graduated to the size of the inheritance,

[1] Woodrow Wilson, *The State*, pp. 613–614. Boston, Heath, 1911, rev. ed.

but never in the measure which nullifies right of inheritance. The State endows persons only for past or prospective public service as in the case of a royal family or men of distinguished merit. Persons who are endowed with a living are a small minority.

941. Concerning the second class, we have already seen that even limited slavery deserves to be reprobated (§ 486). The abnormal and unfortunate, the mentally or physically deficient cannot make a living for themselves and must depend on others. They depend, first, upon their own families; if this help is insufficient, then upon private charity. Since these sources of help are inadequate today, the major burden of supporting the unfortunate devolves upon the State. It is a task that must be done, and since other agencies are inadequate, it goes by default to the State. In meeting this obligation, however, the State must avoid monopolizing action which would dry up charitable feeling, responsibility, and initiative among private persons.

942. Since the vast majority of men fall into the last class, working for a living by bodily or mental toil is of momentous importance both for the individual and the common good.

THESIS LXX. Every man has a right to remunerative work if he can live only by such work.

By living we understand not merely keeping body and soul together but living in a human way.

PROOF

Every man has a right to the necessary means of living. But to live as a man, remunerative work is usually absolutely necessary. Therefore, a man has a right to remunerative work if he can live only by work.

943. A man has two alternatives as far as work is concerned: either he works independently and himself reaps the products of his labor, or he makes a contract with another person in which he hands over his productive labors and receives a wage in exchange.

The chief moral concern of the independent worker — the farmer, merchant, entrepreneur, professional man — should be observance of commutative justice; in particular, he should be careful to render a just equivalent in goods or services for income received. The law of just price especially applies to him. Since in this class are found the more able or at least the more fortunate and usually the shrewder and more industrious, there is no great danger that they will fail to gain a livelihood. Hence, social action to secure a livelihood for them has seldom been necessary, except occasionally in the case of farmers for whose benefit a legal price of farm products has been established or subsidies granted. The socialistic tendency is to eliminate all independent workers. The evil of such action has been dwelt upon. Since the widest possible distribution of property among private owners constitutes a strong bulwark of an enduring State, that legislation would be unsocial which would make taxes so high that small businesses could not operate, or which would make all professional men servants of the State.

The bulk of men are dependent workers. In medieval times the dependent worker lived by status; that is, a person was born into a fixed social and economic position and although he had little opportunity of rising from his status, he was economically secure in what he had. Having surrendered the security of status with its fixed but certain income, modern man takes his energies into the commodity market and bargains with an employer for the best possible return in exchange. To make a living, then, he must secure (*a*) adequate remuneration and (*b*) sufficient remunerative work must be available.

B. Remuneration

944. To gain a living the workman has two alternatives: he may be a partner or an employee. If he is a partner, he shares both the profits and the losses, and assumes commensurate share of commercial risk. If he is an employee, he has no general responsibility, and for services rendered receives a wage at regular intervals. At present, real partnership is impractical for the vast majority of workmen because they cannot afford the risk of partnership; they have no capital to cushion losses and they need money at frequent intervals.

945. Concerning the employer-employee system wherein the employer assumes the risks, takes the net profit, and gives the worker a regular wage the main moral question is, *What constitutes a just contract between employer and employee.* After the marriage contract, the wage contract is the most important. It is the basis of modern economy.

The requisites of a just contract between employer and employees are three: (*a*) both parties must be free to enter it; (*b*) the employer must give a wage equivalent to service rendered; (*c*) the employee must render service commensurate with wages received.

946. The first requisite requires no discussion. We begin, then, with the question of a just wage. Since labor capacity is a marketable commodity we must find its true exchange value. In an ethical treatise one cannot state the just price of any marketable ware in a precise computation of dollars and cents. Therefore, in this discussion a *principle* of natural equity must be sought which a person may apply to a concrete wage situation in order to discover whether a just wage is being paid. The inquiry is restricted to the normal adult male who regularly gives up his full working day to an employer.

We have seen that exchange value depends fundamentally upon utility, proximately upon the common estimation of those who buy and sell the commodity in question (§ 604 ff.). What, then, is the value of a man's labor capacity and how do people estimate it?

THESIS LXXI. The minimum just wage of the adult male is the family wage.

947. There is an universal conviction, at least among all working people, that a man ought to receive a wage sufficient to support a family. Is this conviction a mere subjective desire? When we examine the fundamental worth of human labor we perceive it to have a very special value, differing from the value of commodities about which men generally bargain. Human labor has a double worth, one intrinsic to the worker himself, the other extrinsic to the hirer of that labor.

948. The intrinsic value of human labor. There is something noble about human labor because it shares the dignity of the human person. Man has an eternal destiny toward which he moves by fulfilling his moral obligations. This he cannot do unless he acquires the material necessities of living. The means given him as a free being for securing a living are his mental and physical energies. Hence a man's labor capacity has definite intrinsic value to himself: it is the natural means by which he is to live as a man. Between a man's work and the satisfaction of his needs there is an immediate relation. This, then, is a just equation: labor capacity equals human needs supplied in a human way.

The needs of the normal adult male extend to many more goods than those necessary for individual well-being and development. It is nature's intent that he be the head of a family. To this nature vehemently urges him, and once he has a family, nature lays upon him the inescapable duty of nurturing it. His dependents also are to live a human life. The workman, therefore, must supply his family at least with decent frugal comfort. Today human living will include decent habitation with privacy, sanitation, and ordinary conveniences; wholesome food; sufficient rest and leisure to enjoy family life; reasonable recreation for health of mind and body; a small surplus for emergencies such as sickness or death. In the concrete, the aggregate of these things vary according to circumstances of time, place, custom, and civilization.

949. Justice, therefore, is not satisfied if an employer, considering merely the extrinsic utility to himself of a workman's labor, fails to pay a family wage. He sins against commutative justice because he fails to satisfy for the *full* value of the labor which he accepts; he sins also against social justice whenever injustice against families is so widespread, that society suffers notable detriment.

PROOF

950. The family wage is due in commutative justice. Commutative justice demands that a workman receive a wage equivalent to the total value of his labor.

The total value of a workman's labor includes not only extrinsic value to an employer but primarily intrinsic value to the workman. His labor is the means nature gives him to live as a man.

The only wage which compensates for intrinsic value of labor is one that supplies a workman's needs as a family head. Nature intends the adult male to be a family head and to provide for its present and future needs. Unless the family head does this, he is not living as a man.

951. The family wage is due in social justice. If a family wage is not generally available, a workman has a choice of (*a*) not getting married; (*b*) drastically limiting his family; (*c*) having a family of insufficient means. All three are contrary to the social good.

a) It is morally detrimental for both individuals and State if many young and vigorous men are prevented from marrying.

b) A serious curtailment of the birth rate is obviously bad for the State. Curtailment of offspring usually involves positive contraception.

c) If the income of the family head is insufficient, either some of the essentials of life must be foregone, or this income must be supplemented by labor on the part of the wife and children or by relief. It is bad for society if many families must forego essentials of human living because health, education, or morality will suffer. Dire poverty is a common breeding ground of crime. If economic necessity compels a wife to work outside her home, her duties to the home will suffer. If immature children are compelled to work long hours, their health may be affected and they may be deprived of a suitable education. Dependence on relief ought never to be a normal thing in any family. Finally, a community of workmen receiving a family wage is the true backbone of industrialized civilization because they provide a steady market for consumable goods.

952. Corollary I. The fact that a workman agrees to take less than a living wage does not make the contract just. If sheer necessity presses him to accept an unfair contract, he is a victim of injustice. The employer who offers less than a living wage with a take-it-or-leave-it attitude is taking unfair advantage of his own superior economic situation.

Corollary II. The principle of minimum wage holds for married and unmarried alike. The essential value of labor is present even though *per accidens* the workman does not exercise his right to marry. In practice it would be impossible to discriminate without creating deep discontent. The younger unmarried men should be in a safe economic position to marry when the opportunity presents itself. They should be able to save against the heavy initial expense of matrimony. The economic advantage of the older unmarried men could be balanced by special taxes.

C. Equity to the Employer

953. In many discussions on the wage contract the workman's obligation is ignored. It is assumed that the employee gives a just return for salary received. It is true that he has usually done so. The normal man has the capacity to do a good day's work. This work will be valuable to the employer if the employer has selected a profitable type of business, runs it efficiently, fits the workman to the work for which he is qualified and sees to it that he does what is expected of him. Therefore, since the employer has consistently been the stronger party to the contract, he has been quite able to exact his right. It is, however, possible that he may be prevented from exacting his right by the unjust demands of labor unions.

954. Besides exacting specified quality and quantity of work the employer's rights are claimed to be (*a*) reasonable profit, and (*b*) direction or management. As to the first, the underlying supposition is that some profit exist. The reasonableness of profit has been proved in our rejection of socialism (§ 522). It is a gross exaggeration of the rights of workmen to claim that profits of industry, except those required to repair and replace capital goods, belong to workmen. Workers are only a partial cause of profits gained.

955. In a simple arrangement in which one or a few individuals are both owner and manager, the principles, "The thing perishes to the owner" and "The thing increases to the owner," are clearly applicable. This situation is a private affair of commutative justice, which may be tempered by an employer's knowledge of the needs, merits, or sudden hardships of his employees. The old moralists defined reasonable profit in these circumstances as that which is necessary to maintain the employer in his state of life. This definition is no longer helpful because one may doubt if there are now *fixed* states in life. State in life is

generally proportioned to income, but the fact that a man begins life with a yearly income of ten thousand dollars is no pressing reason why he must always enjoy that income. The better definition would seem to be that reasonable profit compensates the businessman for these factors: (*a*) financial risk undertaken; (*b*) cost of educational preparation; (*c*) foresight, ingenuity, courage, and industry which must be exercised to make the enterprise efficient. To evaluate these factors on a specific percentage basis would be impossible. Many variable circumstances of unforeseen loss and occasional good luck enter into business. One may conclude, therefore, that the small businessman who has done justice to his associates and customers, has given his employees a living wage, and has paid his taxes may cheerfully pocket all net profit, be it much or little.

956. Today, however, the situation is not quite so simple. The modern corporation presents many complications. Thousands of stockholders are the owners. But the owners do not manage: management is in the hands of a small, powerful group whose equity in a business is often negligible. Thousands are employed who are totally unknown to ownership and for the most part to management. Since many of these corporations are spread through many localities and dominate the economic lives of many thousands, their fortunate or unfortunate condition affects the common public good. Although they are private societies in name, they are semipublic in fact. Hence the laws of social justice should to a greater or less extent govern their operation.

Their co-operative purpose is making money, and to this end three distinguishable elements contribute essential shares: (*a*) ownership, which makes the effort possible by risking its capital; (*b*) management, which supplies intelligent direction; (*c*) labor, which supplies the rest by efficient execution of direction. Who, then, should benefit by the goods and money socially produced? Equity indicates that benefits belong to those who help to produce them and in proportion to the value of their contribution. Injustice has been done in this respect, for sometimes stockholders have received no dividends and workers have not been paid adequate wages. Who, then, shall estimate the value of the contribution of ownership, management, and labor? If the decision rested with ownership alone or management alone or labor alone, each would be grossly biased in its own favor. The only recourse is free and equitable agreement. Equity would be destroyed if one party abused the strength of its position to secure more than its rightful share. If the execution of the agreement, or unforeseen circumstances tend to the detriment of any of the parties, a new contract should be drawn. In determining the terms of a new contract each party should have a *proportionate voice.* One of the chief functions of occupational groups described in the Appendix would be the insuring of justice in such contracts. If occupational groups do not exist, or if private agreements cannot be reached, the State, as impartial arbiter, may legislate to regulate prices, wages, and profits. It is undesirable that the State should do this, however, except in grave emergencies.

957. An employer may say that to him the value of a man's work does not equal the wage which he should have to pay. The employer is free not to hire such a person, but if he hires him he should pay a living wage. The man's labor has that value to himself, and in the contract of sale price is not to be determined by the buyer alone. The employer may continue to object that the prices he receives in his business do not allow him to pay a living wage. The answer is that wages of labor should be a primary charge upon merchandise so that prices received do not determine wages but wages paid should determine prices to be asked.

958. Regarding employers who habitually pay less than a living wage several comments are pertinent. (*a*) Employers who take large profits from their business and leave less than a living wage for their employees are maintaining a species of economic slavery. (*b*) If the reason why employers fail to pay a living wage is that they could not otherwise maintain their businesses, several different cases must be distinguished. (*i*) If this inability is due to temporary reverses, owners and employees could agree to take a proportionate loss until business revives. (*ii*) If this inability is permanent, due to poor management, lack of enterprise and efficient methods, that employer ought to go out of business. No man's profits should be founded on injustice. (*iii*) If a business does not make enough to pay living wages because it is overwhelmed with *unjust* burdens of tariffs and taxes, or because it is compelled to sell its products at unjustly low prices, they who cause such conditions — monopolists, financial leaders, or lawmakers — are guilty of grievous wrong. If private initiative cannot remedy the situation — and usually it cannot — the social good demands that governmental regulation provide conditions which make it possible for an honest business to operate at reasonable profit and pay a living wage. This practical ideal every government in an industrial age should unceasingly labor to achieve.

959. If profit still shows after a firm has paid a living wage, has given reasonable dividends, and has reserved funds for replacement of capital goods and future needs, may the workers claim a share in it?

If all the items mentioned have been taken care of justly and efficiently, no further profit should be possible. But if in extraordinarily fortunate circumstances such profit exists, workers may claim a share, *if they have been admitted to partnership*. Except for a few persons with considerable savings to invest in their own firm, workers are not now partners; but the way to some type of partnership could be opened to them. This could be effected through an occupational group which would regulate the rewarding of faithful service. Both individual firms and business in general would benefit because hope of real reward would stimulate more interest in work, and would offer more incentive to loyalty and fidelity.

960. The second alleged right of the employer is *management*. This has been accepted as an immediate deduction from the nature of ownership which is plenary control of an object in accordance with law. Of late, however, many have raised the issue whether the workingmen should be admitted to a voice in management or not.

If the owner manages his own plant he has an unimpeachable right to run his business without interference from his employees, provided of course that he observes the law. They receive a voice in management only when they rise to partnership.

Complaints about management usually have occurred when ownership and management are divorced. The stockholders do not manage the business they own. Pius XI has called attention to this fact: "Immense power and despotic economic domination is in the hands of a few and these few are frequently not the owners but only the trustees and directors of invested funds who administer them at their good pleasure."[2] But even in these cases the workers have not the right of management.[3] Control belongs to the owner.

However, whether ownership and management are the same or not, the control *must accord with law*. Management must respect the right of workers to human working conditions. What, therefore, the law should be on this point concerns the workingman and he is entitled to a proportionate share in its formulation. Hence, "on the broader level of economic life, in dealing with problems which transcend the individual company, labor and management are equal. But on the plant level such equality may not be demanded as a right."[4] The proper solution of management and like industrial problems lies, not so much in legislation as in a corporate organization of society, especially in democratically operated occupational groups.

---

[2] *Quadragesimo Anno.*

[3] Address of Pius XII, June 3, 1950. *Catholic Mind*, 48 (1950), 508.

[4] John F. Cronin, S.S., *America*, Vol. 83 (1950), p. 462.

D. Means of Securing Workers' Rights

961. The living wage is the most important but not the only aspect of the right to a livelihood. Closely allied are the questions of employment and working conditions. First, sufficient remunerative work must be constantly available. If a man has a living wage for six months and is idle six months, his living is meager. Second, the surroundings of one's work must have an elemental human decency: they should not impair bodily, mental, or moral well-being.

Who is obliged to procure for a man a decent, steady job with a living wage? The economic liberalists answered, "the workman alone." The liberalist was right to the extent that this obligation is primarily individual, but he was completely wrong in denying its social aspect. Society has an obligation to the workman. The good or evil condition of the State is in proportion to its economic well-being which can be secured only by harmonious interplay of many social factors chief among which are wages and employment. In fact, economic well-being is no longer a mere national concern; it is international, as the world-wide stagnation of the early thirties proved. Therefore the State must maintain wages and employment at a healthy level. This obligation was ignored by a society dominated by the economic liberals. Consequently, the workman, as weaker party to the wage contrast, had to accept an unjust bargain. To obtain justice he endeavored to lift himself to a position of bargaining equality with his employer. He used three means: labor unions, strikes, and labor legislation.

E. Labor Unions

962. A *labor union* is an association of workmen whose purpose is to safeguard and promote the industrial rights of workmen. Since the individual is powerless to bargain with an employer on a basis of equality, he has recourse to collective action. All the workmen of a given plant or craft or industry unite into a corporate whole which bargains with the employer on behalf of all.

The economic children of Adam Smith and Jeremy Bentham forbade such unions. Although associations of employers, professional men, and other classes might flourish, unions of laboring men were condemned by courts as conspiracies.[5] Many Victorians looked askance at the union as a manifestation of socialistic spirit. A tremendous struggle ensued for the recognition of the union principle. This was not a mere contest of

[5] Arthur M. Schlesinger, *The Age of Jackson*, 166, 194, Boston, Little Brown, 1945.

words carried on in newspapers or debating halls but one of broken heads and copious bloodshed. Positive law, like the National Labor Relations Act of the United States, formally recognized the labor union and enjoined employers from interfering with workmen's right to organize and bargain collectively. The underlying ethical principle is simple.

THESIS LXXII. Labor unions are legitimate associations. Their aims and methods should conduce to the general welfare of society.

PROOF OF PART I

963. Whoever has a right to an end also has the right to the just and necessary means to that end. Workers have a right to a livelihood and labor unions are at present just and necessary means to that end.

It is eminently just and in accord with man's social nature for individuals to band together to obtain a common natural right by collective action.

Unions are necessary means because without them workmen have been helpless and were unable to achieve a decent livelihood.

PART II

964. Labor unions were a long time coming into their own. Having won emphatic recognition from the law and a place of real power, they ought not now abuse that power. It would be a sad mistake if their conduct served as an illustration of the old adage, Put a beggar on horseback and he will ride to the devil. Although the primary end of a labor union is the good of its membership, this end must be achieved in a manner that preserves the rights of employers and public.

Such is the downward trend of human nature that amazing evils have grown up in the wake of labor unions. Some unions have fallen into the hands of racketeers and have become tools of extortion. Leaders have conducted the union for their personal advantage, imposed unjust burdens upon employers, and under pretext of upholding union regulations have outraged common sense. Unions have waged jurisdictional disputes and called needless strikes. They have been callous to the rights of employers so that employees, knowing that they could not be discharged, have failed to do proper work.

Even the best unions seem to operate upon the principle that upon the expiration of each labor contract they must wring more concessions from management.[6] Constant adherence to this principle means that the limits of justice will eventually be overstepped. Since every wage increase, granted at the demands of the unions, has been passed on by the management to the public, one wonders how long the process of spiraling wages and prices can continue without harm to the common good. The harm could be inflation, the exaltation of manual skills above mental skills, the depression of a liberal profession such as teaching.

PROOF OF PART II

965. Associations which in large measure control economic peace should be conducted with a view to the general interests of the community at large. Society is an organism wherein the good condition of a part should be subordinated to the general well-being of the whole.

Labor unions are such associations. They may be private in name but they are public in fact. A large percentage of the population depends on their honest and efficient functioning. In so far as they fail to secure justice for their membership and override just claims of employers and public, so will economic peace or strife result.[7]

966. N.B. I. Labor unions ought to be incorporated and subjected to reasonable regulation. Fitting responsibility can thus be placed upon them. As far as possible, democratic procedures in the conduct of union affairs should be mandatory. An accounting of funds should be made to the membership. Excessive fees should be abolished. Unionism's greatest need is honest and statesman-like leadership.

N.B. II. Has the individual worker an obligation to belong to a labor union? He is not obliged to join a racketeering union or one which is a cloak for subversive activity. If an honest union is available he ought to join it for two reasons. First, the livelihood of all workmen depends

[6] The story is told of the great labor leader, Samuel Gompers, that when negotiations for the settlement of a strike had reached an impasse, he was querulously asked, "Just what exactly do you want, Mr. Gompers?" And he gave the laconic reply, "More." Labor still seeks more. Cf. *Time*, January 2, 1950, p. 28 and August 4, 1952, p. 20.

[7] Labor unions should heed the advice given to the International Labor Organization by Pius XII, November 20, 1954: "The labor movement cannot rest content with material success, with a more perfect system of guarantees and assurances or with a greater measure of influence on the economic system. It cannot visualize its future in terms of opposition to other social classes or of the excessive ascendancy of the state over the individual. The goal it pursues must be sought on the very plane on which the [International Labor Organization] places it, that is to say, on the plane of universality . . . in a social order where material prosperity is the result of the sincere collaboration of all for the welfare of all and serves as a support for the higher values of culture and, above all, for the indissoluble union of minds and hearts" (*The Pope Speaks*, Fourth Quarter, 1954, 372).

on their power of collective bargaining and this in turn depends on union organization. Second, since labor benefits derive from union organization, it would not be fair for an individual to have the advantages of the union and yet refuse to share its responsibilities.

N.B. III. Ought the State enact into law the union shop (all workers must belong to the union which is the collective bargaining agent in any plant) and the checkoff (compulsory collection of union assessments by employers)? Although the individual has an obligation to join a good union, this obligation is inoperative until the rights of employers have been made more secure and both evil unions and the abuse of the union shop and the checkoff have been eliminated.

Right-to-work laws, which forbid the union shop to be the subject of negotiations between labor and management, are highly controversial. Insofar as they aim at preventing the unions from tyrannizing individuals they are commendable; insofar as they aim at weakening the principle of collective bargaining or at rendering the unions impotent they are objectionable.

F. Strikes

967. A strike is a concerted stoppage of work by some or all the employees in an establishment or industry, along with an appeal to public opinion, in order to enforce the assent of employers to specific demands of workmen. The *direct strike* is the walkout of workmen laboring under the same industrial grievance. The *sympathetic strike* is the walkout of workmen who themselves have no grievance but who wish by their strike to help other workmen who are striking. The *general strike* is the universal walkout of all workmen in the State.

Since the strike is a form of industrial war, the same set of principles which governs the morality of war applies to the strike.

1. *The Direct Strike*

968. Is the strike intrinsically evil? (*a*) *Quitting work* is not immoral because a workman may stop working for an employer unless he has made a contract to work for a definite period. (*b*) In a *concerted quitting of work*, organization does not add an immoral element. What men may lawfully do individually, they may combine to do. If a labor union is under contract not to strike for a definite period of time, and if the owners are keeping their part of the bargain, to strike during that period is a serious violation of commutative justice. (*c*) *Appeal to public opinion* is reasonable. If one refrains from slander and abuse, he has every right to present to the public the justice of his cause.

969. Therefore the strike is not in itself immoral, and workmen may be justified in striking if the following conditions are fulfilled.

a) *They must have a true grievance.* To permit the evils consequent upon the strike, a proportionately justifying cause must exist. Workmen have a right to collective bargaining, just wages, decent hours and working conditions. But no union is justified in striking for trivial reasons: apart from denial of *serious* right, the strike is unjustifiable. Jurisdictional strikes, for instance, are an outrage upon the employer and public.

b) *All other means of remedying the grievance must have been used but to no avail.* If the dispute can be settled by direct negotiations, arbitration, or remedial legislation, the union is morally bound to use these means.

c) *There must be a sound prospect of success, and the good to be achieved must outweigh the evils to be endured by employer, public, and workmen.* If the resultant evils to the community overbalance advantages to be won by workmen striking, they are obliged not to strike. This is true of policemen, firemen, and the like with whose uninterrupted service the public good is closely linked.

d) *The means chosen to promote the strike must be legitimate.* No matter how just their cause, workmen may not resort to injustice to achieve their ends. Injustice here includes the sit-down strike, the slow-down strike, and use of violence.

970. The *sit-down strike* is theft of the owner's property. Courts which tolerate the practice abet serious wrong.

The *slow-down strike* is the violation of a labor contract. Workmen are paid for a full day's work and deliberately fail to render it.

Strikers may not destroy property or do violence to strike-breakers or fellow workers who refuse to join the strike. Even though nonstrikers or strike-breakers may be co-operating in injustice on the part of the employer, forceful defense of private right must be left to the State. To allow strikers to engage in violence is to say that private persons may engage in civil disturbance or wage war. The common public good comes before the good of workmen.

2. *The Sympathetic Strike*

971. The principle immediately at issue is charity, namely, strikers with a just cause may be helped by the strike of workers who have no grievance. At the time when rights of workingmen were quite generally disregarded, the occasion of applying the principle of charity did arise. Now, however, when working conditions have greatly improved, it may

be doubted if the facts occur which justify application of the principle. First, there is no *general* condition of injustice to correct. Second, satisfied workers may not exercise charity to their fellow workers when by doing so they will be unjust to their employers. Here justice ranks above charity.

It is right for workers to forward the interests of their class. But the presumption of fact is not that justice is always on the side of workers, that employers are habitually unjust. While the adoption of the policy that workers must *always* respect the picket line of strikers is likened to the principle that the ordinary citizen need not investigate the justice of his country's act of going to war, nevertheless, in particular labor disputes it may be perfectly clear that the workers are wrong. To respect a picket line in such a case is a demand neither of justice nor charity.

3. *The General Strike*

972. Stoppage of all work would be so disastrous to the common good that it is difficult to imagine the benefits which would justify such an upheaval. Indeed the general strike is one of the instruments of communism for fomenting world revolution. However, a harassed people could resort to it in place of revolution in order to stop an unjust war or be rid of an iniquitous government.

973. Strikes are a crude and not too efficient remedy for industrial injustice. As J. F. Cronin says: "The aftermath of a long bitter struggle . . . is unpleasant, no matter who wins the strike. If the union succeeds it is likely to adopt in retaliation an autocratic, suspicious, and uncooperative attitude. If the strike is broken, the workers become sullen, resentful."[8] Before the enactment of labor legislation, strikes may have been an evil to be tolerated. The good sought by strikes is better obtained by appeal to public opinion and through public opinion to law. Strikes and violence only weaken the force of legitimate appeal. The process of law and remedial legislation is a slower but more reasonable and eventually a more effective method of obtaining industrial justice than the direct action of strikes. Once sufficient legislation that safeguards workmen's right to a livelihood is honestly enforced, their right to strike becomes latent.

G. Labor Legislation

974. The most intelligent employers have recognized that their primary

[8] John F. Cronin, *Economics and Society*, p. 217. New York, American Book Co., 1939.

asset is a contented working force and hence have voluntarily offered their workers satisfactory conditions.

For the most part, however, concessions from employers have been forced. Official labor has aimed at solidifying the gains of particular workmen and has endeavored to make them available to all workers by translating them into law of the land.

This difficulty arises. May the State pass labor legislation or does legislation of this kind trespass upon strictly private rights? Because the pestilential influence of economic liberalism still affects so many people, many legislators make grudging assent to labor laws. They tolerate them because they consider them a trend of the times, not because they see any moral or social principle underlying them. Nevertheless there is a principle behind them and it is this: the State must protect natural rights; and if particular classes of individuals experience special difficulty in securing a right, they are entitled to special protection from the State. Since the workman has a right to livelihood and to live as a man in his work, and since his weakness has often made him the victim of injustice, he is entitled to special protection from the State. Furthermore, from the standpoint of the general welfare, one can hardly say the State has a sound economy when a good proportion of the populace lacks a decent living.

975. In protective legislation of this kind, the State may not despoil employers, nullify genuine property rights, or make the common good subservient to the clamor of workers. The interest of no class, neither management nor labor, should dominate the State: the common good is above all class interest.

The State has not overstepped the bounds of justice by legalizing unions and upholding the right of collective bargaining, nor by putting a ceiling on hours and a floor under wages. These measures have done something to bring a living wage within reach of workmen but the awful specter of unemployment has not been removed. Partial alleviation of this problem has been attempted by direct relief laws and unemployment compensation, but so far no modern state has permanently solved the difficulty.

The fundamental reason for this failure is that the solution of the problem does not primarily belong to the State. It is given to the State to solve because now, on account of the atomization of society, no other social institution is capable of dealing with it. However, the whole problem of livelihood could more easily be dealt with by occupational groups whose nature is explained in the Appendix.

II. PROMOTIVE LEGISLATION

976. In the concrete it is sometimes difficult to draw the line between protective and promotive legislation. One type of legislation merges into the other: elements of both may enter the same law. In the preceding section of this chapter we saw that legislation may be initiated for the protection of strict right, for example, the right to livelihood, and once the right is secured, promotive legislation may introduce additional benefits. By protective legislation the State makes secure the essential rights without which persons do not live a human life. By promotive legislation it seeks to enhance the good life. The notion, if not the name, of protective legislation is negative, for it forbids the spoliation of right: the notion of promotive legislation is positive, for it advances some social good.

The area of human goods extends in ever widening circles from an inner core of right to further desirable things, not strictly necessary but conducive to human betterment. In the physical order, once men are sure of life, health, and a living, they may think of improved medical service, recreational facilities, better housing, faster transportation, and communication. In the intellectual order provisions may be made for greater facilities for the dissemination of truth and more educational and aesthetic opportunities. In the moral order, legislation may promote the practice of greater virtue, the enrichment of personality, the standing and influence of religion. The possibilities of human advancement, though not infinite, are indeed very great.

977. What part may the State have in social advance? The State may initiate, foster, or take over any project for human betterment if two conditions are fulfilled. First, its action must be socially necessary or useful. An act of the State is socially necessary when the common good demands it and the State alone can perform it; it is socially useful when it promotes the common good and the State can perform it more efficiently than any private agency; it is socially harmful when the State supplants and absorbs legitimate private endeavor. Second, the State must grant all the citizens equal access to this benefit. Unless all citizens share, the public good is subordinated to private or class interest.

It is impossible to discuss every item that may fall into the category of promotive legislation — which is properly the field of political science and sociology. We shall take up, however, a most important topic which illustrates not only the promotive function of the State but also the manner in which its function fuses with its protective role.

Public Education

978. Every modern civilized State gives careful attention to, and expends enormous sums on, every phase of education. Extreme care and attention is given to the planning and future expansion of the State's part in education. Very great good or evil will come to future generations from the way in which these programs are executed. Therefore, it is of the utmost importance that the State's philosophy of education be in accord with the Natural Law.

On account of the educational policy of totalitarian States, a new philosophy of education is receiving wider acceptance. This philosophy holds that nothing limits the action of the State in education but its own good pleasure. A steadily mounting tide of State encroachment upon exclusively private domain is being accepted as normal: too many people think that they are helpless to resist the ground swell of universal statism.

The basic part which the Natural Law gives the State in education has already been stated in our proof that the essentials of education belong to parents. Therefore the role of the State is subordinate to parental right and duty. The State's educational function, then, is deduced from the primary rights of parents and its own protective and promotive duty.

THESIS LXXIII. The State has the duty of safeguarding the right of children to receive an education from their parents and providing parents with the means of education when their own resources are inadequate. It must likewise remove public hindrances to education such as subversive teachings and unusual incitements to vice. Although the State has a right to demand that the common good be suitably provided for in the training of youth, nevertheless State monopoly of education is unnecessary and unjust.

979. State educational policy depends on the double end of the State. The primary duty of the State is to *safeguard the rights* of its members. In the field of education the following rights undoubtedly exist: (*a*) The child has from nature a right to receive proper preparation for life. (*b*) Parents have from nature an exclusive obligation and right to educate their children. (*c*) The Church has a charter from God to teach His revelation and a mandate to insist with Christian parents that their children be instructed in the faith and formed to Christian morality.

These rights the State must protect but it may not enumerate teaching among its natural functions because, first, by Natural Law this function belongs to parenthood alone; second, the State has not received as has the Church a divine mandate to teach.

The secondary duty of the State is to supply for the common good what private initiative and effort is unable to effect. Hence, when schools become necessary instruments of education, and when parents are unable to supply these themselves, the State must come to their aid. In conducting schools, however, the State is only the delegate of parents, whose primary rights it may not absorb.

For reasons of the common good, the State has a right to exact a certain amount of learning, culture, or technical skill from its citizens and may require parents to provide this for their children. But this right does not empower the State to set up an exclusive educational monopoly.

PART I

980. **The State has the duty of safeguarding the right of children to receive an education from their parents.** In order to protect the child's right when parents are neglectful, the State must compel parents to fulfill their obligation. This does not mean that as soon as parental neglect is discovered the State may take over the care of children. The State must first bring pressure to bear upon the parents to acquit themselves of their task. Only after parents have shown themselves manifestly incompetent or evil, and when no resources of private charity are available to rescue the child, may the State as a last resort assume full responsibility for the child's upbringing. Public assistance should not be sought if private remedies are available.

It must be stressed that children not only have a right to an education but especially to receive that education from their parents. No human agency, private or public, not even the State or the Church, may interfere with the essential order established by nature between parent and child.

PROOF

981. If children have an inalienable right to an education and if parents alone have the function of imparting it, then in the event of neglect or interference, the State must protect the educational rights both of children and of parents. But children have an inalienable right to an education and parents alone have the right to impart it. Therefore

the State has the duty of safeguarding the right of children to receive an education from their parents.

PART II

982. **The State has the duty of providing parents with the means of education when their own resources are inadequate.** Although education is primarily and directly a domestic duty, it may become secondarily and indirectly a matter of public concern. First, the quality of the home product necessarily affects the common good. Second, parents may laudably desire for their children training which they cannot furnish without social action.

Until quite recent times general education was a purely domestic matter. The preparation for life which a child received depended upon the good will and resources of the head of the family. This is still the situation in many places.

Within the past one hundred years, public opinion in western civilization recognized illiteracy as detrimental to the common good, and decided that a common elementary intellectual training should be made available to *all* future citizens. This policy necessitated the erection of a vastly increased number of schools. The efficient way to provide these new instruments of common education was public taxation. Hence, in the civilized world our complicated system of public schools arose.

983. As Part I of this thesis is a practical application of the principle that the prime function of the State is to protect the rights of its members, so the ethical principle of Part II is this: If individual effort is insufficient to procure some human good, the common effort of the State supplies the want. Therefore, if and when schooling becomes necessary for training the young, and families cannot supply schools, then the State ought to provide schools and teachers in a way suited to the legitimate wishes of parents. Public assistance, however, must be only of such kind and measure as to supply for a genuine private deficiency. Where privately conducted schools are sufficient and function efficiently, public schools are not needed and should not be built.

PROOF

984. The State has a duty to supply means necessary for public welfare which private initiative cannot supply. But private initiative sometimes cannot supply schools and schooling necessary for the public welfare. Therefore the State has the duty of supplying them whenever private initiative is insufficient.

PART III

985. The State has the duty of removing public hindrances to education such as subversive teachings and public incitements to vice.

This particular duty of the State in the field of education follows from the obligation of the State to promote the public welfare and from a correct understanding of what constitutes the public welfare.

It is absurd to say that the State has no concern about the morals of its citizens, or that morality is strictly a private affair. It is true that many human acts have no public aspect but many acts do affect society. No man lives in a social vacuum; good and evil example touches everyone both as individuals and as citizens. Hence, the State is to promote morality at least to the extent of removing gross incitements to evil that allure the ordinary person. Since youth is especially susceptible to wrongdoing, it is deserving of special public protection. The State, therefore, should aim at producing such a moral tone in society that parents do not find unusual difficulties but are rather assisted in the moral training of their children.

986. At this point we might give thought to the question of *State censorship*. Liberalism has made censorship a hated word. But what does the word really mean? A censor is one who authoritatively designates as right or wrong private or public words or acts of others, permitting the right, suppressing the wrong. Are there circumstances in which the State is a legitimate censor? Although no one questions the right of State censorship in war, and many persons have applauded the State's abuse of this right, there is a furious outcry against censorship of teaching.

The issue, then, is this: Where do teaching and incitements to vice touch the public welfare and how is the regulation of them to be reconciled with private right?

987. **Teaching.** Concerning the deposit of faith, it is clear that God's revealed word and the truths necessarily connected therewith are completely outside the province of any secular power. These truths have been especially entrusted by God to the keeping of the Church. The teaching of nonrevealed truth may affect the general welfare from the point of view both of the individual and the State.

a) *False teachings affect the individual.* It has been proved that the Natural Law forbids man to inflict moral injury upon his neighbor (§ 489). To indoctrinate one's neighbor with pernicious principles of conduct is to do him moral injury, because such indoctrination seriously interferes with the prosecution of his last end. In the case of children, the injury is even graver because fundamental errors ingrained during childhood usually defy all later attempts at eradication.

b) *False teachings affect the State.* Errors concerning social intercourse, the nature and function of the State, and natural religion are directly harmful to the welfare and stability of the State. It has, therefore, a right to protect itself against error which is likely to produce civil disorder.

Since State and individual have a right to be immune from moral injury, the State, as guardian of right, may and ought to suppress teachings which *seriously* violate these rights.

988. **But are not freedom of the press, freedom of speech, and freedom of teaching fundamental rights of the individual which no State may abrogate?** Every right is limited by the just counterclaims of other persons. Hence, the right to speak, teach, and write freely must necessarily be limited by the right of individual and State to be protected from error. Freedom may easily degenerate into license. The object of freedom may only be the true and the good. To call moral evil and falsity the objects of freedom is a perversion. When, therefore, the pursuit of such a perversion works extensive harm to others and imperils the public welfare, the civil power may lawfully interfere.[9]

Hence an editor, writer, or teacher has no more permission to write, say, or teach anything he pleases, than he has in his private or public conduct to act as he pleases. As moral goodness should be the norm of his conduct, so truth alone should be the norm of his intellectual utterances. Thought and its expression, of themselves, deserve no greater freedom than any other kind of activity. The State may prevent a radical from assassinating its king; why may it not suppress the writings of a pamphleteer advocating the same? The State may stop a man from having two wives; why may it not prevent him from publishing a book favoring the practice? Mrs. Bertrand Russell[10] advocating free love can work greater mischief to the State than the private vices of a public official.

989. But who is to judge the truth or falsity of the utterances of a writer or teacher? Academic freedom claims that the writer or teacher alone is the competent judge. A false principle is involved in this answer, namely, no objective norm of morality or any kind of truth exists, and all truth is subjective. If we apply this principle universally very great harm must come to society. Certainly where truth is elusive, where only probabilities may be found, where merely the better or more expedient

[9] "Nobody can justify in principle, much less in practice, a claim that there exists an unrestricted right of anyone to utter anything he likes at anytime he chooses." Walter Lippmann, *The Public Philosophy*, 124, Boston, Little Brown, 1955.

[10] Mrs. Bertrand Russell, *The Right to be Happy*, Chap. VI, pp. 260–261. Garden City, 1927.

thing is at issue, all men must be allowed widest freedom of expression. But not all truth is elusive: there are plain objective dictates of the Natural Law upon which rest the foundations of civic order. The public welfare can be seriously imperiled by writings and teachings counter to the Natural Law. These the State may and ought to suppress. To deny that the State can correctly define pernicious teaching is tantamount to denying the State the power of enunciating the Natural Law; it is to infer that the State has not the knowledge requisite for making any law.

Censorship is a right which a government may easily abuse by tyrannically suppressing all criticism of its acts and by branding as subversive any theory of rule contrary to that by which it operates. But neither the possibility nor the fact of abuse destroys the reality of right: they merely indicate the need of restraint in the exercise of right.

990. Other public impediments to sound rearing. Every age has its peculiar public dangers to youth. Our age must cope with indecent dress; pornographic motion pictures; licentious art and theatrical exhibitions; easy access to drugs, intoxicating liquor, houses of debauch; lack of parental supervision; broken homes. The dangers which threaten youth may vary, but the principle concerning them remains, namely, the State is bound to suppress public impediments to the virtue of youth, the removal of which is possible and would not create greater evil.

PROOF

991. The State is obliged to defend itself and its members from moral injury. But subversive teachings and public incitement to vice inflict moral injury both on the State and its youth. Therefore the State is obliged to suppress subversive teachings and public incitement to vice.

PART IV

992. The State has a right to demand that the common good be suitably provided for in the training of youth. As the promoter of the public welfare the State may make definite claims in the educational field. Thus in troubled periods the existence of the State may absolutely require military training. The State may rightfully insist on this; for example, in medieval England sons of knights had to learn to fight on horseback, sons of commoners were required to learn to use the long bow. On this latter point there was reiterated legislation. A nation whose welfare depends on an efficient navy may insist that many of its youth be trained in navigation and similar arts. Modern civilized States demand a certain minimum of intellectual culture; for instance, all children are expected to know how to read, write, and use simple arithmetic processes. Many nations insist that future citizens be imbued with the spirit of the nation, have some knowledge of its past, its traditions, its chief laws and institutions, and foster genuine love for the true interest of their country.

PROOF

993. The State may command whatever genuinely advances the public welfare. But the suitable preparation of youth for their responsibilities as citizens genuinely advances the public welfare. Therefore, the State may command suitable preparation of youth for their responsibilities as citizens.

PART V

994. **State monopoly of education is unnecessary and unjust.** Since the State furnishes means of education which parents cannot, the danger arises that, having assumed the major financial burden of schooling, the State will also monopolize education, according to the adage that whoever pays the piper calls the tune.

Because the State has an appreciable stake in the correct formation of future citizens, one may erroneously conclude that the State is by nature an educator; that it has an exclusive right to form the young, to say who shall or shall not engage in the profession of teaching, to determine the skills and doctrines to be taught and the textbooks to be used; that all children must attend State schools.

A totalitarian regime always institutes a dictatorship over education. The reason is plain. Not even such a government may completely flout public opinion. Rather it must shape public opinion to its own bent, and nothing is more effective than domination of young minds.

PROOF

995. State monopoly of education is (*a*) *unnecessary* because it involves the State in needless tasks; it is (*b*) *unjust* because it is an invasion of private right.

Needless tasks. Whole classes of citizens are willing and able to manage the education of their children without help from the State.

In private educational institutions adequate provisions can be made for public interests because, if a parent is responsible, he will see to it that his children are trained in citizenship and learn to love their country. If he refuses to do so, the State has ample means to compel him other than taking over all education.

Invasion of private right. The State cannot assume a monopoly of education without overriding prior rights of parents. Nature intends parents to have an exclusive and inalienable right to educate. Their inalienable right arises from the exclusive responsibility which they must absolutely fulfill. The violation of this right is a serious offense against commutative justice.

996. N.B. A State monopoly would also violate the Church's right and hinder its task of teaching God's revelation. As an independent and perfect society, the Church in no way depends on the State for its essential activities. In accordance with the divine command given it to teach, it may found schools and all institutions of learning helpful to its purpose. To claim that it may do so only by sufferance of the State is a serious perversion of right order.

Corollary. Appeals for State assistance in education should be made only when parental and private resources are inadequate.

READINGS

Aristotle, *Politics*, VII, 13–17.
Australian Hierarchy, "Standard of Living," *Catholic Mind*, 52 (1954), 745–755.
Bardes, G. F., *Distribution of Profits in the Modern Corporation*. Washington, Catholic University, 1951.
Bishops of Glasgow, "Principles Governing the Just Strike," *Catholic Mind*, 54 (July, 1956), 418–420.
Brown, L. C., "Right to Work Legislation," *Catholic Mind*, 53 (1955), 606–614.
Bunting, J. W., ed., *Ethics for Modern Business Practice*. New York, Prentice-Hall, 1953.
Carr, R. K., "National Security and Individual Freedom," *Yale Review*, 42 (June, 1953), 496–512.
Chamberlain-Schilling, *The Impact of Strikes*. New York, Harper, 1954.
Cronin, J. F., *Catholic Social Principles*, 64–165, 257–554. Milwaukee, Bruce, 1950.
Curran, F. X., *The Churches and the Schools*. Chicago, Loyola, 1955.
Dempsey, B. W., "The Worker as a Person," *Review of Social Economy*, 12 (1954), 16–24.
Donahue, C., "Freedom and Education," *Thought*, 27 (1952), 542–560; 28 (1953), 209–233; 29 (1954), 555–573.
Duff, E., "Living Wage," *Social Order*, 5 (1955), 294–298.

Evans-Ward, ed., *The Social and Political Philosophy of Jacques Maritain*. New York, Scribner's, 1955.
Farrell, W., "Freedom of Speech and Speech for Freedom," *From an Abundant Spring*. New York, Kenedy, 1952.
Grace, E. A., "Wages and Prices," *Studies*, 45 (1956), 15–22.
Grosschmid, G. B., "Pesch's Concept of the Living Wage in Quadragesimo Anno," *Review of Social Economy*, 12 (1955), 147–155.
Hierarchy of Quebec, *The Problem of the Worker in the Light of the Social Doctrine of the Church*. Montreal, Palm, 1950.
Johnston, H., *Business Ethics*, 141–294. New York, Putnam, 1956.
Keller, E. A., *The Case for Right-to-Work Laws*. Chicago, Heritage, 1956.
Kirk, R., *Academic Freedom*. Chicago, Regnery, 1955.
Lacroix, J., "The Concept of Work," *Cross Currents*, 4 (1953–1954), 236–250.
Leo XIII, encyclical letter, *Rerum Novarum*.
McCarthy, J., "The Obligation of the Employer to Provide Decent Working Conditions," *Irish Ecclesiastical Record*, 72 (1949), 542–545.
Mueller, F. M., "Some Thoughts on the Problem of Family Wages," *Social Justice Review*, 48 (1955), 120–123, 202–204, 236–240.
Murray, J. C., "Literature and Censorship," *Catholic Mind*, 54 (1956), 665–677.
Pius XI, encyclical letter, *Quadragesimo Anno*.
Pius XII, "Ideals for the Business Man," *The Pope Speaks*, III (1955), 45–53.
——— "Truth, Charity, and the Critic," *The Pope Speaks*, III (1955), 55–62.
Smith, W. D., *Handbook of Elementary Law*. 2 ed. St. Paul, West, 1939.
Sutherland, A. E., "Private Government and Public Policy," *Yale Review*, 41 (1952), 405–420.
Todd, J. M., ed., *The Springs of Morality*, 164–186. New York, Macmillan, 1956.

Chapter XXIX THE EXECUTIVE AND JUDICIAL POWERS

997. No one can deny that a government possesses legislative, executive, and judicial powers. However, because of occasional but inevitable overlapping of these functions, but more so because of dislike of analytical and traditional classifications and worship of the "empirical and positive," there is a tendency to substitute the terms "social control and public service" for the "legislative, executive, and judicial functions." However, as in the case of Aristotle's divisions of government, this classification stands up because it resolves governmental power into its simplest elements and separates things objectively distinct. "Social control and public service" are favorite terms with authors who regard collectivism as the sole desirable form of government.

998. Whether these powers ought to be separated in practice or united in one person or governing body is easily settled in ethics. The Natural Law neither commands nor forbids separation of powers because efficient government is possible under either arrangement. Whether separation or concentration, and how much of either, is better for this particular State will depend upon many circumstances chief of which are political maturity and historic background. The chief argument for concentration is efficiency. The argument for separation is that it is the safest means of preventing tyranny.

999. In a State where the three powers are separated, the legislative power is the most important from several points of view. It may be called the mind of the State. By its laws it creates moral obligation among citizens and establishes general norms binding the executive and judiciary. A State cannot exist without good laws.

But from the viewpoint of actual realization of the State's end, the executive power is paramount. The best of laws which are not made to work are of little avail. In a crisis the very existence of the State will depend upon the sheer strength of the executive arm. Great dignity attaches to the supreme executive as the historic successor of the monarch in whom all power once was vested. The executive, then, may be called the will of the State — its concentrated compelling force. Its most primitive function is maintenance of order among its citizens and protection against foreign aggression. Its most inclusive duty is to carry into effect the laws of the legislature and the decisions of the judiciary.

I. THE EXECUTIVE POWER

1000. Executive functions fall into three classes: diplomatic, military, and administrative. *Diplomatic* action is conduct of official business with other States. *Military* activity includes whatever pertains to the defense of the State. *Administrative* activity is a catchall term referring to all governmental activities which are not strictly legislative or judicial, diplomatic or military. By administration the executive not merely enforces the law without which there can be no orderly civil life, but also provides those public services necessary for public prosperity.

1001. It is usually conceded that the supreme executive office should be held by one person according to the axiom, "To deliberate is the function of many, to act of one." The individual executive cannot pass on his responsibilities; he must stand or fall upon his own performance. A plural executive, however, has functioned efficiently, for example, in Switzerland. In cabinet government, where the prime minister is but *primus inter pares*, the real executive is the entire cabinet.

1002. If a separation of powers is constitutionally required, an overlapping and interchange of legislative and administrative power is inevitable. Since legislation cannot provide for every detail, the administration must be empowered to make ordinances which have practically the effect of law. The executive must have wide power, especially in the time of war. On the other hand, through its committees, the legislature investigates administrators, holds them to an accounting, and, if the committee is permanent, makes itself the ultimate source of authority in the matter. Finally, the laws which actually govern will not include all that are found in statute books but merely those which are enforced. In large measure, laws are made in their enforcement.

1003. In determining the outstanding obligations of the executive, we must distinguish the executive who is total sovereign, or monarch, from the executive who does not possess legislative and judicial supremacy. According to the theory that the monarch is the fount of all authority in the State, he is not subject to any positive law of his own or his predecessor's making. For one cannot simultaneously and under the same circumstances be both superior and subject. According to the same theory, therefore, he is bound only by the Natural Law which compels him to devote himself to the common good even at the expense of his own happiness. Hence came the notion, felicitously phrased by Selden[1] and immortalized by the masterful exposition of Blackstone,[2] that the king can do no wrong. The original meaning is that the monarch is above all positive human law. However, not even the most intransigent defender of the divine right of kings would ever have interpreted the phrase in the words of Sophocles: "Kings are happy in many things but mainly in this that they can do and say whatever they please."[3] Even the monarch must keep the Natural Law. Later the phrase came to mean that as the unbiased distributor of justice, the king cannot constitutionally be supposed capable of injustice. The sole remnant of this idea found in American jurisprudence is the concept that the government is not liable for the wrongful or unauthorized acts of its officers: you cannot sue the government without its consent.

1004. But is the monarch really free of positive law? It is undeniably true that the spiritual monarch, the pope, is above all purely ecclesiastical law, but it ought not absolutely be said that the secular monarch is free of civil law. First, even the most absolute monarchs have been subject to the immemorial customs of their realms. Second, the primary depositary of sovereign powers is the people themselves. Since the monarch's authority is delegated, it is subject to the limitations contained in the original grant of power. Third, the common good may demand the monarch's good example, that is, since he is the visible symbol of the entire State, his conduct ought to represent all individuals keeping the law. His actions, however, are not reviewable by courts of his creation: he is accountable only to the people civilly united.

1005. A monarch is feasible in a State which is in the process of development. In a mature nation, however, one expects separation of powers and the limited executive. The obligations of the limited executive are summarized in the phrase — carry out the law. The obligation is negative, for he may never violate law in the pursuit of governmental business. To do so renders him guilty of malfeasance. The positive aspect of the executive's obligations consists in accomplishing what the law demands to be done. If a particular situation is not covered by positive enactment, the Natural Law must guide the executive. In

[1] John Selden, *Opera Omnia*, "Table Talk," in Vol. III, Part II, p. 2038. Londini, Wilkins, 1726.

[2] Sir William Blackstone, *Commentaries on the Laws of England*, Bk. I, Chap. 7, II (246).

[3] *Antigone*, 506–507.

pursuit of diplomatic and military duties, especially in time of war, he requires reasonable latitude of action.

II. THE NATURE OF JUDICIAL POWER

1006. In the concrete, absolute separation of legislative, executive, and judicial powers is impossible. The reason is that government is a practical science and an art with a single aim — advancement of the public good — and hence its three co-ordinate powers constitute one brotherhood working side by side with mutual toleration and co-operation.

Thus, when the executive vetoes a proposed law, or the supreme judiciary invalidates a law, each is exercising legislative power. When the legislature passes a bill of attainder, it acts in a judicial capacity. At times some executive commissions in the United States exercise all three functions. In England, Parliament has become the ultimate depositary of all governmental powers. It makes the laws; it appoints the ministers who exercise the executive power; its House of Lords is the last court of judicial appeal.

1007. Because of this interchange of governmental functions, some authors today say that it is impossible to define the three powers with rigid accuracy. Their essential differences, however, are quite discernible to one who has learned to recognize when one branch of government is exercising a function which theoretically belongs to another. Marshall said, "the legislature makes the law, the executive enforces the law, and the judiciary construes the law."[4]

The primary end of the State is maintenance of the juridic order. This it does, first, by enunciating the general norms of justice. This action is legislation. Second, it pronounces justice in the concrete, that is, when a dispute of sufficient importances arises, the State decides with which of the disputants right and justice lie. This is the exercise of *judicial power*, which is authority to resolve a complaint that justice has been violated in some particular.

1008. Marshall's emphasis upon the judiciary's power to construe the law led him to the far-reaching conclusion that final explanation of the law is to be sought not from the mind and intention of the legislator but in the interpretation of the judge. Pushed to its logical conclusion, this doctrine means that the law is what the courts determine it to mean, and unless the legislator by subsequent law can overturn

[4] Henry Wheaton, *Reports of Cases Argued and Adjudged in The Supreme Court of the United States*, Bk. VI, Vol. 10, Wayman *vs.* Southard, 46, p. 43. Newark, N. J., Lawyers' Co-operative Publishing Co., 1882.

judicial sentences, the judiciary becomes the master of the State. To have the final word on what the law means is effectively to be a law-maker. The power, therefore, which the American judiciary has assumed of invalidating acts of legislature is truly a legislative function. The State may be satisfied that the judiciary play this part, but one must not therefore confuse it with the essential function of judicial power. St. Augustine aptly remarks: "Once laws are established and sanctioned, it must not be allowed to the judge to judge them but to judge according to them."[5]

Disputes requiring judicial solution are reduced to two categories: (a) cases in which a petitioner seeks against injustice a remedy to be found chiefly in the *Natural Law;* (b) cases in which the remedy against injustice is sought in *established positive law.* The first are handled in courts of equity, the second in courts of law.

1009. Courts of Equity. The term *equity* has two meanings in the moral sciences.

a) Among moralists it means the same as ἐπιείκεια, or benign interpretation which indicates that the law does not urge in this instance. St. Thomas speaks of the special virtue of equity. "Legislators," he says, "keep their minds on what usually happens and frame their law for that; yet in some cases the keeping of the law is against the equality of justice and the common good. In such cases it is evil to abide by the law and good to overlook the words of the law and follow the course dictated by a regard for justice and public expediency. And this is the end of equity."[6] Equity, then, is the tempering of positive law to meet the requirements of universal justice. St. Thomas also says, "Legal justice is directed according to equity. Hence equity is a kind of higher rule of human acts."[7]

b) Among lawyers equity means that natural, evenhanded justice which should exist between contending parties. The term arose from cases which formal positive law did not embrace and to decide which the judge had to resort to natural justice. If, on account of mode of procedure, mandatory regulations, or for any other reason, courts of law are unable to grant a remedy against injustice, a petitioner has recourse to a court of equity.

The main concern of those who administer justice in any court ought not to be forms of law but equality of justice. Justice ought not to be

---

[5] *De Vera Religione,* XXXI, 58.

[6] *Sum. Theol.,* II–II, 120, 1.

[7] *Ibid.,* II–II, 120, 2.

defeated by technicalities. Legalism is a poor substitute for justice. Too often legalism has been the refuge of scoundrels.

1010. **Courts of law** include all other regularly established tribunals whose function is to determine whether customary or statute law has been violated. In these courts, although private persons at times accuse others of violations of commutative justice, the pre-eminent petitioner is the State accusing citizens of violations of legal justice. Since the end of the State's action is the infliction of penalty for violating the law, the fundamental question arises, *By what right may the State punish?*

III. POWER OF PUNISHMENT

1011. St. Thomas says that the acts of law are four, namely, to command, to prohibit, to permit, and to punish.[8] While the majority of men have admitted that punishment is a legitimate function of civil authority, there have been vociferous dissents from time to time. Man's increasing sensitiveness tends to result in the avoidance of every kind of pain. Thus the theory which holds that moral evil is bodily disease contends that the evildoer should be cured but not punished. We are also told that once a bad act is done, to punish is only to add one evil to another. Abuses of punishment and stupid modes of punishment are pointed to as arguments for the abolition of all punishment. Some social historians decry it as a nasty form of revenge, a survival of primitive retaliation. Upon what basis of reason, then, does punishment stand?

1012. **Punishment is the authoritative deprivation of good, operating on some wrongdoer against his will, in order to wipe out a fault committed.** Although anyone can reward, the right to punish belongs only to authority: it is an essential means to the purposes of authority. Punishment is essentially the withdrawal of good from one whose evil act has shown him unworthy of that good. When punishment is inflicted it is not willed as an evil to the person punished but as a good — a requisite for the maintenance of order. When the evildoer willingly assumes a penalty for his fault, he is not undergoing punishment but he offers satisfaction. Only the unwilling are punished. Every punishment must be for a fault already committed: it cannot be inflicted merely to prevent a future fault. The essence of retributive justice is, No fault, no punishment.

1013. The justification of punishment is found in its purpose, which is the inviolable maintenance of the good of which law is the expression and guardian. The end of punishment is practically the same as the

[8] *Ibid.*, I–II, 92, 2.

end of sanction, for punishment is the application of sanction. Laws are buttressed by sanctions to prevent violation. Once a law is broken, punishment must follow; otherwise sanction loses its power to protect law. Second, once the offender is punished, he is inclined to correct himself and keep the law lest punishment be repeated. Civil law, however, does not intend the amendment of the delinquent primarily for his own good but for the common good — the good estate of law observance. Finally, every true exception to law, if tolerated, becomes a precedent, and precedent tends to perpetuate itself and become the rule. Hence every act against law is destructive of law so that the common good must demand the enforcement of law. Enforcement is to be achieved not only by preventive measures — the threat of punishment if the law is broken — but after a law has been broken, law must demonstrate that it does not tolerate that act. Order demands the cancellation and undoing of a violation of the law. This cannot be done by pretending that what actually happened did not happen but by concrete proof to the lawbreaker that he cannot profit by such conduct. Self-preservation demands that law exact such expiation. It is just that they who choose evil should have evil as their portion.

1014. Civil authority should concern itself chiefly with devising and so administering punishment that the best possible observance of law will result. It should look to the deterring and corrective value of a penal code. The expiatory aspects of punishment are usually too much for the imperfect justice of men. In the main, this may safely be left to the perfect knowledge and justice of God.

IV. CAPITAL PUNISHMENT

1015. Justice requires that the State punish no more severely than the good to be obtained requires. May the State go to the extent of taking life for crime?

From the most ancient times it has been taken for granted that the State possesses the power of the sword. The codes of ancient peoples known to history and the customs of primitive peoples now surviving make provision for this form of punishment, although there is no unanimity as to the reasons for inflicting it.

In Genesis we read, "Whosoever shall shed man's blood, his blood shall be shed: for man was made to the image of God."[9] In the Mosaic law death was mandatory for homicide, willful assault upon one's father or mother, cursing one's parents, manstealing, bestiality. A significant

[9] Gen. 9:6.

sentence occurs in the book of Exodus, "Wizards thou shalt not suffer to live."[10] A wizard or witch is one who is so bent on attaining some purpose that he sells himself to the powers of evil and thereby becomes an enemy of the whole human race.

1016. The old codes mention only a few atrocious crimes as deserving of death, but it usually happened that in the course of time these laws were interpreted to include many other offenses. Thus in the oldest days of Rome parricide alone was punishable by death but gradually other crimes were similarly dealt with through the device of calling them parricide. Western Europe, whose jurisprudence was founded in Roman law and usage, witnessed a similar multiplication of causes for the death penalty, until in the reign of George III, Blackstone could lament that one hundred and sixty actions were deemed worthy of death by English law.[11] Thus one could be hanged for cutting down a tree, robbing a rabbit warren, stealing from a dwelling goods worth forty shillings or from a shop goods worth five shillings, counterfeiting the stamps used in the sale of perfumes, and the like.

With the growth of the liberal idea a clamor arose for the removal of the abuses of the death penalty. Much was done to debrutalize criminal codes. Modern sentimentalism, however, has gone a step farther and demands complete abolition of the death penalty. The arguments for abolition are familiar enough, and some States have acceded to the demand.

THESIS LXXIV. The State has the right to punish some criminals with death.

1017. The principle at issue is that of self-defense on the part of the political community. As the individual has a right to kill an unjust aggressor, so the State may cut off one whose crime has made him a gangrenous member of society. The power is necessary for the prevention of horrendous crime. Even when capital punishment has been abolished by statute, the right of inflicting it has not been destroyed. It has merely become latent because the State thinks it can attain the purpose of this punishment by other means. But no government can totally renounce the power of the sword. It is impossible to imagine the articles of war of any nation which do not contain death penalties. Beccaria[12] says that death penalties may be invoked in time of tremendous upheaval but

---

[10] Exod. 22:18.

[11] *Commentaries on the Laws of England,* Bk. IV, Chap. I, p. 18.

[12] Cesare B. Beccaria, *An Essay on Crimes and Punishments,* Chap. XXVIII, p. 76. Dublin, Exshaw, 1777, 5 ed.

never in peace. The experience of the race says that the need of capital punishment exists both in war and peace.

PROOF

1018. The State has a right to every action which is not intrinsically evil and is both expedient and strictly necessary for the maintenance of the State.

The execution of certain criminals is *not intrinsically evil.* The taking of human life is not always wrong. Otherwise one could not adequately defend himself against unjust attack. What is always wrong is the taking of *innocent* life on human authority.

Capital punishment is expedient at least in the case of willful murder. There are two reasons. (*a*) A crime which inflicts irreparable damage requires the ultimate of punishment. The canon of Rhadamanthus quoted by Aristotle says, "If a man have done to him what he has done to others that is the straight course of justice."[13] (*b*) If the death penalty does not exist there is danger that the people either make their own lynch law or engage in blood feuds.

Capital punishment is strictly necessary. (*a*) It is necessary for the protection of society against incorrigibly dangerous malefactors and enemies of the State. Neither banishment nor life imprisonment will always be effective. (*b*) The motives inciting to atrocious crime — revenge, jealousy, greed, and lust — are constantly present in society. Hence the abiding need for a counterpoise. The only suitable counterpoise is the knowledge that the crime will be followed by swift conviction and death. A death penalty which is enforced does keep these crimes to a minimum. There are very few homicides in Great Britain as compared to the United States. Murder is punished by death in Great Britain but in the United States only an infinitesimal number of the persons guilty of homicide ever pay the death penalty. "In 1938 only eighty-four cases of homicide were known to the police (in Britain). In thirty the murderers committed suicide, leaving fifty-four cases to be solved. Thirty-seven were convicted or found insane, ten were acquitted usually on the ground that the act did not constitute murder."[14] During the same year, however, authorities in the United States reported that there were 8799 incidents of homicide of which they were aware.

[13] *Nicomachean Ethics,* V. 5, 1132b.

[14] A. L. Goodhart, in the *Outpost,* No. 64, Aug., 1945.

[15] *Statistical Abstract of the United States, 1940,* p. 86.

READINGS

St. Thomas, *De Regimine Principum,* I, 7–15.
Anderson-Weidner, *American Government,* 4 ed., 575–766. New York, Holt, 1953.
Aristotle, *Politics,* V, 10–12.
Cahn, E., ed., *Supreme Court and Supreme Law.* Bloomington, Indiana University, 1954.
Corwin, E. S., ed., *The Constitution of the United States, Analysis and Interpretation,* 371–646. Washington, Government Printing Office, 1953.
——— *The Constitution and What It Means Today.* Princeton, Princeton University, 1948.
Gabriel, R. H., ed., *Hamilton, Madison and Jay on the Constitution,* 136–189. New York, Liberal Arts, 1954.
Gettell, R. G., *Political Science,* rev. ed., 331–371. Boston, Ginn, 1949.
Hyde, L. M., "Essentials of a Modern State Judicial System," *Notre Dame Lawyer,* 30 (March, 1955), 227–244.
Lippmann, W., *The Public Philosophy,* 3–112. Boston, Little Brown, 1955.
Millspaugh, A. C., *Toward Efficient Democracy.* Washington, Brookings, 1952.
Month, "The Death Penalty," 201 (June, 1956), 325–329.
Ogg-Ray, *Essentials of American Government,* 7 ed., 284–319, 343–358. New York, Appleton-Century-Crofts, 1952.
Pius XII, Allocution to the Auditors, Officials *et al.* of the Sacred Roman Rota, October 2, 1945. Acta Apostolica Sedis, 37 (1945), 256–262.
——— "Crime, Punishment and Rehabilitation," *The Pope Speaks,* First Quarter, 1955, 17–39.
——— "The Criminologist and His Important Service to Society," *The Pope Speaks,* Fourth Quarter, 1954, 361–367.
Shotwell, J. T., ed., *Governments of Continental Europe,* 121–135, 155–170, 413–416.
Swisher, C. B., *The Growth of Constitutional Power in the United States,* Chicago, University of Chicago, 1946.
Thiefry, M., "Retribution or Rehabilitation: Should Man Cease Judging and Punishing?" *Theology Digest,* 1 (1953), 98–101.
Wilson, W., *Constitutional Government in the United States,* 54–81, 142–172.

Chapter XXX THE DUTIES OF CITIZENS

1019. In the foregoing description of the responsibilities of government, we have sketched the rough outlines of distributive justice, that is, the good which is due from the State to its members. We turn now to the demands which legal justice makes upon the members of the State.

We shall call members of the State *citizens.* Without entering into any of the technical differences between subjects, citizens, naturalized foreigners, and resident aliens, we understand by a citizen a person who owes primary allegiance to the laws of a given State and is entitled to its minimal civic privileges. We say "primary allegiance" because, when a citizen is absent from his own State, he generally owes a secondary allegiance to the laws of the place where he resides. We say "minimal civic privileges" because, although all citizens may not equally participate in civic life by voting, sitting on juries, being eligible for public office, and the like, yet there is a least common denominator of civic standing. If a person falls below this level, as does a slave and felon, he is not a citizen. Certainly all who are born within the territorial jurisdiction of a given State and permanently reside there ought to have citizenship rights, except those whose criminal conduct justly forfeits them.

1020. *Patriotism,* which Samuel Johnson caustically defined as the last refuge of a scoundrel,[1] epitomizes the relations of citizen to State. The bond is piety. This is readily understandable if a State is small and its members are one's own kind. Even though the modern State is much more than the family outgrown, the same relation of piety exists between it and its citizens. For as piety binds man to the family, the first of natural societies, so also it ties him to the State, the perfect natural society.

Patriotism is not unreasoning sentiment, nor is it the preference for one's own people which begets contempt for outsiders. It is not prejudice or bias which regards one's own way of life as necessarily superior to that

[1] Boswell's *Life of Johnson,* April 7, 1775.

of all foreigners, and ridicules all strange customs, and considers one's own national acts upright and honorable but those of one's enemy vile and immoral. Nor is patriotism jingoism, the truculent nonsense that one's nation can dominate whom it pleases. Rather it is the *well-ordered love of one's State and of one's fellow citizens.* Here the object of love is not one's native soil. The object of love is primarily one's fellow citizens; it is also the moral person, the State. Some people have said that it is impossible to love an abstraction. That impossibility fades before the cold fact that men do — even by dying for it. Like all real love, this love must include benevolence and beneficence. That is a pernicious patriotism which proclaims, My country, right or wrong. This sentiment presupposes that national welfare, convenience, and prestige are above all moral law; that the State, dealing with other States, has moral license to do whatever it has the force or guile to accomplish. This attitude is one of the scourges of modern life. It has substituted the State for God and the worship of country for religion. Well-ordered love remains within the bounds of reason.

1021. As piety in the family comprises both justice and charity, it includes the same in the State. The good which the citizen strictly owes the State is laid down by *legal* or civic justice. It is aptly called legal justice because law prescribes what the welfare of the State demands of individuals. It may also be called *civic* justice so as to distinguish the common good peculiar to the State from that of the family or the human race at large. The duties of the true patriot are not limited to what law prescribes: he will come forward, as occasion demands, and freely give of his own to the common need. This is a kind of social charity.

In their civic capacity all members of the State are either public officials or private citizens. In what particulars of legal justice and social charity does the Natural Law bind both classes to advance the welfare of the State?

I. THE PUBLIC OFFICIAL

1022. In a broad sense the public official is a person who regularly performs some public service. In this sense a fireman or policeman would be called a public official. In the strict sense, a public official is a person who has been permanently (as opposed to transiently) invested by law with *authority* to perform some function of government. All public officials have authority — power to impose obligation — and most of them formally enter upon it by taking an oath to exercise it faithfully. Inasmuch as a public official is bound to serve the public welfare he is a *servant of the people;* inasmuch as in a legislative, executive, or judicial capacity he can create, declare, or impose moral obligation he is not a servant but a *lawful superior of the people.*

The over-all obligation of the public official is fulfillment of the duties of his office prescribed by positive and *Natural* Law. This requires not merely punctilious observance of the letter of positive law but intelligent effort to grasp its spirit and attain the purpose which it intends. Hence every official must have latitude of discretion to fit the imperfection of positive law to the requirements of natural justice. He should be convinced that the State and all officers of government are bound by the Natural Law, and that the laws of morality, not mere expediency and legality, should govern his official acts. He should abhor the sentiment, attributed by a biographer to Justice Holmes, that moral conceptions do not belong in a court of law.[2]

The demands of legal justice fall most heavily upon the public official: to him opportunities for exercising social charity more readily occur. To serve the public good, therefore, as the Natural Law indicates, he must measure up to the following requirements.

1023. a) *The public official must subordinate his private interests to public welfare,* that is, in his official capacity the public good should be his paramount concern. His official acts must be motivated not by personal but public considerations. He ought not to create useless jobs in order to take care of relatives, friends, or political hangers-on. In the selection of necessary help, he ought not, for personal or party reasons, choose people so incompetent that they would not give the State an adequate return for salary received. He may not use public money nor the official working time of civil servants to secure his re-election or advance party interests. The personal advantages of office, such as salary, perquisites, prestige, and the like, should be only incidental, not primary considerations. He is unfit for public trust who seeks or uses public office primarily as a means of advancing his fortunes or satisfying his desire for power.

1024. b) The public official must be *incorruptible.* Corruption is stealing public funds, receiving bribes for acting unjustly, seeking gifts, moneys, or advantages other than lawful salary for performance of public duties. Even if this last form of graft may not always be forbidden by positive law, it constitutes grave temptation to partiality, warped judgment, and undue bias in favor of "benefactors." Hence the Natural Law forbids special gifts taken by compact to do some just and legal act (the official has already contracted so to act and cannot twice sell

[2] Catherine D. Bowen, *Yankee from Olympus,* p. 388. Boston, Little Brown, 1944.

that for which he has already contracted); any gift or advantage calculated to influence his official acts and be an obstacle to the equitable discharge of his duties.

The official who defrauds the State or an individual of what belongs to them in *commutative justice* owes restitution. A bribe given for an act which the official is bound by his office to perform must be restored for the reason stated above.

On the restoration of bribes there is a curiosity of casuistry that may not be passed over. A probable opinion holds that a judge who takes a bribe for the passage of an unjust sentence may keep it once he has passed the venal sentence. "The reason is that the judge has fulfilled his part of the evil contract and has actually given the briber something which he (the briber) looked upon as worth the money he paid."[3] This opinion is unacceptable. First, let us suppose that a judge at the same sitting gave two judgments, one just and the other unjust, for both of which he has been bribed. Both acts were evil, the second more so than the first. Because the first sentence was just, he would be obliged to restore the bribe. Because the second sentence was unjust, he would be, according to this opinion, in a better moral situation regarding that bribe than regarding the first bribe; for he would have no obligation of restoring the second bribe. The worse act would produce less inconvenient consequences. Therefore by violating commutative justice the bribed judge would be better off *morally* than by observing justice. But this conclusion contradicts the truth that one may not violate the moral law and morally profit thereby even *accidentally*. Second, the doctrine of evil contract, explained in § 583, cannot apply here. When we admit that a person — say a prostitute — may keep the price of an evil act bargained for, we presuppose that the evildoer has some measure of exclusive dominion over the thing or service rendered, and is not disposing of what belongs to another. Here the venal judge is not selling personal service but *public justice*. It is not his to bargain for. Hence he may no more keep the price of perverted justice than he may pocket the price of public lands which he might fraudulently sell.

1025. c) The official must be *impartial*. Since the official bears the majesty of the State, he must act toward his fellow citizens as the State is bound to act. The State stands to its members in a twofold role: custodian of commutative justice and dispenser of public helps. In relation to the State as custodian of justice, all citizens are equal and their rights deserve equal protection. Hence persons who approach

[3] E. F. Healey, *Moral Guidance*, 290–291. Chicago, Loyola University Press, 1942.

an official on business pertaining to commutative justice are to be treated with exact justice, without prejudice, or partiality. The official cannot be a respecter of persons.

When the question arises of the sharing of common benefits, equality before the law does not mean that one person is to receive the same as another. What a person is to receive by way of distributive justice depends on his need and deserving. The strong and wealthy, who are well able to look after themselves, require no special protection, but the poor and ignorant, whose rights are liable to be curtailed by their stronger and less scrupulous neighbors, usually do. Legislators, therefore, ought to bear in mind that there is a constant need for setting up legal barriers to prevent the exploitation of the little man by a monied power. The distribution of bonuses and rewards ought to be made upon a basis of merit and service rendered to the State.

1026. d) The official must be *diligent*, that is, he must give to public responsibilities the energy and time which their importance requires. By oath of office he has contracted so to act. A person who renders decisions affecting the public good should do so only after commensurate investigation and reflection. It is a pernicious custom to allot public office, as a prize for service rendered a victorious political party, to a person who may turn over the real burden of his office to some deputy and himself be free to pursue his own personal, financial, and political interests. When a "political job" becomes synonymous with sinecure, the public weal is bound to suffer. An official who does that for which he has no authority and which is contrary to law is guilty of *malfeasance*. When he does that for which he has authority but does it in a wrongful or injurious manner, he commits *misfeasance*. When he fails to do what the law commands him to do, he may be punished for *nonfeasance*.

1027. e) The official must have *knowledge* adequate to his responsibilities. Although honesty and common sense may suffice in certain county or municipal jobs, greater and more technical knowledge is required of public officials charged with greater responsibilities. For the functions of the State have grown in complexity with the increased complexity of modern life; its action extends into more details of life so that human well-being has become more dependent than ever before upon the folly or wisdom of the State's activities. Although a public servant need not be a sociological, economic, or financial expert, he must have a sound social philosophy and fundamental grasp of the major problems facing the people. This he cannot have without a certain minimum of technical knowledge. Bills have too often been drawn up by an interested lobby and turned over for passage to legislators who could not evaluate them upon their intrinsic worth.

II. THE PRIVATE CITIZEN

A. Obedience to Law

1028. The first obligation of the private citizen is obedience to every law, and the presumption is — until rebutted by positive proof — that all laws are just. By law the State commands the contribution which the individual is to make to the common good. The State's power to command necessarily implies the individual's obligation to obey.

What virtue does the citizen sin against who violates the law of the State? If the violated law is *declarative positive law*, that is, a declaration or clearer elucidation of the Natural Law, that virtue is violated whose practice this law demands. Whoever violates the State's law against libel, rape, assault, and the like sins against commutative justice — the husband who fails to support his family sins against piety and commutative justice. These laws are positive only in their mode of proposal and can never be merely penal laws.

All other laws — *determinative positive law* — bind in virtue of legal justice and will be directly binding in conscience or merely penal according to the norms set down in § 924 ff.

1029. Some particular laws give rise to problems of conscience. First among these we note *laws of compulsory military service*. In time of war or grave danger of war they are gravely binding because they then express the Natural Law commanding citizens to preserve the State. May a person evade them in time of peace? He may not fraudulently evade them, that is, by lying or bribery. If, however, he can avoid service by nonsinful means he is free to do so, whenever such laws in peacetime are an obstacle to the common good. They often impose too great a burden and in the long run they are incitements to war.

1030. The second type of law which may cause problems of conscience is the tax law. The citizen has an immediate obligation from the Natural Law to support the State financially. The reason is that the State cannot operate without money and since it can get a sufficiency only from its citizens, they must supply it. Every citizen, therefore, in proportion to his financial capacity owes monetary contribution to the State. Positive law must clarify this natural obligation, determine capacity to pay, and fix the manner, amount, and time of each one's contribution. This is done by the ordinary tax laws of a nation. A person, therefore, who consistently flouts tax laws and evades all payment of taxes offends against piety. Usually this is a serious offense for he simply fails to support the State.

With what exactness does tax legislation enunciate the Natural Law? The answer depends upon the justice of the law and the intention of the legislator. If the tax law is just, it binds in conscience except in the instances when the legislator intends merely penal law.

1031. With respect to the first condition, a tax law is just if it is required by the common good. Justice means that the State may not be excessive in its demands. The State should conduct its business with reasonable efficiency: it should not undertake tasks which do not fall within its competence. When the State seeks too much revenue, it is asking for that to which it has no claim. Taxes fall on persons or on things. Hence a person should be taxed in proportion to his ability to pay. It is distributive justice that from him who has much, much be required. In choosing things to tax, the State should observe a like proportion of distributive justice. Luxuries should be taxed before necessities. The materials of one business should not be singled out rather than those of another, but each industry and its materials should be taxed upon a basis of cost to the State or exempted because of benefits conferred. Thus automobiles are taxed because of the roads maintained for them: private schools should be exempt because of public service rendered. The norm for choosing an object of taxation should not be the ease of collecting the tax or lack of opposition to it, but equitable distribution of civic burden.

1032. The second condition depends on whether modern governments intend their tax laws to be merely penal. Because a person is disgruntled with government, disapproves of its political principles, or imagines that it discriminates against members of his party, race, or religion, he may not conclude that all its tax laws are merely penal. Unless the government clearly spurns an appeal to conscience, the presumption is for an appeal to conscience.

1033. Certain facts of modern life, however, seem to rule out this presumption. First, tremendous penalties are often attached to tax evasion. Second, taxes are collected with cold efficiency. The government does not wait to collect some taxes from the citizen but compels the employer to deduct taxes from one's salary before the employee even receives it. Third, there is the complexity and multiplicity of tax law. Some tax laws are so involved that a layman often requires expert advice to know how to obey them. Every person pays many taxes; perhaps not overt taxes but certainly hidden ones. For everyone is a consumer. Every consumer of goods and services pays hidden taxes, because sellers of these things have so raised prices that the buyer always absorbs the tax charges of the seller. On account of income taxes, sales taxes, luxury taxes, corporation taxes, surplus profit taxes, social security taxes there are few money transactions which do not contain a hidden tax payment.

1034. Do then tax laws today bind in conscience? The matter is obscure. One cannot appeal to authentic interpretation because the secular State has never said that it does not intend an appeal to conscience. Doctrinal interpretation helps little, for moralists are far from agreeing on this thorny question. Custom, which is the best interpreter of law, in this country and on this point is nonexistent. There was a time when men of upright conscience regarded as binding in conscience those taxes which were of long standing and which people paid without protest. But the flood of new taxes, the conviction that the government is asking too much, the sight of wholesale evasions, the increased number of persons who repudiate moral obligation in the matter — all this causes good men to doubt the morally binding force of even those taxes about which their fathers never doubted. Men of upright conscience are in a minority. If, then, the majority of their fellow citizens have shrugged off the moral obligation of a positive law, it would be unjust to say that the minority are still bound to observe it under pain of sin. A plausible case, therefore, can be made for the position that tax laws are merely penal.

1035. The doubts, however, are not about principle but fact. From the conflicting views of the situation this seems to emerge: the conscientious man is convinced that in general he is obliged in conscience to pay taxes because he cannot disregard the admonition of Scripture: "Render to all their due, tribute to whom tribute is due, taxes to whom taxes are due."[4] He is convinced that if by and large he meets his tax assessments, he may without guilt evade one or another tax when chance allows, provided he does not resort to fraud, bribery, or lying. He likens himself to the habitual train rider, that is, if occasionally he gets a free ride, it has been more than compensated for by all the fare he has *already paid.*

1036. Since taxes bind in conscience, *must the evader of taxes make restitution?* If the obligation of paying taxes is from commutative justice, the answer is in the affirmative; if it is only from legal justice, the answer is *no.* Some authors hold for commutative justice and restitution. Since we may not presume but must certainly prove obligation to exist, the burden of proof rests upon the claimants for restitution. Their

[4] Rom. 13:7.

proofs are not convincing. Some authors seem to think that whenever money is involved, the matter automatically pertains to commutative justice.[5] This is not true. In this case, the money demanded by the State does not belong to it until it has been collected. Before collection the State has a *jus ad rem* to it: only after collection does it have a *jus in re*. A *jus ad rem* does not found a title to restitution. Furthermore, appeal is made to an implied contract between the government and the people. Perhaps in feudal days there was an explicit contract by which the prince pledged himself to conduct the government and the people promised him support, but, since feudalism is dead, no evidence of a natural contract so binding government and people can be adduced.

1037. There are two instances, however, wherein the tax evader owes restitution. First, he owes restitution if he bribes a tax collector. The collector has an explicit contract to collect, and, if he deliberately fails to take what is due, he violates his contract and owes restitution to the State in the amount which be failed to collect. The briber has formally co-operated in the act of injustice. Hence upon him and the corrupt official rests jointly the obligation of making restitution. If the official cannot or will not make restitution, the entire burden falls upon the briber.

Second, the tax evader must make restitution if the amount he fails to pay is so great that it causes the tax rate to go up. Because he has failed to pay his share, others must pay more. His wrongful act has injured them. The Natural Law requires that he undo the harm done to them.

1038. When does the obligation to pay taxes begin? In times of great distress the good citizen will spontaneously offer of his goods to the common cause, but ordinarily the tax obligation does not begin until a person has received an official bill from the State. It is the common understanding that the officials of the State are to fix the definite sum which each person is to pay: only after this has been determined does the obligation to pay begin.

But is one obliged in conscience to volunteer information concerning his taxable property, for example, must a man in the absence of specific request tell the government that his income is now such that he is liable for income tax? Some authors say that he is[6] so obliged because (*a*) the law commands him to give this information, and (*b*) not to tell is equivalent to nonpayment. This conclusion is overrigid. It asks too much of human nature. It is the common understanding of upright

[5] Ryan-Boland, *Catholic Principles of Politics*, p. 201. New York, Macmillan, 1940.
[6] *Ibid.*, p. 203.

men that it is for the government to discover this information by itself. Certainly this provision of the income-tax law is purely penal, for men obey it simply because of the heavy penalties for disobedience.

1039. In making declarations of taxable goods a person must be strictly truthful. To pretend that an incomplete declaration is a complete declaration is a lie; if the false declaration be attested to by oath, a person commits perjury. It is claimed that, if a custom generally prevails of minimizing one's taxable goods, one who follows such a practice does not violate veracity.[7] This statement may easily be misunderstood. It is correct if it refers to a *genuine custom,* in other words, if the practice of minimizing is truly general and tacitly accepted by the government. In that case, an actual income of ten thousand dollars is expected to be reported, say, as eight thousand dollars and whoever makes such a declaration is truthfully responding to the mind of the questioner. The statement, however, is incorrect if there is no genuine custom and it is quite problematic whether such a custom is ever established. And before it would be established, a great deal of lying and perjury would have been done.

It is most odious that the State compels its citizens to swear to the truth of income-tax returns. Here the secularized State is playing the game of "Heads I win, tails you lose." In many instances the modern State abjures its own natural obligation of religion but in this case it invokes religion for its own financial profit. Swearing to income-tax returns is unnecessary because the matter is not serious enough to demand invocation of religion. Besides, it is scandal of the weak, for it needlessly exposes too many people to the proximate occasion of perjury.

B. Reverence

1040. Superior excellence demands that it be recognized and that, as occasion offers, some outward token of submission to it be accorded. This is reverence. The State has in regard to its citizens superior excellence because it can impose moral obligation on them. Reverence, therefore, is due from citizens to the symbols representing the State's majesty and the public officials sharing in the State's authority.

In a democracy people are inclined to minimize this duty. The democratic citizen often takes the attitude that he is just as good a man as any public official; that the official has been voted into his job by his fellow citizens, and, as a servant of the public, has no claim to extraordinary consideration. This is a false understanding of civic equality. A private citizen is not the civic equal of a public official: the latter is his

[7] Vermeersch, *Theologia Moralis,* Vol. II, No. 567, *editio prima.*

superior. Because the official is a bearer of public authority, he is entitled, though he be a rascal, to respect for the office which he holds.

C. Civic-Mindedness

1041. Law observance and reverence do not quit the patriot of civic duty. Charity dictates that he give of himself and his goods to the State in its needs, provided he does not grievously burden himself thereby. There is evident room for social charity in times of calamity and extraordinary need. When war, pestilence, famine, earthquake, fire, flood, sedition, and the like, are seriously menacing the State, the good citizen comes forward unasked to contribute his share to warding off the danger. Patriotism, however, is not a garment to be put on for intermittent occasions and then, like a military uniform, to be laid away until the next emergency. Daily, enduring need exists in the State which legislation can never supply, namely, need for constant social activity on the part of citizens. Other things being equal, the State is sound and flourishing in proportion to the active share which citizens take in public life. Its good condition depends on well-informed, vigilant, and publicly active citizens.

As a man must devote time, thought, and energy to his family, so every citizen must give of himself to the State. Whoever merely refrains from breaking the law is a good citizen only in a negative way. If he never bothers about public interests, he scarcely contributes his full share to the public good. Private apathy eventually spells public decay. Hence the good citizen ought to be civic minded or *public spirited*, that is, he should have constant interest in, and manifest practical devotion to, the welfare of the State.

1. *Knowledge of Public Affairs*

1042. To be public spirited a citizen must have *some knowledge of public life and affairs*. No one can take a helpful part in community life unless he has a practical knowledge of the fundamental law of the land. This knowledge should extend to the basic institutions and spirit of the State; to an evaluation of the outstanding characters in public life; to something more than hazy notions about the large contemporaneous problems with which legislation must grapple. An intelligent grasp of the trends and needs of the times is required in a democracy for two reasons: first, democracy is government by public opinion; for wise rule, public opinion must be enlightened. Second, democracy summons its citizens to share in government; hence the uninformed person is an inefficient citizen.

2. *Vigilance*

1043. The public-spirited citizen is *vigilant*. He observes the course of government and is courageous to protest, when protestation will avail, against incompetence or corruption in government. He is jealous of any infringement of the natural, civil, and political rights which government guarantees him as man and citizen. His natural rights to life, liberty, marriage, property, good name, freedom of conscience have already been established. They do not come from the State nor can the State take them away. There is no need of explicit reference to them in the fundamental law of the State, because one takes for granted that the State exists to protect them.

1044. By *civil rights* we mean freedom and immunities explicitly confirmed to the citizen by statute or fundamental law whose immediate purpose is the welfare of the individual. In the amendments to the Constitution of the United States are enumerated the chief civil rights of American citizens. They are freedom of religion, of speech, of the press, of peaceable assembly; the right to keep and bear arms in accordance with the laws of the states; freedom from the billeting of soldiers in private homes in times of peace; freedom from punishment by bill of attainder or ex *post facto* law; recourse to the writ of habeas corpus under ordinary circumstances; security against unreasonable searches, seizures, and warrants; the right to a hearing before a grand jury in all federal cases involving serious crime; immunity from double jeopardy for the same offense and from acting as witness against oneself; the right not to be deprived of life, liberty, or property without due process of law; the right to just compensation for the taking of private property for public use; the right in criminal cases to a speedy and public trial by jury, to be confronted by witnesses and obtain witnesses, and to the assistance of counsel for defense; the right in civil cases involving more than twenty dollars to a trial by jury; freedom from excessive bail and fines, from cruel and unusual punishments, from involuntary servitude except as a punishment for crime; the right to the equal protection of the laws in all states, to enjoy the privileges and immunities of all the states, to be protected against law impairing the obligation of contracts, to sue and be sued in the courts, and to a republican form of government. It is explicitly stated in the ninth amendment that the enumeration of certain rights in the Constitution shall not be construed to deny or disparage other rights retained by the people.

Although maintenance of civil rights redounds first to the benefit of individuals, nothing more surely makes for security and stability of the State. That State will always be vigorous in which individual liberty flourishes. Nowhere are citizens more ready to defend the State than in a land where tyranny is impossible.

Political rights exist not for the individual but for the public good. They consist in the capacity of private citizens to participate in government. They are not strictly rights but rather privileges.

3. *Use of Political Privileges*

1045. The public-spirited citizen *makes constant* use *of his political privileges.* Political privilege is a favor, over and above one's strict civil right, permanently granted by sovereignty to the citizen. The favor is sometimes an exemption from the common law granted to an individual or group but it is usually a concession of a direct or indirect share in governing given to the whole body of citizenry. As subject to law, the citizen has no natural right to make or administer law but once law allows participation, he rightly considers this his political right.

1046. *Jury service* is a political privilege. The patriotic citizen when summoned to it does not shirk it on the mere plea of private business. This contribution to public life he ought to make even at the cost of some private inconvenience.

A jury is a body of men sworn to declare the existence or non-existence of the essential *facts* under dispute in a judicial process. The juryman must be impartial and disinterested. Hence, if a person has a bias in a given case, or has already formed an opinion concerning it, he should not serve in that case. The law itself disbars from the jury relatives and dependents of litigants.

The juryman's verdict should be based on evidence presented, but this does not mean that justice should be abandoned for the sake of legality. In criminal cases, if the evidence leaves reasonable doubt of the defendant's guilt, the juryman must vote for acquittal, unless he has private and certain knowledge of a defendant's guilt whose acquittal would bring great harm to the State. If evidence convicts the defendant, the juryman may acquit if he has private knowledge of innocence. In either case the private knowledge must be certitude, not feeling or unfounded intuition. In civil suits, if evidence is inconclusive, he must favor the party whose right is more probable. If there is equal probability in a case involving possession of a right or good, he should generally favor the possessor.

1047. Furthermore, the public-spirited citizen *votes.* Today voting is a serious duty. Whether a nation will have good or bad laws, an upright or corrupt administration depends on the voters. Extremely grave issues are laid before them. An apathetic electorate is an invitation to tyranny. A person, therefore, who is able to vote but never votes, is guilty of serious omission. In particular cases where serious issues are involved, a proportionately grave inconvenience is required to excuse from wrongdoing a person who does not vote.

The motive of every vote should be the public welfare. In casting his ballot, the citizen should never be swayed by personal profit, mere whim, religious or racial bias but solely by consideration of which of the conflicting issues or candidates is better for city, state, or nation. Although political parties serve a useful civic purpose, their interests should be kept subordinate to the public good.

1048. The voter should learn to evaluate candidates and to recognize who among them has the qualties necessary for public life. To be elected, a candidate should possess three qualities: correct principles of government, aptitude for public life, and public integrity. The policies of a candidate must give clear indication of promoting peace and prosperity in the community. An honest man, who has false notions of the domination of one class in society or of the omnicompetence of government, can do more civic harm than a venal politician whose theories of government accord with the Natural Law. A candidate must have or be able to acquire efficiency in handling public business. There are intelligent and upright men who, because they totally lack political sense, could not succeed in public office. The candidate must give promise of serving the public faithfully, industriously, and beneficially. A man's private vices do not necessarily render him unfit for public office. Although it is likely that a man, immoral in his private actions, will also be immoral in the public acts, there have been able kings, legislators, and administrators whose private lives were far from edifying but whose public service was almost irreplaceable.

4. *Social Charity*

1049. Finally, *social charity* will suggest that, without assuming too heavy a burden and in the measure which his personal obligations permit, the public-spirited citizen give time, thought, personal service, or material resources to private or semipublic institutions which truly alleviate the sufferings of the needy or promote civic betterment.

READINGS

Anderson-Weidner, *American Government*, 4 ed., 309–378. New York, Holt, 1953.
Aristotle, *Politics*, III, 1–5.

Carr, R. K., *Federal Protection of Civil Rights*, 211–268. Ithica, Cornell, 1947.
Commager, H. S., *Majority Rule and Minority Rights*. New York, Smith, 1950.
Connery, J. R., "The Right to Silence," *Marquette Law Journal*, 39 (1955), 180–190.
Cranny, T., *The Moral Obligation of Voting*. Washington, Catholic University, 1952.
Dumbauld, E., *The Bill of Rights*. Norman, University of Oklahoma, 1957.
Graham, G. A., *Morality in American Politics*. New York, Random, 1952.
Harte, T. J., *Papal Social Principles*. Milwaukee, Bruce, 1956.
King, W. J., *Moral Aspects of Dishonesty in Public Offices*. Washington, Catholic University, 1949.
Land, P. S., "Evading Taxes Can't Be Justified in Conscience," *Social Order*, 5 (1955), 121–125.
McWilliams, R., "The Privilege Against Self-Incrimination," *Catholic Mind*, 52 (1954), 613–622.
Montgomery, J. D., ed., *The State Versus Socrates*. Boston, Beacon, 1954.
Ogg-Ray, *Essentials of American Government*, 80–132. New York, Appleton-Century-Crofts, 1952.
Pius XII, "The Christian in Government," *The Pope Speaks*, Autumn, 1956, 247–250.
Schneider, H. W., *Three Dimensions of Public Morality*. Bloomington, Indiana University, 1956.
Suarez, *De Legibus*, V, 13–18.
Swisher, C. B., "The Delineation of Personal and Civil Rights," *Georgetown Law Journal*, 44 (1956), 395–406.
Voorhis, H. J., *The Christian in Politics*. New York, Association Press, 1951.
Wright, J. J., *National Patriotism in Papal Teaching*, 3–93. Westminster, Newman, 1943.

Chapter XXXI INTERNATIONAL ETHICS

1050. Having examined the mutual relations of the State and its citizens, the next point for study is the conduct of States with respect to one another and to international society. It will help in our consideration of international problems if we further refine the concept of statehood in terms of adequate inter-State relations. Since the State is an outstanding moral person and acts upon the international scene, we put the problem thus: What is required and is sufficient to constitute an *international person?*

I. THE INTERNATIONAL PERSON

A. What Is an International Person?

1051. According to Holland, "The normal international person is a State which not only enjoys full external sovereignty, but is also a recognized member of the family of nations. States which vary from this type either by being defective in sovereignty, or by having no place in the family of nations, are abnormal international persons."[1] By the family of nations he means the Christian nations and those others which the Christian nations choose to admit within the circle of their intercourse.

1052. Holland's first condition, plentitude of sovereignty, is absolutely necessary for every international person. To be capable of adequate relations with members of the community of nations, a State must itself have political self-sufficiency. This is sovereignty which means that the State is accountable to no other State either in relations with its own citizens (internal sovereignty) or in relations with other States (external sovereignty). All authorities agree that any political body which lacks something of internal or external sovereignty fails in self-sufficiency and is not to be accounted as capable of adequate relations with those units which possess full sovereignty.

[1] Thomas Holland, *Jurisprudence,* 13 ed., p. 395. Oxford, Clarendon, 1937.

The second proffered requisite for international standing, membership in the group of nations which has inherited the Christian tradition, we reject. The western nations are so secularized that they are only nominally Christian. The ninteenth-century notion of a *restricted* comity of nations has been abandoned. All that the Natural Law demands for international relationship is plentitude of sovereignty. Every sovereign State is capable of international intercourse, and in justice and in charity should be accorded corresponding standing.

1053. There are political societies, like nascent colonies, which are incapable of exercising full sovereignty. A weak State may conceivably turn to a stronger State for real protection and in return give over to its protector direction of its foreign affairs. Other states have renounced sovereignty to become members of a Federal Union. Since these societies do not have plenitude of sovereignty, they are neither *de facto* nor *de jure* international persons; they are not upon a footing of international equality with sovereign States; they do not have the international rights and duties of sovereign States. *Therefore the international person is each State that possesses full sovereignty.*

1054. When the world is at peace the number of *de facto* sovereign States can be accurately computed. But does this number represent an objectively just situation? The international scene is a curious melange of principle and expediency. Hence several interrelated problems arise: (*a*) Does each sovereign State include in its membership all the groups and only the groups which should rightly form this civic union? (*b*) Ought some political societies which do not now possess full sovereignty be accorded it and treated as fully competent International-Persons? The first problem deals with the Theory of Nationalism and the Rights of Minorities; the second with suppressed States.

B. The Theory of Nationalism

1055. In the nineteenth century the doctrine of nationalism was evolved especially by Italian writers like Mancini.[2] The theory distinguishes between *population*, or those persons actually subject to a particular government, and *nationality*, a large group of persons characterized by special traits of body and mind, and united by similar language, customs, and ancestry. A population may consist of several nationalities or parts of nationalities, as Austria did before 1914. A nationality may be divided among several populations as were the Poles before 1914. According to this theory, a population is an artificial unit; a nationality

[2] P. S. Mancini, "*Della Nationalita come Fondamento del Dritto delle genti,*" in his *Dritto Internazionale Prelegioni*, pp. 5–64. Napoli, Marghieri, 1873.

is the sole natural unit. According to the extreme statement of the theory every nationality has a right to form a State which will include all the members and only the members of that nationality, the rights of all other States notwithstanding. For example, all people of Italian nationality subject to France, Italy, and Switzerland should be incorporated into one purely Italian national State. State and nationality must be coterminous. Hardly anyone, however, would now defend the doctrine in this form. A modified version contends that, if international agreements are not violated, each nationality, capable of autonomy, may demand it when it judges autonomy necessary for national purposes and when it has the strength to effect it. Its ability to accomplish this must be left to the trial of arms.

1056. The principle of nationality is not a precept of the Natural Law. Nature does not indicate that only those people who spring from a common stock should be united in one State. There are three reasons for our denial. First, consent is the sole juridic cause of the State. Nationality, therefore, can be, at most, a remote cause, that is, a factor dispositive to consent, but it is by no means so overwhelming a factor that it must always demand consent. There can be stronger dispositive factors to consent than nationality, namely, local proximity, mutual need, common history, long-enduring habits of acting together. Second, nationality is often so vague and uncertain that it cannot constitute the determining norm of who should belong to a given State. Who can adequately distinguish and classify all the nationalities? Third, the principle advanced is provocative of perpetual discord. To put this theory into effect would disrupt peace everywhere. The change could not be effected without universal war. Some nationalities are so hopelessly spread out and intermingled with others that separation and relocation could not be humanely effected. Some nationalities are too small to constitute a sovereign State: others, which have never constituted a State, may yet be incapable of self-rule. Finally, even if the nationalities could be distinguished and separated too many old ties would be rudely severed, too many claims to lands and cities would still be bandied about; and so the delimitations of nationalities would still remain so vague that no one could guarantee that this new arrangement of States would be any more productive of concord than that which obtains at present.

C. Rights of Minorities

1057. A situation may exist in which a nationality is morally obliged to remain attached to the State of which it now forms part, for example, Scotland to the Kingdom of Great Britain. Separation would mean economic ruin of the separated nationality, foment civil wars, seriously prejudice the rights of the rump State, and the like. However, while retaining its old allegiance and ancient loyalty, the nationality has a right to preserve its language, customs, and national characteristics. These things are an estimable good which men prize. This right, however, ought not to be so exaggerated as to inflict grave injury on the State of which it forms part.

Above all, such a nationality has a right to equitable treament at the hands of the dominant group. "Dominant" is an invidious word suggesting a stronger party which exploits a weaker party. In no State should there be a dominant group in that sense: all groups have an equal right to share in the benefits of the State.

D. Suppressed States

1058. Although nationalism makes exaggerated claims and is provocative of disturbance, it does express valid protest against many existing injustices. There are nationalities, clearly distinguishable, which have inhabited easily definable areas for centuries, and which once constituted sovereign States. Their sovereignty was violently taken away by some more powerful State acting in its own selfish interests. Ought sovereignty be restored to such suppressed nationalities?

1059. The answer must rest on two ultimate principles, namely, consent and human welfare. If a suppressed nationality is located close to the dominant nation, if the political ties binding them are of long standing as in the case of the Welsh and the English, if forcible suppression is happily ended and human welfare is being promoted by their union, the people *de facto* consent. They are obliged to. Nationality has in it a fair amount of vanity and romanticism. It is silly for a people, because of "old forgotten things and battles long ago," to sigh for a chimerical independence. For time has healed the breach between conqueror and conquered and made of them a united population. This, however, is the rarer instance.

1060. The more usual case is this. Distance separates the two parties; the loss of sovereignty is of fairly recent date; the subordinate people are economically exploited; they are not permitted to make vital decisions affecting their welfare; their legitimate national aspirations are thwarted as inimical to the interests of the dominant State. The victims of such an arrangement do not consent but grudgingly bear a foreign yoke because they must. They rightly aspire to be masters in their own house, because *a given people is usually the best judge and the most efficient procurer of its own welfare.* We may say of States what is true of individuals, namely, no one takes better care of a person than himself.

II. THE INTERNATIONAL COMMUNITY

1061. Do the international persons form a natural society? First, the human race, taken as a whole, is a natural community. This follows from the physical oneness of the race and its common social purpose. The agreement of ancient and modern writers is overwhelming. According to Aristotle "man is a political animal. And therefore, men . . . are brought together by their common interests in proportion as they severally attain to any measure of well-being. This is certainly the chief end, both of individuals and of states."[3] Plutarch sums up the doctrine of Zeno that "we are to consider all men to be of one community and polity and we should have a common life and one order for us all."[4] Cicero says that "the oneness of the races of the world must be regarded as a law of nature."[5] Marcus Aurelius says that a man is a citizen "of the highest state of which all other states are but as households."[6] St. Augustine says, "After the state or city comes the world, the third circle of human society."[7] According to Suarez "there is a certain natural form of community, brought about solely through the conformity of its members in rational nature. Of this kind, is the community of mankind, which is found among all men."[8] Erasmus,[9] Gentili,[10] and Vitoria[11] expressed similar views. Science, in the person of Darwin,[12] and revelation, in the teaching of St. Paul,[13] concur in assigning a single origin to the human race.

The units in this natural community are not individuals but States, as is clear from St. Thomas: "Wherever there are many governments ordained to one end, there ought to be one universal government over the particular governments; because in all the virtues and arts . . . there is an order according to the order of ends. . . . One congregation or community contains another; just as the community of a province

[3] *Politics,* III, 6, 1278b.
[4] *Moralia,* IV, 329A.
[5] *Tusculan Disputations,* I, xiii, 30.
[6] *Meditations,* III, xi.
[7] *The City of God,* XIX, vii.
[8] *De Legibus,* I, 6, 18.
[9] *The Complaint of Peace,* 77–81. London, 1795.
[10] *De jure belli,* I, xv.
[11] *De Potestate Civili,* no. 21.
[12] The last sentence of *The Origin of Species.*
[13] Acts 17:25–26.

contains the community of a city; and the community of a kingdom contains the community of a province; and the community of the world contains the community of a kingdom."[14]

III. THE EXISTENCE OF INTERNATIONAL LAW

1062. The natural society of the community of nations must be directed to its end by law. Since this natural society exists it must have authority and as a political society it can exercise authority only through law. So important a community can be directed in no other way. The members of this society must live an ordered co-operative life and social order on a world-wide scale can be had only through law. The only other alternative is force and force eventually means war which is destructive of the community. Hence, as individuals would live an unsocial life unless they submit to the law of the State, so States in relation to one another would lead an inhuman existence unless they submit to international law.

1063. The chief objection which purports to show that international law is not true law but an ineffectual kind of morality comes from the notion of sovereignty advocated by John Austin.[15] His argument is that since law is the command of the sovereign, and since no power stands above the sovereign State, the State is not subject to law.

The Austinian notion of sovereignty is the result of the effort to explain the political facts of the seventeenth century. Then monarchic absolutism was universal. The monarch or sovereign was looked upon as the untouchable person who had all political power and was the proprietor of the territory of the State. His political pre-eminence gradually passed to the parliament and then to the plurality of the electorate. Consequently the sovereignty which was once attributed to the monarch is claimed by the State. Hence today "sovereignty" is often used to designate either the depositary of absolute power in a dictatorship or the strongest influence within a democracy whose wishes ultimately prevail. So from the concept of a superior person within the realm who was above the law, men have turned to the concept of the sovereign State. "A sovereign state at the present time claims the power to judge its own controversies, to enforce its own conception of its rights . . . to treat its nationals as it sees fit, and to regulate its economic life without regard to the effect of such regulations upon its neighbors."[16]

[14] *In IV Sent.*, d. xxiv, q. III, a. 2, ad 3um.
[15] W. Jethro Brown, *The Austinian Theory of Law*, p. 51. London, Murray, 1906.
[16] J. L. Brierly, *The Law of Nations*, 4 ed., p. 48. Oxford, Clarendon, 1950.

We must free the concept of sovereignty from all undue accretions. The idea that sovereignty is also proprietary right has long ago been exploded. Furthermore, sovereignty is a political, not a sociological thing. It is not that power in society whose will ultimately prevails. To attempt to locate such a power in a democracy is a hopeless task. Sovereignty is the public legitimate organized authority which the State has at its disposal for the attainment of its end. This authority is limited by Natural Law and positive international law.

THESIS LXXV. Every State both in regard to its own citizens and to other States is subject to the Natural Law. As a member of the community of nations it is subject to positive international law.

PART I

1064. The State has moral obligations and the persons who act officially for the State must conform their public actions to the Natural Law.

PROOF

1065. The activities of a natural society are governed by the Natural Law because the society originates in the Natural Law which also indicates the main outlines of such a society. Hence it would be absurd to say that the activities of such a society are free of that law. We have already shown the principal natural duties of the State with regard to its citizens. When one State deals with another State, one body of men is holding intercourse with another body of men. The intercourse of men with men is controlled by the Natural Law. It is foolish to imagine that men can avoid the commands and prohibitions of the Natural Law by the device of association.

PART II

1066. International law is the sum of rules which States ought to observe in their intercourse with one another. It is not to be confused with *Jus Gentium*, or Law of Nations. In Roman jurisprudence and early Scholastic terminology *Jus Gentium* referred to those tenets of positive law which are practically the same in the codes of particular States. They are obvious applications of the Natural Law which men cannot help but incorporate into their law.[17] While some of them apply to the

[17] See *Sum. Theol.*, I–II, 95, 4; Suarez, *De Legibus*, Lib. II, c. 17.

intercourse of nations as such, most of them concern the relations of man to man and State to citizen. International law is rather *Jus inter Gentes.*

Natural international law consists of laws which immediately flow from the nature of international society and whose validity does not depend upon State agreement or acceptance.

Positive international law is that body of rules which, by express or tacit agreement, governs the inter-State acts of the nations. It is the outgrowth of customs, treaties, and acts which in the course of time have been accepted as precedents and binding upon the community of nations.

PROOF

1067. As soon as a new State is recognized it finds itself bound by an established set of international rules. That these have the force of positive law is clear from this consideration: to have positive law all that is required is a political community and rules which are accepted as binding that community. Furthermore, the nations treat problems of international law in a legal manner and regard international law as producing legal effects.

1068. Corollary. Sovereignty does not mean that the State is free of all law but of the law of another State. Each State is the political equal of every other State but is subordinate to the community of nations.

IV. THE CONTENT OF NATURAL INTERNATIONAL LAW

1069. What does the Natural Law command, forbid, and allow the nations in their intercourse with one another? Since international life is the action and reaction of groups of men toward other groups of men, the same general laws of human conduct — the demands of justice and charity — govern inter-State activity. We shall treat first of international justice; then of international charity.

A. International Justice

1070. A natural juridic order upon the international level exists because the Natural Law confers rights upon States and upon international society. For their preservation and development these moral persons cannot be without rights. Since rights flow from the essence of statehood, and since each State has the same end and function, *each State has equal natural rights.* A prime function of international society is defense of the rights of States. Here we shall explain the chief rights of States and at the end of the chapter speak of the rights or needs of international society.

1. National Existence

1071. When a State begins to exist it acquires a right to be recognized and treated as such by other States. Since existence is the first good, both of individuals and of societies, the State has a right to continue to exist. The reason is that the new State is a natural institution and a necessary means to the welfare of this people. Since statehood is sovereignty, the State's right of self-preservation means the maintenance of unimpaired sovereignty. This principle involves four items of consideration.

1072. a) *The independent existence of a State may not be destroyed.* Although this right is natural, it is not indefeasible; it may yield before the superior consideration of human welfare in two instances: (i) a State may agree to merge with another State or States; (ii) if the security and existence of one State is constantly menaced by an implacably hostile State, the aggrieved State may as a measure of ultimate self-defense destroy the other in the same legitimate manner as the individual may kill in self-defense. So extreme a situation is seldom realized, but it seems reasonable that the Roman government in Britain in the fourth century of our era would have been justified in destroying the political organization of the Picts and Scots, if they had any, and in subjugating them if it could, since that was the only means of stopping their attacks and tranquilizing Britain.

1073. b) *Nor may partial but permanent limitations be imposed upon the sovereignty of one State by another.* Each State has the inherent right to manage its own affairs as it thinks best. If it obeys the Natural Law, it is free to set up the constitution it chooses, make laws which suit it, and enter into treaties as it pleases. Every State with sufficient strength maintains this right against the world. Through weakness and through possession of assets coveted by a more powerful nation, a luckless State has been compelled to allow another State a voice in its foreign and even in its domestic policy.

Immunity from such interference is the *right of nonintervention.* It is an immediate corollary from the concept of sovereignty and is ultimately grounded on human welfare: each State's affairs are best cared for by itself.

The rule of nonintervention is not so ironclad as to admit of no exception. Human welfare sometimes demands an exception. Thus, if the affairs of a State are in deplorable condition or if a people are suffering from inhuman tyranny, international society may step in with a remedy.

1074. c) *Territorial integrity.* In general, no nation may take over part of another's territory. Outside of the lust for economic advantage, nothing is so provocative of friction among the nations as lust for territory.

1075. d) *Freedom from fomentation of sedition.* Every nation is entitled to its own peaceful life as the primary aim of existence.

2. *Respect*

1076. A State deserves honor and courtesy from all other States. The reason is the excellence of the moral person, the State. Application of this principle is found chiefly in treatment of the State's official representatives and of its chief symbols, notably its flag.

3. *Self-Development*

1077. Since the individual has a right to improve himself, the State has the same right; otherwise the State could not fulfill its natural end — the promotion of public prosperity. The State, therefore, has a right to any means of self-improvement which does not injure another State. This right involves access to means of full human living, freedom of communication, increase of dominion.

1078. a) *Access to means of full human living.* If a people could not readily obtain a secure supply of the necessaries of life, they would not form a State, for they would lack elemental economic self-sufficiency. Hence it is taken for granted that each State has the means of subsistence. But if a State wishes to make progress, it needs materials, notably minerals. Since the bounty of nature has been intended for the whole human race, no nation or combination of nations may monopolize the raw wealth of the earth and fix prices which put desirable goods beyond the reach of less fortunate nations. Economic monopoly is the real sore spot in international relations. From the envy of the have-nots for the haves arise wars. Lasting peace is possible only upon a foundation of equitable economic opportunity among the nations.

1079. b) *Freedom of communication.* Nations that wall themselves off from international intercourse quickly cease to make progress. Interchange of goods and ideas is the essential requisite for advancement. No State, therefore, may be prevented from friendly intercourse with the nations of the earth. So also a State would ordinarily do wrong which refused communication with the outside world or forbade it to its subjects. The right of intercourse, however, does not include a strict "Right of Legation," that is, a duty existing in all other States of receiving its official representatives. A nation refusing to receive the ambassadors of another country may violate charity but not justice.

This right also includes the peaceable use of the natural means of communication — the high seas and the common airways.

1080. c) *Increase of dominion.* Increase of dominion is the extension of a State's jurisdiction over any new territory which is not already subject to another State. Occupation is a good title both of proprietary dominion and of jurisdiction. For its occupation to be valid, the State must fulfill three conditions. (i) By a *public* act the State must lay claim to the land. The private act of a citizen who discovers it and makes some of it his private possession is not sufficient. (ii) The State must effectively control the land. Mere discovery and claim are not enough: what it cannot control does not pass into its jurisdiction. (iii) The land must belong to no other State, barbarous or civilized. If barbarous people are settled on the land and have their own self-sufficient polity, they constitute a legitimate State even though it is not reckoned among the family of nations. No civilized State is justified in forcing foreign jurisdiction upon it. The right of a barbarous State to exist is as good as that of a civilized State. *There is no such thing as naked right of conquest:* force cannot of itself found a right. The legitimate mode of exercising the right to increase dominion is colonization.

1081. Colonization. A colony is a group of citizens who have left their own land to people another and whose government is subject to the mother country. Where a colony is established on land which is merely overrun by nomads, the colonizing power must not make it impossible for the nomads to live. If a colony is set up in a land which heretofore was too sparsely inhabited to have a government, the rights of the aboriginal inhabitants to their *private* holdings in land and the like must be respected. Even though their titles are not recorded in a courthouse, they are as valid as those recognized among civilized men.

The powers of a colonial government are determined by the mother country. As the colony increases and its need for the protection of the mother country decreases, the management of its affairs may more and more be left to itself. As a son in the family ultimately achieves emancipation from paternal rule, so a colony, fully self-sustaining, is entitled to complete independence when it chooses to exercise it.

4. *Treaties*

1082. A *treaty* is a public contract between two or more sovereign States. It is quite distinct from a private contract between States, for example, the purchase by the Chinese Government of the Brazilian legation buildings in London. As private persons may exchange rights by contract so may States. Treaty making is but an expansion of the right of intercourse.

To bind a nation, a treaty must be an act of the Sovereign. Constitutional law determines where the treaty-making power lies in a government.

Treaties derive their binding power from the Natural Law alone. No agencies of positive international law exist upon which treaties could depend for binding force, interpretation, execution, or reparation. It is, therefore, a general precept of the Natural Law that *agreements made among the nations must be kept.* They bind in commutative justice.

1083. Practically the same requirements for validity and liceity hold for treaties as for private contracts (§ 576 ff.). The outstanding difference between treaties and private contracts is that the individual can appeal to a court to declare an agreement invalid or even to rescind a contract initially good, but the State cannot. No court exists competent to invalidate treaties. Must, then, a State absolutely observe every treaty which it signs? Let us distinguish between treaties willingly and unwillingly entered upon.

1084. a) *May a State refuse to honor a treaty which it has been compelled to accept?* In general, it may not be left to a State later to repudiate, on the score of no consent, a treaty which it had been forced to accept. The reason is that, if this practice were allowed, no treaties would have binding force. Hence, if the terms of the treaty are just, the unwilling signatory is clearly bound to fulfill them. If the injustice is only doubtful, the treaty likewise must be observed. However, if the terms are palpably unjust, no treaty exists no matter how solemn the formalities which inaugurated it. The reason is that what is unjust cannot be the object of any contract. The oppressor State is morally obliged to renounce its claims under the agreement and to repair all injury effected by it. The aggrieved State has no obligation in commutative justice to fulfill its part. Hence, if it can avoid performance without provoking war, it is justified in doing so. If it cannot do so without disturbing international peace, the common good demands that the unjust agreement be kept, especially if the issues involved are not of paramount importance. However, a State's obligations to the fellowship of nations cannot ask too much of it, for example, to observe terms which would lead to loss of independence, acute misery of its people, or spoliation of the fundamental means of development.

1085. b) *May a State void a treaty which it has freely entered into?*

Treaties cease to bind for the same reasons that private contracts lapse: mutual consent, impossibility of performance, extinction of one party, and the like. The question which arises here is whether there are any circumstances in which a State may lawfully denounce a treaty initially valid and remaining such to the moment of its repudiation?

According to Cronin[18] there is one and only one circumstance wherein a nation may upon its own initiative declare itself freed of treaty obligation, namely, when an implied condition, necessary to impose obligation at the time the treaty is made, no longer holds good. He cites two examples: (i) when one party has substantially failed to live up to its part, the other party may declare itself free of all obligation; (ii) when fulfillment would involve loss of independence for one party—unless the treaty was meant to hold even in such a contingency.

5. *Self-Defense*

1086. The above-mentioned rights must be capable of defense; otherwise they are useless. When, then, any of them are violated or are in danger of infringement, a State may protect its interests by protest, negotiation, arbitration, severance of diplomatic relations, an embargo of trade. *May it resort to violence?* Certainly if national territory is wantonly invaded by hostile force, the citizens themselves, even in the absence of an official armed force, may, if they are able, repel the invader. This is an instance of collective self-defense. The full issue here is, *May one nation go to war with another?*

6. *War*

1087. *War* is the violent attempt of one nation or part of a nation to impose its will upon another similar group. It is *civil war* when the contention is carried on by armed forces within the same nation. There is scarcely anything more destructive of the ends of the State. It is the primary duty of any government to prevent and suppress all civil war. According to international custom, whenever rebels are not only in possession of an army but have a civil political organization sufficient to be responsible for armed forces and quasi-governmental acts, they may be recognized as *belligerents,* that is, capable of waging war according to its accepted laws. The effect of such a declaration is that henceforth the rebels are not to be dealt with as mutineers or pirates; the parent country is freed from all responsibility for what happens within the insurgent lines; neutrals may enter into commercial relations with them.

---

[18] Michael Cronin, *The Science of Ethics,* Vol. II, pp. 658–661. Dublin, Gill, 1909.

Civil wars never begin by a formal declaration of war but by the interruption of regular administration through insurrection.

Among ancient and modern civilized peoples war between *sovereign States* has regularly been initiated by a formal proclamation of hostilities. *Does the Natural Law prohibit or allow a declaration of war?*

1088. If war is intrinsically evil, the Natural Law must forbid it. The immediate object of warlike effort is the destruction of the armed forces of one's adversary which inevitably involves taking human life. Taking human life is not in itself evil; otherwise God could not ordain it in the ordinary course of nature. Nor is taking human life upon human authority intrinsically evil, for it may be justified in personal self-defense or public execution. From its end of work, therefore, war is not condemned. The morality of war is to be determined from motive and circumstances.

On the score of motive we distinguish war of aggression and war of defense. (a) *War of aggression* is the violent endeavor to deprive another people of independence, territory, or the like, for the sake of increasing one's own power and prestige. (b) *War of defense* is the forceful protection of national rights.

a) Aggressive War

THESIS LXXVI. The Natural Law forbids all wars of aggression.

PROOF

1089. The Natural Law forbids the unreasonable suppression of the rights of any State. For nature which grants these rights would contradict itself if it did not forbid all undue interference with them.

War of aggression is unreasonable suppression of the rights of the assaulted State. It is violent trespass upon that State's right to a peaceful existence. The only reasonable use of force against an equal is protection and reparation of right.

Corollary. Except for the one instance noted in § 1072 a right of conquest does not exist.

1090. N.B. It is the hypocritical custom of aggressors to conceal their international assaults with such euphemisms as, "preventive defense," "punitive expeditions," "the white man's burden." There must still exist an appreciable temporal utility to moral principles; otherwise imperialists would not so assiduously try to disguise their aggressions in the borrowed plumage of virtue.

b) *Defensive War*

THESIS LXXVII. Under certain conditions the Natural Law allows the State a war of defense

1091. The same fundamental principles which apply to the use of force by the individual in defense of individual rights we apply here, making due allowance for the difference between individual and State. For a declaration of war or the initiation of hostilities to be justified, these four conditions must be fulfilled.

1092. a) War must be an act of *Sovereign Authority*. The only justification of war is legitimate defense of the State. Hence war may be initiated only by the supreme authority in a State. No individual or subordinate authority may declare war on foreign nationals.

1093. b) War must be an act of *legitimate self-defense*. Not every right of the State is important enough to justify war. The right to be defended must be of surpassing importance. War is too frightfully serious, too fraught with dreadful consequences for all parties involved, ever to be lightly invoked. Two rights alone measure up to this requirement, namely, independent existence and legitimate development. If a State's independence is in danger, if by unjust means it is being economically strangled to death, if its territorial integrity is threatened in a large way, it may go to war. Since war is so horrible, a State may not fight on account of wounded national honor or injustices done to a few citizens abroad. Nor is *mere* punishment an adequate reason. No sovereign State has a right to punish another State, because punishment is the prerogative of a superior. A *fortiori*, it is immoral to fight for more territory; for national revenge or increase of power, profit, and prestige; for balance of power; for the sake of interfering in the internal affairs of a neighbor.

The defense of right here postulated clearly implies that the complaining State is not at the same time doing wrong to its prospective adversary. If it is, the two States are simultaneously the victims and the perpetrators of mutual injustice. The aggrieved nation is justified in going to war only when it has clean hands and has itself ceased from all acts of injustice.

1094. c) There must be *moral certainty* that a State's essential rights are in danger. As a judge may not condemn a man to death unless he is certain of guilt, so a State may not cast the die for war unless it is certain of the justice of its cause. Mere probability of attack is not enough. Since there is a certainly existing obligation to respect the rights of other States and an ever pressing duty arising from the common good of all nations not to disrupt the peace, there is no room here for the application of probabilism. If, however, all the conditions of just war are verified, the injured State — as in the case of personal assault — need not passively await the military attack of its adversary but may itself strike the first blow.

1095. *d*) *War must be the last resort.* Every peaceable means of settling the dispute must first have been tried sincerely and assiduously. Only when no other means are available is violence a justifiable means of safeguarding right. The principle of *proportionate evil* must be fully invoked. Not only must the right to be defended outweigh the evils of war, but government must beforehand ponder all the chances of war. It would be wrong to embark even on a just war without fair prospect of success. And even a successful war may leave a State worse off than if it had refrained from fighting and tolerated certain injustices. In many wars both the victors and the vanquished suffer irreparably.

PROOF

1096. The Natural Law allows the uniquely necessary means of protecting essential rights if this means is not evil in itself. Otherwise the grant of right is illusory.

That defensive war is not in itself evil is proved in § 1088. In certain circumstances war can be absolutely the only way to maintain the right to independence or the essential means of development.

1097. Before an individual takes up arms, how *certain* must he be of the justice of the side for which he intends to fight?

A person may fight for a State other than his own from a motive of charity, that is, for a State which is justly defending its rights and which needs all possible assistance. Mere romantic preference for one side or love of excitement are insufficient reasons. A volunteer must always investigate and be *morally certain* of the justice of the cause for which he fights.

Concerning persons who fight for their own country, different cases must be distinguished.

a) Conscripts and soldiers already in the army when war begins may legitimately presume that their country is right. The justice or injustice of a war will not usually be evident to the common soldier. Nor is he obliged to investigate because such investigation, even if possible, would lead to nothing. When they doubt, they may resolve their doubt by giving their country the benefit of the doubt. Hence they are to obey their commanders. If, however, they are convinced of the injustice of the war, they may not inflict damage on the enemy. Their right of personal self-defense remains, however. The practical solution of the situation is a request for noncombatant service.

b) Whoever volunteers to serve must first satisfy himself that the cause is just.

c) If a State has foolishly or unjustly gone to war, and is in danger of destruction, the State may call upon all citizens to ward off the peril and all competent citizens are obliged to obey.

d) A person who contends that participation in any war is always immoral is deceived. However, if his conscience is invincibly erroneous and he is summoned to active military service, he must follow his conscience and decline active part in the war.

The obligations of individuals may be summarized thus: (i) Statesmen, legislators, and volunteers for a foreign army must be *morally certain* of the justice of their acts. (ii) When the country declares war, the ordinary man may give it the benefit of any doubt, because full information is not available to him, and because his country is most seriously endangered by the mere fact of war.

c) *The Conduct of War*

1098. It is one thing to go to war for a just cause. It is quite another to try to win a war through immoral practices. Once a war starts one cannot say that all is fair in war.

THESIS LXXVIII. In the prosecution of war the Natural Law forbids every action intrinsically evil.

PROOF

Actions intrinsically evil are always and everywhere wrong and hence forbidden by the Natural Law. Therefore they are also forbidden even in the prosecution of a just war.

Corollary. No State may do what is intrinsically evil even to save itself from total destruction.

The chief particular moral problems arising from war are now considered.

(1) *Use of Violence*

1099. According to the theory of *total war* absolutely every energy of a State and its total population are organized to win a war. Consequently all values must be subordinate to military victory, and violence of any kind or quantity may be used against any person or place of the enemy. This theory, however, is based upon a myth and expresses a vicious morality.

1100. The myth is that the warring State is a single, integrated individual, like the "greater man" of Plato, and he is engaged in mortal combat with a similar abstraction. "Uncle Sam" or "John Bull" of the cartoons is pummeling the "Russian bear" or Hitler. This is a false view of the facts. An abstraction, the United States, does not fight another abstraction, Russia. Out of the total population, a very small proportion — the armed forces — endeavors to dissolve the armed forces of the enemy. Another small portion of the population co-operates in the war effort. To date no nation has ever realized an all-out effort for war.

Total war is vicious morality because it is defeative of absolute human ends. It rests upon the presuppositions that the State is the absolute being, that the end of life is the fulfillment of the objectives chosen by a government, that all human values must be subordinate to military victory. To say, however, that the moral law is subordinate to military victory is blasphemy because the moral law is God commanding us to promote the necessary ends of human existence, forbidding us to defeat them. Second, total war is evil because it claims unlimited freedom of action. But war, at best, is a concession granted under most stringent conditions. Besides demanding a just cause for war, the moral law limits warlike activities by declaring who may be subjected to violence and what kind and amount of violence are legitimate.

1101. What persons may be objects of military force? The ancients believed in total war so that any male of the enemy could be assailed and any woman appropriated. But Christian teaching, which holds that it is always wrong directly to kill an innocent man, evolved the distinction between the combatant, who may be assailed, and the noncombatant, who may not be assailed. But why may even the combatant be assailed? asks the pacifist. The only justification is that a State is defending itself against an unjust party and authorizes certain persons to use violence in its name to suppress the unjust party. Hence a soldier, as representative of his nation defending its right, may directly assail an enemy soldier because he is a guilty party, a co-operator with the unjust aggressor. This distinction of guilty and innocent is of Natural Law: without it war has no rational meaning and is utterly immoral.

While the distinction between guilty and innocent is clear enough in the abstract, it may be difficult to apply it according to the convention that the combatant is the man in uniform and the noncombatant is the civilian. Who then is the modern combatant?

1102. A combatant is one who *immediately* co-operates in military effort. Two essentials are involved, namely, military effort and immediate co-operation. Military effort is force under the control of the State. Since war may be the act only of the State, particular warlike acts must be controlled by the State's authority. The State may not summon forth violence against an enemy which it cannot direct. To do this is to encourage the perpetration of every sort of crime and to help in the dissolution of society's bonds. A combatant, then, is first, one who is authorized to fight as are all members of the armed services. The unauthorized person who kills an enemy combatant, except in self-defense, is an assassin. A combatant is also any civilian who temporarily or permanently renders *immediate* aid to military effort. Persons who do so permanently ought to be aggregated to the armed forces. Civilians, who only remotely and indirectly promote military effort, are not to be classified as combatants and their persons and homes may not be the objects of direct attack. First, direct attack is out of proportion to the indirect violence which they offer the enemy. They are not immediately attacking the person of their enemies; therefore, their persons should be immune from direct attack. Second, to allow direct attack upon such persons is a dangerous threat to the whole human race. Such persons may be prevented from doing war work by bombing the factories in which they work; by destroying the raw materials, means of transportation and communication, and the like, which they use; by taking them prisoner, but *not by a directly aimed attack upon their person.*

1103. Modern conditions perhaps require adjustment of the convention which identifies the combatant with the man in uniform. It seems more realistic to say that combatants are the members of the armed forces and all who *directly* co-operate with them. Since, however, war is but a grim concession and life is still a sacred thing, the burden of proof lies upon those who would depart from the received tradition and greatly enlarge the category of combatant. After liberal allowances have been made for enlarging the number of combatants, there will still remain in the civil population vast numbers of the innocent. Children, old people, the sick, and they who must care for them, far from helping the war effort, may be said to retard it. During World War II a detailed analysis of persons and occupations in the United States was made and the conclusion was that two thirds of the civilian population should be considered innocent noncombatants.[19] Furthermore, "however completely all efforts be directed toward attaining the purposes of the war, the

[19] John Ford, *Theological Studies,* September, 1944, pp. 283–286.

distinction between combatants and noncombatants (which the doctrine of total war denies) keeps coming back as an exigency of war itself. The combatant cannot fight unless there is someone who is not fighting but keeping the civil life of the country in efficient running order by attending to the works of peace (farming, etc.)."[20]

1104. The moral principle governing every use of violence is that *a person should use no more violence than is requisite to make his right secure.* To go beyond that point is to be guilty of unjust aggression. There is a limit to the quality and quantity of violence, even in war. As for quality, a State may not employ weapons which inflict useless suffering. Weapons are tools of defense intended to crush the aggression of an enemy, not to inflict pain for the sake of pain. By positive agreement the majority of the nations have agreed not to use poisons, poisonous gases, and bacteria. The over-all good of the human race is an added reason for the observance of this convention. As for quantity of violence, once an individual enemy is incapable of resistance through wounds, sickness, lack of weapons, and the like, or is genuinely willing to surrender, violence against him must cease. To kill a wounded or surrendered enemy is murder. To refuse to take prisoners is, equivalently, murder except when an enemy feigns surrender the more easily to inflict damage. In that case soldiers may take every precaution to insure their safety. Prisoners must be humanely treated and when peace is concluded they must be returned to their homes.

1105. Bombing. It is a legitimate act of war to bomb directly any military target. The term, military target, includes not only armed personnel and purely military installations, but roads, railways, every kind of communication and transportation, factories, warehouses, government buildings — anything which directly subserves a military purpose. Killing noncombatants in air raids may never be directly willed but only permitted according to the principle of double effect. To bomb a purely civilian area for the sake of terrorizing the enemy into subjection is merely mass murder.

An open city is one which contains nothing of direct military value. Hence it is immune from air attack. If, however, a belligerent disperses his factories among private homes and uses these as arsenals of war, they automatically become legitimate military targets.

1106. The moral difficulty concerns area *bombing.* In bombing a large area where military and nonmilitary objectives stand next to each

[20] Guido Gonella, A *World to Reconstruct,* tr. by T. L. Bouscaren, p. 159. Milwaukee, Bruce, 1944.

other, it will often be impossible to take precautions against hitting nonmilitary targets. Such is the lamentable chance of war. If it is possible to take these precautions, there is a strict moral obligation to do so, for noncombatants have definite rights that must be respected. To take no precautions to avoid hitting churches, hospitals, schools, historical monuments, civilian homes when such precautions are militarily possible, is equivalent to direct attack. Such indiscriminate bombing is immoral. So also is the blanket order to raze a large city.

1107. What is the morality of dropping a single *atomic bomb* which devastates a tremendous area? The answer will depend upon what is in that area. For the act to be good, the area must contain a preponderance of particular military objectives and the military good to be effected must be proportioned to the damage done to noncombatants. To consider atomic bombing merely as an act of total war, as the body blow of one global giant against another, is to forget the pertinent human rights of many thousands of persons. To attack an overwhelmingly civil population with this weapon is simply the direct slaughter of thousands of innocent people. Nor may the action be justified on the ground of bringing war to a speedy end. The best of ends never justifies immoral means.

The introduction of such terrible weapons returns us to our most fundamental issue — the use of violence. Is there a moral obligation to refrain from such stupendous violence? Should the making of such weapons be stopped?

If use of certain weapons becomes a direct threat to the existence of the human race or certainly entails return to barbarism, all nations are obliged to forego use of such weapons and an individual nation would have to suffer abridgment of its rights rather than let loose such calamities on the human race. But this threat does not exist at present.

Can destructive weapons be produced which could imperil all men? If so, the Natural Law must forbid their use, for the over-all good of the human race has precedence over the good of any nation. Such a situation is a possibility, not a present actuality.

There can be no moral obligation on man to cease delving into the secrets of nature on the ground that new discoveries may be misused. We may not put limits to intellectual investigation. Because more stupendous forms of violence may be discovered, the moral obligation of being master of that violence grows apace. This mastery can be achieved only by man learning to live with man. It is injustice which he must conquer rather than sink his knowledge of atomic energy to the bottom of the sea.

(2) *Enemy Property*

1108. Since a most effective mode of national defense is to deprive one's enemy of the sinews of war, it is legitimate for the State to seize or destroy any public or private property of the enemy that has a military value. *Property which has no military value must be left untouched.* It should be carefully noted that what is conceded by the Natural Law is *a right of use in self-defense.* These uses are reduced to two: seizure and destruction.

a) *Seizure of enemy property.* The right to take and use enemy property does not by *Natural Law* include the right of permanent possession. Holland[21] is wrong when he calls enemy property a *res nullius,* a thing which may be occupied. The reason is that no kind of force — not even military force — may found a title of ownership or of any kind of right. By *Natural Law,* therefore, when hostilities end, all seized properties automatically revert to their former owners: the enemies' right of use has lapsed.

But must we not recognize a right of booty and prize? From ancient times soldiers have acted as though all enemy goods become the property of the captor and have endeavored to keep what they forcibly took. Agreements among the nations, however, have clarified the issue, and upon *agreements* now in force rests the right of booty and prize. A careful distinction is made between public and private property.

Whenever *public* immovable property falls into the hands of the enemy, he has the use and usufruct of the same. Movable public property is simply appropriated by the enemy occupier. What is taken on land is booty; on sea, is a prize. Title vests not in the individual captors but in the sovereign. He, however, may transfer something of his right to his military in order to encourage them. In the case of prizes, title does not pass until a prize court has passed a sentence of condemnation. Treaties may provide special immunity for churches, museums, works of art, and the like.

It is forbidden to take *private* property except in "cases dictated by the necessary operations of war." When private property is requisitioned it must be paid for or a receipt given, to be honored later by one's own government or the enemy. Combatants who appropriate things for their *personal gain* are looters. Trophies or souvenirs are not loot.

b) *Destruction of enemy property.* Whatever has military value to the enemy is liable to destruction. After property has been destroyed in war, is there an obligation of restitution? If a man uses another's

[21] Thomas Holland, *Jurisprudence,* 13 ed., p. 216, Oxford, Clarendon, 1937.

property to save his life and that property is damaged, the user owes nothing in strict justice, for his use has been just. So if a belligerent *in a just war* destroys enemy property he owes no reparations. An unjust belligerent, victor or loser, owes reparations according to his ability to pay.

(3) *Rights of Neutrals*

1109. During the past century the nations accepted as a rigorous precept the principle that a nonbelligerent must act impartially toward the parties to a war. A neutral was to refrain from immediate military aid to either party and prevent within its jurisdiction any such act on the part of anyone whatever. Positive agreements defined immediate military aid. This conception of neutrality was the outcome of the teaching of Grotius on just and unjust wars. Grotius said that whenever a State initiates an unjust war it should be put down by all other States as a malefactor. This was inconvenient doctrine when wars were so frequent. This inconvenience, however, was avoided by saying that the justice of a sovereign's action was left to the conscience of the sovereign, that disinterested parties were incapable of determining the justice of their neighbors' quarrels, and consequently, when war arose, nonbelligerents had to keep a strictly hands-off attitude. The elaborate system of neutrality, based on positive agreements, was quite thoroughly shattered by the ruthless conduct of two World Wars. However, there is still a neutrality which is of Natural Law; for a State still has a right to keep out of war. Furthermore, no belligerent may repudiate treaties with a neutral, move troops across its territory, interfere with a neutral's *peaceful* intercourse with other belligerents, compel a weak nation to enter a war against its best interests. A just belligerent may not solicit aid by promises which are unjust to fulfill. To induce a neutral into an unjust declaration of war is to co-operate immediately in its guilt.

(4) *Reprisal*

1110. A reprisal in war is retaliatory action taken by one belligerent upon the serious violation of the law by the enemy in order to induce him to keep the law. Until World War I reprisal took the form of a specific action intended to correct a specific offense. Thus the United States closely confined some Confederate prisoners because some Union prisoners had been mistreated. Unlimited reprisal was not admitted. For the belligerents of 1914, however, the limit to be put upon reprisals was military expediency. Reprisal crackled upon reprisal until practically the whole system of conventional usages, especially in regard to the rights of neutrals upon the seas, disappeared.

Reprisal, as a means of self-protection, is allowable but it cannot be unlimited. It may never extend to doing that which is evil in itself. "If one general kills in cold blood some hundreds of prisoners who embarrass his motions, his antagonist may not be justified in staining himself by a similar crime, nor may he break his word or oath because the other had done so before."[22] It is murder to take hostages from a civilian population and execute them because unidentifiable persons are making attacks upon the enemy occupier. If, however, the enemy act has been merely the violation of a treaty, for example, not to use privateers, the other State is freed from observing that treaty.

(5) *Lying*

1111. Lying is as wrong in war as in peace. There is, however, a recognizable difference between lying and legitimate deception of the enemy. To fabricate atrocity stories and father them upon the enemy in order to rouse world opinion against him is a serious injustice.

(6) *Blockade*

1112. Blockade is a legitimate means of subduing enemy troops. "If civilians suffer, it is not intended that they should suffer; it is their misfortune, and is due to the fortune of a just war that they happen to be in the same place as their army."[23]

(7) *Terms of Peace*

1113. The terms of peace must be just. Since the only justifying reason for war is vindication of right, once that has been fully secured, the victor must rest. To impose harsh terms which take away necessary rights of a beaten nation is injustice, for even in military defeat a nation retains rights. After a just war the victor may claim compensation for damages sustained, yet his bill for reparations may not condemn the people of the losing side to misery. Both justice and charity demand that the victor follow a policy of live and let live.

(8) *Punishment of Enemies*

1114. May the victor punish the vanquished, that is, both the nation as a whole and individual enemies guilty of serious offenses? Punishment is a deterrent, a correction, and an expiation of crime. It is inflicted on

[22] Theodore Woolsey, *Introduction to the Study of International Law*, 6 ed., p. 211. New York, Scribner's, 1901.

[23] Henry Davis, *Moral and Pastoral Theology*, Vol. II, p. 122. New York, Sheed and Ward, 1936.

the guilty to prevent further crime, to change their evil disposition, and to restore the order of justice disturbed by wrongdoing. The fullness of this power is found in the authority of the State with regard to its own subjects. Are the defeated nation and its nationals also subject to it?

An unjust State is subject to the deterrent and corrective power which each State has for the prevention and reparation of inter-State wrongs. In the vindication of its rights the wronged nation may take measures which will prevent the enemy from repeating his wrong. The victorious State may strip the enemy of the means of future aggression, put individuals to death if the future safety of the State certainly warrants it, and, as a last resort, destroy the enemy government and subject the people to itself (cf. § 1072). "If the victor deals with persons who are alien to humanity and religion, these he may rightfully compel to change conduct which is contrary to nature."[24]

1115. But the heart of punishment is expiation. Only one who has jurisdiction over the offender may exact it. Since punishment is one of the four acts of law,[25] no expiatory punishment is allowed which does not arise from authority and law.

By what authority then may a victor exact expiation from the vanquished? In the extraordinary circumstances cited above where the victor acts as national sovereign toward the vanquished, he may try individuals for violations of existing international and municipal law, or deliver them to another State for trial in the place where the crime was committed. Apart from so unusual a situation the authority of a State is inadequate. Since all States are equal and since one State has not ordinary jurisdiction over the national of another State, what is required for the punishment of international criminals is the authority of international society. Without doubt this authority exists and has been intermittently exercised.

1116. What does positive international law indicate concerning the punishment of war criminals? Suarez[26] found the justification of international punishments in the *Jus Gentium* — those conclusions from the Natural Law which the nations of his time had agreed should govern their inter-State acts. The binding force of the *Jus Gentium* depends on consent. Remove consent and a formerly accepted practice no longer holds. During the two centuries prior to 1945, however, the nations by contrary doctrine and practice withdrew consent from this tenet of the

---

[24] Alberici Gentilis, *De Jure Belli*, Lib. III, C. XI, p. 558, Hanoviae, Haeredes Antonii, 1612.

[25] *Sum. Theol.*, I–II, 92, 2.

[26] *De Legibus*, II, xix, 8.

Jus Gentium. As for doctrine, modern jurisprudence is positivistic, rejecting the Natural Law upon which the *Jus Gentium* rests, teaching the absolute sovereignty of the State, accepting as internationally binding only explicit agreements. In the Hague Conventions it was agreed that *in the actual conduct of the war* commanders in the field could punish with death certain offenses against the laws of war. The purpose of this power is the protection of the armed forces. But concerning punishments to be inflicted after war is concluded, every modern international convention is silent. As for practice, the heads of nations and the commanders of armies have been untouchable. No court would assume jurisdiction over a foreign sovereign unless he voluntarily submitted to it nor would it try foreign nationals who do not reside within its territory without the consent of their own government. Prior to World War I, the termination of war automatically meant an amnesty for all persons who might be charged with wrongful acts of war. At the end of World War I the Allies gave the German government a list of German citizens to be handed over to the Allies for trial. The German government replied that compliance with the demand was abdication of its sovereignty. It proposed instead to try these persons in a special court of its own. The Allies accepted the proposal as in keeping with current international procedure.

The trials at Nuremberg at the end of World War II were a complete cleavage from all modern precedent. This precedent, however, may now be assumed to be part of positive international law. For the principles of jurisdiction and legal punishment, asserted by the judgment of the principal Nuremberg tribunal, were reaffirmed by the United Nations in 1947; in 1950 its International Law Commission formulated these principles in seven precise statements (cf. *American Journal of International Law*, Vol. 44 [1950], Supplement, pp. 125–134).

1117. In the absence of implicit or explicit agreement, does the Natural Law immediately confer authority to punish? Suarez[27] denies this but De Lugo,[28] Vitoria,[29] and other sixteenth-century Scholastics assert it. Indeed De Lugo holds that in the absence of municipal authority even a private person may assume the role of punisher. Bellarmine says: "A prince who has just cause for war bears the character of judge with regard to another prince who has injured him."[30] Does right reason demand that a just victor be *ipso facto* endowed with authority to punish?

[27] *Ibid.*

[28] *De Justitia et Jure,* Disp. X, Sect. ii, n. 81.

[29] *De Jure Belli,* No. 19, no. 57.

[30] *Disputationum Roberti Bellarmini Tomus Secundus,* De Laicis, C. XV, p. 667. Ingolstadii, Adami Sartorii, 1601.

An affirmative answer extracts too much from the doctrine of self-help. Once the victor is secure in his right, the end of self-help has been attained. Does orderly living demand that he then be allowed to punish? Certainly not for the securing of his own good. The only justifying reason for the grant of authority to punish is the good of international society. It seems that the common good would be more often hindered than helped by the assertion of such jurisdiction. For it is unfair that the same party be both accuser and judge; no one is a good judge in his own case. Furthermore, increased strife, contention, and desire for revenge on the part of the punished may well be feared from the application of this doctrine. However, clear instances can arise when appalling crimes are committed and the very existence of international society demands that they do not go unpunished. In such cases there would be an extraordinary and temporary grant of authority to States which are able and disinterested enough to pass just judgment on international criminals.

Since the issue is obscure in Natural Law it requires clarification by positive law. Indeed the prevalence of international crime requires the organization of international justice in a positive manner. The order of daily life forbids the individual to punish his assailants and compels him to seek redress from municipal law. The nations should follow a similar procedure. When individuals constitute themselves ministers of divine retribution, civic order perishes. When the nations follow a similar procedure on the international scene, peace is but a preparation for war. A visible international authority with proper jurisdiction over the inter-State acts of the nations should be constituted to legislate against and punish international crime (cf. § 1123 ff.).

B. International Charity

1118. Many persons who admit the relation of natural justice among States deny the existence of a duty of international charity. However, just as charitable obligation binds individuals, so it binds groups. Group life and group action do not strip men of their essential human characteristics and needs. As the needs which one individual cannot supply for himself ought to be charitably supplied by other individuals, so similarly group needs are to be supplied by other groups. Men remain men as members of a nation.

THESIS LXXIX. The Natural Law commands States to exercise charity toward other States.

PROOF

1119. The practice of charity is essential to human well-being. If it is not exercised, men in need lack a human living. Man lives a social life in order that his needs may be supplied by other men.

States are obliged to practice that which is essential to human living. Hence they fail in their natural function of supplying a completely human life to the needy when they neglect charity.

States do not satisfy this obligation by practicing charity merely to their own members. To restrict charity to one's own people, is to deny the true basis of charity, namely, possession of a common nature and destiny. If there is a duty of charity to some men, there is a duty of charity toward all men.

1120. The general rule of international charity finds a number of particular applications.

a) A nation fighting a righteous war may be aided by another nation.

b) *Immigration.* Nations which have living space and resources to spare ought not to close their doors against all foreigners, especially people from nations which are overcrowded and have limited resources. The prudent charity of all nations could provide reasonable remedies for situations of this kind. If they did, we would have fewer wars.

c) *Tariffs.* In protecting one's own financial and industrial security one nation may not exact excessively high dues or enter into commercial agreements with a favored few which deprive many other nations of equitable opportunities to secure raw materials, set up needed industries, or market their products. As in the individual State one class may not make laws which benefit this class to the hurt of other classes, so in international dealings a combination of States ought not enter into cartels which permanently impoverish less fortunate States. Justice as well as charity may thus be violated. The intricate problems here involved can be settled only when all nations sit down in conference and draw up economic agreements which give a fair chance to all. The nations form one human family.

1121. d) *Intervention.* The liberals of the nineteenth century proclaimed an absolute rule of nonintervention which permitted of no exception, namely — no outsider, individual or nation, may interfere in the internal affairs of a sovereign State for any reason whatever. This principle doubtless arose as a protest against the Holy Alliance, a combination of European powers bent on defeating any attempt to overthrow monarchy in any country. Nonintervention, however, is too narrow an understanding of sovereignty and, when adhered to rigidly, violates true charity. Sovereignty is not an end in itself; it is but a means to human welfare. Hence the rights of sovereignty must be tempered by considerations of the human welfare of the people in whose interest sovereignty exists. If one State has been long and grievously afflicted by another, if the people are revolting against intolerable tyranny, if a State is vainly trying to suppress a revolt injurious to national or international welfare, if a State has been convulsed by endless anarchy — in a word, if a people are overwhelmed by a tremendous evil which is definite, certain, and irremediable by themselves, they may call upon outsiders, individuals or States, to help them. These outsiders have an obligation in charity to assist, if assistance does not bring upon them evils of similar magnitude.

The fact that this principle of charity has been and may again be abused does not refute its existence, nor does the difficulty of deciding when it actually applies. The existence of inhuman and irremediable evil can be determined with certitude. It remains only that the intervening State have an upright motive, which is the good of the people in need. The mode and duration of intervention must likewise be determined by the same unselfish motive.

1122. e) *Patriotism and internationalism.* No State develops real patriotism by encouraging either disdain for all foreigners or hatred for a particular rival. It is wrong for a father to allow his children constantly to disparage or cherish enmity for his neighbor's children. Likewise in a State, unreasonable ill feeling for foreigners should positively be discouraged. It is true that the State cannot control the thinking and private conversation of its citizens. Nevertheless, no acts of the State should lend approval to uncharitableness; officials should promote sentiments of good will toward all nations; the citizen in his formative years should be taught that he is a member not only of this nation but also of the whole human race. Patriotism which does not develop into sane internationalism is defective. Certainly that isolationism is to be reprobated which disclaims any social obligation to the rest of the world. A man is naturally a member not only of a family and a nation, but also of that larger society, the human race.

V. INTERNATIONAL SOCIETY JURIDICALLY ORGANIZED

1123. Social justice defines our obligations to all natural societies and among these we must include the race at large. In it all the elements of a functioning society, save one, are present: namely, a plurality, which is the nations of the world; a common end, which is temporal happiness to be attained by all States and the ultimate satisfaction of human sociability; a partial conspiration toward this end by many men of good will; the common bond of *natural* international duties. All that is lacking is *juridical organization* with authority to direct and compel the nations to co-operate unto the common good of all. *Must this final step be taken?* Is there a moral obligation binding the States to constitute positive international authority and to obey it?

THESIS LXXX. The States are now obliged to erect a positive international authority possessing the institutions necessary to regulate by law the international acts of the nations and attain the end of international society.

1124. Every kind of social obligation does not apply at all times in history. In primeval times the only social obligations which a man had pertained to his family. At that time the familial organization was all that men required. After families had grown into patriarchal septs and tribes, the need of a superfamilial organization became apparent. The State, which had not been thought of, gradually became a necessity. The tribes who lived in the same territory could have no lasting peace and chance of progress unless they organized a political union. As the idea of the State and its function became clear, the heads of families little by little surrendered to the State many of their responsibilities and prerogatives.

1125. For countless generations the State has been the ultimate unit in social organization. For centuries the story of the race was a record of the scattering of men across the earth into remote regions whence communication and contact with many others was impossible. In that isolated situation men had no need of an organization over and above the State. Let it be noted that the outstanding contribution of the State to human progress was *intra*national peace. The instrument was law. By subjecting the individual to visible authority in his dealings with other men, blood and tumult gave way to comparative peace and order.

1126. But now the uninhabited parts of the earth have been occupied, and the old isolating barriers have disappeared, because modern transportation and communication have made all nations neighbors. As a result, the international contacts and interdependencies of all States have increased a thousandfold. Unfortunately, however, these relations have not been subjected to competent authority: the impress of compelling law has not been made upon them. The ultimate arbiter of international disputes has not been law but force. From this lack of law has flowed widespread misery. Whenever the Natural Law is inadequate it must be supplemented by positive law. If the mere precepts of the Natural

Law fail to effect order in so increasingly important a department of human activity, does human welfare cry out for the creation of a visible social authority which will submit to law the international acts of all States? As the social acts of individuals are subject to the law of the State, must the international acts of States themselves become subject to positive law?

1127. Since law can come only from legitimate authority, the nations must consent to establish international authority. To be effective, this authority must be able not merely to suggest and advise but to make and enforce laws governing inter-State activity. The erection of this authority will involve on the part of the nations the surrender of some of their sovereignty. Retaining supreme control of purely domestic matters, the State would hand over to this supranational authority ultimate control of foreign affairs. Unlimited national sovereignty is not an end in itself. It is less than man and hence for man. When it ceases to promote human welfare it must give way to an arrangement that will.

The fact is that the national State in many respects has ceased to be self-sufficient. Acute human problems have arisen because political readjustments have not yet been made to fit the factual situation. Of course the national sovereignties are loathe to part with anything of their power, but so too in the days of the nascent State, heads of families did not like to yield anything to the tribal king.

PROOF

1128. States are obliged to do that which the welfare of their people imperatively demands. The welfare of all peoples demands positive international authority capable of regulating the international acts of all nations. In the present system of unlimited national sovereignties the welfare neither of particular people nor of the whole human race is sufficiently provided for.

a) *The welfare of individual nations is at stake.* It is an anachronism to say that today each nation is adequately self-sufficient. First, when international war arises what single nation can isolate the war or maintain a strict neutrality or when attacked adequately protect its people? Second, economically and financially no nation can get along without the co-operation of the rest of the world.

b) *The welfare of the human race is at stake.* The important social acts of man require regulation and supervision by positive law; otherwise social life is impossible. Ample regulation on local, regional, and national levels is provided by State law. On the international level there is little law. So long as international relations did not deeply affect the daily lives of men, lack of positive international authority was of small consequence. But now the economic life of the world is one. Unfortunately, however, international commerce and finance are conducted as undercover war. When the tension becomes too great, world-wide war results.

Grave political injustice, such as denial of self-rule, diminution of the sovereignty of weaker nations, rape of territories, are maintained by force. These injustices, coupled with national jealousies and economic rivalries, are the seeds of potential conflict. The sole arbitrament to date has been war. So frightfully devastating have become the weapons of war that the very existence of the race will be endangered by further development and use of them. With more deadly gases, easier diffusion of bacteria, and more destructive hydrogen bombs in prospect, international war must be eliminated. State authority embodied in the law of national kings did suppress petty war: the only hope of eliminating or at least lessening the frequency of international war is international authority and law.

1129. N.B. It is not necessary that this supranational authority be a single world State to which the nations of the world would be subject as the States of the union are subject to the United States. Such a power might prove to be a Frankenstein. For if control of that power got into the hands of evil men — and communists are now plotting to build precisely such a power — the present democracies could well fear the loss of their liberties and the prosperous nations would be reduced to the level of the poorer nations. An omnipotent world executive presents the problem of, Who will watch the watchmen?

The problem, however, should not be given up as insoluble. We may draw some hope from the past. For what contemporary of the all-powerful sixteenth-century sovereign would have dreamed that some day he would be stripped of his power and that they who now exercise it in his place would be held accountable to the community for their wise use of it? Admitting that no satisfactory answer to the problem of how an adequate international law is to be effectively enforced, we must await the unfolding of events and remember that the State did not issue full blown from the blueprint of some philosopher like Athene from the head of Zeus. We see only the beginnings of the juridical organization of international society. What definitive form it will take no one can tell with certainty. We may speculate, however, that the form of international society will be shaped not only by the needs but also by the weakness and vice of mankind.

READINGS

American Catholic Philosophical Association Proceedings, "The Natural Law and International Relations," 1950.
Brierly, J. L., *The Law of Nations*. Oxford, Clarendon, 1950.
Cook, T. I., "Theoretical Foundations of World Government," *Review of Politics*, 12 (1950), 20–55.
Corbett, P. E., *Law and Society in the Relations of States*. New York, Harcourt Brace, 1951.
Eppstein, J., ed., *The Catholic Tradition of the Law of Nations*. Washington, 1935.
——— *Code of International Ethics*. Westminster, Newman, 1953.
Ford, J. C., "The Morality of Obliteration Bombing," *Theological Studies*, 5 (1944), 261–309.
Kelly, G., "Notes on Moral Theology," *Theological Studies*, 12 (1951), 56–59.
Kenny, J. P., *Moral Aspects of Nuremberg*. Washington, 1949.
Levi, W., *Fundamentals of World Organization*. Minneapolis, University of Minnesota, 1950.
Nussbaum, A., *A Concise History of the Law of Nations*. New York, Macmillan, 1954.
Oppenheim, L., *International Law*, 7 ed., by H. Lauterpacht. London, Longmans, Green, 1952.
Pius XII, "International Community and Religious Tolerance," *The Pope Speaks*, First Quarter, 1954, 64–71.
——— "International Penal Law," *Catholic Mind*, 52 (1954), 107–120.
——— "International Reconciliation," *The Pope Speaks*, Winter, 1955, 315–326.
Schiffer, W., *The Legal Community of Mankind*. New York, Columbia, 1954.
Sorokin, R. A., *The Reconstruction of Humanity*. Boston, Beacon, 1948.
Stratmann, F. M., *War and Christianity Today*. London, Blackfriars, 1956.
Sturzo, L., *Nationalism and Internationalism*, 174–308. New York, Roy, 1946.
Suarez, *De Bello*.
——— *De Legibus*, II, 17–20.
Svarlien, O., *An Introduction to the Law of Nations*. New York, McGraw-Hill, 1955.
Thompson, K. W., "The Study of International Politics," *Review of Politics*, 14 (1952), 433–467.
Wandycz, P., "The Theory of International Relations," *Review of Politics*, 17 (1955), 189–205.
Wilson, G. G., *Handbook of International Law*, 3 ed. St. Paul, West, 1939.
Wright, R. F., *Medieval Internationalism*. London, Williams and Norgate, 1930.
Zammitt, P. N., "The Need of International Society," *The Thomist*, 18 (1955), 71–87.
Zizzamia, A., "Catholicism and Internationalism," *Thought*, 28 (1953), 485–527.

Appendix

OCCUPATIONAL GROUPS

When treating of the organic nature of the State in § 844 we spoke of occupational, or vocational groups. A more detailed explanation of their nature, function, and benefit is in order. In the past occupational groups have assured men their livelihood. They could do so again. Furthermore, they would help in solving the grave economic-moral problem of today and would ease the burden of grievously overladen government.

I. THE NATURE OF AN OCCUPATIONAL GROUP

It accords with man's social instincts freely to form societies the better to achieve a desirable end. Since a man's job is of such consuming importance, it is natural that those who have the common interest of the same kind of work combine to protect their livelihood and improve themselves in their work. Such a combination of men is an occupational group. There is no advantage in haggling over the name to give it: call it occupational or vocational. By the reality we mean a *spontaneously organized, semipublic, autonomous society, intermediate between the family and the State, composed of absolutely all who engage in the same type of labor, trade, or profession, whose purpose is the economic well-being and professional excellence of its members.*

This organization must be established by the people themselves. It may not be superimposed on them by the State. For then it would be artificial and lack that natural development it must have if it is to serve men's economic needs. As an arm of the State, it would only be doing administrative work in the name of the State; and State administration of economics is to be avoided. To succeed, this society must be non-political; otherwise it can never perform the autonomous social function of which it is capable.

The occupational group must be semipublic, that is, it is not to be a private society like a labor union. Since its purpose is to secure economic order, justice, and peace for its members — a good which so closely touches the common good — it should have a public character, but since rule would remain in the hands of private citizens, we call it semipublic.

As the municipality has a certain competence and autonomy in political matters which it receives by charter from the State, so this association should be constituted by the State as a corporation and given autonomy and responsibility in the economic order. Its general task would be to produce economic order within the State and to establish and enforce rules to which a man must conform if he wishes to follow a given occupation.

At this suggestion economic liberals raise a keening howl: this corporation would be the death of individual initiative. We agree that it would be the death of unreasonable initiative, as is all law and regulation, but it is time that unsocial and unreasonable activities in the economic field were strongly curbed and economic activity brought back to where it belongs — to the service of society. The occupational group means giving economics that discipline without which orderly activity is impossible. A man does not have to be a doctor, but if he elects to be one, he ought to conform to the ethics of the profession. No one has to live in New York City, but whoever chooses it as his residence must obey the city ordinances. So also if a man wishes to become a printer or manufacturer of textiles, should he not conform to norms governing the printing and textile businesses? But this is fascism, the liberals cry. There is a big difference between fascism and this. Fascism is discipline imposed from without; this discipline is from within, voluntarily agreed to by the members of the group. The economic world requires order and discipline, and who can better say what disciplined order in the printing and textile businesses is than the common voice of those who work at them every day?

The immediate end of a corporation will be the good condition of a particular occupation, for example, the shipping industry. Its ultimate end is the economic welfare and professional betterment of its members. These purposes are realized when the members enjoy a satisfactory economic and professional standing, that is, a real livelihood and a status proportionate to their function and merits; when harmony exists within individual firms, that is, when both employers and employees co-operatively work together for the good of the firm; when order prevails among the firms within the organization.

The corporation also stresses the professional consideration of a job well done. Men are happy at their work when they have ambition to excel at it and serve the community. The corporation can perform a mighty service by giving a business something of the stature of a profession. The primary purpose of the great professions, medicine, law, and the sacred ministry, is service of the community. Personal financial considerations are secondary, because, if a man serves the community, he is assured a decent living. Is it possible that business be raised to an approximate level? The root evil of business is that its total motive is gain. Service to the community scarcely gets lip service. Why could not these values be more proportionately adjusted? Selling clothes and providing amusement are a service to the community—not so noble as healing pain but an appreciable service. Why could not the social and hence the moral aspect of the activities be duly considered by their purveyors? If they did so, women's swimming suits and stage productions would seldom be a pitfall to entrap the peccable onlooker. When pride in one's work and service to the community are considered almost as important as personal gain, that greed which knows no bounds is strongly shackled. Tie down greed, and economic evils tend to disappear.

II. THE FUNCTION OF AN OCCUPATIONAL GROUP

Depending on the size of a country, each occupation would be organized locally, regionally, and nationally. To each corporation the State would grant jurisdiction which is economic and social. (a) *Economic* jurisdiction means authority to put order into the production and distribution of goods and services by adapting them to the needs of consumers. (b) *Social* jurisdiction means regulation of the professional conduct of the members. Within its proper sphere the corporation could regulate, administer, discipline, and represent. Once the occupations are properly organized, harmony and co-ordination must be established between them. This could be done by a general economic council composed of representatives of all of them. This body would be competent to advise the State upon economic matters of national importance, but it would not constitute an economic congress parallel to the political congress. It would be nonpolitical and never dominate the State, because government must be aloof from, and above, every interest but the common good.

The cry goes up, This is a Planned Economy. Assuredly, every activity must follow some pattern if it is to achieve its end. Digestion and reproduction, for example, obey rather rigid laws of nature. So also economics must follow some kind of reasoned planning. If chaos is not to continue, there must be economic planning. It will be done. Who is to do it? Leaders of finance, bureaucrats, or democratically controlled occupational groups united in a supreme economic council? The world has had too woeful an experience with the economic decisions of the rugged individualists who control the credit of the world. Enough has already been said about the undesirability of State-planned economy. The fumbling attempts of bureaucrats to regulate daily economic life during World War II has shown that they seldom have the technical experience nor the mental viewpoint requisite to make practicable judgments in these matters. As the horse's shoes are still best put on by the blacksmith, they are best capable of making economic decisions whose daily lives are immersed in these things and whose living immediately depends thereon.

III. BENEFITS OF OCCUPATIONAL GROUPS

Society today labors under three major handicaps: (a) lack of economic order; (b) social injustices; (c) need of organic social life. The occupational groups will not bring on the millennium, but in all three difficulties they have a notable contribution to offer.

a) Occupational groups will produce *economic order*. No better solution to the anarchy of production has yet been offered. If production is controlled by social need and not unlimited profit, production becomes more stable and employment steadier. An end will be put to unbridled competition with its unholy offspring of monopolistic gouging. While this system imposes reasonable supervision of private enterprise, supervision will be done by those closest to business and hence most competent to do it wisely. Occupational groups will prevent the calamity of the destruction of private enterprise.

One of the bitterest complaints against the prevailing system is the over-all control of business and industry by anonymous and irresponsible finance. After asserting that control of wealth has gone into the hands of a few directors of invested funds, Pius XI says: "This power becomes particularly irresistible when exercised by those who, because they hold and control money, are able also to govern credit and determine its allotment, for that reason supplying, so to speak, the life blood to the entire economic body, and grasping, as it were, in their hands the very soul of production, so that no one dare breathe against their will. This accumulation of power, the characteristic note of the modern economic order, is a natural result of limitless free competition, which permits the survival of those who are the strongest, which often means those who fight most relentlessly, pay least heed to the dictates of conscience."[1]

In a corporative arrangement the mere fact that a man has available capital will not suffice to put him into a business. Since the corporation

[1] *Quadragesimo Anno.*

itself will determine who engages in the business, how much is to be produced, and what is reasonable profit, it will be impossible for a man to go into an industry looking for large quick returns: he will be able to do business only on the terms which the corporation establishes. Money will be the servant of industry; industry will no longer be the servant of money. Unlimited opportunities for investment and unlimited competition will no longer exist.

b) Occupational groups will help remove *social injustices*. Unlimited competition offers tremendous prizes of very great wealth to a few persons with the inevitable consequence that many people fail to get a living. Hence arises a proletarian class, that is, large masses of workers without productive wealth and economically dependent on a small class owning all the instruments of production. The corporation would scale down the size of the prizes at the top so as to permit all the members of the corporation a living. This would mean the gradual disappearance of the proletariat. Since the little man would make a living wage and would be secure against unemployment, he could, if he is thrifty and progressive, rise to a status of small ownership and a share in the profits.

Social classes based upon possessions are now hostilely arrayed against each other: capital against labor, employer against employee. The corporation would not be *against* anyone but *for* all its membership. This would accomplish two things. First, with enormous profits no longer possible to a few persons, tremendous contrasts of extreme wealth and utter dependence would not be normal.

Second, amicable co-operation would be demanded of all, because all employers and employees would belong to the same organization. This fact would result in the due recognition of the part which labor plays in the production of wealth. The stigma attaching to labor would be removed and a man's social status would not depend on his possessions but on the value of his social function to society.

c) Occupational groups will offer *social organization*. With each corporation functioning under a supreme economic council, dependent on civil authority, the State would have the organic form which it now lacks and a tremendous weight of needless tasks would be lifted from government. Each business and industry would take care of its own personnel by providing cultural and recreational opportunities, unemployment insurance, old age pensions, and all the other desiderata of modern sociology. The State would then be free to regain its natural function of supreme arbiter and dispenser of justice. It would no longer take sides; it would be neither prolabor nor procapital, but the impartial guardian of the good of all.

INDEX